From Plassey to Partition and After

Praise for the Second Edition

"With ten imprints in as many years, Bandyopadhyay's book has by now established itself as perhaps the most widely read and taught general history of modern India. Extensively researched and clearly written, it now comes with a succinct and helpful post-Partition survey for the research student, bringing the story of the successes and failures of the Indian nation up to date."

Shahid Amin, Professor of History, University of Delhi and author of *Event, Metaphor, Memory: Chauri Chaura, 1922–1992*

"Bandyopadhyay's book is comprehensive, lucid, closely attentive to findings of recent academic research, and scrupulously fair in representing many contentious debates that have occurred in the field. With a new chapter that summarises developments since Partition and Independence, it will continue to be valuable to students, teachers and interested readers."

Partha Chatterjee, Professor of Anthropology and South Asian Studies Columbia University

Praise for the First Edition

"The best and most objective account of the period."

Ramachandra Guha, author of *India after Gandhi: The History of the World's Largest Democracy*

"*From Plassey to Partition*...stands out as the very best of the recent batch of general histories of modern India.... [O]ne can only be struck by the impressive range and depth of Bandyopadhyay's scholarship."

Tony Ballantyne, *New Zealand Journal of Asian Studies*

"Accessible and thorough, this laudable textbook will find place in every undergraduate's essential reading list and in every history library."

Partho Datta, *The Book Review*

"[This book] takes into account the materialistic factors in [its] analysis, which makes [it] more comprehensive than many others."

M. Abul Fazl, *Dawn*

From Plassey to Partition and After

A History of Modern India

SECOND EDITION

SEKHAR BANDYOPADHYAY

Orient BlackSwan

FROM PLASSY TO PARTITION AND AFTER

ORIENT BLACKSWAN PRIVATE LIMITED

Registered Office
3-6-752 Himayatnagar, Hyderabad 500 029 (Telangana), INDIA
e-mail: centraloffice@orientblackswan.com

Other Offices
Bengaluru, Bhopal, Chennai, Ernakulam, Guwahati, Hyderabad,
Jaipur, Kolkata, Lucknow, Mumbai, New Delhi, Noida, Patna, Vijayawada

First published 2004
Reprinted 2004, 2006, 2007, 2008
First Orient Blackswan impression 2009
Reprinted 2010, 2011, 2012, 2013, 2014
Revised edition 2015
Reprinted 2015, 2016

ISBN: 978 81 250 5723 9

Maps Cartography by
Sangam Books (India) Private Limited, Hyderabad

Printed in India at
Yash Printographics
Noida

Published by
Orient Blackswan Private Limited
1/24 Asaf Ali Road
New Delhi 110 002
e-mail: delhi@orientblackswan.com

For
Sohini
and her generation

Contents

List of Maps

Preface to the Second Edition

This book has been in print for the last ten years, and in this past decade thousands of students, scholars and general readers have used it. And I have received overwhelmingly positive feedback from a wide range of people from different corners of the world—all telling me how much they liked and benefited from this book. I was pleased to see that so many people liked my idea of India being a pluralist nation with many voices.

However, I also received a complaint that the book ended abruptly in 1947. The year no doubt constituted a watershed in the history of the Indian nation, but it did not mark the end of its history; the story of nation-building only entered a new phase after 1947. I completely agree. To rectify that incompleteness, I have now added a new chapter on postcolonial India. In keeping with the new chronological coverage of the book, I am also slightly changing its title to *From Plassey to Partition and After*.

However, I am also aware that the discerning reader may detect another imbalance in this new chapter. In contrast to the rest of the text, it is more selective, as it tries to capture almost seventy years of complex history in one chapter. But I think I have covered all the major events and historical trends of this period. Also it is difficult to write about a time in which you are living and some of the historical actors are your contemporaries. While absolute objectivity is impossible to achieve, I have tried to be as balanced as possible in my narrative. My intentions have never been to hurt or hate anyone.

The other major challenge of writing on this period is the existence of a vast body of literature, contributed not just by historians, but by scholars from multiple disciplines, most notably by political scientists. I have tried to cover as much as possible within the limited time I had at my disposal. I must also admit that I would not have been able to traverse as much intellectual ground as I did without the help of a talented political scientist, Dr Hilal Ahmed of Centre for the Study of Developing Societies, Delhi. He came to our institute in Wellington as a visiting fellow in 2013 and helped me in planning this chapter—by alerting me to the literature, suggesting a viable structure and interrogating my arguments. Without his assistance I would not have been able to write this chapter so quickly, as my numerous administrative responsibilities allow me very little time for serious academic work these days. My sincere thanks go to Hilal for his intellectual and personal friendship. I am also thankful to my student, Benjamin Kingsbury, for updating the appendix.

I should also thank my publishers; without their incessant pressure, encouragement and support, I would not have ventured to write this new chapter. My family as usual has been helpful and supportive, as they have continued to bear with my workaholic habits. As usual, if there is any error, the responsibility is entirely mine.

14 October 2014

SEKHAR BANDYOPADHYAY
New Zealand India Research Institute
Wellington

Preface

This book proposes to present in eight thematic chapters a general history of India under British rule. It focuses more on the Indian people, than on the colonial state or the "men who ruled India". It highlights the perceptions of the ruled, their cultural crises and social changes, their rebellion, their search for identity and their attempts to negotiate with a modernity brought to them through a variety of colonial policies. Above all, it narrates the story of how the Indian nation was gradually emerging, with all its contradictions and tensions, under the domineering presence of Western imperialism.

In recent years there has been a tremendous outpouring of research publications in this area. And therefore, it is time to relate these specialised research findings and theoretical interventions to the whole story. Tucked away in my island abode down under—separated from my primary sources by thousands of miles—I thought this would be an ideal project for me. This book tries to provide, on the one hand, a story with adequate empirical details needed by students for history courses and by general readers. On the other hand, acknowledging that there can be multiple interpretations of a historical event, the narrative is consciously situated within its proper historiographical context. The book, in other words, summarises the findings and conclusions of an enormous body of research literature that has been produced in the last two decades or so on the colonial history of India. However, although it presents a synthetic history, it does not offer an eclectic view. The narrative has carved its way carefully through the undulated terrains of Indian historiography. Sometimes, it has taken sides, sometimes it has treaded a middle path, but on occasions it has also been innovative and unorthodox. In other words, it refers to the debates and critically examines them to arrive at its own conclusions about the establishment and functioning of colonial rule and also the emergence of a pluralist and polyphonic nationalism in India.

The book begins with a discussion of the political transformation of India in the eighteenth century, marked by the decline of the Mughal empire at the one end and the rise of the British empire on the other, and in between them a period of uncertainty, dominated by some powerful regional successor states that emerged because of a decentralisation of Mughal authority. It then discusses the ideology behind empire building, the historical controversies about the nature of British imperialism, the way a colonial economy unfolded itself and impacted on the Indian society. Then come the responses of the Indian people, their cultural adaptations, social reforms, and finally, their armed resistance, the most violent manifestation of which was the revolt of 1857. The chapters following this discuss the rise of modern nationalism in India, the controversies about its nature, its transformation under the Gandhian leadership, and the emergence of mass politics under the aegis of the Indian National Congress. This narrative seeks to take the discussion of nationalism beyond that constricted discursive space where nation-state is situated at the centre and the existence of a homogeneous nation is uncritically accepted and it is supposed to have spoken in one voice. This book acknowledges the historical significance of the mass movement against colonial rule—the largest of its kind in world history in terms of its sheer scale—but shows that the masses rarely spoke in one voice. If Congress represented the mainstream of nationalism in India that found fulfilment in the foundation of the Indian nation-state, there were several powerful minority voices too, such as those of the Muslims, non-Brahmans and dalits, women, workers and peasants, who had different conceptions of freedom, which the mainstream nationalism could not always accommodate. In this nationalist movement dalit concerns for the conditions of citizenship, women's yearning for autonomy, peasants' and workers' longing for justice jostled unhappily with Congress's preoccupation with political sovereignty. The celebrations of independence in August 1947 were marred by the agonies of a painful and violent partition, signalling the stark reality of Muslim alienation. This book, in other words, is mindful of the diversities within unity, and narrates the story of a polyphonic nationalism where different voices converged in a common struggle against an authoritarian colonial rule, with divergent visions of future at the end of it. The making of this pluralist nation in India is a continually unfolding story that does not end where this book finishes, i.e., at the closing of the colonial era. Nevertheless, the end of colonial rule constitutes an important watershed, as after this the contest for 'nation-space' acquires new meanings and different dimensions. The present endeavour however remains modest in its scope and focuses only on the colonial period of that continuing saga of adjustment, accommodation and conflict.

While writing this book, if there is one single text of historical writing that has influenced me most, it is Sumit Sarkar's *Modern India, 1885–1947* (1983), which I have used extensively as a source of information as well as ideas, of course, not always agreeing with all his views. I have acknowledged the debt in the text as far as possible, but the debt is far too much that I can possibly acknowledge formally in every detail. I have also used some other books quite extensively, primarily as sources of information. Mention must be made of the works of S.R. Mehrotra (1971), Philip Lawson (1993), David Hardiman (1993), Geraldine Forbes (1998) and Ian Copland (1999). However, ultimately, this book projects my own understanding of Indian history. And as there is no unpositioned site of historical knowledge, this narrative is coloured by my own preferences and predilections—or in plain words, by my views on Indian nationalism, which will be self-evident in the narrative. I offer no apology for that. However, no interpretation, as we all now acknowledge, is absolute. For other interpretations, readers may follow the bibliography given at the end of this book.

I am indebted to many for writing this book, which has been taking shape in my mind for a very long time. My first and foremost debt is to my students over the last twenty-five years, at Calcutta University in India and at Victoria University of Wellington in New Zealand. They have heard earlier versions of many chapters of this book in their class lectures and tutorial discussions. Through their questions and comments they have constantly challenged me to think about Indian history in newer ways, and in the process have enriched my understanding of the subject. It is also time to acknowledge my longstanding intellectual debt to my teachers from whom I had my lessons of history. I had the privilege of being trained by some of the most eminent historians of modern India, like the late Professors Amales Tripathi and Ashin Das Gupta and Professors Benoy Bhushan Chaudhuri, Arun Dasgupta, Barun De, Nilmoni Mukherjee and Rajat Kanta Ray, all of whom have left their marks on my understanding of Indian history. Some of my friends, Rudrangshu Mukherjee, Parimal Ghosh, Samita Sen, Subho Basu and Rajat Ganguly have read various sections of the manuscript and have given their valuable suggestions. Gautam Bhadra has been generous as ever in sharing with me his incredible bibliographic knowledge. I am also thankful to my former colleagues at Calcutta University with whom I discussed many of my ideas in their early formative stage. My present colleagues in the History Programme at Victoria University of Wellington presented me with a collegial and intellectually stimulating working environment, without which I would not have been able to write this book. I also wish to thank the Research Committee of the Faculty of Humanities and Social Sciences at Victoria University of Wellington for sponsoring the project with generous research and travel grants, and also the staff of the Victoria University library for supplying me innumerable books and articles used in this book through its inter-library loan system. Special thanks are also due to several people at the Orient Longman: to Sonali Sengupta who first put the idea of this book into my head, to Nandini Rao who sustained my enthusiasm over the years by maintaining her faith in the project, and to Priti Anand who finally made this book possible. I am also indebted to the anonymous reader for pointing out some significant omissions in the manuscript and for making some valuable suggestions for improvement. And finally, I am immensely grateful to Veenu Luthria, whose meticulous editing has saved me from a lot of embarrassment.

My family as usual has been enormously supportive. My parents have always been sources of inspiration for me. My wife Srilekha ungrudgingly took the responsibility of looking after the household, tolerated my endless grumblings, encouraged me constantly and kept a watchful eye on the progress of this book. My daughter Sohini, with her growing interest in history, has been a source of inspiration in many ways than she knows. It is to her and to other young minds, keen to learn about the historic struggles of the people of India, that this book is dedicated.

Despite my best efforts there will certainly be many errors in the book, for which I alone remain responsible.

Glossary

abwab	extra legal charges exacted by landlords
adalat	court
ahimsa	non-violence
akhra	gymnasium
amil	revenue official
amla	zamindari official
anjuman	local Muslim association
ajlaf	Muslim commoners
atma sakti	self strengthening
ashraf	Muslim respectable class or elite
ashram	Hindu religious organisation
atrap	Muslim commoners—same as *ajlaf.*
azad	free; liberty
azad dastas	guerrilla bands
babu	a disparaging colonial term for educated Bengalees
bahas	Muslim religious meeting
bakasht	land where permanent tenancies had been converted into short-term tenancies
bhadralok	Bengali gentlemen, belonging to upper caste
bhadramahila	Bengali gentlewoman
bhaichara	brotherhood
bhakti	devotional religion
chapatis	flattened wheat bread
chakri	office job
charkha	spinning wheel
chaukidari	system of village ward and watch
chauth	one-fourth of the revenue claimed by the Marathas
cutchery	a court of law; a zamindar's court or office
dadan	advance
dadani	merchants who procured goods by paying advances to primary producers

dal(s)	faction(s)
Dal Khalsa	Sikh religious organisation initiated by Guru Govind Singh
dalam	revolutionary units
dalapati	leader of factions
dalit	oppressed—term used by the untouchables to identify themselves
dalwai	prime minister of the Mysore state
daroga	local police officer
dastak	permits issued by the local councils of the East India Company certifying their goods for the purpose of tax exemption
deshpande	revenue collector
deshmukh	revenue officer
dharma	religion; also, code of moral conduct
Dharmashastra	Hindu religious texts
diku	foreigner—term used by the tribals (Santhals) to identify outsiders
diwan	treasurer
diwani	revenue collecting right
diwani adalat	civil court
durbar	royal court
farman	Mughal imperial order
fatwa	Islamic religious declaration
faujdari adalat	criminal court
fitna	sedition
fituris	a tradition of tribal rebellion
ghatwali	service tenure for village watchmen
garbhadhan	consummation of marriage at the beginning of puberty
giras	customary dues
gomustah	Indian agent of the East India Company
goonda(s)	hooligan elements
Granth	sacred text
gurdwara	Sikh place of worship
harijan(s)	literally, God's children—a phrase used by Gandhi to identify the untouchables
hartal	strike
hundi	bill of exchange
ijaradari	revenue farming system
ijaradar	revenue farmer
ilaka	area

jagir	revenue paying estate distributed among the Mughal aristocrats
jama	estimated land revenue income
janmi	holder of janmam tenure
jat	a personal rank of a Mughal military commander or mansabdar
jatha(s)	Sikh bands of warriors
jati	caste
jatra	rural theatrical performance
jhum	shifting (slash and burn) cultivation
jotedar(s)	intermediary tenure holders
kanamdar/kanakkaran	holder of kanam tenure
karma	action or deed; the Hindu belief that actions in the present life determine a person's fate in the next life
kazi	Muslim judge
khadi	homespun cloth
khalsa	Sikh order of brotherhood
khalisa	royal land
khanazad	hereditary Muslim aristocrats in the Mughal court
khudkasht(s)	peasants with occupancy rights
khutba	Friday prayers in the mosque
kisan	peasant
kotwal	Mughal police official in charge of an urban centre
kulin	some castes among the Brahmans and Kayasthas of Bengal who are considered to be the purest
lathiyal(s)	musclemen who fought with bamboo clubs
mahal	fiscal unit in north India
mahatma	great soul—epithet given to Gandhi by the people of India
masand	a deputy of the Sikh guru
maulavi	Islamic religious teacher
mulgujar	landholding primary zamindar
mansabdar	Mughal military commander/aristocrat
mansabdari	system of organisation of the Mughal aristocracy
Manusmriti	religious text believed to be written by the ancient lawgiver Manu.

meli(s)	anti-feudal demonstrations
mir bakshi	Mughal imperial treasurer
mirasidar	holders of hereditary land rights (mirasi) in south India
misls	combinations of Sikh sardars based on kinship ties
mistri	jobbers
mofussil	small town or subdivisional town
mohalla	an area of a town or village
mufti	Muslim learned person, expert in religious laws
muktiyar namah	power of attorney
mullah	Muslim priest
mushaira	public recital
muttadars	estate holders
nakdi mansabdar	mansabdars who were paid in cash
nankar	revenue free land
nari bahinis	women brigades
nawab	Mughal provincial governor
nazim	official title for the Mughal provincial governors
pahikasht(s)	vagrant peasants
panchayat	village council
pattadar(s)	landowners
patil	village headmen
patni	subinfeudatory tenures
patta	written agreement between the peasant and the landowner
peshkash	fixed amount paid by an autonomous ruler to the Mughal emperor
peshwa	prime minister of the Maratha ruler
pir	Islamic preacher
podu	a tribal term for shifting cultivation prevalent in the Andhra region
praja	nation/subjects/tenants
praja mandal	nationalist people's organisations in the Indian Princely states
prati sarkar	parallel government
pundit	an expert in Hindu religious texts
purdah	a Persian word, literally meaning curtain, used to define the seclusion of Indian women

qaum	community based on common descent
raj	rule
raja	autonomous ruler
Ramrajya	kingdom of the mythical king Rama
rashtra	state
risalas	units of the army of Haidar Ali of Mysore
sahajdharis	non-khalsa Sikhs
sahib	Indian term for the Europeans
sahukar	moneylender
sajjad nishins	custodians of sufi shrines
samiti	association
sanad	Mughal imperial order
sangathan	organisation
saranjam	transferable land rights
sardar(s)	chiefs of Maratha, Rajput or Sikh clans; also the term for jobbers through whom workers were recruited in Indian industries
sardeshmukhi	a term for Maratha revenue demand
sarkar	government; also, rural district
satyagraha	a method of non-violent agitation devised by Mahatma Gandhi
sati	the custom of widows sacrificing themselves on the funeral pyre of their dead husbands
sawar	a numerical rank for Mughal military commanders indicating the number of horsemen they were supposed to maintain
seba dal(s)	volunteer corps
sepoy	Indian soldier in the British army—originating from the Indian word *sipahi*
shakti	primal power
sharif	respectable Muslim
shastra	Hindu religious texts
sharia	Islamic law
subah	Mughal province
sud	a tribal term for foreigners prevalent in the Choto Nagpur region
suddhi	purification; reconversion movement started by Arya Samaj
swadeshi	indigenous political movement to boycott foreign goods and institutions and use their indigenous alternatives

swaraj	self-rule
swaraj ziladish	independent district magistrate
taluqdars	large landlords in Awadh
tankha jagir	hereditary possessions of the Rajput chiefs under the Mughals
tehsildar	subordinate police officer
thana	police station; also unit of police jurisdiction of twenty to thirty square miles
tinkathia	a system that bound peasants to produce indigo in three twentieth part of their land
tufan dal(s)	revolutionary village units
Upanishad	ancient Hindu scripture
ulama	Muslim priests
ulgulan	rebellion of the Mundas
ummah	community based on allegiance to the common Islamic faith
utar	forced labour
vakil(s)	representatives/advocates at the Mughal courts
varna	fourfold division of Hindu society
varnashramadharma	code of conduct maintaining the fourfold division of Hindu society
Vaishnavaites	followers of Vaishnavism
vatan	hereditary land rights
Vedanta	Upanaishads or texts written at the end of the Vedas
Vedas	ancient Indian scriptures
wazir	prime minister
zabt	Mughal system of land measurement
zamindar(s)	landlords
zenana	the women's quarter in the inner part of the house
zillah	administrative district

Abbreviations

AICC	All India Congress Committee
AITUC	All India Trade Union Congress
ATLA	Ahmedabad Textile Labour Association
ASSOCHAM	Associated Chambers of Commerce
AISPC	All India States People's Conference
AIKS	All India Kisan Sabha
BHU	Banaras Hindu University
BPKS	Bengal Provincial Kisan Sabha
BPKS	Bihar Provincial Kisan Sabha
CID	Central Investigation Department
CNMA	Central National Mohammedan Association
CPI	Communist Party of India
CSP	Congress Socialist Party
DK	Dravida Kazhagam
FICCI	Federation of Indian Chambers of Commerce and Industries
GIP	Great Indian Peninsular (Railway)
ICS	Indian Civil Service
INA	Indian National Army
IoA	Instrument of Accession
IJMA	Indian Jute Mills Association
JLA	Jamshedpur Labour Association
KPS	Krishak Praja Party
PCC	Pradesh Congress Committee
RAF	Royal Air Force
RIAF	Royal Indian Air Force
RIN	Royal Indian Navy
RSS	Rashtriya Swayamsevak Sangh
SGPC	Siromani Gurdwara Prabandhak Committee
TISCO	Tata Iron and Steel Company

chapter one

Transition of the Eighteenth Century

1.1. Decline of the Mughal Empire

Founded by Zahiruddin Babur in 1526 and expanded to its full glory by Emperor Akbar in the second half of the sixteenth century, the Mughal empire began to decline rapidly since the reign of its last great ruler Aurangzeb (1658–1707). Even in the first half of the seventeenth century its capital Delhi was considered to be the major power centre in the entire eastern hemisphere; but within fifty years the signs of decline of this mighty empire were unmistakably visible. Some historians ascribe Aurangzeb's divisive policies for this rapid decline—particularly blamed are his religious policies, which alienated the Hindus who constituted the majority of the subject population. His expansionist military campaigns in western India against the two autonomous states of Bijapur and Golconda and against the Marathas are also believed to have sapped the vitality of the empire. But some other historians believe that the roots of Mughal decline lay in institutions and systems intrinsic to Mughal administration, rather than in personalities or specific policies.

There is, however, less dispute about the fact that the process of decline had set in during the time of Aurangzeb and that it could not be arrested by his weak successors. The situation was further worsened by recurrent wars of succession. The Mughal army was weakened, allegedly because of a lamentable dearth of able commanders; there was no military reform and no new technology. This weakening of the Mughal military power encouraged internal rebellions and invited foreign invasions. The Marathas under Shivaji had time and again challenged Aurangzeb's imperial rule. After his death the Maratha plunders increased—in 1738 they plundered even the suburbs of Delhi. This was followed by the Persian invasion under Nadir Shah in 1738–39 and the sack of Delhi, which was a tremendous blow to the prestige of the empire. A brief recovery followed and the first Afghan invasion in 1748 was repelled. But the Afghans under Ahmad Shah Abdali again struck back, took over Punjab and sacked Delhi in 1756–57. To repel the Afghans, the Mughals sought help from the Marathas; but the latter were also defeated by Abdali at the battle of Panipat in 1761. The Afghan menace did not last long, because a revolt in the army forced Abdali to retire to Afghanistan. But the political situation in north India certainly signified the passing of the glorious days of Mughal empire.

Earlier historians like Sir J.N. Sarkar (1932–50) believed that it was a crisis of personality—weak emperors and incompetent commanders were responsible for this downfall of the mighty Mughal empire. But then, other historians like T.G.P. Spear (1973) have pointed out that there was no dearth of able personalities in eighteenth-century India. It was indeed a period marked by the activities of such able politicians and generals as the Sayyid brothers, Nizam-ul-Mulk, Abdus Samad Khan, Zakaria Khan, Saadat Khan, Safdar Jung, Murshid Quli Khan or Sawai Jai Singh. But unfortunately, all these able statesmen were preoccupied more in self-aggrandisement and had little concern for the fate of the empire. So at times of crises, they could not provide leadership and even directly contributed to the process of decline. But this need not be considered as personal failures, as it was more due to the weaknesses inherent in the Mughal institutions, which had evolved gradually in the sixteenth and seventeenth centuries.

The Mughal empire has been described as a "war-state" in its core.[1] It sought to develop a centralised administrative system, whose vitality depended ultimately on its military power. The emperor stood at the apex of this structure, his authority resting primarily on his military might. Below him the other most important element in this structure was the military aristocracy. In the late sixteenth century, Akbar had organised this aristocracy through his *mansabdari* system, which meant a military organisation of the aristocracy, its basis primarily being personal loyalty to the emperor. Every aristocrat was called a *mansabdar*, with a dual numerical rank—*jat* and *sawar*—jat signifying his personal rank and sawar the number of horsemen he was required to maintain. This dual numerical rank also indicated the position of a particular nobleman in the overall Mughal bureaucracy. Sometimes they were paid in cash (*naqdi* mansabdar); but most often they were paid in the form of a jagir or landed estate, the estimated revenue income (*jama*) of which would cover his personal salary and the maintenance allowance for his soldiers and horses. There were two types of jagir—transferable or *tankha* jagir and non-transferable or *vatan* jagir. Most of the jagirs were transferable—the non-transferable jagirs were only a device to incorporate the locally powerful rajahs and zamindars into the Mughal system, by proclaiming their autonomous chiefdoms their vatan jagirs.

Appointment, promotion or dismissal of mansabdars and allocation or transfer of jagirs were done only by the emperor and so the members of the aristocracy only had personal loyalty to the emperor himself. Any form of impersonal loyalty—national, ethnic or religious—could not develop in Mughal India and so the entire imperial edifice stood on a "patron-client relationship" existing between the emperor and the ruling class.[2] The effectiveness and the permanence of this relationship depended on the personal qualities of the emperor and the constant expansion of resources, which explains the constant drive towards territorial conquests in Mughal India. But there were no more conquests since the late years of Aurangzeb, and this was supposedly followed by a period of constant shrinkage of the resources of the empire. This is what ruptured, as some historians argue, the functional relationship between the emperor and the aristocracy, on which depended the efficiency of the imperial administration.

To understand how this diminishing loyalty of the aristocrats could affect the Mughal empire, a close look at the composition of this ruling class is called for. Lineage or ethnic background was the single most important factor in matters of appointment as mansabdars. A great majority of the Mughal nobles were outsiders who had come from various parts of central Asia. But they were gradually Indianised, although this Indianisation took place without any coherent policy of the empire. The aristocracy was therefore divided into various ethno-religious groups, the most powerful among them being the Turani and the Irani groups. Those who came from the Turkish speaking regions of central Asia were called the Turanis, while those who came from the Persian speaking regions of present-day Iran, Afghanistan and Iraq were called the Iranis. The Turanis were Sunnis and the Iranis were Shias, which lent a religious colour to their mutual animosity and jealousy. Though the Mughals belonged to the Turani ethnic lineage, they did not show any personal favour to the Turanis. The other groups among the nobility were the Afghans, Sheikhjadas or the Indian Muslims and the Hindus. The latter group mainly consisted of the Rajputs and Marathas, whose incorporation was because of specific political needs of the empire. After Aurangzeb conquered the two Deccani kingdoms of Bijapur (1685) and Golconda (1689), the noble men who were in the employ of those two kingdoms were absorbed into the Mughal aristocracy and they came to form what is known as the Deccani group. It was primarily during the last years of Aurangzeb, due to the incorporation of the Maratha and Deccani nobles, that the composition of the Mughal aristocracy underwent a dramatic change, which brought to the surface the latent contradictions within its ranks.[3]

The mutual rivalry and competition among these groups of nobles, as it is argued by some historians, came to a head supposedly because of an eighteenth century economic crisis. About four-fifths of the land-revenue income of the Mughal empire was under the control of the mansabdars; but this income was very unevenly distributed. In the middle of the seventeenth century, out of about 8,000 mansabdars, only 445 controlled 61 per cent of the revenue income of the empire.[4] This naturally created jealousy and tension within the aristocracy, particularly when the resources of the empire were stagnant or even diminishing. This economic situation—known as the "jagirdari crisis" of the eighteenth century—has been defined by Satish Chandra in the following words: "The available social surplus was insufficient to defray the cost of administration, pay for wars of one type or another and to give the ruling class a standard of life in keeping with its expectations".[5] This happened because of the unusual increase in the number of mansabdars at a time when the area to be distributed as jagir (or *paibaqi*) remained stagnant or even declined. Revenue collection, particularly in the south, fell far short of the estimated income, diminishing in turn the real income of the jagirdars in disturbed areas. To make matters worse, there was a continuous price rise since the late seventeenth century, as the supply of luxury goods flowed towards the European markets, putting the Mughal aristocracy in further distress.[6] As too many mansabdars were now chasing too few jagirs, many of them had to remain jagirless for years; and even when a jagir was assigned, there was no guarantee that they would not be transferred within a short period. The entire aristocracy, therefore, suffered from a tremendous sense of personal insecurity.

This jagir crisis was not, however, a new phenomenon, as there had always been gaps between collection of revenue and the estimated revenue income of a particular jagir. The crisis increased during the last years of Aurangzeb, mainly because of the Deccan wars. There was now a rise in the number of mansabdars and the political turmoil made the collection of revenue a more difficult task. J.F. Richards (1975) has argued that the problem was to some extent artificial and due to wrong policies of Aurangzeb, who was constantly expanding the size of the royal land or *khalisa*. There was a 23 per cent revenue increase after the conquest of Bijapur and Golconda. But instead of distributing this extra income among his mansabdars, Aurangzeb wanted to use these resources to finance his Deccan campaign. So the newly conquered lands were incorporated into the royal khalisa land, its revenue income going directly into the imperial treasury to meet the salary demands of the soldiers fighting in the south. An opportunity to solve the jagirdari crisis was thus lost and therefore Richards thinks that this crisis was artificial and not due to any real scarcity of resources. He has shown, however, that revenue collections in the Deccan were gradually falling, while Satish Chandra argues that Deccan always was a deficit area. So, it is difficult to say conclusively how the conquest of Bijapur and Golconda would have really solved the jagir problem.

But whether artificial or real, the jagir crisis is believed to have led to an unhealthy competition among the nobles in order to have control over good jagirs. Group politics at the Mughal court became an order of the day, each group wanting to have influence over the emperor to get access to good jagirs. After the death of Bahadur Shah in 1712, the problem reached crisis proportions, as now the low-ranking officials found it real hard to maintain their lifestyle with what they got from their jagirs, as revenue collection became increasingly difficult. The problem intensified further during the reigns of Jahandar Shah (1712–13) and Farruksiyar (1713–19). It did not improve at all during the reign of Muhammad Shah (1719–48), when mansabdari ranks were distributed indiscriminately for political reasons, leading to further inflation in the numbers of aristocrats. To meet their increasing demands, portions of khalisa land were converted into jagir. This measure could not fully solve the problems of the mansabdars, but impoverished the emperor. Nizam-ul-Mulk, after becoming wazir (prime minister) tried to solve the problem through a redistribution of land. But he could not follow it through, because of strong opposition from within the court.[7]

Politicking at the imperial court was at its height during this time. More generally, the Mughal nobility was divided into three warring factions: the Irani group led by Asad Khan and his son Julfiqar Khan, the Turani group, led by Ghazi Uddin Khan, Feroz Jung and his son Chin Qulich Khan (Nizam-ul-Mulk) and the Hindustani group led by the Sayyid brothers, Khan-i-Dauran, some Afghan leaders and some Hindus. These factions were not organised around ethnicity or religion, but more on family ties, personal friendship and above all selfish interests. This faction fighting never went beyond

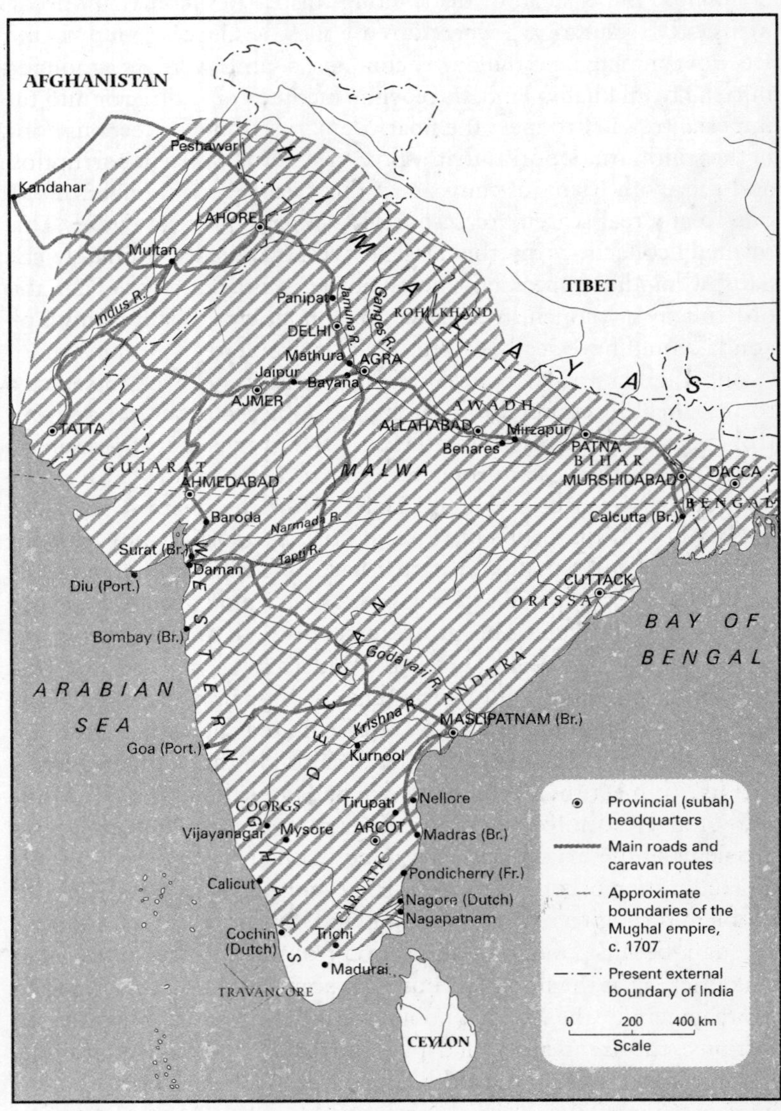

MAP 1: The Mughal empire in 1707

the imperial court, nor lapsed into violent confrontations. No one questioned the divine right of the Timurids to rule; but every group tried to extend their influence over the emperors to control the distribution of patronage. Proximity of any particular group to the centre of power naturally alienated the others and this gradually affected the personal bonds of loyalty between the emperor and his noblemen, as disaffected groups found no reason to espouse the cause of the empire. And what was worse, this resulted in corruption in the army. No mansabdar maintained the required number of soldiers and horses and there was no effective supervision either. This weakening of the army was fatal for the empire, as ultimately the stability of the empire depended on its military might. That the Mughal army was no longer invincible was successfully shown by the Maratha leader Shivaji. This decline of the army became more palpable, as there was no fresh technological input or organisational innovation. The nobles now were more interested in carving out autonomous or semi-autonomous principalities for themselves, which resulted in a virtual fragmentation of the empire.

Recurring peasant revolts in the late seventeenth and the early eighteenth centuries are also believed to have been a major cause of the decline of the Mughal empire and it is not unlikely that the crisis of the ruling elites had something to do with them. An empire imposed from above and its gradually increasing economic pressures were perhaps never fully accepted by the rural society; and the regional sentiments against a centralised power had also been there. Peasant unrest was therefore a recurrent theme in the history of the Mughal state ever since its inception. But fear of the Mughal army always acted as a deterrent and prevented the problem from blowing out of proportion. In the late seventeenth to eighteenth centuries, as the weaknesses of the central power became apparent and the Mughal army faced successive debacles, and at the same time the oppression of the Mughal ruling class increased, resistance to imperial authority also became widespread and more resolute. In most cases, these rebellions were led by the disaffected local zamindars and backed fully by the oppressed peasantry. Eventually the combined pressure of the zamindars and peasants often proved to be too much for the Mughal authority to withstand.

These revolts can be interpreted in various ways. They can be portrayed as political assertion of regional and communitarian identities against an intruding centralising power or as reactions against the bigoted religious policies of Aurangzeb. The latter interpretation seems to be more unlikely, as in the later part of his reign, Aurangzeb was showing more liberalism towards the non-believers and in fact wooing many of the Hindu local chieftains in a cool calculating move to win their loyalty and solve the political problems of the empire by isolating his enemies.[8] But the real reasons behind these revolts, as some historians argue on the other hand, could be found in the property-relations of the Mughal empire. Whether or not the emperor was the owner of all lands in his empire is a debatable issue; but he certainly had an unquestionable right over the income of the land which was collected in the form of land revenue, the amount of which was gradually increasing since the Sultani period. Irfan Habib (1963) has shown that the Mughal land-revenue system rested on a compromise: the peasant was left with sufficient provision for subsistence, while the surplus, as far as possible, was extracted by the state in the form of land revenue. It is not true that the Mughal peasant was left with no surplus at all; for continuing production, he was certainly left with some, while differentiation within the peasantry also indicates that. But on the whole, although larger peasants could withstand the pressure, the smaller peasantry increasingly felt oppressed.[9] Usually in the *zabt* areas (where a detailed land survey was undertaken) the revenue demand was one-third of the produce, but the actual amount varied from region to region. In some areas it was half of the produce and in fertile regions like Gujarat it was as high as three-fourths. Part of it, collected from the khalisa land, went to the imperial treasury, while the larger portion (80 per cent in Aurangzeb's time) went to the jagirdars.

Below the demand of the state and above that of the peasants, there was another kind of demand on the income of the land, and that was the demand of the local landlords or zamindars. There was differentiation among the zamindars.[10] Some of them, like the Rajput chiefs of Rajasthan, were fairly big rajas with considerable local political power. They were incorporated into the Mughal bureaucracy, as in return for a fixed payment (*peshkash*) and loyalty to the emperor, their autonomous power over their own territory or *vatan* was recognised. At the bottom were the *mulgujari* or primary zamindars, who had an independent right over the land and in many cases it was through them that revenue was collected from the peasants and in return they got *nankar* or revenue-free land. Between these two groups were the intermediary zamindars who collected revenue from their own zamindari as well from other primary zamindars. Below the zamindars were the peasants who were also differentiated: the *khudkashts* were peasants with occupancy rights, while the *pahikashts* were vagrant peasants. There were close community relations based on caste, clan and religion between the primary zamindars and the peasants. This was an important source of power for the zamindars, many of whom controlled small armies and forts. The Mughal administration in the interior could not therefore function without their active cooperation. Akbar had tried to turn the zamindars into collaborators; but from the late years of Aurangzeb, particularly after the war of succession (1707–8) following his death, the loyalty of the zamindars definitely began to flounder.[11] In the Deccan, towards the last years of Bahadur Shah's reign, all the zamindars, both primary and intermediary, turned against the Mughal state with the active support of the hardpressed peasantry.[12]

One major reason for the open defiance of the local landlords might have been the increasing oppression of the jagirdars. The earlier emperors tried to keep them in check through a system of rotation. Irfan Habib (1963) has argued that because of this Mughal system, and by taking advantage of it, the jagirdars oppressed the peasantry. As they were frequently transferred, they did not develop any attachment or any long-term interest in the estate and tried to exact as much as possible during their short tenures, without any consideration for the peasants. Their natural oppressive propensities remained within certain limits only because of constant imperial supervision; but this supervisory system totally collapsed in the eighteenth century. The overmighty nobles who could resist or defy transfer, developed local power bases and by using that tried to extract as much as possible. This trend was quite visible in Golconda after its subjugation.[13] Later, in the last years of Bahadur Shah's reign, a number of jagirdars in the Deccan made compromises with the Maratha *sardars* (chiefs) and that arrangement allowed them to collect as much as possible from the peasantry. Sometimes they collected advances from the *amils* (revenue officials), who in turn extorted as much as they could from the peasants.[14] On the other hand, those who were more frequently transferred found the local conditions too turbulent for the collection of revenue. To solve this problem and to squeeze maximum benefit within a short period, they devised the *ijaradari* system, through which revenue-collecting right was farmed out to the highest bidder. The revenue farmer's demand was often much higher than the actual revenue demand and the pressures ultimately moved downward to the primary zamindars and the peasants. During the time of Farruksiyar's reign even khalisa lands were being given over to the ijaradars.

The Mughal compromise is believed to have completely broken down as a result, and the primary zamindars began to defy the Mughal state for their own share of the surplus. In the outlying and more disturbed areas, such as Deccan, zamindari defiance became an order of the day. Even in the heart of Mughal north India in the eighteenth century, there was a widespread tendency among the zamindars to defy the central authority, withhold revenue payment and to resist the Mughal state when it forcibly tried to collect it.[15] Because of their community ties with the peasants, they could easily mobilise them against the Mughal power. For the peasants also, this zamindari initiative solved the problem of leadership, as they often found it difficult to challenge on their own a centralised authority and continue their struggle for a very long time. The peasant grievances in late Mughal period were, therefore, often organised around religious and regional identities. The Maratha sardars took advantage of the peasant grievances; the Jat peasants were mobilised in north India by their zamindars; the Sikhs rose in revolt in Punjab; and the Rajput chiefs withdrew their allegiance in Rajasthan. All these revolts led to the formation of autonomous kingdoms in different parts of the empire, further attenuating the authority of the Mughals. The eighteenth century thus witnessed the rise of a variety of regional states, some of which built on "older local or regional tradition(s) of state formation", others focused on ethnic identity and associated "notions of 'community'".[16] By the end of the century, effective rule of the Mughal emperor was confined only to a narrow stretch around the capital city of Delhi. In 1858 when the English deposed the last emperor Bahadur Shah II, they only ended the fiction of his imperium.

To some historians, however, poverty and economic pressure do not seem to be a wholly adequate explanation for these rebellions and the eventual decline of the Mughal state, since there had been significant regional variations in local economies. The recent 'revisionist' literature, therefore, wants us to move away from this centrist view and to look at the situation from a different perspective—the perspective of the periphery. The Mughal decline, according to this new history, is the result of the rise of new groups into economic and political power and the inability of a distant and weakened centre to control them any longer. In the entire history of Mughal empire there is more evidence of prosperity and growth than of decline and crisis. There is no denying that even in the eighteenth century there had been regions with surplus resources, like for example, Moradabad-Bareilly, Awadh and Banaras; but the Mughal state could not appropriate this surplus and the resources accumulated in the hands of local zamindars.[17] Bengal was another surplus area. In eastern Bengal, vast stretches of forest land was being reclaimed around this time and the settlers of these new areas gave distinct religious and political orientation to their newly established agrarian communities, while the provincial officials could easily carve out for themselves new revenue units around these agrarian settlements.[18] The rising agricultural production in some areas and monetisation of the economy, in other words, made available more resources at the disposal of the zamindars and peasants, and powerful local lineages, who gained distinctively greater advantage and confidence vis-à-vis the imperial centre.[19] Taking advantage of a weakening central control, they now found it more convenient to repudiate their allegiance to a centralised imperial power and assert their autonomy, while still maintaining the cultural and ideological framework of the Mughal state.

Possibilities for such diffusion of power had always been there in Mughal India, it has been argued. There were corporate groups and social classes who enjoyed, despite a supposedly obtrusive central authority, various kinds of rights that constituted, in C.A. Bayly's terminology, their "portfolio capital", which they could invest to reap huge profits.[20] According to this school of history, throughout the Mughal period there had been a constant process of reconciliation and adjustment between the central power and the regional elite. Mughal sovereignty, as Andre Wink has argued, rested on a "balancing system of continually shifting rivalries and alliances." The Mughal system was prepared to accommodate "*fitna*" or sedition, and always tried to incorporate the ascendant localised powers, either indigenous or foreign, into its concept of universal dominion and on the effective functioning of this mechanism of conciliation and coercion depended its continued existence.[21] The Mughal process of centralisation, in other words, left enough space for the continued existence of rival principles of organisation. Frank Perlin, in this context, has talked about the existence of a "'library' of categories and techniques", implying a multiplicity of systems of governance, methods of measurement and techniques of collecting revenue, varying widely in space and time. There was multiplicity of rights, like the concept of vatan in the Deccan, which meant heritable rights that could not be taken away even by kings. Attempts at centralisation could not eliminate those rights in the eighteenth century.[22] So, as Muzaffar Alam sums up the situation, around this time, because of decentralisation and commercialisation, a group of "upstarts" had come to monopolise the resources of the empire at the exclusion of the hereditary Mughal nobility or the *khanazads*.[23] These upstarts were the new regional power elite who rose to prominence in the provinces and successfully contested the centralising tendency of the Mughal state. This group included the jagirdars who defied transfer and thus became local rulers, and the revenue farmers—or the new "entrepreneurs in revenue"—who "combined military power with expertise in managing cash and local trade".[24] "Consistent economic growth and prosperity", rather than poverty and crisis, thus provided "the context of the local political turmoil".[25] The Mughal system, in other words, had always left a space for the rise of powerful regional groups and significant economic and social changes in the eighteenth century brought that possibility into sharper focus. But then these new developments were not properly recognised or accommodated within the system, and hence its eventual demise.

It is difficult to arrive at a convenient middle ground between the 'conventional' and 'revisionist' histories; nor is it easy to dismiss either of them. The revisionist history has been taken to task for underestimating the cohesiveness of the Mughal empire and for ignoring the contemporary Muslim concepts of centralised sovereignty. These critics, on the other hand, have been assailed for clinging on to a mindset that is accustomed to look at the Mughal empire only as a centralised structure.[26] If there is any shared ground at all, as Athar Ali admits in his critique of the revisionist historiography, it is in the common recognition of the fact that the zamindars or the intermediary classes "constituted a centrifugal force" in the Mughal structure.[27] We may, however, conclude by saying that the idea of 'decline' is perhaps an inadequate theme for understanding the eighteenth century in Indian history. The Mughal system continued even long after the de facto demise of the empire, which was followed by the emergence of a number of regional powers. The eighteenth century in Indian history is not a dark age, nor an age of overall decline. The decline of one pan-Indian empire was followed by the rise of another, the intervening period being dominated by a variety of powerful regional states. This century should, therefore, be considered, as Satish Chandra (1991) has argued, as a distinct chronological whole.

1.2. EMERGENCE OF THE REGIONAL POWERS

By 1761 the Mughal empire was empire only in name, as its weaknesses had enabled the local powers to assert their independence. Yet the symbolic authority of the Mughal emperor continued, as he was still considered to be a source of political legitimacy. The new states did not directly challenge his authority and constantly sought his sanction to legitimise their rule. In many areas of governance these states continued the Mughal institutions and the administrative system; where changes occurred—and they did occur, of course—they came rather slowly, to accommodate the altered power relations in the regions. The emergence of these states in the eighteenth century, therefore, represented a transformation rather than collapse of the polity. It signified a decentralisation of power and not a power vacuum or political chaos. These new states were of various kinds with diverse histories: some of them were founded by Mughal provincial governors, some were set up by the rebels against the Mughal state; and a few states which asserted their independence were previously functioning as autonomous but dependent polities.

Bengal, Hyderabad and Awadh were the three successor states of the Mughal empire, in the sense that they were founded by Mughal provincial governors who never formally severed their links with the centre, but virtually exercised autonomy in matters of execution of power at the local level. The province or the *subah* of Bengal gradually became independent of Mughal control after Murshid Quli Khan became the governor in 1717.[28] Initially, Aurangzeb had appointed him the *diwan* (collector of revenue) of Bengal to streamline the revenue administration of the province. Then in 1710 Bahadur Shah reappointed him in this position after a short break of two years. When Farruksiyar became the emperor, he confirmed Murshid Quli in his position and also appointed him the deputy governor of Bengal and governor of Orissa. Later in 1717 when he was appointed the governor or *Nazim* of Bengal, he was given the unprecedented privilege of holding the two offices of nazim and diwan simultaneously. The division of power, which was maintained throughout the Mughal period to keep both the imperial officers under control through a system of checks and balances, was thus done away with. This helped Murshid Quli, who was already known for his efficient revenue administration, to consolidate his position further. He did not of course formally defy Mughal authority and regularly sent revenue to the imperial treasury. Indeed, the Bengal revenue was often the only regular income for the beleaguered Mughal emperors during periods of financial stringency and uncertainty. But behind the veneer of formal allegiance to the Timurid rulers, Murshid Quli began to enjoy a considerable amount of autonomy within his own domain and initiated almost a dynastic rule. He was indeed the last governor of Bengal appointed by the Mughal emperor.

The foundation of Murshid Quli's power was of course his very successful revenue administration, which even in the days of political chaos elsewhere in the empire, made Bengal a constant revenue paying surplus area. It is difficult to determine whether or not he was oppressive or that revenue demand during his period increased significantly; but revenue collection had shot up by 20 per cent between 1700 and 1722. This efficient collection system was operated through powerful intermediary zamindars. Murshid Quli sent his investigators to every revenue-paying area to make a detailed survey and compelled the zamindars to pay in full and on time. For this purpose, he encouraged the development of a few powerful zamindaris at the expense of smaller inefficiently managed zamindaris, while refractory zamindars were punished and some of the jagirdars were transferred to the outlying province of Orissa, their estates being converted into khalisa or royal land.[29]

The period between 1717 and 1726 therefore witnessed the emergence of a few landed magnates. These magnates assisted the nazim in the timely collection of revenue and with his patronage they also expanded their own estates.[30] Indeed, by the time of Murshid Quli's death in 1727, fifteen largest zamindaris were responsible for about half of the revenue of the province. But along with the rise of the zamindars as a new powerful elite in the province, there was also the growing importance of merchants and bankers during this period. Bengal always had a lucrative trade, and the political stability and increase in agricultural productivity during Murshid Quli's period provided further impetus to such trading activities. In the seventeenth century, silk and cotton textile, sugar, oil and clarified butter from Bengal went through overland route to Persia and Afghanistan via a number of north and west Indian distributing centres and on the oceanic route through the port of Hughli to the Southeast Asian, Persian Gulf and Red Sea ports. During the political turmoil of the eighteenth century, traffic through the overland route partially declined, but oceanic trade thrived with increasing investment from the European Companies—the Dutch, the French and the English. During the first half of the century, Europe certainly became the major destination for goods from Bengal, and this had a significant impact on the textile industry in the region. Bengal always enjoyed a favourable balance of trade, with surplus bullion brought in by the European Companies to buy Bengal goods and this was absorbed smoothly into the cash economy and revenue remittance structure. On the Indian side this trade was dominated by a variety of merchants—Hindus, Muslims and Armenians. Some of them were magnates, like the Hindu merchant Umi Chand or the Armenian tycoon Khoja Wajid who controlled a fleet of ships. And they enjoyed a very cordial relation with the state and bureaucracy, as the Mughal state traditionally never tried to squeeze the merchants.[31] On the other hand, the constant pressure on the zamindars to pay revenue in time and its regular remittance to the imperial treasury in Delhi brought powerful financiers and bankers into great demand. They provided securities at every stage of the transaction and enjoyed unprecedented patronage of the governor, thus providing the main supportive pillar of his power. The most significant story of such collaboration was the rise of the banking house of Jagat Seth, who eventually became the treasurer of the provincial government in 1730, with strategic control over the mint. Apart from zamindars, merchants and bankers, Murshid Quli also ensured the loyalty of the officials, by appointing his friends, relatives and loyalists in important positions and driving his potential enemies out of the province—a situation which could not be dreamt of in the heyday of the Mughal empire.[32]

Murshid Quli, however, never did sever his formal connections with the Mughals and continued to send the annual Bengal revenue to Delhi regularly. But within his own domain he acted as an autonomous ruler and in a true dynastic fashion named his daughter's son Sarfaraz Khan his successor. But Sarfaraz was ousted by his father Shujauddin Muhammad Khan (Murshid Quli's son-in-law), who took control of the two provinces of Bengal and Orissa in 1727 and had his position endorsed by the Mughal emperor Muhammad Shah. He too maintained the relationship with the Mughal court, but enjoyed autonomy in matters of local administration, which was supported by the new forces of Bengal politics, the zamindars, merchants and the bankers. By the 1730s, as Philip Calkins argues, "the government of Bengal began to look more like government by co-operation of the dominant forces in Bengal, rather than the imposition of the rule from outside".[33] However, it is also true that this gradual rise in the power of the merchants, bankers and zamindars also meant a relative diminution of the authority of the nazim. This became quite evident in a coup in 1739–40, in which Shujauddin's son Sarfaraz Khan, who had become the new nazim, was ousted by his army commander Alivardi Khan, with the help of the banking family of Jagat Seths and a few powerful zamindars. Sarfaraz had to go not just because he was an inefficient administrator, but because he had alienated the house of Jagat Seth, and had lost the support of a few powerful officials. With his deposition the office of the nazim went to an able military general, Alivardi Khan, who later obtained imperial sanctions for his appointment.

It was Alivardi's reign, which marked a virtual break with the Mughals. All major appointments were now made without any reference to the emperor and finally, the regular flow of revenue to Delhi was stopped. Although there was never any formal defiance of the Mughal authority, for all practical purposes an autonomous administration, free of all sorts of imperial control, had now emerged in Bengal, Bihar and Orissa. The major problems for Alivardi came from outside: he had to face Maratha depredations and Afghan rebellion. The Marathas from the west in their search for a pan-Indian empire invaded Bengal a number of times, causing immense damage to life and property. Ultimately in 1751, Alivardi came to terms with the Marathas by agreeing to pay *chauth* (one-fourth of the revenue) and handing over Orissa. But in the meanwhile some rebel Afghan troops under the leadership of Mustafa Khan had taken over Patna in 1748 and thus had posed another great challenge to his authority. Alivardi eventually succeeded in putting down the Afghans and recovered Patna. However, one major fallout of the Maratha raids was the disruption of Bengal trade, particularly of the overland trade with north and west India. But it was short-lived and the recovery was aided by a massive increase in European trade, both corporate trade of the Companies and private trade of their officials. They could not immediately dislodge the Indian merchants from the market, but it certainly signified the beginning of European dominance in the trading world of Bengal, preparing the ground for an eventual English takeover of the province[34]—a development we shall discuss in detail later. Alivardi died in 1756, nominating his grandson Siraj-ud-daula his successor. But his succession was challenged by two other contenders for the throne, Shaukat Jung (Faujdar of Purnea) and Ghaseti Begum (Alivardi's daughter). This resulted in intense court factionalism, as the overmighty zamindars and commercial people felt threatened by an extremely ambitious and assertive young nawab.[35] This destabilised the administration of Bengal, and the advantage was taken by the English East India Company, which acquired a foothold in Bengal politics through what is popularly known as the Plassey conspiracy of 1757 that ended the rule of Siraj-ud-daula. This story of yet another transition in Bengal politics we shall see in a short while.

The autonomous kingdom of Hyderabad was founded in 1724 by a powerful noble at the imperial court, Chin Qulich Khan, who eventually took the title of Nizam-ul-Mulk Asaf Jah I. Known as the leader of the Turani party, he felt frustrated in court politics due to the haughty assertion of power by the Indian Muslim faction led by the Sayyid brothers, who had emperor Farruksiyar killed and Muhammad Shah installed on the throne as a puppet ruler in 1719.

To save the Timurid rule from being subverted in this way, Nizam-ul-Mulk organised the Turani and Irani noblemen against the Sayyids and ultimately defeated and killed them in 1720. Muhammad Shah was restored to the throne and Nizam-ul-Mulk acted as his wazir from 1722 to 1724. But eventually he found that carving out an autonomous principality in the Deccan for himself was more attractive.

In Hyderabad, Mubariz Khan, the Mughal governor of Deccan, was ruling almost as an independent king. In 1723 the nizam defeated Mubariz and the following year he took over as the Subahdar of Deccan and consolidated his power around Hyderabad. The actual independence of the Hyderabad kingdom may be dated from 1740 when finally the nizam left north India to settle there permanently. He subdued the refractory zamindars and showed tolerance towards the Hindus who had economic power in their hands and as a result, Hyderabad witnessed the emergence of a new regional elite who supported the nizam. By the time of his death in 1748, the state of Hyderabad was a recognisable power in Deccan politics, acknowledging Mughal suzerainty only in a symbolic sense. Coins were still minted in the name of the Mughal emperor; his name also figured in the *khutba* or the Friday prayers. But for all practical purposes, the nizam acted independently, conducting wars, signing treaties, conferring mansabs and making important appointments without any reference to the emperor.

Soon, however, after the death of the first nizam, Asaf Jah I, Hyderabad began to experience a series of crises. While Maratha depredations continued to be a major source of anxiety, a war of succession ensued between his son Nasir Jung and grandson Muzaffar Jung, the advantage of that disunion being taken by the French under Dupleix. Muzaffar emerged victorious from this contest with French support and gave handsome monetary rewards and territorial concessions to the French. But that did not end his problems, as during the subsequent years, the Marathas, Mysore and the Carnatic—all settled their territorial scores against Hyderabad. The situation improved again after 1762 during the period of Nizam Ali Khan, who seized control of the administration and during his long reign lasting up to 1803, he settled border disputes with his neighbours, giving Hyderabad the much desired political stability.

The Hyderabadi administrative system did not try to destroy the indigenous power structures within the territory, but sought to incorporate them into a "patron-client relationship" with the central power. The locally entrenched semi-autonomous rulers were allowed to govern their inherited territories in return for an annual tribute or peshkash paid to the nizam. The locally powerful traders, moneylenders and the military aristocracy also played a crucial role in the Hyderabad polity, by providing valuable financial and military support to the nizam, who emerged as the chief patron within the polity. Under this new administration, the old Mughal institutions were not totally thrown out, but they underwent substantial changes in content. Land revenue was collected through powerful intermediary revenue farmers; but unlike the Mughal practice, there was very little attempt to keep them under control. The jagirs under this new system became hereditary and the mansabdari system only retained a few of its Mughal features. There was also a remarkable change in the composition of the nobility: while the older military aristocracy retained some of its power, some new men with expertise in revenue and financial management rose from lower ranks. On the whole, "power remained widely diffused" in the Hyderabadi administrative structure.[36] By the end of the eighteenth century, Hyderabad represented a relatively new political system with a whole range of new participants, who had diverse origins and social background.

Another Mughal province that became autonomous in the course of the eighteenth century was Awadh. Saadat Khan was appointed the Mughal governor of Awadh in 1722 with the difficult charge of subduing rebellions by the local rajas and chiefs. He accomplished this task within a year and in appreciation, the emperor Muhammad Shah conferred on him the title of Burhan-ul-Mulk. Soon after this, Saadat Khan returned to the capital to consolidate his position in the imperial court, but ended up in a quarrel with one of Muhammad Shah's favourites and was again forced to return to Awadh. Frustrated in court politics, Saadat then decided to build up a power base in Awadh and as a first step had his son-in-law Safdar Jung recognised by the emperor as his deputy governor. The other step towards the establishment of his dynastic rule was to make the office of diwan virtually independent of all imperial control. The revenues of Awadh from then on were handled by a Punjabi Khatri official who functioned under Saadat Khan and never reported anything to the imperial office.

The problem of refractory zamindars in Awadh was solved in time and a new land revenue settlement was introduced with the revenue demand increasing by more than half. The jagirdari system was reformed, with jagirs being granted to the local gentry, while a rich flow of trade kept the province affluent. This resulted in the creation of a new regional ruling elite, consisting mainly of Indian Muslims, Afghans and Hindus who became Saadat's main support base. But the latter kept the communication channels open with the imperial court. Indeed, during this whole period he constantly expanded the frontiers of the Awadh subah, but never without the formal approval of the emperor. He also nurtured his old ambitions in imperial court politics, but only to be frustrated again in 1739–40 when the position of *mir bakshi* (imperial treasurer) went to the nizam, despite the services he had rendered during the invasion of the Persian king Nadir Shah. He considered this a betrayal and in vengeance changed sides to join the Persian invader. But he could not suffer the arrogance and haughty behaviour of Nadir Shah and the day after the occupation of Delhi, in sheer frustration and despondency, he poisoned himself to death. However, by the time he died in 1740, Saadat had certainly developed in Awadh a semi-autonomous regional political system, with vastly reduced financial commitment to, but no formal disjunction with, the Mughal state.

Nadir Shah remained the emperor of India for just two months and he settled the succession question in Awadh by accepting twenty million rupees as peshkash from Safdar Jung. Muhammad Shah later confirmed this appointment and conferred on him an imperial title. But Safdar Jung's opportunities really came when both Muhammad Shah and the Nizam-ul-Mulk died in 1748 and he was appointed wazir by the new emperor Ahmad Shah. Safdar Jung extended his sphere of influence by using the new imperial position, the most important of these gains being the seizure of Farukhabad from the Pathans. But on the other hand, this self-aggrandisement of the wazir soon alienated both the imperial family as well as the court nobles who ultimately contrived his ouster in 1753. The year marked an important turning point in the political history of north India, as Richard Barnett points out, by signifying "the visible secession of Awadh and Allahabad from the remainder of the dwindling empire".[37] The formal connection was yet to be severed fully. After Safdar Jung's death in late 1754, his only son Shuja-ud-daula was again appointed the governor of Awadh by the puppet emperor Alamgir II. And Shuja too successfully maintained the autonomy of the Awadh subah without ever formally defying the symbolic authority of the Mughal emperor. When in December 1759 on the death of Alamgir II, the fugitive crown prince staged his own coronation as Shah Alam II, he named Shuja his wazir. Although this position was merely fictional, Shuja maintained his power within his own domain and was a much sought after ally for both the parties when Afghan leader Ahmad Shah Abdali arrived again in India to engage the Marathas in the Third Battle of Panipat (1761). Shuja joined the Afghan invader to see his local opponents, the Marathas, humbled and weakened; but throughout this confrontation he behaved like an independent partner in an alliance of equals. Within his own domain of Awadh and Allahabad his autonomy and power remained unchallenged till his encounter with the English East India Company in 1764.[38]

Apart from these successor states formed by Mughal governors, the other states that emerged in eighteenth-century India were those founded by rebels against the Mughal state, such as the Marathas, the Sikhs, the Jats and the Afghan kingdoms of Farukhabad and Rohilkhand. Among them it was perhaps only the Maratha state that had the potential to develop into a new pan-Indian empire replacing the Mughals; but that potential was never fully realised because of the nature of the Maratha polity itself. In the seventeenth century it began as a small kingdom in western India, founded by the legendary Maratha chief Shivaji, against stiff opposition from the local Muslim kingdom of Bijapur and the pressure of the mighty Mughal army. Soon after his death in 1680, it was troubled by dynastic factionalism and the constant pressure of the Mughal policy of conquest in the Deccan. Local *deshmukhs* (revenue officers) and zamindars took advantage of the situation by sometimes aligning with the Mughals and sometimes joining hands with the Marathas. Two of Shivaji's sons, first Shambhaji and then Rajaram, ruled briefly and battled incessantly with the Mughal army. When Rajaram died in 1699, one of his queens, Tarabai, began to rule in the name of her infant son Shivaji II; but Aurangzeb's army during this period conquered Maratha forts one after another, keeping Tarabai constantly on the move. From late 1705, however, the tide began to turn against Aurangzeb and when he died in 1707 after forty years of futile warfare in the Deccan, the Marathas still remained to be subjugated.

The Maratha kingdom was, however, certainly weakened and the process was further exacerbated after the release of Shahu, Shivaji's grandson, from the Mughal prison in 1707. There were now two rival contenders for the throne and during the next eight years, Maharashtra was immersed in a full-scale civil war between the forces of Shahu and those of Tarabai, who intended to rule in the name of Shivaji II. The loyalty of the Maratha sardars and deshmukhs shifted constantly between the two Maratha factions and the Mughals, the situation of anarchy becoming all-pervasive by 1712–13. But, helped by a group of new independent sardars, as well as a number of Brahman banking families, and an able Chitpavan Brahman *peshwa* (prime minister), Balaji Vishwanath, Shahu ultimately

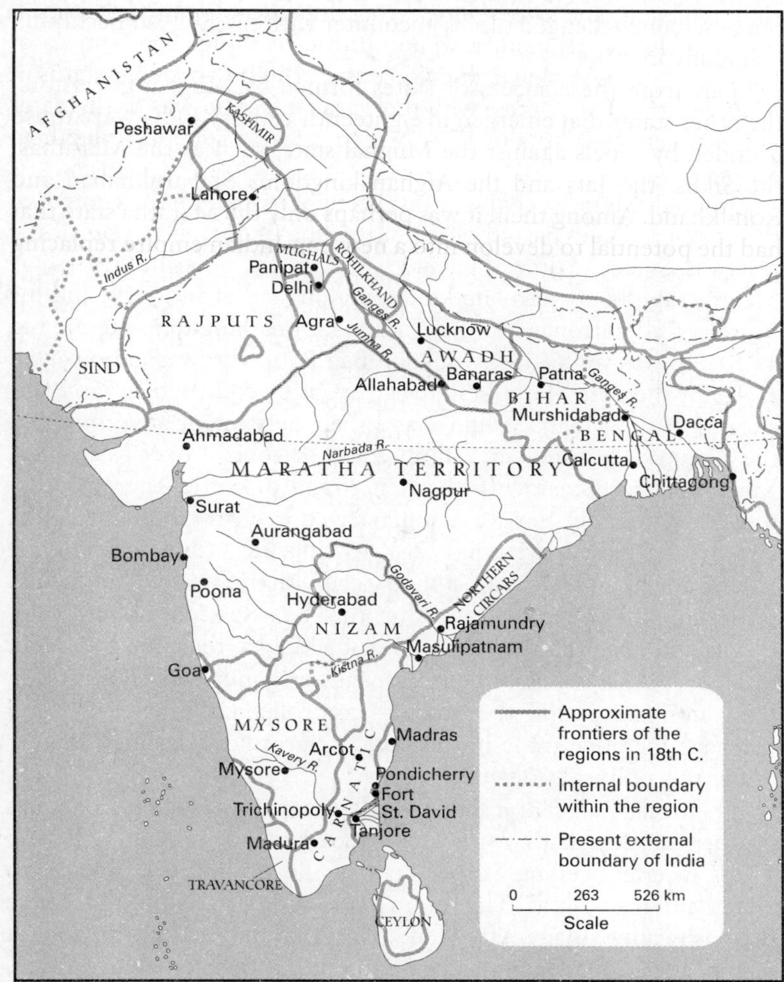

MAP 2: The regional powers of the eighteenth century

emerged victorious from this contest and by 1718–19 he consolidated his position firmly. In 1719, by helping the Sayyid brothers establish a puppet emperor in Delhi, Balaji Viswanath secured for his master a Mughal *sanad* (imperial order) recognising Shahu's right to chauth and *sardeshmukhi* (one-fourth and one-tenth respectively of the government revenue) in the six Mughal provinces of Deccan, chauth of Malwa and Gujarat and an independent status in Maharashtra. The contest with the Tarabai faction was settled later in the Treaty of Warna in 1731, which gave the state of Kolapur to Shivaji II.

Although Maratha civil war was brought to an end, the control of the state gradually passed on from the line of Shivaji to that of the peshwas. Since the time of Balaji Viswanath, the office of the peshwa became rapidly powerful and the fountainhead of authority and the source of all patronage in the entire Maratha kingdom. He died in 1720 and was succeeded by his son Baji Rao, who was in power till 1740. By then the Maratha state had acquired control over large territories of the Mughal empire, and their only major adversary was the Nizam of Hyderabad, as both vied for control over Karnataka, Khandesh and Gujarat. In the first round of battle, the Marathas were defeated; but this was soon avenged in a resounding Maratha victory at Palkhed (March 1728), forcing the nizam to recognise Shahu as the sole Maratha monarch with rights to chauth and sardeshmukhi of the Deccan. After that Baji Rao led military campaigns and acquired the fertile lands of Malwa, reaching Rajasthan by 1729.[39] Meanwhile in Gujarat, Maratha bands collected taxes in the countryside, while the Mughals controlled only the cities[40] and the once lucrative trade in the port of Surat now declined rapidly under this political pressure.[41]

When Baji Rao sent a large Maratha army to Gujarat under his brother, the Mughal governor concluded two treaties in 1727 and 1728, in effect ceding 60 per cent of the revenues of Gujarat to Shahu and his peshwa. The nizam made another attempt to humble the peshwa by allying with some rival Maratha factions in Gujarat (Gaikwad, Dabhade and Kadam Bande); but their combined forces were finally defeated by the peshwa's army in 1731. Some time later Baji Rao's attention was directed towards the coastal plains of Konkan, where by 1736 he gained control over the territories of the Sidis (Abyssinian Muslims) and drove the Portuguese out of Salsette, Bassein and Chaul. Then again he returned to the north and in 1737 attacked Delhi and held the emperor captive for some time. The following year, he defeated a huge Mughal army under the generalship of nizam and the treaty of Bhopal that followed in January 1739 ceded to the peshwa the subah of Malwa and sovereignty over all lands between the rivers Narmada and Chambal. In these territories, however, the Marathas did not try to overturn the local power structure and quickly entered into negotiations with the local zamindars for the payment of yearly tributes. A civilian system of revenue administration took time to emerge in this newly conquered region and this was a feature typical of all Maratha conquests.

After the death of Baji Rao in 1740, Shahu appointed his son Balaji Bajirao, better known as Nana Saheb (1740–61), in his place. More experienced in administration than in military campaigns,[42] he was, however, the most successful among the peshwas. Nana Saheb became the supreme authority in the Maratha polity after the death of Shahu in 1749. This was indeed the peak period of Maratha glory when all parts of India had to face Maratha depredations. In the east, from 1745 onwards Maratha bands under Raghuji Bhonsle of Nagpur regularly raided Orissa, Bengal and Bihar, then ruled autonomously by Alivardi Khan. A treaty in 1751 stopped these raids, as Alivardi surrendered Orissa and agreed to pay Rs. 120,000 as annual chauth payment for the three provinces. Near at home, the Maratha forces regularly raided the nizam's territories in Konkan, exacted tributes, but never succeeded in completely subduing them. In the north, by the treaty of Bhalke in 1751, Salabut Jung, the new nizam, practically ceded the entire control of Khandesh. Further north, the Maratha bands regularly raided the Rajput kingdoms of Jaipur, Bundi, Kotah and Udaipur and the Gond kingdom of Deogarh. They intervened in their wars of succession, exacted annual tributes from their rulers, but never tried to have any permanent conquest in the region. In the face of an Afghan invasion overrunning Lahore and Multan, a treaty in 1752 brought the Mughal emperor under the protection of the Marathas; and a succession dispute in 1753 gave them the opportunity to install their own chosen candidate on the Mughal throne. The Maratha expedition to Punjab was, however, short-lived and soon a Sikh rebellion put an end to Maratha authority in this region. In any case, the Marathas by then had gained mastery over large parts of north India; but there was never any attempt to establish an empire. It was only in Khandesh, Malwa and Gujarat that they tried to put in place some kind of an administration; their conquest elsewhere would seldom go beyond plunder and levying of chauth and sardeshmukhi. As a result, it was difficult to maintain this mastery and soon an Afghan invasion under Ahmad Shah Abdali dealt a deadly blow to Maratha glory.

Abdali, though troubled by lack of discipline in his army, was supported in this contest by a number of other indigenous forces, like the Rohillas and Shuja-ud-daula of Awadh. In the crucial Third Battle of Panipat fought on 14 January 1761, the Maratha forces under Sadasiv Rao Bhao were routed by Abdali, causing about fifty thousand casualties. This marked the beginning of the decline of Maratha power. The peshwa died within weeks and as the young peshwa Madhav Rao tried to gain control of the polity, factionalism among the Maratha sardars raised its ugly head. This faction fighting increased further after Madhav Rao's death in 1772. His uncle Raghunath Rao seized power, but was opposed by a number of important Maratha chiefs. To consolidate his position, he found a new ally in the English, then stationed in Bombay; but this took Maratha history into an entirely different trajectory, as the English had by then emerged as a new contender for power in the turbulent politics of eighteenth-century India.[43]

The Maratha state could not become an alternative to Mughal empire because of its own structure. Its nature was that of a confederacy where power was shared among the chiefs or sardars, like the Bhonsles of Nagpur, Gaikwad of Baroda, Holkar of Indore or Sindhia of Gwalior, all of whom had made their fortunes as military leaders since the days of Shahu. Parts of the Maratha state had been alienated to these military commanders and it was difficult to control these chiefs, who did not like the peshwa regulating their activities. What resulted soon was increasing factional rivalry among the Maratha sardars and although there was always a strong centre, the composition of the inner circle of power changed from generation to generation. At the lower level, as mentioned earlier, there was the existence of heritable vatan rights, like those of the village headmen, *mirasidars* and deshmukhs, which could not be taken away by kings. The regional assemblies of vatandars exercised political power and resolved disputes at a local level, thus representing local loyalties as opposed to any centralised concept of kingship. The Maratha state, in order to establish its control over the territory and consolidate the powerbase of its new ruling class, sought to peripheralise the regional assemblies in the seventeenth and early eighteenth centuries. It tried to replace the horizontal ethos of "brotherhood" of the vatandars with the vertical relationship of service by generously distributing among its clients temporary and transferable land rights or *saranjam* that resembled Mughal jagir. But the old system could not be displaced, as the new system of prebended lordship, as Frank Perlin has argued, often cut across the traditional hierarchies of status. So the same locally powerful Brahman or Maratha individuals now enjoyed a "bundle" of different kinds of rights. Local loyalties and centralised kingship thus continued to exist in Deccan through a continuous process of adjustment and balancing.[44]

There is a significant debate about the relationship between the Maratha state and the Mughal system, as some historians emphasise its rebel nature. Irfan Habib (1963) thinks that it was the outcome of a zamindar revolt against an oppressive Mughal bureaucracy. Satish Chandra (1993) has argued about its regional nature; although Baji Rao made a move towards north India, his major aim was only to establish supremacy in the Deccan. In other words, the Maratha state is often seen as a departure from the Mughal tradition. But some other historians like Andre Wink have argued that the Marathas were also very much within the Mughal tradition, as they had built their power on the notion of sedition or *fitva* (the Deccani corruption of the word *fitna*), which the Mughal state always provided a space for. There was no "rebellion" as such, as "concurrent rights ... constituted sovereignty".[45] Even in the 1770s the Marathas acknowledged the symbolic authority of the Mughal emperor and in Malwa, Khandesh and parts of Gujarat, where they established some sort of administration, it looked very much like the Mughal system. The old terminology was retained and even the differential urban tax rates continued to favour the Muslims. The only difference was that in the Maratha territories there were many civilian revenue collectors, mainly Brahmans, who did not move on to military command, as was the custom in the Mughal system where there was only one unified civilian/military bureaucracy.[46] Other than this, the Mughal tradition remained central to social and political life of the Maratha state system, although, as we have noted earlier, it had to contend continually with local loyalties. Existing political conflicts between warrior families were resolved through a combination of coercion and conciliation, the deshmukhs remaining the co-sharers in the polity and rights being granted for building kingdoms. The Maratha state ultimately declined not so much because of factionalism, but because of the increasing power of the English in the Deccan. It was difficult for the Marathas to resist this efficient army.

Turning to north India in the eighteenth century, we find that the history of the Sikh *Panth* in Punjab was as old as that of the Mughal empire. When Guru Nanak, born in 1469, began to preach his message of inner devotion and equality among all human beings, Babur was founding the Mughal empire. Within the *bhakti* or *sant* tradition of medieval India, this was the beginning of Sikhism, which gradually began to attract millions of devotees and started acquiring its shape and definition under the leadership of the subsequent gurus.[47] Aurangzeb was initially not very hostile to the Sikhs; but as the community grew in size and challenged the central authority of the Mughals, the emperor turned against them and Guru Tegbahadur, the ninth in line, was executed in Delhi in 1675.

The tenth guru, Guru Gobind Singh, took an important step in 1699; he transformed the Sikhs into a military organisation by establishing the brotherhood of *Khalsa*. It was a ceremony in which the guru himself (and not his deputies or *masands*) initiated the disciples, who were obliged to maintain five distinctive insignia—including unkempt hair and carrying of weapons—that would publicly proclaim their identity. Why he did it is a matter of conjecture. One reason possibly was the continuing conflict with the Mughals, which had convinced the gurus, first Guru Hargobind and then Guru Gobind Singh, about the necessity of armed resistance for the defence of the Panth.[48] It was also probably because of the rise of the Jat peasantry among the Sikhs, as carrying arms and resolving disputes through the use of arms were already part of Jat cultural tradition and to which the other components of the Sikh community, the Khatri traders, were not perhaps very averse to.[49] The founding of the Khalsa projected the Sikh community as a militant outfit, although all Sikhs were not necessarily its members. The Jat peasants continued to dominate the Khalsa at the expense of the older Khatri leadership. Their aspiration for equality was further fulfilled when Guru Gobind Singh decided to terminate the position of guru after his death; the power of the guru henceforth was to be vested in the Panth and the *Granth* (sacred texts). Thus, by invoking cultural resources, such as the sacred texts, and prescribing initiation and other life-cycle rituals, the Khalsa sought to provide order in the life of the Sikhs in otherwise uncertain days of the eighteenth century, and in this way tried to construct a distinctive Sikh social and political identity.[50]

Guru Gobind's open quarrel with the Mughals followed a complex trajectory. From about 1696 he tried to carve out an autonomous domain in and around Anandpur, which brought the hostility of the hill chiefs of Himachal Pradesh, who approached the Mughal faujdar for protection. The siege of Anandpur by a combined force in 1704 compelled Guru Gobind to leave; but Aurangzeb, then busy in Deccan, soon reversed the stand and sought to conciliate the guru. After Aurangzeb's death, Guru Gobind met Bahadur Shah at Agra in 1707 and he promised to return Anandpur. However, the new emperor had to appease the hill chiefs as well, and therefore continued to postpone his final decision. In the meanwhile, on

7 October 1708, Guru Gobind was murdered in a conspiracy,[51] and his mantle then fell on one of his followers, Banda Bahadur, who continued the Sikh revolt. The stage of the contest now shifted to Majha (between the rivers Beas and Ravi) and Doab (between rivers Beas and Sutlej) regions, where lived mainly the Jat peasants. Mughal oppression around this time put tremendous pressure on the small zamindars and peasants. Not all of them, it is true, supported Banda Bahadur, whose main supporters were the small mulguzari zamindars of the Jat community. Within a year a large area between the rivers Jamuna and Ravi came under his influence and here he promptly established his own administration, appointed his own faujdars, diwan and kardars, minted a new coin and used his own seal for issuing orders.[52]

In 1710, Bahadur Shah proceeded to Punjab, but failed to crush the Sikh revolt. When Farruksiyar ascended the throne in 1713, he appointed Abdus Samad Khan the faujdar of Lahore and gave him special orders to put an end to the Sikh upsurge. The position of Banda Bahadur had also weakened by then to some extent, because of internal dissension within the Sikh community. Although in general the Jat peasants supported him, some of the Jat zamindars went to the Mughal side, Churaman Jat of Agra being a major example. The Khatri business class from around 1710 also went against the Sikh movement, as political stability and security of trade routes were essential to the smooth running of their business. At the same time, when the Mughals introduced the ijaradari system in Punjab for collecting land revenue, many of the Khatri traders became revenue farmers and this naturally linked their interests to those of the Mughal state. The emperors also tried to take advantage of this internal dissension within the Punjab society, as during the time of Jahandar Shah and Farruksiyar, many Khatris were given high positions within the Mughal nobility. Farruksiyar tried to use Guru Gobind's widow to drive a wedge between Banda and his Sikh followers. This did not necessarily weaken Banda's movement, as oppressive Khatri ijaradars often drove desperate Jat peasants into the rebel's camp. But ultimately in 1715 Banda had to surrender to Abdus Samad Khan. He was taken to Delhi along with some of his close followers; in March 1716 all of them were executed.

The execution of Banda did not mean the end of Sikh power in Punjab, although there was no one immediately available to take up the leadership. But even in spite of the absence of a centralised leadership, roving bands of Sikh rebels took advantage of the breakdown of imperial control in north India to assert their independence, despite the best efforts of Zakaria Khan who had succeeded his father Abdus Samad Khan as the Mughal governor of Lahore. Even the Afghan invader Ahmad Shah Abdali failed to bring Punjab under his command; his governors were soon thrown out and by September 1761 the Sikhs came to control wide regions of Punjab from rivers Sutlej to Indus. Abdali himself came to Punjab in 1765, but retired soon to Kabul without fighting a single battle. The Sikhs once again established their political power in Punjab once Abdali retired from the Indian scene. But at this stage, power in the Sikh polity became more horizontally structured, as *misls*, or combinations based on kinship ties, now held territories as units. Whenever a misl conquered new territory, it was distributed among its members according to the nature of contribution made by each member towards the conquest. The highest share obviously went to the chief, but even the lowest soldier got his own *patti* or a portion of land, which he could enjoy as a co-sharer with absolute freedom.[53] The number of misls thus holding territories in 1770 was more than sixty. Above them was the *Dal Khalsa* with a chosen leader. The misls did unite on occasions, as they did in 1765 against the Afghans.[54] But on the whole, political authority in Punjab remained decentralised and more horizontally dispersed during this whole period until Ranjit Singh, the chief of the Sukerchakia misl, tried to raise a more centralised Sikh state at the end of the eighteenth century.

After repelling the third Afghan invasion under Abdali's successor Zaman Shah in 1798–99, Ranjit Singh emerged as one of the outstanding Sikh chiefs and conquered Lahore. Leading an army with improved artillery and infantry trained by European officers, by 1809 he had brought under his control large areas in the five doabs of Punjab. By the Treaty of Amritsar in that year the English recognised him as the sole sovereign ruler of Punjab. This gave him the opportunity to round his conquests off by ousting the Afghans from Multan and Kashmir and subduing most of the other Sikh chiefs, many of whom were reduced to the status of tribute-paying vassals. By the time of his death, his authority was recognised in territories between the river Sutlej and the mountain ranges of Ladakh, Karakoram, Hindukush and Sulaiman.

Although Mughal and Afghan rules were displaced from Punjab, the new administration which Ranjit Singh or the other Sikh rulers before him had introduced remained, like the Maratha polity, a careful mix between the Mughal system and local traditions. Continuity of Mughal institutions was remarkable in the organisation of administrative divisions, in the nomenclature of officials, as well as in the tax collection system. Trade and commerce flourished in Punjab because a powerful state under Ranjit Singh provided safe passage to traders and their caravans; but still land revenue remained the main source of income for the state. And although the amount of land revenue collection increased, about 40 per cent of it was alienated as jagir.[55] While in the rest of the territories land revenue was directly collected through kardars, this penetration of the state stopped at the village level and did not infringe upon the power of the clans and their chiefs. Local traditional hierarchies and the concept of a centralised monarchical state thus existed in a delicately balanced relationship, or in other words, in the dualism between 'national' and 'local' systems of governance. This process of incorporation and adjustment as a part of the construction of a monarchical state could be seen at the cultural level as well, where the Khalsa attempt to construct an exclusive Sikh identity gradually incorporated the non-Khalsa Sikhs or the *sahajdharis* as well.[56] At the central level of *durbar* politics also Ranjit Singh maintained a careful balance between the powerful Sikh chiefs on the one hand and on the other freshly recruited military commanders from among the peasants of central Punjab and the non-Punjabi nobles, such as the Dogra Rajputs from Jammu.[57] This delicate balancing game functioned well until Ranjit Singh's death in 1839. Within a decade of his death independent Sikh rule disappeared from Punjab, as struggle for power among the mighty Sikh chiefs and the royal family feuds helped the English to take over without much difficulty—a story we will return to in a short while.

In the eighteenth century, a few smaller states, apart from the larger powers described earlier, had also emerged in north India by taking advantage of the weakness of the Mughal empire. The Jat kingdom of Bharatpur is an important example of this. The Jats were an agriculturist and pastoral caste inhabiting the Delhi-Mathura region. Caste affinity with their zamindars brought solidarity within the community and they began to revolt against the Mughal state from the time of Jahangir. The first revolt of the Jat peasants took place in 1669 and the emperor himself had to proceed to suppress this rebellion. In 1686 the Jats revolted again; this time the Mughal imperial commander Bishen Singh Kachhwa achieved some success against them, but failed to curb their power completely. In this way, first the local zamindar Gokla and then Rajaram and Churaman Jat used the discontent of their peasants against the Mughal state and founded the Jat kingdom at Bharatpur. It was Suraj Mal who consolidated Jat power during his reign (1756–63), compelling the

Mughal authorities to recognise him. He successfully withstood a siege by Abdali's army and supported the Marathas in the Third Battle of Panipat. However, as for the organisation of this rebel polity, the Jat state, although founded with the active support of the peasants, continued to retain its feudal character. The state had to depend on the zamindars who held both administrative and revenue powers, and their revenue demands sometimes were even higher than those under the Mughal system. Suraj Mal in the 1750s tried to reduce this dependence on the overmighty kinsmen and members of his caste, began to drive them off from positions of power, tried to raise an army with foreigners and introduced the Mughal system of revenue collection.[58] But this effort at centralisation of power ended with his death in 1763, which was followed by a virtual collapse of the Jat state that stretched at one stage from the Ganga in the east to Agra in the west and from Delhi in the north to Chambal in the south.

A couple of small Afghan kingdoms were also established in north India following the weakening of the Mughal empire. The Afghans, who started migrating to India from the fifteenth century, were bands of roving warlords, who continually moved from camp to camp. During the early phase of Afghan state formation in India in the fifteenth-sixteenth century, the Lodi Sultanate remained only "a pastoral confederation of tribal lords". In the mid-sixteenth century, Sher Shah Suri during his rule in Delhi (1540–45), transformed this horizontal structure of Afghan polity into a vertical relationship based on military service and direct loyalty to the king. Thus tribal principles of equality and inherited rights were replaced with the concept of centralised power, subordination and royal prerogatives. But Sher Shah's rule did not last long and the Afghans continued to operate as a fluid ethnic group of mercenary soldiers in the military labour market of north India.[59] In the eighteenth century, Afghan migration to India increased because of political instability and economic dislocations in Afghanistan. The breakdown of authority in north India that followed Nadir Shah's invasion gave opportunity to another Afghan leader, Ali Muhammad Khan, to establish a petty kingdom of Rohilkhand at the foothills of the Himalayas. But the new kingdom acquired hardly any influence at all, as it suffered heavily at the hands of the neighbouring powers, like the Marathas, Jats, Awadh and later the English. Another independent Afghan kingdom to the east of Delhi in the area around Farukhabad was established by Ahmad Khan Bangash. Both the Rohillas and Bangash helped Ahmad Shah Abdali during the Third Battle of Panipat; but their power declined quickly as Abdali retired from the Indian stage leaving Najib-ud-daula in charge of affairs at Delhi.

Apart from the successor states and the rebel states, which came into existence following the weakening of the Mughal empire, there were also a few principalities, like the Rajput kingdoms, Mysore or Travancore, which already enjoyed considerable amount of autonomy in the past and now in the eighteenth century became completely independent. In the medieval period a number of roving warrior groups thrived in the north Indian military labour market, from where the Mughal army recruited its soldiers. Gradually professional specialisation was offering these people ethnic identities, Rajput being one of them, as social mobility from peasant to Rajput became a frequent occurrence during this period.[60] It was by sixteenth-seventeenth century that the Rajputs came to be organised into about twenty major clans, with their chiefs gradually establishing their centralised control over territory, with the patronage of the Mughal emperors following a policy of indirect rule. Since the time of Akbar, different Rajput chiefs were being incorporated into the Mughal structure as peshkashi zamindars. They paid an annual tribute (peshkash) to the Mughal emperor as a mark of subordination, and enjoyed autonomy in matters of internal administration. Many of them were also given high military ranks within the Mughal army and contributed to the strength of the empire, and in return were given help in their effort to consolidate their own control over their kingdoms. Thus as many of the Rajput chiefs sought to claim centralised authority in their territories, this significantly affected the power relations within the Rajput states based on land ownership. Previously, entitlement to land depended on inherited rights given by the brotherhood of the clan or marriage relations. But now gradually this relationship of "corporate egalitarianism", as Norman Zieglar calls it, was replaced by the hierarchical principles of service and loyalty that entitled clients to pattas on land.[61] However, the displacement was never complete, as the chiefs and their centralising policies were continually challenged by local groups or junior lineages from within the clans. When someone rebelled, he was helped by his own immediate kinsmen and their marriage alliances; but rebels when unsuccessful were usually accommodated within the polity and therefore rebellion happened to be an accepted norm of political behaviour. Even in the early nineteenth century, in a Rajput polity like Sirohi, the darbar remained "a synthesis of the powers of the sovereign and the nobles", and "there was not a single noble . . . whose lineage had not rebelled" in the recent or distant past against the incumbent ruler.[62]

To put it in another way, Rajput polities, to quote Norbad Peabody, "were built on webs of criss-crossing, non-exclusive political relationships that produced state formations that were neither founded on the basis of territorial integrity nor absolute and exclusive political loyalties."[63] And it was within this complex matrix of local loyalties, centralising kingship and clan rivalries that the Rajputs placed their relationship with the Mughals. In the seventeenth century during the time of Aurangzeb the harmonious relationship between the two seemed to break down, though, contrary to popular historical myths, this was not because of religious reactions or Rajput nationalism. Aurangzeb did not discriminate against the Rajput sardars in matters of recruitment; but he could hardly tolerate the continuous territorial expansion of Mewar under Raj Singh at the expense of other Rajput chieftains, as this would contravene the traditional Mughal policy of balance of power. So to contain him, he began to patronise other neighbouring Rajput sardars. The situation actually began to take an ugly turn when he interfered in the succession question of Marwar. After the death of Rana Jaswant Singh, a son was born to Rani Hari, but Aurangzeb refused to recognise him as the new Rana and instead put up Inder Singh as his own candidate for the position. Such interference was not unprecedented, as in the past the Mughal emperors had used clan rivalries and exerted their right to appoint successors to Rajput states. And now, particularly as Marwar was situated in the strategic route between Agra and Ahmedabad, it could not be left in charge of a child ruler. The question of religious difference did not arise, as the Maharani was prepared to accept Sharia and pay a higher peshkash if her son Ajit Singh's claim was recognised. But when this did not happen, the Rathor sardars, ably helped by Mewar, rose in revolt against the Mughal empire.[64]

Mewar's assistance to the warring chiefs of Marwar was to establish its pre-eminence in Rajput politics and not so much to further Rajput nationalism, as Satish Chandra has shown. The other Rajput clans, like the Kachchwas, Haras, Bhattis and the Rathors of Bekanir, did not participate in this revolt of 1680–81; some of them even supported the Mughals. Indeed, the movement soon dissipated due to internal rivalries among the Rajput sardars, each trying to consolidate or expand territorial control at the expense of other clans.[65] In the eighteenth century many of them began to assert their independence vis-à-vis the Mughal empire—their method was to slowly loosen their ties with Delhi and function as independent states in practice. The most powerful of the Rajput chiefs during this period was Sawai Jai Singh of Amber who ruled in Jaipur from 1699 to

1743 and also played a significant role in Mughal politics. In the second half of the eighteenth century, the Rajput polities had to face constant depredations of the Marathas and Afghans, although none of them succeeded in permanently subjugating the region.

In south India the emergence of Mysore as a significant power in the mid-eighteenth century was most spectacular. Originally a viceroyalty under the Vijaynagara empire in the sixteenth century, Mysore was gradually transformed into an autonomous principality by the Wodeyar dynasty. Its centralised military power began to increase from the late seventeenth century under Chikkadevaraja Wodeyar (1672–1704),[66] but it reached its real period of glory under Haidar Ali. A man of humble origin, Haidar had started his career as a junior officer in the Mysore army and gradually rose to prominence. By 1761 he took over political power in Mysore by ousting the corrupt *dalwai* (prime minister) Nanjraj, who had in the meanwhile usurped real power in the kingdom by reducing the Wodeyar king into a mere titular head.

Haidar modernised his army with French experts, who trained an efficient infantry and artillery and infused European discipline into the Mysore army. It was organised on a European model through the system of *risalas*, with a clear chain of command going up to the ruler. Each risala had a fixed number of soldiers, with provision for weaponry and modes of transport and a commander appointed directly by Haidar himself. His power was further consolidated by the subjugation of the local warrior chiefs or hereditary overlords like deshmukhs and *palegars* (poligars), who had until then complete mastery over the countryside through their control over agricultural surpluses and local temples. Haidar, and later his son Tipu Sultan, introduced the system of imposing land taxes directly on the peasants and collecting them through salaried officials and in cash, thus enhancing enormously the resource base of the state. This land revenue system was based on detailed survey and classification of land; sometimes fixed rents and sometimes a share of the produce were collected from different categories of land, such as wet or dry lands, the rate of rent varying according to the productivity of soil. It did not completely dispense with the Mughal institution of jagir, but restricted it to a very small proportion of the available land.[67] Burton Stein has called Tipu's revenue system a form of "military fiscalism", where taxes were collected from a wide base directly by state officials in order to mobilise resources to build up and maintain a large army. This was therefore part of a political project to establish centralised military hegemony by eliminating the intermediaries who were co-sharers of power in a previous segmentary state under the Vijaynagara empire.[68]

Tipu's state in order to expand its resource base provided encouragement for the development of agriculture, such as tax remission for reclamation of wasteland, and tried to protect the peasants from the rapacity of tax collectors. Even his arch enemies had to concede that "his country was the best cultivated and its population the most flourishing in India".[69] Tipu was also interested in modernising the agricultural economy, by repairing old irrigation systems and constructing new ones, by promoting agricultural manufacturing and introducing sericulture in Mysore. He sent ambassadors to France to bring in European technology, went on to build a navy, with ambition to participate in oceanic trade. He launched in 1793 what can be described as a "state commercial corporation", with plans to set up factories outside Mysore. In course of time Mysore state began to participate in a lucrative trade in valuable goods like sandalwood, rice, silk, coconut, sulphur etc. and established thirty trading centres in and outside Mysore in other parts of western India and overseas like Muscat. But his plans of modernisation went far beyond his resources and therefore, Mysore remained, as Irfan Habib argues, "far away from a real opening to modern civilization".[70]

The state of Mysore under Haidar Ali and Tipu Sultan was involved in establishing a centralised military hegemony. Its territorial ambitions and trading interests got it engaged in a state of constant warfare, which overshadowed all other aspects of its history during this period. Haidar Ali had invaded and annexed Malabar and Calicut in 1766, thus expanding the frontiers of Mysore significantly. On the other hand, the boundaries of the Maratha kingdom extended over the coastal areas of Konkan and Malabar, which made conflict with Mysore inevitable. There was also conflict with the other powers in the region, like Hyderabad and then the English, on whom Haidar Ali inflicted a heavy defeat near Madras in 1769. After his death in 1782, his son Tipu Sultan followed his father's policies. His rule came to an end with a defeat at the hands of the English in 1799—he died defending his capital Srirangapatnam. We shall return to that story shortly, but before that it is important to remember that in a significant way Tipu's reign represented a discontinuity in eighteenth century Indian politics, as his kingship, argues Kate Brittlebank (1997), was rooted firmly in a strong regional tradition. Unlike other eighteenth century states which did not challenge the political legitimacy of the Mughal emperor, in a symbolic gesture to proclaim his independence, Tipu issued coins without any reference to the Mughal emperor; and instead of Emperor Shah Alam's name he inserted his own name in the khutba (Friday sermons at the mosques); finally, he sought a sanad from the Ottoman Khalif to legitimise his rule. But he too "did not completely sever links" with the Mughal monarch, who still commanded respect in the subcontinent. Being a "realist" as he was, Tipu recognised Mughal authority when it suited him and defied it when it did not.[71]

Further south, the southernmost state of Travancore had always maintained its independence from Mughal rule. It gained in importance after 1729 when its king Martanda Varma started expanding his dominions with the help of a strong and modern army trained along Western lines and equipped with modern weapons. The Dutch were ousted from the region; the English were made to accept his terms of trade; local feudal chiefs were suppressed; and smaller principalities governed by collateral branches of the royal family were taken over. By the beginning of the 1740s, Varma had constructed a powerful bureaucratic state, which required control over larger resources. He resolved this problem by proclaiming a royal monopoly, first on pepper trade and then on all trade in the prosperous Malabar coast. Some of the profit that the state earned in this way was ploughed back into the community through development of irrigation, transport and communication systems and various other charities.[72] In view of recent researches, this measure in itself does not seem to be a major departure from existing political convention. Although Travancore was not formally within the Mughal system, "royal and noble trade" was becoming an established Mughal tradition since the seventeenth century.[73] Travancore withstood the shock of a Mysorean invasion in 1766 and under Martanda Varma's successor Rama Varma its capital became a centre of scholarship and art. In his death towards the closing years of the eighteenth century the region lost its former glory and soon succumbed to British pressure, accepting a Resident in 1800. However, the internal social organisation of the state, marked by the dominance of the Nair community in administration, landholding and social spheres continued for another fifty years, yielding to the forces of change in the second half of the nineteenth century.[74]

The major characteristic of eighteenth-century India was therefore the weakening of the centralised Mughal empire and a dispersal of political power across the regions. There was in other words, a transformation of the polity, rather than complete collapse.[75] The symbols of Mughal authority were still recognised, the Mughal system also continued, although in some areas its content was substantially changed. Talking about Mughal Bengal, Richard Eaton concludes that "even while central power in Delhi declined, rendering Bengal effectively independent from the second decade of the eighteenth century on, the ideological and bureaucratic structure of Mughal imperialism continued to expand in the Bengal delta".[76] But although the successor states continued Mughal institutions—and perhaps also inherited some of their weaknesses—there were also indications of significant innovation and improvement—both in terms of political rituals and insignia, as also in perfecting mechanisms of resource extraction from agriculture and trade. At a political level all these states continually made adjustments between concepts of centralised kingship and local loyalties, between prebended lordship and hereditary rights, or in more general terms, between centripetal and centrifugal tendencies. This political heterogeneity also favoured the flourishing of a diverse cultural life, where religious strife was not a part of ordinary social life—despite some tension between the Shia and Sunni Muslims in Awadh—and where side by side with orthodoxy, there were also plebeian, syncretistic and rationalist schools of thought, which were patronised by the regional rulers. Thus the devotional religion of Vaishnavism flourished in Bengal,[77] the Firangi Mahal blossomed in Lucknow as a rationalist school of Islamic thought[78] and even after the decline of its main centre at Bijapur the Deccani Sufi tradition and its literary culture survived in Hyderabad and Arcot.[79] If Tipu Sultan found in Islam an enduring ideology of power, he was equally patronising towards the Hindu religious institutions like the Sringeri Math and other Hindu shrines.[80]

On the economic side the eighteenth century was not a period of total stagnation either, as there had been considerable regional variations. Satish Chandra (1991) has talked about the resilience of the economy, as trade, both internal and external, continued without disruption and even prospered. There was now an expanding commercial economy and the revenue farmers and merchants with money power increased their political influence. Indigenous bankers handled considerable amounts of cash and operated extensive financial networks across the country to transfer credit through *hundis*. And as one theory would have it, they were now supposedly favouring the regional elite, rather than the central Mughal authority.[81] There was, in other words, "creation of new wealth and social power in the provinces", which, as C.A. Bayly has argued, resulted in the decline of the centralised Mughal power.[82] There is one significant point that emerges from the recent historiography of eighteenth-century India—that there were regions with considerable amounts of resources, which actually attracted the English and other European traders and triggered off a competition among them for mastery over the subcontinent.

1.3. FOUNDATION OF THE BRITISH EMPIRE

The English East India Company was founded by a royal charter on 31 December 1600, as a joint stock company of London merchants uniting to combat Dutch competition in Eastern trade. It was given monopoly of all trade from England to the East and was permitted, even in an age dominated by mercantilist ideas, to carry bullion out of the country to finance its trade. It was not, however, given any overt mandate at that time to carry on conquest or colonisation. The Company formally started trading in India from 1613 after settling scores with the Portuguese, who had arrived at the scene earlier. A *farman* from Mughal emperor Jahangir gave them permission to establish their factories or warehouses in India, the first factory being set up in Surat in the western coast. In 1617 Jahangir received Sir Thomas Roe as a resident English envoy in his court. This was the modest beginning from where the Company gradually extended its trading activities to other parts of India, with Bombay, Calcutta and Madras emerging by the end of the seventeenth century as three major centres of its activities. Political expansion started from the middle of the eighteenth century, and within hundred years almost the whole of India was under its control.

PJ Marshall (1968) has argued that until 1784 (i.e., the passage of Pitt's India Act), there was no conscious or consistent British policy for political conquest in India. Authority at home remained divided between the Court of Directors of the East India Company and the tenuous regulatory power of the government, with no one seemingly interested in acquiring territories in India until 1784, although by then a large empire had already been acquired. "Thus the growth of territorial empire in India", argues Marshall, "was neither planned nor directed from Britain";[83] it was the initiative of the Company officials operating in India which decided the course of action, despite the absence of any policy directives from London in favour of conquest and colonisation. Marshall acknowledged in an earlier essay that there was considerable commercial expansion during the early eighteenth century and the obvious connection between trade and empire was also hard to ignore.[84] But then, it was the political fragmentation and instability following the decline of the Mughal power that actually facilitated the territorial expansion of the Company. Its history, therefore, needs to be traced in the developments of eighteenth-century Indian politics, where the English were only "responding to these developments and exploiting the opportunities that came their way".[85] In other words, it was developments in the periphery, rather than impetus from the metropole, which thrust upon the Company a career of territorial expansion in India. And even after the 1780s, argues C.A. Bayly, the imperial expansion was primarily motivated by the fiscal and military needs of the Company, rather than interests of trade—the "free traders [being] nothing more than the fly on the wheel".[86]

While it is difficult to deny the importance of "sub-imperialism"[87] of the men on the spot or pressures generated at the periphery as driving forces behind territorial conquests, we may also posit here some telling evidence of engagement of the metropole in the project of empire building in India. There is, first of all, considerable evidence to suggest that from the very beginning use of force to promote trade was an axiom in the practices of the East India Company; its trade was always armed trade.[88] And despite the apparent separation between the Company and the state, the two were intimately interlinked in promoting England's diplomatic goals, as the Company itself owed its privileges, and indeed very existence, to royal prerogative.[89] In English politics, the Company's fortunes suffered reverses during the time of the Stuart monarchs James I and Charles I and also during the Civil War, when its privileges came under severe attack. But the situation began to improve with the restoration of Charles II to the throne of England. To secure wealth and independence for the crown, both he and his brother James II followed an aggressive commercial policy abroad. In real terms, this involved the use of naval power in the Indian Ocean and in the Indian coastal areas, where fortified bases and enclaves in the factory ports were constructed as a part of regular policy, which, in Philip Lawson's words, may be described as "the moral economy of English gunnery in these local markets".[90] The English naval guns during this period could not alter the entire trading pattern of the East; but they prevented the Indian rulers from obstructing or undermining English trade in the local markets.

The relationship between the Crown and the Company was mutually beneficial. In 1660 the Company celebrated the restoration of the Stuart monarchy by offering £3,000 worth of silver plates to His Majesty. In 1661 Cromwell's charter was replaced by one signed by the king and in gratitude the Company directors voted in 1662 a loan of £10,000 for the King. In the subsequent years more loans totaling £150,000 were offered and more charters with additional privileges followed. "King and Company", as John Keay writes, "understood one another well."[91] The initial history of the Presidency system in India is also indicative of Crown's involvement in the colonisation of the country. The island settlement of Bombay, which Charles II received from the Portuguese crown in 1661 as dowry for his bride, was handed over to the East India Company in 1668 for a token annual rental of £10 and it was here that in 1687 the Presidency headquarters of the west coast was shifted from Surat. What is important to note here is that Bombay had been given to Charles through the Treaty of Whitehall, which included a secret provision that it would be used to protect the Portuguese settlements in India. It involved a mutual defence pact against the aggressive and expanding Dutch East India Company, and now even after the handover, that obligation to defend Portuguese positions was happily owned up by the King, and that made the English Company directors immensely grateful, offering a further loan.[92] The growth of the Madras Presidency was also to a large extent because of Cromwell's charter, which provided encouragement for the development of this area. The Calcutta Presidency developed later in the eighteenth century and the London authorities were involved in a major way in its development and defence.[93] But even prior to that, in the 1680s when Aurangzeb became busy in imperial wars, seriously threatening the stability and security of English trade, the East India Company under the leadership of Sir Josiah Child decided to take an aggressive stance in defence of Company's trading interests. Its military weakness at this stage proved disastrous, although, fortunately for the Company, Aurangzeb did not take any retributive action and restored its privileges in return for an apology and a payment of compensation. But defeat does not hide the aggressive intent of the Company, which "became identified with a Stuart monarchy pursuing an equally bold and authoritarian imperial policy around the globe." In the middle of the eighteenth century the Europeans gained "a decided technological edge" over the Indians and this paved the way for victory of what has been described by Philip Lawson as a "policy of aggression and state imperialism by proxy."[94]

After James II was replaced by William and Mary in 1689, the Company once again came under increasing attack in England. The political ascendancy of the Whigs brought the Company's monopoly rights and corrupt practices into question and a rival Company was set up. However, the bill authorising the foundation of the new company was passed by the House of Commons in 1698 only when the promoters of the new company offered a £2 million loan to the state, as against the offer of £700,000 by the old Company wanting a renewal of its exclusive charter. It became clear by this time that the right to trade in the East was "a marketable commodity", and if Parliament granted that right, it was the state which would benefit, instead of King and the Court.[95] By 1709 the anomalies were sorted out, as the two companies merged again and it was widely accepted in London how crucial the financial role of the Company was in strengthening the state and in improving its diplomatic profile in European politics. The eighteenth century thus marked the beginning of self-confident territorial expansion in India, as imperial expansion and the financial strength of the Company came to be integrally connected.[96] It was discussed in the early eighteenth century not only among the Company officials, but also widely among the London public and in the political circles; the foundation of the Company's empire in India was therefore not entirely without direction from London. The relationship between the state and the Company was further streamlined in the 1770s, when the latter agreed to pay £400,000 annually to the state exchequer for its Indian territorial possessions and revenues earned since 1765, and thus gained an official endorsement of its position in India. By this time the Company was being looked at as "a powerful engine in the hands of the Government for the purposes of drawing from a distant country the largest revenue it is capable of yielding." The charters of the Company were seen to be providing for "delegated sovereignty", while the monopoly of trade and territorial possessions were considered to be returns for the public funds and trust invested in the joint stock company "for the benefit of the British nation". The Regulating Act of 1773 resolved the ambiguities involved in the sovereignty issue, by establishing the rights of the state on all territorial acquisitions overseas.[97] If later the London authorities became at all averse to territorial expansion, it was only because of the expenses of wars. They wanted very much to share the resources of an Indian empire, but not the cost of acquiring it or the burden of administering it.[98]

The expansion of the empire in India in the second half of the eighteenth century marked, according to P.J. Cain and A.G. Hopkins, an extension of the "gentlemanly capitalism", upheld by an alliance between landed interests and financial power that was in ascendancy in London after 1688; and that was the reason why "revenue became and remained the central preoccupation" of imperial policy.[99] Cain and Hopkins brought the metropole back into the discussion of imperialism, and it is difficult to deny the importance of Indian revenue resources for financing England's growing internal and overseas trade, and this undoubtedly created the impulse for conquest. But in eighteenth-century India there were a few other significant interests—other than revenue and the Company's trade—which were also involved in determining the specific course of territorial expansion. From the very beginning, the Company's monopoly rights were breached in various ways and in the eighteenth century it rose to crisis proportions. The "interlopers" in the seventeenth century directly defied the Company's monopoly rights by conducting and financing illegal trade between England and the Indian Ocean countries. Efforts to curb their power often led to constitutional crises as in the *Skinner v. The East India Company* in 1668–69, when the House of Lords actually upheld the rights of an interloper.[100] But the problem of illegal trade was actually compounded by the Company's own organisation. Its employees began to involve themselves in the country trade in India in order to supplement their meagre salaries. There were also free merchants, who were not in the employment of the Company, but were allowed to settle in its establishments. The Company used to ignore this trade and even encouraged such private traders, operating in conjunction with the Indian merchants, as long as they did not directly participate in the oceanic trade to and from Europe.

These two types of parallel trading activities, however, soon came into conflict in the second half of the eighteenth century. Whenever the interests of the private merchants clashed with those of the Company, there was cheating, deceit and a whole circle of illicit credit and trading networks, eroding the profits of the Company.[101] Often there was collusion between the private traders and the interlopers and the profit earned through this illicit trade was remitted through bills of exchange drawn on the London office of the Company or the Amsterdam office of the Dutch Company. In the 1750s such remittances through only the English Company amounted to an average of £100,000 annually, which was more than sixty times of the annual salary which these officials earned in Company's service. More critical, however, was the misuse by these private traders of the trading privileges granted by the Mughal authorities to the East India Company. The *dastak* or the permits issued by the local councils of the Company certifying their goods, which were to be charged no duty by the Mughal authorities, were frequently issued by the Company officials to their own Indian agents, thus defrauding the Mughal treasury of enormous amounts of revenue. The Court of Directors tried to stop this malpractice, but with no effect; and soon in the 1750s this became a major cause of friction between the Company and the local Mughal ruler in Bengal, creating the context for the emergence of the Company as the imperial power in India.[102] However, as its empire in India was acquired over a long period of time—nearly one hundred years—a myriad of factors motivated this territorial expansion. As we examine this protracted process in detail, it becomes clear that both pressures from the periphery and impetus from the metropole constantly interacted with each other, and search for revenue, quest for trading privileges and the imperatives of military exigencies all took the driving seat in turn to accelerate the process of territorial conquest and erect in India the most magnificent empire that Britain ever had.

It all started in Bengal, which in the early eighteenth century had become very important in the structure of the Company's trade at the expense of the west coast, particularly Bombay, Surat and Malabar, as Bengal goods came to comprise nearly 60 per cent of English imports from Asia.[103] The Company was moving towards this position gradually. In 1690 Aurangzeb's farman had granted them right to duty-free trade in Bengal in return for an annual payment of Rs. 3,000. The foundation of Calcutta in 1690 and its fortification in 1696 were followed by the grant of zamindari rights in three villages of Kolikata, Sutanuti and Gobindapur two years later. The situation became unstable again at the death of Aurangzeb, but was formalised again by a farman from emperor Farruksiyar in 1717, which granted the Company the right to carry on duty free trade, to rent thirty-eight villages around Calcutta and to use the royal mint. But this farman also became a new source of conflict between the Company and Murshid Quli Khan, the new autonomous ruler of Bengal, who refused to extend its duty free provision to cover also the private trade of the Company officials. The latter therefore took to rampant misuse of dastaks, and the nawab resented the loss of revenue. Apart from this, Murshid Quli also denied permission to the Company to buy the thirty-eight villages and refused to offer the minting privileges. The conflict between the Bengal nawab and the English Company had thus started developing right from 1717.

The outbreak of the Austrian Succession War in Europe in 1740 brought in hostilities between the English and the French Companies to India. In Bengal the new nawab Alivardi Khan kept both of them under control and forbade them from getting involved in any open hostilities. But French victories in south India made the English apprehensive in Bengal as they had very little trust in the power of the nawab to protect them against any French onslaught. Moreover, as it has been shown recently,[104] the English private trade suffered heavily in the 1750s as a result of French competition in collusion with Asian merchants. In 1755, therefore, the English began renovating the fortifications in Calcutta without the nawab's permission and in utter defiance of his authority began to offer protection to fugitives from his court. The conflict assumed critical dimensions when Siraj-ud-daula became nawab in 1756 and threatened the lucrative English private trade by stopping all misuse of dastaks. The more immediate issues of discord were the grant of asylum to Krishna Ballabh who was charged with fraud by the nawab and the new fortifications at Calcutta—both of which posed a challenge to the authority of the nawab and were critical to the issue of sovereignty. When the Company failed to listen to warnings, Siraj showed his strength by taking over the factory at Kasimbazar. Governor Drake believed that he could avenge this defeat by force and ignored the nawab's overtures for a diplomatic reconciliation. This was followed by Siraj's attack on Calcutta and its capture on 20 June.

This precipitated a crisis, as Robert Clive now arrived with a strong force from Madras. The English fear about Siraj's friendship with the French and apprehension that their trading privileges would be cut down led to the destruction of Hughli and a French defeat at Chandernagore. Apprehensive of an Afghan attack under Abdali, Siraj now preferred a negotiated settlement; but a confident Clive decided on a coup d'etat. The confident servants of the Company in Calcutta were not prepared to tolerate a young tyrannical nawab threatening to destroy their trading privileges and trying to squeeze out a source of fabulous fortunes.[105] There was already a disaffected faction at the nawab's court, consisting of merchants, bankers, financiers and powerful zamindars, like the Jagat Seth brothers, Mahtab Rai and Swarup Chand, Raja Janki Ram, Rai Durlabh, Raja Ramnarain and Raja Manik Chand, who felt threatened by the assertion of independence by a young nawab enthusiastically trying to reorder the balance of power in his court. There was also a natural communion of interests between the Indian mercantile community and the European traders, as many of the Indian merchants were operating in collaboration with the English Company and private traders, acting as their *dadani* merchants supplying them textiles from the interior in exchange for advances or *dadan*. Many of the Indian merchant princes had been prefering English ships for carrying their cargo, and this in fact resulted in the gradual decline of the port of Hughli, giving its place of pride to Calcutta.[106] So a collusion of the two groups was not unlikely and what followed as a result was a conspiracy to replace Siraj with Mir Jafar, his commander-in-chief, who was the choice of the Jagat Seths, without whose support any coup d'etat was virtually impossible. The question whether there was already a conspiracy in existence at the Murshidabad court and the English took advantage of that or it was the English who hatched up the conspiracy—a question over which historians have fought their futile polemical battles—is less important. What is important is the fact that there was a collusion, which resulted in the Battle of Plassey (June 1757), in which Siraj was finally defeated by Clive. It was hardly more than a skirmish, as the largest contingent of the nawabi army remained inactive under Mir Jafar's command. But it had profound political impact, as fugitive Siraj was soon captured and put to death and the new nawab Mir Jafar became a puppet in the hands of the English. The Battle of Plassey (1757) thus marked the beginning of political supremacy of the English East India Company in India.

What followed hereafter is often referred to as the "Plassey plunder". Immediately after the war the English army and navy each received the hefty sums of £275,000 for distribution among their members.[107] Apart from that, between 1757 and 1760, the Company received Rs 22.5 million from Mir Jafar; Clive himself got in 1759 a personal jagir worth £34,567. So far as the Company was concerned, it brought in a major change in the structure of its trade. Prior to 1757 the English trade in Bengal was largely financed through import of bullion from England; but after that year not only bullion import stopped, but bullion was exported from Bengal to China and other parts of India, which gave a competitive advantage to the English Company over its European rivals.[108] On the other hand, for the Company officials Plassey opened the gates to make personal fortunes, not only through direct extortion, but also through rampant abuse of dastaks for their private trade. So after some time Mir Jafar found it difficult to meet the financial demands of the Company and was removed from the throne to be replaced by his son-in-law Mir Kasim in October 1760. But conflict arose again over the misuse of trade privileges by the Company's servants. Unable to stop the misuse of dastaks, the new nawab abolished internal duties altogether, so that the Indian merchants could also enjoy the same privilege. The English, however, did not like this display of independence and as a retaliatory measure, again replaced him with Mir Jafar.

In December 1763 Mir Kasim fled from Bengal and tried to form a grand alliance with the Mughal emperor Shah Alam II and Shuja-ud-daula of Awadh. The emperor was in the region since 1758, when as a crown prince he had fled from the nasty politics of the Delhi court and tried to carve out for himself an independent kingdom in the eastern provinces. In December 1759, hearing about his father's assassination, he proclaimed himself the emperor and appointed Shuja his wazir. When Mir Kasim fled to him for refuge, it was only after long and tortuous negotiations that the two agreed to proceed against the English; Shuja's support was secured after he was promised Bihar and its treasury, along with a payment of Rs 30 million at the successful completion of the mission. But their combined army was routed at the Battle of Buxar (1764), as an eighteenth-century Indian army with its segmentary social organisation was in serious disadvantage against a technically efficient English army with a unitary command. What followed the English victory at Buxar is however more important. The Company treated the defeated Mughal emperor with respect, because of his continuing symbolic significance in eighteenth-century Indian politics. Indeed, not before 1857 the British ever formally repudiated the sovereignty of the Mughal emperor. In return, by the Treaty of Allahabad of 1765, Shah Alam granted the Company the *diwani* (revenue collecting rights) of Bengal, Bihar and Orissa—in other words, absolute control over the lucrative resources of the prosperous Bengal subah. The British Resident posted at the court of Murshidabad hereafter gradually by 1772 became the locus of real administrative power in the province and thus it was in Bengal that the system of indirect rule as a policy of the Company's imperial governance was first initiated.[109] Awadh had to stand the pressure of the Calcutta Council's lack of resources. According to the treaty, Shuja-ud-daula had to pay Rs. 5 million; the nawab and the Company would henceforth defend each other's territories; a British Resident would be posted in his court and the Company would enjoy duty free trading rights in Awadh—a clause which in later years created fresh tensions and prepared the grounds for the annexation of Awadh itself.[110]

As eastern India thus came under control of the Company by 1765, the context for expansion in the south was provided by the Anglo-French rivalry. The French were the last among the European powers to arrive in India; but they were the first to conceive the ambitious project of building a territorial empire in this subcontinent.

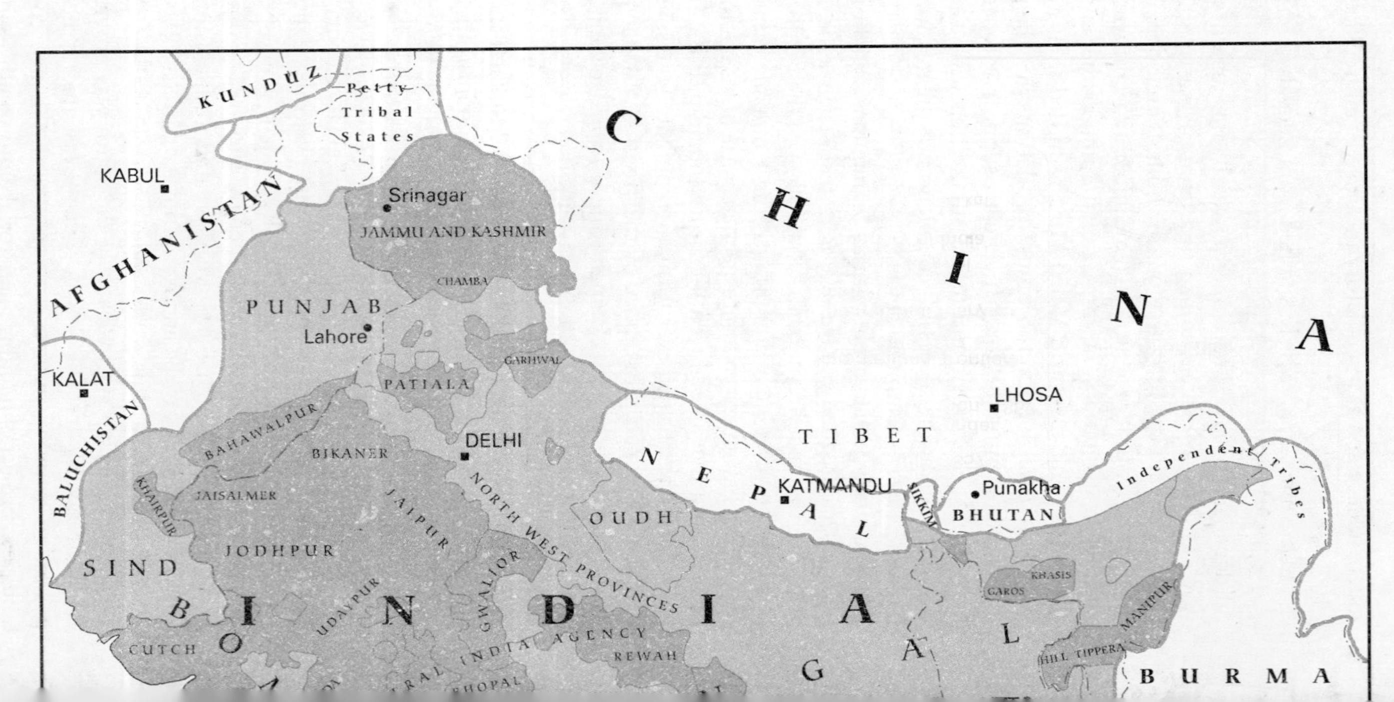
CHINA
KUNDUZ
Petty Tribal States
KABUL
AFGHANISTAN
Srinagar
JAMMU AND KASHMIR
CHAMBA
PUNJAB
Lahore
GARHWAL
PATIALA
KALAT
BALUCHISTAN
BAHAWALPUR
BIKANER
DELHI
KHAIRPUR
JAISALMER
JAIPUR
NORTH WEST PROVINCES
OUDH
JODHPUR
SIND
GWALIOR
UDAYPUR
INDIA
AGENCY
REWAH
BHOPAL
CUTCH
TIBET
LHOSA
NEPAL
KATMANDU
SIKKIM
Punakha
BHUTAN
Independent Tribes
KHASIS
GAROS
MANIPUR
HILL TIPPERA
BURMA

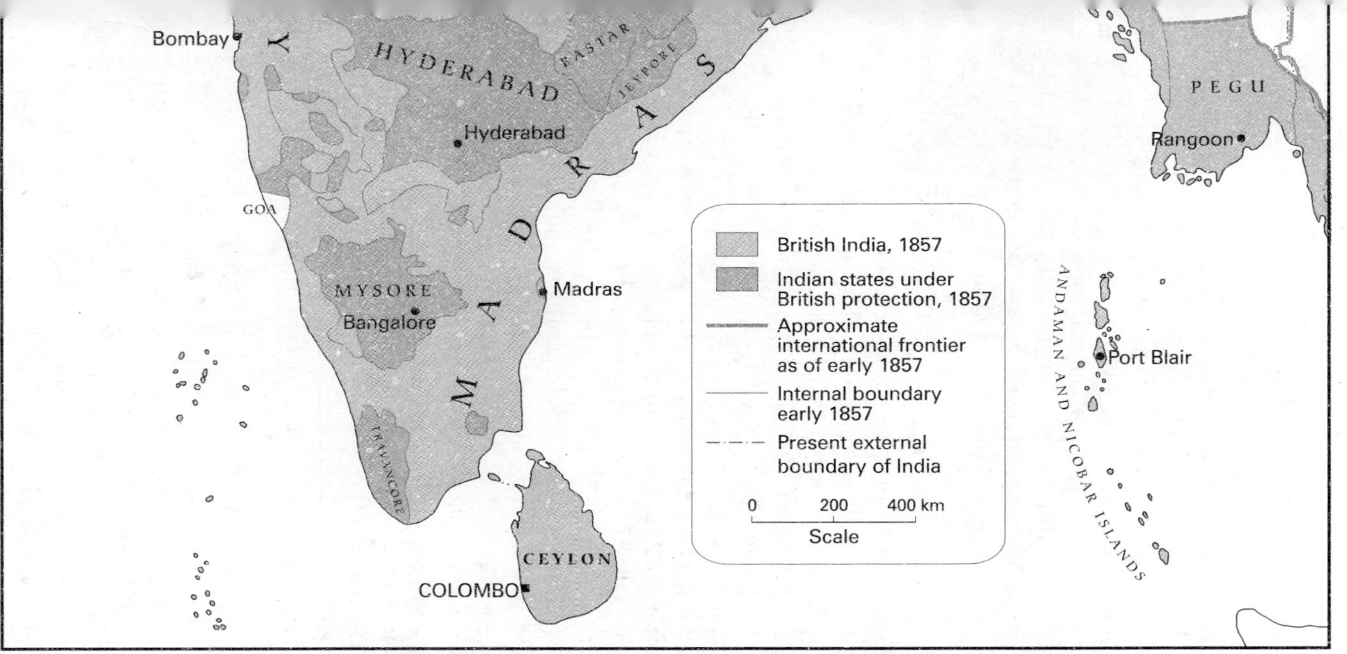

MAP 3: British territories in India in 1857

Their main centre at Pondicherry was founded in 1674 and was raised to great political prominence by Dupleix, the most illustrious French governor general in India. He first became the governor of the French settlement of Chandernagore in Bengal in 1731 and within ten years French trade from this centre increased appreciably. Dupleix was a workoholic, who detested India, but made a personal fortune through involvement in a profitable private trade. In 1742 he got charge of Pondicherry and started working immediately to improve its trade and more significantly, to embark on a political career.[111] It was he who had first showed the way of intervening in disputes of the Indian rulers and thereby acquiring political control over vast territories[112]—a technique which was later perfected by the English Company, their main European trading rival in the Indian scene. The outbreak of the Austrian Succession War in Europe in 1740 provided the immediate context for the political conflict between the two European rivals in India. Their hostility in Bengal had been contained by the effective intervention of Alivardi Khan. But in the south, the French position was strengthened by the arrival of a fleet from Mauritius and this resulted in an attack on the English position in Madras. With the surrender of Madras the first Carnatic war began, as the English appealed to the Nawab of Carnatic for protection. The nawab sent a force against the French, but it suffered an ignominious defeat. At this stage the French position was also weakened by the differences between Dupleix and Admiral La Bourdaunairs, who returned to Mauritius after surrendering Madras. In September 1746 Dupleix led a second attack on Madras, which capitulated and this was followed by a siege of Fort St. David, a minor English possession to the south of Pondicherry. But before this could drag on any further, the end of hostilities in Europe by the Treaty of Aix-La-Chappelle brought an end to the first round of Anglo-French conflicts in India as well. The English possessions in India were returned, while the French got back their North American possessions.

Political complexities arising from dynastic feuds in India provided the context for the second round of Anglo-French conflict in the south. The succession disputes at both Carnatic and Hyderabad provided the French Governor General Dupleix an opportunity to intervene in Indian politics and secure thereby important territorial and financial concessions. The French supported Chanda Sahib for the throne of Carnatic and Muzaffar Jung for that of Hyderabad, while the English supported their rival candidates. Both the French candidates emerged victorious and Muzaffar Jung, the new Nizam of Hyderabad, granted substantial territorial concessions to the French in the form of a jagir in the Northern Sarkars, Masulipatam and some villages around Pondicherry and significant control in his court through the appointment of a French agent. This alarmed the English; a strong force arrived from Calcutta under Robert Clive and the Second Carnatic War began in 1752. The English this time emerged victorious: Clive's occupation of Arcot was followed by the release of Muhammad Ali, who was now placed on the throne of Carnatic.

Dupleix tried to retrieve French position; but the French government became displeased with him, particularly because of the financial losses, and he was recalled in 1754. His failure against the English can be explained in terms of various factors, such as his own wrong moves and miscalculations, the lack of support from the French government and the Company, the French anxiety to retain their possessions in North America and also the fundamental weakness of France in colonial struggles, as demonstrated also in later warfare. But the policies of Dupleix and the advantages he had gained in India were not jettisoned immediately. He was replaced by Godeheu, who signed a treaty with the English in 1754. The treaty left the French in possession of territories around Pondicherry and Karikal, important posts in Carnatic, the four Northern Sarkars and controlling influence at the Hyderabad court.[113] The French power in the south was thus far from over yet.

The outbreak of the Seven Years' War in Europe between England and France in 1756 provided the context for the third and decisive round of Anglo-French conflict in south India. The French position by now had been significantly weakened by financial difficulties, as even the soldiers remained unpaid for months. The apathy of the French government was shaken at the outbreak of European hostilities and a strong force was dispatched under Count de Lally. Yet the French lost their positions in India one after another: first fell Chandernagore in Bengal; then when Bussy was recalled to help Lally in the Carnatic, the Northern Sarkars were exposed to an attack from Bengal; the fall of the Sarkars together with that of two other old settlements of Masulipatam and Yanam ended French influence in the Deccan. The English fleet returned from Bengal and inflicted heavy losses on the French in August 1758; and all the French strongholds in the Carnatic were lost. Lally's siege of Madras had to be withdrawn and the Nawab of Carnatic paid for the campaign. The most decisive battle of the Third Carnatic War was the battle of Wandiwash in January 1760. In May Pondicherry was seized and it capitulated in January 1761, once again the Carnatic nawab paying for the campaign. Mahe in Malabar coast and the last two forts in Carnatic—Jinji and Thiagar—fell in the same year. The French were now without a toehold in India.

A number of factors can be cited to explain this ultimate and decisive French defeat—e.g., the rashness and arrogance of Lally, who had managed to alienate nearly all the French officers at Pondicherry, the acute shortage of money which hindered military operations, the recall of Bussy from the Deccan and above all, the superiority of the English navy, their ready supply of money and their new self-confidence. By the Peace of Paris in 1763 France got back all the factories and settlements that it possessed in India prior to 1749, with the only proviso that it could not any more fortify Chandernagore.[114] But the balance of power in India had by now decisively changed with the steady expansion of power of the English Company. The French East India Company was finally wound up in 1769 and thus was eliminated its main European rival in India. It was now also the *de facto* master of Carnatic, although the Treaty of Paris had assured the nawab his entire possessions. His nominal sovereignty was respected till 1801; then, after the death of the incumbent nawab, his territories were annexed and his heir was pensioned off. Hyderabad too virtually became dependent on the English and the nizam in 1766 gave them the Northern Sarkars in return for military support against his overmighty neighbours. The Anglo-French rivalry by bringing in Crown troops to India in significant numbers considerably enhanced the military power of the English East India Company vis-à-vis the other Indian states. The balance of power in India had now begun to tilt decisively in its favour.

This brings us to the question of the Company's relationship with the other Indian rulers. The Indian states in the eighteenth century were perpetually involved in mutual conflicts. Their urge for territorial expansion was for gaining control over new resources, because internally in many areas a limit had been reached for extraction of fresh revenue. Politically each one was trying to establish supremacy over others and the English were looked upon as a new force in this power game. Combining as a nation against an alien power was beyond the imagination of the Indian princes in the eighteenth century political context. It was no wonder, therefore, that often they entered into diplomatic alliances with the Company in order to turn the balance of power in their favour in their contests against neighbours. This rivalry between the Indian states offered an opportunity, while commercial interests provided a sufficient motivation for

English intervention in local politics. However, as the following story would suggest, the Company was not just responding to opportunities, as suggested by some historians; it was also showing great deal of initiative in creating those opportunities to intervene and conquer, as insecure frontiers or unstable states were often construed as threats to free flow of trade. It is true that for a short period after the passage of the Pitt's India Act in 1784 there was parliamentary prohibition on imperial expansion, and the major thrust of the policy of the Board of Control and the East India Company during this time was to protect British possessions and promote trading interests through a careful balance of power between the Indian states, thus reducing imperial military liabilities. But that cautious policy was jettisoned when Lord Wellesley arrived as governor general in 1798, with a dream of conquest and a lust for personal glory. The policy of balance of power no longer worked in India, he decided even before arriving in the country, and so what was needed was empire. Napoleonic invasion of Egypt in the summer of 1798 offered him a useful tool to soften London's resistance to expansion, although he never believed for a moment that there was any danger of a French invasion of British India either over land from Egypt or a naval attack round the Cape of Good Hope. However, to assuage London's concerns he evolved the policy of 'Subsidiary Alliance', which would only establish control over the internal affairs of an Indian state, without incurring any direct imperial liability. Wellesley's personal agenda for expansion was also buttressed by a change of personnel in the Anglo-Indian diplomatic service favouring such a forward policy. As Edward Ingram has argued, Wellesley was "not formulating a policy in response to local conditions but trying to create the conditions necessary for the attainment of his objectives. . . . If Indian politics were turbulent, he described them as threatening, if they were tranquil, he ruffled them." However, authorities in London were not gullible or innocent observers in this imperial drama either. They sanctioned all the aggressive moves in pursuance of the most important objective of British foreign policy since 1784, i.e., protecting British India against all threats from its European rivals. Wellesley was recalled in 1805 only when his wars of conquest landed the Company's administration in India in a serious financial crisis.[115]

Within this context, it does not become difficult to understand why the political power of Mysore under Haidar Ali and Tipu Sultan appeared to be a security threat to the English position in Madras and in the Carnatic. In course of a few years, Mysore's boundaries had stretched from the Krishna in the north to the Malabar coast in the west, which inevitably brought it into conflict with its Indian neighbours, notably Hyderabad and the Marathas. And the two were often in collusion with the English, who suspected Mysore's friendship with the French. But this threat perception was more an "illusion" than real, as there was now very little chance of a possible French revival in India or a French attack from outside.[116] Mysore's control over the rich trade of the Malabar coast was also seen as a threat to English trade in pepper and cardamom. In 1785 Tipu declared an embargo on export of pepper, sandalwood and cardamom through the ports within his kingdom; in 1788 he explicitly forbade dealings with English traders. The interests of the private Company merchants now inevitably dictated a policy of direct political intervention to protect their commercial interests.[117] But most significantly, Tipu Sultan was trying to build in Mysore a strong centralised and militarised state, with ambitious territorial designs and a political aspiration to control south Indian politics. This made him the most potent danger to the as yet vulnerable Company state in the south. Young army officers like Thomas Munro and Alexander Read could see that the "mercantilist state" of Mysore represented the same kind of hegemonic ambition as those of the Company state in the south and therefore could never be relied upon in any arrangement of indirect rule based on the principle of balance of power among the Indian states. Hence, although the civilian administration in Madras vacillated, they concurred with Governor Generals Lord Cornwallis and later Lord Wellesley that Mysore needed to be eliminated.[118]

There were four rounds of battle (1767–69, 1780–84, 1790–92, and 1799) between the Company and Mysore, before the latter could be finally taken over in 1799. In the first Anglo-Mysore War, the Marathas and the nizam were with the British against Haidar Ali; in the second, they joined hands with Haidar against the British. But again the two powers sided with the British in 1790 when the latter under Lord Cornwallis declared war on Tipu Sultan who had lately attacked their ally, the Raja of Travancore. At the end of this war the Company annexed Dindigul, Baramahal and Malabar. A few years later, the spectre of a French resurgence and Tipu's secret negotiations with them gave a pretext to Lord Wellesley to move decisively for the final round of colonial aggression. In 1799 Srirangapatnam, the capital of Mysore, fell to the Company, while Tipu died defending it. Mysore, then once again placed under the former Wodeyar dynasty, was brought under the 'Subsidiary Alliance' system of Lord Wellesley. This meant an end to the independent state of

Mysore. Under this system, it would not henceforth enter into any relationship with other European powers; a contingent of Company army would be stationed in Mysore and the provision for its maintenance would come from its treasury. Part of Mysore territory was given to the nizam who had already accepted a 'Subsidiary Alliance'; and parts of it, such as Wynad, Coimbatore, Canara and Sunda, were directly annexed by the Company.

Meanwhile, the sudden growth of the Company's cotton trade with China through Bombay from Gujarat made them concerned about the security of Deccan, then under the control of the Maratha confederacy. A succession dispute provided the first opportunity for intervention, as Raghunath Rao, who had his nephew Peshwa Narayan Rao killed in a conspiracy, now faced combined opposition of the Maratha sardars and began to look at the British in Bombay as a possible new ally. In March 1775 Raghunath Rao's forces were defeated in Gujarat, and a combined British army from Madras and Bombay arrived in his rescue. An inconclusive treaty of Purandar in 1776 offered a number of concessions to the Company in return for its withdrawal of support for Raghunath Rao. But the treaty was not ratified by the authorities at Bengal and war was resumed again in 1777. By now the Maratha forces had regrouped under Nana Fadnis, Sindhia and Holkar and inflicted a crushing defeat on the British at Wadgaon (1779). The latter however got the revenue of southern Gujarat, as a strong contingent arriving from Bengal forced the Gaikwad to surrender it. This was the period that witnessed the rise of Nana Fadnis to the political centrestage of the Maratha polity. By 1781 he and the Bhonsle family had formed a grand alliance with the nizam and Haidar Ali against the British. But the inconclusive First Anglo-Maratha War came to an end in 1782 through the Treaty of Salbai, which committed the Marathas once again to friendship with the Company and also to a confrontation with Mysore.

The Maratha state was, however, in a deplorable condition by now, due to the bitter internal rivalry between the sardars. Nana Fadnis had made the peshwa virtually powerless. In 1795 the frustrated peshwa committed suicide and the succession dispute that followed put the entire Maratha polity into utter confusion. The new peshwa Baji Rao II wanted to get rid of Fadnis and sought allies in different quarters. With the latter's death in 1800 the confusion deepened even further. While Daulat Rao Sindhia supported the peshwa, the Holkar's army started plundering his territories in Malwa. A desperate peshwa once again looked at the Company for help. In the meanwhile, with the arrival of Wellesley, there had also been a remarkable change in British attitudes towards the Indian states: Hyderabad, as we have already seen, had accepted a 'Subsidiary Alliance' and Mysore was crushed in 1799. So, this brought the Company face to face with the Marathas, the only remaining significant indigenous power in the subcontinent. After Holkar's army defeated the peshwa's forces and plundered Poona in October 1802, the peshwa fled to the British in Bassein and in 1803 was obliged to sign a 'Subsidiary Alliance'. Surat was handed over to the Company, while the peshwa agreed to pay for a British army and consult a British Resident stationed in his court. Hereafter, Baji Rao was escorted to Poona and installed in office; but this did not mean an immediate end to independent Maratha power.

This in fact marked the beginning of the Second Anglo-Maratha War (1803–5), as Holkar soon put up a rival candidate for peshwaship and looked for allies. Lord Wellesley and Lord Lake on the other hand fielded a large army and for the next two years battle continued at different fronts across the Maratha territories. In the end, treaties of subordination were imposed on a number of tributaries of the Marathas, like the Rajput states, the Jats, the Rohillas and the Bundellas in northern Malwa. Orissa was taken control of, while the treaty with the Sindhia secured the British all his territories north of Jamuna including Delhi and Agra, all his possessions in Gujarat and claims over the other Maratha houses. The treaty also forbade other Europeans from accepting service in any Maratha army and made the British arbiters in any dispute between the Maratha houses. But even this did not mean the final demise of the Maratha power!

The wars, on the other hand, meant huge expenses for the Company, and the Court of Directors, already dissatisfied with the forward policy of Lord Wellesley, recalled him in 1805. Lord Cornwallis was reappointed as the governor general in India with specific instructions to follow a policy of non-intervention. This allowed the Maratha sardars, like Holkar and Sindhia, to regain some of their power, while their irregular soldiers, known as the Pindaris, plundered the countryside in Malwa and Rajasthan. The situation continued for some time till the arrival of Lord Hastings as the governor general in 1813. He initiated the new policy of "paramountcy", which privileged the interests of the Company as a paramount power over those of other powers in India and to protect such interests the Company could legitimately annex or threaten to annex the territories of any Indian state.[119] Peshwa Baji Rao II around this time made a desperate last attempt to regain his independence from the

English by rallying the Maratha chiefs. This led to the Third Anglo-Maratha War (1817–19) in which Holkar's army and the Pindaris were thoroughly crushed; the British took complete control over the peshwa's dominions and peshwaship itself was abolished. Significant parts of the territories of Bhonsle and Holkar were also ceded to the Company, while they entered into alliance of subordination.[120] The English East India Company had now complete mastery over all the territories south of the Vindhyas.

In north India too there had been by now significant acquisition of territories. Ever since the victory at Buxar and the Treaty of Allahabad, Awadh was serving as a buffer state between the Company's position in Bengal and the turbulent politics in north India, particularly imperilled by Maratha depredations. British strategic interests in Awadh were secured by the stationing of a Resident at the court of Lucknow in 1773 and the positioning of a permanent British garrison in Awadh, to be paid for by Nawab Shuja-ud-daula through the payment of a subsidy. Soon, however, this became a contentious issue, as the amount of subsidy demanded by the Company increased gradually. To meet this increasing demand, the nawab had to impose more taxes, which soured his relationship with the taluqdars. This was the prime reason for more political instability in the state, which eventually became a pretext for direct annexation. Warren Hastings, who became the governor general in 1774, had first argued that the best way to ensure regular payment of the subsidy was to annex those territories of Awadh whose revenues were equal to the amount of subsidy. Distraught by the French and Mysore wars, the Company's desperate need for money at this stage was amply revealed in the demands imposed on Chait Singh of Banaras, his inability to pay and his subsequent deposition in August 1781. The crisis was also manifested in the bizarre saga of extortion, under direct instruction from Warren Hastings, from the Begums of Awadh, who still controlled the treasures of Shuja, ostensibly to pay the mounting debt of the nawab to the Company.

So annexation of Awadh was clearly on the cards for quite some time and Wellesley gave it a concrete shape in 1801, when the nawab expressed his apprehension that he might not be able to pay the subsidy. There were other reasons too. Ever since the Treaty of Allahabad, Nawab Shuja-ud-daula had been complaining about the rampant abuse of the Company's duty free trading rights by the European private traders and their Indian *gomustahs*. The Company's authorities only half-heartedly tried to control it, as it was beyond their power to restrain these merchants. Moreover, Awadh had become crucially important for expanding British seaborn trade from Bengal. In the last decade of the eighteenth century, there was an expanding demand for indigo in London, and about three-fifths of its total export from India came from Awadh. By the beginning of the nineteenth century, Awadh raw cotton became another chief item of supply to China market to keep the imperial balance of trade in favour of Britain.[121] In this context, the high rate of taxes imposed by the nawab on exports from Awadh even after the treaty of 1788, signed during the time of Lord Cornwallis to ensure "free trade", was certainly an irritant.[122] Annexation seemed imminent when with the arrival of Lord Wellesley there was a clear tilt in Company's policies in favour of vigorous expansion.

The first opportunity for intervention was provided in 1797 by the death of Nawab Asaf-ud-daula, who had succeeded Shuja in 1775. The English refused to recognise the claim of his son to succeed and put the late nawab's brother Saadat Ali Khan on the throne. As a price, the latter agreed to transfer a few territories and pay a staggering annual subsidy of Rs. 7.6 million. Yet, this did not solve the problem, as the new nawab, though willing to pay subsidy, was not prepared to accept British interference in his administration. In 1801, Wellesley, therefore, sent his brother Henry to impose on him a treaty, which resulted in the annexation of half of Awadh as a permanent payment of the subsidy. In real terms, this amounted to the cession of Rohilkhand, Gorakhpur and the Doab, which yielded a gross revenue of Rs. 13,523,475—almost double the amount of the subsidy.[123] Wellesley justified his action in terms of high moral argument, i.e., to save Awadh from incurably bad native administration;[124] but it is difficult to separate this issue from the revenue and commercial demands of imperialism.[125] What is more significant, the problem did not end there. The arrangement of 1801 did not end British extortion, though it was meant to be a final payment of subsidy. The office of the Residency in Lucknow gradually developed into an alternative centre of power within Awadh, fabricating its own constituency of courtiers, administrators and landlords, bought off with various kinds of favours and extra-territorial protection. The Resident thus systematically isolated the nawab, undermined his political and moral authority and reduced his military capabilities.[126] When Lord Dalhousie finally annexed the remainder of Awadh in 1856 on grounds of misgovernment, it was only a logical culmination of a long-drawn out process.

The only other major power now left in north India were the Sikhs of Punjab. The consolidation of Sikh power had taken place under Ranjit Singh in the late eighteenth century (1795–98). During his lifetime there was no major tension with the British; but after his death Punjab became politically unstable. A number of people ascended the throne in quick succession and the whole region was plunged into prolonged and bloody succession battles. But what contributed to these family feuds and court conspiracies was the breakdown of the delicate balance of power that Ranjit Singh had carefully maintained between the hereditary Sikh chieftains and the upstarts, and between the Punjabi and Dogra nobles from Jammu in the royal court. Corruption in the bureaucracy and the internecine strife among the sardars put the Punjab economy into shambles. In the countryside, revenue demands increased after 1839 due to the rise in the cost of the army, resulting in zamindar resistance to revenue collection. On the other hand, the kardars increased their extortion of the landed zamindars and continued to defraud the central treasury. The developments only encouraged centrifugal tendencies within the Punjabi society.[127] The commercial classes were disenchanted by political disruptions and the whole situation offered opportunities to the British to intervene.

To tell the story briefly, when Ranjit Singh died in 1839, he had nominated his son Kharak Singh to be his successor. He was not known to be a very able administrator and became dependent on his Dogra wazir Raja Dhian Singh. The relationship was initially cordial, but soon the maharaja tried to clip his wazir's wings by patronising the anti-Dogra faction in his court. But the wazir fought back, allied himself with the maharaja's son Nao Nihal Singh, but before this could go much further, Kharak Singh died in 1840, followed immediately by the death of his son in an accident. Now the throne was contested by Sher Singh, one of the six living princes, and Maharani Chand Kaur, the widow of Kharak Singh, who laid a claim on behalf of her unborn grandchild to be born to Nihal Singh's widowed wife. In this contest Sher Singh was supported by the Dogra faction, while the Maharani's claim was upheld by the Sindhanwalia chieftains, who were collaterals of the royal family. Both the candidates appealed to the Company for support, but the latter decided not to interfere. Sher Singh ultimately became the maharaja through a bizarre conspiracy hatched by the Dogras, and once again became dependent on the overmighty Dogra wazir, Raja Dhian Singh. However, as it had happened earlier, after a short while the maharaja sought to reduce the power of his wazir and began to align with his adversaries in the court, like the Sindhanwalias and other hereditary chiefs. But the strategy backfired, as the Sindhanwalias now had their revenge by getting him murdered in 1843 along with his son, and also wazir Dhian Singh. But soon the table was turned again by the latter's son Raja Hira Singh Dogra, who won over a section of the army, destroyed the Sindhanwalias and put up Ranjit Singh's youngest son five year old Dalip Singh on the throne, with himself taking on the wazir's office.

Palace intrigues and rivalries among the sardars did not end there. But now the Khalsa army became a power unto itself and began to control Punjabi politics. During Sher Singh's reign the army had established regimental committees or *panchayats*, which had direct access to the maharaja. These panchayats now began to demand more and more concessions from the darbar, and Hira Singh could survive only by making larger grants to the army. But this could not go on for long as anti-Dogra sentiments began to rise among the army and the hereditary chieftains. Hira Singh was assassinated in December 1844, whereupon Dalip Singh's mother Maharani Jindan became the Regent and her brother Sardar Jawahir Singh became the wazir; but he remained for all practical purposes a puppet in the hands of the army. It was this political rise of the Khalsa army, its new experiments with democratic republicanism, and the prospect of there being no stable government in Lahore that made the British concerned about Punjab. In the early nineteenth century the Company wanted to maintain the Sikh state as a buffer between its north Indian possessions on the one end and the Muslim powers in Persia and Afghanistan on the other. But continuous political instability made that scheme unworkable and so many in the early 1840s began to think of the inevitability of an Anglo-Sikh confrontation. Preparations for this on the British side began in 1843, and as the situation did not stabilise, and when Jawahir Singh was executed by the army in September 1945, Lord Hardinge decided that the time for a showdown had arrived. He declared war on the state of Lahore on 13 December 1845 and the first Anglo-Sikh war began.[128]

Failure of leadership and treachery of some of the sardars led to the defeat of the formidable Sikh army. The humiliating treaty of Lahore in March 1846 resulted in the English annexation of Jalandhar Doab; Kashmir was given to Raja Ghulab Singh Dogra of Jammu, as a reward for his allegiance to the Company. The size of the Lahore army was reduced, and an English army was stationed there. Dalip Singh was to retain his throne, but was to be advised and guided by an English Resident. Another treaty in December removed Maharani Jindan from the position of Regent, formed a Regency Council and gave the English Resident at Lahore extensive authority to direct and control the activities of every department of state. But the ultimate British aim was full annexation of Punjab, which was achieved by Governor General Lord Dalhousie after the victory in the Second Anglo-Sikh War in 1849. The immediate pretext for aggression was the rebellion of two Sikh governors, Diwan Mul Raj of Multan and Sardar Chattar Singh Atariwala and his son Raja Sher Singh of Haripur. In the first two rounds of battle at Ramnagar in November 1848 and at Chillianwala in January 1849, the British suffered heavy losses. But this was soon reversed in February-March, as the rebel sardars surrendered one after another. On 29 March 1849 Maharaja Dalip Singh signed the document of annexation; Punjab hereafter became a province of the East India Company's empire in India.[129]

Other parts of India were also gradually coming under direct or indirect control of the Company during the nineteenth century, as empire itself—or more precisely, the security of the empire—became an argument justifying further imperial expansion. The authorities in India, particularly the military establishment, continually anticipated dangers from outside as well as from within to the security of the Indian empire, and the best guarantee of security they believed was a vigorous display of the power of the sword. This argument swept aside all the cautionary attitudes that the Company directors in London might have had against further territorial aggression. Lord Amherst came to India as governor general with a clear mandate to ensure peace and eschew expensive imperial wars, but came to face a growing crisis with Burma in the northeastern borders of Bengal. The Burmese monarchy had been showing expansionary tendencies since the second half of the eighteenth century, when it subjugated Pegu, Tenasserim and Arakan and then in the early years of the nineteenth century extended its influence in Manipur, Cachar and finally Assam. These moves in the past did not always lead to annexation and so the earlier governors general chose to ignore them. But in 1822–23 the Anglo-Indian military elite began to argue, after a lull in imperial warfare for about six years, that the internal enemies of the empire were drawing encouragement from the audacious incursions of the Burmese. So the Burmese needed to be treated a lesson, preferably through a vigorous display of power.[130] Hence in 1824–28 began the Company's First Burma War, which brought the annexation of Assam and Nagaland in northeastern India as well as Arakan and Tenasserim in Lower Burma. In 1830 Cachar was added to Company's territory; Coorg was later annexed in 1834 by Lord Bentinck.

If Burma was a threat in the northeast, Russo-phobia before and after the Crimean War (1854–56) provided a prime motive for British expansion towards the northwest. Lord Auckland fought the first Afghan War in 1838–42 to install indirect rule by restoring a deposed king on the Afghan throne; and Lord Ellenborough took over Sind in 1843. However, it was during the time of Lord Dalhousie (1848–56) that expansionist tendencies became most manifest during Company's regime. By using his "Doctrine of Lapse", i.e., the policy of annexing the territories of Indian rulers who died without a male heir, he took over Satara (1848), Sambalpur and Baghat (1850), Udaipur (1852), Nagpur (1853) and Jhansi (1854). The Second Burma War (1852–53) resulted in the annexation of Pegu, while in 1853 he took over Berar from Hyderabad to secure the payment of subsidy for the Company's army. Thus by 1857 the Company had annexed about 63 per cent of the territories of the Indian subcontinent and had subordinated over 78 per cent of its population.[131] The remaining territories were left in charge of Indian princes, who were relied upon after 1858 for ensuring the loyalty of their people to the British Raj. Its policies by now had shifted from those of annexation to that of indirect rule.[132] Quite often, however, the princely states had to experience intensive British intervention, although formally no more annexation occurred (see chapter 2.4 for more details on princely states and indirect rule).

To sum up our discussion, whether intended by the government at home or crafted by the East India Company's servants on the spot—supposedly sucked into a career of conquest by the political crisis of eighteenth century India—the link between commercial and political expansion is not difficult to discern in the story of imperialism in India in the late eighteenth and early nineteenth centuries. By way of identifying the continuities in British imperial history, Gallagher and Robinson (1953) argued that the British policy should be summed up as "trade with informal control if possible; trade with rule when necessary". It may be pointed out, however, that differences between such analytical categories are rather dubious; it was from attempts to secure trade benefits through informal control that the necessity to secure direct rule arose more often. The considerable growth of private trade and the expansion of the activities of free merchants had been dependent on the growth of British power and this created possibilities of conflict. Indian rulers were constantly pressurised to grant immunities and concessions and in the end, such successive demands corroded the authority of the Indian states. It was possible for the Company to effectively exert pressure because of the rivalry among the Indian rulers and factionalism within their courts, which prevented the formation of a joint front. The dream of Nana Fadnis to forge a confederacy of Indian princes pitted against British power never really actualised.[133]

Thus for the Company, commerce provided the will to conquer and the political disunity provided the opportunity; now there was the question of capacity to conquer an empire. In spite of the Mughal decline, the successor states were not weak, though in terms of military organisation and technology, their armies were backward in comparison with the European forces. The Anglo-French rivalry brought in Crown troops to India at an unprecedented scale and this increased British military power, indicating a greater positive input of the metropolis in the affairs of the Indian empire. But what was more significant, the Company at this stage decided to raise its own army in India, to be disciplined and commanded by European officers. The size of this Company army steadily increased, giving it a decisive military edge over its political adversaries. On the other hand, the new army itself became a reason for fresh demands on the Indian rulers and hence the perpetual tension about the amount and payment of subsidies. The Company's obsession with stable frontiers, as a necessary precondition for smooth operation of trade, was another motivation behind conquest, as one annexation brought them to more unstable frontiers, which necessitated more conquests. However, it was also the army establishment—that devoured the largest share of the Indian revenues—which deliberately created and reinforced such an environment of scare that continually anticipated threats to the security of the empire either from an allegedly militarised Indian society or from outside. Conquest therefore became a self-perpetuating and self-legitimising process, justifying the maintenance of a vast military establishment (for more on the army, see chapter 2.4).

The success of the East India Company also depended on its capacity to mobilise greater resources than its rivals. The soldiers fighting at the frontline for the Company's army were better fed and regularly paid in contrast to those servicing the Mughal successor states. The Indian bankers who controlled and transferred large sums of money through hundis, seemed to have been preferring the Company as a more trustworthy creditor than the unstable Indian princes.[134] The Company gradually reduced this dependence and turned it upside down by establishing control over the revenue resources, which became vital for financing trade as well as further conquests. Revenue considerations got the Company involved in administration and thus there was the progression from military ascendancy to dominion of territory—from indirect rule to direct annexation. This approximates closely to the point made by Cain and Hopkins about the primacy of revenue in the functioning of British imperialism in India. The politically emerging alliance at home between land and money, they argue, created the notion of power being centred in land and hence the preoccupation of the Company-state with "the need to raise revenue as well as to keep order", which determined the course of much of the later annexations and consolidation of British rule in India.[135] The consanguinity between revenue, commerce and military exigencies in the process of British imperial expansion in India is a point too obvious to miss; it is futile to debate over their relative importance. It is also difficult to deny that from the late eighteenth century the colonial state was being fashioned by the ideologies and values of Georgian England, using state power to garner the fruits of capitalism, to protect the liberal benefits of freedom of trade or right to property and to secure markets for commodities at home and abroad.[136] Both at ideational and functional levels, the pressures from the periphery and the interests of the metropole worked in conjunction in conquering and administering the empire in India. It is in the next chapter that we will discuss in more detail how these political debates in England actually informed the modes of imperial governance in India.

NOTES

1. Richards 1993: 282.
2. Pearson 1976.
3. Athar Ali 1966.
4. Qaisar 1965.
5. Chandra 1973: xiv.
6. Athar Ali 1975.
7. Malik 1977.
8. Chandra 1993.
9. Raychaudhuri 1982.
10. Hasan 1969.
11. Richards 1976.
12. Alam 1974.
13. Richards 1975.
14. Alam 1974.
15. Siddiqi 1973.
16. Alam and Subrahmanyam 1998: 59, 68.
17. Alam 1986.

18. Eaton 1993.
19. Richards 1993: 295–96.
20. Bayly 1983.
21. Wink 1986: 27, 34 and passim.
22. Perlin 1985: 435, 452 and passsim.
23. Alam 1986.
24. Bayly 1987: 9.
25. Alam 1991: 68.
26. See Wink–Habib debate in *The Indian Economic and Social History Review*, 1989, 26 (1): 363–72.
27. Athar Ali 1993: 703–6.
28. See Karim 1963 for details.
29. Calkins 1970.
30. Sinha 1962.
31. For more on trade see Prakash 1976, 1988; Chaudhury 1995 and Subramanian 2001.
32. Calkins 1970; Marshall 1987.
33. Calkins 1970: 805.
34. See Subramanian 2001; for an opposing view Chaudhury 1995.
35. Marshall 1987: 75 and passim.
36. Leonard 1971: 575 and passim.
37. Barnett 1980: 40.
38. See Barnett 1980 for details.
39. See Gordon 1993 for details.
40. Wink 1986: 115–29.
41. Das Gupta 1979.
42. Jagadish N. Sarkar 1976.
43. For more details on the Marathas see Gordon 1993.
44. See Perlin 1985: 450–64.
45. Wink 1986: 31–33, 154.
46. Gordon 1993: 145.
47. McLeod 1968.
48. Singh 1963: 1.
49. McLeod 1976.
50. Oberoi 1994: 66–69.
51. Grewal 1990.
52. Alam 1986: 134–55.
53. Oberoi 1994: 73.
54. See Grewal 1990 for details.
55. See Banga 1978 for details.
56. Oberoi 1994: 86, 90.
57. Major 1996: 30–31.
58. Bayly 1987: 22, 152.
59. Kolff 1990: 32–37, 58.
60. Ibid: 58, 71 and passim.
61. Zieglar 1998: 257–64
62. Vidal 1997: 46–47.

63. Peabody 1996: 206.
64. Athar Ali 1961.
65. Chandra 1993.
66. Stein 1985.
67. Habib 2000: xxi–xxiii.
68. Stein 1985: 392–93, 402–5.
69. Quoted in Sheik Ali 2000: 64.
70. Habib 2000: xxxv and passim; also see Stein 1985: 403.
71. Brittlebank 1997: 73.
72. Das Gupta 1967.
73. Alam and Subrahmanyam 1998: 26.
74. Jeffrey 1994: xviii–xix.
75. Alam 1986.
76. Eaton 1993: 312.
77. See Chakrabarty 1985 for details.
78. Robinson 2001: 14 and passim.
79. Eaton 1978: 290–91.
80. See Habib 1999.
81. Leonard 1979.
82. Bayly 1987: 11.
83. Marshall 1998: 498.
84. Marshall 1975a.
85. Marshall 1998: 506.
86. Bayly 1989: 10.
87. For more on this concept, see Gallagher and Robinson 1961.
88. Chaudhuri 1978.
89. Hunter 1899–1900, 1: 256.
90. Lawson 1993: 49.
91. Keay 1991: 131.
92. Ibid.
93. Lawson 1993: 47–48.
94. Ibid: 50–51.
95. Keay 1991: 182.
96. Cain and Hopkins 1993: 323–24.
97. Sen 1998: 80, 126–27.
98. Fisher 1993: 13.
99. Cain and Hopkins 1993: 321.
100. Lawson 1993: 45.
101. Watson 1980.
102. See Marshall 1976: 109–12; Sen 1998: 79–81.
103. Lawson 1993: 66–70 and passim.
104. Chaudhury 2000: 80 and passim.
105. Ibid; Marshall 1987: 91.
106. See Subramanian 2001.
107. Marshall 1976: 165.
108. Gupta 1962.
109. Fisher 1991: 50.

110. Barnett 1980; Fisher 1991: 378.
111. Gardner 1971: 54–55.
112. Sen 1971: 27.
113. See Sen 1971 for details.
114. See ibid for details.
115. For a detailed discussion on Wellesley, see Ingram 1981: 115–91; quotation from 117–18.
116. Sen 1971: 23.
117. See Nightingale 1970.
118. Stein 1989: 19, 24, 349.
119. Fisher 1993: 19.
120. See Gordon 1993 for details.
121. Mukherjee 1982.
122. Marshall 1975b.
123. Barnett 1980.
124. Marshall 1975b.
125. Mukherjee 1982.
126. Fisher 1991: 384–86.
127. For details, see Major 1996: 53–57.
128. For more details, see ibid: 40–74.
129. For details, see Singh 1966: 2; Grewal 1990.
130. For this argument see Peers 1995: 149–53.
131. Details in Fisher 1993: 21–24 and passim.
132. Metcalf 1965.
133. Ray 1998: 519–20.
134. Subramanian 1995.
135. Cain and Hopkins 1993: 321–28.
136. Sen 1998: 130.

chapter two

British Empire in India

2.1. The Imperial Ideology

Since the conquest of Ireland in the sixteenth century, the English gradually emerged as the "new Romans, charged with civilizing backward peoples" across the world, from Ireland to America and from India to Africa.[1] This imperial history of Britain is periodised into two phases, the "first empire" stretching across the Atlantic towards America and the West Indies, and the "second empire", starting from around 1783 (Peace of Paris) and swinging towards the East, i.e., Asia and Africa. The details of structural or ideological disjunctures and interfaces between the two empires are not relevant here, but it suffices to say, that from the late eighteenth century there was a greater acceptance of a territorial empire based on the conservative values of military autocracy, hierarchy and racial insolence.[2] As British patriotism gradually developed in the eighteenth century, it was closely associated with the grandeur and glories of having overseas territorial possessions. In a post-Enlightenment intellectual environment, the British also started defining themselves as modern or civilised vis-à-vis the Orientals and this rationalised their imperial vision in the nineteenth century, which witnessed the so-called 'age of reform'. In other words, British imperial ideology for India was the result of such intellectual and political crosscurrents at home. Sometimes, "sub-imperialism"[3] of the men on the spot, regarded by some as the "real founders of empire",[4] and pressures from the ruled—in short, the crises in the periphery—led to adjustments and mutations in the functioning of that ideology. The nature of the imperial connection also changed over time; but not its fundamentals.

For several years, it is argued, the government of the East India Company functioned like an "Indian ruler", in the sense that it recognised the authority of the Mughal emperor, struck coins in his name, used Persian as the official language and administered Hindu and Muslim laws in the courts. Lord Clive himself had recommended a system of "double government" as a matter of expediency, under which the criminal justice system would be left in the hands of nawabi officials, while civil and fiscal matters would be controlled by the Company. This policy of least intervention, which had emanated from pure pragmatism to avoid civil disturbances, did not, however, wane rapidly when such situations ceased to exist, although the Company officials were then required to get involved much more deeply in the administration. The Anglicisation of the structure of this administration began, but it progressed, as it seems, gradually. It was not, in other words, a revolutionary change, as the officials looked at themselves "as inheritors rather than innovators, as the revivers of a decayed system".[5]

The idea of this "decayed system" however originated from a teleological construction of India's past. The early image of India in the West was that of past glory accompanied by an idea of degeneration. There was an urge to know Indian culture and tradition, as reflected in the endeavours of scholars like Sir William Jones, who studied the Indian languages to restore to the Indians their own forgotten culture and legal system—monopolised hitherto only by the learned pundits and maulvis (Hindu and Islamic learned men). By establishing a linguistic connection between Sanskrit, Greek and Latin—all supposedly belonging to the same Indo-European family of languages—Jones privileged India with an antiquity equal to that of classical West. This was the beginning of the Orientalist tradition that led to the founding of institutions like the Calcutta Madrassa (1781), the Asiatic Society of Bengal (1784) and the Sanskrit College in Banaras (1794), all of which were meant to promote the study of Indian languages and scriptures. One should remember, however, that while discovering India, primarily through analysis of ancient texts, these Orientalist scholars were also defining Indian "tradition" in a particular way that came to be privileged as the most authentic version or true knowledge, for it was legitimated by the power of the colonial state. Some scholars like Eugene Irschick have argued that contrary to the supposition of Edward Said (1978) that Orientalism was a knowledge thrust from above through the power of the Europeans, it was produced through a process of dialogue in which the colonial officials, Indian commentators and native informants participated in a collaborative intellectual exercise. One could point out though that even when Indians participated in this exercise, they seldom had control over its final outcome. However, while emphasising the importance of the Indian agency, Irschick does not deny the most important aspect of this cognitive enterprise, that Orientalism produced a knowledge of the past to meet the requirements of the present, i.e., to service the needs of the colonial state.[6]

Orientalism in practice in its early phase could be seen in the policies of the Company's government under Warren Hastings. The fundamental principle of this tradition was that the conquered people were to be ruled by their own laws—British rule had to "legitimize itself in an Indian idiom".[7] It therefore needed to produce knowledge about Indian society, a process which Gauri Viswanathan would call "reverse acculturation". It informed the European rulers of the customs and laws of the land for the purposes of assimilating them into the subject society for more efficient administration.[8] It was with this political vision that Fort William College at Calcutta was established in 1800 to train civil servants in Indian languages and tradition. The Orientalist discourse, however, had another political project, as Thomas Trautmann (1997) has argued. By giving currency to the idea of kinship between the British and the Indians dating back to the classical past, it was also morally binding the latter to colonial rule through a rhetoric of "love". "Every accumulation of knowledge", Warren Hastings wrote in 1785, "is useful to the state: . . . it attracts and conciliates distant affections; it lessens the weight of the chain by which the natives are held in subjection; and it imprints on the hearts of our own countrymen the sense and obligation of benevolence."[9] But if the Orientalist discourse was initially premised on a respect for ancient Indian traditions, it produced a knowledge about the subject society, which ultimately prepared the ground for the rejection of Orientalism as a policy of governance. These scholars not only highlighted the classical glory of India—crafted by the Aryans, the distant kin-brothers of the Europeans—but also emphasised the subsequent degeneration of the once magnificent Aryan civilisation. This legitimated authoritarian rule, as India needed to be rescued from the predicament of its own creation and elevated to a desired state of progress as achieved by Europe.

Hastings's policy was therefore abandoned by Lord Cornwallis, who went for greater Anglicisation of the administration and the imposition of the Whig principles of the British government. Lord Wellesley supported these moves, the aim of which was to limit government interference by abandoning the supposedly despotic aspects of Indian political tradition and ensuring a separation of powers between the judiciary and the executive. The state's role would only be the protection of individual rights and private property. The policy came from a consistent disdain for "Oriental despotism", from which Indians needed to be emancipated. Despotism was something that distinguished the Oriental state from its European counterpart; but ironically, it was the same logic that provided an "implicit justification" for the "paternalism of the Raj".[10] From the very early stages of conquest, the Company state tried to curb the local influence of the rajas and zamindars, the local remnants of the Mughal state, in order to ensure a free flow of trade and steady collection of revenues. And ostensibly for that same purpose, it took utmost care in surveying and policing the territory and insisted on the exclusive control over the regalia of power, e.g., flag, uniform, badges and seals.[11] This indicated the emergence of a strong state, based on the premise that natives were not used to enjoying freedom and needed to be emancipated from their corrupt and abusive feudal lords. Men like William Jones typified such paternalist attitude exhibited by many British officers at that time. Radical at home, attracted to the glorious past of India and its simple people, they remained nonetheless the upholders of authoritarian rule in India.[12] One purpose of the Fort William College was to prevent the spread of the ideas of freedom preached by the French Revolution. Javed Majeed (1992), therefore, sees no apparent contradiction, but a gradual evolution of a conservative ideology in the ideas of Jones since his arrival in India. This conservatism, of which Edmund Burke was the chief exponent, was related to domestic politics in England facing the threat of Jacobinism. The Georgian state had to consolidate public support at home by manipulating ceremonies and enhancing the popular profile of the monarchy. The issue of uniqueness of cultures, requiring change or not, tied in an unmistakable way the questions of reform at home and in India. The process of Anglicisation and the regulative administration under Cornwallis and Wellesley reflected this conservatism of the time.

As Eric Stokes (1959) has shown, two distinct trends were gradually emerging in the Indian administration of the East India Company, although they were not totally unrelated. There was, on the one hand, the Cornwallis system, centred in Bengal, and based primarily on the Permanent Settlement. Lord Cornwallis introduced Permanent Settlement with the hope that the rule of law and private property rights would liberate individual enterprise from the shackles of custom and tradition, and would bring in modernisation to the economy and society. But Thomas Munro in Madras, and his disciples in western and northern India, such as Mountstuart Elphinstone, John Malcolm and Charles Metcalfe, thought that the Cornwallis system did not pay heed to Indian tradition and experience. Not that they were averse to the rule of law or separation of powers; but such reforms, they thought, had to be modified to suit the Indian context. Some elements of the Indian tradition of personal government needed to be maintained, they believed; the role of the Company's government would be protective, rather than intrusive, regulative or innovative. So Munro went on to introduce his Ryotwari Settlement, with the intention of preserving India's village communities. But ultimately his aim was to consolidate the Company's state in the south by expanding its revenue base, where land taxes would be collected directly from the peasants by a large number of British officers, an idea he had borrowed from the "military fiscalism" of Tipu Sultan's Mysore (see chapter 1.2).[13] Both the systems, it therefore appears, were based on the same fundamental principles of centralised sovereignty, sanctity of private property, to be protected by British laws. Munro believed, as Burton Stein argues, that part of India should be indirectly governed; but he insisted that the traditional Indian forms of government would function well if "directed by men like himself, knowledgeable and sympathetic, with great and concentrated authority". This authoritative paternalism rejected the idea of direct political participation by Indians.[14] Respect and paternalism, therefore, remained the two complementing ideologies of the early British empire in India. And significantly, it was soon discovered that imperial authoritarianism could function well in conjunction with the local elites of Indian rural society—the zamindars in Bengal and the mirasidars in Madras—whose power was therefore buttressed by both the Cornwallis system and the Munro system, both of which sought to define and protect private property. If the Awadh taluqdars lost out, their angst caused the revolt of 1857; and after the revolt they were again restored to their former positions of glory and authority.[15]

If Cornwallis was a little restrained and conservative, it was partly out of the expediencies of administering a newly conquered territory, and at the same time raising sufficient revenue to pay for the Company's annual investments. The situation began to change with further conquests and pacification. Around 1800 the Industrial Revolution in Britain created the necessity to develop and integrate the Indian markets for manufactured goods and ensure a secured supply of raw materials. This required a more effective administration and the tying up of the colony to the economy of the mother country. There were also several new intellectual currents in Britain, which preached the idea of improvement and thus pushed forward the issue of reform both at home and in India. While the pressure of the free trade lobby at home worked towards the abolition of the Company's monopoly over Indian trade, it was Evangelicalism and Utilitarianism, which brought about a fundamental change in the nature of the Company's administration in India. Both these two schools of thought asserted that the conquest of India had been by acts of sin or crime; but instead of advocating the abolition of this sinful or criminal rule, they clamoured for its reform, so that Indians could get the benefit of good government in keeping with the "best ideas of their age". It was from these two intellectual traditions "the conviction that England should remain in India permanently was finally to evolve".[16]

Evangelicalism started its crusade against Indian barbarism and advocated the permanence of British rule with a mission to change the very "nature of Hindostan". In India the spokespersons of this idea were the missionaries located at Srirampur near Calcutta; but at home its chief exponent was Charles Grant. The principal problem of India, he argued in 1792, was the religious ideas that perpetuated the ignorance of Indian people. This could be effectively changed through the dissemination of Christian light, and in this lay the noble mission of British rule in India. To convince his critics, Grant could also show a complementarity between the civilising process and material prosperity, without any accompanying danger of dissent or desire for English liberty. His ideas were given greater publicity by William Wilberforce in the Parliament before the passage of the Charter Act of 1813, which allowed Christian missionaries to enter India without restrictions.[17] The idea of improvement and change was also being advocated by the free-trade merchants, who believed that India would be a good market for British goods and a supplier of raw materials, if the Company shifted attention from its functions as a trader to those of a ruler. Under a good government the Indian peasants could again experience improvement to become consumers of British products. Fundamentally, there was no major difference between the Evangelist and the free-trade merchant positions as regards the policy of assimilation and Anglicisation. Indeed, it was the Evangelist Charles Grant who presided over the passage of the Charter Act of 1833, which took away the Company's monopoly rights over India trade.

This was also the age of British liberalism. Thomas Macaulay's liberal vision that the British administrators' task was to civilise rather than conquer, set a liberal agenda for the emancipation of India through active governance. "Trained by us to happiness and independence, and endowed with our learning and political institutions, India will remain the proudest monument of British benevolence", visualised C.E. Trevalyan, another liberal, in 1838.[18] It was in this atmosphere of British liberalism that Utilitarianism, with all its distinctive authoritarian tendencies, was born. Jeremy Bentham preached that the ideal of human civilisation was to achieve the greatest happiness of the greatest number. Good laws, efficient and enlightened administration, he argued, were the most effective agents of change; and the idea of rule of law was a necessary precondition for improvement. With the coming of the Utilitarian James Mill to the East India Company's London office, India policies came to be guided by such doctrines. Mill, as it has been contended, was responsible for transforming Utilitarianism into a "militant faith". In *The History of British India,* published in 1817, he first exploded the myth of India's economic and cultural riches, perpetuated by the "susceptible imagination" of men like Sir William Jones. What India needed for her improvement, he argued in a Benthamite line, was an effective schoolmaster, i.e., a wise government promulgating good legislation. It was largely due to his efforts that a Law Commission was appointed in 1833 under Lord Macaulay and it drew up an Indian Penal Code in 1835 on the Benthamite model of a centrally, logically and coherently formulated code, evolving from "disinterested philosophic intelligence".[19]

The Utilitarians differed from the liberals in significant ways, especially with regard to the question of Anglicisation. This was the time that witnessed the Orientalist–Anglicist debate on the nature of education to be introduced in India. While the liberal Lord Macaulay in his famous Education Minute of 1835 presented a strong case for the introduction of English education, Utilitarians like Mill still favoured vernacular education as more suited to Indian needs. In other words, dilemmas in imperial attitudes towards India persisted in the first half of the nineteenth century. Although gradually the Anglicists and Utilitarians were having their day, the old dilemmas were not totally overcome, and the epitome of this dilemma was Lord Bentinck, himself. An ardent follower of Mill, he abolished sati and child infanticide through legislation. He believed in the Utilitarian philosophy that legislation was an effective agent of change; and the concept of rule of law was a necessary precondition for improvement. But at the same time, he retained his faith in Indian traditions and nurtured a desire to give back to the Indians their true religion. The official discourse on the proposed reform of sati was, therefore, grounded in a scriptural logic that its abolition was warranted by ancient Hindu texts.[20] The Indian Penal Code drafted in 1835 could not become an act until 1860. The dilemmas definitely persisted in the mid-nineteenth century, in spite of Lord Dalhousie's determination to take forward Mill's vision of aggressive advancement of Britain's mission in India.

It was Victorian liberalism in post-1857 India that certainly made paternalism the dominant ideology of the Raj. The traumatic experience of the revolt convinced many in England and in India that reform was "pointless as well as dangerous"[21] and that Indians could never be trained to become like Englishmen. Not that the zeal for reform totally evaporated, as it was amply represented in the Crown Proclamation of 1858, in the patronage for education, in the Indian Councils Act of 1861 and in the Local Self-government Act of 1882, which in a limited way moved towards sharing power with the Indians. But on the other hand, veneration for Indian culture was definitely overshadowed by a celebration of the superiority of the conquering race. Bentinck's dithering attitudes were now replaced by the authoritarian liberalism of James Fitzjames Stephen, who succeeded Macaulay as the new law member in the viceroy's council. He not only emphasised India's difference, but also asserted India's inferiority. Such ideas in the nineteenth century were further strengthened by the rise of racial sciences in Victorian England, which privileged physical features over languages as the chief markers of racial identity. This racial anthropology could not accommodate the idea of an ancient Indian civilisation into its theory of dichotomy between the civilised white-skinned Europeans and the dark-skinned savages. Hence the story of invading white Aryans founding the Vedic civilisation through a confrontation with the dark-skinned Indian aborigines was invented, a theory constructed by "consistent overreading" of evidence and "a considerable amount of text-torturing".[22] To put it more directly, this new Orientalist discourse—contributed not just by Sanskritists, but by a whole range of observers, ethnologists and civilians—eventually produced an essentialist knowledge of a backward caste-ridden Indian society; it was this knowledge of the Indian "essences" which rationalised authoritarian colonial rule.[23] All discussions about India's eligibility for self-rule were dismissed as sentimental, and racial distancing as well as avowal of privileges for the rulers triumphed over the earlier liberal visions of similarity and assimilation.[24] If reforms were introduced, they were more in response to articulate political demands of the Indians (see chapter 6.1).

However, it needs to be pointed out here that statements of racial superiority of the rulers were not for the first time being made in the mid-nineteenth century. If we look at the actual functioning of the empire, such statements were made rather loudly since the late eighteenth century, when Cornwallis transformed the Company's bureaucracy into an "aloof elite", maintaining physical separation from the ruled. British soldiers were forbidden to have sexual relations with Indian women and were confined to army cantonments, where they would be quarantined from infectious diseases as well as Oriental vices. Moreover, the Company's civil servants were discouraged from having Indian mistresses, urged to have British wives and thus preserve—as one official put it before a parliamentary select committee in 1830—"the respect and reverence the natives now have for the English". Any action undermining that respect, Henry Dundas, the president of the Board of Control had argued as early as 1793, would surely "ruin our Indian empire".[25] Such overt statements of physical segregation between the ruler and the ruled as an ideology of empire were quite clear in the very way the human environment of the imperial capital city of Calcutta developed in the eighteenth century. "The process worked in an overall setting of dualism, basically a feature of all colonial cities, between the white and the black town".[26] This phenomenon of dualism reflected on the one hand, the conquerors' concern for defence and security, but on the other, their racial pride and exclusivism. In the early eighteenth century, this spatial segregation along racial lines had been less sharply marked, as there was a White Town and a Black Town, intersected by a Grey Town or an intermediate zone, dominated by the Eurasians or East Indians, but accessible to the natives as well. The position of the Eurasians—the children of mixed marriages—continually went down in the imperial pecking order since 1791, when they were debarred from covenanted civil and higher-grade military or marine services. The racial polarisation of colonial society was now complete. By the early nineteenth century, "the social distance" between the people and the ruling race became an easily discernible reality in Calcutta's urban life.[27]

However, during the first half of the nineteenth century along with racial arrogance, there was also a liberal optimism, as expressed in Lord Macaulay's ambition to transform the indolent Indian into a brown sahib, European in taste and intellect—but not quite a European; he would be "more brown than sahib", to use Ashis Nandy's cryptic expression.[28] It was this optimism that was shattered by the rude shock of 1857. From the very beginning in colonial discourses Indian subjecthood was likened to childhood and effiminacy that required tutoring and protection; but now it was also equated with primitivism, which justified imperialism on the arrogant assumption of the superiority of culture.[29] The Imperial Assemblage of 1877, which resolved the ambiguity of sovereignty by proclaiming Queen Victoria the Empress of India, manifested in unmistakable terms what Bernard Cohn has called the "British construction of their authority over India".[30] It established a new social order where everyone, from people to princes, were situated in a hierarchy, and the viceroy became the central locus of power. The Ilbert bill controversy in 1883 marked the ultimate victory of the authoritarian trends and racial arrogance of the colonisers. The bill—proposed by a liberal viceroy, Lord Ripon, intending to give jurisdiction to Indian judges over Europeans—had to be toned down under pressure from non-official Englishmen as well as the bureaucracy. It was this authoritarian imperial order that Indian nationalism had to confront in the early twentieth century.

2.2. PARLIAMENT AND THE EMPIRE

In mid-eighteenth century, when Company Raj was gradually being established in the subcontinent, the difficulties of communication with England gave the Company's servants a free hand in India to behave like their own masters. There was misinformation and lack of interest about Indian affairs in Britain. And as a result, before 1784, thinks P.J. Marshall (1975a), new policies were hardly ever initiated from London. But although the "sub-imperialism" of the Company's men on the spot had been an important motivating factor behind much of the territorial conquests in India, the relationship between the state and the Company was much more complex than what was implied by that fact. Not only the Company's existence depended on the renewal of the charter, but right from the seventeenth century, the Company's servants in India acted on the concept of "delegated sovereignty", and there were clear instructions on how to divide the booty between the Company and the royal troops, if the latter participated in any joint campaign. The Company had to depend on the successive governments in London for various matters, and the latter was ever ready to provide it in exchange for hefty subscriptions to the state exchequer. There were always a few MPs with East Indian interests and the ministers used the Company's resources for expanding the scope of their patronage. The Company was also an important element in the city politics of London, about which the government was always keenly concerned. The conflicts between the parties within the Company often got aligned with wider political configurations within the Parliament. As the rumours about the growing riches of the Company began to spread, there was even greater eagerness on the part of the government to have a share of it. There had been government interventions in the Company's affairs in 1763 and 1764, paving the way for a parliamentary intervention in 1766, over the rights of the state to the revenues of the territories conquered with the help of the royal army. The result was the Company agreeing to pay £ 400,000 to the government annually.[31] Thus, right from the beginning, the British state participated in and profited from the empire; it is difficult to argue that it was acquired "in a fit of absence of mind". One could, however, say that the empire was acquired "without the national cognizance", by a "small number of Englishmen who had not the least illusion about what they were doing".[32]

Although the state was profiting from the empire, the question was how to control it. The need to impose greater parliamentary control over the Company's affairs increased during the decades after Plassey, because of a growing concern about mis-government of the Indian affairs by the corrupt servants of the Company. Much of this "corruption" was the result of these officials being caught in the complex exchange nexus of trade and governance in eighteenth-century India. Exchange of gifts and pleasantries for political favour and trading concessions were accepted norms of the uneven power relationships between the political elites and the traders. But what was natural in the northern Indian political milieu, was anathema to the Western moral discourse of imperial rule.[33] The debate grew bitter, as the English gentry became jealous of the East Indian "Nabobs" indulging in conspicuous consumption to force their way into English society. As the Company's empire in India expanded, the British government also felt that it could no longer be allowed to remain outside the ambit of the state. In 1772, Edmund Burke claimed that it was "the province and duty of Parliament to superintend the affairs of this Company".[34] Governors General in India, like Clive or Hastings, also desired to forge some kind of formal constitutional relationship with the Crown, which would buttress their power and legitimise their authority. There was of course no political will yet to impose any direct control over the Company affairs in India, except in matters of defence and internal order and establishment of sovereignty was still being considered to be too drastic a measure. The existing abuses were therefore to be corrected by attacking the Company's servants, but not the Company itself. Lord Clive in 1773, and Warren Hastings in 1786, were tried unsuccessfully for misconduct and, later in 1806, Lord Wellesley had to go through the same ordeal.

A Select Committee of the Parliament was, however, appointed in April 1772 to inquire into the state of affairs in India. There were some important constitutional problems to be resolved: how, for example, the relationship between the British government and the Company with its possessions in India was to be defined; how would the Company's authorities in Britain exert control over its servants in India; or, how a single centre of power could be devised for the far-flung possessions in India. The immediate occasion for such considerations was provided by the Company's application for a loan, which raised suspicion about mismanagement of resources in India. The stories about the rich resources of Bengal and the fabulous wealth brought home by the Company officials did not go well with the fact that the Company was facing a financial crisis. There were, therefore, concerns about the lowering of moral standards, which might also bring in corruption in British politics. Adam Smith, and his book *An Inquiry into the Nature and Causes of the Wealth of Nations*, brought in a new school of economic thinking that condemned companies enjoying exclusive monopolies. Free enterprisers were striving to have a share of the profits of the India trade and wanted to put an end to the monopoly rights of the Company. The Parliament, however, decided on a compromise; some sort of control over Indian affairs was established, but the Company was allowed to continue its monopoly of Eastern trade and the Directors of the Company were given control of the Indian administration.

However, a trend was thus set. The next important step to control the Company's administration in India came in the shape of the Regulating Act of 1773, which formally recognised parliamentary right to control Indian affairs. The Court of Directors of the Company would henceforth be obliged to submit all communications received from Bengal about civil, military and revenue matters in India to the British government. Apart from that, territories in India were also subjected to some degree of centralised control. The status of governor of Bengal was raised to that of governor general, to be assisted by a council of four members. They were given the power to superintend and control the presidencies of Madras and Bombay in matters of waging war or making peace with the Indian states, except in emergency situations. The governor general and his council were under the control of the Court of Directors, whom they were supposed to send dispatches regularly. A Supreme Court was established in Calcutta, while the legislative powers were vested in the governor general and the council. The act was by no means satisfactory, as it failed to streamline Indian administration, while the supervision of the British government remained ineffective due to problems of communication. The administration in India was hampered by the disunity in the council and disharmony between the council and the governor general. The provincial governors took advantage of the wide manoeuvring space they had been offered by the vague wordings of the act and the ambiguities in the jurisdiction of the Supreme Court and the council created serious conflicts between competing authorities. All these obscurities and indeterminate character of the act, it seemed, arose from Parliament's inability to define properly the issue of sovereignty in India. An Amending Act of 1781 defined more precisely the jurisdiction of the Supreme Court, but did not address the other anomalies.[35]

A corrective came in the shape of Pitt's India Act of 1784. But it too was a compromise: the Company's territorial possessions were not touched, only its public affairs and its administration in India were brought under more direct government control. A Board of Control consisting of six members was constituted and would include one of the secretaries of state, the chancellor of the exchequer and four privy councillors. It would "superintend, direct and control all acts, operations and concerns" related to "the civil or military government or revenues of the British territorial possessions in the East Indies".[36] The orders of the board became binding on the Court of Directors, which was required to send all its letters and dispatches to the board for its perusal. The Court of Directors retained its control over commerce and patronage, but only with the approval of the Crown could it appoint its principal servants in India, such as the governor general, governors and the commander-in-chief. The government of India was placed under the governor general and a council of three, thus giving greater power to the former. The presidencies of Madras and Bombay were subordinated to the governor general, whose power over them was now enlarged and more clearly defined. The governor general in council in his turn was subordinated to the Court of Directors and the Board of Control. Thus a clear hierarchy of command and more direct parliamentary control over Indian administration was established.

But the arrangement still had too many defects. The first and foremost was the provision of two masters for the governor general—the Court of Directors and the Board of Control—which gave virtual autonomy to the man on the spot. The governor general could easily play his two masters one against another and act at his own discretion. But on the other hand, a factious council and the inability of the governor general to override its decisions could often make him ineffective, particularly as his right to use the army had been curbed. An Amending Act of 1786 corrected these anomalies. It gave the governor general right to override his council in extraordinary situations and authorised the Court of Directors to combine the two offices of governor general and commander-in-chief, resulting in Warren Hastings for the first time enjoying the two positions simultaneously. An effective and authoritarian instrument of control was thus put in place, which continued till 1858 with only little modifications.[37]

The Charter Act of 1793 renewed the charter of the Company for twenty years, giving it possession of all territories in India during that period. In Indian administration, the governor general's power over the council was extended and the Governors of Bombay and Madras were brought more decisively under his control. A regular code of all regulations that could be enacted for the internal government of the British territories in Bengal was framed. The regulation applied to all rights, person and property of the Indian people and it bound the courts to regulate their decisions by the rules and directives contained therein. All laws were to be printed with translations in Indian languages, so that people could know of their rights, privileges and immunities. The act thus introduced in India the concept of a civil law, enacted by a secular human agency and applied universally. William Wilberforce had wanted to include two more clauses into the act: one would declare that the purpose of British rule in India would be to work towards the moral and spiritual uplift of the Indians and the other would allow entry of appropriate persons, such as teachers and missionaries, into India to achieve that imperial goal. Both the clauses were, however, dropped, but only till the next renewal of the charter.

In 1808 the House of Commons appointed a committee of investigation, which submitted its report in 1812. The free traders in the meanwhile had become dominant in British politics and were demanding free access to India. This would bring, they argued, capital and skills, and with the establishment of industries and introduction of new agricultural techniques, it would result in development and improvement for India. The Benthamite reformists and the Evangelicals too tried to influence British politics and British policies in India and they gained a decisive voice when the Evangelist Charles Grant was elected to the Court of Directors. The Charter Act of 1813 incorporated in a significant way all these aspirations for change in Britain's India policy. It renewed the Company's charter for twenty years, and during that period it was allowed to have its territorial possessions. But at the same time the act asserted the "undoubted sovereignty of the Crown of the United Kingdom" over the Indian territories.[38] The Company was also deprived of its monopoly of trade with India, although its monopoly of China trade was left untouched for another twenty years. And in addition to that, Christian missionaries were henceforth to be allowed to enter India, subject only to obtaining a licence either from the Court of Directors or the Board of Control.

The Charter Act of 1813 was thus an important benchmark in the push towards westernisation of India. When the charter was again due for renewal in 1833, there was a fresh and more widespread agitation in Britain for the abolition of the Company and a direct takeover of the Indian administration by the government. The political atmosphere in Britain at that time was also fully charged with enthusiasm for reform, as the Reform Act of 1832 had just been passed. A parliamentary inquiry was held, and the Act of 1833, which followed from its recommendations, became a landmark in the constitutional history of India. The Company's monopoly of tea trade with China was now abolished and henceforth it was meant only to have political functions, and here too the Indian possessions of the Company were to be held in trust for the British Crown. The President of the Board of Control now became the Minister for Indian Affairs, while the board was empowered to superintend all administrative affairs in India. The Governor General of Bengal became the Governor General of India, who would, in consultation with his council, control all civil, military and revenue matters in the whole of India. With the extension of territories and influx of British settlers into India, there was need for uniform laws. The governor general in council was, therefore, empowered to legislate for the whole of British territories in India and these laws were to be applicable to all persons, British or Indian. A law member was added to the council (Lord Macaulay) and a law commission was instituted for codification of laws. The Company's services in India were thrown open to the natives; but there was no provision for their being nominated to the covenanted services.

Although in India during all these years demands were being raised for the abolition of the Company rule, the British government was not yet so sure about such a measure. The charter of 1833 was renewed in 1853, but this time not for another twenty years. The Company was allowed to retain the Indian possessions "in trust for Her Majesty, her heirs and successors until Parliament shall otherwise provide", thus keeping the door ajar for a future takeover. The act also provided for the separation of the executive and legislative functions of the governor general's council by adding new members for legislative purposes. And the Company's control over appointments was curtailed by the introduction of competition for the recruitment of the Indian Civil Service. Already deprived of its commercial privileges, the Company hereafter hardly ever controlled policies in India. Since the act did not give it the right to govern for the next twenty years, the House of Commons with greater ease could formally abolish Company administration in India in 1858, the immediate occasion for this final stroke was of course provided by the revolt of 1857, which shall be discussed in the next chapter. The revolt made the English people more aware of the Indian situation and generated popular support for the perpetuation as well as reorganisation of British rule there. Since 1833, many English traders and settlers had also developed a vested interest in India and their persistent complaint was that the Company had been neglecting their interests. In other words, both at home and in India there had been now considerable pressure for the abolition of the Company Raj and the establishment of Crown rule.

However, in terms of the administrative structure, the Government of India Act of 1858, which followed the pacification of the revolt, meant more continuation than change. It replaced the President of the Board of Control with a Secretary of State for India, who became "in subordination to the cabinet, the fountain of authority as well as the director of policy in India".[39] He was to be advised by a Council of India, consisting of fifteen members, seven of whom were to be selected from the now superseded Court of Directors. The Governor General of India, who would henceforth be known as the Viceroy, would retain all his powers, but instead of a dual control, he would be answerable only to the secretary of state. Continuity was also maintained in the structure of the civil service, and the same recruitment examination introduced in 1853 was carried on. India thus passed from Company rule to Crown rule, which meant ironically the rejection of a liberal promise of reforming India in order to prepare her for self-government. It meant, in other words, a "symbolic endorsement of British permanence in India".[40] The liberal zeal for reform and change had by this time died down and in the aftermath of revolt one could discern in every aspect of British policy in India what Thomas Metcalf has called a "new attitude of caution and conservatism".[41] There was now an assertion of the racial superiority of the ruling race, which, as mentioned earlier, carefully distanced itself from the subject society in order to formalise a more authoritarian regime. Indians were held to be 'tradition-bound' and therefore beyond reform to live up to the high moral standards of the West. And trust was reposed in their 'natural leaders', the landed gentry and the aristocrats, who were restored to prominence, in the hope of securing their loyalty. The situation, which Anand Yang (1989) has described as the "Limited Raj" where the colonial regime depended on local power elites like zamindars for the administration of the interior, was indeed contributing to the foundation of a more authoritarian Raj.

2.3. EXTRACTING LAND REVENUE

Since the grant of diwani for Bengal, Bihar and Orissa in 1765, the major concern of the East India Company's administration in India was to collect as much revenue as possible. Agriculture was the main basis of economy and the main source of income and hence, although the nawabi administration was retained with Muhammad Reza Khan acting as the Naib Diwan for the Company, several land revenue experiments were introduced in haste to maximise extraction. And here they did not want to take any chances. So, although native officials were in charge of collection, European officers of the Company were given supervisory authority over them, and their corruption as well as lack of understanding of the local situation led to complete disorganisation of the agrarian economy and society in the diwani provinces within a few years. The devastating famine of 1769–70, in which about one-third of the Bengal population was wiped off, was but only one indication of the prevailing chaos. The Company directors, unable to pay their shareholders the expected amounts of dividend, began to look for reasons for falling revenues and the devastations of famine. They found an easy "scapegoat" in Reza Khan, who was arrested on false charges of corruption and embezzlement. But the real reason for his removal was the desire of Warren Hastings, the newly appointed Governor of Bengal, to get rid of Indians altogether from the administration of revenue and make the British the sole controller of the resources of the province.[42] In 1772, he introduced a new system, known as the farming system. European District Collectors, as the nomenclature suggested, were to be in charge of revenue collection, while the revenue collecting right was farmed out to the highest bidders. About the periodicity of the settlements, a number of experiments were made, but the farming system ultimately failed to improve the situation, as the farmers tried to extract as much as possible without any concern for the production process. The burden of revenue demand on the peasants increased as a result and often it was so onerous that it could not be collected at all. The net outcome of this whole period of rash experimentation was the ruination of the agricultural population. In 1784, Lord Cornwallis was therefore sent to India with a specific mandate to streamline the revenue administration.

PERMANENT SETTLEMENT

Cornwallis realised that the existing system was impoverishing the country, ruining agriculture and was not producing the large and regular surplus that the Company hoped for. Company's trade also suffered, because of the difficulty in procuring Indian goods for export to Europe. Production of silk or cotton, two of the Company's major export items, was mainly agro-based, while decline in agriculture also affected handicraft production. It was thought, therefore, that the only way to improve this situation was to fix the revenue permanently. Indeed, it was since 1770, i.e., even before Cornwallis arrived, that a number of Company officials and European observers, like Alexander Dow, Henri Patullo, Philip Francis and Thomas Law were advocating for the land tax being permanently fixed. Despite their various ideological orientations, they shared a common faith in the Physiocratic school of thinking that assigned primacy to agriculture in a country's economy. These ideas went into the making of the Permanent Settlement of 1793, which introduced in Bengal the policy of "assessment for ever".[43] This would reduce, it was hoped, the scope for corruption that existed when officials could alter assessment at will. The landlords would invest money in improving the land, as with the state demand being fixed the whole of the benefit from increased production and enhanced income would accrue to them. The Company would get its taxes regularly and when necessary, as Cornwallis thought, it could raise its income by taxing trade and commerce. The land revenue, since it was going to be fixed in perpetuity, was also to be fixed at a high level—the absolute maximum. So taking the assessment for the year 1789–90 as the standard, it was fixed at Rs. 26.8 million (approximately £3 million). While according to P.J. Marshall, the revenue demand in 1793 was just about 20 per cent higher than what prevailed before 1757,[44] in B.B. Chaudhuri's calculation, it "nearly doubled" between 1765 and 1793.[45]

The other problem for the Company was to decide as from whom the revenue was to be collected. The nawabs used to collect it from the zamindars. Some of them were big landlords who controlled large areas and had their own armed retainers; in 1790 twelve big zamindari houses were responsible for paying more than 53 per cent of the land revenue assessment in Bengal.[46] Others were smaller zamindars, who paid revenue either directly to the state or through the bigger zamindars. Peasants undertook cultivation and paid the zamindars at customary rates, which often varied from subdivision to subdivision and sometimes extralegal charges called *abwabs* were collected as well. By 1790, however, the Company's administration had profoundly confused this situation by retaining some zamindars and replacing others by new revenue farmers. In terms of assessment too, the old customary rates were ignored and by the time Cornwallis arrived, a complete confusion prevailed in this area. Being a member of the landed aristocracy of Britain and imbued with the idea of improving landlordism, his natural preference was for the zamindars. They were expected to invest for the improvement of agriculture if their property rights were secured. There were also other practical reasons: it was easier to collect revenue from a small number of zamindars than from the innumerable peasants, which would require a large administrative machinery; and finally, it would ensure the loyalty of a powerful class of the local population. So the Permanent Settlement in 1793 was made with the zamindars. Every bit of land in Bengal, Bihar and Orissa became a part of a zamindari or estate and the zamindar had to pay the tax fixed upon it. If he did so, then he was the proprietor or owner of his zamindari: he could sell, mortgage and transfer it; land could also be inherited by heirs. But failure to pay the revenue would lead to the confiscation of the zamindari by the government and its sale by auction; the new purchaser would then have the ownership right on it. This was the so-called creation of private property in land; the magic of private property, it was widely hoped, would bring in the desired improvement in agriculture.

The Permanent Settlement vested the land ownership right in the zamindars, who previously enjoyed only revenue collecting right. Therefore, those who lost out in this settlement were the peasants, who were left at the mercy of the zamindars. Their customary occupancy right was ignored and they were reduced to the status of tenants. The provision of *patta,* or written agreement between the peasant and the zamindar providing a record of the amount of rent to be paid, was rarely followed by the zamindars. Nor was it liked by the peasants who always feared to lose in any formal record of rights and obligations. The burden of high revenue assessment was thus shifted to the peasants, who were often also called upon to pay illegal cesses. The subsequent regulations of 1799 and 1812 gave the zamindars the right to seize property of the tenants in case of nonpayment of rent without any permission of a court of law. It is no wonder, therefore, that as a cumulative effect of this support to the coercive power of the zamindars, the condition of the actual cultivators declined under the Permanent Settlement.

Though the settlement was pro-zamindar, they too had to face a number of difficulties. As Daniel Thorner has argued, creation of private property in land was a misnomer, as the absolute ownership was retained by the imperial authority.[47] The zamindars had to pay a fixed amount of revenue by a particular date (the so-called 'sun-set' law), failure leading to the sale of the zamindari. Often they found it difficult to collect the rent, as demands were too high and there were the uncertainties of nature. The result was the frequent sale of zamindari estates: between 1794 and 1807 land yielding about 41 per cent of the revenue in Bengal and Bihar was sold out in auction; in Orissa between 1804 and 1818, 51.1 per cent of the original zamindars were wiped off because of auction sales.[48] This of course meant the collapse of most of the old zamindari houses; but contrary to the old myths, those who bought these estates were not exactly 'new' men in the Bengal agrarian society. The old zamindaris were parcelled out by their own *amlas* (zamindari officials) and rich tenants or by the neighbouring zamindars among themselves.[49] And some of the old houses, such as the Burdwan raj, survived by resorting to the novel method of subinfeudation that complicated the tenurial structure to an absurd level.[50] These subinfeudatory *patni* tenures, which sometimes proliferated up to twelve grades between the zamindar and the peasants, increased the demand on the latter. In 1859 and 1885 there were tenancy legislations, which to some extent protected the tenants by recognising their occupancy rights. This was the time when the Company Raj had transformed itself into a self-confident territorial state trying to penetrate deeper into the economy and society and co-opt wider sections of the population.[51] But zamindari power remained largely unrestrained and their alliance with the Raj unaltered.

The new legal reforms could not provide any relief to the poor cultivators. These reforms on the other hand only strengthened the position of a group of powerful rich peasants—the *jotedars*—who are believed to have been actually controlling landholding at the village level, as argued by Rajat and Ratnalekha Ray (1973, 1975), while the zamindars enjoyed only the revenue collecting right. Beneath all the changes effected by colonial policies, the Rays argue, the power of this class and their control over the rural society remained unaffected and herein lay the basic continuity of the rural social structure in colonial Bengal. This 'jotedar thesis', however, came under serious attack in a monograph by Sugata Bose (1986) who found such jotedar domination confined only to northern Bengal. In the rest of the region he discovered two other distinct modes of peasant economy—the peasant landholding-demesne labour complex in the west and the peasant small holding system in eastern Bengal. In both the regions he found the power of the zamindars continuing unhindered till the 1930s, a position which has found support also in the works of Akinobu Kawai (1986–87) and Partha Chatterjee (1984a). In a subsequent essay in defence of the 'jotedar', Rajat Ray (1988) conceded the fact that the zamindars probably retained some of their influence and authority in rural Bengal till about the 1930s, but there still existed all along a section of substantial peasants who yielded considerable power in the Bengal countryside. This modified position has found partial corroboration in two subsequent works. Nariaki Nakazato (1994) has shown the existence of a powerful jotedar-haoladar class in certain districts of central and eastern Bengal in the late nineteenth and early twentieth centuries. This did not mean, however, as he argues, a demise of the old zamindari system, as the interests of the two classes were complementary to each other and not necessarily antagonistic. In western Bengal, on the other hand, in Midnapur district for example, Chitta Panda (1996) has detected only unqualified decline of the zamindars, who were losing out to a class of rich peasants who dominated the land market, rural credit and the trading networks. Both Nakazato and Panda, however, argue emphatically that there was more change than continuity in the agrarian structure of post-Permanent Settlement Bengal. And, as we shall see in the next chapter, these changes, which almost uniformly affected the poor peasants, perennially excluded from any control over land and power, resulted in a series of peasant revolts.

RYOTWARI SETTLEMENT

Lord Cornwallis expected that his Permanent Settlement, or the zamindari system, would be extended to other parts of India as well. When Lord Wellesley came to India, he and Henry Dundas of the Board of Control equally shared a faith in the Bengal system, and in 1798 Wellesley gave orders for its extension to Madras Presidency. Here the problem was to find a sizeable zamindar class as in Bengal; but still between 1801 and 1807 the Madras authority introduced it in large areas under its control. The local poligars were recognised as zamindars, and in other areas, where such people could not be found, villages were aggregated into estates and were sold in auction to the highest bidders. But before this could go on very far, in British official circles there was growing disillusionment with the Permanent Settlement, which provided for no means to raise the income of the government, while the increased income from land was being garnered by the zamindars. This distrust for the large landlords was also partly the result of Scottish Enlightenment, which insisted on the primacy of agriculture and celebrated the importance of the yeoman farmer within the agricultural societies. Such ideas obviously influenced Scottish officials like Thomas Munro and Mountstuart Elphinstone, who took the initiative to change the Company's revenue administration.[52] This was also the time when Utilitarian ideas had begun to influence policy planning in India, and among them David Ricardo's theory of rent seemed to be hinting at a revision of the existing system.[53] Rent was the surplus from land, i.e., its income minus the cost of production and labour, and the state had a legitimate claim to a share of this surplus at the expense of the unproductive intermediaries, whose only claim was by virtue of their ownership right. The theory provided, therefore, an argument to eliminate the zamindars and appropriate a larger share of the increasing income from the new acquisitions of land. But theories alone hardly guided policies in India.[54] A more powerful reason for a new settlement was the perennial financial crisis of the Madras Presidency, worsened by the rising expenses of war. This was the genesis of the Ryotwari Settlement in Madras Presidency.

The Ryotwari experiment was started by Alexander Reed in Baramahal in 1792 and was continued by Thomas Munro from 1801 when he was asked to take charge of the revenue administration of the Ceded Districts. Instead of zamindars they began to collect revenue directly from the villages, fixing the amount each village had to pay. After this they proceeded to assess each cultivator or ryot separately and thus evolved the Ryotwari System. It created individual proprietary right in land, but it was vested in the peasants, rather than in the zamindars, for Munro preferred it to be "in the hands of forty to fifty thousand small proprietors, than four or five hundred great ones".[55] But Munro's system also made a significant distinction between public and private ownership. In David Ludden's words: "it defined the state itself as the supreme landlord, and individual peasants landowners who obtained title by paying annual cash rents, or revenue assessments, to the government".[56] This was, as it evolved eventually, a field assessment system, as rent payable on each field was to be permanently assessed through a general survey of all lands.

And then annual agreements were to be made between the government and the cultivator, who had the choice of accepting or rejecting the agreement. If he agreed, he would get a patta, which would become a title to private property and if no cultivator was found, the land might lie fallow. The system, therefore, in order to be attractive and equitable, required a detailed land survey: the quality of soil, the area of the field and the average produce of every piece of land had to be assessed and on the basis of that the amount of revenue was to be fixed. But this was the theory; in practice the estimates were often guesswork and the revenue demanded was often so high that they could only be collected with great difficulty or could not be collected at all. And the peasants were to be coerced to agree to such unjust settlements. So the Ryotwari system was almost abandoned soon after Munro's departure for London in 1807.

But around 1820 the situation began to change as Thomas Munro returned to India as the governor of Madras. He argued that Ryotwari was the ancient Indian land-tenure system and therefore best suited to Indian conditions.[57] This reference to the past was however in the interest of the empire. He believed that the British empire needed a unified concept of sovereignty and the Ryotwari system could provide a foundation for that. The security and administration of the empire needed, as his experience in the Ceded Districts revealed, the elimination of the overmighty poligars and collection of revenue directly from individual farmers under the supervision of British officers. He therefore justified his position by arguing that historically land in India was owned by the state, which collected revenue from individual peasants through a hierarchy of officials paid through grant of *inam* land. The power of this landlord-state rested on military strength and when that declined, the poligars appropriated land and thereby usurped sovereignty. This process of alienation needed to be reversed now.[58] In arguing this, he briskly set aside the contrary observations by men like Francis Ellis who argued that property right was traditionally conferred on the community or tribes and that family had a variety of rights to the community assets. Munro at the same time insisted that this system would reduce the revenue burden for farmers, while it would yield larger amount of land revenue for the state, as no intermediaries would be having a share of the surplus.[59] And London was happy too as this system would place authority and power directly in British hands in a way which the Cornwallis system would never hope to achieve.[60] The Madras government was chronically short of funds and so it decided to introduce the Ryotwari Settlement in most parts of the presidency;

but gradually it took quite different forms than the one which Munro had visualised. It raised the revenue income of the government, but put the cultivators in great distress. In many areas no surveys were carried out and the tax of a ryot was assessed on an arbitrary basis, based on village accounts. Known as the *putcut* settlement, the revenue to be paid by a ryot was fixed on his entire farm, not on each field, which might have varying irrigation facilities and therefore different levels of productivity. And where the survey was actually undertaken, it was often "ill-conceived and hastily executed", resulting in over-assessment.[61] Contrary to Munro's insistence that the cultivator be given freedom to take as much or as little land as he chose to, this "right of contraction or relinquishment" was effectively dropped by 1833.[62] The cultivating peasants were, therefore, gradually impoverished, and increasingly indebted and could not invest for the extension of cultivation. Except for Coimbatore, there was practically no land market in Madras, as buying land would mean paying extortionate land revenue.

The Ryotwari system did not also eliminate village elites as intermediaries between the government and the peasantry. As privileged rents and special rights of the mirasidars were recognised and caste privileges of the Brahmans respected, the existing village power structure was hardly altered, and indeed even more strengthened by the new system.[63] This whole process was actually supported by a colonial knowledge, collaboratively produced by officials and Tamil writers, that the mirasidars of good agricultural castes, like the Vellalas, were the original colonists and good agriculturists. Such stereotypes made such traditional village elites as the mirasidars pivotal to the British ideal of a sedentary agricultural community.[64] The latter therefore could gradually position themselves comfortably in the subordinate ranks of the revenue establishments, and some of them bought lucrative and large tracts of irrigated land after getting their official appointments.[65] These revenue officials after 1816 combined in themselves both revenue collection and police duties in the countryside. This enhancement of power inevitably resulted in coercion, bribery and corruption by the subordinate officials of the Collectorate, which were revealed in abundant and gory details in the Madras Torture Commission Report in 1855, indicating the need for effective reform.[66]

It was from this year that a scientific survey of land and a fresh assessment of revenue were undertaken, resulting in decline in the real burden of tax. It was decided that the revenue rate would be half of the net value of the produce of the land and the settlement would be made for thirty years. The reformed system was introduced in 1864, immediately leading to agricultural prosperity and extension of cultivation. This was interrupted by two famines in 1865–66 and 1876–78; yet, as Dharma Kumar asserts, "recovery was faster in the Presidency as a whole". She also argues that contrary to prevalent myths, "statistics . . . fail to support the view that land was increasingly passing into the hands of rich farmers and moneylenders". Inequality increased only in the prosperous and irrigated areas, such as the Godavari delta; elsewhere it declined. There is also no evidence, she affirms, that indebtedness was resulting in widespread dispossession. Debts varied in nature, while absentee landlordism, except in Tirunelveli, declined everywhere else. However, where the tenants existed, there was hardly any protection for them in the entire presidency.[67]

The impact of the Ryotwari system on the agrarian society of Madras can be looked at in different ways. As a number of recent micro-studies have revealed, by redefining property rights, it actually strengthened the power of the village magnates where they did exist, and thus intensified social conflict. However, it is also true that this impact had wide regional variations, depending on the existing social structures and ecological conditions. David Ludden's study of the Tirunelveli district,[68] for example, shows how the locally powerful mirasidars manipulated the system to get privileged rents and convert their collective rights into individual property rights. The Madras government since 1820 showed absolutely no interest in protecting the rights of the tenants, despite their active but futile resistance to mirasidari power. However, mirasidars in the wet zones, Ludden argues, did much better than their counterparts in the dry or mixed zones. Willem van Schendel's study of the Kaveri delta in Tanjavur (Tanjore) district also shows "the golden age" of the mirasidars, who entrenched their control over land and labour and thus "intensified the polarisation of local society". Their power eroded somewhat in the second half of the nineteenth century, because of greater social and economic differentiation within their community and the older families giving way to new commercial groups. But this by no means marked the end of mirasidari power in local society.[69] Among other Tamil districts, the situation was largely similar in the wet taluks of Tiruchirapalli (Trichinopoly), while in South Arcot and Chingleput such privileged landownership rights were being increasingly challenged by the actual cultivators. In other vast areas of Tamilnad, however, where there was abundance of cultivable land, the situation was dominated by a large number of owner-cultivators and a small group of middle landowners.[70] In the Andhra districts of the Madras Presidency too the Ryotwari system promoted differentiation within the peasantry. By the beginning of the twentieth century, there was an affluent group of big landholders—whom A. Satyanarayana calls "peasant-bourgeoisie"—who controlled large farms and leased out surplus lands to landless tenants and sharecroppers. The intermediate strata also did well and lived under stable economic conditions. On the other hand, the poor peasants, who constituted the majority of the rural population, lived in squalid conditions, were exploited by rich ryots, creditors and lessors, were forced to hire themselves despite wretched conditions and remained tied to small plots of land.[71]

The Ryotwari system in the Bombay Presidency had its beginning in Gujarat after its annexation in 1803, and then when the peshwa's territories were conquered in 1818, it was extended to those areas as well under the supervision of Munro's disciple, Mountstuart Elphinstone. Initially, in these areas the British had been collecting revenue through the desmukh and the village headmen or the *patil*. But this did not yield as much revenue as they hoped for, and hence from 1813–14 they began collecting directly from the peasants. The abuses that characterised the Madras system soon appeared in Bombay too, as the revenue rates that were fixed turned out to be extraordinarily high. With frequent crop failures and sliding prices, peasants either had to mortgage their lands to moneylenders or abandon cultivation and migrate to neighbouring princely states where rates were lower. A land survey was therefore undertaken by an officer called R.K. Pringle, who classified the land and fixed the revenue at 55 per cent of the net value of the produce. The scheme, first introduced in the Indapur taluk in 1830, was soon found to be faulty and abandoned. It was replaced in 1835 by a reformed 'Bombay Survey System' devised by two officers G. Wingate and H. E. Goldsmid. It was a practical settlement aiming at lowering the demand to a reasonable limit where it could be regularly paid. The actual assessment of each field depended on what it paid in the immediate past, expected price rise, the nature of soil and location. This new assessment began to be made in 1836 on the basis of a thirty years settlement and covered most of Deccan by 1847.

The impact of the Ryotwari Settlement on the agrarian society of western India is the subject of a major historical controversy, as it gave rise to a rural uprising in Bombay Deccan in 1875. Historians like Neil Charlesworth (1985) do not think that the Wingate settlements actually introduced between 1840 and 1870 caused any dramatic change in western India. It reduced the village patil to the status of an ordinary peasant and a paid employee of the government. But the erosion of his power had started in pre-British days, and British rule "was merely completing a process already in full motion." And the settlements did not universally displace all village elites either; in Gujarat the superior rights of the *bhagdars, narwadars* and the Ahmedabad taluqdars were respected, and as a result, in these regions "greater political and social stability was guaranteed." It was only in central Deccan that a power vacuum was created, which offered opportunities for a greater active role for the Marwari and Gujarati banias. And for the peasants, the new settlements "were making revenue assessment less burdensome and inequitable". If they became massively indebted by the middle of the nineteenth century, such indebtedness was indeed "long-standing", not because of the land revenue demands, and did not in itself result in any large-scale alienation of land, as the Marwari creditors had little attraction for the cultivator's land.[72] H. Fukazawa also endorses this interpretation and asserts that: "There is no evidence that land was increasingly being bought up by traders and moneylenders".[73] Ian Catanach thinks that dispossession and land transfer from agriculturists to non-agriculturists did occur in Deccan in mid-nineteenth century, but this did not necessarily cause the Deccan riots.[74] But on the other hand, Ravinder Kumar and Sumit Guha have argued that a significant social upheaval was being caused by Ryotwari Settlement which undermined the authority of the village headmen and thus caused a status revolution in the Maharashtra villages, and that discontent ultimately propelled into the Deccan riots.[75] We will discuss this controversy in greater detail in chapter 4.2, when we will be looking at the Deccan riots of 1875. What perhaps can be observed here is that the social effects of the Ryotwari system, both in Madras and in Bombay, were perhaps less dramatic than those of the Permanent Settlement. But it is difficult to argue a case for "continuity", as the older forms that continued were now "differentially enstructured by imperialism".[76]

MAHALWARI SETTLEMENT

The 'village community', which some of the early Western observers from Charles Metcalfe to Henry Maine spoke so eloquently about, figured neither in the Permanent Settlement nor in the Ryotwari system. However, when these two systems were being worked out, vast stretches of territory in north and north-western India were overrun between 1801 and 1806. This region, once the heartland of the Mughal empire, stretching from the Himalayan foothills to the central Indian plateau, including the Ganga-Jumna Doab, formed the North-Western Provinces. In the agrarian structure of this area, there was on the one hand, a small group of magnates, known as the taluqdars. Nurul Hasan has described them as the "intermediary zamindars", who "contracted with the state to realise the revenue of a given territory". There were on the other hand, a large group of "primary zamindars", who were the "holders of proprietary rights over agricultural as well as habitational lands". Included in this group were both the small owner-cultivators and also the large proprietors of several villages.[77] With the Bengal model in mind, the British initially proceeded to collect revenue from the taluqdars, who by the end of the eighteenth century included two distinct social groups. On the one hand there were the locally entrenched "rulers of the lineage-dominated principalities" and on the other, the Mughal jagirdars, revenue officials and tax-farmers who had instituted themselves as "de facto rajas or taluqdars".[78]

These initial short-term settlements, eventually to be made permanent, were based on artificial and faulty estimates of the productivity of the newly conquered lands, and therefore revenue assessments in many cases were abnormally high. Many of the big taluqdars resisted the new regime and its high revenue demand, and were liquidated with utter ruthlessness. Many were driven off and their mud fortresses razed to the ground. In other cases, defaulting estates were sold off by the government. As a result, by 1820, many of this "inchoate magnate class of upper India", as Eric Stokes described them, had "either lost their position entirely or were left in a shrunken condition".[79] The land sold in auction was often bought by the amlas and tehsildars, who used their local knowledge and manipulated their power to buy some of the best properties in the area. In the Banaras region, for example, about 40 per cent of land had changed hands by the middle of the nineteenth century and they went into the possession of, as Bernard Cohn gives the list, "under civil servants and their descendants, and to merchants and bankers". These people came to constitute a "a new class of landlords", who were outsiders to the village community and had different attitudes to the land.[80] But on the other hand, as Thomas Metcalf has argued, since land market was imperfect (often there were no buyers) and frequently the new purchasers had to leave the former owners in charge, in few cases only the land actually changed hands. The situation created nevertheless a scare that land was passing into the hands of non-cultivating classes, Holt Mackenzie in 1819 describing it as a "melancholy revolution"; for in his judgement only the village coparcenary bodies were the "sole owners of the land".[81]

So from taluqdars British preference now shifted to the 'primary zamindars' and village communities. Mackenzie's recommendations were incorporated in the Regulation VII of 1822, which provided for a detailed field-to-field survey for revenue assessment. Settlement was to be made with the village community or with a taluqdar where available; and in addition to the rights of the proprietors, the rent to be paid by the resident cultivating peasants was also to be ascertained and recorded. Thus taluqdars were not completely eliminated; but where possible joint proprietary right in land was vested in the village communities. The refractory and oppressive nature of the taluqdars and the need to maximise revenue as well as protect the rights of the peasant proprietors to ensure the improvement of agriculture, rather than the influence of the Ricardian theory of rent, prompted the making of the Mahalwari Settlement. But the new settlement from the very beginning was enmeshed in confusion, and corruption, as in practice it was virtually impossible to implement. The survey, which was at the core of the new arrangement, failed, because it was too complex to be carried out with the existing administrative machinery. The obvious result was over-assessment, based on "idiosyncratic estimates".[82] The situation was worsened by the agricultural depression of 1828. Arrears started mounting, land remained uncultivated; buyers were difficult to find. Some reforms had become clearly necessary, which came in the Regulation XI of 1833.

The revised system, as worked out by another civilian, R.M. Bird, provided for a detailed survey to assess the revenue of an entire *mahal* or fiscal unit, based on the net value of potential produce of the field. The total revenue thus fixed was then to be shared by the members of a co-sharing body. The state was to appropriate two-thirds of the net income of the land and the settlement was to be made for thirty years. But the village settlements, started by Bird and completed by James Thomason, were again based on imperfect survey, inaccurate calculations and therefore over-assessment. And they were marked by an unconcealed hostility towards the taluqdars, whom Bird considered to be a "host of unproductives". Many of them were dispossessed and pensioned off with a cash allowance; and so effective was this policy that it nearly "flatten[ed] the whole surface of society", as the Lt. Governor of the province commented in 1842 after Bird's retirement.[83] But this did not mean the ushering in of a golden age for the village communities, which were ruined by high revenue demand, mounting debt burden, arrears of revenue and the resulting sales of their properties and dispossession through decrees of the civil courts. Land in many cases passed into the hands of moneylenders and merchants, more so in the commercialised districts. Whether this meant a fundamental social upheaval is open to question, as in many cases the formal sale of properties did not effect any real change in the structure of landholding in the villages, as the new purchasers could hardly do anything without the original owners. But, as Thomas Metcalf concedes, "one can hardly say that 'nothing happened'".[84] The grievances of the rural society of north India were soon to be expressed rather loudly and violently in the revolt of 1857, as we shall see in the next chapter.

Thus by the middle of the nineteenth century the Company's administration had devised three systems of land revenue administration, creating private property in land and conferring that proprietary right on three different groups—the Permanent Settlement was made with the zamindars, the Ryotwari Settlement with the ryots or peasant proprietors and the Mahalwari Settlement with the village community. The latter system was extended to Punjab and central India when those regions were conquered subsequently, while the Ryotwari system was introduced in Sind, Assam and Coorg. The zamindari system was tried in the northern districts of the Madras Presidency where zamindars could be found. According to a rough estimate, in 1928–29 about 19 per cent of the cultivable land in India was under zamindari settlement, 29 per cent under Mahalwari settlement and 52 per cent under Ryotwari system.[85] A common feature of all the settlements, as we have noted, was over-assessment, as the primary aim of the Company's government was to maximise revenue income. The results were arrears of payment, mounting debt, increasing land sales and dispossession. Contrary to received wisdom, modern research has established that the effects of these changes were less spectacular than once imagined, and had significant regional variations, as the land transfers could not fundamentally alter the structure of landholding everywhere. The agrarian society thus proved to be more resilient than once thought to be. But the groups and classes that survived had substantially different rights, obligations and powers. These changes and grievances generating from there were amply reflected in the series of agrarian disturbances that marked the first century of British rule in India, which we shall examine in the next chapter.

2.4. THE APPARATUS OF RULE

As the empire grew in size and its resources needed to be controlled, so did the need for an efficient and authoritative administrative system increase. Initially there was respect for Indian tradition and no attempts were made to impose European ideals. But soon this mid-eighteenth century construction of a "rational" Asia began to wane, as the conquerors felt the need to assert sovereignty and exert control to ensure a steady flow of revenue. The idea of cultural particularism gradually began to lose ground in the face of Evangelical attacks and the Utilitarian zeal for reform. The idea of improvement led to the introduction of British principles of justice and uniformity under a civil authority exercised by British personnel. Good laws and sound administration, it was hoped, would lead to the freeing of individual initiative from despotism, irrational customs and traditions. This would give free and full scope for capital and labour and place due emphasis on individual rights and ownership. The Utilitarians advocated the 'Rule of Law' for India, while a uniform system of administration throughout the conquered territories also suited British interests. Till 1813 the Company acted more like a traditional Indian ruler, avoiding innovation or intervention, but keeping nonetheless a vigilant eye on extracting agricultural surplus. But this scenario gradually changed under the ideological pressure of the intellectual movements mentioned above and also because the Industrial Revolution in Britain necessitated an integration of the markets throughout India and her development as a source for agricultural raw materials. All this required an unequivocal assertion of sovereignty, much greater penetration into Indian economy and society and control over Indian trade not only with Britain but with other countries as well.

JUDICIAL SYSTEM

The grant of diwani in 1765 gave the East India Company the right to collect revenue in Bengal, Bihar and Orissa, but the nawabi administration and the Mughal system remained in place. The practical implications of this dual administration were however very little, as the authority of the nawab was overtly and systematically undermined by the Company, while maintaining for some time to come the fiction of Mughal sovereignty. The judicial administration of the subah remained initially in the hands of the Indian officers between 1765 and 1772 and the Mughal system was followed in both civil and criminal justice. Clive appointed Muhammad Reza

Khan to represent the Company's civil jurisdiction; as Naib Nazim he also administered the criminal jurisdiction of the nawab. However, this acceptance of the indigenous system depended to a large extent on the colonisers' understanding and interpretation of it. The Mughal system was never centrally organised and depended to a large extent on the local faujdars and their executive discretion. Although the *sharia* or the Islamic law was referred to for legitimation, its application varied widely depending on the seriousness of the case and the interpretation of the *muftis* and *kazis*. The focus of this system was more on mutual resolution of conflict rather than punitive justice (except in cases of rebellion), and punishment when meted out often depended on the status of the accused. To many Company officials this system looked like one marked by unusual laxity and they attributed it to an eighteenth century degeneration when the zamindars and revenue farmers had allegedly usurped judicial authority. These people were thought to be driven more by considerations for pecuniary benefit than justice and this led to the complaint about the "venality" of the justice system. It was therefore argued by 1769 that there was need for some sort of direct or overt European supervision to ensure a "centralization of the judicial prerogative" retrieved from the hands of the zamindars and revenue farmers, and thereby to assert Company's sovereignty.[86] So when Warren Hastings took charge as governor in 1772, he decided to take full control of the justice system and he had no doubts whatsoever as to why he should: through such a measure, he reasoned, "the people of this country would be accustomed to the Company's sovereignty".[87] One major reason for arresting Reza Khan in 1772 and for keeping him in confinement without trial for nearly two years was to get rid of the most powerful obstacle to this project of eliminating Indian agents from the administration of justice. It was Khan who was continually insisting on Mughal sovereignty and the supremacy of Islamic laws. Even after his acquittal, Hastings pleaded with the Company directors not to restore him to his former position.[88]

Under the new system of 1772, each district was to have two courts, a civil court or *diwani adalat* and a criminal court or *faujdari adalat*. Thus the Mughal nomenclature was retained, and the laws to be applicable were Muslim laws in criminal justice and the Muslim or Hindu laws in adjudicating personal matters, such as inheritance, marriage etc. This division of the topics of law was evidently in accordance with the English system, which left such matters as marriage, divorce, property, religious worship or excommunication, in the jurisdiction of the Bishops' courts, where the law applicable was the ecclesiastical law.[89] The civil courts in India were to be presided over by the European District Collectors, and they were to be assisted by maulvis and Brahman pundits interpreting indigenous laws for their understanding. There would be an appeal court in Calcutta, which too would be presided over by the president and two members of the council. The criminal courts were to be under a kazi and a mufti, but they were to be supervised by the European collectors. The appeal court, the Sadar Nizamat Adalat, was removed from Murshidabad to Calcutta; Reza Khan had already been dismissed and now the control of the court was vested in the president and council members. However, the legal fiction of nawabi sovereignty was still maintained, as all their orders were sent to the nawab for his final sanction. In reality, Hastings personally supervised the criminal justice system until 1774, when he finally acknowledged his failure to improve law and order situation and reluctantly accepted the Court of Directors' decision to reappoint Reza Khan at the head of the nizamat adalat, which was once again moved back to Murshidabad.[90]

In civil justice system further changes took place between 1773 and 1781, partly in response to the demands of revenue collection and partly in deference to the Whig principle of separating executive functions from the administration of justice. According to the plans worked out by Hastings and Sir Elijah Impey, the chief justice of the Calcutta High Court, district collectors were divested of their judicial duties. In the area of civil justice, instead of district courts, initially six provincial courts, later replaced by eighteen *mofussil* courts were created and they were to be presided over by only the European covenanted officers of the Company, who would be designated 'Judges' for this purpose. For some time the new Supreme Court, created by the Regulating Act of 1773, acted as an appeal court; but its conflict with the Supreme Council over definition of jurisdiction led to the confinement of its authority to the city of Calcutta and to matters related to factories dependent on Fort William. In its place the Sadar Diwani Adalat was now reconstituted to serve as an appeal court, with Sir Elijah himself taking over its superintendence in 1780. Along with this Europeanisation, which was the most dominant and visible feature of the judicial reforms of this period, there was also another coherent trend, and that was towards systematisation or institutionalisation of the civil justice system. The Code of 1781 prescribed specific rules and regulations to be followed in all the civil courts down to the lowest level and all judicial orders were henceforth to be in writing. The major problem that hindered certainty and uniformity in the system was that of conflicting and varying interpretations of indigenous laws, as Brahman pundits, for example, often gave divergent interpretations of the various schools of *dharmashastra* and sometimes their opinions on the same law varied widely from case to case. To reduce this element of uncertainty, a committee of eleven pundits compiled, at the behest of Hastings, a digest of Hindu laws in 1775, and it was translated into English by N.B. Halhed in 1776 for the purpose of lessening the dependence of European judges on their indigenous interpreters.[91] A code of Muslim laws was also compiled by 1778. With this standardisation of law, the practice of law now needed professional expertise that could only be expected from a specially trained group of people, the 'lawyers'. Thus, in its effects, the reforms of the Hastings era "tended to centralise judicial authority, and reduce administration to a system."[92]

There was a certain reversal of this system in 1787, when once again the collector was given the duty of administering civil justice. It was Lord Cornwallis and his Code of 1793 that finally set the rule of separating revenue collection from administration of civil justice as a safeguard for property rights against abuse of power by revenue officials and their agents. The new system provided for a hierarchy of courts from zillah (district) and city courts to four provincial courts and the Sadar Diwani Adalat with appellate jurisdiction. All the courts were to be headed by European judges, with provision for appointment of 'native commissioners'. The criminal justice system was also completely overhauled, as the district magistrates complained to Cornwallis about the anomalies of Islamic laws and the corrupt practices at the criminal courts. But more importantly, it was felt that such an important branch of administration could no longer be left in charge of an Indian.[93] The faujdari adalats, which until then functioned under Naib Nazim Reza Khan, were therefore abolished and replaced by courts of circuit, headed by European judges. The office of the Naib Nazim itself was abolished and the Sadar Nizamat Adalat was brought back to Calcutta and placed directly under the supervision of the Governor-General-in-Council. The jurisdiction of these criminal courts did not extend to the British-born subjects, who remained under the jurisdiction of the Supreme Court at Calcutta. The entire judicial reform of Cornwallis therefore spoke of one thing—a total exclusion of Indians from the whole system, which became less ambiguous in its authoritarian and racially superior tone.

The Cornwallis regulations were extended to the province of Banaras in 1795 and to the Ceded and Conquered Provinces in 1803 and 1805 respectively. But the Bengal system based on the assumptions of a permanent settlement with the zamindars, faltered seriously in Madras, where it was introduced because of Lord Wellesley. By 1906 it was clear that in a Ryotwari area, where the collector had to function also as a Settlement Officer and assess revenue, and where there was no such powerful class as the zamindars of Bengal, the separation of revenue collection and magisterial and judicial powers posed serious problems. On Thomas Munro's insistence, the Court of Directors in 1814 therefore proposed a different system for Madras, which included provisions for greater Indianisation of the system at the lower levels (village panchayats, district and city courts) and the union of magisterial, revenue collection and some judicial powers in the office of the collector. Fully introduced in Madras by 1816, it was later extended to Bombay by Elphinstone in 1819.

Certain unresolved issues remained in the area of judicial administration however. Apart from the question of Indianisation, there was the issue of codification of laws, which would establish a uniform judicial administration and civil authority throughout British India. These issues were not raised until the governor-generalship of Lord Bentinck and the Charter Act of 1833. The act, first of all, threw open judicial positions to Indians and provided for the appointment of a law commission for codification of laws. By this time the collectors had once again resumed magisterial authority and some judicial power. The law commission appointed under Lord Macaulay completed the task of codification by 1837, but it had to wait until after the revolt of 1857 for full implementation. The Code of Civil Procedure was introduced in 1859, the Indian Penal Code in 1860 and the Criminal Procedure Code in 1862. The new codes, as Radhika Singha has argued, sought to establish "the universal principles of jurisprudence", based on "a notion of indivisible sovereignty and its claims over an equal abstract and universal legal subject".[94] But this institutionalised justice system, it needs to be mentioned here, was to be applicable only in British India. In the vast regions that remained within the princely states, whose size and efficiency varied widely, the judicial administration was usually run by a motley amalgam of British Indian laws and personal decrees of the princes, who also acted as the highest judicial appellate authority. But they too were subjected to constant imperious supervision of the British Residents and Political Agents stationed in their court (for more details see section on Residents and Paramountcy).[95]

In British India, however, the judicial administration now looked significantly different from what it was under the Mughal rule, and these changes the ordinary Indians found hard to comprehend.[96] While previously they had access to a variety of judicial procedures, now they were subjected to a streamlined system. Although initially in personal matters traditional Hindu and Muslim laws were applied, the judicial interpretations made the laws often look very different and incomprehensible to the indigenous people. Justice now became distant, not just physically, because of the geographical distance from the district courts, but also psychologically, as the indigenous people did not understand the complex judicial procedures, dominated by a new class of lawyers. As a result, justice also became expensive. And as the huge number of court cases started piling up, for most people justice became inordinately delayed, sometimes even by fifty years. But there were elements of "continuity" too, particularly in the first century of British rule. In most cases the way Hindu personal laws were interpreted by Brahman pundits that these only benefited the conservative and feudal elements in Indian society. It was only the public side of the law that upheld the idea of freeing the individual from the shackles of status.[97] But here too there were problems, as the colonial system retained a considerable terrain for judicial discretion, based on the argument of cultural particularism or civilisational inferiority of the indigenous people. The concept of equality before law often did not apply to the Europeans. If there was greater movement towards equality in civil justice system, racial privilege for the rulers remained in place in various forms in the criminal courts.[98] And there were significant domains of activity, for example, those of the police and the army, which remained unaffected by this colonial definition of the 'Rule of Law'.

POLICE

When the East India Company took over diwani in 1765, the Mughal police system was under the control of the faujdars, who were in charge of their *sarkars* or rural districts; the *kotwals* were in charge of the towns, while the village watchmen were paid and controlled by the zamindars. This system continued for some time under the authority of Muhammad Reza Khan acting as the Naib Nazim with his station at Murshidabad. But the old system could hardly function effectively, as the growing power of the Company had thoroughly undermined the authority of the nawab. Crime rates began spiraling upward after the famine of 1770, and the general state of 'law and order' declined day by day with an alarming rise in the rate of crime against property. For the Company officials, like other departments, the police administration too seemed to be in need of European supervision, as every crime was a direct affront to their authority. The faujdari system continued with minor modifications until 1781, when the faujdars were finally replaced by English Magistrates. The zamindars retained their police duties, but were made subservient to the magistrates.

But this limited reform of Warren Hastings could not solve the problem, as the establishments of the magistrates proved to be too inadequate for the purpose, while the zamindars abused the system and freely took advantage of its weaknesses. So Lord Cornwallis in 1793 decided to divest the zamindars of their policing duties, and instead divided the districts into thanas or units of police jurisdiction of twenty to thirty square miles, each placed under a new officer called *daroga*, who was to be appointed and supervised by the magistrates. The daroga thus became a new instrument of control for the Company's government in the diwani provinces, or as the peasants looked at them, as the local representatives of the "aura and authority of the Company Bahadur ".[99] A new and alien element in the countryside, they could hardly ignore the powerful local-landed magnates, who retained much of their extra-legal coercive powers and in most cases made alliances with them. By the nineteenth century the daroga-zamindar nexus thus emerged as a new instrument of coercion and oppression in Bengal rural life. But on the other hand, when the resourceful contestants for power in the countryside, the zamindars and the planters, both having posses of mercenaries or *lathiayals* at their command, got embroiled in fierce battles for territories, the ill-equipped and poorly provided darogas stood as helpless onlookers.[100] Therefore, when the regulation was extended to Banaras in 1795, Jonathan Duncan, the Resident at Banaras, made further modifications to make the tehsildars, who were to be in charge of the policing units, more subservient to the magistrates and the zamindars more responsible for crime prevention in their estates. The daroga system was extended to Madras in 1802 and the tehsildari system to the Ceded and Conquered Upper Provinces in 1803 and 1804 respectively. But everywhere the system produced devastating results because, as Thomas Munro diagnosed, it was "not founded in the usages of the country".[101]

Whenever the system failed and the law and order situation deteriorated, the colonial authorities searched for reasons, and the easy scapegoats to be found were the native subordinate officers who were stereotyped for their alleged lack of morality and integrity. So the Cornwallis system was scrapped within a few years. The tehsildars were divested of police duties in 1807, the daroga system was formally abolished in 1812, and the supervision of the village police was vested in the collector, who was now responsible for revenue, police and magisterial functions at the same time. This extreme concentration of power led to other problems. The subordinates in the revenue department, who were now in charge of revenue collection as well as supervision of rural policing, became the new agents of oppression and coercion. This was revealed, for example, in the report of the Madras Torture Commission appointed in 1854.[102] In Bengal, on the other hand, where there was no subordinate establishment in the Collectorate offices, because of the Permanent Settlement, the darogas were retained and allowed to perform police duties, although after 1817 they were placed under a more regulatory regime closely supervised by the District Magistrates. But such patchy reforms were hardly satisfactory and the colonial state clearly needed an appropriate and uniform police system that would assert its authority, secure property and ensure the introduction of its version of the 'rule of law' throughout the empire.

The new model was first experimented in Sind when it was conquered by Sir Charles Napier in 1843. Discarding the previous practice of trying to adapt the indigenous systems to the needs of the colonial state, he created a separate police department with its own officers, following the model of the Royal Irish Constabulary, which he found to be ideally suited to the colonial conditions. It needs to be mentioned here that while English political opinion remained ideologically averse to the idea of a professional police force, it was in Ireland, in view of the growing sectarian and peasant movements, that a regular police force was created in 1787 as an apparatus of colonial intervention.[103] Under this model, which was now applied to Sind, the whole territory was to be under the supervision of an Inspector General, while the districts would have their own Superintendents of Police, answerable to both the Inspector General and the District Collector, representing the civilian authority. While the rank and file were to be Indians, the officers were to be invariably Europeans. The Sind model, which was found to be adequately suited to tackle any political agitation, was later introduced in Punjab when it was conquered in 1849, and later, with various modifications to Bombay in 1853 and Madras in 1859. The Madras system provided for a military police and a civilian unarmed force, both subservient to the civilian authority of the Collector-Magistrate in the districts. But in the meanwhile, the revolt of 1857 had shaken the foundations of British rule and had made it more conscious of the need of an effective machinery for collecting information and policing the empire. The Police Commission appointed in 1860 provided for a basic structure of a police establishment for the Indian empire that was enacted in the Police Act of 1861. And that structure, with only minor adjustments, remained unchanged for the next century of British rule.[104]

In the new organisation military police was eliminated and the civilian police was organised on a provincial basis, with the inspector generals answerable to the provincial governments, and the district superintendents to the collector. Thus the entire police organisation was placed under the control of the civilian authorities, and for a long time the positions of the inspector general were filled in by civil servants. The district superintendents were to be in charge of rural police, the daroga becoming the subinspector, thus solving the age-old problem of integrating rural police into the imperial structure. In this way the police organisation established a well-defined hierarchy of command, from which Indians were systematically excluded. The Police Commission of 1902 provided for the appointment of educated Indians to the position of officers in the police force; but they "stopped in rank where the European officer began".[105] Thus, distrustful of the Indian subordinates and subservient to the civilian authorities, the Indian police system was tellingly reflective of its colonial nature. Although not a police state in a conventional sense, thinks David Arnold, a "Police Raj" gradually emerged between the revolt of 1857 and the transfer of power in 1947.[106] Faced with recurrent peasant rebellions and mounting political resistance, the police became the foremost tool of repression in India, with the colonial state retaining total monopoly over its coercive power. And if a situation ever went out of hand, there was always the army to take control.

ARMY

The evolution of the Company's army was integrally connected to the development of its Indian empire. In the eighteenth century, Royal forces, particularly the navy, were often dispatched to India on lease to the Company to help it out at times of trouble, but this created problems, particularly in the relationship between the King's army officers and the civilian authorities of the Company. So from very early on there was an attempt to raise a permanent Company's army in India.[107] The tradition of recruiting peasant armies had been developing in north India since the sixteenth century and this created what Dirk Kolff (1990) has called a "military labour market". During the Mughal period, the distinction between this peasant army and the civilian population was never very clearly marked. It was in the eighteenth century that the rulers of some of the north Indian successor states, like the Nawab of Awadh and the Raja of Banaras, refined this recruitment system and raised sophisticated trained peasant armies distanced from the civilian communities.[108] It was this tradition that the East India Company appropriated as it started recruiting its own army, which came to be known as the sepoy (from *sipahi* or soldier) army. The French had first initiated this tradition of recruiting an Indian army in 1721–29. And it was against the backdrop of Anglo-French wars in south India that in 1748 Captain (Major?) Stringer Lawrence—who had brought in the Royal naval reinforcement to rescue the beleaguered English Company—first began the drive towards recruiting a permanent Indian army for the English Company. It was renewed by Lord Clive after the defeat of the Bengal nawab in 1757. This sepoy army was to be trained and disciplined according to European military standards and commanded by European officers in the battlefield. Some of these officers including the commander-in-chief were King's officers, while the majority were nominated by the Company directors by way of distributing patronage. In the early nineteenth century by legislation twenty thousand Royal troops were to be stationed in India and paid for by the Company, ostensibly as a strategy to subsidise Britain's defence expenditure in the post-Napoleonic era.[109] In addition to that the size of the Company's Indian army also increased continually and as its territory expanded beyond Bengal, the military labour market from where it recruited extended as well. The number of sepoys rose from 82,000 in 1794 to 154,000 in 1824 to 214,000 in 1856.[110]

"Indeed, the recruitment of the East India Company's army", Seema Alavi argues, "was central to the development of the Company's political sovereignty",[111] which rested on a monopoly of power. The army therefore claimed the largest share of the Company's expenditure in India, and also it was crucial to effective collection of revenue—a situation that Douglas Peers has called "military fiscalism". The army not only conquered territories, it also protected the empire against real or imagined internal threats; it handled peasant rebellions against high revenue demands, made alliances with Indian elites, collected information about Indian society and economy. It was thus considered to be the most important apparatus of rule for the Company's administration in India. To a large extent, however, this sense of importance was generated by the army itself. A number of military ideologues argued incessantly that India was in a perpetual state of war, given the militarised state of her society and the inherent volatility of the political situation. This "Anglo-Indian militarism", as Peers argues, created constant pressures for conquests, generated a sense of self-importance for being the ultimate guarantee of the empire's security and stability and thus sustained its claims to autonomy and unrestrained expenses.[112]

The recruitment of the Company's army in the eighteenth century was not just building on the existing traditions of the north Indian military labour market; those traditions were being adapted to British imperial preferences. The recruitment system, for example, endorsed the traditional British preference for peasants as best potential recruits and followed the colonial stereotypes that wheat-eating Indians rather than the rice-eating groups were physically more suitable for the job, although such ethnic stereotyping became a much more important factor in army recruitment in the late nineteenth century rather than in the eighteenth. During the initial formative phase, Hastings did not want to disturb the existing caste rules in the affairs of the army. So the Company's army consisted mainly of upper caste Brahman and Rajput landed peasants from Awadh and the Rajput and Bhumihar-Brahman peasants from north and south Bihar—both wheat-eating regions. These people joined the Company's army because the pay, allowances, pension and resettlement provisions offered by the Company were much better than those offered by the regional states, and what was most important, salaries were paid regularly. The deliberate policy of respecting caste, dietary, travel and other religious practices of the sepoys fostered a high caste identity of the Company's army. By joining it many of the upcoming socially ambitious castes—like the Bhumihar-Brahmans—could fulfill their aspirations for social mobility. Cornwallis, despite his preference for Anglicisation, did not disturb this specific organisation of the army, and as a result, the Company came to possess a high caste army, which was prone to revolt when their social privileges and pecuniary benefits were cut from the 1820s. As the Company's territories expanded to the west beyond the Bengal frontiers into the mountainous Jungle Terai, in the 1770s and then into the Ceded and Conquered Districts in 1802 there was another attempt to recruit from among the hill tribes. While in the plains the Company ran permanent recruitment centres, in the hills recruitment was made through local notables and payment was offered through the Mughal system of *ghatwali* service tenures. The defeat of the Indian states, particularly of Mysore in the late eighteenth and of the Marathas in the early nineteenth centuries created another vast reservoir of surplus armed manpower to recruit from; but the Company's army could not absorb all the disbanded soldiers of the Indian princes. Then from 1815 there was another experiment to recruit Gurkha soldiers from among the Nepalis, Garwahlis and Sirmouri hillmen. A skilful blending of the Nepali martial tradition and European training and discipline made the Gurkhas the most trusted soldiers in the British army.[113]

Thus as the empire expanded, the Company's army came to incorporate a variety of social groups and a number of military traditions, which had to be accommodated in a careful balancing game and power had to be shared with the local elites. Within these circumstances while the Bengal army remained more high caste in character, the Bombay and Madras armies became more heterogeneous. In the 1820s, when the empire attained stability with the weakening of most of the Indian powers, and Company's finances ran into trouble, the contradictions of this balancing game became apparent. In the following decade there were attempts to streamline the army administration, the main purpose of which was to have more rigorous control over the sepoys and their families. The reforms of the 1830s, which aimed at levelling the differences and promoting a universal military culture, as Alavi shows, created discontent among the sepoys. This unhappy feeling particularly showed in the Bengal army, as the reforms infringed upon the sepoys' high caste status and disturbed the power relations within which they were located. In the 1840s, therefore, the disaffection of the Indian troops found articulate expressions from time to time and these incidents prepared the backdrop for the mutiny in the Bengal army in 1857, which shall be discussed in the next chapter.

After the mutiny there was a lot of rethinking about the constitution and recruitment strategies for the Indian army. The Peel Commission which was appointed to look into the military affairs of India recommended that "the native army should be composed of different nationalities and castes, and as a general rule, mixed promiscuously through each regiment."[114] Therefore, during the next few years regiments which had mutinied were disbanded, castes were more evenly mixed across the regiments, recruitment remained focused on Punjab which remained loyal during the mutiny, and the regional elements like the Punjab, Hindustan, Bombay and Madras, were carefully kept separate. The recruitment strategies were further streamlined in the 1880s when the colonial knowledge of Indian ethnicity and racial stereotypes were deployed to evolve the theory of "martial races". Certain groups, such as the Pathans of the North-West Frontier Province, the Jats of Punjab, the Rajputs of north India or the Gurkhas of Nepal, were identified as ideally suited for the job, because of their martial background or racial status, i.e., being of Aryan Kshatriya stock. These groups were thought to be warlike, trustworthy, but at the same time intellectually deficient, so that they could fight but not lead. This gave the European commanding officers a sense of security. As David Omissi calculates, by 1914, "about three-quarters of the Indian infantry came from Punjab, Nepal or the North West Frontier Province."[115] The peasants from these social groups joined the army primarily because it was a lucrative career. On the other hand, their loyalty was ensured by the army administration by deliberately encouraging their respective religious traditions and their sense of honour, which kept them devoted to the master whose "salt" they had eaten. The valorising of warrior self-image communicated through uniforms and other insignia, and the idea of shaming themselves and their communities through dishonourable deeds or cowardice remained important parts of a carefully cultivated army culture. This loyalty of the army was important for the stability of the Raj, as it was used more against internal threats to security than against external foes. Except for a brief Russian threat through Afghanistan in the 1880s, the British empire in India did not face any external danger to its security. Yet a large army was maintained—quarter of a million in peace time—devouring 40 per cent of the central revenue. The "British Raj", writes, David Omissi, "was a garrison state".[116]

In the administration of this garrison state the relationship between the civilian and military authorities remained always a sticky point ever since the beginning of the Company's army. In order to establish civilian authority over the army, the Charter Act of 1793 very clearly gave the ultimate control over all matters of war and peace to the Board of Control. The commander-in-chief was made subservient to the governor general, but the functional relationship between the two, despite various safeguards, worked well only when there was good personal understanding between them. Often the pressure of the army was too much for the civilian authorities to withstand. Lord Amherst was pressurised by the army into a belligerent foreign policy, while William Bentinck had serious problems in his dealings with his commander-in-chief.[117] This relationship continued to be unpleasant during the period of Crown rule, and became ugly during the notorious Curzon–Kitchener controversy in 1904/5. The commander-in-chief, Lord Kitchener, wanted to abolish the position of the Military Member in the viceroy's council and centralise control and command of the army in his own hands. Viceroy Lord Curzon objected to it and when the home government offered a compromise formula of reducing the powers of the Military Member without abolishing the position, he offered his resignation. To his surprise, the resignation was quickly accepted, indicating the power of the army establishment. But Kitchener too did not have his way fully. In 1905 the position of the Military Member was abolished and the commander-in-chief became directly responsible to the viceroy's council. But the crucial financial control of the army was not left in his hands; for this a separate Military Finance Department was created, with a civilian chain of command going up to the Finance Member of the Council. This system remained in place until the end of colonial rule.[118]

In the late nineteenth and early twentieth centuries, the army remained, as before, the most effective instrument of coercion. It provided guarantee of stability to the Raj against all sorts of civil disturbances, for example, nationalist agitations, workers' strikes, peasant movements or communal riots. The police were not always suitable to handle these situations, as the policemen lived in the communities and therefore were susceptible to social coercion and exposed to ideological influences. The army, on the other hand, was quarantined in the garrisons spread across India, deliberately kept at a low level of literacy and insulated from all political influences. The army was not used frequently for the purpose of policing the country, as frequent use would reduce its effectiveness and blunt its demonstration impact. But the civilian administrators knew that it was always there at times of grave emergencies. In such situations, and there were more of them in the 1920s and 1930s, usually British troops were preferred, as since 1857 till almost the end of the colonial period one British soldier was maintained to two or three Indian sepoys. But in a vast country like India colonial order could not be maintained without the collaboration of the latter, who remained steadfast in their loyalty to the King-emperor. Except on two occasions—one in 1907 during the Canal Colony agitations in Punjab and then again in 1920 during the Sikh gurdwara movement—the sepoys were never touched by the political agitations. This was the main reason why there was so much bureaucratic opposition to the Indianisation of the command chain in the army. Training and appointment of Indian officers started hesitatingly and selectively in

1931 after the first Round Table Conference. The issue was given full consideration only in the 1940s as a delayed concession to the nationalists under the pressure of the military needs of World War Two. But it was already too late to win the sympathies of the Indians. In the subsequent years the composition of the army officer corps completely changed and many of the Indian officers became attracted to the cause of Indian nationalism.[119] Visible signs of this cracking of the loyalty of the Indian army, we will argue in the last chapter, was one of the main reasons why the Raj had to end its career in 1947.

INDIAN CIVIL SERVICE

The civilian bureaucracy, which controlled the army by pulling the financial strings if not anything else and ran the Indian empire with its help, were meant only to implement policies framed at home. But the distance between London and India, the difficulties of communication and their command over information from the field gave them a considerable amount of discretion and initiative. As a result, as Clive Dewey observes: "In their heyday they were the most powerful officials in the empire, if not the world".[120] It was "a patronage bureaucracy" at the outset, as the method of recruitment, as outlined by the India Act of 1784 and the Charter Act of 1793, was only through nomination by the members of the Court of Directors of the Company, who would sign a declaration that they had not received any money for offering this favour. Various factors also compelled them to nominate from outside their immediate family circles. Yet, corruption and inefficiency gradually crept in, and the educational background as well as abilities of the recruits were found to be extremely uneven. As Bernard Cohn calculated, between 1840 and 1860, "fifty to sixty extended families contributed the vast majority of civil servants who governed India".[121] And from this service, Indians were carefully excluded, as no position worth an annual salary of £500 or more could be held by them.

The expansion of empire, however, increased the responsibilities of governance and required an efficient bureaucracy, trained in Indian languages and laws. Lord Wellesley, who arrived in India in 1798 with a grand imperial vision, wrote in his minute of 1800 that the Indian empire "should not be administered as a temporary and precarious acquisition".[122] What he wanted was adequate training for the European civil servants. At Fort William College in Calcutta the civil servants from all the presidencies took three years of training before getting their civil posting. But the college did not continue for long, as Wellesley soon lost the favour of the Court of Directors, and the latter feared that such a training programme might result in the loyalties of the civil servants shifting from London to Calcutta. So in 1802 Fort William College was closed; it would continue there only as a language school. In its place, in 1805 the East India College was established at Hertford near London; it was moved to Haileybury in 1809. All candidates nominated by the Court of Directors were to have at this college two years of training and only if they passed the final examination would they secure an appointment to civil service in India. It is difficult to fathom how much influence this education actually had on the subsequent behaviour of the civil servants in India, as this training, following Lord Macaulay's recommendation, was essentially based on a generalist curriculum, which, except the language component, had practically nothing of relevance to India. But Haileybury College developed among the Indian civil servants a sense of camaraderie—or indeed, a sense of belonging to an exclusive club.

By the 1830s, however, the administrative responsibilities of the bureaucracy in India had increased immensely, as the District Collector had once again combined in his office the revenue collecting responsibilities, magisterial authority and also some judicial powers. In the newly conquered territories—the so-called 'non-regulation' provinces—such as Punjab or Assam, the powers and responsibilities of the district officers were even greater. Along with that, functions of the state were also gradually extending to newer areas of activities. This brought in greater impersonalisation and a more elaborate hierarchy in the bureaucratic structure, requiring more able administrators. It was, therefore, felt around this time that the existing patronage system could not bring in adequate number of able personnel for such onerous administrative responsibilities. What was needed was competition to attract the best minds from the rising middle classes of England. The Charter Act of 1833 introduced competition for recruitment; but it was limited competition among the candidates nominated by the directors and therefore could not improve the situation. Finally, the Charter Act of 1853 introduced the principle of open competition; civil servants for India were henceforth to be recruited through an examination open to all "natural born subject of Her Majesty". The Haileybury College was abolished in 1858 and the Civil Service Commission henceforth recruited civil servants through an examination held annually in England. The steel frame of a centralised bureaucracy thus came of age in India in response to the needs of an empire that had by now established itself on firm grounds.

It was no wonder, therefore, that in this administrative structure the Indians were accommodated, if at all, only in subordinate positions, known as the Uncovenanted Civil Service. After 1813 under Warren Hastings a gradual process of Indianisation of the subordinate services had begun, mainly in the judiciary. Later Lord Bentinck advocated inclusion of Indians for orientating administration to local needs; the other reason might have been the question of expenses. A regulation in 1831 gave more power and responsibility to the Indian judicial officers; but the top echelon of the Covenanted Civil Service still remained closed to the Indians. The introduction of competitive examination in 1853 technically opened the gates to the Indians; but they were still effectively barred, as the recruitment examination was held only in England. And in spite of repeated petitions from the Indian nationalists in the late nineteenth century, the opposition of the European bureaucracy prevented the holding of a simultaneous examination in India. Yet the government could neither ignore the nationalist demands and so the compromise formula was the introduction in 1870 of a 'Statutory Civil Service'. It meant that Indians of ability and merit could be nominated to a few positions hitherto reserved for the European covenanted civil servants. But as Lord Lytton's predilections were clearly in favour of the aristocracy, Indians chosen for such positions were usually those with respectable family background or belonging to the indigenous princely families.

It was Lord Ripon who realised the political importance of the Indian middle classes and argued that their continued exclusion from administration might eventually spell danger for the empire. He, therefore, preferred a simultaneous competitive examination in India, which would allow the entry of educated Indians of merit and ability into the Covenanted Civil Service. But the proposal met with a concerted opposition of the European bureaucracy, who clearly felt threatened by the prospect of sharing power with the Indians. Indeed, in the late nineteenth century following the revolt of 1857, the European covenanted civil servants in India suffered from a profound sense of insecurity, which issued from aristocratic criticism at home, Liberal democratic attacks in the Parliament and the growing political protests of the educated Indians. They loathed therefore any idea of sharing power with the Indians and tried to scuttle the Local Self-government Act in 1882 and then in racist conjunction with the Anglo-Indian commercial community, opposed covertly, and often even overtly, the Ilbert bill in 1883–84. They objected the very idea of introducing the principle of election in India and obstructed the proposed Indianisation of the civil service on the basis of a "mythical rationale" of "inefficiency" that was used to legitimise their own monopoly of power.[123]

The structure of the civil service was ultimately reformed in 1892, on the basis of the recommendations of a Public Service Commission submitted five years ago. The new regulations retained the exclusive status of the covenanted civil service and called it the Indian Civil Service (ICS). The Uncovenanted Civil Service, on the other hand, was to shed its derogatory epithet and was to be called the Provincial Civil Service. The Statutory Civil Service was abolished, and in its place certain higher positions which were previously preserved for the ICS were now to be filled in through promotion from the Provincial Civil Service. The Indians could still enter the ICS through the open examination held in London; but their representation in this service remained abysmally low—just about 15 per cent in 1922. But then it was from this year that the proportion of representation in the civil service began to change.

In response to the nationalist demands, the Government of India Act of 1919 finally provided for a separate, not simultaneous, recruitment examination to the ICS to be held in India; and under its provision, the first examination was held in Allahabad in February 1922. As a result, by 1941 the Indians outnumbered the Europeans in this charmed circle of Indian Civil Service. If the period between 1858 and 1919 was that of "bureaucratic despotism",[124] when the will of the civil servants used to run the government, this tendency somewhat diminished after the gradual democratisation of the polity since 1919. But even after 1937, when Indian ministers took office in the provinces, the administration was virtually run by the civil servants, because of their superior knowledge at the ground level and their informal alliances with the local power structure. However, the gradual Indianisation of the civil service also reduced its value as an apparatus of authoritarian rule for the empire and paved the way for a transfer of power. On the other hand, this Indianisation made it possible for the continuation of the tradition into the period after independence,[125] when the service only changed its nomenclature into the Indian Administrative Service.

RESIDENTS AND PARAMOUNTCY

While the steel frame of the Indian Civil Service ruled British India, about two-fifths of the territory of the Indian subcontinent were under 'indirect rule' of the Company and later the Crown. Until then indigenous princes ruled, but the British Residents and Political Agents governed. As the nature of the East India Company's function in India changed from commercial to political, the role of the commercial agents, who were placed at the courts of various Indian states to look after the Company's trading interests, also transposed into that of Residents handling the political relations between the Company Raj and the Indian princes. The system of Residency, as Michael Fisher has argued,[126] was unique, as it was not to be found in existing European imperial tradition and differed from the Mughal system of *vakils*. The latter were employed by the client states and Mughal nobility to represent them at the imperial court and the same system was replicated by the successor states. The Residency system involved a redefinition of sovereignty, which was encoded in the new terminology of 'Paramountcy', under which the Indian states were left with "domestic sovereignty", while sovereignty beyond their borders lay with the Company as the superior imperial power. The actual terms of the subordinate sovereignty of the Indian states varied from case to case, depending on the status of the princes and the circumstances within which treaties with them had been signed. But in effect, "British practice often reduced some of these very 'sovereigns' to the de facto status of puppets or virtually confined them within their own palaces".[127]

As the Company's imperial expansion progressed in India, for reasons of resources—both financial and manpower—it preferred to keep many of the Indian states under indirect rule, rather than trying to control and administer them directly. The choice depended on many factors. The states which were not in a position to challenge the military power of the British were left to themselves; those situated in remote corners or on hostile terrains were also left alone; while those that did have little arable land, and therefore limited prospect of revenue returns, held little attraction for direct conquest.[128] The policy was also subjected to various ideological push and pulls, responding to conservative pressure for disengagement, aggressive pleas for direct annexation and pragmatic reasoning for indirect control. The evolution of the Residency system therefore underwent various ups and downs.

Michael Fisher has identified three distinct phases in the evolution of indirect rule in India until the revolt of 1857. The first phase (1764–97) starts with the initial placement of the Company's Residents at the courts of Murshidabad, Awadh and Hyderabad after the Battle of Buxar (1764). The Company's authorities were not yet confident and clear-visioned about its forward policy in India, and so the development of the Residency system during this period was halting, and the role of the Residents rather restricted and cautious. This initial hesitation was, however, decisively gone in the second phase (1798–1840), which was marked by aggressive expansionism, championed by Lord Wellesley (1798–1805) and his policy of Subsidiary Alliance (see chapter 1.3 for details). The role of Residents also changed during this period from that of maintaining diplomatic relations to that of indirect control, and in many cases the Residents themselves facilitated further territorial expansion. This trend was temporarily halted by the recall of Wellesley and the coming of Lord Cornwallis with a mandate to follow a policy of non-interference. But after his death, British officials in India again embarked on a mission of territorial expansion, and many of the newly conquered territories were left to be indirectly controlled by the Residents. This growth went on unabated until 1841, when the abortive Afghan campaign (1838–42) for the first time failed to establish indirect British rule in Afghanistan. The third phase (1841–57), therefore, saw the ascendancy of the idea of "consolidation", rather than expansion, which had now reached its physical limits in India. During this period, therefore, we find a policy shift towards direct annexation, spearheaded by Lord Dalhousie's forward policies (for example, 'Doctrine of Lapse'), which saw the takeover of a number of Indian states like Awadh, Jhansi, Nagpur, Satara and a number of Punjab states. These contributed to the grievances that flared up in the revolt of 1857.[129]

The revolt of 1857, therefore, constitutes an important watershed in the evolution of British policies towards the Indian states. It was not only diagnosed that the annexation policies had contributed to the revolt, but it was also found that territories under indirect rule were less affected by the disturbances than those under direct rule. And not only that, states like Gwalior and Hyderabad rendered valuable service in containing the conflagration. So, as India passed into the hands of the Crown, the Queen's Proclamation of 1 November 1858 made a commitment to "respect the rights, dignity and honour of the native princes as our own". Lord Canning reassured them against possible extinction of their dynasties by issuing 150 'adoption' sanads recognising their adopted heirs.[130] But that did not mean that the Indian states were to be left unreformed, as the British often assumed a greater responsibility for the welfare of the princely subjects. The Raj, therefore, argues Ian Copland, "dedicated to grooming the princes as 'natural allies'". This reformist mission

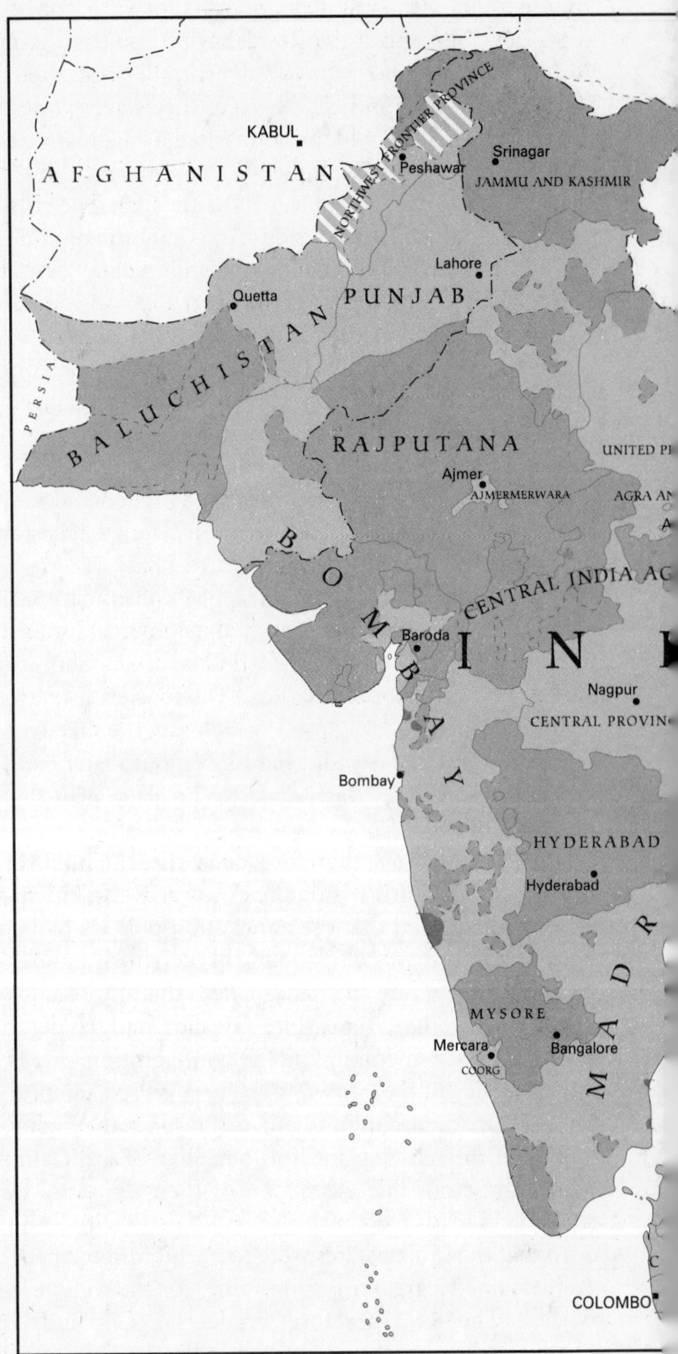

MAP 4: British India and the princely states, c. 1904

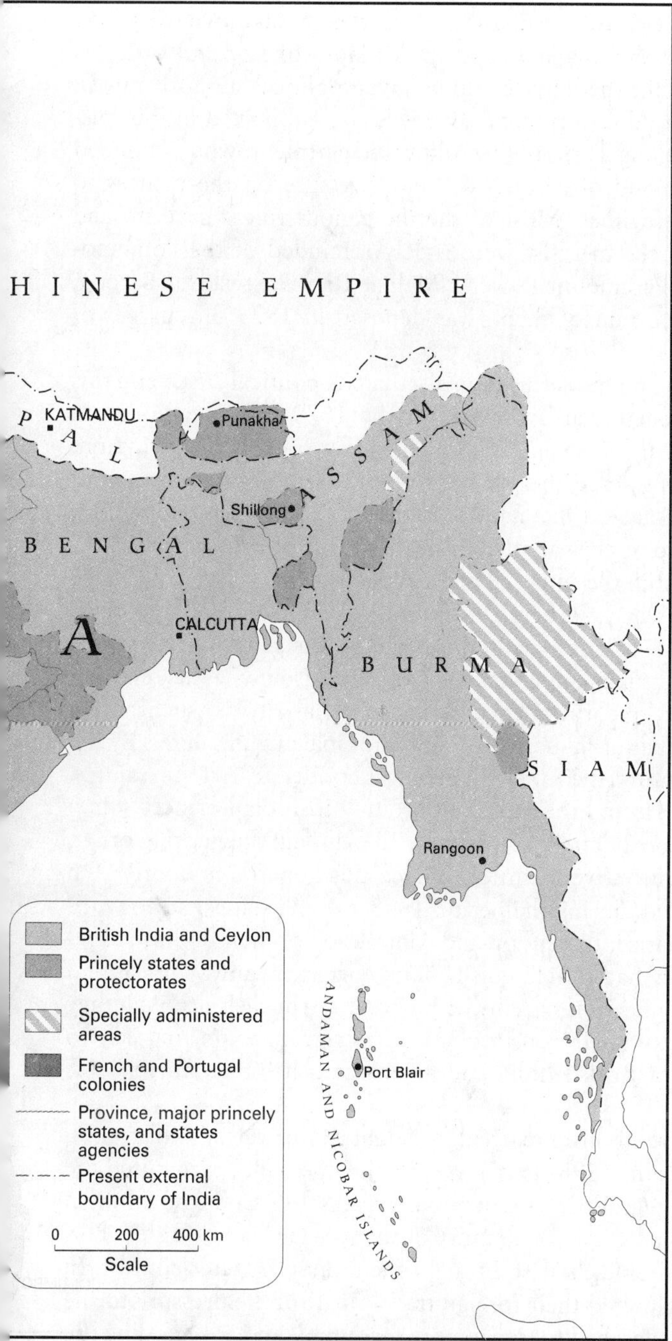
HINESE EMPIRE
KATMANDU
PAL
Punakha
ASSAM
Shillong
BENGAL
CALCUTTA
A
BURMA
SIAM
Rangoon
ANDAMAN AND NICOBAR ISLANDS
Port Blair
British India and Ceylon
Princely states and protectorates
Specially administered areas
French and Portugal colonies
Province, major princely states, and states agencies
Present external boundary of India
0
200
400 km
Scale

became a dominant official policy with the coming of Lord Mayo (1869–72) as viceroy. He discovered a certain breakdown of *durbari* authority, which contributed to the collapse of law and order in many states. But the latter could be given political support only in return for "good government". He was also supported in this mission by the Young Turks in the Political department, who continued to put subtle and often not so subtle pressure on the princes to reform their regimes. Most of the indigenous rulers gave in, and those who chose to resist were rudely reminded of the "omnipotence of the Paramount Power". Malhar Rao Gaikwad of Baroda, the most important of them, was deposed in 1875 on charges of "gross misrule".[131]

But reform and modernisation also had its political costs, and this became evident towards the end of the 1870s when nationalism gradually began to surface in British Indian politics. Lord Lytton, therefore, considered the princes to be the true representatives of traditional India and the 'natural leaders' of the Indian people. But they were also to be reminded of the grandeur of British power and be placed within the imperial order, which at this stage, as we have seen (chapter 2.1), was being institutionalised into an elaborate hierarchy. This association with the princes also gave the Raj some amount of legitimacy, and that was another reason why this relationship was duly incorporated into the imperial rituals, such as the Imperial Durbar of January 1877 and the table of gun salutes. By the twentieth century, the King-emperor was entitled to 101 gun salutes, the Viceroy 31, and the more important 113 Indian princes somewhere between 21 and 9 gun salutes. To maintain the pecking order, the minor princes were entirely denied this imperial honour.[132] On the other hand, during the period 1878–86, the states had to withstand systematic intervention and contraction of their domestic sovereignty. They had to relinquish control over the railway tracks and other communication systems within their territories, although they had to pay for their construction, refrain from exporting salt to other parts of British India and accept British Indian currency as legal tender.

This interventionism reached its height during the administration of Lord Curzon (1898–1905). He, on the one hand, recognised the princes as integral parts of imperial organisation and invited them with due honour to the grand Coronation Durbar of 1903. But, on the other hand, he also brought them under stricter control. In 1900 he prohibited their foreign travel; in 1902 he pressurised the Nizam of Hyderabad to sign a more favourable treaty regarding the administration of Berar; he forced the princes to pay more for the Imperial Service Troops; deposed a number of rulers and brought sixty-three states under temporary British administration. No wonder, as Scindia of Gwalior later confessed, that the princes simply hated "the tyranny" of Curzonian paternalism. The "Shackles of Paramountcy", as Copland describes the situation, were eased somewhat as Lord Minto took over as the viceroy and found the princes effective and willing allies in his fight against political extremism. As a quid pro quo, he promised to respect their internal autonomy, and in an historic speech at Udaipur on 1 November 1909, announced his new policy of laissez-faire. However, the officers in the Political department often did not share the viceroy's wisdom. If the new policy was meant to isolate the states from the political currents then sweeping British India, it was meant to be "subordinate isolation". And things remained like that until the outbreak of World War One, which once again brought in a policy change vis-à-vis the princely states.[133]

One important question remains to be answered at this stage and that is about the rights and obligations of the princes under the Paramountcy and how were they supervised by the overbearing Residents. The responsibilities and privileges of the princes were in all cases defined in treaties between them and the Company, the obligations of the latter being inherited subsequently by the Crown. The provisions of these treaties varied according to the circumstances in which they were signed, the status of the princes and the size of their states; but there were certain generalities too and the treaties in many cases were later revised as well to bring in more uniformity. To begin with, all the princes recognised the Company and later the Crown as the suzerain power, relinquished their right to enter into diplomatic relations with or declare war against any other state or to employ any other European or American, agreed to direct all their communications with the outer world through the British agents, pay for a contingent of Imperial Service Troops and contribute militarily when there was need for military assistance for the defence of the empire. They had to relinquish sovereignty over the railway tracks running through their territories, and share control over post and telegraph and other communication systems with the Raj. In return, they were to be protected against external aggression and internal revolt, and enjoy internal autonomy. They maintained small police forces for enforcing law and order and spent very little on public facilities for their subjects, such as healthcare or education. If some states did spend on modernising such institutions as a mark of status, and if some other larger states like Baroda, Mysore, Travancore or Cochin, introduced some constitutional changes, they were exceptions, rather than the rule.

However, the internal autonomy of the princes was in practice seriously constrained by the overbearing presence of the Residents in the case of larger states and the Political Agents to the governor general in the cases of smaller states. The Resident, as Michael Fisher defines his position, stood at "the intersection between the indigenous Rulers and the British".[134] They controlled all communications between the two and from time to time exerted the supremacy of the latter over the former. He often tried to promote good government in the states, gave solicited and often unsolicited advice to the rulers on various internal matters and sought to control all important appointments, particularly those of the ministers through whom this informal but not so subtle control was exerted. Often they took advantage of the minority status of the rulers to extend their direct control over the affairs of the states through Councils of Regency. These Residents and Agents were members of either the Foreign Department of the Government of India, or the Political Department of the Bombay government. In 1914, the Foreign Department was split into two: a Political Department looked after the Indian states and a Foreign Department concentrated on the frontier regions and the Persian Gulf states.[135]

Although the Political Department, for various historical reasons, did not attract men of high intellectual capabilities,[136] it was on their personalities and attitudes that the nature of such interventions actually depended. Often they stretched official policies to suit their visions of supervisory role, and sometimes even openly deviated from them. It is true that the princes also tried to co-opt, appropriate and manipulate the political officers to their advantage; sometimes they used the organisational divisions within the British administration to retain their autonomy.[137] Some even resisted the intrusive Residents and the presumptuous Paramount power; one such example was Malhar Rao of Baroda mentioned earlier. Another glaring example was Salar Jung, the ambitious Anglophile minister of the Nizam of Hyderabad, who not only proclaimed Hyderabad's status of a semi-independent ally of the British Crown, and asserted his master's rights over Berar, but also resisted an uneconomical railway project thrust upon him by the British for military reasons. But with his death in February 1883 Paramount power was asserted again in Hyderabad in its full vehemence. Most other lesser princes succumbed to the relentless pressures of the representatives of

Paramountcy even without any semblance of resistance. As Bharati Ray puts it, within a few decades since Lord Canning and Sir Charles Wood at the India Office gave a new orientation to the Raj's policy to the Indian states, their status changed from "semi-independent allies of the Company, into . . . feudatories of the Crown".[138]

The colonial intrusion into the ways of governance in princely India also brought significant changes in the existing social equilibrium in the states, as the previous balance of power was continually redefined under the new regimes. Such social change, however, took different directions in different regions. In the case of Sirohi, a small kingdom in Rajasthan, Denis Vidal (1997) has shown how a dynamic system of power sharing in the durbar between the ruler and the nobles belonging to various lineages within the dominant clan was disturbed by the colonial intervention in favour of the ruler; and so was disturbed the relationship between the ruler and the mercantile groups, who were systematically marginalised from the state administration. As the ruler tried to assert his authority, with the patronage of the British, the other groups resisted. The nobles did not like their jagirs being surveyed for higher revenues and the merchants detested the various judicial reforms that went against their interest. But their traditional means of resistance were now delegitimised or indeed "criminalised" and suppressed, sometimes even with armed intervention. Such crises could not be solved as they were in the past to the satisfaction of all the parties, affecting in the process the interconnections between different sections of the local population.[139] An almost similar situation could be seen in Alwar, also in Rajasthan, where the local ruler in the process of erecting the structures of a modern centralised state ruptured his traditional relationship with the Rajput elites. The latter were reduced from their status of co-sharers of power to that of subordinate subjects.[140] On the other hand, in the far south, in the state of Travancore we come across a different kind of reorientation of the balance of social power. Pressurised by the Madras government—which in turn was being continually prodded by the Christian missionaries—Travancore since the 1860s underwent an elaborate programme of modernisation, executed energetically by a versatile Dewan, T. Madhava Rao. This involved among other things, the introduction of Western education, the state services being thrown open to talent, and finally the establishment of the Sri Mulam Popular Assembly to curtail the political influence of the palace coteries. This cut into the power structure of Travancore and by early twentieth century had far-reaching social consequences, marking the beginning of—to use Robin

Jeffrey's words—a "movement from inherited to achieved status". In other words, the existing caste society was given a thorough shake up, as the dominance of the Nairs in state politics, their near monopoly over administrative positions and other sinews of power were now effectively challenged by the upwardly mobile enterprising dalit groups like the Ezhavas and the local Syrian Christians.[141] The local societies in the princely states continually experienced the encounter of two contending systems of values. The one authorised by the power of the colonial state threatened to displace the locally rooted traditions and tended to alter the social structure in a more fundamental way than we sometimes allow.

2.5. EMPIRE AND ECONOMY

We have already seen how over the years in the late eighteenth and the early twentieth centuries the colonial state had been perfecting its system of surplus extraction from the agricultural economy of India. Now another question remains to be discussed—a question that has been so intensely debated by historians: did India under British rule experience any economic development at all? As an entry point to this discussion, we may first look at India's economic obligations to the empire and how did it fulfill them. It has been argued that it was after the pacification of the revolt of 1857, that the "classical colonial economic relationship" between Britain and India gradually emerged.[142] The Indian empire was supposed to pay for itself and at the same time the country's resources were meant to be available in the imperial cause. India had to provide a market for Britain's manufactured goods, and serve as a source of agricultural raw materials. Till the end of the nineteenth and the beginning of the twentieth century, India fulfilled many of her imperial obligations successfully. It served as a major market for British industries, like cotton, iron and steel, railways, machinery etc. At the time of World War One, Indians consumed 85 per cent of cotton piecegoods produced at Lancashire and 17 per cent of British iron and steel production was absorbed by the Indian railways.[143]

Until World War One, there was no import duty, which could possibly offer any sort of protection to any of the Indian industries, and this was, as A.K. Bagchi has noted, "quite contrary to the trend in the rest of the world, including the British Dominions".[144] Even after 1919, when policies were meant to change under the 'Fiscal Autonomy Convention', successive recommendations of the Indian Tariff Boards to raise cotton duties, were successfully thwarted by the Lancashire lobby, which fought for "our rights" in India, which was considered to be "an important imperial asset".[145] Apart from that, India was also a field for British capital investments in railways and agency houses; the Government of India had to ensure the payment of interests on guaranteed railway stock and debt bonds and meet its annual home charges. This invariably increased India's public debt. On the other hand, India's export trade with other countries helped Britain to overcome its own problems of balance of payment deficit with them, particularly with Europe and North America. Finally, Britain could use the Indian army to maintain its far-flung empire across the world, the entire expenses being borne by the Indian tax payers. Military expenditure had been the greatest single burden on Indian revenues, accounting for almost one-third of the budget.[146] No wonder, India was considered to be the most precious "jewel" in the imperial crown of the British monarch.

In the process of fulfilling these imperial obligations, India was being drained out of her wealth, so complained the early nationalists. There were several pipelines through which this drainage allegedly occurred, and these were interest on foreign debt incurred by the East India Company, military expenditure, guaranteed interest on foreign investments in railways, irrigation, road transport and various other infrastructural facilities, the government purchase policy of importing all its stationery from England and finally, "home charges" or paying for the secretary of state and his establishment at the India Office in London, as well as pay, pension and training costs for the civilian and military personnel—or "the men who ruled India". The actual transfer of money took place through the sale of "Council Bills", which were sold in London in sterling to purchasers of Indian goods who received Indian rupees in exchange. It was often pointed out by the votaries of empire that the phenomenon of drainage was exaggerated; a modern historian would put the amount of drainage at £17 million per annum in the late nineteenth and early twentieth centuries, and point out that this "represented less than 2 per cent of the value of India's exports of commodities in that period".[147] But though a small amount, as the Indian nationalist Dadabhai Naoroji argued, what was being drained out was "potential surplus" that could generate more economic development if invested in India.[148] The other imperial argument was that some of this expenditure was to encourage economic development in India in the way it had happened in the West. India was brought into the larger capitalist world market and that was in itself a progress towards modernisation. Much of the foreign loans and investments were for the development of infrastructure, for integrating internal markets and, therefore, for the modernisation of the Indian economy itself. Some of the recent historical writings point out that the fact still remains that India was not transformed into a full-fledged capitalist economy. As in the case of agrarian economy, so also in other sectors, British policies failed to foster growth. And this was due to the colonial nature of those policies, i.e., the policy of gearing up the colonial economy to the needs of the economy of the mother country. To what extent British policies can be held responsible for macro-economic changes in India remains, however, a contentious issue, as a revisionist view claims that on the whole "colonial India experienced positive economic growth". But this growth, it is admitted, varied widely in both time and space. In other words, there were periods of growth (for example, 1860–1920) and regions of prosperity (such as Punjab, coastal Madras and western Uttar Pradesh), and a generalised view of colonial policies cannot explain these regional and periodic variations. But where stagnation prevailed, it was to a large extent because the government did not do as much as it should have by investing in resource generation, such as irrigation, education and healthcare. The revisionist view acknowledges that it was the presence or absence of these critical resources, which determined regional development or lack of it.[149]

So what was the track record of the colonial state in matters of generating resources in India? There was, first of all, limited colonial initiative to develop agricultural production, except the construction of some irrigation canals in parts of northern, north-eastern and south-western India, i.e., in non-Permanent Settlement areas where there was scope for enhancing land-revenue rates. It is possible to argue that between 1900 and 1939, the area under irrigation almost doubled; but that was only in absolute terms. In relative terms, in 1947 when the British empire ended its long career in India, only a quarter of the total cropped area was under public irrigation system. While we may try to put the blame on technological bottlenecks, social issues and local power rivalries for this lack of progress in extending irrigation facilities, the real reason was that public investment in this sector was guided only by the profitability factor and extreme contingencies, such as prevention of famines.[150] So public irrigation facilities remained hopelessly inadequate, creating only a few pockets of relative prosperity; and even in those areas, irrigation favoured only the more prosperous among the peasantry, as canal rates were very high. As Imran Ali has shown for Punjab, the canal colonies became the model of commercial agriculture in Asia, but the new prosperity that accrued even after paying high water rates, was shared only by limited social groups, such as a few agricultural castes and some medium and large-sized landlords, while the poor continued to labour as tenants-at-will.[151] So in general, although the development of irrigation resulted in some improvement in productivity and some other technological innovations, these profited only the privileged peasants and helped the production of cash crops in certain pockets. It is difficult to dispute the fact that "in the aggregate agricultural yields were largely static in colonial India", and between 1920 and 1947, especially the production of food crops lagged far behind the rate of population growth.[152] Near-famine conditions were therefore not rarities in India during the British period and in 1943 two to three million people perished in a major famine in Bengal (see chapter 8.2).

Commercialisation of agriculture, which favours differentiation within the peasantry, capital accumulation and production for the market, is considered to be a sign of progress towards capitalist agriculture. In the Indian case, however, the initiative often did not come from within the peasant society and the benefits did not accrue to them either. In the case of indigo in eastern India, it was directly fostered by the Company's government when in 1788 it offered advances to ten pioneer planters trying to grow indigo in Lower Bengal by using West Indian methods. Since then indigo industry never functioned as a proper plantation economy, as with no right to buy land until 1829, the planters had to persuade, and later force, the local peasants to accept advances to produce indigo in their lands. This created enough scope for friction, because demand remained uncertain, and it was with an eye on the needs of the remittance trade, rather than the requirements of English textile manufacturers, that the amount of production was monitored. The system became more exploitative and coercive day by day, leading to the indigo rebellion in 1859–60.[153] As for other crops, there is a persistent view that the peasants were "forced" to cultivate cash crops because of high revenue demand, the necessity to pay revenue and rent in cash and above all for debt servicing. This view is refuted by the fact that there was always a positive correlation between the price of a crop and the cropped acreage, indicating profit motive behind the peasants' decision for preferring a particular cropping pattern.[154] But at the same time it was only the rich peasants who could go for cash crops and they too remained immensely vulnerable to the fluctuations in the market. In western India, for example, cotton cultivation grew in response to the cotton boom in the 1860s caused by the American Civil War. It created a pocket of prosperity in the Deccan cotton belt, which disappeared very soon after the end of the war and was followed by a famine and agrarian riots in the 1870s. Jute cultivation in eastern India developed as the peasants failed to meet the subsistence necessities and hoped to earn more by cultivating the "golden crop". So an economic motive was certainly there in peasants' decision to shift to jute cultivation. But as Sugata Bose has shown, the primary producers could hardly reap the benefit of the boom in jute market between 1906 and 1913, as "jute manufacturers and exporters [majority of whom were British] were able to exercise their monopsony power as purchasers of raw jute", leaving the jute growers no space to bargain for prices.[155]

So how can the impact of commercialisation of agriculture on Indian peasant society be assessed? By way of commenting on this question, Tirthankar Roy has argued that: "It is possible that the capitalists captured most or all of the increase in value-added. The rich may have become richer. But that does not mean that the poor got poorer. For, total income had increased."[156] One could argue however that if the rich got richer and the poor remained poor (though not poorer) or became just marginally better off, that was not a very happy state of development either. In other words, commercialisation of agriculture did not benefit the majority of the peasants, although it would be hasty to conclude that it signified a "transition" from pre-capitalist to capitalist mode of production marked by the rise of a powerful rural capitalist class and the proletarianisation of the peasantry.[157] The jute economy crashed in the 1930s and was followed by a devastating famine in Bengal in 1943. It is difficult to establish a direct connection between commercialisation and famines, even though cash crops in some areas might have driven out foodgrains from the better quality land, with consequent impact on output.[158] But even if this had happened, it was an extremely localised phenomenon, as on the whole food crops and cash crops were produced simultaneously. When colonial rule came to an end, food crops were still being grown in 80 per cent of the cropped acreage.[159] But on the whole, as noted earlier, the aggregate production of food crops lagged behind population growth. In view of this, the claim of some historians that growth of trade and integration of markets through development of infrastructure actually increased food security and contained the chances and severity of famines in colonial India[160] remains at best a contentious issue, particularly in the context of the Bengal famine of 1943, which was preceded by a long period of consistently declining per capita entitlement of rice in the province (more on this famine in chapter 8.2).[161]

Railways are considered to be another contribution of British rule towards the development of modern economic infrastructure. "India became", writes a modern historian, "a nation with its local centres linked by rail to each other and to the world".[162] Yet, the very way the railways were constructed makes it clear that its main purpose was to serve the interests of the empire, rather than the needs of the Indian economy. In 1853 Lord Dalhousie took the decision to construct railways in India mainly to facilitate army movements. Gradually there arose another need to integrate the Indian market to open it to British imports, i.e., to connect the port cities to the internal markets and sources of raw materials. So British capital investments were invited with 5 per cent guaranteed interests to be paid, if necessary, from Indian revenues. The companies were given free land with ninety-nine years lease, after the expiry of which the line would become government property. But any time before that—even a few months before the expiry of the lease—the companies could return the lines to the government and claim full compensation for all capital expended. In other words, they could enjoy 5 per cent guaranteed profit for ninety-eight years and then get back all their capital. This made the railway projects, as Sabyasachi Bhattacharya describes them, "an instance of private enterprise at public risk". It was quite natural, therefore, that between 1858 and 1869 Indian railways would attract capital investments to the tune of £70,110,000.[163] The main purpose of this railway construction was to tie up the Indian hinterland in the interest of foreign trade, rather than favour Indian economic development. The construction planning favoured this goal, as it connected the internal markets with the ports, but provided no interconnection between the internal market cities. The preferential freight charges also betrayed this motive: there were less freight charges for bulk manufactured goods travelling from the ports to the interior and raw materials from the interior to the ports, than vice versa.[164] Apart from this, the multiplier effect of the railway construction boom benefited British economy, as machinery, railway lines, and up to a stage even coal was imported from England. The transfer of technology remained confined to low technology areas, such as plate-laying, bridge-building or tunnelling, while in the 'hitech' area the expertise that was imported was never Indianised to develop "a truly national technology".[165] And in certain cases the construction work disturbed ecology, subverted the natural sewage system, and in Bengal for example, created malaria epidemic in the nineteenth century.[166]

About the railways the nationalists often complained of constant drainage of wealth through payment of guaranteed interests, which encouraged a lot of wasteful construction. The government also invested directly in railway construction, mainly in the frontier regions to meet the needs of army movement or for "famine lines" in scarcity areas. The nationalists' main objection was against the selection of priority areas for such public investments, as many of them believed that irrigation would have been a more suitable area for such investment promising higher social benefits. For a colonial government looking for profits, there was obviously less incentive for investment in irrigation. Thus the railways, as it seems, did not encourage Indian economic development as it did in industrialising Europe. Although agriculture was relatively favoured, it did not become a growth sector either. But nevertheless, when the British left, in 1946/47 there were 65, 217 kilometres of railway tracks in India, covering 78 per cent of the total area.[167] The railways had also encouraged the construction of feeder roads and a few other strategic roads interconnecting different regions of India. This did certainly integrate the Indian market to some extent and provided a cheaper mode of transportation for both people and goods, which were taken advantage of by the Indian businesses at a later stage after Independence. And finally, the railways certainly had significant social and cultural impact on Indian society and nation;[168] but those were, one should remember, the unintended results of British imperialism.

The other nationalist complaint against the empire was about its adverse impact on Indian handicraft industries, which at the beginning of British rule in the mid-eighteenth century used to supply about a quarter of all manufactured goods produced in the world[169] and constituted chief export items of European trade. Following the industrial revolution, not only did this export demand gradually evaporate, but colonial rule opened the Indian markets for British manufactured goods and led to "deindustrialisation" or destruction of indigenous handicraft industries, reducing the number of people dependent on secondary industries. Initially, the British imported goods, mainly woollen textiles, had a limited market in India; but then industrial revolution changed the scenario. The preferential tariff policies between 1878 and 1895 were meant to solve a crisis in British industrial economy, which could be overcome by having a captive market in India, now being integrated by the railways. Thus, disappearance of export demand as well as invasion of the home market by cheap manufactured goods from England resulted in the destruction of craft industries. For India its obvious outcome was increasing pressures on land and pauperisation.

However, some modern economic historians have questioned this nationalist thesis. They argue, first of all, that the rate of deindustrialisation, if it did occur at all, is difficult to quantify, because of the paucity of reliable data and also multiple occupations of the Indian artisans, many of whom were often involved in agriculture as well. And if the cotton weavers are supposed to be the chief victims of this onslaught of cheap Manchester produced cotton textile, there is enough evidence to suggest that the Indian handlooms continued to produce coarse cotton cloth for the poorer consumers at home well up to 1930s, when they were overtaken only by the Indian mill produced goods.[170] Some other recent researches, however, reveal that the nationalist position might not have been so incorrect after all, as the available statistical data from Gangetic Bihar clearly show that the proportion of industrial population to total population of that region declined from 18.6 per cent in 1809–13 to 8.5 per cent in 1901. Greater fall was in the percentage of weavers and spinners, whose proportion to the total industrial population declined drastically from 62.3 to 15.1 per cent during the same period.[171]

That does not bring the "deindustrialisation" debate to a convenient conclusion, for it has been shown further that while employment declined, real income per worker in industry increased between 1900 and 1947 and this did not indicate overall regress in the industrial situation. This rising industrial income was not certainly due to the intervention of modern industries in India, but, as Tirthankar Roy has argued, because of increasing per worker productivity in the crafts. This was achieved through technological specialisation and industrial reorganisation, such as substitution of family labour with wage labour within the small-scale industry, which was mostly the case in the handloom textile sector.[172] As Roy further suggests, there is also evidence of "a significant rise in labour productivity" in other small-scale industries as well, resulting from a process which he describes as "commercialisation". It included producing for non-local markets, a shift from local to long distance trade, evolution of infrastructure and institutions to support that change and shifts in consumer and producer behaviour as a consequence of that. These factors helped artisanal industry, but did not lead to successful industrialisation, with the necessary structural changes and economic development.[173] The basic occupational structure in the subcontinent remained substantially unchanged between 1881 and 1951, with agriculture providing for 70 per cent, manufacturing 10 per cent and services 10–15 per cent. Modern manufactures grew rapidly only after World War One; but the rate of increase in the over all income from the secondary sector before World War Two was only 3.5 per cent per annum, not "fast enough to set India on the path of an industrial revolution".[174]

One of the reasons behind this lack of overall economic development was that the colonial state in the nineteenth century was far from just a "night watchman", as supposed by Morris D. Morris (1968). Officially the British government was committed to a laissez-faire policy, but actually it was a policy of discriminatory intervention, which amounted to, as one economic historian has described them, "non-market pressures exerted by the government".[175] Such pressures successfully nudged out Indian entrepreneurs like Jamsetjee Jeejeebhoy[176] or Dwarkanath Tagore,[177] who still mistakenly believed in the idea of partnership. Since 1813 when Indian trade was freed from the monopoly of the East India Company, India came to be considered as a lucrative field for British private capital investment, chiefly in railways, jute industry, tea plantation and mining. Indian money market was dominated by the European banking houses. One major reason why the Indian entrepreneurs failed and their European counterparts thrived was the latter's greater access to and command over capital, facilitated by their connections with the banks and agency houses, while the Indians had to depend on their kins, families and castemen.[178] On the other hand, British economic interests in India operated through the Chambers of Commerce and the Managing Agency Houses, which influenced government policies and eliminated indigenous competition. The managing agencies, controlled by the British "merchant adventurers", offer an interesting story of economic domination of expatriate capital. These were private partnership firms, which controlled through legal contracts a host of jointstock companies, with no obligations to their shareholders. Thus a large firm like Andrew Yule would control about sixty companies in 1917. They preferred racial exclusivism and autonomy, and resisted all attempts at integration. On the eve of World War One, there were about sixty such agency houses, dominating jute industry, coal mining and tea plantations, controlling 75 per cent of the industrial capital in India and almost half of the total industrial employment.[179] So whatever industrialisation that did occur was mostly, though not exclusively, through British capital, with the profits being regularly repatriated. And the major factors that favoured this development were the discriminatory official policies.

An ideal example of such economic favouritism was the tea plantation in Assam, which was developed in 1833, directly under the sponsorship of the government, seeking to reduce import of expensive tea from China. Later, plantations were transferred to individual capitalist ownership, and here native investors were deliberately ignored. The Inland Emigration Act of 1859 secured them a steady supply of labour, by preventing the migrant workers from leaving the plantation sites. Tea industry remained dominated by British capital until the 1950s; so was coal mining in eastern India. The development of jute industry in Bengal is another interesting saga that needs to be recounted here. Jute as a cheap substitute for flax was developed in the early nineteenth century and Bengal remained the chief supplier of raw jute for the industries in Dundee. In 1855 the first jute mill was started in Bengal, and then closeness to sources of raw materials and cheap labour gave it a competitive edge over the Scottish industry. The opening of the Australasian markets in the late nineteenth century, World War One and the wartime demand hike gave the industry a real push. The amount of paid up capital in jute industry increased from 79.3 million in 1914–15 to 106.4 million in 1918–19, to 179.4 million in 1922–23. Bulk of the capital invested was British capital, organised through the Indian Jute Mills Association (IJMA), which controlled output in order to maintain high prices. The profitability of the industry continued until the Great Depression, when both exports and net profits began to decline.[180]

However, this dominance of expatriate capital notwithstanding, from the 1920s some Calcutta-based Marwaris, who had made money as traders and shroffs, began to intrude into this exclusive sphere and started investing in jute industry. First, through buying stocks and lending money, many of the Marwaris got themselves elected to the boards of the European managing agencies. And then, people like G.D. Birla and Swarupchand Hukumchand set up their own mills in 1922. This marked the beginning of Indian jute mills around Calcutta, as in this decade one Armenian and six Indian mills were started, accounting for over 10 per cent of the loomage. In the 1930s this position was further consolidated, as some mills dared to operate outside the control mechanism of the IJMA, thus challenging the hegemony of expatriate capital in this industry. This Marwari stranglehold was gradually extended to other sectors, like coal mines, sugar mills and paper industry. Between 1942 and 1945, they began to take over some of the European companies, so that by 1950, argues Omkar Goswami, they were "poised to take over almost all the older industries in the region" which had hitherto been dominated by European capital.[181] While Tomlinson would ascribe this development to the flight of expatriate capital because of decolonisation,[182] Goswami would give more credit to Marwari entrepreneurial skills.

The real success of the Indian industrialists, however, came in the cotton industry of western India. Until the beginning of World War One imported textiles dominated Indian markets. This import considerably declined during the war—more than halved between 1913–14 and 1917–18—partly because of the transport dislocations caused by the war and partly due to 7.5 per cent import duty on cotton textiles imposed in 1917. The Japanese competition was not so serious yet, while on the other hand, excise duty on Indian textiles remained static at 3.5 per cent. In addition, there was the military demand and the call for 'Swadeshi', proposing a boycott of foreign goods and the use of their indigenous alternatives. Cotton industry existed in India before World War One, and along with the European managing agencies, certain traditional trading communities like the Gujarati banias, Parsis, Bohras and Bhatias, who made money through export trade with China, had maintained their presence in this sector. But as opportunities contracted and their subordination in export trade of raw cotton became more constrictive, they began to diversify into manufacturing as a strategy for survival. The development of cotton industry went through three distinctive phases. It had its early beginning in Bombay in the 1870s and 1880s; its diversification beyond Bombay began in the 1890s, first to Ahmedabad, and then to other centres like Sholapur or Kanpur, its major expansion coming after World War One and in the 1920s; the third phase of its development came in the 1930s when it withstood the initial pressures of depression and then began to expand. The industry remained dependent on foreign collaboration for imported machinery, chemicals and technological expertise. But technology was not the most crucial factor behind its growth, which depended on three things, as Rajnarayan Chandavarkar has identified them, i.e., "relentless improvisation in the use of old machinery, the manipulation of raw materials and the exploitation of cheap labour."[183] Although import of cheap Japanese goods threatened its growth temporarily in the 1930s, by the time of World War Two, the Indian cotton industry had established "an unchallenged monopoly over its vast domestic market and began competing with Lancashire in foreign markets".[184]

Iron and steel industry, under the leadership of Tata Iron and Steel Company (TISCO), began at the turn of the century under direct government patronage. Because, here the monopoly of the Birmingham steel industry had already been broken by continental steel, except in matters of government and railway orders. Revision of store purchase policy during World War One and protection after the war provided a real push to the growth of TISCO. But during World War Two, when there was another opportunity for expansion, the government showed "a strange unconcern".[185] But by then (1938–39) TISCO was producing on an average 682,500 tons or 66 per cent of the steel consumed in India. Apart from cotton textiles and steel, the other industries that developed during the inter-war period were shipping, coal, paper, sugar, glass, safety matches and chemical industries. It is true that protection after World War One, motivated by fiscal compulsions and the need for a local power base, stimulated growth in a number of manufacturing industries in India. But their growth potential was limited to domestic market alone, which remained consistently depressed, given the massive poverty of the Indian population. The situation could only improve through effective government intervention, which was not forthcoming (more on industrialisation and industrialists in chapter 7.3).

If the government policies and the stranglehold of British capital inhibited Indian enterprise in certain sectors, recent researches show that below the westernised enclave and above the subsistence economy of the peasants, there was an intermediate level—the bazaar—where Indian businessmen and bankers continued to operate. This tier consisted of the sectors where either the returns were too low or risks too high to attract European investors, who "confined themselves to sure bets" or the exclusive spheres protected by the empire.[186] This phenomenon which Rajat Ray has called the "imperial division of economic space",[187] provided a sphere of operation, though less rewarding and more risky, for the enterprising communities from Gujarat, Rajasthan or Tamilnadu. The recent microstudy of Bihar by Anand Yang shows how the bazaar provided a profitable ground for the operations of the indigenous merchants-cum-bankers from the mid eighteenth century right up to the period of the Gandhian movements in the twentieth.[188] Some of these indigenous firms took advantage of the new opportunities of the empire, such as the railways and telegraph, and ran sophisticated and fairly integrated business networks that covered the whole of the subcontinent. These firms later expanded overseas to China, Burma, Straits Settlement, Middle East and East Africa. It was these operations which generated indigenous capital, which was later invested in industries after World War One, when the imperial economic policies began to slacken due to multifarious pressures, both financial and political. India's underdevelopment was therefore not due to any lack of entrepreneurial skills.

This brings us back to the point where we began, i.e., India's economic and financial obligations to the empire and how did it fulfill them till the end of the imperial connection. Between 1880 and World War One successive financial crises showed that India was incapable of shouldering the financial burden of serving the empire. The financial crises were due to various reasons, such as greater Indian demands for a share of resources. Development of an articulate political opinion made any increase in internal taxation rate a risky proposition. There were also the macro-economic factors, like fluctuating exchange rates, trade depressions etc. or the vagaries of nature. These led to the weakening of the imperial goal and resulted in greater devolution of power. Gradually import tariffs were imposed against British textile, which virtually amounted to a protection for Indian industries. There was also a shift in British industrial economy and the Indian market lost its importance for the growth sectors in British economy. British investments in Indian capital market also declined, so did the use of Indian army for the defence of empire. The Indian army could still be used, but the cost had to be borne by London or by the dependent colony, which needed it. Thus, gradually India's role in the greater imperial structure was subordinated to its own domestic requirements. The imperial goal and ideology were muted to accommodate pressures built up in India, both financial and political. This diminution of imperial economic interests in India is regarded by some historians as a major factor behind the decision to transfer power. We shall examine that claim in detail in the last chapter.

NOTES

1. Metcalf 1994: 3.
2. For details, see Marshall 1999 and C.A. Bayly 1999.
3. For a detailed discussion on this concept, see Gallagher and Robinson 1961.
4. Stokes 1978: 26.
5. Stokes 1959: 1.
6. Irschick 1994: 6–13, 191–204 and passim.
7. Majeed 1992: 22.
8. Viswanathan 1989: 28.
9. Quoted in Trautmann 1997: 17.
10. Metcalf 1994: 8.
11. Sen 1998: 104 and passim.
12. Mukherjee 1968: 141.
13. Stein 1985.
14. Stein 1989: 351–53.

15. Reeves 1991: 11–12.
16. Hutchins 1967: 5–6.
17. Details in Embree 1962.
18. Quoted in Stokes 1959: 47.
19. Quotations in Majeed 1992: 163, 193.
20. Mani 1998.
21. Metcalf 1994: 53.
22. Ibid: 208 and passim.
23. For more on this argument see Inden 1990.
24. For details see Stokes 1959: 288–310.
25. Ballhatchet 1980: 2–3, 96–97.
26. Sinha 1978: 7.
27. Ballhatchet 1980: vii, 97 and passim.
28. Nandy 1998: viii.
29. Ibid.
30. Cohn 1992: 208.
31. Sutherland 1952.
32. Hutchins 1967: 84.
33. Sen 1998.
34. Quoted in Marshall 1968: 57.
35. Misra 1959: 18–23.
36. Marshall 1968: 132.
37. Misra 1959: 27–34.
38. Quoted in Marshall 1968: 31.
39. Spear 1965: 229.
40. Hutchins 1967: 99.
41. Metcalf 1965: 323.
42. Khan 1969: 294, 297–349.
43. For more details see Guha 1963.
44. Marshall 1987: 123, 141–44.
45. Chaudhuri 1982: 88.
46. Islam 1979: 2–3.
47. Cited in Dhanagare 1991: 32.
48. Chaudhuri 1975: 5–6.
49. Islam 1979; R. Ray 1979.
50. Raychaudhuri 1969; Islam 1988.
51. Robb 1997: 83 and passim.
52. Bayly 1989: 85.
53. Stokes 1959.
54. Bhattacharya 1992: 119.
55. Quoted in Beaglehole 1966: 8.
56. Ludden 1985: 104.
57. Beaglehole 1966: 80ff.
58. Stein 1989: 99, 106, 125–26, 207.
59. Ludden 1999: 160.
60. Stein 1989: 191.

61. Mukherjee 1962: 116.
62. Bandopadhyay 1992: 138–39.
63. Mukherjee and Frykenberg 1969: 220–225.
64. Irschick 1994: 194–200 and passim.
65. Ludden 1985: 83, 90, 105–7.
66. Arnold 1986a: 20.
67. Kumar 1982: 230– 37; 1965: 179.
68. Ludden 1985.
69. van Schendel 1991: 81–85.
70. Bandopadhyay 1992: 270–71.
71. Satyanarayana 1990: 113–14, 135–36.
72. Charlesworth 1985: 48–49, 62–69, 83–86, 96–106.
73. Fukazawa 1982: 198.
74. Catanach 1970: 20.
75. Kumar 1968; Guha 1992.
76. Stein 1992: 28.
77. Hasan 1969: 24–27.
78. Reeves 1991: 5–6.
79. Stokes 1982: 40–41.
80. Cohn 1987: 336–37.
81. Metcalf 1979: 56–58.
82. Metcalf 1979: 59 and passim.
83. Reeves 1991: 8.
84. Metcalf 1979: 135 and passim.
85. Bhattacharya 1989: 47.
86. For details, see Singha 1998: 1–27.
87. Quoted in Majumdar 1960: 308.
88. Khan 1969: 294, 341.
89. Derrett 1968: 233.
90. Khan 1969: 344–49.
91. Derrett, 1968: 239–40.
92. Misra 1959: 240.
93. Chattopadhyay 2000: 35.
94. Singha 1998: viii.
95. Ramusack 1978: 19.
96. See Cohn 1987: 463–82.
97. Washbrook 1981: 650–54.
98. Singha 1998: 30, 289–93.
99. Chattopadhyay 2000: 109.
100. For details see ibid: 102–20.
101. Quoted in Arnold 1986a: 18.
102. See ibid for details.
103. Bayly 1989: 131.
104. See Arnold 1986a for details.
105. Bayley 1969: 49.
106. Arnold 1986a: 230–31.

107. Cohen 1971: 5–6.
108. Alavi 1995: 10–34.
109. Peers 1995: 47, 52– 53.
110. Cohen 1971: 7–8, 32.
111. Alavi 1995: 4.
112. Peers 1995: 1–14, 54–67.
113. For these and more details on the Company army, see Alavi 1995.
114. Quoted in Cohen 1971: 38.
115. Omissi 1994: 44.
116. Ibid: 192–93.
117. Peers 1995: 66–67.
118. Cohen 1971: 22–27.
119. For these and more details on the army after 1860, see Omissi 1994.
120. Dewey 1993: 1.
121. Cohn 1987: 521.
122. Quoted in Misra 1977: 66.
123. For details, see Spangenberg 1976: 347 and passim.
124. Misra 1977.
125. See Potter 1986.
126. Fisher 1991: 67.
127. Ibid: 444.
128. Ramusack 1978: 10.
129. Fisher 1991: 44–59.
130. Copland 1999: 16–17.
131. Copland 1982: 123–52.
132. Ramusack 1978: 12, 22– 24.
133. For details, see Copland 1999: 20–21, 30–32.
134. Fisher 1991: 29.
135. For details, see Ramusack 1978: 4–9, 17–22.
136. See Copland 1982: 78–87.
137. For details see Fisher 1991.
138. See Bharati Ray 1988: 164 and passim.
139. For details see Vidal 1997.
140. Mayaram 1997: 56–58.
141. Jeffrey 1994: 241 and passim.
142. Misra 1999: 20–21; Tomlinson 1979: 1–6.
143. Misra 1999: 21.
144. Bagchi 1972: 48.
145. B. Chatterji 1992: 350.
146. Tomlinson 1979: 27–28.
147. Ibid: 17.
148. Sarkar 1983: 27.
149. For more details on these two views, see Roy 2000: 12–18, 89–100, and passim; quotation from p. 14.
150. Whitcombe 1982: 677–78.

151. Ali 1988: 158–205, 235–44.
152. Tomlinson 1993: 32.
153. Kling 1966: 18–19 and passim.
154. Roy 2000: 90–94.
155. Bose 1986: 63, 72.
156. Roy 2000: 93.
157. For more on the "transition" debate, see Chaudhuri 1996.
158. Charlesworth 1982: 25.
159. Roy 2000: 88.
160. For more on this view, see Roy 2000: 86–89.
161. For more on the Bengal famine see Greenough 1982.
162. Hurd 1982: 737.
163. Bhattacharya 1971: 105–6.
164. Bhattacharya 1989: 131–33.
165. See Derbyshire 2001: 277–303.
166. Samanta 2002: 36–37.
167. Hurd 1982: 739–40.
168. For more details see Kerr 2001.
169. Tomlinson 1993: 101.
170. Vicziany 1979; Tomlinson 1993: 102–9.
171. Bagchi 1976a; Bagchi 1976b.
172. Roy 1993.
173. Roy 1999: 22 and passim.
174. Ray 1994: 7–8.
175. Bhattacharya 1982: 293.
176. Siddiqi 1982.
177. Kling 1976.
178. Chandavarkar 1998: 50.
179. Misra 1999: 4–7, 19–26.
180. Chakrabarty 1989: 36–37.
181. Goswami 1985: 226 and passim.
182. Tomlinson 1981.
183. Chandavarkar 1998: 30–73; quotation from p. 56; also see Chandavarkar 1994: 239–77.
184. R.K. Ray 1979: 73.
185. Ibid: 84.
186. Bagchi 1987: 72.
187. Ray 1994: 17.
188. Yang 1998.

chapter three

Early Indian Responses: Reform and Rebellion

3.1. Social and Religious Reforms

The early policy of the East India Company was that of non-intervention in Indian social matters. Along with pragmatism that demanded continuation of existing systems, there was also a respect for traditional Indian culture that expressed itself in Warren Hastings's policy of Orientalism. It meant, as we have discussed in the previous chapter, an attempt to learn about Indian culture through a study of scriptures in Sanskrit and Persian languages, and to use that knowledge in matters of governance. The result of this endeavour was the establishment of the Asiatic Society of Bengal, the Calcutta Madrassa and the Sanskrit College at Banaras. Knowledge about the subject population, their social customs, manners and codes were regarded as a necessary prerequisite for developing permanent institutions of rule. Hastings's policy to govern the conquered in their own ways and resist Anglicisation thus reflected Orientalist ideological preferences and also political pragmatism.

Since the end of Hastings's tenure there was a gradual move towards cautious intervention in Indian social institutions. What contributed to this shift, as we have seen earlier, were several ideological influences in Britain, such as Evangelicalism, Utilitarianism and free trade thinking. While the Utilitarians began to talk of appropriate social engineering and authoritarian reformism, the Evangelists argued about the necessity of government intervention to liberate Indians from their religions that were full of superstitions, idolatry and tyranny of the priests. The free trade thinkers too wanted government intervention to free Indian economy from the shackles of tradition to ensure a free flow of trade. But the Company's government was still tentative about interfering for fear of adverse Indian reaction. It could not do so unless a section of the Indian society was prepared to support reform. Such a group that would support wide ranging social reforms in India was soon to emerge through the introduction of English education, which became therefore the first and the most important area of intervention and innovation for the Company's state in India.

English education was introduced in India in the eighteenth century through the charity schools run in Calcutta, Madras and Bombay for the education of the European and Anglo-Indian children. The Company supported these schools in various ways, but did not take any direct responsibility for the education of the indigenous population until 1813. Charles Grant's advocacy of English education to be introduced in India fell on deaf ears before the Charter Act of 1793 for fear of political unrest. His major concern was however about the misrule of the Company officials. The real hegemony of the British, he thought, could be established in India through a display of the superior moral and ethical values of the West as manifested in its Christian heritage. Christian instruction was the best guarantee against rebellion, as it would rescue the natives from their polytheistic Hinduism and make them parts of the assimilative project of colonialism.[1] But the missionaries still remained banned from entering India for another twenty years. Despite the ban, the missionaries continued to use various ingenuous means to arrive in the country and work for the dissemination of Western education, which they believed, would lead to proseylitisation. Thus, while the Protestant missionaries started working from the Danish station in Madras from the early eighteenth century, the Srirampur Danish settlement near Calcutta became, towards the end of the century, the refuge of three Baptist missionaries: Dr William Carey, Ward and Joshua Marshman. Apart from running a printery and translating the Bible into local languages, they also ran schools for both boys and girls. Unless they directly offended the religious sensibilities of the local population, the Company's government tolerated such missionary activities, the number of which before 1813 was however very small.[2]

The real beginning of Western education in India can therefore be dated from the Charter Act of 1813, which not only allowed the missionaries to travel to India, but provided for the allocation of one hundred thousand rupees per year for two specific purposes: first, "the encouragement of the learned natives of India and the revival of and improvement of literature; secondly, the promotion of a knowledge of the sciences amongst the inhabitants of that country".[3] This was unprecedented in an age when publicly funded education was not in vogue even in England. The immediate concern of the Parliament in forcing the Company into this commitment was once again the corruption and degeneracy of its officials in India; but beyond that, there was also an agenda for greater territorial control. The officials rampantly exploited the country as they viewed it as a temporary territorial possession, argued Charles Grant.[4] So greater commitment to the development of the natives would provide a greater sense of security or in other words, a sense of duty to the people would lead to the development of a context for greater consolidation of power. But this decision did not immediately decide the nature of education to be provided for the Indians, as this specific clause 43 was rather vague in its language and was open to interpretation. In official thinking in India, the Orientalist thoughts were still powerful, having received strong support in a then recent Minute of Lord Minto, the governor general between 1806 and 1813. The new General Committee of Public Instruction was dominated by the Orientalists, who interpreted the clause to mean advancement of Indian classical literature and the sciences of the land. The programme they chalked out was for the establishment of a Sanskrit College in Calcutta, two more Oriental Colleges at Agra and Delhi and patronage for the *tols* and *madrassas* as institutions of indigenous learning.

In the meanwhile, however, public attention in India was steadily being drawn away from this tradition of indigenous classical learning. Christian missionaries and European individuals like David Hare, started opening schools in all parts of India, where English became the medium of instruction. And then the Calcutta School Book Society and later Calcutta School Society (started in 1819) began to promote vernacular schools for elementary education. The tide seemed to shift decisively in the other direction when Raja Rammohun Roy sent a memorandum to the governor general protesting against the founding of the Sanskrit College in Calcutta. Roy represented a generation of Indians who believed that modernisation of India would come through English education and the dissemination of knowledge of the Western sciences. The balance finally tilted in favour of the Anglicists when William Bentinck, a Utilitarian reformist, took over as governor general in 1828 and Thomas Babington Macaulay was appointed the law member in his council in 1834. The latter was immediately appointed the President of the General Committee of Public Instruction. On 2 February 1835 he issued his famous Minute on Indian Education, which became the blueprint for the introduction of English education in India. Full of contempt for Oriental learning, Macaulay's Minute asserted that "a single shelf of a good European library was worth the whole native literature of India and Arabia". What he advocated, therefore, for the Indians was an education in European literature and sciences, inculcated through the medium of English language. Such an education, he argued, would create "a class of persons between us and the millions whom we govern, a class of persons Indian in blood and colour, but English in taste, in opinions, in morals and intellect".[5] Bentinck immediately endorsed his proposals in an executive order of 7 March 1835, and did not budge from this position despite loud protests from the Orientalists. Thus, as Sabyasachi Bhattacharya has put it, a new education system was introduced in India, in which the task of producing knowledge was assigned to the metropolitan country, while its reproduction, replication and dissemination were left for the colonised people.[6] This was the beginning of the new modernisation project for India.

English education, as Gauri Viswanathan has argued, was present in India in various forms before 1835. But while previously English was studied in a classical fashion primarily as a language, the new shift was towards the study of literature as a medium of modern knowledge. English literature, it was believed, was an ideal representation of English identity, sanitised and abstracted from the more immediate history of exploitation and oppression. Moreover, it would inculcate an appropriate training in morality, ethics and correct behaviour, and thus incorporate a group of natives into the structure of colonial rule, which was the main political agenda of Anglicism.[7] The major feature of this new English education policy was therefore the theory of "downward filtration". It was not meant for the masses, but for "the rich, the learned, the men of business", as C.E. Trevalyan described them,[8] as they already had a literate tradition, had eagerness as well as means to learn and above all had sufficient leisure. Once these men were trained, they could act as teachers and through them elementary education would percolate downward through regional languages, at much less public expenditure. Thus the whole indigenous society would benefit from Western knowledge and superior moral and ethical ideals.

The reports of William Adam, recommending improvement of vernacular education through indigenous village schools were, therefore, ignored for being impractical and expensive. The same model—of promoting English education and higher education at the expense of classical and vernacular learning as well as elementary education—was extended also to the Bombay and Madras Presidencies. However, in the North-Western Provinces, Thomason, an enthusiastic civilian, experimented with vernacular elementary schools and he was so successful that Lord Dalhousie later recommended its extension to Bengal and Bihar. In 1854, Charles Wood's Education Dispatch also signalled a similar shift away from the downward filtration policy, as it recommended the extension of vernacular elementary education, which was endorsed by Dalhousie's administration. However, even in this shifting focus towards elementary mass education it is not difficult to see a concern for the political economy of the empire that rested on the idea of division of labour. This policy proposed that while a relatively small group of highly educated Indians would be needed to man the subordinate positions in the administration, the wider population should also have "useful and practical knowledge" in order to become good workers, capable of developing the vast resources of the empire, and also become good consumers valuing the superior quality of British goods requiring a market. So while elementary and technical education was advocated for the masses, higher education was also given a further boost in 1857 through the creation of three universities in Calcutta, Bombay and Madras on the model of the University of London, which was found to be most suited to colonial conditions. Secondary schools, where the medium of instruction was still English, proliferated under the liberal grants-in-aid scheme, with missionary and private Indian initiatives. But these schools were required to charge fees, as free education, it was argued, would not be properly valued.[9] The scheme was replaced in 1859 by Secretary of State Stanley's idea of an education rate; and vernacular elementary education suffered most as a result.

The Indian Education Commission in 1882 tried unsuccessfully to resolve the problem of duality in the education system by seeking to readjust the balance between higher English literary education for a few and elementary and technical education for the masses. "It is desirable", its report said, "that the whole population of India should be literate." And to ensure such general literacy it recommended "special funds" to be set apart particularly for the education of backward communities".[10] Yet, such backward groups as the vast community of dalits or the untouchables, continued to be excluded from state schools, as their presence would drive away the higher caste pupils, who were meant to be the main target population for the colonial education system. This exclusion happened with the active support of the colonial bureaucracy, succumbing in the name of practicality to the pressures of the conservative sections of the Indian elite, many of whom had by now become grass-roots level functionaries of the empire.[11] British education policy thus endorsed and supported differentiation in Indian society. By 1885 there was in India, according to B.T. McCully's calculation, "an English-educated class of about fifty-five thousand natives";[12] but in 1881–82 out of a total population of more than 195 million, only a little more than 2 million had attended elementary schools.[13] The impact of this differentiation on social and political development of India was indeed far-reaching.

It was with various motives that English education was introduced in India and its continuous expansion sustained. For missionaries, it was supposed to open the gates for proselytisation of the Indians. For Utilitarians it was the ultimate fulfillment of Britain's imperial mission; "imparting education to natives is our moral duty", said Lord Moira in 1815.[14] On the other hand, East India Company from the beginning of the nineteenth century was seeking to reduce the cost of governing India by Indianising the subordinate positions in the administrative structure, particularly in the judicial and revenue branches. Manning the administration exclusively with Englishmen was no longer financially feasible, nor it was politically expedient. A proper education in English—"the language spoken by the ruling class", as Macaulay defined it—was, therefore, a means to train them for such subordinate public services. However, speaking like the Englishmen was not enough, they had to think and behave like Englishmen as well. This pedagogic enterprise of imperialism, therefore, was to inculcate a spirit of loyalty among its Indian subjects who would believe in its providential nature and its civilising mission. Gauri Viswanathan has argued that the colonial education system deployed English literary studies in its curriculum as "an instrument for ensuring industriousness, efficiency, trustworthiness, and compliance in native subjects."[15] But as a moral study it did not function as effectively in India as it did in England, firstly because there were not enough material rewards for liberal education in India. But more seriously because the educated Indians selectively adopted this knowledge and deployed it to interrogate colonial rule itself (see chapter 4.3). So the colonial regime could never abandon the policy of using direct force to uphold its hegemony, and maintained for this purpose elaborate police and army establishments throughout the period. But its social control was certainly buttressed, as K.N. Panikkar argues as well, "by an illusion created by ideological influences", which always remained the central concern of the imperial educational enterprises.[16] The Indians who were attracted to English education were predominantly Hindu upper-caste males from middle and lower income groups, who were economically very hard-pressed due to changes of the time. For most of them, education had a functional utility: it was a means of survival in difficult times, a tool for achieving economic prosperity and getting power, rather than just a pathway to intellectual enlightenment. However, when that material expectation faltered, it was their knowledge which became their best weapon for confronting an authoritarian colonial state, a story we will return to in the next chapter.

Protagonists of English education like B.T. McCully argued long time ago that "English education brought the native youth in contact with a body of thought which openly questioned many of the fundamental assumptions upon which the fabric of traditional values rested".[17] More precisely, we may identify this new "body of thought" as post-Enlightenment rationalism, which came to define "modernity" for a select group of educated Indians. They began to look at their own society through a prism ideologically constructed by such concepts as reason, utility, progress and justice. In 1893 Rabindranath Tagore noted the emergence of a "public" in India, which was not yet matured, but keen to debate publicly—through their newspapers and voluntary associations—various issues affecting the well-being of their society. In other words, there was the rise of a civil society, though very limited it was, but articulate in defending its rights, while locating its identity in an Indian tradition.[18] But this tradition, it was also felt, needed reform, because within this specific colonial ideological context, all existing social practices and religious notions appeared to be signs of a decadent feudal society that had to be remodelled according to the values of a bourgeois social order. In other words, 'Enlightenment' seemed to be the "panacea" for all the evils and backwardness that Indians were being blamed for.[19] For this new elite, striving to move forward in a new global order intellectually defined for them by colonialism, "science" now became "a universal sign of modernity and progress" and came to constitute, as Gyan Prakash has suggested, an authoritative "language of reform".[20] Although the colonial state would not provide scientific education for the Indian masses, intellectuals like Rammohun Roy proposed for his countrymen an education system that would focus on Western sciences. In Calcutta, in 1825, a Society for Translating European Sciences was set up, followed by the establishment of the Society for the Acquisition of General Knowledge in 1838. This movement, which saw the development of scientific education as the key to national improvement, reached a major milestone when the Bengali intellectual Mahendra Lal Sircar established in 1876 the

Indian Association for the Cultivation of Science. And if this discourse was first started by a small circle of enlightened Calcutta elite, it was soon universalised, as it spread to other provinces through the development of a new print culture. In north India, for example, the Banaras Debating Club founded in 1861, the Aligarh Scientific Society founded in 1864 by Sayyid Ahmed Khan and the Bihar Scientific Society started in 1868, contributed to this discourse on the power of science, which then began to pervade the new territories of Hindi literary movements and Hindu revivalist campaigns.[21]

However, the problem was to translate this scientific rationalist mentality of an elite into an effective social reform agenda affecting and involving the larger public. This new mentality had first become most conspicuous among the students of Henry Vivian Derozio, a 'Eurasian' teacher at the Hindu College in Calcutta, who developed among his pupils a spirit of free thinking. This controversial group, known as the Young Bengal, became notorious in their own times for their individual social rebellion, manifested through wining and dining in forbidden meat. But what was more important about them was that they posed an intellectual challenge to the religious and social orthodoxy of Hinduism. It was they who formed in 1838 the 'Society for the Acquisition of General Knowledge', where they discussed various aspects of Western science, and stood for a number of social reforms, such as the prohibition of caste taboos, child marriage, *kulin* polygamy or the ban on widow remarriage. Yet, they could not usher in the desired age of reform. Their total faith in the British and in English education, their rationalism and scientism derived from the West set them apart from the masses of Indians and they never succeeded in organising any social movement in support of their proposed reforms. Their professed "atheism", which was so avowed at the initial phase, declined soon, and their social radicalism too showed signs of backsliding, as they grew older and became established in society. Thus, ultimately, as Sumit Sarkar concludes, the Young Bengal, the followers of Derozio, "left little distinctive or permanent impression on the plane of religion and philosophy" in nineteenth-century India.[22]

The challenge of the other Indian reformers of this period was to rediscover reason and science in their own civilisation, and to reposition the modernisation project within a cultural space defined by Indian tradition. These new intellectual stirrings created a reform mentality that did not reject Indian tradition, but sought to change certain 'unreasonable' aspects of Hindu society, which did not conform to their new 'rationalist' image of a glorious Indian past. This provided legitimacy to the reform agenda of the Utilitarian reformers like William Bentinck. But since this mentality was still confined to a small circle of English educated elite, the reform programme could hardly be expected to succeed. Indeed, in the early nineteenth century a series of social reforms followed, being mainly reform from above through government fiat. And as expected, these reforms remained on paper in most cases, as there was never any attempt to develop a modern social consciousness from below. Lord Wellesley, for example, in 1803 banned the religious custom of child sacrifice at Sagar Island in the Bay of Bengal.[23] But although this ritual practice was stopped, the less visible social practice of female infanticide continued unabated in western and northern India, where landowning high-caste families, practising hypergamy, found it difficult to get suitable grooms for their daughters or pay high amounts of dowry and resorted to clandestine killing of female offsprings at the time of birth. The British authorities sometimes tried to persuade them, and after 1830 sought to coerce them to desist from the practice, with little tangible effect. The talks of a legal ban were halted by the revolt of 1857, and were kept on hold until 1870, when finally the Female Infanticide Act was passed by the Viceroy's Council. But even after that the census authorities reported abject neglect of female children, resulting in high mortality that could not be detected or prevented by the law.[24]

The greatest achievement that Lord Bentinck is remembered for is the prohibition of sati or self-immolation of widows on the funeral pyres of their dead husbands. It was a social practice prevalent in India from ancient times; but as a modern researcher confirms, it "has always been very much the exception rather than the rule in Hindu life".[25] During the Mughal period, it was practised only by the Rajput princely families in central India and Rajasthan and in the kingdom of Vijaynagara in south India. During the British period in the late eighteenth and early nineteenth centuries, the practice was revived on a wider scale in areas, which experienced the highest rate of development under British administration, i.e., the capital city of Calcutta and districts around it. Here it became popular not only among the upper castes, but also among the peasant families of lower and intermediary castes, who achieved social mobility and then sought to legitimise their new status by imitating their caste superiors.[26] Apart from this sociological reason and the religious notion of an ideal wife who would follow her husband in life and in death, the other factor was the greed of the relatives, which the new prosperity of the families had possibly engendered. The practice had become most widespread in those areas where the *dayabhaga* school of personal Hindu law was applicable. As compared to the *mitakshara* school, it allowed the widow relatively greater right to inherit her deceased husband's property. Although the Christian missionaries had first started attacking the institution, it was a strong abolitionist campaign under Raja Rammohun Roy that gave the movement its real momentum. Finally, Governor General Bentinck prohibited sati in 1829 by a government regulation, which could not be overturned by a Hindu petition from the anti-abolitionist Dharma Sabha to the Privy Council in 1830. But although the incidence of sati declined gradually after the regulation, the idea and the myth of sati persisted in popular culture, despite the modernist critique of the western-educated middle classes and the reformist zeal of the colonial administration. The idea was continually reaffirmed through epics, ballads and folktales, to reappear again in public life as late as in 1987 in the much publicised sati of Roop Kanwar at village Deorala in Rajasthan.[27]

Even more ineffective was the other reform movement of the mid-nineteenth century that sought to promote widow remarriage. Its main protagonist, Iswarchandra Vidyasagar, like his predecessor Rammohun Roy, also looked to the colonial state for a piece of legislation. The Hindu Widows' Remarriage Act of 1856, which legalised such marriages, could not however make this practice socially acceptable. On the contrary, as Lucy Carroll has argued, the legislation was intrinsically conservative in character, as on remarriage it disinherited the widow of her deceased husband's property, and thus endorsed the Brahmanical norm of rewarding only "the chaste, prayerful widow".[28] The movement ended in what Vidyasagar's biographer Asoke Sen has called an "unavoidable defeat".[29] He failed to see many widows remarried, as for that he needed social consent, which could not be generated by the power of the colonial state. As a result, not only the practice of widow remarriage remained rare and exceptional among the educated classes in Bengal, but in the next few decades the taboo came to be further universalised and it became a forbidden practice even among the lower orders.[30]

The situation was no different in western India where as early as 1841 an anonymous Maharashtrian Brahman reformer had advocated remarriage of infant widows as a measure to control their sexuality and make their reproductive capacity socially useful. The movement to promote widow remarriage spread among the Western educated middle classes in the 1860s and the debate between the reformers and their detractors also became sharper and bitter. In 1866 Vishnushastri Pandit started a society for the encouragement of widow-remarriage, while his opponents also formed a rival organisation. In 1870, the reformists suffered a set back when in a public debate in Poona, they were found to be at fault by Sankaracharya of Kavir Math and many of them accepted the ritual of penance. Although there were exceptional widows, like Pandita Ramabai, who made her mark in Maharashtrian public life (more on her in chapter 7.5), the movement for the remarriage of widows ended in a whimper, as by the end of the century only thirty-eight widows had been remarried, and in those cases too, the couples were subjected to enormous social pressure and ostracism. And now, the prohibition on widow remarriage became even more widespread, as it became also a lower-caste social practice, despite non-Brahman social reformer Jotirao Phule's spirited attacks on enforced celibate widowhood.[31]

In the Telugu-speaking areas of Madras Presidency, the reform movement in support of widow remarriage was started by Veerasalingam Pantulu, who founded in 1878 a Society for Social Reform for this purpose. The first widow remarriage in the region was officiated by him in 1881 in his hometown Rajahmundry, in the face of stiff opposition. Gradually, support for the reform increased and in 1891 a Widow Remarriage Association was formed with the patronage of the prominent citizens of the town.[32] But this enthusiasm notwithstanding, by this time only three such marriages had been arranged by the reformers.[33] The situation varied widely from region to region, for in Haryana, where the practice of widow remarriage was already in vogue at a large scale, the new act provided such marriages with legitimacy and further social acceptance.[34] The colonial legislation for reform, in other words, had a very uneven impact on Indian society. In Bengal, Vidyasagar continued his reform movement, directing it against polygamy and later child marriage and finally secured an Age of Consent Act in 1860 that fixed the age of consent for the consummation of marriage at ten years for women. It was raised to twelve by another legislation in 1891 (more details in chapter 5.2); but as census statistics show, child marriage continued to be a widely practiced social custom among all the castes, high and low alike, well into the twentieth century.[35]

Reform from above, more specifically through legislation, remained ineffective in other areas too, where it was directed against specific or organised religious or social practices. The British conquest of the Deccan and central India by the beginning of the nineteenth century created the reformist urge to establish pax Britannica in those unsettled territories. But that became a difficult proposition as the disbanding of armies by the Indian chiefs and the general contraction of job opportunities increased the rate of crime, particularly robbery, by roving armed gangs. To this was added the official distrust for the wandering monastic orders, which challenged the very British ideal of a settled tax-paying peasant community. Hence all these various peripatetic groups were stereotyped into a colonial construct, called *thugs,* who were believed to have been members of a "fraternity" traditionally involved in robbery and ritual killings in the name of religion. The campaign against *thugee* was initiated in the 1830s in assertion of the same humanitarian mission of British paramountcy championed by Lord Bentinck. The purpose of the campaign, as Radhika Singha has argued, was not to root it out through education or regeneration of the indigenous society; the "Thuggee" Act (XXX) of 1836 and the Thuggee Department were simply aiming at policing and prosecuting gangs seen as perpetrating a crime in the name of religion. But it proved to be a difficult task. In 1839, Sir William Sleeman, the architect of the campaign, claimed that thuggee as an organised system had been exterminated. In reality what happened was that he realised the difficulty of prosecuting various groups of peripatetic mendicants on charges of thuggee. He therefore preferred to try more flexible strategies for policing such communities.[36]

Legalistic reforms were even more ineffective against less visible or less organised social customs that remained parts of peoples' everyday culture for centuries. An ideal example of this was the abolition of slavery in 1843. Slavery had been abolished in Britain in 1820, and in India the colonial administrators continued to detect its existence in various forms. The agrarian relations in India were complex, marked by numerous structures of labour dependencies, many of which, viewed through the post-Enlightenment "lens of the freedom-unfreedom opposition",[37] looked like slavery in British eyes. The Charter Act of 1833, therefore, instructed the government of India to abolish slavery, and parliamentary pressure continued to mount until its legal abolition. But since the actual forms of bondage differed, particularly so far as agrestic slavery was concerned, the impact of the legal ban was also very limited. Caste, customs and debt kept the agricultural labourers bonded to their landlords in various ways and for a very long time to come.

It is interesting to note that women's status became the main focus of the reforming activities of the colonial state as well as of the educated Indians. To a large extent it was the result of a comparative civilisational discourse of the colonial period. In other words, when civilisations were ranked, one of the major criteria was the position of women, and it was here that the Indians were increasingly under attack by the Western observers, from missionaries to civilians. To put it differently, Indian civilisation was despised because it assigned such a low status to women. This gender question was a key issue for James Mill condemning Indian civilisation in his *The History of British India*.[38] So the Indian intelligentsia also responded to this civilisational critique by advocating and supporting reforms to improve the status of women in Indian society. Such reforms, as we have seen, affected only a few women belonging to their own classes and that too in a very restricted way, as these women remained recipients of male patronage and never became involved in these reformist projects as conscious subjects of their own history. This early nineteenth-century public discourse on reform thus not only had limited impact on society as a whole, it also signified the patriarchal control of the educated Indian males over the private sphere or the domestic arena reserved for women.[39] It is simplistic to suggest that the great reformers of the nineteenth century were not concerned about the welfare of women; but the reforms were not just for women, and we will return to this topic in a short while.

Another response of the educated Indian elite to such civilisational critiques was to reform Hinduism from within in the light of post-Enlightenment rationalism. This phenomenon is often celebrated in the older historiography as the "Bengal Renaissance" or the "Nineteenth Century Indian Renaissance". Although the use of the term "renaissance" is problematic, this cultural movement essentially involved attempts to discover rationalism in India's past and thus to reposition her religious and philosophical traditions within the critical terrain of reason. The movement was started in Bengal by Raja Rammohun Roy who is often described as the father of modern India. He was one of those upper-caste gentry whose power and position had been enhanced by the Permanent Settlement and other opportunities opened up by colonial rule. Rammohun imbibed rationalism from his early training in the eighteenth-century Perso-Arabic literature. Eventually, he studied Vedantic monism and after his migration to Calcutta in 1815 was exposed to Christian Unitarianism. Such intellectual influences motivated him to contest the missionary claim of superiority of Christianity; his answer was to reform Hinduism in the light of reason, by going back to its purist form as enshrined in the *Vedanta* texts. He condemned idolatry, priestcraft and polytheism and translated the *Upanishads* into Bangla to demonstrate that ancient Hindu scriptures themselves propagated monotheism.[40]

Roy's first organisation, Atmiya Sabha, founded in Calcutta in 1815, eventually took the shape of Brahmo Samaj in 1828. It emerged as a major religious movement of the middle-class educated Bengalis, based on the essential principle of monotheism. After Roy's death in 1833, the leadership of the Brahmo movement was taken over by Debendranath Tagore who provided the movement with a better organisational structure and ideological consistency.[41] But the movement was actually taken out of the limited elite circles of Calcutta literati into the district towns of east Bengal by Bijoy Krishna Goswami and Keshub Chandra Sen in the 1860s. Goswami bridged the gap between Brahmoism and the popular religious tradition of Vaishnavism, while Sen's specific focus was to reach larger numbers of non-Westernised Bengalis in the eastern Gangetic plains and to take the movement outside Bengal to other provinces of India.[42]

If missionary activities had been one major contribution of Keshub Sen to the Brahmo movement, the other contribution was a renewed attention to social reforms. He brought in some amount of radicalism into the movement, by attacking caste system, by focusing on the question of women's rights, by promoting widow remarriage and inter-caste marriages, and by raising the issue of caste status of the Brahmo preachers, a position hitherto reserved for the Brahmans alone. But this radicalism also brought the first rift within the Brahmo movement. Basically, as Meredith Borthwick has shown, it was a schism between Keshub's followers, for whom social progress and reform were more important than anything else, and the followers of Debendranath, who preferred to maintain their identification with Hindu society.[43] The former in 1866 established their Brahmo Samaj of India, while the latter sought to retain their identity under the rubric of Adi (original) Brahmo Samaj. These developments signified the perennial dilemmas of Indian modernisation, which continuously sought to be rooted in Indian traditions. This rift was, as it became clear soon, more about an identity crisis than about any fundamental difference of ideology: while some of the Brahmos wanted to define themselves as separate from the Hindus, others began to seek a position within the great tradition of Hinduism.

The crisis deepened and the chasm expanded when the Brahmo Marriage Act was passed in 1872; it legalised Brahmo marriages, which allowed inter-caste and widow marriage, but only if the contracting parties declared themselves to be non-Hindus. As a result, the act never became very popular. Sen himself later retreated from his radical position, condemned the act for promoting "God-less marriages"[44] and later came closer to the Hindu ascetic Rama-krishna Paramahansa. This gradually led to another rift in the Brahmo Samaj in 1878. When Sen arranged the marriage of his minor daughter with the Maharaja of Cooch Bihar, his followers parted company and formed the Sadharan Brahmo Samaj. In 1881 Sen formed his Naba Bidhan (New Dispensation) and started moving towards a new universalist religion. But by this time successive ideological rifts and organisational divisions had weakened the Brahmo movement, confining it to a small elite group. And then it succumbed to a neo-Hindu aggressive campaign for "revivalism", rather than "reformism", as a bold assertion of Hindu identity vis-à-vis the West (more in chapter 5.2).

In western India, reformism began in the early nineteenth century in two different ways. One was the Orientalist method of exploring and translating ancient Sanskrit texts and rediscovering in them the glories of Indian civilisation. The most notable scholar-reformers involved in this project were K.T. Telang, V.N. Mandalik and above all, Professor R.G. Bhandarkar.[45] The other trend was represented by the more direct method of social reform attacking such institutions as caste system or prohibition of widow remarriage. This was undertaken by a number of individuals like Mehtaji Durgaram Mancharam, Karsondas Mulji, or Dadoba Pandurang, who were involved in organisations like Manav Dharma Sabha, founded in 1844, or the Paramhansa Mandali, founded in 1849. The latter organisation followed the iconoclastic radical tradition of the Derozians in Bengal; but in order to avoid any frontal confrontation with the wider community, they operated like a secret society. Revelation of its membership in 1860, therefore, quickly led to its demise, leaving very little achievement to its credit.[46] However, in the meanwhile, Western education had made headway in Maharashtra and the Gujarat region, creating a critical core group looking for reform. In such a context, the two visits of the Bengali Brahmo missionary Keshub Chandra Sen to Bombay in 1864 and 1867 had a profound impact. Indeed, as a direct consequence of that, the Prarthana Samaj (Prayer Society) was founded in Bombay in 1867. Although its founder president was Atmaram Pandurang, the real spirit behind it was Mahadev Gobind Ranade, who was ably assisted by Bhandarkar and N.G. Chandavarkar. K.T. Telang, who attended the samaj services regularly, never became a member. All the leading personalities in this new organisation were Western educated Marathi Brahmans. As for its philosophy, like the Brahmo movement, the Prarthana Samaj also preached monotheism, denounced idolatry, priestly domination and caste distinctions. Later it developed a syncretism and connected itself to the Maharashtrian bhakti tradition.[47]

The Prarthana Samaj maintained its distinction from the Brahmo movement of Bengal. The most notable distinction was in its cautious approach in contrast to the relatively more confrontational attitudes of the Bengali Brahmos. "The peculiar feature of the movement in [Bombay] Presidency", Ranade pointed out, was that its goal was "not to break with the past and cease all connection with our society".[48] The reforms it sought were to come gradually, not cataclysmically, wrecking the structure of the society. Modernisation, in other words, was to be accommodated within the cultural space of tradition, without signalling a sharp break. It was this gradualist approach, which made Prarthana Samaj relatively more acceptable to the larger society. Branches were opened in Poona, Surat, Ahmedabad, Karachi, Kirkee, Kolhapur and Satara. Its activities also spread to south India where the movement was led by the Telugu reformer Veerasalingam Pantulu. By the beginning of the twentieth century, there were eighteen branches in the Madras Presidency.[49] But on the other hand, this cautious approach also brought the Prarthana Samaj face to face with its first crisis. In 1875 Swami Dayanand Saraswati visited Gujarat and Maharashtra and offered the possibilities of a more radical and self-assertive religious movement. A group of Samaj members, under the leadership of S.P. Kelkar, felt attracted to the Swami's Aryan ideology, and broke away. Although the dissident group later came back to the fold of Prarthana Samaj, this marked the beginning of a different kind of religious politics in western India, which was marked more by cultural chauvinism than reformism.

This rupture in the tradition of reform came through the religious movement started by Swami Dayanand Saraswati, who founded his Arya Samaj in 1875. Dayanand invoked the authority of the *Vedas* as the most authentic Indian religious texts, and sought to purge Hinduism of all its post-Vedic accretions. It is difficult to ignore the Western Orientalist touch in his discourse that tried to project Hinduism as a "religion of the book", like Christianity and Islam.[50] But what is more important, in his aggressive response to the West, he fully appropriated the Western intellectual discourse of reason and science and deployed them against his adversaries. He claimed that the Vedas alone contained "scientific truths", and therefore, the religion based on these texts was superior to Christianity and Islam.[51] On the authority of the Vedas, he attacked idolatry, polytheism, ritualistic religion dominated by the Brahman priests, condemned child marriage and stood for widow remarriage, inter-caste marriages and female education.[52] Interestingly, these were the reforms that the Western reformers were advocating! He also denounced untouchability, and repudiated caste system (for more on this see chapter 7.2); but at the same time, he upheld the fourfold varna division, thus retaining the core of the Indian social organisation.[53] His aggressive reformism failed to convince the orthodox Hindus, or even the Brahmos, and remained marginal in eastern and western India; but it received warm acceptance in Punjab and the North-Western Provinces. At the time of his death in 1883 there were Arya Samaj branches all over this region and it was from this time on that the movement became more and more popular and also more aggressive. The moderates among his disciples, who chose to focus on education and community work, were gradually marginalised after 1893, while a militant group under Pandit Guru Dutt and Pandit Lekh Ram launched a militant campaign for preaching the religion of the Vedas, attacking the Muslims and retrieving lost ground by initiating *suddhi* or reconversion of those who were lost to the three proselytising religions of Christianity, Sikhism and Islam. And then in the 1890s, the Arya Samaj became intensely involved in the cow-protection movement, thus moving decisively from reformism to revivalism, a topic that we will return to in chapter 5.

What needs to be focused here though are some of the special features of these social and religious reform movements of the nineteenth century, which made such transformation possible. These movements, first of all, had remained confined to a narrow social space, as the reformist spirit appealed only to a small elite group, who were primarily the economic and cultural beneficiaries of colonial rule. In Bengal, the reform movement involved only a small number of Western educated elite who were known by the general term *bhadralok* (gentlefolk). These were the "new men" who had made money as junior partners of the English officers and free merchants, consolidated their position as small landholders under Permanent Settlement and later took advantage of English education to fill in the various new professions and subordinate administrative positions. Socially, they were mostly Hindus, and though caste was not a major criterion for membership, most of them belonged to the three higher castes, Brahman, Kayastha and Baidya.[54] The Brahmo movement was almost exclusively patronised by these groups, and although it spread from Calcutta to district towns and to other provinces, it remained alienated from the masses. The reformers never even tried to take the reform to the people, as the language of reform, the chaste Sanskritised Bengali prose of Rammohun Roy for example, remained incomprehensible to the uneducated peasants and artisans.[55] Similarly in western India, the members of the Prarthana Samaj were the English educated Chitpavan and Saraswat Brahmans, some Gujarati merchants and a few members of the Parsi community.[56] In 1872 the Samaj had only sixty-eight members and about 150–200 sympathisers.[57] And in Madras Presidency, where English education made much slower progress and caste domination of the Brahmans remained unshaken, the reform ideas took longer to appear.[58] Indeed, the general high caste character of the reform movements of the early nineteenth century explains to a large extent the relative silence on the caste question. Untouchability as an issue of social reform had to wait until the beginning of the twentieth century and the arrival of Mahatma Gandhi in Indian public life after World War One (more on this in chapter 7.2). Lacking in a broad social base, the reformers of the early nineteenth century thus exhibited an intrinsic faith in the benevolent nature of colonial rule and relied more on legislation for imposing reform from above. There was very little or no attempt to create a reformist social consciousness at the grass-roots level, where religious revivalism later found a fertile ground.

Equally important is the colonial character of the reforms, as the Indian reformers' positions in a significant way mirrored the colonial mind and therefore also the ambivalence of the colonial policy planners. The dominant colonial assumption of the time was that religion was the basis of Indian society and this religion was encoded in the scriptures. This colonial perception assumed a total submission of the indigenous society to the dictates of the scriptures. Social evils were thought to be the results of distortion of scriptures by self-seeking people, in this case the cunning Brahman priests who had a monopoly over this textual knowledge. The civilising mission of the colonial state was thus seen to lie in giving back to the natives the truths of their own little read and even less understood *shastras*. Lata Mani (1998) has argued that the whole debate over sati was grounded in scriptures: the colonial government decided to prohibit it only when it was convinced that the custom was not enjoined by the scriptures. As the colonial rulers gave supreme importance to scriptures, the Indian reformers too, as well as their detractors, referred to ancient religious texts to argue their respective cases. The brutality or the irrationality of the custom, or the plight of women, whom the reform was intended for, were lesser concerns in a debate, which was more on the definition of tradition. In Mani's words, "women are neither subjects nor objects but, rather, the ground of the discourse on *sati*; . . . women themselves are marginal to the debate".[59] The same thing can be said of the debate on widow remarriage,[60] and later, on the prohibition of female infanticide.[61] The scriptures, lately valorised by the Orientalists, thus provided legitimacy for social reforms and women were denied agency in their own emancipation (more discussion on the women's isses in chapter 7.5).

This brings us to the inner tensions of colonial modernity, as it is not proper to say that the Indian reformist discourses just reflected some colonial formulations. The early writings of Rammohun Roy are indeed full of "humanistic pleas" to ameliorate the conditions of Indian womanhood.[62] He talked of scriptures when advocating the abolition of sati, as that was how he could sell his reform to a cautious colonial government and to a reticent Hindu society reluctant to accept change. But this traditionalism notwithstanding, his "clinching arguments", as Tapan Raychaudhuri has pointed out, "anticipate[d] the idiom and stances of contemporary feminism".[63] Roy's rationalism was indeed pre-colonial. In his early writings in Persian he had taken a totally rational approach to religion that nearly amounted to a negation of religion itself. However, after his contact with Christianity and Western free-trade thinking in Calcutta, he became more moderate or perhaps more ambivalent.[64] One has to admit that a sharp tradition/modernisation dichotomy is not intellectually conducive to understanding the process of reform in nineteenth-century India.[65] The perceptible ambivalence in the position of the reformers was clearly the outcome of a colonial context. Against the claims of a totalising influence of the colonial discourses, one may point out that no hegemony is ever that absolute that it allows no space for autonomy. Although Indian modernisers looked towards the colonial state for support and direction and post-Enlightenment rationality shaped their visions, they could neither leave their tradition, nor forget their Indian identity. The Indian modernisation project therefore always felt a compulsion to construct a modernity that would be located within Indian cultural space. To summarise their position in Christophe Jaffrelot's words, they "undertook to reform their society and its religious practices in order to adapt them to Western modernity while preserving the core of Hindu tradition."[66] It was through this project that the cultural essence of Indian nationhood, its difference from the colonising West, were gradually imagined by the Indian intelligentsia. However, the inherent ambivalence or tensions within this cultural enterprise later made it appear weak and rendered it vulnerable to the more aggressive assertion of tradition in the late nineteenth century. This later cultural movements too, as we shall see, were involved in a complex intellectual project of interrogating and adjusting at the same time to the colonial constructs of Indian tradition.

3.2. PEASANT AND TRIBAL UPRISINGS

When the elites of the Indian society were busy in initiating religious and social reforms to change their society from within to answer the moralistic critiques of the West, the rural society was responding to the imposition of colonial rule in an entirely different way. In contrast to the urban intelligentsia, who were also the chief beneficiaries of colonial rule, the response of the traditional elite and the peasantry, who were losing out as a result of colonial impositions, was that of resistance and defiance, resulting in a series of unsuccessful attempts at restoring the old order. Not that peasant revolts were unknown in Mughal India; indeed, they became endemic in the first half of the eighteenth century as the rising revenue demands breached the Mughal compromise and affected the subsistence provisions of the peasants, and the Mughal provincial bureaucracy became ever more oppressive and rigorous in collecting it (chapter 1.1). The tendency became even more pervasive as the colonial regime established itself, enhanced its power and introduced a series of revenue experiments, the sole purpose of which was to maximize its revenue income. Resistance to colonial rule was therefore as old as the rule itself.

In the late eighteenth and early nineteenth centuries the revenue reforms of the Company's government had fundamentally affected and altered the Indian rural society. To get an overview of this new structure we may follow the general model developed by Daniel Thorner and D.N. Dhanagare,[67] allowing of course, possibilities of variation in different regions. The first group in this model consisted of landlords holding proprietary rights over large estates, usually consisting of several villages. They were an absentee rentier class with little or no interest in land management or improvement of agriculture. The second group consisted of rich peasants, who could again be subdivided into two subgroups, i.e., the rich landowners and rich tenants. The first group held proprietary right in land, but usually in the same village and took personal interest in cultivation, if not actually participated in it. The rich tenants, on the other hand, had substantial holdings, enjoyed security of occupancy rights and paid nominal rents to their landlords. The third group consisted of middle peasants, who could again be subdivided into: (a) landowners of medium-size holdings or self-sufficient peasants who cultivated with family labour and (b) tenants with substantial holdings paying higher rents than the other privileged tenants. The fourth group included the poor peasants, i.e., the landowners with small holdings not sufficient to maintain their families, tenants with small holdings with little or no tenurial security and the sharecroppers or tenants at will. The last or fifth group, according to Dhanagare, consisted of the landless labourers.

The structure described above is, however, an arbitrary classification based on production relationship and not all the categories could be seen in all the regions. More generally, it was a pyramidal agrarian society, with 65 to 70 per cent of the agricultural population being non-owners of land. These complexities of the agrarian social structure actually developed more fully in the late nineteenth century rather than in the pre-1857 phase. During the latter period, very broadly, to follow David Hardiman's taxonomy, the Indian agrarian society could be fitted into three categories: the rural magnates who were gradually building on their power as landlords, the rich peasants or peasant farmers and the poor peasants.[68] It is often argued that the rich or the middle peasantry, being more independent, were always potentially the more radical elements to initiate and sustain peasant rebellions. But in the late eighteenth or early nineteenth-century India, the land reforms and the high revenue demands of the Company's government had so severely affected the entire rural population that all sections of the peasantry in different parts of the country participated in a series of violent protests. So here we will talk about "peasants"—rather than any finer divisions among them—who rose against the Company Raj and all those who stood for it or benefited from it.

During the first century of British rule there were, first of all, a series of uprisings which Kathleen Gough has called "restorative rebellions", as they were started by disaffected local rulers, Mughal officials or dispossessed zamindars. In most cases they were supported by the local peasants, whose primary goal was to reinstate the old order or restore the existing agrarian relations. One could mention in this regard the revolt of Raja Chait Singh and other zamindars of Awadh in 1778–81, followed by that of the deposed nawab of Awadh, Vizier Ali in 1799.[69] The troubles here continued into the 1830s, particularly in the northern and southern parts of Awadh, causing problems for the revenue collectors. Then followed a rebellion of the Bundela Rajput chieftains in 1842, disrupting agriculture and endangering trade routes in the region for few years. In the south, in the Tirunelveli district of North Arcot and the ceded districts of Andhra, between 1799 and 1805 the Madras government faced stiff resistance from the local chiefs called the poligars. While the Company's government treated them as just zamindars holding military service tenures, in local peasant societies they were regarded as sovereigns inheriting power from the pre-Muslim Vijaynagara kingdom. So when they put up resistance to the Company's troops, they were openly supported by the local peasant societies and were even treated as folk heroes.[70] Also in the south, there was the revolt of Pazhassi Raja which rocked Malabar in 1796–1805, followed by the insurrection of Velu Thampi, the prime minister of the Travancore state, who commanded a large army of professional soldiers and peasant volunteers. All these armed rebellions were, however, put down eventually by the British army. In some cases the rebels were later reinstated with more lenient revenue terms. But more generally, they were suppressed with what Gough calls "exemplary savagery".[71]

The peasants themselves often on their own initiative offered resistance to British rule. The Rangpur rebellion of 1783 in the northern districts of Bengal is an ideal example of such opposition. In the early days of revenue farming system, the peasantry was oppressed by the revenue contractors and company officials, imposing high revenue demands and often collecting illegal cesses. The worst offenders were revenue contractors like Debi Singh or Gangagobinda Singh, who had unleashed a reign of terror in the villages of Rangpur and Dinajpur districts. The peasants initially sent a petition to the Company's government asking for redress. But when their appeal for justice went unheeded, they organised themselves, elected their own leader, raised a huge army, equipped themselves with primitive bows, arrows and swords and attacked the local *cutchery* (a court of law), looted grain stores and forcibly released prisoners. Both Hindu and Muslim peasants fought side by side and stopped paying revenue. The rebels sought to legitimise their movement by invoking what Sugata Bose has called "the symbols of the pre-colonial state system". They called their leader "nawab", started their own government and levied charges to meet the costs of their movement. On Debi Singh's appeal, the Company's government under Warren Hastings sent troops to put down the rebellion. Its brutal suppression was, however, followed by some reforms in the revenue farming system.[72] Similarly in the south, the final overthrow of Tipu Sultan and reinstatement of the old ruling dynasty of Mysore brought in enhanced revenue demands that fell ultimately on the peasants. Rampant extortion by corrupt officials further aggravated their desperate situation, motivating them to rise in open rebellion in 1830–31 in the province of Nagar. Here too the rebels elected their own leaders, defied the authority of the Mysore rulers and ultimately bowed down to the advancing British troops.

In many of the peasant movements of this period, religion played an important role in providing a discursive field within which the peasants understood colonial rule and conceptualised resistance. In other words, their religion defined their ideology of protest. The earliest of these was the Sanyasi and Fakir rebellion, which rocked northern Bengal and adjacent areas of Bihar between 1763 and 1800. The Dasnami Sanyasis, known for their martial tradition, were involved in landholding, moneylending and trade in raw silk, piecegoods, broad cloth, copper and spices. The Madari Fakirs, who traced their origin from the Sufi order initiated by Sha-i-Madar, enjoyed rent-free tenures and retained armed followers during the Mughal days. Both these groups of armed wandering monks were affected by the Company's high revenue demands, resumption of rent-free tenures, and commercial monopoly. And then, their ranks were inflated by the sufferers from the famine of 1769–70, a large number of aggrieved small zamindars, disbanded soldiers and the rural poor. The remarkable philosophical affinity between the two religious orders, their mutual relationship, organisational network and communication with the followers, facilitated mobilisation of the rebels.[73] However, what made the conflict inevitable was the Company-state's unwillingness to tolerate such wandering bands of armed monks, who would seriously challenge its cherished ideal of a settled peasant society in Bengal that would regularly pay revenue without resorting to resistance.[74] Therefore, from the beginning of the 1760s until the middle of 1800s recurrent confrontations between the Sanyasi-Fakirs and the armed forces of the East India Company took place in a wide region of Bengal and Bihar and the number of participants rose up to fifty thousand at the height of insurgency, which however began to decline after 1800. But soon another movement developed in the Sherpur pargana of Mymensingh district in east Bengal, where Karim Shah and later his successor Tipu Shah started a new religious movement among the

Hinduised tribals like the Garos, Hajangs and Hadis. As the Company's rule consolidated itself in this region and the zamindari system became more firmly entrenched under the Permanent Settlement, the peasants' grievances rose against the illegal abwabs exacted by the zamindars and the new revenue settlement effected by the Deputy Collector Dunbar. In such circumstances, around 1824 Tipu's *Pagalpanthi* sect held out a promise of a new regime and just rents. The new spirit gradually spread over the whole region and took the shape of an armed insurrection, which had to be crushed with the help of the army in 1833.[75]

Simultaneously in another part of Bengal a religious movement called Tariqah-i-Muhammadiya was developing under the leadership of Titu Mir. Starting his career as a hired muscleman for the local zamindars, he later went to Mecca, and was initiated by Sayyid Ahmad Barelwi. He came back to preach Islam in a 250-square-mile area in the northern part of the district of 24 Parganas on both sides of the rivers Jumna and Ichhamati. His followers came mainly from the poor Muslim peasants and weavers, who were organised into a community with distinctive dress and beard as markers of identity. As this self-assertion of the peasantry challenged the established relations of power, the local zamindars tried to curb them in various ways, by imposing, for example, a tax on beard. Titu Mir and his followers defied the existing authority—as represented by the local zamindars, the indigo planters and the state—established their own regime, started collecting taxes and struck terror in the region. The government ultimately had to mobilise the army and artillery and on 16 November 1831 blew off Titu's bamboo fortress to crush his movement.[76]

Around the same time, another religious movement called the Faraizi movement developed among the peasants of eastern Bengal, under the leadership of Haji Shariatullah. The Tariqah movement described above owed its origin to the school of the eighteenth century Sufi saint Shah Waliullah of Delhi and derived its inspiration from Shah Sayyid Ahmad of Rae Bareli, the followers of whom were commonly known in colonial parlance as 'Wahabis'.[77] The Faraizi movement, on the other hand, was indigenous in origin. It sought to purify Islam by purging all un-Islamic beliefs and practices and by signifying Koran as their sole spiritual guide. The importance of this movement lay in its social roots, as the rural Muslim poor of east Bengal united under this religious sect and revolted against landlords, indigo planters and the British rulers. Although Hindu landlords felt the main brunt of their angst, Muslim landlords did not feel safe either.[78] When Shariatullah died in 1839, his son Dudu Mian took over the leadership and mobilised the peasantry around an egalitarian ideology. Land belonged to God, he declared, collecting rent or levying taxes on it was therefore against divine law.[79] He built a network of village organisations in the districts of Faridpur, Bakarganj, Dacca, Pabna, Tippera, Jessore and Noakhali. He held local courts as alternatives to British judicial institutions, and collected taxes to meet the expenses of his movement. Violent clashes with the zamindars and planters occurred throughout the 1840s and 1850s. There was a temporary lull in the movement after Dudu Mian's death in 1862, but then it was renewed again at a different scale by his successor Naya Mian in the 1870s (see chapter 4.2 for more details).

A similar peasant movement of the 1840s and 1850s where religion played an important role was the Moplah uprising in the Malabar region of south India. The Moplahs (or Mappilas) were the descendents of Arab traders who had settled in this region and had married local Nair and Tiyar women. Later their ranks inflated through conversion of lower caste Hindus like the Cherumars, a slave caste whose emancipation under the Slavery Abolition Act of 1843 had put them in greater social problems.[80] Gradually the Moplahs became dependent on agriculture and turned into a community of cultivating tenants, landless labourers, petty traders and fishermen. When the British took over Malabar in 1792, they sought to revamp the land relations by creating individual ownership right in land. The traditional system stipulated an equal sharing of the net produce of the land by the *janmi* (holder of *janmam* tenure), the *Kanamdar* or *Kanakkaran* (holder of *kanam* tenure) and the cultivator. The British system upset this arrangement by recognising the janmi as absolute owners of land, with right to evict tenants, which did not exist earlier, and reduced other two categories to the status of tenants and leaseholders. Apart from that, over-assessment, a huge burden of illegal cesses and a pro-landlord attitude of the judiciary and the police meant that the "peasantry in Malabar", writes, K.N. Panikkar, "lived and worked in conditions of extreme penury entailed by the twin exactions of the lord and the state".[81]

A series of incidents therefore occurred in Malabar throughout the nineteenth century, which registered the protest and resistance of the rural poor to acts of oppression and exploitation.[82] But the most important aspect of this agrarian relations was that the majority of the janmi were high-caste Hindus and the peasants were the

Muslim Moplahs. Within this social matrix, the traditional Muslim intellectuals, like Umar Qazi of Veliamkode, Sayyid Alavi Tangal and his son Sayyid Fazal Pookkoya Tangal of Mamburam and Sayyid Sana-Ullah-Makti Tangal, played an important role in revitalising a popular ideological domain where religion and economic grievances intermingled to produce a mentality of open resistance. Mosques became the centres of mobilisation and the targets were the Hindu janmi, their temples and the British officials who came to their rescue. Three serious incidents occurred in Manjeri in August 1849, in Kulathur in August 1851—both in south Malabar—and in Mattannur in the north in January 1852. British armed forces were deployed to suppress the revolt. The repressive measures restored peace for about twenty years, but then the Moplahs rose again in 1870 and the events followed a similar trajectory (see chapter 4.2).

Some of the peasant rebellions in pre-1857 India were participated exclusively by the tribal population whose political autonomy and control over local resources were threatened by the establishment of British rule and the advent of its non-tribal agents. The Bhils, for example, were concentrated in the hill ranges of Khandesh in the previous Maratha territory. British occupation of this region in 1818 brought in the outsiders and accompanying dislocations in their community life. A general Bhil insurrection in 1819 was crushed by the British military forces and though some conciliatory measures were taken to pacify them, the situation remained unsettled until 1831 when the Ramoshi leader Umaji Raje of Purandhar was finally captured and executed. The Bhils' local rivals for power, the Kolis of Ahmadnagar district, also challenged the British in 1829, but were quickly subdued by a large army contingent. The seeds of rebellion however persisted, to erupt again in 1844–46, when a local Koli leader successfully defied the British government for two years.[83] Another major tribal revolt, the Kol uprising of 1831–32, took place in Chota Nagpur and Singbhum region of Bihar and Orissa. In these areas, they used to enjoy independent power for centuries. But now British penetration and imposition of British law posed a threat to the power of the hereditary tribal chiefs. And the Raja of Chota Nagpur started evicting tribal peasants by farming out land to outsiders for higher rents. This settlement of non-tribals and constant transfer of land to merchants and moneylenders—generally referred to as the *sud* or outsiders—led to a popular uprising, as their plea for justice failed to move the authorities. The forms of rebellion consisted of attacks on the properties of the outsiders, but not their lives. Plunder and arson, in other words, were the chief modes of peasant protest, while the rate of killings was negligible. But the rebellion "wiped off the Raj from Choto Nagpore in a matter of weeks".[84] The British army had to move in to quell the disturbances and restore order.

The most effective tribal movement of this period was, however, the Santhal *hool* (rebellion) of 1855–56. The Santhals lived scattered in various districts of Cuttack, Dhalbhum, Manbhum, Barabhum, Chota Nagpur, Palamau, Hazaribagh, Midnapur, Bankura and Birbhum in eastern India. Driven from their homeland, they cleared the area around the Rajmahal Hills and called it *Damin-i-koh*. They were gradually driven to a desperate situation as tribal lands were leased out to non-Santhal zamindars and moneylenders. To this was added the oppression of the local police and the European officers engaged in railroad construction. This penetration of outsiders—called dikus by the Santhals—completely destroyed their familiar world, and forced them into action to take possession of their lost territory. In July 1855, when their ultimatum to the zamindars and the government went unheeded, several thousand Santhals, armed with bows and arrows, started an open insurrection "against the unholy trinity of their oppressors—the zamindars, the mahajans and the government".[85] The insurrection spread rapidly and in a wide region between Bhagalpur and Rajmahal the Company's rule virtually collapsed, spreading panic in government circles. At this stage the Santhal rebels were also being actively helped by the low caste non-tribal peasants. This invited brutal counter-insurgency measures; the army was mobilised and Santhal villages were burnt one after another with vengeance. According to one calculation, out of thirty to fifty thousand rebels, fifteen to twenty thousand were killed before the insurrection was finally suppressed.[86] Henceforth, the British government became more cautious about them and the Santhal inhabited areas were constituted into a separate administrative unit, called the Santhal Parganas, which recognised the distinctiveness of their tribal culture and identity.

The peasant rebellions described above are only the more prominent ones in a long list of other similar movements that took place across the subcontinent. Any generalisation about their origins and nature is risky. Yet, in a very broad sense it can be said that the changing economic relations in the colonial period contributed to peasant grievances and their anguish found expression in these various rebellions. Indian peasant economy in pre-colonial period was based on a subsistence ethic. The state collected the surplus, but in an environment of scarcity the peasants would not normally protest if they were left with enough provision for their subsistence. The pre-colonial Mughal compromise, as described earlier (chapter 1), broke down in the eighteenth century, as surplus extraction became more vigorous. This affected the peasants' subsistence provisions and resulted in recurrent peasant revolts; the colonial revenue system only strengthened that process. But there was more change than continuity in the colonial agrarian economy, as we have seen in the previous chapter. Colonial endeavour to draw Indian economy into the world capitalist system and attempts to develop capitalist agriculture had in many cases a devastating impact on agrarian relations. Creation of property right in land and consequently of a land market resulted in the replacement of customary production relationship with contract. With the growth of comercialisation, tribute was gradually replaced by profit as the dominant mode of surplus extraction; but the process of transformation was never complete. As tribute and profit continued to exist side by side, the net result was the breakdown of all familiar norms of agrarian relations.

The colonial rule resulted in what Ranajit Guha has called the "revitalization of landlordism".[87] Due to the changes in property relations, the peasants lost their occupancy right and were turned into tenants-at-will, which meant a great transformation in their status. Not until 1859 the British government looked at the tenancy issue and did anything to protect their rights. The high land revenue demand of the state could therefore easily be passed on to the peasants; the corrupt practices and the harsh attitudes of the revenue officials added to their miseries. The landlords' power to oppress the peasants was greatly expanded by British law. Their military power was not actually curbed and continued to be exerted through the zamindar–daroga nexus, while the new courts and the lengthy judicial processes added further to their coercive authority. The landlords came to be looked at as agents of oppression, protected by the state; grievances against the landlord therefore turned easily against the British as well. The landlords were more interested in extraction rather than in capitalist enterprise, as they too were under constant pressure of the sunset laws and the burden of high revenue demand of the state. The development of land market resulted in a growing rate of land alienation and what accentuated the process was the new credit nexus. The high land revenue demand increased the peasants' need for credit and that enhanced the power of the moneylenders and merchants over the rural society. Growing indebtedness led to eviction from land, which passed on to the hands of the non-cultivating classes. In the words of Ranajit Guha, the landlords, moneylenders and the state thus came to constitute "a composite apparatus of dominance over the peasant".[88]

The tribal peasants had some special reasons to be aggrieved. They lived at the periphery of the settled Hindu peasant societies and enjoyed autonomy of culture, which was based on an egalitarian ethos. Over the period, their gradual Hinduisation had been bringing them under the oppression of the ritual hierarchy; and then the extension of the British land revenue system fully destroyed the autonomy of the tribal world. They were drawn into the larger economic nexus, as the tribal lands passed into the hands of the non-tribal oppressive agents—the zamindars and the moneylenders. And the new forest regulations appeared as encroachments on their natural rights. The imposition of British rule, in other words, resulted in the loss of their autonomous domains of power, freedom and culture. The destruction of their imagined golden past by the intruding outsiders—the suds and dikus—led obviously to violent outbursts.

These peasant and tribal uprisings of the early colonial period have been looked at in different ways. The British administration considered them as problems of law and order; the rebels were portrayed as primitive savages resisting civilisation. The nationalists later on tried to appropriate the peasant and tribal histories for the purposes of anti-colonial struggle and projected them as the pre-history of modern nationalism. Eric Stokes, the historian, would call them "primary resistance, that is, a traditional society's act of violent defiance, from which usually follows the imposition of colonial rule in response".[89] Others like D.N. Dhanagare would regard the peasant rebellions as "pre-political", because of their lack of organisation, programme and ideology.[90] Ranajit Guha, on the other hand, has argued that "there was nothing in the militant movements of ... [the] rural masses that was not political".[91]

The rebellions that we have described previously were not apolitical acts; they constituted political action that demonstrated, although in different ways, the political consciousness of the peasantry. As Ranajit Guha (1994) has shown, they exhibited, first of all, a clear awareness of the relations of power in rural society and a determination to overturn that structure of authority. The rebels were quite conscious of the political sources of oppression, and this was demonstrated in their targets of attack—the zamindars' houses, their grain stocks, the moneylenders, the merchants and ultimately the state machinery of the British, which came forward to protect these local agents of oppression. A clear identification of the enemies was matched by an equally clear marking of the friends. What we often find in these peasant rebellions is a redefinition of the relationship of the oppressed to the language, culture and religion of the dominant classes, although the protests took myriad forms. The rebellions were political action, different from crime, because they were open and public. The Santhals gave ample warning in advance; the Rangpur leaders imposed a levy for insurrection on the peasantry. There were public conferences, assemblies, and planning which definitely spoke of a programme. There were grand ceremonies of rebel marches. The public character was reinforced by drawing on the corporate labour activity, as the Santhals characterised the rebel actions as their traditional hunting activity; but now hunting had acquired a new political meaning.

As for the leadership of these peasant rebellions, it came from the ranks of the rebels themselves. Since the leaders belonged to the same cultural world of the peasants and tribals whom they led, they could provide more effective leadership. The mobilisation took place along community lines, an exception being the Rangpur uprising. The colonial rural societies experienced varying degrees of tension between class, caste, ethnic and religious groups, which were articulated in a violent condition of oppression and poverty in the countryside. Religion in many cases provided the bond of unity among the poorer classes and the leaders were the holy men who promised a new millennium to be achieved through supernatural means.[92] In pre-capitalist societies, where class-consciousness was ill developed and class ideology absent, religion provided an ideology for rebellion. The holy leaders referred to the loss of a moral world and thus expressed the anxieties of the peasants in religious idioms. Religion thus provided legitimacy to their movements. In such revolutionary messianism, the charismatic leaders were thought to be endowed with magical power; their empowering was thus an act of God. The rebellion was therefore divinely ordained and legitimised through reference to a higher authority. This provided both an ideology as well as motivation for peasant action. These peasant rebellions also differed from modern nationalism. The spread of the rebellion depended on the rebels' own perception of space and ethnic boundary; it was most effective within the geographical area within which that community lived and worked. The Santhals' battle, for example, was for their 'fatherland'; but sometimes ethnic ties extended across the territorial boundaries, as in Kol insurrection we find the Kols of different regions rose in revolt simultaneously. The rebels' own perception of time played a significant role as well.

There is often an evocation of history in the conception of a "Golden Age" in a distant past.[93] An urge for the restoration of that imagined golden past provided an ideology for peasant action, the Faraizi and Santhal rebellions being prime examples of that.

Apart from the more organised movements described earlier, violent armed rebellions, social banditry or general "lawlessness" were endemic in the first century of British rule in India. Indeed, the boundary between revolt and collaboration was quite thin, as apparent collaborators often nurtured sense of disaffection and hatred for the alien rulers. The Calcutta bhadralok, for example, who had reposed their faith in the British empire and therefore were zealously critical of the peasant rebels, also raised the issue that the loyal Santhals had not taken up arms against the king without any reason.[94] And like the peasantry, the lower classes of the urban society were equally articulate in their protest. Grain riots and resistance against the monopolistic activities of the grain dealers and interventionist British officials took place in western Hindustan and Delhi in 1833–38. There were rice riots in Vellore and southern India between 1806 and 1858 against threats of conversion to Christianity. The decline of handicraft industry as a result of free trade imperialism resulted in urban revolts by artisan groups in Calcutta in 1789, in Surat in the 1790s and 1800s and in Rohilkhand and Banaras between 1809 and 1818. These revolts were not always directly anti-colonial movements, but were all related to the policies and conditions of colonial rule.[95] However, the most powerful and potentially the most dangerous act of resistance to Company's rule in India was the revolt of 1857.

3.3. THE REVOLT OF 1857

The year 1857 witnessed armed revolts in parts of central and northern India, as a result of which effective British rule nearly collapsed in these regions until the spring of 1858, when order was restored again by the advancing imperial forces. The revolt witnessed an extraordinary amount of violence unleashed on both sides. As British rule had "meticulously constructed a monopoly of violence", it was retorted with an equal amount of counter-violence of their subjects. If the British counter-insurgency measures included public execution of the rebels, blowing them off from cannons and indiscriminately burning native villages, the rebels also massacred white civilians—women and children included—without mercy. The Kanpur massacre of 27 June 1857 was in this sense an act of "transgression" in being the indigenous violence of the colonised breaking that monopoly of violence of the colonisers.[96] The revolt ended the rule of the East India Company, as after its pacification in 1858 by an act of parliament the Indian empire was taken over by the British Crown. The revolt, for long mistaken to be a mere mutiny of the Indian sepoys in the Bengal army, was indeed joined by an aggrieved rural society of north India. Its causes, therefore, need to be searched for not only in the disaffection of the army, but in a long drawn process of fundamental social and economic change that upset the peasant communities during the first century of the Company's rule.

The Company's government while raising a standing army since mid-eighteenth century respected the traditions and customs of the indigenous communities and a high caste identity of the army was deliberately encouraged. This was particularly true of the Bengal army, which had a predominantly high caste character, mainly consisting of Brahmans, Rajputs and Bhumihars, whose caste rules, dietary and travel restrictions were scrupulously respected by the army administration, under instructions from Warren Hastings. However, from the 1820s things began to change, as army reforms were initiated to introduce a more universalised military culture. As the reforms in the 1820s and 1830s sought to establish a tighter control over the army administration and began to curtail some of the caste privileges and pecuniary benefits, there were acts of resistance, which continued into the 1840s (for details on the army, see chapter 2.4). These incidents prepared the backdrop for the mutiny of 1857, the early signals of which could be detected in late January when rumours started circulating among the sepoys in Dum Dum near Calcutta that the cartridges of the new Enfield rifle, lately introduced to replace the old 'Brown Bess' musket, had been greased with cow and pig fat. Since the cartridges had to be bitten off before loading, it confirmed the sepoys' old suspicion about a conspiracy to destroy their religion and caste and convert them Christianity. The cartridge rumour, which was not entirely devoid of truth, spread like wildfire in various army cantonments across the country. Although the production of those cartridges was stopped immediately and various concessions were offered to allay their fears, the trust that had been breached could never be restored. On 29 March in Barackpur near Calcutta, a sepoy with the name of Mangal Pande fired at a European officer and his comrades refused to arrest him when ordered by their European superiors. They were soon apprehended, court martialled and hanged in early April, but the disaffection of the sepoys could not be contained. In the following days, incidents of disobedience, incendiarism and arson were reported from the army cantonments in Ambala, Lucknow and Meerut, until finally, the Meerut sepoys started the revolt on 10 May. They rescued their arrested comrades who had previously refused to accept the new cartridge, killed their European officers and proceeded to Delhi, where on 11 May they proclaimed the ageing Mughal emperor Bahadur Shah Zafar the Emperor of Hindustan.[97] From Delhi the uprising soon spread to other army centres in the North-Western Provinces and Awadh and soon took the shape of a civil rebellion, as disgruntled rural population lent a helping hand. On 19 June Lord Canning, the despondent governor general, wrote: "In Rohilcund and the Doab from Delhi to Cawnpore and Allahabad the country is not only in rebellion against us, but is utterly lawless".[98]

The mutiny mainly affected the Bengal army; the Madras and the Bombay regiments remained quiet, while the Punjabi and Gurkha soldiers actually helped to suppress the rebellion. It should, however, be remembered that maximum number of Indian sepoys were in the Bengal regiment and if we look at total numbers, almost half of the Indian sepoys of the East India Company had rebelled.[99] The composition of the Bengal army was much to blame, as it had minimal British military presence, which later was considered to be a capital error. Moreover, the high-caste background of the sepoys in the Bengal army, mostly recruited from Awadh, gave them a homogeneous character. They were nurturing for a long time a number of grievances: their religious beliefs had lately come into conflict with their new service conditions; their salary level dropped; they suffered discrimination in matters of promotion and pension. To make matters worse, in 1856 a set of new service rules were introduced, which abolished their extra allowance for service outside their own regions. Service abroad was considered to be prejudicial to their caste rules, but expansion of the British empire made that unavoidable. Their refusal to serve in Burma, Sind or Afghanistan met with reprisals and dismissal.

To the discontent with service conditions was added a constant fear that the British were determined to convert them into Christianity. The presence of missionaries, the rumours about mixing cow and pig bone dust with flour and finally the controversy about the cartridge for Enfield rifles—all fitted nicely into a conspiracy theory. The annexation of Awadh in 1856 had a special adverse effect on the morale of the Bengal army, as about seventy-five thousand of them were recruited from this region. Sir James Outram had already cautioned Dalhousie that "every agricultural family in Oudh, perhaps without exception, ... sends one of its members into the

British army".[100] The annexation of Awadh shook the loyalty of these sepoys, as it was for them an ultimate proof of untrustworthiness of the British. Moreover, as sepoys were peasants in uniform, they were anxious about the declining conditions of the peasantry due to the summary settlements in Awadh. The revolt was preceded by about fourteen thousand petitions from the sepoys about the hardships relating to the revenue system.[101] In other words, it was not just because of the "cartridge" that the sepoys threw in their gauntlet and rose in open rebellion against the British.

It is much more difficult to explain the civilian revolt that accompanied the mutiny. As colonial rule had a differential impact on Indian society, the latter's responses were also widely variegated. First of all, regions and people who were beneficiaries of colonial rule did not revolt. Bengal and Punjab remained peaceful; the entire south India remained unaffected too. On the other hand, those who revolted had two elements among them—the feudal elements and the big landlords on the one end and the peasantry on the other. Different classes had different grievances and the nature of grievances also varied from region to region. So far as the feudal elements were concerned, their major grievance was against the annexations under Lord Dalhousie's 'Doctrine of Lapse' which derecognised the adopted sons of the deceased princes as legal heirs and their kingdoms were annexed. In this way, Satara (1848), Nagpur, Sambalpur and Baghat (1850), Udaipur (1852) and Jhansi (1853) were taken over in quick succession. This amounted to British interference in the traditional system of inheritance and created a group of disgruntled feudal lords who had every reason to join the ranks of the rebels. Finally, in February 1856 Awadh was annexed and the king was deported to Calcutta. The annexation did not merely affect the nawab and his family, but the entire aristocracy attached to the royal court. These deposed princes in many cases offered leadership to the rebels in their respective regions and thus provided legitimacy to the revolt. Thus, Nana Sahib, the adopted son of Peshwa Baji Rao II, assumed leadership in Kanpur, Begum Hazrat Mahal took control over Lucknow, Khan Bahadur Khan in Rohilkhand, and Rani Lakshmibai appeared as the leader of the sepoys in Jhansi, although earlier she was prepared to accept British hegemony if her adopted son was recognised as the legitimate heir to the throne. In other areas of central India, where there was no such dispossession, like Indore, Gwalior, Saugar or parts of Rajasthan, where the sepoys rebelled, the princes remained loyal to the British.

The other elements of rural society that joined the ranks of the rebels were the landed magnates or the taluqdars. The annexation of

Awadh was followed by a summary settlement in 1856, which led to the dispossession of a number of powerful taluqdars. The settlement was made with the actual occupiers of the land or village coparcenaries to the disregard of all other proprietary rights, in the same way as it was done a little while ago in the North-Western Provinces. The prime motive was to gain popularity among the agricultural population and get rid of the unwanted middlemen who stood between the peasants and the government. As a result, in Awadh the taluqdars lost about half of their estates; they were disarmed and their forts demolished, resulting in a considerable loss of status and power in local society. In the eyes of law they were now no different from the humblest of their tenants.[102] Awadh, therefore, became the hotbed of discontent of the landed aristocrats and so was the North-Western Provinces, where too many taluqdars had lately been dispossessed. As the revolt started, these taluqdars quickly moved into the villages they had recently lost, and significantly, they faced no resistance from their erstwhile tenants. Bound by ties of kinship and feudal loyalty, as Thomas Metcalf has argued, the villagers were happy to acknowledge the claims of their lords and joined hands against their common enemy, the British.[103]

The peasants joined the rebellion because they too were hard hit by the inordinately high revenue demands of the state. In Awadh for example, the revenue assessment overall was reduced, but there were pockets of over-assessment, and here the taluqdars' losses resulted in a "talukdar-peasant complementarity" of interests.[104] The same situation existed in the North-Western Provinces too, where Mahalwari Settlement had been made with the village mulguzars. These village proprietors who were the supposed beneficiaries of the new land revenue system, were not satisfied either, because of high land revenue demand. It was the owner-cultivators, rather than the rent-receiving landlords, who felt the burden of over-assessment more severely than others and increased public sales of landed rights were the index of this extraordinary pressure, which became a major cause of the revolt. Where agriculture was insecure, high revenue demands inevitably drove the peasants into debt and eventually, dispossession, the new civil courts and the legal system contributing to this process.[105] In 1853 in the North-Western Provinces alone, 110,000 acres of land were sold in auction and therefore, when the revolt started, the baniya and the mahajan and their properties became the natural targets of attack by the rioting peasants. "Thus the sale of land", as S.B. Chaudhuri summarises the situation, "not merely uprooted the ordinary people from their small holdings but also destroyed the gentry of the country, and both the orders being the victims of the operations of British civil law were united in the revolutionary epoch of 1857–58 in a common effort to recover what they had lost".[106]

The story was not perhaps that straightforward, as Eric Stokes (1980) has drawn our attention to the complexities of the situation. It should be remembered, first of all, that not all taluqdars suffered under the British revenue system. In many areas the proprietary rights circulated among the traditional landed castes and often new landed magnates emerged from the declining castes; in some cases official positions gave advantage to local men in public land sales. These successful taluqdars, whom Stokes has called "the new magnates", could adjust well to the current situation both in Awadh and in the North-Western Provinces, and not only did they not revolt, but they exerted a sobering influence on their respective communities. Not all peasants suffered equally either. Those in the fertile and irrigated areas could more easily withstand the burden of over-assessment than those in the backward regions. In the latter areas again, it was more a sense of relative rather than absolute deprivation, which was the main cause of resentment. While some groups of peasants reeled under pressure, they could not take it easily that their caste brethren were prospering in the neighbouring canal tracts with profitable cash crop agriculture.

It was again in the backward regions that the peasants were seemingly more vulnerable to the pressures of the moneylenders or mahajans and were more likely to lose possession of their land. Yet, it is doubtful whether there was any direct correlation between indebtedness and revolt; in fact, Stokes has argued about an inverse relationship between the two. Dry lands with high revenue assessments were hardly attractive to the outside banias or mahajans. They took possession of land only where there was expansion of cash cropping. In such cases very little actual physical dispossession took place, as the motive was more political, i.e., to take control of the peasant producers, rather than the land itself. Therefore, the backward and "thirsty" tracts with high revenue demands, where the intrusion of the mahajans was the lightest, became most prone to outbreak of violence during the revolt. Also where caste brotherhoods or *bhaicharas* were powerful, the pressure of the mahajans was better resisted. And here social homogeneity and collective power became crucial factors in promoting rebelliousness among the peasantry. Community ties among the Gujars or Jats, Rajputs or Sayyids, became major factors in determining the effectiveness of the peasant rebellion. Perhaps, the only common trait that pervaded all the layers of rural society was a suspicion of British rule, allegedly threatening their religion. The social reforms of the earlier period indirectly created this environment and the Christian missionaries directly contributed to it. The Hindus and the Muslims were equally affected and therefore, Hindu–Muslim unity was all along maintained during the revolt. No single causal explanation can be provided for this widespread outbreak of violent protest among the agrarian population of north India. What Eric Stokes has established, writes C.A. Bayly, is that: "The Indian Rebellion of 1857 was not one movement, . . . it was many".[107]

Another contentious issue about the revolt of 1857 is its nature and the debate over it started almost instantaneously as it happened. Some contemporaries thought it was a Muslim conspiracy to restore the Mughal empire; but there was not much evidence to support that. The more dominant contemporary official interpretation of the events was that it was primarily a mutiny of the sepoys, the civilian unrest being a secondary phenomenon, which happened as the unruly elements took advantage of the breakdown of law and order. Some of the later Indian historians too, like S.N. Sen, in his officially sponsored centennial history of the revolt, have echoed the same colonial argument. "The movement began as a military mutiny", Sen argued; and then "[w]hen the administration collapsed the lawless elements ... took the upper hand".[108] R.C. Majumdar's thoughts are also identical: "What began as a mutiny", he thinks, "ended in certain areas in an outbreak of civil population", which was sometimes organised by self-seeking local leaders and sometimes was only "mob violence" caused by the breakdown of the administrative machinery.[109] But differing views from across the political spectrum were also being voiced since the time of the revolt itself. "Is it a military mutiny, or is it a national revolt?"—asked Benjamin Disraeli in the House of Commons on 27 July 1857. Karl Marx in the summer of 1857 expressed the same doubts in the pages of *New York Daily Tribune*: "what he [John Bull] considers a military mutiny", he wrote, "is in truth a national revolt". It was V.D. Savarkar who drafted the revolt of 1857 directly into the historiography of Indian nationalism by describing it, in a 1909 publication, as the "Indian War of Independence", a war fought for "*swadharma* and *swaraj*".[110] Although this claim was vigorously denied by both Sen and Majumdar, it received serious academic support in 1959 from S.B. Chaudhuri, who saw in the revolt "the first combined attempt of many classes of people to challenge a foreign power. This is a real, if remote, approach", he thought, "to the freedom movement of India of a later age.[111]

The debate has been going on since then, with a growing consensus gradually emerging that the revolt of 1857 was not a nationalist movement in the modern sense of the term. In 1965 Thomas Metcalf wrote: "There is a widespread agreement that it was something more than a sepoy mutiny, but something less than a national revolt".[112] It was not "national" because the popular character of the revolt was limited to Upper India alone, while the regions and groups that experienced the benefits of British rule remained loyal. There were also important groups of collaborators. The Bengali middle classes remained loyal as they had, writes Judith Brown, "material interests in the new order, and often a deep, ideological commitment to new ideas".[113] The Punjabi princes hated the Hindustani soldiers and shuddered at the thought of a resurrection of the Mughal empire. On the other hand, those who rebelled, argued C.A. Bayly, had various motives, which were not always connected to any specific grievance against the British; often they fought against each other and this "Indian disunity played into British hands."[114] There was no premeditated plan or a conspiracy, as the circulation of chapatis or wheat bread from village to village prior to the revolt conveyed confusing messages. The rebellion was thus all negative, it is argued, as the rebels did not have any plan to bring in any alternative system to replace the British Raj. "[I]n their vision of the future the rebel leaders were hopelessly at odds", writes Metcalf; some of them owed allegiance to the Mughal emperor Bahadur Shah, others to various regional princes. "United in defeat, the rebel leaders would have fallen at each other's throats in victory".[115]

This so-called "agreement" described above has, however, been seriously questioned by a number of historians in recent years. It can hardly be denied that among the rebels of 1857 there was no concept of an Indian nation in the modern sense of the term. Peasant actions were local affairs bound by strictly defined territorial boundaries. Yet, unlike the earlier peasant revolts, there was now certainly greater interconnection between the territories and the rebels were open to influence from outside their *ilaqa* (area). There was coordination and communication between the rebels from different parts of north and central India and there were rumours afloat which bound the rebels in an unseen bondage. A common feature shared by all of them was a distaste for the British state and disruptions it brought to their lives. Anything that stood for the authority of the Company, therefore, became their target of attack. They all felt that their caste and religion was under threat. Like the sepoys of Jhansi, rebels everywhere fought for their "*deen* [faith] and *dharam* [religion]"—to restore a moral order, which had been polluted by an intruding foreign rule.[116] As Gautam Bhadra puts it: "It was the perception and day-to-day experience of the authority of the alien state in his immediate surroundings that determined the rebel's action".[117] Yet, although unknown to each other and also perhaps separated by their different experiences, they were nonetheless pitted against the same enemy at the same historical conjuncture. "They took up arms", writes Ranajit Guha, "to recover what they believed to have been their ancestral domains".[118]

But what did this domain actually mean? The idea of domain, in terms of geographical or social space, was perhaps now larger than the village or their immediate caste or kin group. As Rajat Ray has argued, they were trying to free "Hindustan" of foreign yoke. There was remarkable religious amity during the revolt, as all agreed that Hindustan belonged to Hindus and Muslims alike.[119] The rebels of 1857 wanted to go back to the old familiar order and by this they did not mean the centralised Mughal state of the seventeenth century. They wanted to restore the decentralised political order of eighteenth century India, when the provincial rulers functioned with considerable autonomy, but all acknowledged the Mughal emperor as the source of political legitimacy. When Birjis Qadr was crowned by the rebel sepoys as the King of Awadh, the condition imposed on him was to recognise the Mughal emperor as the suzerain authority.[120] Delhi, the Mughal capital and Bahadur Shah, the Mughal emperor acted as symbols of that familiar world, and on this there was no dispute among the rebels. In his most recent book, C.A. Bayly has discovered in the rebellion of 1857 "a set of patriotic revolts". What the rebels demanded, he writes, "was the restoration of the Indo-Mughal patrias within the broader constellation of Mughal legitimacy, animated by mutual respect and a healthy balance between lands and peoples".[121] As the revolt made progress, even among the so-called collaborators there was no uncritical acceptance of British rule. The profession of loyalty, for example, by the Calcutta intelligentsia was not without dilemma, as they too were feeling what the *Hindoo Patriot* described, the "grievances inseparable from subjection to a foreign rule". The paper aptly summed up the dilemma: "This loyalty, it may be true, springs nearer from the head than from the heart".[122] Thus, conscious voices of dissent and disaffection against foreign rule, if not always an avowed yearning for liberation, ran across the different sections of population in India in 1857–58. In recent years, the pendulum of historical interpretation of 1857 has moved considerably to the opposite direction.

The other important question about the character of the revolt is whether or not it was an elitist movement. Some historians like Judith Brown think that during the revolt the feudal elements were the decision makers and that much of the revolt was determined and shaped by the presence or absence of a thriving magnate element committed to British rule, for it was only they who could give the revolt a general direction.[123] Eric Stokes goes on to conclude that: "Rural revolt in 1857 was essentially elitist in character".[124] This position, however, trivialises the role of the masses. So far as the feudal lords were concerned, in many cases they were reluctant to assume leadership and were indeed pushed by the rebels. Bahadur Shah was taken by surprise when approached by the rebel sepoys, and only with great hesitation did he agree to be their leader. Nana Sahib in Kanpur—as it was later revealed in the confession of his close confidante Tantia Topi—was seized by the rebel sepoys and was threatened with dire consequences; he did not have much choice other than joining hands with the rebels.[125] And the Rani of Jhansi was actually threatened with death if she did not assist the sepoys or collaborated with the British.[126] The initiative for the revolt and even its effectiveness did not really depend on the feudal leadership.

So far as the taluqdars were concerned, it is true that in many areas peasants followed their leaders, because of the existence of a pre-capitalist symbiotic relationship between the two classes. But the role of the taluqdars varied widely from region to region. In Awadh, for example, as Rudrangshu Mukherjee has shown, taluqdar participation was never universal: some of them remained loyal, some became turncoats, others followed a middle course and some submitted at the sight of the approaching British troops.[127] In many areas the peasants and the artisans forced the taluqdars to join the revolt, while in some cases, the masses insisted on carrying on the revolt even after the taluqdars had made peace with the British. And above all, the main initiative came from the sepoys, the peasants in uniform, who now had shed their uniforms to merge with the peasants again. Almost everywhere in central and northern India, the rising in the army barracks soon spread to the neighbouring villages; caste and ethnic ties of the sepoys also connected them to the peasant communities. Almost everywhere, rebel action was preceded by conferencing and panchayat meetings or open gatherings of large number of rebels. And finally the chapatis, which circulated rapidly between villages in geometrical progression conveying divergent meanings to different peoples, stood as a symbol or an omen, rather than index or cause, of an impending crisis.[128] It is difficult to ignore the evidence of autonomous mobilisation of the peasantry in the rebellions of 1857–58.

The rebellion was suppressed with brutal force. Lord Canning gathered British troops at Calcutta and sent them to free Delhi. On 20 September 1857, Delhi was finally recaptured and Bahadur Shah Zafar was imprisoned and later deported; but this did not yet mean the end of the rebellion. Very slowly Banaras, Allahabad and Kanpur were taken over, the rebels fighting for every inch of territory and the British unleashing an unmitigated reign of terror in the countryside. The arrival of fresh British troops at Calcutta in October decisively tilted the balance against the rebels. Between the spring of 1858 and the beginning of 1859, British troops gradually recovered Gwalior, Doab, Lucknow and the rest of Awadh, Rohilkhand and the remainder of central India. The contemporary colonial explanations for the defeat of the sepoys and of the rural rebels highlighted British bravery, their superior national character, better leadership qualities and effective military strategies, as against the lack of unity, discipline and order among the rebels. Some of the earlier Indian historians too believed in the same theory. Modern historians would, however, point out that the British won as they committed unlimited men and resources to reclaim their empire, while the sepoys suffered from a desperate scarcity of cash. The ordinary rural rebels in the true fashion of a peasant army were only equipped with primitive weapons and most of them were not even trained soldiers. They were facing the British army, which not only had control over most sophisticated weapons, but who were the masters of practically the whole of India, had the backing of a centralised bureaucracy and had access to an efficient communication system. Furthermore, as Stokes has argued, the rebel sepoys showed a remarkable "centripetal impulse to congregate at Delhi", which prevented the rebellion from spreading as much as it could. So when by March 1858 Delhi and Lucknow fell, the rebellion entered its dying phase.[129] The extremely localised nature of the uprisings helped the British to tackle them one at a time. By the beginning of 1859 all was over.

The revolt of 1857 is in many ways an important watershed in Indian history. First of all, it ended the rule of the East India Company. Even before peace was fully restored in India, the British parliament passed on 2 August 1858 an Act for the Better Government of India, declaring Queen Victoria as the sovereign of British India and providing for the appointment of a Secretary of State for India who would be a member of the cabinet. The act was to come into effect on 1 November and on that day the Queen issued a Proclamation, which promised religious toleration and proposed to govern Indians according to their established traditions and customs.[130] Bernard Cohn has summarised what this constitutional change meant for the status of British rule in India: "In conceptual terms, the British, who had started their rule as 'outsiders', became 'insiders' by vesting in their monarch the sovereignty of India.'[131] The proclamation provided for the ordering of the relationship between the monarch and her representatives in India, their Indian subjects and the princes, all of them being neatly fitted into an elaborate imperial hierarchy. Apart from this, there were other far-reaching changes resulting from almost one year of bloody racial warfare. The sepoys were charged with a serious breach of trust and this in general made all the Indians suspect in the eyes of the British, both in India and at home. The stories of sepoy atrocities raised the clamour for punishment and retribution and if the saner elements like Viceroy Lord Canning tried to restrain this hysteria, he soon earned the derisive epithet of "Clemency Canning" from his own countrymen and requests were sent to the Queen for his recall. Although this madness subsided gradually, it left a lasting imprint on British-Indian relations in the subsequent period. Racial segregation from now on became firmly entrenched, as Indians were regarded not only different, but also racially inferior. What is more important, the earlier reformist zeal of a self-confident Victorian liberalism now evidently took a back seat, as many believed now that Indians were beyond reform. This new mood, which Thomas Metcalf has called the "conservative brand of liberalism", rested upon the "solid support of the conservative and aristocratic classes and upon the principle of complete non-interference in the traditional structure of Indian society".[132] This conservative reaction evidently made the empire more autocratic and denied the aspirations of the educated Indians for sharing power. This, therefore, also made the empire more vulnerable, as from this frustration of the educated middle classes arose modern nationalism towards the end of the nineteenth century.

NOTES

1. Viswanathan 1989: 71–74.
2. Nurullah and Naik 1971: 30–39.
3. Quoted in Ghosh 1995: 20.
4. Viswanathan 1989: 25–27.

5. Quoted in Ghosh 1995: 31–33.
6. Bhattacharya 1998: 7.
7. Viswanathan 1989: 20, 45, 93.
8. Quoted in Misra 1978: 151.
9. Viswanathan 1989: 146–48.
10. Quoted in Singh 1998:115.
11. See Constable 2000 for details.
12. McCully 1966: 177.
13. Ghosh 1995: 88.
14. Quoted in Singh 1998: 108.
15. Viswanathan 1989: 93.
16. Panikkar 1995: 9.
17. McCully 1966: 217.
18. For more on this point, see Ray 2001: 33–39.
19. Panikkar, 1995: 8.
20. Prakash 1999: 60, 71 and passim.
21. See Prakash 1999 and Panikkar 1995 for details.
22. Sarkar 1985: 26.
23. Spear 1965: 203.
24. Vishwanath 1998.
25. Hawley 1994: 3.
26. Ray 1975: 3–5.
27. See Nandy 1994b: 138–142.
28. Carroll 1983: 379.
29. Sen 1977: 6.
30. Bandyopadhyay 1995: 8–9.
31. O'Hanlon 1991: 67–69; Chakravarti 1998: 81–94.
32. Forbes 1998: 24–25.
33. Heimsath 1964: 87–88.
34. Chowdhry 1995: 40.
35. Bandyopadhyay 1990: 119.
36. Singha 1998: 168–93; also see Pinch 1996: 7–8; Gordon 1969.
37. Prakash 1992: 16.
38. Chakrabarty 1994: 53–54.
39. Ramusack 1990: 154.
40. Sarkar 1981: 5–6.
41. Jones 1994: 4.
42. Kopf 1979: 224–28, 317–27.
43. Borthwick 1978: 57.
44. A.P. Sen 1993: 46.
45. Dobbin 1972: 248–49.
46. Tucker 1976: 325–27.
47. Dobbin 1972: 249–52; Tucker 1977.
48. Quoted in Heimsath 1964: 108.
49. Jones 1994: 143.
50. Van der Veer 1994: 65.

51. Prakash 1999: 93–94.
52. Details in Jones 1976.
53. Jaffrelot 1996: 15.
54. Mukherjee 1993: 128–38.
55. Bhattacharya 1975.
56. Jones 1994: 141.
57. Dobbin 1972: 252.
58. Heimsath 1964: 110–12.
59. Mani 1998: 79.
60. Bandyopadhyay 1995.
61. Vishwanath 1998.
62. Sarkar 2000: 248.
63. Raychaudhuri 1995: 49.
64. Sarkar 1975.
65. R.K. Ray 1975.
66. Jaffrelot 1996: 14.
67. Dhanagare 1991: 14–15.
68. Hardiman 1993: 4–5.
69. Gough 1979: 94–97.
70. Bayly 1987: 172.
71. Gough 1979: 97.
72. Bose 1993: 145–46.
73. Details in Dasgupta 1992.
74. Pinch 1996: 24–25.
75. Van Schendel 1985; Bhadra 1994.
76. Bhadra 1994: 232–99.
77. Ibid 238–41.
78. Ahmed 1996: 39–41, 45.
79. Kaviraj 1982: 90.
80. Dhanagare 1991: 56–57.
81. Panikkar 1989: 48.
82. Dale 1975: 228–32.
83. Sumit Guha 1999: 96–102.
84. Sumit Guha 1994: 162.
85. Natarajan 1979: 140.
86. Ibid: 145.
87. Guha 1994: 7.
88. Ibid: 8.
89. Stokes 1980: 123.
90. Dhanagare 1991: 82.
91. Guha 1994: 6.
92. Fuchs 1992: 22–24.
93. Ibid: 11.
94. Bandyopadhyay 1997b: 19.
95. Bayly 1987: 177–78.
96. Mukherjee 1998: 23 and passim.

97. Taylor 1997: 31–49.
98. Quoted in Metcalf 1965: 49.
99. Chandra et al. 1989: 31.
100. Quoted in Chaudhuri 1957: 14.
101. Khaldun 1986: 17.
102. Mukherjee 1984: 40, 57, 159–60.
103. Metcalf 1965: 68.
104. Mukherjee 1984: 62.
105. Stokes 1986: 218– 19.
106. Chaudhuri 1957: 21.
107. Bayly 1986: 226.
108. Sen 1957: 398–418.
109. Majumdar 1963: iii.
110. Embree 1963: 5, 21, 39, 41.
111. Chaudhuri 1957: 297.
112. Metcalf 1965: 60.
113. Brown 1994: 90.
114. Bayly 1987: 183.
115. Metcalf 1965: 61.
116. Tapti Roy 1993: 213.
117. Bhadra 1985: 275.
118. Guha 1994: 318.
119. Ray 1993: 133–82.
120. Mukherjee 1984: 136; 1998: 64.
121. Bayly 1998: 88.
122. Quoted in Bandyopadhyay 1997b: 22–23.
123. Brown 1994: 92.
124. Stokes 1980: 185.
125. Mukherjee 1998: 62–63.
126. Roy 1993: 210.
127. Mukherjee 1984: 157.
128. Ranajit Guha 1994: 239–46.
129. Stokes 1986: 49–50.
130. Taylor 1996: 113, 277.
131. Cohn 1992: 165.
132. Metcalf 1965: viii.

chapter four

Emergence of Indian Nationalism

4.1. Historiography of Indian Nationalism

Most historians of Indian nationalism have argued that the Indian political nation, in a modern sense of the term, did not exist prior to the establishment of British rule. Whether or not such a nation lay unselfconsciously embedded in Indian civilisation and then gradually evolved through history is a point that nationalist leaders and historians have incessantly debated over. Most recently, Prasenjit Duara has crtiqued such formulations as "teleological model of Enlightenment History" that gives the "contested and contingent nation" a false sense of unity.[1] There is, however, as of now, little disagreement that the Indian nationalism that confronted British imperialism in the nineteenth century, and celebrated its victory in the formation of the Indian nation-state in 1947, was a product of colonial modernity (see chapter 3.1 for more discussion on this). As the self-professed mission of the colonisers was to elevate the colonised from their present state of decadence to a desired state of progress towards modernity, it became imperative for the latter to contest that stamp of backwardness and assert that they too were capable of uniting and ruling themselves within the structural framework of a modern state. So the challenge of nationalism in colonial India was twofold: to forge a national unity and to claim its right to self-determination. India has been a plural society, everyone agrees, with various forms of diversity, such as region, language, religion, caste, ethnicity and so on. It was from this diversity that "a nation [was] in making" (*sic*), to use the phrase of Surendranath Banerjea, one of the earliest architects of this modern Indian nation. Agreement among historians, however, stops here. How did the Indians actually "imagine" their nation is a matter of intense controversy and ongoing debate.

At one end of the spectrum, Partha Chatterjee would argue that nationalism in India, which was assigned a privileged position by its Western educated political leadership, was a "different", but a "derivative discourse" from the West.[2] Ashis Nandy also thinks that Indian nationalism as a response to Western imperialism was "like all such responses, shaped by what it was responding to". The alternative version of universalism, rooted in Indian civilisation and propounded by men like Rabindranath Tagore or Mahatma Gandhi—the "counter-modernist critic[s] of the imperial West"—was rejected by the Western educated middle-class India. While the alternative vision could unite India at a social rather than political level by accepting and creatively using difference, the Indian nationalists accepted the Western model of nation-state as the defining principle of their nationalism.[3] C.A. Bayly (1998), on the other hand, has recently searched for the "pre-history of nationalism". Indian nationalism, he thinks, built on pre-existing sense of territoriality, a traditional patriotism rationalised by indigenous ideas of public morality and ethical government. But how those regional solidarities were consolidated into a broader cultural notion of India through their encounter with colonial rule and with each other is an issue of vigorous contestation. There were various influences and various contradictions in that process, various levels and forms of consciousness. It is difficult to construct a one-dimensional picture out of this virtual chaos. Yet, since a nation-state was born, attempts have been made to reconstruct its biography. This does not of course mean that outside this grand narrative of the evolution of mainstream nationalism that asserted its dominance in the formation of the Indian nation state, there were no alternative narratives of envisioning the nation.

The early nationalist school, as well as some of its later followers, while studying this process of nation-building, focused primarily on the supremacy of a nationalist ideology and a national consciousness to which all other forms of consciousness were assumed to have been subordinated. This awareness of nation was based on a commonly shared antipathy towards colonial rule, a feeling of patriotism and an ideology rooted in a sense of pride in India's ancient traditions. This school, in other words, ignored the inner conflicts within Indian society—which among other things, led to its division into two nation states—and assumed the existence of nation as a homogeneous entity with a single set of interests. In opposition to this, a new interpretation emerged in the Anglo-American academia and Rajat Ray has rather loosely labelled it as the "neo traditionalist" school.[4] This new interpretation echoed the old imperialist assertion of authors like Valentine Chirol, that politicisation of Indian society developed along the lines of traditional social formations, such as linguistic regions, castes or religious communities, rather than the modern categories of class or nation. The most important catalysts of change in this context were the institutional innovations of the colonial state, notably the introduction of Western education and political representation. These new opportunities intersected with the traditional Indian social divisions and created a new status group—the Western-educated elite, which drew its members from the existing privileged indigenous collectives, such as the bhadralok in Bengal, the Chitpavan Brahmans in Bombay or the Tamil Brahmans of Madras. The backward regions or the underprivileged groups that remained outside this limited political nation had no access to the modern institutional life of colonial India, within the confines of which the messages of early Indian nationalism reverberated. This went on until the end of World War One, when for the first time Mahatma Gandhi flung open the gates of constitutional politics to initiate the new era of mass nationalism.

If the 'neo traditionalist' historians studied Indian politics within the framework of the province, a few others have tracked these divisions further down to the level of localities. These latter writings, which have come to be identified as the 'Cambridge School',[5] have questioned the ontology of a unified nationalist movement, and have traced instead only a series of localised movements in colonial India. As imperialism was weak, since it could not function without the help of Indian collaborators, nationalism that grew out of contestation with it was weak as well; it was nothing more than a battle between the two men of straws. As imperial rule depended on Indian collaborators, there was competition among them for favour of the colonial rulers. This led to emergence of various interest groups, which started to expand their constituencies as the British introduced local self-government and electoral system to rope in more collaborators. The national movement was led by these self-seeking leaders entirely to pursue their narrow individual or clannish interests. Leaders at various levels were tied through patron-client relationships and it was through these vertically structured loyalty networks that they bargained with the British for power and patronage. This school, in other words, completely derecognises the role of a nationalist ideology and seeks to explain nationalist politics in terms of a competition—collaboration syndrome. India was not a nation, but an aggregate of disparate interest groups and they were united as they had to operate within a centralised national administrative framework created by the British.[6] This cynical view of history, which took the mind and emotion out of its analysis and followed a narrow Namierite model, reduced nationalist movement to the state of "Animal Politics", as Tapan Raychaudhuri has described it.[7] This model of interpretation is, however, no longer subscribed to even by its one time enthusiastic champions. C.A. Bayly's book *Origins of Nationality in South Asia* (1998), referred to earlier, is a reminder of that significant historiographical shift.

By contrast to this rather constricted political explanation of nationalism, the orthodox Marxist school sought to analyse the class character of the nationalist movement and tried to explain it in terms of the economic developments of the colonial period, primarily the rise of industrial capitalism and the development of a market society in India. It identified the bourgeois leadership, which directed this movement to suit their own class interests and neglected the interests of the masses and even to some extent betrayed them. This narrow class approach and economic determinism of the early Marxists like R.P. Dutt and Soviet historian V.I. Pavlov were qualified in later Marxist writings of S.N. Mukherjee, Sumit Sarkar and Bipan Chandra. Mukherjee pointed out the complexities of nationalism, its multiple layers and meanings, the importance of caste along with class and the simultaneous use of a traditional as well as a modern language of politics.[8] Sarkar showed the non-bourgeois background of the Indian educated classes and argued that they acted as "traditional" intellectuals, unconnected with the processes of production, responding to world ideological currents like liberalism or nationalism and "substituted" for the as yet inert masses of India.[9] In his later book, *Modern India* (1983), Sarkar has warned us that "class and class-consciousness are analytical tools which have to be used more skillfully and flexibly". He recognises the legitimacy of nationalism, but does not ignore the "internal tensions" within it. There were two levels of anti-imperialist struggles in India, he contends, the one elite and the other populist. One need not ignore either of the two, but look at the "complex interaction of these [two] levels" through which was produced "the pattern of continuity through change" that constituted the dominant theme of the period.[10]

Bipan Chandra and a few of his colleagues have given Marxist interpretation a distinctly nationalist orientation in their collective enterprise, *India's Struggle for Independence* (1989). They argue that Indian nationalist movement was a popular movement of various classes, not exclusively controlled by the bourgeoisie. In colonial India they demonstrate two types of contradictions. The primary contradiction was between the interests of the Indian people and those of British rule; but apart from that, there were also several secondary contradictions within the Indian society, between classes, castes and religious communities. As the anti-colonial struggle made progress, the secondary contradictions were compromised in the interest of the primary contradiction and in this way the hegemony of a nationalist ideology was established. But the nationalist movement was not the movement of a single class or caste or a religious community, and leaders like Gandhi or Jawaharlal Nehru recognised that India was not a structured nation but a nation in the making. There were various groups with conflicting interests and hence the need for constant compromises to avoid class, caste or communal conflicts and to bring all those disparate groups under one umbrella type leadership. As a result, the Indian nationalist movement became a peoples' movement, though all the secondary conflicts were not satisfactorily resolved.[11]

A brave new intervention in this debate came in 1982 when the first volume of the *Subaltern Studies*, edited by Ranajit Guha, was published, with a provocative opening statement: "The historiography of Indian nationalism has for a long time been dominated by elitism". This "blinkered historiography", he goes on to say, cannot explain Indian nationalism, because it neglects "the contribution made by the people *on their own*, that is, *independently of the elite* to the making and development of this nationalism".[12] This radical Marxist school, which derives its theoretical inputs from the writings of the Italian Marxist, Antonio Gramsci, thinks that organised national movement which ultimately led to the formation of the Indian nation-state was hollow nationalism of the elites, while real nationalism was that of the masses, whom it calls the 'subaltern'. There was a "structural dichotomy" between the two domains of elite politics and that of the subalterns, as the two segments of Indian society lived in two completely separate and autonomous, although not hermetically sealed, mental worlds defined by two distinct forms of consciousness. Although the subalterns from time to time participated in political movements initiated by the bourgeoisie, the latter failed to speak for the nation. The bourgeois leadership, Ranajit Guha argued in a later essay, failed to establish its hegemony through either persuasion or coercion, as it was continually contested by the peasantry and the working class, who had different idioms of mobilisation and action, which the nationalist movement failed to appropriate. The new nation-state established the dominance of this bourgeoisie and its ideology, but it was a "dominance without hegemony".[13]

This particular historiographical strand has, however, undergone considerable shifts in recent years, with the focus moving from class to community, from material analysis to the privileging of culture, mind and identity. Complaints have been raised by its one time stalwart contributor Sumit Sarkar about the "decline of the subaltern in *Subaltern Studies*".[14] This is because gradually its focus has expanded from an exclusive preoccupation with forms and instances of subaltern protest to an incorporation of the politics of the colonial intelligentsia as well. "Elite and dominant groups can also have a subaltern past", argues Dipesh Chakrabarty as a justification for this shift in focus.[15] It has been argued, following Edward Said (1978), that their subalternity was constituted through the colonisation of their mind, which constructed their subjectivity. As for an understanding of nationalism of these subordinate colonial elites, the most important contribution has come from Partha Chatterjee. His earlier assertion was that nationalism in India was essentially a "different" but "derivative discourse" from the West that developed through three distinct stages: the "moment of departure" when the nationalist consciousness was constructed through the hegemonising influence of the "post-Enlightenment rationalist thought", the "moment of manoeuvre" when the masses were mobilised in its support, and the "moment of arrival" when it became "a discourse of order" and "rational organization of power".[16] This theory has been further developed in his later book *The Nation and Its Fragments* (1993), where he has argued about two domains of action of this intelligentsia—the material and the spiritual. In the inner spiritual domain they tried "to fashion a 'modern' national culture that is nevertheless not Western" and here they refused to allow colonial intervention; it was here that nationalism was already sovereign. In the outer material world, defined by the institutions of the colonial state, there was however little scope for them to avoid the influence of Western models. In the outer world the Indian elite contested the colonial rule of difference, while in the inner domain they sought to homogenise Indian society by producing consent and dominating the space of subaltern dissent. So the two domains of elite and subaltern politics should now be studied not in their separateness, Chatterjee persuades us, but in their "mutually conditioned historicities".[17]

The subaltern view of nationalism—or what is now being described as a major strand in "postcolonial" theory—has witnessed further development in Gyan Prakash's most recent book *Another Reason* (1999), where he has argued—in partial revision of Chatterjee—that "[t]here was no fundamental opposition between the inner-sphere of the nation and its outer life as a nation state; the latter was the former's existence at another, abstract level".[18] The fashioning of the nation-state in India was no mere emulation of the Western model, as thought by Chatterjee, but a rethinking and critiquing of the Western modernity from the vantage point of India's spiritual-cultural heritage, combined with a scientific approach. This state, as contemplated by leaders like Jawaharlal Nehru, would be guided by the Indian principles of ethical conduct that privileged collective good, and in this sense, it would not be a "Western import". However, this very reliance on the state emanated from their failure to achieve national unity, which they had only visualised at a discursive level. Thus, as Prakash argues, "[t]he nation-state was immanent in the very hegemonic project of imagining and normalizing a national community" and herein lay the contradiction of Indian nationalism.[19]

Outside these particular schools mentioned earlier, which are more or less clearly definable, there are, however, a whole range of other writings that have looked at Indian nationalism from diverse ideological vantage points and historiographical perspectives. Indian nationalism, in other words, is an intensely contested discursive terrain from where it is difficult to arrive at a dialectical middle ground or evolve an eclectic view that would be acceptable to all. If British rule sought to colonise Indian minds, the Indians also selectively appropriated, internalised and manipulated that colonial knowledge to mount their own resistance to colonial hegemony. But if mainstream nationalism assumed the existence of a homogeneous nation that supposedly spoke with one voice, there have been persistent claims about exclusion, silences and suppression of discordant voices, such as those of women[20] or dalits.[21] In other words, it is now argued by an ever-increasing group of historians that the forms of anticolonial resistance and the ideologies that went behind them were visualised or constructed in multiple ways. It is difficult to deny the truth in Ania Loomba's observation that here "the 'nation' itself is a ground of dispute and debate, a site for the competing imaginings of different ideological and political interests".[22] India was a plural society and therefore Indian nationalism was bound to have many voices, as different classes, groups, communities and regions interpreted their 'nation' in various, sometimes even contradictory, ways. Indians had many identities, like class identity, caste identity, religious identity and so on; at different historical conjunctures different identities were articulated and intersected with each other. As the colonial state sought to reinforce and substantialise these fissures, the Indian nationalists tried to publicise an alternative discourse of integration. Jawaharlal Nehru talked about "the old Indian ideal of a synthesis of differing elements and their fusion into a common nationality".[23] Such a romantic assumption of fusion was, however, to avoid the hard realities of conflict and contradiction. Such complacency and failure to accommodate difference in the imagining of a national culture excluded some groups from the project of nationalism and the unity that was achieved proved to be fragile and hence so much dependence on a centralising nation-state. However, this critique need not take us to what Sugata Bose and Ayesha Jalal have warned us against, i.e., "[e]xulting over fragment" and "sliding into mindless anti-statism".[24]

Instead of denying the existence of the nation at an emotional level, we will consider it as a site of political contestation. The normalising tendency of the mainstream nationalism notwithstanding, this dominant version of the nation was repeatedly contested from inside. But here a question remains: is this contestation incapable of resolution, or as Homi Bhabha has claimed, such "forces of social antagonism or contradiction cannot be transcended or dialectically surmounted"?[25] Or may be, we should not posit that question at all! For, to expect a final resolution and everyone living happily ever-after, is to think of an end of history. On the contrary, nation building is always a process of continuous adjustment, accommodation—and contestation. It is from this historiographical position of recognising the multiplicity of responses, rather than assuming any unilinearity of progress, that we will look at the emergence of nationalism in post-1857 India. We will focus on the different levels at which this consciousness was developing and try to analyse how such various forms of consciousness intersected and interacted with each other, how they viewed contradictions within Indian society and also defined their variegated contestatory positions vis-à-vis their common oppressive 'Other', the colonial regime.

4.2. AGRARIAN SOCIETY AND PEASANT DISCONTENT

In post-1857 India we witness first of all a continuation of some of the earlier forms of protest against various oppressive aspects of colonial rule, the tribal and peasant movements being the foremost among them. We have already discussed various aspects of peasant ideology and their political consciousness (chapter 3.2), many of these trends being present in the later period as well. But these later movements acquired some new features as well. First, we find in this period a greater awareness of colonial policies, laws and institutions among the peasantry, both tribal and non-tribal. And what is more important, some of them even embraced those institutions, the law courts for example, as an extended and legitimate space for venting their anger or for seeking redress to existing injustices. The other important feature was the growing involvement of the educated middle-class intelligentsia as spokespersons for the aggrieved peasantry, thus adding new dimensions to their protests and linking their movements to a wider agitation against certain undesirable aspects of colonial rule. The nature of this outside intervention in peasant movements has been a subject of intense debate. Ravinder Kumar, on the one hand, would think that these middle-class leaders performed an important and effective function as "a channel of communication, between rural society and the administration", at a time when the traditional channels and methods had become ineffective.[26] Ranajit Guha, on the other hand, has described the nineteenth century middle-class attitude to peasants as "a curious concoction of an inherited, Indian style paternalism and an acquired, western-style humanism". Their actions at every stage betrayed their innate collaborative mind and revealed "the futility of liberalism as a deterrent to tyranny".[27] But whatever might have been the nature or impact of this middle-class mediation, this was nonetheless a new feature of nearly all the peasant movements in the second half of the nineteenth century.

One of the major events in which the old and new features of peasant movements were equally visible was the indigo rebellion in Bengal in 1859–60. The oppressive aspects of the indigo plantation system (see chapter 2.5) had been the targets of peasant protest in the central and eastern Bengal for a long time. In 1832 in Barasat, the followers of Titu Mir had given the local indigo planters the fright of their lifetime. Almost around the same time the Faraizi movement under Dudu Mian in eastern Bengal had the indigo planters as one of their selected targets of attack. The oppression of the planters increased in the second half of the nineteenth century as indigo lost its economic importance as an export item and the Union Bank, which was the chief financier for the planters, failed in 1847. The oppressed peasantry continued to bear with the coercive planters for a while, but their attitudes changed when in May 1859 a sympathetic John Peter Grant took up office as the Lieutenant Governor of Bengal and with his encouragement some of the district officers—though not all—began to take a pro-peasant position, thinking that the coercive methods of the planters went against the ethos of free enterprise.

The indigo disturbances started in the autumn of 1859 when peasants refused to accept advances from the planters in a wide region in the districts of Nadia, Murshidabad, and Pabna. The Jessore peasants joined hands in the spring sowing season of 1860, by which time the entire delta region of Bengal had become affected. As the planters' men tried to coerce the peasants to sow indigo, they met with stiff resistance and sometimes their Indian agents were subjected to organised social boycott. The substantial peasants and village headmen provided leadership. The local zamindars, who resented the European planters usurping their prime position of power in the countryside, often sympathised with the ryots, sometimes even offering leadership; but soon they lost control of the situation. The panic-stricken pro-planter lobby in Calcutta had a temporary legislation passed in March 1860, compelling the peasants to fulfill their contractual obligations to sow indigo. The courts were flooded with such cases and some of the overzealous magistrates forced the peasants to cultivate the hated crop. But Grant refused to extend the legislation beyond its life of six months and forbade the magistrates to compel peasants to accept advances to cultivate indigo. The peasants also took their cases to courts, which were inundated with such law suites. The movement at this stage turned into a no-rent campaign and as the planters sought to evict their defaulting tenants, the latter went to court to establish their right as occupancy ryots under the Rent Act X of 1859.

In this whole episode another important feature was the intervention of the educated middle classes and some of the European missionaries. Dinabandhu Mitra published in September 1860 a play in Bengali called *Neel Darpan* (literally, 'blue mirror'), which depicted the atrocities of the indigo planters in the boldest possible colour. The play was translated into English by the famous Bengali poet Michael Madhusudan Dutta and was published by Rev. James Long of the Church Missionary Society to bring it to the notice of the liberal political circles in India and London. For this, Long was tried for libel in the Calcutta Supreme Court and was fined Rs. 1,000 with a jail sentence of one month. His conviction enraged the Calcutta literati, as the Indian press, particularly the *Hindoo Patriot* and *Somprakash* took up the cause of the indigo peasants, and the British Indian Association came to their side as well.[28] Although their appeal was to the liberal political opinion among the imperial bureaucrats and it betrayed their unflagging faith in British justice system,[29] these middle-class protagonists, however, succeeded in bringing the peasants' issue to the wider arena of institutional politics and this resulted in a growing pressure on the planters to behave. By 1863, the movement was over, as by that time indigo cultivation, which was itself an anachronism before its dissolution began, had almost disappeared from Bengal.

But indigo plantation survived in the backyard of the empire, in the "relatively remote and backward region" of Bihar, where the oppressive system was allowed to continue without much government interference. Indeed, after the disturbances of 1859–60, much of the indigo investment from Bengal shifted to Bihar, where it continued to grow until an artificial dye was invented in 1898. But still the industry continued into the twentieth century, even experiencing a brief revival during World War One. There were instances of resistance in Darbhanga and Champaran in 1874 and then again in 1907–8, by the indigo cultivators under the leadership of rich or substantial peasants. But these movements were suppressed by the planters and their musclemen, with only occasional mild intervention from the government, which could secure for the peasants only some limited concessions.[30] Indigo plantation in Champaran had to wait for Gandhi's intervention in 1917 for its complete demise (see chapter 6.2).

In Bengal—where the spirit of rebellion had been kindled among the peasants of eastern and central districts, particularly where the Faraizi movement had prepared a moral ground for greater righteousness—dissent and resistance persisted through to the closing decades of the nineteenth century. The next most important event was the forming in 1873 of the Agrarian League in the Yusufshahi pargana of Pabna district, where the oppression of a few new landlords pushed the peasants to the threshold of tolerance. In this area, the rate of rent had been continually going up, along with the illegal cesses or abwabs.[31] But the main grievance of the peasantry was against the concerted attempts of the landlords to destroy their occupancy rights by denying them leases in the same plot of land continually for twelve years, which would entitle them to the protection of the law (Rent Act X of 1859). The movement, which was mainly spearheaded by the substantial peasants, but aided by the lower peasantry as well, remained largely non-violent and within the bounds of law, with a profound faith in the British justice system. Indeed, the peasant ambition was to become the true subjects of the Queen; they formed the Agrarian League to raise money to take the landlords to courts, which were inundated with rent suites.[32]

What was more important, the Pabna experiment was repeated soon in other districts of eastern and central Bengal where the zamindars had recently resorted to what Benoy Chaudhuri has described as "high landlordism", i.e., defying all laws in the management of their estates, enhancing rent at their will, imposing illegal abwabs and persistently trying to destroy the occupancy rights of the substantial peasants. Agrarian leagues came up in Dacca, Mymensingh, Tripura, Bakarganj, Faridpur, Bogra and Rajshahi districts, where civil courts were choked with rent suites. Although some leaders were Hindus and there was remarkable communal harmony, these were also the regions where Faraizi movement had a large following and Naya Mian, the son of Dudu Mian, was himself active in organising the agrarian combination in Mehendigunge in 1880. As a result of the movement, agrarian relations in Bengal became sharply polarised, and the mounting tension accelerated the passage of the Bengal Tenancy Act of 1885. It provided for relatively greater protection of occupancy rights of the substantial peasants who leased land in the same village (not just the same piece of land) continuously for twelve years. But the rights of the lesser peasantry remained undefined as before. The other interesting feature of the Pabna uprising and its aftermath was the ambivalence of the educated middle classes. The Calcutta native press, which had been able to take an unequivocal position against the European planters, now was divided when the oppression of the indigenous landlords was under attack. The same *Hindoo Patriot*, along with the *Amrita Bazar Patrika*, took an overtly pro-landlord position, while *Bengalee* and the Anglo-Indian press ridiculed them when their grandiose reports on peasant violence turned out to be mere landlord propaganda.[33] This was a dilemma which the middle-class Indian nationalists suffered from since the beginning of their career and which they never succeeded in overcoming completely.

Peasant protest against landlord oppression was not confined to Bengal alone. The fight of the Moplah peasants against their jenmis continued in Malabar (see chapter 3.2), while in Sitapur district of Awadh and in Mewar in Rajasthan peasants resisted rent enhancements and imposition of illegal cesses by their landlords in 1860 and 1897 respectively.[34] Religion still played a large role in peasant rebellions as before; in Punjab, for example the attempts to purify Sikhism led to the Kuka revolt in 1872. In all these regions the tradition of peasant militancy continued into the first decade of the twentieth century, ultimately merging into the larger Gandhian tradition of mass movement in 1921. This merger, of course, was not without its own tensions, given the perennial dilemmas of the middle-class leadership (see chapter 6).

In Maharashtra, on the other hand, the peasants had another enemy to fight against; here they clashed head-on with their moneylenders. Although contemporary colonial officials and some recent historians have referred to these events of 1875 as the Deccan Riots, the peasants looked at it as a revolt or *band*, and thus, as David Hardiman has argued, "incorporated their uprising into a long tradition of *revolt* in Maharashtra".[35] It took place, as Ravinder Kumar tells us, because of a "redistribution of social power in the villages of Maharashtra".[36] The roots of discontent lay in the changing relationship between the Maratha Kunbi peasants and the *sahukar* moneylenders. The sahukars used to lend money to the Kunbi peasants in the past, but were never interested to take more intimate control of the village economy. The introduction of the ryotwari system, however, changed the situation, as each peasant individually needed more credit, and the creation of property right in land and the courts protecting such rights created a land market and hence there was now more demand for land. The moneylenders now lent money by mortgaging the peasants' land at a high interest rate and in case of failure to repay, he took possession of the land through a decree of the court. Caste prejudices prevented the moneylenders from touching the plough; so the same land was now leased out to their former owner-cultivators, who thus became tenants in their own land. The amount of land transfer that took place in Maharashtra during this period and to what extent that caused the riots are of course matters of controversy. Ian Catanach (1993) agrees that there were land transfers, but does not accept Ravinder Kumar's position that it was the main reason behind peasant discontent. Neil Charlesworth, on the other hand, completely dismisses this factor, as he believes that only about 5 per cent of the cultivable land in Deccan had passed on to the hands of the Marwari or Gujarati moneylenders at the time of the riots.[37] But one has to admit that this small proportion of land was the most fertile in the whole region and their loss would therefore be much resented.[38]

A situation for open conflict was soon created when the government increased the revenue rates in 1867 on grounds of extension of cultivation and rise in agricultural prices. In the taluka of Indapur, the increase in revenue demands was on the average of 50 per cent, but in some villages it was as high as 200 per cent. Charlesworth thinks that the new taxes were hardly the reasons behind the riots, as villages most affected by the disturbances in the Ahmadnagar district did not face any tax revision at all, while some of the revised talukas remained completely passive during the whole period. But even then, one can hardly ignore the fact that these new rates were announced at a time that could not have been more inappropriate. The cotton boom in Deccan, created by the artificial demand generated by the American Civil War, had just crashed after the end of the war. The peasants were impoverished and were bound to become hopelessly indebted; the rise in revenue in such a situation would inevitably increase panic.

The Kunbis made appeals for a revision of the new rates; but their traditional leadership had been completely out of touch with the new institutions and their novel demand for a new rational and legal language of communication. The Poona Sarvajanik Sabha, the new association of the middle-class intellectuals, now intervened and presented in 1873 a "Report" or a case for a revision of the revenue rates. It also sent volunteers to the villages to arouse the Kunbi peasants against the new rates. Pressurised by this, as Ravinder Kumar argues, the Bombay government now granted a major concession, that in case of a failure to pay revenue, first the movable properties of a peasant would be attached; his land would be put up for auction only if his movable properties proved to be insufficient. This concession actually became the source of conflict between the peasants and moneylenders, as the latter in 1874 refused to offer credit to the peasants to pay their land revenue because of what they thought a lack of sufficient security. But the riots of 1875 were not the result of this single factor, as Kumar further argues; they stemmed from a combination of factors, such as the dislocation of the economy by the American Civil War, an ill-conceived revision of land tax, agitation initiated by the Poona Sarvajanik Sabha and finally the longstanding hostilities between the Kunbi peasants and the moneylenders.

The riots first broke out on 12 May 1875 at a village called Supe in Bhimthadi taluka and soon it spread to other villages in Poona and Ahmadnagar districts. A wide area, about sixty-five kilometres north to south and a hundred kilometres east to west was affected by the disturbances. Everywhere the Gujarati and Marwari moneylenders were attacked, not simply because they were "outsiders", but because they were thought to be more avaricious. They also lived in the villages and therefore were more exposed to such attacks, unlike the Brahman moneylenders who usually resided in better-protected cities. What is more significant, there was very little violence against the person of the sahukars; only their debt bonds were seized and destroyed. Moreover, violence was resorted to only if there was resistance in handing over these legal documents. This very feature distinguishes these riots from the average genre of "grain riots" engineered by poverty-stricken peasants. The rioters had clearly identified their target, an instrument of oppression and dominance, and thus seemed to have been quite aware of the new institutional framework of power relations within which they had of late found themselves locked in. And if the British had not acted promptly in suppressing the revolt, the rioting spirit was highly likely to have spread to the whole of Maharashtra. The Bombay government acted promptly in preventing the recurrence of such rioting; the peasants were protected against such future land grabbing through the Deccan Agriculturists Relief Act of 1879.

What is important, however, is the fact that in the second half of the nineteenth century and in the first half of the twentieth, such occurrences of peasant protests against moneylenders were quite common throughout India, as colonial rule had significantly altered the relationship between the two groups in the political economy of the village. And everywhere we find similar patterns of peasant behaviour, i.e., little violence against persons, but destruction of the legal debt bonds of the moneylenders. This happened in Saharanpur district of western UP in 1857, in Nasik in 1868, in the ghat regions between Bombay and Poona in 1874, in Ajmer district of Rajasthan in 1891, in Punjab in 1914 and in east Bengal in 1930.[39] Very clearly such disturbances were the reactions of Indian rural society against the adverse impact of the British land system, the laws of property right and courts, which appeared as alien impositions from above that tended to turn their world upside down.

However, it was not just the symbols of British rule or changes brought about by it that were being targeted by the peasants; there were also overtly anti-British peasant movements, particularly in the ryotwari areas. Along with the attacks on moneylenders, there were also no-tax campaigns in a wide area of Maharashtra Deccan in 1873–74 in response to the revenue hike by the Bombay government in the 1860s and 1870s. Although the government on this occasion offered some concessions, it refused to tone down the built-in inflexibility of its tax system. So when again in 1896–97 there was a crop failure resulting in a severe famine, there was no remission of revenue, leading to a widespread no-tax campaign, particularly in the coastal districts of Thane and Kolaba. In Khandesh and Dharwar districts, the sahukars refused to pay the land tax as there was a harvest failure, and the peasantry withheld payment of all taxes. One of the major features of the movement, as Hardiman notes, was its strength in relatively more prosperous regions which were least affected by the famine. This was an "agitation of landlords and rich peasants", while the mediation of the urban leadership from Bombay and Poona played a significant role too, inviting strong-arm tactics from the government. By the end of 1897 it was all over. But peasant unrest erupted again in 1899–1900 in Gujarat, which suffered from a bad harvest and famine. Led once again by the richer peasantry, Kheda, Surat and Broach districts witnessed nearly a universal refusal to pay land taxes; but here the outside urban leadership could not play any important role. Here too, the government broke the movement by coercion and threat of confiscation of the defaulter's property.[40]

A more direct and effective confrontation between the peasants and the colonial state took place in 1907 in Punjab, where in the Chenab Canal Colony the local government proposed to introduce a new law which would control the lives of the settlers more intimately. It proposed to control inheritance of land in the canal settlements, fine all those who would break the canal colony regulations and enhance the water taxes. Peasants were organised by their more educated members to protest against the draconian law; mammoth public meetings were held and petitions were sent. At this stage, the involvement of Lajpat Rai and Ajit Singh, the two leaders of the Lahore Indian Association, and the support of the Singh Sabha and Arya Samaj, enlarged the scope of the movement both vertically and horizontally. The peasants held large demonstrations and withheld the payment of all taxes; riots broke out in large cities like Amritsar, Lahore and Rawalpindi. The Punjab government initially misjudged the magnitude of the tension and mistook it to be instigated entirely by outsiders. So it deported Rai and Singh and banned all public meetings; but that did not lead to any abatement of unrest, which now affected the army, as Punjab was the most important catchment area for army recruitment. So ultimately on 26 May, Viceroy Minto vetoed the new act and the measure had a miraculous effect on the peasantry, who hailed it as "a vindication of British justice".[41] In peasant consciousness, the distant ruler was still the saviour, while the enemy was the corrupt official closer at home. Such ambiguity notwithstanding, they fought against what they thought to be unjust taxes or undesirable interference in their traditional way of life. In this, Punjab was no exception. No tax campaigns were reported in this period from different parts of India—from Awadh in the north in 1879, from Cambay state in Gujarat in the west in 1890, from Tanjore district in the south in 1892–93 and from Assam in the northeast in 1893–94.[42]

Along with the unrest among the settled agriculturists, the earlier tradition of millenarian movements among the tribal peasants also continued well into the post-1857 period, a major example of this tradition being the Munda *ulgulan* of 1899–1900, under the guidance of a charismatic religious leader, Birsa Munda. The alienation of Munda land and the advent of dikus had spurred an agitation under their leaders in 1890–95. This movement gradually came under the leadership of Birsa, who for two years mobilised the Munda tribal peasants from a wide region in Chota Nagpur in Bihar, by promising to protect them from an apocalyptic disaster. Rumours spread about his occult powers, ability to heal diseases and perform miracles. In tribal imagination, he appeared as a messiah who could turn British bullets into water. He took them on a pilgrimage to Munda holy places and on the way held large public meetings, talking about a golden past or *satjug* that was gone and the dark *kaljug* that had befallen, when the Munda land or *disum* was ruled by Queen Mandodari, the wife of the demon King Ravana—probably a metaphor for the Raj under Queen Victoria.[43] What came out in these meetings was the tribal peasants' antipathy towards the foreigners, the dikus—the landlords and the moneylenders and their patrons, the sahibs (Europeans)—both officials and Christian missionaries. The grounds were thus prepared for a massive anti-colonial tribal uprising that started during the Christmas of 1899. It targeted churches, temples, policemen and other symbols of the new regime and was finally defeated by the government forces. What was important, however, about the Munda ulgulan was their greater awareness of the wider political realities of the colonial state. Tribal territoriality notwithstanding, Birsa's ambitions were no longer localised. The aim of his movement was not merely to drive out the dikus, but "to destroy their enemies and put an end to the British Raj" and establishing in its place "a Birsa Raj and a Birsaite religion".[44] It was this political awareness and ability to connect to the broad picture that was new in the late nineteenth century tribal movements.

Another new feature of the tribal peasant life of this period was the "unquiet woods", as Ramchandra Guha has described it (1991). The people in the woods became restless as government regulations threatened to deprive them of their customary user rights on forest resources. The attention of the British was drawn to the vast forestry of India in 1806, primarily because of the imperial demand for oak timber needed for shipbuilding for the Royal Navy. And then the rapid construction of railways in the mid-nineteenth century and the huge demand for sleepers that it created, made conservation of forests a major concern for the colonial state. In 1864 a forest department was started, followed by a Government Forests Act passed in 1865. It was further tightened by the Indian Forests Act of 1878, which established complete government monopoly over Indian forestlands. Needless to say, this imperial need to reserve forests for commercial timber production went against the previous unhindered customary user rights of the tribal peasants and impinged on their principal sources of livelihood. The act divided the forestlands in India into three categories: "reserved", "protected" and "unclassified". The "reserved" forests were under complete government monopoly where felling of trees was totally prohibited; from the "protected" forests the traditional right holders could collect timber for personal use, but not for sale. Initially they could do it free of cost; but gradually the government imposed and then enhanced user charges.[45]

By 1900, 20 per cent of India's land area had come under government forest administration, which not only redefined property rights there, but also threatened the customary ecological balance. This change imperilled two groups of tribal peasants, the hunter-gatherers and those who depended on *jhum* (slash and burn) cultivation, and their resistance to forest laws became endemic in the second half of the nineteenth century in practically all parts of India. To give a few examples, commercial forestry and the game laws that accompanied it, prohibiting subsistence hunting, threatened the Chenchus of Hyderabad with virtual extinction and they took to banditry. On the other hand, the Baigas of central India, the Hill Reddis of Hyderabad and the Bison Marias of Bastar continued with their hunting rituals in defiance of the laws. The government attempted to stop jhum cultivation, because it was considered to be a primitive method of agriculture and against the interests of commercialisation of forests; but these attempts met with various kinds of resistance. The Baigas often migrated to neighbouring areas, thus depriving the government of a useful source of labour. Sometimes, they refused to pay taxes or defiantly resorted to shifting cultivation in prohibited zones. The Saora tribals of the Ganjam Agency, on the other hand, often got involved in frontal confrontation with the state by clearing reserved forests for jhum and courting arrests for the violation of laws.[46]

The state monopoly and commercial exploitation of forests also brought outside intruders into the tribal territories, many of whom used a considerable amount of coercive power to exploit the tribal peasants. This situation in turn brought stiffer resistance, as it happened in the Gudem and Rampa hill tracts of Andhra Pradesh, inhabited by the Koya and Konda Dora tribes. The first few rebellions or *fituris* in this region between 1839 and 1862, were initiated by the local *muttadars* or estate holders, who found their power curbed and rights denied by the intrusion of the new outside control. However, in the late nineteenth century some other changes took place that brought the masses of tribal peasants into the Rampa rebellion of 1879. As the commercial use of forestry began, and the construction of roads opened the hills to commercial penetration, traders and sahukars from the plains came to the mountainous regions and gradually took hold of tribal lands by confiscating properties of the indebted peasants and muttadars. The prohibition of shifting cultivation (*podu*), restrictions on the use of forest resources and a new tax on toddy tested the tolerance levels of the peasants and they looked to the muttadars for leadership.

The fituri broke out first in Rampa in March 1879, and then spread to the neighbouring regions in Gudem. The major targets of attack were the mansabdars, the British and their police stations and the trader-contractors from the plains. The leadership was provided by the muttadars, but in many cases this elite participation was secured by mass pressure and arm-twisting. The villagers supported the rebels in many ways as they were in general opposed to the government; but the fituri of 1879–80, as David Arnold argues, never took "the form of a mass uprising or jacquerie", for mass participation was neither required nor necessary, as the goal of the rebels was only to cleanse the hills of outsiders, and not to take their rebellion beyond their demarcated territory.[47] The British armed intervention restored order in the region by December 1880, but fituri was revived again six years later in 1886 in Gudem, when religion played a significant role, giving it the character of a messianic or millenarian movement. The tradition of fituri survived in the hills of Gudem and Rampa, but by the 1920s it was seeking to extend to the outer world by trying to connect itself to the wider tradition of Gandhian mass movements (see chapter 6.3).

In the princely states too, where the local rulers tried to enforce restrictions on shifting cultivation, the tribal peasants resisted such efforts. The Marias and Murias of Bastar in 1910 openly attacked the police stations and killed foreigners and could be brought under control only when a British army contingent was called in. The tribal peasants on the fringes of settled agricultural areas were affected equally by forest laws. This was particularly true in the hill areas where terraced farming predominated, accompanied by animal husbandry as a substitute source of income. Such deprivation obviously brought resistance in various forms. In Madras Presidency, for example, forest crimes increased manifold; in Travancore, the peasants refused to cooperate with the forest department officials. In the Thane district of coastal Maharashtra the protest took a violent turn,[48] while in the Jungle Mahal in Midnapur district of Bengal, the Santhal peasants looted village markets and fisheries.[49]

In the Himalayan forest tracts of UP, in Tehri Garhwal, which was a princely state and in Kumaun, which was a British administered territory, the local peasants' anger against forest laws was vented in a number of interesting ways. In Tehri Garhwal, the peasants followed the old tradition of *dhandak*, which was protesting against the tyranny of the officials and appealing for justice to the sovereign. When the local raja tried to enforce stricter conservancy laws, the peasants protested in 1886 and then again in 1904. Some concessions from the raja failed to satisfy the peasants and in December 1906 they became violent in their protest against the local conservator and the raja had to appeal to the British for assistance. In Kumaun, the protests were directly against the British, as the peasants resisted the system of *utar* or forced labour and the tyrannous forest management. Mostly this protest was of a non-confrontational nature, like the defiance of law, theft of timber, incendiarism and finally, purposefully firing the reserved forests.[50] In the forests of central India too, where the consistent colonial policy was to transform the forest tribes like the Bhils either into settled agriculturists or into a servile labour force, the tribals resisted such efforts in various ingenuous ways.[51] The Bhils of the Dangs in western India had under the pressure of the British discontinued around 1840s their usual raids on the villages of the plains of Khandesh to claim their customary *giras* (dues), as a mark of asserting their shared sovereignty. Instead, they were now paid directly by the British, but they lost in the process their hold over the forestland. Although there was no sustained overt protest and the Bhils seemed to have accepted the centrality of the Raj in their daily existence, yet they could not completely reconcile themselves to this alienation and subjection, as the memories of a Bhil raj persisted. Such memories from time to time were manifested in protest movements, such as those in 1860, 1907, 1911 and 1914, when they defied the local representatives of the state, destroyed their documents, ransacked forest department offices or set fire to forests.[52] Similar forms of resistance could also be found in the forest areas of Punjab, where peasants resorted to unauthorised felling, lopping and grazing, deliberate firing and attacking the symbols of new forest management, like the forest guards or the boundary lines.[53]

Even when there was no overt resistance, use of such tools of protest, which James C. Scott (1985) has described as the "weapon of the weak", has not been uncommon in peasant history. Absence of direct violent resistance, therefore, did not always mean a general approval of an undesirable world order. And when protests did occur, the colonial government often showed a patronising attitude towards the 'wild' tribes—stereotyped as the 'noble savage'—who were believed to be honest, sincere, brave, but simple folk, who could be easily manipulated by the deceitful plains people. So when rebellions occurred in the hills, these were often looked at as instigated by outsiders and the rebels were sometimes depicted as "naughty boys making a disturbance in the schoolroom when they believed the school master's attention was momentarily diverted".[54] But the rebellions were suppressed ruthlessly nonetheless, as they posed challenges to colonial mastery and were likely to be taken advantage of by the nationalists. The tradition of tribal resistance, for example, survived in the hills of UP, to be appropriated later in the 1920s by the wider stream of Gandhian mass politics, as it happened also in Midnapur in Bengal or the Gudem-Rampa region of Andhra Pradesh (see chapter 6.3).

In post-1857 India peasant and tribal revolts occurred in all parts of the country; but they remained disjointed or isolated and localised movements. To a large extent, this was due to the complex class structure in Indian agrarian society, which had great regional variations. As discussed earlier also, economic categories sometimes coincided with and sometimes cut across the cultural categories of religion and caste. Peasants identified themselves more with their cultural groups rather than with the economic category of class. Some historians have argued that it was 'community' and not class, which was the main focus of the peasants' mental world. It was their religious or caste identity, which defined their position in this world, and therefore it was easier to mobilise the peasantry along these lines.[55] Sometimes class and community organisations converged in rural societies, particularly when religious or ethnic boundaries neatly coincided with class cleavages. Peasant mobilisation was easier in such situations; but it would become problematic when class and cultural divisions cut across. Caste or religious affinity between the oppressor and the oppressed sometimes minimised the possibility of conflict; in other cases caste or religious identity of one group of rebels alienated the other possible participants in the rebellion. However, it is also a fact that community organisations often proved to be useful tools for peasant mobilisation; on such occasions it was a source of strength rather than weakness.

The series of peasant uprisings that took place throughout the nineteenth and the early twentieth centuries seriously contested the hegemony of the colonial state. The Indian National Congress after the advent of Gandhi tried to harness this force for its struggle against British rule. But Ranajit Guha has argued that peasant movements of the earlier period should not be looked at as the "prehistory of the 'Freedom Movement'"; they have a history of their own.[56] As we have mentioned earlier, controversies exist over the question of leadership or about the connections between the two levels of politics, that of the elites and the subalterns. In the late nineteenth century a section of the Western-educated middle class were trying to project themselves as the leaders of the nation, representing the grievances and interests of all sections of the Indian population, the peasants included. Guha and other subaltern historians have argued that peasants were capable of organising themselves and could articulate their own grievances; intervention of the outside elite leaders was only to appropriate these movements for their own political benefits. Only rarely such middle-class leaders exhibited the same radicalism as that of the peasantry. A major exception perhaps was Vasudeo Phadke, who in 1879 gave leadership to an armed peasant revolt in the villages to the southwest of Poona. But everywhere else, as Hardiman has emphasised, their "enterprise was carried on in a spirit of compromise and timidity".[57] But despite this alleged frailty, these urban middle-class leaders performed an important role: they tried to connect the localised and isolated peasant and tribal movements to a wider struggle against the undesirable aspects of colonial rule. They acted as crucial channels of communication between the peasants and the colonial state—a role, which the traditional peasant leadership was no longer equipped enough to perform effectively. But they had their dilemmas too, for although they empathised with the suffering peasants, they did not want to see their familiar world disordered. These dilemmas and their ambivalence we will understand better if we look at their social background and ideological inclinations.

4.3. THE NEW MIDDLE CLASS AND THE EMERGENCE OF NATIONALISM

Nationalism at an organised level at the top, as against peasant anticolonial resistance described above, emerged in India in the late nineteenth century. The rise of nationalism, it is often argued, was favoured by industrialisation, urbanisation and print capitalism. And nationalism in the developing world of Asia and Africa, as Benedict Anderson (1983) tells us, is supposed to have followed one or the other model developed in the West. This theory, which denies intellectual agency to the people of Asia in shaping their own history, has recently come under criticism from a wide variety of ideological positions. Partha Chatterjee, for example, has argued that if the West defined subjectivity and prescribed our predicament, and also imagined for us the forms of our resistance to colonial regimes, then what was really left for us to imagine? He argues therefore that long before the political struggle for power began, the Indian society was imagining its nation in a private cultural sphere, even though the state was in the hands of the colonisers. It was here that they imagined their own domain of sovereignty and constructed an Indian modernity that was modern but not Western.[58] It was from here, i.e., from this cultural construction of a space for autonomy in the early nineteenth century, that Indian nationalism started its career.

C.A. Bayly, on the other hand, has traced the roots of Indian nationalism to its pre-colonial days; it emanated from what he describes as "traditional patriotism", which was "a socially active sentiment of attachment to land, language and cult" that developed in the subcontinent long before the process of Westernisation (read modernisation) had begun.[59] In India of the eighteenth and early nineteenth centuries, such sentiments were emerging on a regional basis as homeland was being defined by various terms like *desh*, *vatan* or *nadu*, where identities were gradually taking shape with the development of regional languages and religious affiliations. But although regionally centred at Bengal, Maharashtra, Awadh or Mysore, their isolation broke down through various means of communication. The political legitimacy of the Mughal empire was recognised throughout Hindustan, which was thought to be the abode of both Hindus and Muslims; and cultural barriers melted down through commercialisation and regular pilgrimages. As the East India Company established its hegemony, Bayly argues, this traditional patriotism manifested itself through various indigenous critiques of foreign rule deviating from the established ethical traditions of good government and through irate reactions to Christian missionary propaganda. Finally, it burst forth through numerous acts of resistance, participated by both the princes and the commoners, culminating in the revolt of 1857. After the revolt, a modern sector of politics gradually evolved in India, through rapid spread of education, development of communication systems, such as the railways and telegraph, and the emergence of a new public space created by the colonial institutions. Although "old patriotism" did not completely die out during this period, it was significantly reworked and reshaped—if at this point we may go back to Chatterjee—to create a new colonial modernity that was different from that of the West. We may trace here very briefly the initial phase of that complex and ongoing transformatory process that tried to fuse together, not always seamlessly though, all theose regional, local and fragmentary identities into a modern 'nation'.

The political history of India in the post-1857 period—when the political contest with the colonial regime began at a more modern institutionalised public space—is multifaceted. First of all, in colonial policies a conservative reaction set in after the revolt of 1857. Attempts were made to rehabilitate and strengthen the landed aristocracy, deemed to be the "natural" leaders of the people. They could "alone command the allegiance of the masses" and could therefore be the reliable allies of a vulnerable colonial state.[60] The Imperial Durbar of 1877, where Queen Victoria assumed the title of the Empress of India, and which Lord Lytton, the then viceroy, organised in great splendour and pomp, despite famine conditions occurring in some parts of the country, gave the place of precedence to the native princes in the new imperial social order.[61] Apart from them, big zamindars from now on began to play a prominent role within the colonial administrative set up. The British Indian Association was the first major voluntary organisation in India founded in 1851 in Calcutta, representing primarily the local landlord interests. It began to play a prominent role after the Indian Councils Act of 1861, which provided for limited Indian representation in the legislative councils. Members of this association were usually nominated to the legislative councils and their dominance continued until the Act of 1892 introduced limited electoral system. But although "old" elements continued to dominate this organisation, it was also new in many respects and performed some very new roles.

For example, unlike its predecessor the Landholders' Society that had many non-official Anglo-Indians among its members, the British Indian Association was exclusively Indian in its membership. And it was created on the eve of the renewal of the Charter of the East India Company to send petitions to the British parliament to express the legitimate demands of the Indian subjects. It initially tried to coordinate the efforts of the three presidencies in this regard by opening up branches in Bombay and Madras. But regional barriers ultimately stood in the way, as two other similar associations, the Madras Native Association and the Bombay Association, came into existence in 1852 for the same purpose. The three presidency associations sent three separate petitions to London, but—interestingly—

all of them made almost identical demands. What they wanted was a greater participation in the administration of their own country and what they complained against were the perplexing "dual system" of government, expensive and incompetent administration, legislations unresponsive to the feelings of the people, high taxation, salt and opium monopolies and the neglect of education and public works. They were not against British rule as such, but felt, as the Calcutta petition made it clear, that they had "not profited by their connection with Great Britain, to the extent which they had a right to look for".[62] Thus, the educated members of the landed gentry who headed these associations were contributing to the evolution of a modern sector in Indian politics. But their agitation over charter was treated with "almost contemptuous indifference" by the authorities in London; as Mehrotra tells us, the new Government of India Act of 1853 incorporated none of their demands. For, ironically, it was not the educated Indians, but the uneducated and uninformed that the Raj was expecting its gravest danger from.[63]

This official assumption of an unquestionable loyalty of the landlords and educated Indians was premised on the latter's self-professed faith in the providential nature of British rule and their scornful attitude towards the peasant rebellions of the first half of the nineteenth century and later disapproval of the revolt of 1857. But this was a misconception, to say the least. For behind this loyalism there was also a growing awareness of the ignominy involved in their state of subordination. The unabashed show of loyalty by the Calcutta literati during the revolt of 1857 also came with a sense of dilemma; as the *Hindoo Patriot* wrote in an introspective editorial: "This loyalty . . . springs nearer from the head than from the heart".[64] It was from the early nineteenth century that the Calcutta intellectuals had begun to criticise what they considered to be certain undesirable aspects of colonial rule. Rammohun Roy started a modest constitutional agitation on such demands as the separation of powers, freedom of the press, trial by jury and the Indianisation of the services,[65] many of these issues being later taken over by the members of the Young Bengal. In 1841, at a meeting of the short-lived Deshahitaishini Sabha [Society for the Amelioration of the Country], a young Derozian, Saradaprasad Ghosh noted with angst that "our deprivation of the enjoyment of political liberty is the cause of our misery and degradation".[66] The precocious image of an empire based on interracial partnership nurtured by an earlier generation of Dwarkanath Tagore, was ruthlessly shattered by the controversy over the so-called "Black Acts", which proposed to place the British born subjects under the criminal jurisdiction of ordinary courts from which they were previously exempt. The act was passed in 1850, but was put on hold for fear of a white rebellion. The controversy around it, however, drove a wedge between the two racial elements in colonial society. The same year, despite united protests from the Hindus of Madras, Nagpur and Calcutta, the government went ahead with the Lex Loci Act, which gave the Christian converts the right to inherit their ancestral properties. The act, the Hindus widely believed, would open floodgates to Christian conversion.

The growing racial tension, threat of conversion and the reforming zeal of the Benthamite administrators made the educated Indians stand back and have a hard look at their own culture. This resulted in a process, which Bernard Cohn (1987) has described as the "objectification" of culture, with the educated Indians defining their culture as a concrete entity that could easily be cited, compared, referred to and used for specific purposes. This new cultural project, which partly manifested itself through the social and religious reforms of the nineteenth century (see chapter 3.1), was encoded in the word "Renaissance". Its purpose was to "purify" and "rediscover" an Indian civilisation that would be conformant with the European ideals of rationalism, empiricism, monotheism and individualism. It was meant to show that Indian civilisation was by no means inferior to that of the West, but in one sense, in its spiritual accomplishments, was even superior to it. Evidence of this search for a superior national culture could be found in the development of a patriotic regional literature in Bangla, Marathi, Tamil, Telugu and Hindi, in the evolution of new art forms, in the search for purer forms of classical music and in the construction of new ideals of womanhood. All of these were projected as modern, but were predicated upon the spiritual superiority of the Indian past. In other words, as already mentioned, this movement was meant "to fashion a 'modern' national culture that is nevertheless not Western".[67] This sense of pride in the spiritual essence of Indian civilisation, as opposed to the material culture of the West, not just helped Indians reorganise and sanctify their private spheres of life; its ideological inspiration also motivated them to confront the colonial state in a newly emerging public space. This, in other words, provided the ideological foundation of modern Indian nationalism that developed in the late nineteenth century.

This ideology was, of course, not without contradictions, as the sense of pride in the spiritual heritage was often reduced to an uncritical and obscurantist defence of all customs and practices of the past. And what was more important, this nineteenth century invention of the Indian tradition, as Vasudha Dalmia argues, conveniently "bypass[ed] the long stretch of Muslim rule" to present an idealised form of Indian/Hindu tradition rooted in classical Sanskrit texts that were now put to modern usage.[68] This created an identity that was inclusive and exclusive at the same time; it united the Hindus in opposition to an alien rule, but alienated the Muslims, non-Brahmans and the untouchables. This problematic of Indian nationalism, which is referred to as Hindu "revivalism"—often thought to be the genesis of "communalism"—will be discussed in greater detail in chapter 5.

The evolution of Indian nationalism might not have been the result of Western modular influences in the same way as Benedict Anderson had thought, but the role of Western education was important nevertheless, as it produced a critical public discourse conducive to its growth. If this education was designed to colonise the mind of the Indian intelligentsia and breed in them a sense of loyalty, the latter also selectively appropriated and manipulated that knowledge of domination to craft their own critique of colonialism. But this critical consciousness was unevenly shared by groups of Indians, as education itself had an extremely uneven growth. Higher education began to grow rapidly in India after universities were established in the three presidencies in 1857 and education became a free enterprise in 1882. The number of students in arts and professional colleges grew fourfold, from 4,499 in 1874 to 18,571 in 1894.[69] The total number of students under instruction was a little over four million in 1896–97; the number more than doubled by 1920.[70] But this growth was highly uneven, and obviously it had a bearing on the uneven development of political consciousness in the various regions of India. The three coastal presidencies of Bengal, Bombay and Madras, as the available statistics suggest, witnessed wider expansion of education than the heart of north India then constituted into three provinces, i.e., the North-Western Provinces and Awadh, Punjab and the Central Provinces. Within the presidencies again, certain communities were more advanced than the others were. In Bengal, higher education was monopolised by the bhadralok belonging mainly to the three higher castes of Brahman, Kayastha and Baidya; in Bombay it remained mostly confined to Chitpavan Brahmans and the Parsis; in Madras, among the Tamil Brahmans and the Aiyangars. Again in Bengal, the Bengalees were far ahead of the Oriyas, Biharis and Assamese; in Bombay, the Marathi speaking regions were ahead of the Gujarati speaking areas and in Madras, the Tamil speaking areas surged ahead of the Telugu and Malayalam speaking regions. And in general, the Hindus were far ahead of the Muslims and among the Hindus, a significant proportion of the lower castes and untouchables remained excluded from education. Those who went for higher education were coming from the middle or declining gentry whose income from land was dwindling, forcing them to look for subsidiary sources of income. For them government employment was the obvious choice; but in this sector, where the domination of the Europeans and Eurasians was quite palpable, Indians were confined only to subordinate positions and were poorly paid. Independent professions, like teaching, engineering, medicine and above all the legal profession became their next desirable option; but here too supply soon outstripped demand.

The situation described above undoubtedly created frustration and as Anil Seal argued, engendered a spirit of "increasing competitiveness" between various groups and regions.[71] But nationalism did not grow out of material frustration alone, and to say that competition forestalled unity is to simplify a much more complex scenario. Obviously, the differential growth of education impacted on the level of political activities in different regions, i.e., the presidencies with higher level of education were politically more articulate than the provinces. But this happened because western education here exposed many more students to a variety of ideological influences that helped create a critical discourse that held the colonial state under stringent scrutiny. If English education was introduced initially to inculcate a spirit of loyalty (see chapter 3.1),[72] it also exposed Indians, to quote A.R. Desai, to the "rationalist and democratic thought(s) of the modern west".[73] These ideas came to constitute an ideological package, which Dipesh Chakrabarty has called "political modernity", consisting of such concepts as "citizenship, the state, civil society, public sphere, human rights, equality before the law, the individual, distinctions between public and private, the idea of the subject, democracy, popular sovereignty, social justice, scientific rationality, and so on."[74] Not that the colonial regime offered all these to its subjects; but they were projected as ideal milestones on the road towards progress. The educated Indians now deployed these same ideas to construct their own critique of an autocratic and arrogant colonial state, and mixed with an emotional patriotic belief in the superiority of Indian culture and civilisation, this helped them to formulate conscious theories of nationalism. The *Hindoo Patriot* in June 1857 described the Indian as "strong enough . . . in mind and knowledge to assert his right of citizenship."[75] In July 1878 the

Indian Mirror averred more firmly that "We fight for our rights in India". In September that year a public meeting in Calcutta was even more explicit; its resolution put forth in no uncertain words "the claims of the people of this country to the rights of British citizenship".[76] The Indian patriots of the late nineteenth century were not questioning the imperial connection. But Her Majesty's loyal subjects were also gradually turning into conscious citizens, demanding their rights from an authoritarian colonial state. A rapidly growing print culture circulated such ideas across the subcontinent; by 1875 there were about four hundred Indian owned newspapers, published in both English and the regional languages, with an estimated readership of 150,000. These newspapers, as S.R. Mehrotra writes, "broke down internal barriers and encouraged inter-regional solidarity".[77]

In the second half of the nineteenth century, the educated Indians had many reasons to be concerned about their rights being trampled by the colonial state. It started with the continuing threats of Christian conversion, encouraged by the passage of the Lex Loci Act in 1850, protecting the right of a convert to inherit ancestral property. But more importantly, when in the 1860s and 1870s various parts of India were experiencing a series of natural calamities and outbreak of famines, the Government imposed an income tax in 1860, without giving Indians any control over the expenditure of this revenue income. The Indian Councils Act of 1861 had provided for the inclusion of a very limited number of non-official Indian members in the governor general's council; but they could not introduce any bill without the prior sanction of the governor general, who also had, over and above this, the all important power of veto. The income tax under strong nationwide protests was withdrawn in 1865, to be surreptitiously reimposed again in 1867 in the guise of a "certificate tax" of 1 per cent on all trades and professions. The next year, it was converted again into a full-fledged income tax, and the rates went on increasing to reach $3^1/_8$ per cent in 1870. The same year another colonial policy incensed the educated Indians, particularly in Bengal. As the Anglo-Indian press started a propaganda that higher education only bred discontent and disaffection, the government in a resolution on 31 March 1870 proposed to cut back funding for English education in Bengal, allegedly to rechannel funding to promote mass education through vernaculars. The educated Indians were dismayed to find that increased taxation and fund cuts for higher education came at a time when the government continued to spend excessively on army, the "home charges" and other public works serving the imperial needs.

The municipal reforms of the 1870s introducing limited principles of election were a concession to the educated Indians. But this was soon counterbalanced when in 1876 the maximum age for sitting the Indian Civil Service examination was lowered from 21 to 19 to the disadvantage of the Indians; their older demand for a simultaneous examination in London and India still remained unfulfilled. By far the most vicious attack on the educated Indians came from Lord Lytton who came to India as viceroy in 1876. He passed in 1878, against the advice of his own law member, the Vernacular Press Act, designed basically to gag the Indian press, which had become critical of the colonial policies. The act provided for a deposit from all printers and publishers of regional language newspapers, which was to be forfeited and their machinery confiscated if they published anything objectionable. The act at once became the target of a vehement countrywide agitation of the educated Indians and their various associations, and they found an unexpected patron in Gladstone who raised a furore in the British parliament. The same year, i.e., in 1878, Lytton also passed a new Arms Act, which introduced a licensing system throughout India for possessing firearms, but exempted the Europeans and Eurasians from its coverage. In an environment like this, the victory of the Liberal Party in Britain in 1880 brought great joy and expectations among the Indians. Lytton resigned and a liberal Lord Ripon came to India as the new viceroy; but the conservative mindset of the colonial bureaucracy did not change.

Though Ripon proceeded cautiously, some of his early measures restored faith among the Indians in the liberal tradition of England. In 1882 the Vernacular Press Act was repealed and the Arms Act was modified to eliminate the undesirable racial exemptions. In a Resolution in May 1882, the liberal viceroy proposed to introduce local self-government in India; by the end of 1884, as S. Gopal has shown, "the mosaic of local self-government covered almost the whole of British India".[78] This happened despite persistent opposition of the Indian Civil Service and the India Council in London. But all hell was let loose when C.P. Ilbert, the law member in his council, introduced on 2 February 1883 what is known as the infamous Ilbert Bill. It proposed to give Indian district magistrates and session judges the power to try European offenders in the *mofussil* (small towns), as they already did in the presidency towns. The ugly face of Anglo-Indian racism now revealed itself in the "white mutiny" that followed, as the British born subjects shuddered at the very thought of being tried by a native Indian. The bill was bitterly opposed not just by the non-official Anglo-Indians, but also by a large section of the British officials, including Rivers Thompson, the Lieutenant Governor of Bengal, who reportedly condemned the bill for "ignoring race distinctions" in order to "establish equality" by "a stroke of pen".[79] The liberal promise of racial equality could not so easily be disavowed, as it was enshrined in Queen Victoria's Proclamation of 1858. The plea for the preservation of racial privileges was therefore coded in a gendered language. The "effeminate babu", it was argued, was not fit to preside over the trial of a "manly Englishman", nor could he be expected to honour the dignity of white women, as they did not respect women in their own household.[80] The controversy made it crystal clear to educated Indians that racial equality was something, which they could not expect from the present regime. This became more evident when in January 1884 Ripon ultimately succumbed to the pressure and withdrew the bill, substituting it with a milder compromise formula, which somehow sought to preserve the principle by adding a provision of trial by a mixed jury in such cases involving European offenders.

The Ilbert bill controversy was the last straw that politically conscious educated Indians could take, as it made them painfully aware of their subordinate position in the imperial power structure. The counter demonstrations, which they staged, and the press propaganda war that raged on this occasion constitute an important benchmark in the history of the evolution of modern political activities in India. But in the meanwhile, another major change in the organised political life of India had started taking place: the older associations controlled by a landed plutocracy were being gradually replaced by new associations dominated by middle-class professionals. In Calcutta, the British Indian Association controlled by the zamindari elements, came to be looked at as an exclusive body torn by internecine strife. It came increasingly under challenge from the new educated professional classes, which ultimately formed on 26 July 1876 a new organisation, called the Indian Association, under the leadership of Surendranath Banerjea, with the avowed ambition of "representing the people". In Bombay, the Bombay Association had a new lease of life when in 1876 Naoroji Ferdunji and Dadabhai Naoroji returned from London and gave new life to the dying organisation. But it too faced challenge from a younger generation of Western-educated leaders like M.G. Ranade, P.M. Mehta and K.T. Telang and from the establishment of rival associations, such as the short lived Western Indian Association. Its major challenge, however, came from Poona, the traditional capital of Maratha culture and a centre of old patriotism. It was here that on 2 April 1870 a new organisation, called the Poona Sarvajanik Sabha, was established to represent the wishes of the people and within one year its members collected signed *muktiyarnamahs* or power of attorneys from seventeen thousand people giving it a true representative character. By contrast, in Madras, political activities remained at a low ebb after the demise of the Madras Native Association in 1862. It was only after 1884, i.e., after an interval of more than two decades, that political life in this presidency again started vibrating with the foundation of the Madras Mahajan Sabha. Outside the presidencies too, organised political life revolved round the new associations, like the Lahore Indian Association in Punjab or the Allahabad Peoples' Association in the United Provinces.[81]

It should be remembered, however, that the sprouting of new associations did not automatically mean the demise of the older forms of politics; the two idioms of politics, the modern and the traditional, coexisted side by side for a much longer period. The older ways survived in various forms, in Bengal for example, as S.N. Mukherjee (1971) has shown, it did in the form of *dals,* which were dominated by absentee landlords or *dalapatis* (leaders of the dals). They presided over informal but effective social networks spanning from Calcutta to the countryside, acting as an apparatus of social control. The dals took position in support of or in opposition to various public issues; any strict line between the conservatives and progressives or between the modern and the traditional became difficult to draw. The same Raja Radhakanta Deb and his Dharma Sabha, who were so vehemently opposed to the abolition of sati, supported with enthusiasm the spread of female education. This dal system continued with varied degrees of effectiveness till about the end of the nineteenth century. Then, as John McGuire has noted, capitalist development gradually weakened its social bonds and its control mechanism. "Yet this process of disintegration was long and complex".[82] And Bengal was no exception in witnessing this dichotomy; in the United Provinces too social impulses were channeled through the older "Caste and communal associations" which became platforms for the ventilation of the grievances of a wide variety of people. The older organisations in a new colonial context acquired new importance, as they had to confront "a more intrusive and supposedly representative government" In the towns, therefore, as C.A. Bayly has found, "the old connections and the new organizations:" came to be "more closely bunched together".[83]

The newness of this politics of the second half of the nineteenth century, however, lay in the new demands that were being raised.

These were sometimes of a local or regional character; but most often they were of national significance. The new associations demanded, among other things, Indian representation in the legislative council, separation of the executive and judicial functions of the government, Indianisation of the civil service, and for that purpose simultaneous Indian Civil Service examination in India and England, imposition of import duties on cotton goods, reduction of expenditure on 'home charges' and costly foreign wars, like the Afghan wars of 1878–79, rationalisation of the financial relations between India and England, and the extension of the Permanent Settlement to other parts of British India. They also protested against the imposition of income tax, the draconian Vernacular Press Act and the racist Arms Act. Apart from raising such public issues, which concerned all Indians across the regions, these associations also took interest in the affairs of the peasantry. Their involvement in the indigo riots in Bengal, in the Deccan riots in Poona and in the protests against water tax in the Chenab Canal Colony in Punjab has already been mentioned. Some of these organisations, like the Poona Sarvajanik Sabha, were involved in a variety of social work among the peasantry, like mobilising famine relief or organising arbitration courts. Through such mediation, the Indian peasants, so far locked away in their localised existence, were being gradually connected to a wider national contest with colonial rule. These associations were, of course, not overtly anti-British, as many of them sent messages of loyalty to Queen Victoria on the occasion of the Delhi Durbar. They were fighting for limited reforms, but nevertheless, they exhibited a new public awareness. They were demanding equality and representative government—above all, a share in the administration of their own country—and this is where the new politics differed from the earlier phase of landlord-dominated politics.

But the educated professional leadership of this new politics also suffered from a few dilemmas, which originated from the social composition of this class. As observed earlier, they came mostly from the priestly and literary castes, who previously held a monopoly control over proprietary right in land. In a way, English education and new professions provided for the extension of the sphere of dominance for essentially the same dominant classes; it was only in Bombay that we witness the emergence of a commercial bourgeoisie. So the professionals in most parts of the country retained a connection with land and therefore also fought for landlord interests. This was revealed in the united Indian opposition to the Bengal

Tenancy Bill in 1885, which proposed to protect the occupancy rights of the peasants and to restrict the right of the landlord to raise rent arbitrarily; the bill was passed by official majority. These hard to conceal dilemmas evoked mixed reactions from the British. The colonial government in the late nineteenth century recognised the political importance of the new educated class. Particularly, liberal viceroys like Lord Ripon realised that it was essential to provide a fair field for their legitimate aspirations and ambitions and convert them into friends of the Raj. But his more conservative successor Lord Dufferin took a different view and contemptuously called them "babu" politicians, representing only a "microscopic minority". After the Indian Councils Act of 1892, which introduced in a limited form the principle of election to constitute the legislative councils, the new professional class in terms of political prominence superseded the landed aristocracy; but they could never completely ignore the landed magnates. The colonial state, therefore, could confidently claim itself to be the real champion of the interests of the masses.

The limitations and contradictions of early nationalism were visible in other areas too, as many of these high-caste Hindu leaders could not totally overcome their social conservatism. Their attempts to construct a nationalist ideology premised on the notion of a golden Hindu past instantly inspired a wide range of people; but this also alienated some others. The social debates brought in a schism in the Poona Sarvajanik Sabha between the two leaders and their followers—the more conservative B.G. Tilak on the one hand and the liberal reformist G.K. Gokhale on the other. The controversy over the Age of Consent Act (1891), which proposed to raise the age for the consummation of marriage for women from ten to twelve, centred around the argument that the British had no right to interfere in Hindu social and religious life (more in chapter 5.2). Indian nationalism thus came to be associated with the defence of Hindu religion against foreign interference and the patriotic literature both in Bengali and Marathi started defining Indian nationalism in terms of Hindu imageries. These developments certainly alienated the Muslims from this stream of nationalism, as a new consciousness was developing among them as well. They too were defining their own self-interests in opposition to those of the Hindus and colonial policies further encouraged such Hindu-Muslim schism. As the Arya Samaj started the cow protection movement, this communal conflict began to acquire a mass dimension. Large-scale communal riots rocked northern India from the 1870s, constituting certainly a new phenomenon in Indian history. The eighteenth century concept of Hindustan being equally shared by the Hindus and Muslims alike, was gradually receding in the face of an emerging communal exclusivism in the nineteenth, paving the way for a violent contest for territory in the twentieth (more details in chapter 5.2).

This communal estrangement in north Indian society had another important dimension. The Brahmans and the other high-caste Hindus, who dominated new education, professions, and new associations, did not do anything to enlist the support of the lower castes and the untouchables. Yet, despite this apathy and indifference, there were unmistakable signs of enlightenment and social awakening among these lower castes, resulting from colonial educational policies, Christian missionary philanthropy as well as their own initiative. This inspired them to construct alternative political ideologies based on anti-Brahman sentiments, around which powerful movements were organised by the untouchables and the non-Brahman castes in Maharashtra and Madras, aiming primarily at their own advancement. They looked at the emerging nationalist movement as a conspiracy to establish Brahmanic hegemony over the new colonial institutions and viewed colonial government as their patron and liberator (more details in chapter 7.2). Thus, the political project of imagining an Indian nation from the top had to confront from the very beginning the difficult issue of diversity and difference. The administration obviously took advantage of such contradictions in colonial society and further encouraged them in order to create more impediments for the budding Indian nationalists who, in spite of all their weaknesses and limitations, were raising some unpleasant questions for the Raj. It was in this context that Indian National Congress was born in 1885 and during the subsequent years it dominated Indian nationalist movement, trying with mixed successes to resolve these contradictions.

4.4. FOUNDATION OF THE INDIAN NATIONAL CONGRESS

The Indian National Congress, which was destined to play a dominant role in India's struggle for independence, was formed at a national convention held in Bombay in December 1885, under the presidency of W.C. Bonnerji. A retired British civil servant A.O. Hume was crucially involved in this process, as it was he who toured across the subcontinent, talked to prominent political leaders in Bombay, Madras and Calcutta and persuaded them to meet at a national conference that was initially supposed to meet at Poona.

The outbreak of cholera deprived the Marathi town of this privilege, which was now passed on to the more cosmopolitan colonial city of Bombay. But whatever might have been the historic significance of this first meeting, Hume's involvement in it gave rise to a lot of controversy regarding the origins of Congress. The safety-valve theory or the conspiracy theory, which was deduced from this simple fact, was for a long time subscribed to by all shades of historians, in the right, left and centre. It was even accepted by some of the stalwarts of nationalist movement. In recent researches, however, it has been thoroughly discredited.

The theory originated from William Wedderburn's biography of Hume published in 1913. Wedderburn, another ex-civil servant, wrote that in 1878 Hume had come across seven volumes of secret reports which showed that there had been seething discontent among the lower classes and a conspiracy to overthrow British rule by force. He became disturbed, met Lord Dufferin and together they decided to establish an organisation with educated Indians. This would serve as a safety valve by opening up a line of communication between the rulers and the ruled and would thus prevent a mass revolution. The Congress was in this way the creation of British rule. This safety-valve theory was believed by the earlier nationalist historians; the imperialist historians used it to discredit Congress and the Marxist historians developed a conspiracy theory from this. R.P. Dutt, for example, wrote that Congress was born through a conspiracy to forestall a popular uprising in India and the Indian bourgeois leaders were a party to it. In the 1950s these safety valve or conspiracy theories were proved to be wrong. First of all, those seven volumes of secret reports have not been traced in any of the archives either in India or London. Historians argue that given the structure of British information system in the 1870s, it was highly unlikely that so many volumes of secret reports could have existed. Except in Wedderburn's biography of Hume, nowhere else any reference to the existence of such reports could be found, and he too mentioned that they were supplied to Hume by religious gurus, and were not procured from any official sources. Then the opening up of Lord Dufferin's private papers in the late 1950s cleared up the confusion by exploding the myth of Dufferin's sponsorship of the Congress or Hume. He had indeed met Hume in Simla in May 1885, but did not take him seriously and then gave definite orders to the Governor of Bombay to be cautious about the delegates who were going to meet in his city. Both he and Lord Reay, the governor of Bombay were suspicious and disapproved of the proposed meeting, as they thought that they were going to start in India something like a Irish Home Rule League movement. Soon after the formation of the Congress, Dufferin was openly castigating Congress for its dubious motives. In 1888, he criticised it for representing a "microscopic minority" and this statement, if not anything else, explodes the safety valve or conspiracy theory. Historians now more or less agree that the story of seven volumes of secret report was a fiction created by a friendly biographer Wedderburn to portray Hume as a British patriot who wanted to save the British empire from an impending crisis. So, as Bipan Chandra comments, "it is high time that the safety-valve theory ... was confined to the care of the *mahatmas* from whom perhaps it originated!"[84]

The fact that Hume played a crucial role in the foundation of the Congress, however, remains, although this role might have been grossly exaggerated in the safety valve or conspiracy theories. In reality, Hume was a political liberal, who certainly had a clear idea about growing discontent among the Indians. Therefore, he visualised an all India organisation, which would represent Indian interests and would act as something like Her Majesty's Opposition. He got in touch with Viceroy Lord Ripon and offered his full support for his liberal reform programme, particularly his plan of introducing local self-government, which he knew his conservative colleagues would try to derail to their own peril. After Ripon's departure, he embarked upon a project of linking up his wide contacts among the educated Indians in order to bring them into a national organisation as a legitimate forum for venting their grievances. But even if Hume had not taken any initiative, in India of the 1870s and 1880s the formation of a national organisation was clearly in the air.

As we have seen already, groups of educated Indians were politically active in the three presidencies and they had established new associations which had begun to fight for civil liberties and organised countrywide agitations on various national issues. Protests against missionary interventions and against the Lex Loci Act of 1850 were voiced from different parts of India simultaneously. In 1867 there was a nationwide agitation against the proposed income tax and in support of a demand for balanced budget. Then in 1877–80 a massive campaign was organised around the demand for Indianisation of the civil services and against Lord Lytton's expensive Afghan adventures, the cost of which had to be met from Indian revenues. The Indian press and associations also organised an orchestrated campaign against the notorious Vernacular Press Act of 1878. In 1881–82 they organised a protest against Plantation Labour and Inland Emigration Act, which condemned the plantation labourers to serfdom. Finally, a major nation-wide agitation was launched again in 1883 in favour of the Ilbert Bill, which had shaken the educated Indians' faith in the righteousness of British rule. In 1885 there was an all-India effort to raise a National Fund, which would be used to promote political agitation in India and England. The same year, the Indians fought for the right to join the volunteer corps so long restricted to Europeans alone and then organised an appeal to British voters to vote for those candidates who were friendly towards India. The main initiative for organising such agitations came from the presidency associations, the Indian Association being the most articulate of them all. But they were not confined to the presidency towns alone. The other provincial towns, like Lahore, Amritsar, Meerut, Kanpur, Aligarh, Poona, Ahmedabad, Surat, Patna or Cuttack, were equally affected by agitations that were launched on what clearly appeared to be some national issues. Western education and English language had formed a bond between these regional elites, while a community of suffering remained conducive to the germination of a new political consciousness across the regional barriers.

All these demands raised by the associations remained unfulfilled and this all the more convinced the regional leaders about the need for an all-India organisation. While informal contacts between leaders from various cities were not lacking in any period, attempts to establish a formal forum were also made a number of times. The earliest of such endeavours to forge all-India links was in 1851 when the British India Association of Calcutta tried to open branches in other two presidencies with a view to send a joint petition to British parliament on the eve of the renewal of the Company's Charter. Again on the occasion of the Delhi Durbar in 1877, the Indian journalists who were invited to this extravaganza took the opportunity to form a Native Press Association. They elected S.N. Banerjea, the leader of the Indian Association and the editor of *Bengalee*, as its first secretary and resolved to meet once or twice every year to discuss issues related to press and the country. The Indian Association organised a national conference in Calcutta in 1883 and another was scheduled in December 1885. Again in Madras in 1884, through the private initiative of a member of the Theosophical Society, delegates from different parts of India met on the sideline of the society's annual convention, to discuss the necessity of a national organisation. So the emergence of a national body was clearly on the cards, although mutual jealousies that thwarted such attempts in 1851 had not been completely removed either. There was still the need for a mediator who could bring all these regional leaders together under one organisational umbrella. Hume was ideally suited for this role, as his supra-regional identity made him acceptable to all the regional leaders. He was also acceptable for his known liberal political opinions.

The Indian National Congress, which was thus born in December 1885, tried from the very beginning to eliminate such regional differences. The first Congress declared that one of its major objectives would be the "development and consolidation of those sentiments of national unity". The decision to hold the Congress session every year in different parts of the country and to choose the president from a region other than the one where the session was being held, was meant to break the regional barriers and misunderstandings. In 1888 it was decided that no resolution would be passed if it was objected to by an overwhelming majority of Hindu or Muslim delegates; a minority clause figured prominently in a resolution adopted in 1889 demanding reform of the legislative councils. The avowed objective of all these endeavours was to create a forum through which the politically conscious people of different regions of India could unite. It was meant to be organised in the way of a parliament and the sessions were conducted democratically.[85] It represented, in a true sense of the term, the modern politics in India and obviously therefore, it signalled the coming of a new trend in Indian public life.

At the same time, the Congress from the very beginning suffered from some important weaknesses, the most significant of them being uneven representation and total exclusion of the non-elite groups of Indian society. The composition of the delegates at the first Congress reflected almost accurately the changing patterns of organised political life in India, the Western educated professional groups gradually taking the lead over the landed aristocrats. Geographically, within the overall ascendancy of the presidencies, Bengal was gradually slipping from its leadership position, which was being taken over by Bombay, surging ahead of all other regions. The first meeting of the Indian National Congress in 1885 was attended by seventy-two non-official Indian representatives and they included people apparently from various walks of life, or belonging to "most classes", as claimed by the official report of the Congress. There were lawyers, merchants and bankers, landowners, medical men, journalists, educationists, religious teachers and reformers. If we look at their regional distribution, thirty-eight came from Bombay

Presidency, twenty-one from Madras, but only four from Bengal, as the Indian Association had convened its own national conference in Calcutta almost at the same time and the Bengal leaders were told of the Bombay conference only at the very last moment. Apart from the presidencies, seven representatives came from the four principal towns of North-Western Provinces and Awadh and one each from the three towns of Punjab.[86] It was in other words, despite lofty claims, a gathering of professionals, some landlords and businessmen, representing primarily the three presidencies of British India. In their social composition too, the members of the early Congress belonged predominantly to the high caste Hindu communities and this pattern continued unchanged for more than two decades of its existence.[87] This limitation of participation did not fluster the members of the Congress, as they complacently claimed to represent the whole nation; but it obviously put some constraints on their programmes, which we will discuss in greater detail in the next chapter.

In its political behaviour, quite expectedly, the Indian National Congress in its early career was never a radical organisation, as the culture of open opposition to the government had not yet taken roots. So they were cautious reformers seeking to alleviate certain unpleasant aspects of what Surendranath Banerjea described as the "un-British rule" in India and their method was sending prayers, petitions and memoranda. W.C. Bonnerji, the president of the first Congress, made it clear at the very outset that it was not "a nest of conspirators and disloyalists"; they were "thoroughly loyal and consistent well-wishers of the British Government".[88] This explains why the founders of the Congress had to involve A.O. Hume in their project. His association would assuage official suspicion and this was crucial, as Gokhale, another stalwart of the early Congress, wrote in 1913, any attempt by the Indians to form an all India organisation would immediately attract the unfriendly attention of the authorities. "If the founder of the Congress had not been a great Englishman", he wrote, "the authorities would have at once found some way or the other to suppress the movement". Thus, to use Bipan Chandra's analogy, "if Hume and other English liberals hoped to use Congress as a safety-valve, the Congress leaders hoped to use Hume as a lightning conductor".[89] In this way the Congress movement started in India as a limited elitist politics for limited reforms. But nevertheless, it represented a new and modern trend in Indian political tradition. Despite its limitations, it sought to forge an overarching national unity and raised a very important political demand: "the basis of the government should be widened and the people should have their proper and legitimate share in it".[90] It was from here that the mainstream of Indian nationalist politics began to flow. Given its limitations and inherent contradictions, it was bound to face contestation, which we will discuss in due course.

NOTES

1. Duara 1995: 4.
2. Chatterjee 1986: 42.
3. Nandy 1994a: 3–4 and passim; also 1998.
4. Ray 1980: 16–26; as examples of this school of thought, see Rudolph and Rudolph 1967, Broomfield 1968, Low 1968, Irschik 1969, Rothermund 1970, Dobbin 1972, Gordon 1974.
5. See for example, Gallaghar, Johnson and Seal 1973, Johnson 1973, Bayly 1975, Baker and Washbrook 1975, Washbrook 1976.
6. Seal 1973.
7. Raychaudhuri 1979.
8. Mukherjee 1996: 104–19.
9. Sarkar 1973.
10. Sarkar 1983: 11.
11. Chandra et al. 1989: 22–30.
12. Guha 1982: 1–3, emphasis in original.
13. Guha 1992.
14. Sarkar 1997.
15. Chakrabarty 1998: 475.
16. Chatterjee 1986: 43, 50–51.
17. Chatterjee 1993: 6–7, 13 and passim.
18. Prakash 1999: 202.
19. Ibid: 202, 212 and passim.
20. See, for example, Visweswaran 1997: 84–85 and passim.
21. See, for example, Aloysius 1997: 2 and passim.
22. Loomba 1998: 207.
23. Quoted in Oommen 2000: 3.
24. Bose and Jalal 1998: 10.
25. Bhabha 1990: 5.
26. Kumar 1968: 175–76.
27. Guha 1993: 64–65, 74–76.
28. Kling 1966.
29. Guha 1993:73–77.
30. Hardiman 1993: 17–18.
31. Chaudhuri 1967.
32. Sengupta 1974.
33. Sengupta 1979.
34. Hardiman 1993: 23– 26.
35. Hardiman 1996: 219, italics in original.
36. Kumar 1968: 151 and passim.

37. Charlesworth 1972: 408.
38. Hardiman 1993: 34.
39. Hardiman 1993: 37–38.
40. Ibid: 40–44.
41. Barrier 1993: 251.
42. Hardiman 1993: 46.
43. Ranajit Guha 1994: 292.
44. Singh 1983: 199, 201.
45. Bhattacharya 1992: 127–28.
46. Gadgil and Guha 1993.
47. Arnold 1986b: 133.
48. Gadgil and Guha 1993.
49. Dasgupta 1994.
50. Guha 1991.
51. Guha 1999.
52. For details, see Skaria 1999.
53. Bhattacharya 1992.
54. Quoted in Skaria 1999: 272.
55. Chatterjee 1984a.
56. Guha 1994: 4.
57. Hardiman 1993: 50, 52.
58. Chatterjee 1993: 5–7.
59. Bayly 1998: 79.
60. Metcalf 1964: 323–24.
61. Cohn 1994: 180,189.
62. Quoted in Mehrotra 1971: 61.
63. Ibid: 76–78.
64. Quoted in Bandyopadhyay 1997b: 23.
65. Sarkar 1981.
66. Quoted in Sarkar 1985: 31.
67. Chatterjee 1993: 6.
68. Dalmia 1997: 15.
69. Misra 1978: 302.
70. Basu 1974: 100.
71. Seal 1968: 25.
72. For this argument, see Viswanathan (1989)
73. Desai 1959: 144.
74. Chakrabarty 2000: 4.
75. Quoted in Bandyopadhyay 1997b: 26.
76. Quoted in Mehrotra 1971: 290–91.
77. Ibid: 110–11, 281.
78. Gopal 1953: 110.
79. Quoted in Ray 1984: 26.
80. For more on this, see Sinha 1995: 33–63.
81. See Mehrotra 1971 for details.
82. McGuire 1983: 35.

83. Bayly 1975: 14–15, 17.
84. Chandra, et al. 1989: 70 and passim for details on this.
85. Ibid: 74–75.
86. Mehrotra 1971: 412.
87. Ghosh 1960: 24–26.
88. Quoted in Mehrotra 1971: 413.
89. Chandra, et al. 1989: 81.
90. Quoted in Mehrotra 1971: 413.

chapter five

Early Nationalism: Discontent and Dissension

5.1. The Moderates and Economic Nationalism

Congress politics during the first twenty years of its history is roughly referred to as moderate politics. Congress at that time was hardly a full-fledged political party; it was more in the nature of an annual conference, which deliberated and adopted resolutions during the "three day *tamashas*" and then dispersed. Its members were mostly part-time politicians, who were successful professionals in their personal lives—a thoroughly Anglicised upper class who had very little time and commitment for full-time politics. There had been some distinct phases in moderate politics, but on the whole, there was an overall uniformity in their objectives and methods of agitation. The moderates were primarily influenced by Utilitarian theories, as Edmund Burke, John Stuart Mill and John Morley had left a mark on their thoughts and actions. The government should be guided by expediency, they believed, and not by any moral or ethical laws. And the constitution was to be considered inviolable and hence repeatedly they appealed to the British parliament complaining about the Government of India subverting the constitution. They did not demand equality, which seemed to be a rather abstract idea; they equated liberty with class privilege and wanted gradual or piecemeal reforms. British rule to most of them seemed to be an act of providence destined to bring in modernisation. Indians needed some time to prepare themselves for self-government; in the meanwhile, absolute faith could be placed in British parliament and the people. Their complaint was only against "un-British rule" in India perpetrated by the viceroy, his executive council and the Anglo-Indian bureaucracy—an imperfection that could be reformed or rectified through gentle persuasion. Their politics, in other words, was very limited in terms of goals and methods. They were secular in their attitudes, though not always forthright enough to rise above their sectarian interests. They were conscious of the exploitative nature of British rule, but wanted its reform, not expulsion. As Dadabhai Naoroji, one of the early stalwarts of this politics, put it in 1871: "In my belief a greater calamity would not befall India than for England to go away and leave her to herself."[1]

Therefore, within the constitutional field, the moderate politicians never visualised a clinical separation from the British empire; what they wanted was only limited self-government within the imperial framework. They wanted first of all the abolition of the India Council which prevented the secretary of state from initiating liberal policies in India. They also wanted to broaden Indian participation in legislatures through an expansion of the central and provincial legislatures by introducing 50 per cent elected representation from local bodies, chambers of commerce, universities etc. They also wanted new councils for North-Western Provinces and Punjab and two Indian members in the Viceroy's Executive Council and one such member in each of the executive councils of Bombay and Madras. The budget should be referred to the legislature, which should have the right to discuss and vote on it and also the right of interpellation. There should also be a right to appeal to the Standing Committee of the House of Commons against the Government of India. Thus their immediate demand was not for full self-government or democracy; they demanded democratic rights only for the educated members of the Indian society who would substitute for the masses.

The expectation of the moderate politicians was that full political freedom would come gradually and India would be ultimately given the self-governing right like those enjoyed by the other colonies as Canada or Australia. With an intrinsic faith in the providential nature of British rule in India, they hoped that one day they would be recognised as partners and not subordinates in the affairs of the empire and be given the rights of full British citizenship. What they received in return, however, was Lord Cross's Act or the Indian Councils Amendment Act of 1892, which only provided for marginal expansion of the legislative councils both at the centre and the provinces. These councils were actually to be constituted through selection rather than election: the local bodies would send their nominees from among whom the viceroy at the centre and the governors at the provinces would select the members of the legislative councils. The budget was to be discussed in the legislatures, but not to be voted on. The opposition could not bring in any resolution, nor demand a vote on any resolution proposed by the government. The Government of India was given the power to legislate without even referring to the legislatures, whose functions would be at best recommendatory and not mandatory. Very few of the constitutional demands of the moderates, it seems, were fulfilled by this act.[2]

So far as the reformation of the administrative system was concerned, the first demand of the moderates was for the Indianisation of the services. An Indianised civil service would be more responsive to the Indian needs, they argued. It would stop the drainage of money, which was annually expatriated through the payment of salary and pension of the European officers. More significantly, this reform was being advocated as a measure against racism. What they demanded actually were simultaneous civil service examination both in India and London and the raising of the age limit for appearing in such examinations from nineteen to twenty-three. But Charles Wood, the president of the Board of Control, opposed it on the ground that there was no institution in India, which could train the boys for the examination. The Public Service Commission, appointed under Charles Aitchison, recommended the raising of the maximum age, but not simultaneous examination. In 1892–93 under the initiative of William Gladstone, the House of Commons passed a resolution for simultaneous examination, though the secretary of state was still opposed to it. But at the same time the maximum age for examination was further lowered to the disadvantage of the Indians. Soon Gladstone was replaced by Lord Salisbury and the whole matter was buried there (see chapter 2.3 for more details).

Another sore point in this area was the military expenditure. The British Indian army was being used in imperial wars in all parts of the world, particularly in Africa and Asia. These and the Indian frontier wars of the 1890s put a very heavy burden on the Indian finances. The moderates demanded that this military expenditure should be evenly shared by the British government; Indians should be taken into the army as volunteers; and more and more of them should be appointed in higher ranks. All of these demands were however rejected. Commander-in-chief Roberts abhorred the idea of volunteer service, as he feared that the Maratha and Bengali volunteers, disaffected and untrustworthy as they were because of their association with nationalism, would surely find their way into the army and subvert its integrity. Similarly, the demand for appointing Indians in commissioned ranks was rejected, as no European officer would cherish the thought of being ordered by an Indian commander. The British government agreed to share only a small fraction of the military expenditure, less than £1 million in all. The higher exchange rates reduced the amount even further, and so the burden on the Indian finances remained the same. The other administrative demands of the moderates included the extension of trial by jury, repeal of the arms act, complaint against over-assessment of land revenue and demand for the extension of the Permanent Settlement, demand for the abolition of salt tax and a campaign against the exploitation of the indentured labour at the Assam tea gardens. All these demands represented a plea for racial equality and a concern for civil rights and also perhaps reflected a concern for the lower orders, though of a very limited nature. But it is needless to mention that none of the demands were even considered by the colonial administration.

However, despite all these setbacks, the most significant historical contribution of the moderates was that they offered an economic critique of colonialism. This economic nationalism,[3] as it is often referred to, became a major theme that developed further during the subsequent period of the nationalist movement and to a large extent influenced the economic policies of the Congress government in independent India. Three names are important to remember in this respect: Dadabhai Naoroji, a successful businessman, Justice M.G. Ranade and R.C. Dutt, a retired ICS officer, who published *The Economic History of India* in two volumes (1901–3). The main thrust of this economic nationalism was on Indian poverty created by the application of the classical economic theory of free trade. Their main argument was that British colonialism had transformed itself in the nineteenth century by jettisoning the older and direct modes of extraction through plunder, tribute and mercantilism, in favour of more sophisticated and less visible methods of exploitation through free trade and foreign capital investment. This turned India into a supplier of agricultural raw materials and foodstuffs to and a consumer of manufactured goods from the mother country. India was thus reduced to the status of a dependent agrarian economy and a field for British capital investment. The key to India's development was industrialisation with Indian capital, while investment of foreign capital meant drainage of wealth through expatriation of profit. This "drain theory" was in fact the key theme of this economic nationalism. It was argued that direct drainage of wealth took place through the payment of home charges, military charges, and guaranteed interest payment on railway investments. The burden became heavier because of the falling exchange rates of rupee in the 1890s and was compounded by budget deficits, higher taxes, and military expenditure. In Naoroji's calculation this huge drainage amounted to about £12 million per year, while William Digby calculated it to be £30 million. In average, this amounted to at least half of the total revenue income of the British Indian government. This directly impoverished India and stultified the process of capital formation. High land revenue demands led to land alienation and impoverishment of the peasantry, while absence of protective tariff in the interest of the British manufacturers hindered Indian industrialisation and destroyed the handicraft industry. This led to overburdening of agriculture and further impoverishment; the cycle was completed in this way. Naoroji calculated the per capita income of the Indians to be Rs. 20, while Digby's calculation was Rs. 18 for 1899. The government did not accept this calculation: in 1882 Ripon's finance secretary calculated it to be Rs. 27, while Lord Curzon in 1901 calculated it to be Rs. 30. The famines and epidemics of this period however told a different story. To quote Dadabhai Naoroji again, "materially" British rule caused only "impoverishment"; it was like "the knife of sugar. That is to say there is no oppression, it is all smooth and sweet, but it is the knife, notwithstanding."[4]

So, to rectify this situation what the moderates wanted was a change in economic policies. Their recommendations included reduction of expenditure and taxes, a reallocation of military charges, a protectionist policy to protect Indian industries, reduction of land revenue assessment, extension of Permanent Settlement to ryotwari and mahalwari areas, and encouragement of cottage industries and handicrafts. But none of these demands were fulfilled. Income tax, abolished in the 1870s, was reimposed in 1886; the salt tax was raised from Rs. 2 to Rs. 2.5; a customs duty was imposed, but it was matched by a countervailing excise duty on Indian cotton yarn in 1894, which was reduced to 3.5 per cent in 1896. The Fowler Commission artificially fixed the exchange rate of rupee at a high rate of 1 shilling and 4 pence. There was no fundamental change in the agricultural sector either, as colonial experts like Alfred Lyall believed that Indian agriculture had already passed through its stationary stage and had entered the modern stage of growth and hence there were more signs of progress than recession. The moderate economic agenda, like its constitutional or administrative agenda, thus remained largely unrealised.

This nationalist economic theory may appear to be a contentious issue for economic historians (see chapter 2.5), but construction of this economic critique of colonialism at this historical juncture had its own political and ethical significance. This economic theory by linking Indian poverty to colonialism was trying to corrode the moral authority of colonial rule, and also perhaps by implication challenging the whole concept of paternalistic imperialism or British benevolence. In this way the moderate politicians generated anger against British rule, though because of their own weaknesses, they themselves could not convert it into an effective agitation for its overthrow. The moderate politicians could not or did not organise an agitation against British rule, because most of them still shared an intrinsic faith in the English democratic liberal political tradition. So their appeal was to the liberal political opinion in England; their method was to send prayers and petitions, to make speeches and publish articles. By using these tools of colonial modern public life they tried to prepare a convincing "logical case" aimed at persuading the liberal political opinion in England in favour of granting self-government to India, But this political strategy, which the more extremist elements in the Congress later described as the strategy of mendicancy, failed to achieve its goals. The failure of moderate politics was quite palpable by the end of the nineteenth century and their future was doomed as the less sympathetic Tories returned to power in Britain at the turn of the century. Nevertheless, the moderates created a political context within which such an agitation was to develop later on.

There were also other contradictions in moderate politics, which made it more limited and alienated from the greater mass of the Indian population. This was related to the social background of the moderate politicians who mostly belonged to the propertied classes. The first conference of the Indian National Congress in 1885 was attended by seventy-two non-official Indian representatives who included people belonging, as it was claimed, to "most classes", such as lawyers, merchants and bankers, landowners, medical men, journalists, educationists, religious teachers and reformers.[5] But despite the preponderance of the new professionals, the British Indian Association of the landowners maintained a cordial relationship with the Congress for the first few initial years and remained its major source of finance. About 18.99 per cent of the delegates who attended the Congress sessions between 1892 and 1909 were landlords; the rest were lawyers (39.32 per cent), traders (15.10 per cent), journalists (3.18 per cent), doctors (2.94 per cent), teachers (3.16 per cent) and other professionals (17.31 per cent). Among the lawyers again many were related to landlord families or had landed interests.[6] The Congress, therefore, could not dispense with landed aristocrats and could not consequently take a logical stand on peasant questions. They demanded extension of the Permanent Settlement only in the interest of the zamindars and opposed cadastral survey in 1893–94, though it was meant to protect the peasants from the manipulations of the zamindars and their intriguing amlas. The small pro-tenant lobby within the Congress led by R.C. Dutt was soon outmanoeuvred, as their opposition in 1898 to the pro-zamindar amendment to the Bengal Tenancy Act of 1885 put them in a difficult situation. Opposition to the Punjab Land Alienation Bill in 1899 also betrayed their pro-landlord sympathies. Representation of the commercial classes among its members also prevented Congress from taking a pro-working class position. They were opposed to factory reforms like the Mining Bill, which proposed to improve the living condition of women and children and restrict their employment under certain age. They also opposed similar labour reforms in Bombay on the plea that they were prompted by Lancashire interests. However, they supported labour reforms for Assam tea gardens, as capitalist interest involved there was of foreign origin,[7] happily forgetting that the Indian mill owners in Bombay exploited their labourers in no less flagrant ways. Finally, their advocacy of indigenous capitalism as a panacea for Indian poverty revealed their true colours. It was the pro-landlord and pro-bourgeois policies of the early Congress politicians that allowed the colonial government to project itself as the real protector of the poor.

These early moderate politicians were also mainly Hindus, barring the notable exception of the Bombay politician, Badruddin Tyabji. Between 1892 and 1909, nearly 90 per cent of the delegates who attended the Congress sessions were Hindus and only 6.5 per cent were Muslims and among the Hindus again nearly 40 per cent were Brahmans and the rest were upper-caste Hindus.[8] This social composition inevitably resulted in social orthodoxy, as social questions were not to be raised in the Congress sessions till 1907. More crucial however was the question of mobilising the Muslims, as the Congress demand for elected councils was not liked by prominent Muslim leaders like Sir Sayyid Ahmed Khan, who feared that this would mean Hindu majority rule—the dominance of the frail-bodied Bengalees—to the disadvantage of the Muslim minority.[9] In response to this, in its 1888 session, Congress passed a rule that no resolution would be accepted if an overwhelming majority of Hindu or Muslim delegates objected to it. In 1889 in its resolution demanding reform of legislatures, a clause was added recommending proportional representation of the minorities.[10] But these symbolic gestures did not remove the apprehension of the Muslims, while the crucial silence of the Congress during the cow-killing riots of 1893 added further to such misgivings. Congress was not directly involved in the cow-protection movement, nor did it sympathise with this cause; but by speaking against it, they felt, they might lose the support of the Hindu constituency. Its silence was misinterpreted—for legitimate reasons—as concurrence; and as John McLane has shown, Muslim participation in Congress sessions began to decline rather dramatically after 1893.[11] Yet there was no major Congress endeavour to bring the Muslims back into its fold. The Congress politicians suffered from a sense of complacency as no rival Muslim political organisation worth its name developed until 1906.

The moderate politics thus remained quite limited in nature, in terms of its goals, programmes, achievements and participation. Lord Dufferin, therefore, could easily get away with his remark at the St. Andrew's Day dinner at Calcutta in November 1888 that Congress represented only a "microscopic minority" of the Indian people. Yet, despite this limited representation, the historical significance of the early Congress lay in the fact that by providing an economic critique of colonialism and by linking Indian poverty to it, the moderate politicians had constructed a discursive field within which the subsequent nationalist attack on colonialism could be conceptualised. It was because of the failures of the moderate politics that an extremist reaction was soon to develop in Congress politics to lead to what is often referred to as the notorious Surat Split of 1907. The reunification of the Congress and the expansion of the political nation had to wait for the arrival of Gandhi and World War One.

5.2 Hindu Revivalism and Politics

Political extremism in the second half of the nineteenth century was not just a reaction to moderate failures; it drew its inspiration and ideology from a cultural and intellectual movement that developed simultaneously with and parallel to moderate politics of the Indian National Congress. The movement is vaguely referred to as "Hindu revivalism", which generally meant, despite the existence of various strands and contradictory tendencies, an attempt to define Indian nation primarily in terms of Hindu religious symbols, myths and history. Religion was never totally detached from politics in India, nor was it ever exclusively confined to private space. But so far as public discourses on religion were concerned, one has to make a distinction between two different trends within it, i.e., between reform and revival. The reform movements, in which a number of moderate politicians were involved, essentially attempted to bring changes in Hindu social organisation and practices from within to bring them into conformity with the new rationalist ideas of the West. The creation of the National Social Conference as an adjunct body to the National Congress in 1887 is an indication of this mentality. Although religion was kept deliberately out of its agenda, the issues it discussed and reforms it recommended to various provincial organisations had strong religious implications. These movements were both influenced by Western post-Enlightenment rationalist ideas and were also responses to the challenge of Westernising forces and their critiques of Hindu civilisation. It was this second aspect of reformism that eventually led to revivalism. For, to many Indians, reform—which was often backed by the colonial government—appeared to be an inadequate response or indeed a surrender to Western critics and imported rationalist ideas. Nationalism and reformism seemed to be contradictory ideas, as Charles Heimsath (1964) has argued, and this led to the growth of anti-reformism, based on a sense of pride in everything Indian. This is what is often referred to as revivalism, marked as it was by a conceptualisation of a glorious Hindu past, believed to have been degenerated under Muslim rule and threatened by the British. This glorification of Hindu civilisation over Islamic or Western often boiled down to attempts to exalt and rationalise Hindu institutions and practices, sometimes even to the point of offering articulate resistance to urgent social reforms. The late nineteenth century witnessed the gradual weakening of the reformist trend and the strengthening of such revivalist forces. But this revivalism was not just obscurantism, as it had a strong political overtone, dictated by the historical need of sculpting a modern Indian nation.

Among the reformist organisations the Brahmo Samaj in Bengal, which was more modernist in its approach, was weakened after the 1870s by internal dissent and divisions. This was followed by the emergence of the Ramakrishna-Vivekananda movement in the 1880s. While Brahmo Samaj's appeal was to intellect, that of Ramakrishna Paramahansa, the Brahman sage at Dakshineswar near Calcutta, was to the mind and emotions. Completely untouched by Western rationalist education, he offered simple interpretations of Hinduism, which became immensely popular among the Western-educated Bengalees, tormented by their subjection to the drudgery of clerical jobs in foreign mercantile or government offices. Ramakrishna's teachings offered the possibility of an escape into an inner world of bhakti, despite the binding disciplines of alien jobs. Thus, although in his teachings there is hardly any direct reference to colonial rule, there is however an open rejection of the values imposed by Western education and the routine life of a time-bound job or *chakri*.[12] The educated middle class in the nineteenth century often found the domain of reason to be oppressive, as it implied the historical necessity of the "civilising" colonial rule. Therefore, in the teachings of this uneducated saint at Dakshineswar, this subordinated middle class found the formulation of a new religion, which—to use Partha Chatterjee's phrases—"appropriated", "sanitized" and "classicized" the popular traditions into a national religious discourse.[13]

Ramakrishna was not a revivalist per se, for he inculcated a form of religious eclecticism, which did not however involve the preaching of an open and fluid syncretism. There are various ways to achieve god, he argued; but one must stick to one's own path in a world of fairly rigid divisions. Ramakrishna's catholicity therefore soon came to be projected as an essence of Hinduism and became for his disciple, Vivekananda, a ground for claiming the superiority of Hinduism over all other religions.[14] It was Vivekananda who infused into this discourse a missionary zeal. He condemned the other reform movements as elitist and invoked the ideal of social service. The best way to serve god, he emphasised, was to serve the poor people. He founded therefore the Ramakrishna Mission in 1897 as a philanthropic organisation. To describe him as a revivalist is to ignore the "universalistic" aspects of his teachings.[15] Nevertheless, the fact that he drew inspiration from the Vedantic tradition, followed some of the orthodox Hindu rituals, exhibited an intrinsic faith in the glories of Hindu civilisation and nurtured a belief that it had degenerated in recent times, made it possible for the revivalists to appropriate him. His evocation of Hindu glory mixed with patriotism, which sought to restore the masculinity of the Indian nation denied to them by their colonial masters, had a tremendous impact on the popular mind. His message was therefore misused and misinterpreted to give a revivalist slant to nationalism in Bengal. His evocation of the glories of a Hindu past was popularised, while his trenchant condemnation of the evils of Hinduism was conveniently forgotten. His philanthropic activities were hardly ever emulated; his criticism of the Brahmanical and gender oppression was scarcely ever taken seriously. But he became the "patron prophet" for a whole generation of extremist leaders and militant revolutionaries, dreaming the resurrection of a glorious Hindu India.

Gradually an intellectual tendency developed in Bengal that sought to legitimise any defence of Hindu traditions as a respectable and acceptable response to the challenge of Western civilisational critiques. At a more obscurantist level, Sasadhar Tarkachudamoni began to invent precedents in ancient India for every modern scientific discovery of the West. Not that he was out there to reject or discredit modern science, but tried to show that everything the modern West claimed to have invented was already known to Indians long ago. This he believed was the only way to evoke respect for Hinduism among a Western-educated middle class devoted to the goddess of reason. The whole campaign took the form of an "aggressive propaganda" through a number of regional journals and organisations like Bharatvarshiya Arya Dharma Procharini Sabha, committed to the idea of reviving the Aryan religion, as expounded in the *Vedas, Tantras* and *Puranas.*[16] On the other hand, there was the more sophisticated intellectual tradition of Bankim Chandra Chatterjee, portraying the mythical figure Krishna as the modern politician and a nation builder. It was in his novel *Anandamath*, published in 1882, that he invented an icon for the nation, the Mother Goddess, identified with the motherland. And the song *Bande Mataram* (Hail mother) which he composed in exaltation of this once beautiful mother, became the anthem of nationalist movement in India. But the way he imagined this icon shows that although taken from the repertoire of Hinduism, it was nonetheless highly unorthodox.[17] Without a revival of the religion of the nation there was no good possible for India, he believed. But this was not the orthodox ritualistic Hinduism he was talking about, but a "reconstituted Hinduism", the more rationalistic dharma, that was regenerative and not obscurantist. In him, therefore, we find quite an "unprincipled use of Hinduism", a recognition of its elasticity, and its immense internal diversity, which made it possible to stretch its resources to accomplish a task that it was never asked to achieve, i.e., to imagine a history that would unite a nation against foreign domination.[18]

In Maharashtra, the Ranade-Telang school of reform and their Prarthana Samaj had been following a cautious policy of social reform along the lines of "least resistance". But by the 1890s they came to be assailed both by the radicals and the orthodox elements. Behramji Malabari's 1884 "Note" on child marriage leading to enforced widowhood, led to a countrywide debate on the prohibition of child marriage. This social institution had by then become an issue of public debate as a result of a court case in 1884–88, in which Rukhmabai, a twenty-two year old Hindu woman belonging to the carpenter caste, was taken to Bombay High Court by her husband Dadaji, because she refused to recognise his conjugal rights. She was married as an infant and after eleven years of separate living, she argued, that unconsummated marriage was no longer binding on her as an adult. She lost the case, which dragged on for four years, and was threatened with imprisonment, which she avoided through a compromise. Dadaji was, however, a mere pawn in this case, through which the Hindu orthodoxy strived to assert the rights of patriarchy and preserve their preferred way of life. On the other hand, important reformists formed the Rukhmabai Defence Committee, of which Malabari was an important member.[19] Intellectual reformist opinion now exerted a moral pressure on the British to pass the Age of Consent Bill in 1891 to prevent early consummation of marriage (*garbhadhan*). The first act against child marriage had been passed in 1860 and it prohibited consummation of marriage for a Hindu girl below ten years of age; the new act only proposed to raise that age of consent from ten to twelve. The earlier act had been passed without much opposition, but the new one provoked a powerful orthodox Hindu backlash, which had a much wider mass base than the reformist movement. Conservative and obscurantist sentiments now converged with the nationalist argument that foreign rulers had no right to interfere with the religious and social customs of the Indians. However, just government intervention was not the issue, as during the same period, Hindu orthodox opinion seldom hesitated to accept government legislation against cow slaughter. And just then in the Rukhmabai case it was the British legal system, which the Hindu orthodoxy was using to assert its rights. This proposed intervention, as it has been argued, sought to invade that sacred inner space, the family and the household, which the Hindu society had always regarded as impenetrable or inviolate, a sovereign space that could not be colonised. But now the Hindu males were about to lose even this last "solitary sphere of autonomy", and therefore, "a new chronology of resistance" was to begin from here.[20] The response to this reform was intense and violent.

In Maharashtra the movement was led by Bal Gangadhar Tilak and his Poona Sarvajanik Sabha, in alliance with the Poona revivalists, who frequently invoked Hindu, Brahman and Maratha glory. As early as January 1885 Tilak had been organising meetings to oppose government intervention in marriage customs and now he proposed that education rather than legislation was the most legitimate method of eradicating the evil. The debate however reached furious proportions towards the end of 1890, after the reported death of an eleven-year-old girl Phulmoni from sexual abuse by her husband twenty-nine years older than her. As the reformist pressure increased for a legislation, the orthodox Marathi journals *Kesari* and *Mahratta* strongly upheld the conservative view about the garbhadhan ceremony, which required the Hindu girls to be married before reaching puberty, but consummation had to await puberty. Any interference with this custom would put Hinduism in danger—that was the essence of all opposition arguments.[21] And this propaganda spread as far as Bengal, where despite the disapproval of people like Bankim Chandra or Vivekananda, the orthodox elements like Sasadhar Tarkachudamoni and others raised a furore in the pages of *Bangabasi*.[22]

This cacophony of obscurantist propaganda tended to drown the reformist voices like that of Professor R.G. Bhandarkar of the Poona Deccan College. Following the Orientalist cognitive tradition of textualising Indian culture, he showed through meticulous research on the *dharmashastras* that marriages after puberty were allowable and not opposed to Hindu religious laws. We should remember, however, that men like Tilak in their personal lives were hardly ever obscurantists, as his own eldest daughter remained single till the age of thirteen.[23] But in this debate they found a powerful self-confident rhetoric against foreign rule. As Tanika Sarkar argues, the "Hindu woman's body" became the "site of a struggle that for the first time declare[d] war on the very fundamentals of an alien power-knowledge system." However, in this protest against Western reformism and rationalism, the pain and tears of the child wives were completely forgotten.[24] There is one interesting point to note here: all the divergent positions on the Consent debate—like the previous social reform debates of the early nineteenth century—converged at one point. The reformers, their detractors, as well as the colonial state—all agreed that the question of child marriage and its consummation belonged to the realm of religion, which, as Mrinalini Sinha has argued, had long been recognised as an autonomous space for "native masculinity". Indeed, the masculinist anxieties in England generated support for the opponents of the reform; yet the government in India decided to take a pro-reform interventionist position because of the specific political imperatives of the time.[25] Therefore, despite all opposition, the Age of Consent Bill was passed on 19 March 1891, though, as both the reformers and their opponents soon realised, it had little more than "educative effect". But this debate set an interesting trend. While on the one hand, reformism had become a part of the nationalist discourse, the anti-reformists and orthodox elements also received immense publicity.[26] And what is more significant, Hinduism now became a useful rhetoric for organising a more articulate and sometime even militant opposition to foreign rule.

The use of orthodox Hindu religious symbols for political mobilisation took a more militant form in north India through the Arya Samaj and the cow-protection movement, which led to widespread communal violence in 1893. Arya Samaj was established in 1875 by Dayanand Saraswati. Gradually, it found a fertile ground in Punjab and the North-Western Provinces. It offered a sharp criticism of the existing Hindu practices, like idolatry, polytheism, child marriage, widow celibacy, foreign travel, dominance of Brahmans and caste-system. Indeed, what it inculcated was an aggressive assertion of the superiority of ancient Indian religion, based on the *Vedas* over all other faiths. Because of this element, the movement was later absorbed into the dominant pan-Hindu revivalist framework. As Peter Van der Veer argues, the reformist Arya Samaj and their orthodox critics found a common ground in their "defense of the Hindu nation".[27] This happened after Dayanand's death in 1883, under his disciples. Kenneth Jones (1976) has shown that aggressiveness increased as a result of Christian missionary activities, which introduced religious competitiveness into the social atmosphere of Punjab. They began to preach the supremacy of the Arya *dharam* (religion), Arya *bhasha* (language) and the *Aryavarta* (land) and their propaganda was mainly directed against the Muslims and the Christians. As a direct response to Christian proselytising activities, the Arya Samaj developed the concept of suddhi, which aimed at reconversion from Christianity, Islam and Sikhism. The moderate group within the Samaj was gradually marginalised by 1893, and the militant group became dominant. They came closer to other orthodox groups and were involved in violent confrontations with the Muslims. The tension reached its peak on the issue of cow protection.

The importance of cow was always recognised in Indian society, as the economy moved from pastoral to agricultural orientation. But in ancient time cow was not regarded as sacred or inviolable; veneration for cow increased during the medieval period when the rate of cow slaughter increased phenomenally. The Muslim practice of cow sacrifice at the Bakr-Id festival further increased Hindu veneration of cow as a sacred symbol.[28] But it was never a cause of communal conflict in earlier times, not even in early colonial period. The earlier religious disturbances arose on local issues and subsided quickly. It was only in the late nineteenth century that the communities began to define their boundaries more closely and began to display more communal aggressiveness. The Hindus clearly lacked organisational integration and therefore Hindu mobilisation took place around the symbol of cow, which communicated a variety of cosmological constructs relevant to both the Brahmanical and devotional traditions of Hinduism.[29] Cow, in other words, was a generally acceptable symbol across regional, linguistic and denominational barriers. It was first the Kukas, a reformist sect among the Sikhs, who took up the cow-protection issue in 1871 in order to galvanise their movement and win more support. They were involved in some violent incidents trying to stop cattle slaughter by the Muslims and invited in the process ruthless repression from the government.[30] In the 1870s however the cow protectionist sentiments rapidly spread in Punjab, North-Western Provinces, Awadh and Rohilkhand. The Arya Samaj converted this sentiment into an organised all-India movement. The mobilisation took place through the establishment of the Gaurakshini Sabhas (cow protection societies), which became most strong in the Hindu dominated areas like Bihar, Banaras division, Awadh, eastern Allahabad, and later on in Bengal, Bombay, Madras, Sind, Rajputana, and the Central Provinces.[31]

During Dayanand's time the cow-protection movement was not overtly anti-Muslim and by providing economic and nationalist arguments he also tried to rationalise the movement and gave it a certain amount of respectability. But gradually it became an issue of communal rivalry as the debate over the legal ban on cow slaughter arose. For the Muslims, a cow was cheaper than a sheep or goat for sacrificial purposes. Cow slaughter also had a political meaning for them; it meant a symbolic assertion of freedom from Hindu supremacy. The issue was fought at the modern institutional level of municipalities, legislatures, press and political meetings. By the middle of 1893 the provocations and counter provocations reached its peak, leading to the outbreak of the first riot in Mau in Azamgarh district over the rival interpretations of a legal ban on cow slaughter. The riots rapidly spread over a wide region; thirty-one riots took place in six months in Bihar and the North-Western Provinces. These were led by the zamindars and religious preachers and followed by the peasants. The mass participation was sometimes the result of social coercion; but sometimes it was also spontaneous. Market networks were used to ensure participation.[32] The series of violent incidents culminated in a riot in Bombay involving the working classes. And although outwardly against the Muslims, the spirit of discontent, as the government suspected, was definitely anti-British; the cow-question was merely a war cry to arouse the lethargic Hindus.[33]

John McLane thinks that the riots showed an "expanded sense of community membership" breaking down class and geographical barriers.[34] Immediately after 1893, communal tension subsided. The cow-protection movement also lost its momentum, although it continued in some areas for some more time. This shows that cow itself was perhaps not important; it was being used as a symbol for community mobilisation. There was an increasing need for such mobilisation along community lines, as constitutional questions were now being discussed, new competitive institutions were being created. In such an environment of competition, there was need for both the communities to mobilise along communal lines in order to register their collective presence in the new public space, and the cow served as a handy symbol. Gyanendra Pandey (1983) has shown that the cow-protection movement did not yet indicate a complete communal polarisation of Indian society. The construction and articulation of the communal category was entirely in the interest of the elites, while various other groups participated with various other motives. The zamindars by leading the gaurakshini sabhas tried to reassert their social power that had been slipping away from their hands because of the various changes instituted by colonial rule. The peasant participants came mainly from the Ahir community, who had been socially mobile and, therefore, had to legitimise their new status by projecting their Hinduness. This did not mean that the barriers of class had been dismantled or permanently effaced. On other occasions they fought against their Hindu zamindars along with other Muslim peasants. And apart from that, there were many regions, which were not at all affected by the cow-protection sentiment. But the movement put an unmistakable Hindu stamp on the nationalist agitation. Congress, though not directly involved, remained silent and even patronising. After the Nagpur session of the Congress in 1891, the gaurakshini sabha held a large meeting within the Congress pavilion, attended by Congress delegates and visitors. Prominent cow protectionist leaders like Sriman Swami attended the Allahabad Congress in 1893,[35] while other well known Congress leaders like Tilak were closely associated with the local gaurakshini sabhas.[36] This alienated the Muslims from Congress politics, as Muslim representation in Congress sessions declined drastically after 1893.[37]

If cow protection drew the lines between the two religious communities in north India, these lines were further reinforced by skilful manipulation of other available cultural symbols, such as language.[38] The Hindi–Urdu controversy began in the North-Western Provinces and Awadh sometime in the 1860s, but it was revived with great enthusiasm in 1882 when it also spread to other Hindi-speaking regions of north India, such as Punjab and the Central Provinces.

The movement acquired greater intensity in the 1890s with the foundation of the Nagri Pracharani Sabha in 1893 in the holy city of Banaras. Truly speaking, Hindi and Urdu, spoken by a great majority of people in north India, were the same language written in two scripts; Hindi was written in Devanagri script and therefore had a greater sprinkling of Sanskrit words, while Urdu was written in Persian script and thus had more Persian and Arabic words in it. At the more colloquial level, however, the two languages were mutually intelligible. But since Urdu was officially recognised, there was a concerted campaign to get Nagri recognised for all official purposes as well and the movement proceeded through a literary campaign, memorialising the government and editorialising in the local language press. Leading literary figures like Bharatendu Harischandra, by upholding the classical Sanskrit heritage of the Hindi language emphasised its high status and antiquity, but in the process purged it of its local and popular traditions.[39] But most significantly, in course of this cultural campaign, Hindi came to be identified with the Hindus and Urdu with the Muslims, although many Hindus like the well-established Kayasthas were still in favour of using Urdu as an official language. The association of leaders like Madan Mohan Malaviya with this campaign gave it an obvious political colour. In April 1900, a Resolution of the Government of North-Western Province and Awadh gave Nagri an equal official status with Urdu, and this, as Christopher King argues, stirred up the protagonists of Urdu to offer an emotional defence of their language.[40] They now formed the Anjuman Taraqqi-e-Urdu (Society for the progress of Urdu), as some of them believed that this official measure would eventually lead to the complete extinction of their language. Although this euphoria over the controversy subsided after some time, language henceforth became an important component of the cultural project of nationalism in India.

In the wake of the cow-protection riots, there were also other more overt attempts to use Hindu religious and historical symbols for the purpose of political mobilisation. In Maharashtra, Tilak's next project, to borrow a phrase, was "the political recruitment of God Ganapati".[41] Ever since the days of the peshwas, the Hindu deity of Ganapati or Ganesh used to enjoy official patronage in this region. It was a deity that was equally respected both by the Chitpavan Brahmans and the non-Brahman lower castes; but Ganapati puja was always a domestic or family affair. In 1893, however, following the Bombay riots generated by the cow-protection movement, Tilak and other Chitpavan Brahmans of Poona decided to organise it as an annual public festival and to imbue politics in it, as a means to bridge the gap between the Brahman-dominated Congress and the non-Brahman masses. Alleging government partiality for the Muslims, he urged the Hindus of Poona to boycott their Muharram festival and participate in a public celebration of the puja of Lord Ganapati. In 1894 to further consolidate the group aspect of the festival, he introduced certain innovations, like the installation of large public images of the god and an introduction of the *mela* movement in which singing parties, comprising twenty to several hundred singers at times, sang political songs to communicate the message of nationalism to wider masses. As a result, the Hindus who previously participated in the Muharram festivals in previous years, now largely boycotted it and flocked to the Ganapati festival. And then from 1895 the festival began to spread from Poona to every other part of Deccan; by 1905 seventy-two towns outside Poona celebrated Ganapati festival.

Celebration of Hindu mythical or historical symbols and opposition to reformism now became an accepted practice in Poona politics. Ranade's National Social Conference, which used to meet every year at the Congress session, was finally driven out at the Poona session in 1895 by the rival faction led by Tilak. In 1896, Tilak introduced another festival, called Shivaji festival, to commemorate the coronation of Shivaji Maharaj, who "upheld our self respect as Hindus, and who gave particular direction to our religion".[42] Although the Bombay government did not immediately view these festivals as a direct threat to British rule, it did inspire a number of revolutionaries. The Chapekar brothers, for example, who killed Rand, the hated Superintendent of the Plague Commission, were associated with the Poona Ganapati festival and with Tilak.[43] Two other revolutionaries, Ganesh and Vinayak Savarkar, also wrote inflammatory songs for the Ganapati festival at Nasik. Thus, although the Ganapati festivals were not directly connected with the revolutionary movement, they acted as important vehicles for disseminating such ideas and training a cadre for such groups. From 1900 onwards, these festivals became overtly political, and it was because of this militant tone that the government virtually suppressed them by 1910. But to what extent the festivals had been able to disseminate the political message is open to question. On the non-Brahmans the political content of the Ganapati festival had very little impact, while the Muslims were directly alienated by it.[44] And the Shivaji cult was to be put to an entirely different political use by the non-Brahman leaders like Jotirao Phule to construct a separate identity of their own (see chapter 7.2).

But despite its limitations, Hindu revivalism became by now an established political force, more closely associated with the extremist reaction against the reformist moderate Congress politicians. Madras was no exception either, as here Hindu reaction to missionary activities and conversion arose in the 1820s in the form of Vibhuti Sangam (Sacred Ashes Society) which preached reconversion of the radicalised Shanar Christians. Then in the 1840s came the Dharma Sabha, mainly patronised by the Brahmans and high-caste Hindus. The two organisations stood for conservative resistance to change, rigid adherence to *varnashramadharma* and caste exclusiveness.[45] With the establishment of the Theosophical Society in 1882, Hindu revivalism gained strength in Madras, as it stimulated the interest of the educated Indians in the history and culture of their country. It was further reinforced after the arrival of Annie Besant, who also formed the linkage with nationalism and Congress politics.

Nationalism in this way came to be associated with Hindu religious revivalist ideas in the late nineteenth and early twentieth centuries. But there are certain problems involved in its history, as this modern idea of "Syndicated Hinduism" was to a large extent the construction of nineteenth-century Western hermeneutics.[46] The term "Hinduism" was used historically to convey a wide variety of meanings: in a general sense, it meant anything "native" or "Indian"; in a narrower sense it indicated the high culture or religion of India, especially those of Aryan, Brahmanical or Vedic origin.[47] When in the late nineteenth century, Indians were asked to identify their religious status in the census returns, Hinduism in popular perception was still not recognisable as a religion with definable boundaries. In 1881, in the column for 'religion', instead of 'Hindu', many of them mentioned their sect or caste; such problem of definition continued to haunt the census authorities at least until 1901.[48] This Hinduism, therefore, appears to be a colonial construct, not bound by any specific doctrinal definition or not historically attached to any community identity. The idea of a homogenised Hinduism was constructed, as Ashis Nandy has argued, by the "cultural arrogance of post-Enlightenment Europe, which sought to define not only the 'true' West but also the 'true' East".[49] The colonial ethnographic studies and census reports gave a concrete definable shape to this concept of religion as community (see discussion in 5.4), and a section of the westernised Indians internalised it into their collective consciousness and developed it into a self-definition. In emulation of their martial rulers and their religion, they sought to revive an emaciated

Hinduism as an effective antidote against alien cultural intervention that continually stereotyped the colonised society as effeminate.[50] The term revivalism itself remained problematic, as it did not mean resurrecting a forgotten and obsolete past, but reconstituting the past in the service of the present. Many of the social practices and symbols that were being "revived" or defended, were already continuing or were in existence in collective memory.[51] And not all social customs of the past were being revived either; there was only a selective absorption of specific aspects of the past and adapting them to the present-day needs of nation building.[52] Some of these so-called revivalist leaders and intellectuals were actually caught between the mythical past and a rationalist present and their "unhappy consciousness" sought to resolve this dilemma by taking shelter in an "imaginary history".[53]

Partha Chatterjee has called this phenomenon the central problematic of early Indian nationalism. In conceiving nationalism, the Indian nationalists were obviously influenced by ideas from European bourgeois experience; but Indian nationalism did not develop only because of Western modular influences. As we have already seen (chapter 4), the Indian nationalists felt compelled to talk in terms of an opposing paradigm; they invoked the past as an alternative to colonial rule. This provided for a "viable cultural foundation of nationhood".[54] But this particular mode of conceptualisation, we must point out, had also some inherent contradictions and consequent dangers. First of all, as it has been pointed out, this very construction of cultural nationalism was prompted by Orientalist cognition that located Hinduism in a high textual tradition. The tendency here was "to turn Hinduism into an organized religion" based, like Christianity, on a recognised text—*Vedas* for Dayanand and *Bhagavadgita* for Vivekananda—thus marginalising the more liberal and open ended folk traditions.[55] And when this reconstituted Hinduism became the foundational idea for imagining a nation, that "Hindu nationalism", as Christophe Jaffrelot has convincingly argued, "largely reflect[ed] the Brahminical view of the high caste reformers".[56] This particular cultural discourse of nationalism therefore failed to appeal to the non-Brahman and lower caste masses of India (more on this in chapter 7.2). It also used the past very selectively and readily accepted, often uncritically, the Orientalist stereotype of "medieval Muslim tyranny and decline" as against "ancient Hindu glory".[57] This inevitably led to the unhappy consequence of alienating the Muslims who became suspicious of Hindu majority rule. This nationalism, which grew in strength in the late nineteenth century, was thus beset with contradictions from the very beginning.

Not only were the Muslims alienated by this militant brand of Hinduism, it has been argued by Richard Fox that the articulation of a distinctive Sikh identity through an organised Singh Sabha movement in the late nineteenth century was directly the result of the Arya Samaj campaign in Punjab, particularly of its attacks on Guru Nanak.[58] It is perhaps simplistic to argue that the Singh Sabhas came up only in response to the challenge of the Arya Samaj, but it will be pertinent here to have a brief discussion on this movement as it belonged to the same cultural politics of identity formation in the late nineteenth-century India. There were in fact many reasons behind the rise of this movement, such as the emergence of a small Sikh elite in the nineteenth century and their indignation about relative exclusion of the Sikhs from education and employment in Punjab, the influence of the Brahmo Samaj and Anjuman-i-Punjab, the proselytising activities of the Christian missionaries, the colonial stereotyping of the Sikh identity and their "decline", official control of the Sikh holy places and so on. The first Singh Sabha was started in Amritsar in 1873 and another in Lahore six years later. Between 1880 and 1900, 115 Singh Sabhas were founded mostly in Punjab, but some also in other parts of India and abroad. The main theme of this movement, as in the case of Hindu revivalism, was the perceived notion of decline of the Sikhs and the necessity to retrieve the image of Tat Khalsa or pure Sikhs, as it was prevalent in the eighteenth century during the heyday of Sikhism. The cultural movement involved a purification of Sikhism by purging all popular elements and impurities such as the influence of polytheism and idolatry, often openly visible in the holy shrines. It also emphasised the maintenance of the 5 k's or the external symbols of Sikh identity, performing the authentic Sikh life-cycle rituals as enjoined in the Sikh manual of conduct or the *Rahit-nama*, refraining from participation in all popular religious festivals and pilgrimages, reclaiming the sacred space by establishing control over the holy shrines and purging them of all signs of idolatry, and finally, making the Gurmukhi script and the Punjabi language the most authentic symbols of Sikh identity. Not all Sikhs agreed with this universalised version of Sikh identity; but this very claim that the Sikhs were a distinct and homogeneous community—separate from both the Hindus and Muslims—had significant implications for imagining the Indian nation at the beginning of the twentieth century.[59]

5.3. THE RISE OF EXTREMISM AND THE SWADESHI MOVEMENT

When the failure of moderate politics became quite apparent by the end of the nineteenth century, a reaction set in from within the Congress circles and this new trend is referred to as the "Extremist" trend. The moderates were criticised for being too cautious and their politics was stereotyped as the politics of mendicancy. This extremism developed in three main regions and under the leadership of three important individuals, Bepin Chandra Pal in Bengal, Bal Gangadhar Tilak in Maharashtra and Lala Lajpat Rai in Punjab; in other areas extremism was less powerful if not totally absent.

Many causes are cited to explain the rise of extremism. Factionalism, according to some historians, is one of them, as at the turn of the century we observe a good deal of faction fighting at almost every level of organised public life in India. In Bengal there was division within the Brahmo Samaj and bitter journalistic rivalry between the two newspaper groups, the *Bengalee*, edited by moderate leader Surendranath Banerjea and the *Amrita Bazar Patrika*, edited by the more radical Motilal Ghosh. There was also faction fighting between Aurobindo Ghosh on the one hand and Bepin Chandra Pal and Brahmabandhab Upadhyay on the other, over the editorship of *Bande Mataram*. In Maharashtra there was competition between Gokhale and Tilak for controlling the Poona Sarvajanik Sabha. The contest came to the surface when in 1895 Tilak captured the organisation and the following year Gokhale started his rival organisation, the Deccan Sabha. In Madras three factions, the Mylapur clique, the Egmore clique and the suburban elites fought among each other. In Punjab, the Arya Samaj was divided after the death of Dayanand Saraswati, between the more moderate College group and the radical revivalist group. One could argue therefore, that the division in Congress between the moderates and the extremists was just faction fighting[60] that plagued organised public life everywhere in India around this time. But the rise of extremism cannot be explained in terms of factionalism alone.

Frustration with moderate politics was definitely the major reason behind the rise of extremist reaction. The Congress under moderate leadership was being governed by an undemocratic constitution. Although after repeated attempts by Tilak a new constitution was drafted and ratified in 1899, it was never given a proper trial. The Congress was also financially broke, as the capitalists did not contribute and the patronage of a few rajas and landed magnates was never sufficient. The social reformism of the moderates, inspired by Western liberalism, also went against popular orthodoxy. This came to the surface at the Poona Congress of 1895, when the moderates proposed to have a national social conference running at tandem with the regular sessions of the Congress. More orthodox leaders like Tilak argued that the social conference would split the Congress and the proposal was ultimately dropped. But more significantly, moderate politics had reached a dead end, as most of their demands remained unfulfilled and this was certainly a major reason behind the rise of extremism. This increased the anger against colonial rule and this anger was generated by the moderates themselves, through their economic critique of colonialism.

The Curzonian administration magnified this nationalist angst further. Lord Curzon (1899–1905), a true believer in British righteousness, had the courage to chastise an elite British regiment for its racial arrogance against native Indians.[61] But he was also the last champion of that self-confident despotic imperialism of which Fitzjames Stephen and Lytton Strachey were the ideologues. He initiated a number of unpopular legislative and administrative measures, which hurt the susceptibilities of the educated Indians. The reconstitution of the Calcutta Corporation through the Calcutta Municipal Amendment Act of 1899 reduced the number of elected representatives in it; the Indian Universities Act of 1904 placed Calcutta University under the most complete governmental control; and the Indian Official Secrets Amendment Act of 1904 further restricted press freedom. Then, his Calcutta University convocation address, in which he described the highest ideal of truth as essentially a Western concept, most surely hurt the pride of the educated Indians. The last in the series was the partition of Bengal in 1905, designed to weaken the Bengali nationalists who allegedly controlled the Congress. But instead of weakening the Congress, the Curzonian measures acted as a magic potion to revitalise it, as the extremist leaders now tried to take over Congress, in order to commit it to a path of more direct and belligerent confrontation with colonial rule.

The goal of the extremists was *swaraj,* which different leaders interpreted differently. For Tilak it meant Indian control over the administration, but not a total severance of relations with Great Britain. Bepin Pal believed that no self-government was possible under British paramountcy; so for him swaraj was complete autonomy, absolutely free of British control. Aurobindo Ghosh in Bengal also visualised swaraj as absolute political independence. However, for most others swaraj still meant self-rule within the parametres of British imperial structure. The radicalisation was actually visible in the method of agitation, as from the old methods of prayer and petition they moved to that of passive resistance. This meant opposition to colonial rule through violation of its unjust laws, boycott of British goods and institutions, and development of their indigenous alternatives, i.e., *swadeshi* and national education. The ideological inspiration for this new politics came from the new regional literature, which provided a discursive field for defining the Indian nation in terms of its distinct cultural heritage or civilisation. This was no doubt a revivalist discourse, informed by Orientalism, as it sought to invoke an imagined golden past and used symbols from a retrospectively reconstructed history to arouse nationalist passions. This was also a response to the gendered discourse of colonialism that had established a teleological connection between masculinity and political domination, stereotyping the colonised society as "effeminate" and therefore unfit to rule. This created a psychological compulsion for the latter to try to recover their virility in Kshatriyahood in an imagined Aryan past, in order to establish the legitimacy of their right to rule.[62] Historical figures who had demonstrated valour and prowess were now projected as national heroes. Tilak started the Shivaji festival in Maharashtra in April 1896 and soon these ideas became popular in Bengal, where a craze for national hero worship began. The Marathas, Rajputs and Sikhs—stereotyped in colonial ethnography as 'martial races'—were now placed in an Aryan tradition and appropriated as national heroes. Ranjit Singh, Shivaji and the heroes culled from local history like Pratapaditya and Sitaram, even Siraj-ud-daula, were idolised as champions of national glory or martyrs for freedom. Vivekananda made a distinct intervention in this ideological discourse by introducing the idea of an "alternative manliness", which combined Western concepts of masculinity with the Brahmanic tradition of spiritual celibate ascetism. A physical culture movement started with great enthusiasm with gymnasiums coming up in various parts of Bengal to reclaim physical prowess; but the emphasis remained on spiritual power and self-discipline that claimed superiority over body that was privileged in the Western idea of masculinity.[63] The Indian political leaders also looked back to ancient Indo-Aryan political traditions as alternatives to Anglo-Saxon political systems. The Indian tradition was described as more democratic with strong emphasis on village self-government. The concept of dharma, it was argued, restricted the arbitrary powers of the king and the republican traditions of the Yaudheyas and Lichchhavis indicated that the Indian people already had a strong tradition of self-rule.[64] This was directly to counter the colonial logic and moderate argument that British rule was an act of providence to prepare Indians for self-government.

Indeed, at this stage, this was the central problematic of Indian nationalism. The moderates had wanted the Indian nation to develop through a modernistic course; but modernism being a Western concept, this meant an advocacy of the continuation of colonial rule. The extremists, on the other hand, sought to oppose colonial rule and therefore had to talk in terms of a non-Western paradigm.[65] They tried to define the Indian nation in terms of distinctly Indian cultural idioms, which led them to religious revivalism invoking a glorious past—sometimes even unquestioned acceptance and glorification of that past. But their Hinduism was only a political construct, not defined by any definite religious attributes. As the nineteenth-century Englishmen claimed ancient Greece as their classical heritage, the English-educated Indians also felt proud of the achievements of the Vedic civilisation.[66] This was essentially an "imaginary history"[67] with a specific historical purpose of instilling a sense of pride in the minds of a selected group of Indians involved in the process of imagining their nation. Some of the leaders, like Tilak or Aurobindo, also believed that this use of Hindu mythology and history was the best means to reach the masses and mobilise them in support of their politics. The veteran moderate politicians refused to accommodate these new trends within the Congress policies and programmes, and this led to the split in the Congress in its Surat session in 1907.

But before going into the bizarre story of the Surat split in the Congress (1907), we may look into the history of the Swadeshi movement in Bengal (1905–11), which may be described as the best expression of extremist politics. The movement began as an agitation against the partition of Bengal in 1905, which Lord Curzon had designed as a means of destroying political opposition in this province. The Bengal Presidency as an administrative unit was increasing in size with the accretion of territories through conquest and annexation. As a result, its frontiers at one point extended to Sutlej in the northwest, Assam on the northeast and Arakan on the southeast. The presidency was indeed of an unwieldy size and therefore the necessity to partition Bengal was being discussed since the time of the Orissa famine of 1866. In 1874 Assam was actually separated with 3 million people, while three Bengali-speaking areas, i.e., Sylhet, Goalpara and Cachar, were also added to it. Safeguarding the interests of Assam, rather than weakening Bengal, seemed to have been the more important consideration behind the policy decision at this stage.[68] Hereafter, making Assam a viable administrative unit came to occupy British administrative attention. In 1892 there was a proposal to transfer the entire Chittagong Division to Assam; in 1896 William Ward, the then Chief Commissioner of Assam again proposed the transfer of the districts of Dacca and Mymensingh, so that Assam could become a Lieutenant Governor's province with a separate civil service cadre. But the scheme was not favoured at that time; only the Lushai Hills were transferred in 1897 and the rest of the scheme was shelved.

When Lord Curzon arrived in India and went on a tour of Assam in March 1900, the scheme was resurrected again, as the European tea garden planters demanded a maritime outlet nearer than Calcutta to reduce their dependence on the Assam-Bengal railways. In 1901 the partition of Bengal seemed more urgently required as the census in that year revealed that Bengal population had reached 78.5 million. Curzon drew up a scheme in his Minute on Territorial Redistribution in India (19 May/1 June 1903), which was later published as the Risley Papers on 3 December 1903. It proposed the transfer of Chittagong Division, Dacca and Mymensingh districts to Assam and Chota Nagpur to the Central Provinces; Bengal would receive in return Sambalpur and the feudatory states from Central Provinces and Ganjam district and the Vizagapatnam agency tracts from Madras. In the subsequent months the scheme gradually expanded, although secretly, through additions to the list of transferred districts. The final scheme was embodied in Curzon's dispatch of 2 February 1905 to the Secretary of State Broderick, who reluctantly accepted it without even a proper parliamentary debate. The partition of Bengal was formally announced on 19 July and implemented three months later on 16 October 1905. It meant the creation of a new province of Eastern Bengal and Assam, consisting of all the districts in Chittagong, Dacca and Rajshahi divisions, as well as Hill Tippera, Malda and Assam. The new province would contain a population of 31 million, of which 18 million would be Muslims and 12 million Hindus, while the remaining province of Bengal would be having a population of 54 million, 42 million Hindus and 9 million Muslims. The Bengali Hindus would be outnumbered by the Muslims in the new province, and they would be a linguistic minority in the old, which would contain large numbers of Hindi and Oriya speaking population.

It was these demographic peculiarities of the two provinces, which raised new questions: was the partition really for administrative efficiency? The Curzonian administration obviously defended the scheme on administrative grounds: it would reduce the excessive administrative burden of the Bengal government; this would also solve the problem of Assam which would become a lieutenant governor's province with a separate civil service cadre; there would be substantial commercial benefits, as the interests of the tea gardens, oil and coal industries would be safeguarded; the Assam planters would be having a cheaper maritime outlet through the port of Chittagong; and the Assam-Bengal railways, which was so vital to the economic development of north-eastern India, would be brought under a single administration. But, as Sumit Sarkar points out, all these arguments seem to have been fallacious[69]; indeed, administrative considerations were uppermost in the colonial mind only until 1903 and not after that. Had the partition been purely on administrative grounds, then the government would have accepted the alternative proposals offered by a number of civil servants suggesting more logical partition plans based on linguistic division rather than religious division of the population. But Curzon rejected all these proposals on political ground that linguistic unity would further consolidate the position of the Bengalee politicians. So we should look for the real reasons of partition in the political prejudices of the colonial government.

Indeed, it was the anti-Bengalee feelings of the colonial bureaucracy, which Curzon was initiated into even before he became the viceroy, and a desire to weaken this politically articulate community, which seem to have provided the prime motive behind the partition. Home Secretary Herbert Risley made this point clear in his note of 7 February 1904. "Bengal united is a power", he argued; "Bengal divided will pull in several different ways. That is perfectly true and is one of the merits of the scheme." Curzon further believed that Congress was manipulated from Calcutta by its "best wire-pullers and . . . frothy orators"; so any measure to dethrone Calcutta and encourage alternative centres of activity and influence would also weaken the Congress. He was convinced that the "best guarantee of the political advantage of our proposal is its dislike by the Congress".[70] The partition would also serve another purpose. As the Memorandum of Lord Minto (5 February 1906), who had succeeded Curzon as the new viceroy, and the Resolution of October 1906 of Sir Lancelot Hare (the second Lt. Governor of East Bengal and Assam) indicated, this would destroy the virtual "class rule" by the Bengali bhadralok, or the landowning, moneylending, professional and clerical classes, belonging mostly to the three Hindu upper castes of Brahman, Kayastha and Baidya. They had monopolised education and employment to the virtual exclusion of all other communities and this was the main source of their political power.[71] So the antidote to bhadralok power was to encourage the development of other communities, in this case it was the Muslims who captured the attention of the colonial rulers.

A large concentration of Muslim population in the eastern districts of Bengal was first pointed out by Dr Francis Buchanan through his sociological and statistical surveys in the nineteenth century. In 1836 Adam's report on vernacular education also pointed out a similar demographic phenomenon. The first census of 1872 revealed that 49.2 per cent or nearly half of the population of Bengal were Muslims and they lived mainly in the eastern, central and northern districts. There was, in other words, a clear geographical divide along the river Bhagirathi: eastern Bengal being dominated by the Muslims, western Bengal by the Hindus and in central Bengal the two communities balanced each other. And not only that, this Muslim population was overwhelmingly rural in character and about 90 per cent of them belonged to agricultural and low service groups. As early as 1896, it was being pointed out, therefore, that a new province in eastern Bengal would unite the significant Muslim population and would reduce the politically threatening position of the Hindu minority in undivided Bengal. Curzon, in his Dacca speech in February 1904, defined this policy in more categorical terms; in the new province of East Bengal the Muslims would enjoy a unity, which they never enjoyed since the days of the old Muslim rule. The final draft of the partition scheme, prepared in September 1904, also emphasised that in course of time Dacca, the headquarters of the new province, would assume the character of a provincial capital where Muslim interests would be strongly represented if not become predominant.[72] No wonder, the Muslims in eastern Bengal gradually rallied round the partition scheme.

But the partition instead of dividing and weakening the Bengalees, further united them through an anti-partition agitation. Indeed, what the Curzonian administration had ignored was the emerging Bengali identity which cut across narrow interest groups, class, as well as regional barriers. Greater geographical mobility, evolution of a literary language in the nineteenth century and the modern communication agencies like the regional newspapers had already introduced a powerful narrative text for such horizontal solidarity. The economic condition of the province at the turn of the century also had created a charged situation. The famines and epidemics of the 1890s had shattered the faith in the providential British connections. The narrowing opportunities for the educated Bengalees, the rising prices fuelled by consecutive bad harvests in the early twentieth century made life miserable for the middle classes. At this juncture the partition instead of dividing the Bengali society, brought into existence a "swadeshi coalition" by further consolidating the political alliance between the Calcutta leaders and their east Bengali followers, which according to Rajat Ray, was "nothing less than a revolution in the political structure of Bengal society".[73] The agitation against the partition had started in 1903, but became stronger and more organised after the scheme was finally announced and implemented in 1905. The initial aim was to secure the annulment of partition, but it soon enlarged into a more broad-based movement, known as the Swadeshi movement, touching upon wider political and social issues. Sumit Sarkar (1973) has identified four major trends in Bengal Swadeshi, namely, the moderate trend, constructive swadeshi, political extremism and revolutionary terrorism. Periodisation of these trends, he argues, is not possible as all the trends were present more or less simultaneously throughout the period.

To summarise Sarkar's exposition here, the moderates began to criticise the partition scheme ever since it was announced in 1903. Assuming that the British would be amenable to arguments, through prayers, petitions and public meetings they sought to revise the scheme in its formative stage. But when they failed to do so and the partition was announced in 1905, they took the first initiative to transform the narrow agitation into a wider swadeshi movement. For the first time they went beyond their conventional political methods and Surendranath Banerjea at a meeting in Calcutta on 17 July 1905 gave a call for the boycott of British goods and institutions. At another mass meeting at Calcutta Town Hall on 7 August a formal boycott resolution was passed, which marked the beginning of the swadeshi movement. This was also the first time that the moderates tried to mobilise other than the literate section of the population; some of them participated in the national education movement; some of them even got involved in labour strikes. But their political philosophy remained the same, as they only sought to pressurise British parliament to secure an annulment of partition and could not conceptualise boycott as a step towards the regeneration of national economy or start a full-scale passive resistance. As a reaction, a new trend developed with emphasis on self-reliance, village level organisation and constructive programmes to develop indigenous or swadeshi alternatives for foreign goods and institutions. By 1905, as Sarkar demonstrates, two main currents were visible in this extremist trend: a non-political constructive swadeshi with strong emphasis on self-development endeavours and political extremism with its emphasis on passive resistance.

The Bengal extremists were initially more inclined to constructive programme which included amateurish attempts to manufacture daily necessities, national education, arbitration courts and village organisation. It was from the 1890s that attempts were made to organise swadeshi sales through exhibition and shops. The Bengal Chemical was started as a swadeshi enterprise in 1893 and then another factory was started in 1901 to manufacture porcelain. National education movement started with Bhagabat Chatuspathi (1895) of Satischandra Mukherjee, the Dawn Society (1902–7), the Saraswat Ayatan of Brahmabandhab Upadhyay (1902) and the Santiniketan Ashram of Rabindranath Tagore (1901). The emphasis was on non-political constructive programmes or a self-strengthening movement before the political agitation, with importance attached to religious revivalism, as Hindu religion was expected to become the bond of unity for the whole nation. Rabindranath Tagore emerged as the main ideologue of this constructive swadeshi, although revivalist ideas figured in his writings only between 1901 and 1906. In his "*Swadeshi Samaj*" address, delivered in 1904, he outlined the constructive programme of self-help or *atmasakti*, and after July 1905 this became the creed of the whole of Bengal, with swadeshi enterprises like textile mills and handlooms, match and soap factories and tanneries coming up everywhere. National education movement moved forward with the establishment of national schools and the founding of the Bengal National College and School in August 1906. The Swadesh Bandhab Samiti in the district of Bakarganj claimed to have settled 523 disputes through its eighty-nine arbitration committees by August 1906.

But it was also around 1906 that this trend came to be criticised by the political extremists like Aurobindo Ghosh, Bepin Chandra Pal or Brahmabandhab Upadhyay, who argued that without freedom no real regeneration of national life was possible. The movement hereafter began to take a new turn. Its goal no longer remained the mere abrogation of the partition, but complete independence or swaraj, and in this sense the movement could not be considered in any way to be an expression of narrow Bengali sub-nationalism. The programme at this stage included four things: boycott of British goods and institutions, development of their indigenous alternatives, violation of unjust laws and violent agitation if necessitated by British repression. As Sarkar argues, this anticipated the Gandhian programme, minus of course his insistence on non-violence. This political programme obviously required mass mobilisation and religion was looked at by leaders like Aurobindo Ghosh as a means to reach the masses. Religious revivalism therefore was a main feature of this new politics. *Bhagavadgita* became a source of spiritual inspiration for the swadeshi volunteers and Hindu religious symbols, usually *sakta* imageries, were frequently used to mobilise the masses. But, as Barbara Southard (1980) has shown, this also alienated the Muslims and failed to attract the lower caste peasants, many of whom were *Vaishnavites*.

The other method of mass mobilisation was to organise *samitis*. Prior to the banning of the five principal samitis in 1909 they were engaged in various forms of mobilising efforts, such as moral and physical training, philanthropic work, propagation of the swadeshi message, organisation of the swadeshi craft, education, arbitration courts etc. But these mass mobilisation efforts ultimately failed as the membership of the samitis did not extend much beyond the ranks of educated bhadralok and this high caste Hindu gentry leadership alienated the lower caste peasantry by often using their coercive power. And not just physical coercion that was used; the Swadeshi leaders rampantly deployed the tool of social coercion or social boycott—exerted through caste associations, professional bodies and nationalist organisations—to punish collaborators or to produce consent among the reluctant participants.[74] The latter's reluctance was often because of the divergence of interests with those of the leaders who claimed to represent them. Swadeshi alternatives were often more expensive than British goods; national schools were not adequate in number. Moreover, some of the lower-caste peasants, like the Rajbansis in north Bengal or the Namasudras in the east, had developed around this time aspirations for social mobility and self-respect, which the Swadeshi movement, devoid of any social programme, failed to accommodate or even recognise.[75] The other method of mass mobilisation of the swadeshis was to organise labour strikes, primarily in the foreign owned companies. But here too the nationalists could penetrate only into the ranks of white-collar workers, while the vast body of Hindustani labour force as well as the plantation labour remained untouched by such nationalist efforts.[76] It was primarily because of this failure of mass mobilisation that the boycott movement failed to affect British imports into India.[77] By 1908 political extremism had definitely declined, giving way to militant nationalism. But certainly another contributory factor behind this decline was the Surat Split of 1907.

The all-India political alignments in 1906–7 could be best described as in a state of confusion. The Bengal moderates cherished their connection with the Bombay group, but local politics imposed upon them a more radical course, as they wholeheartedly denounced the partition and supported boycott, swadeshi and national education. These radical tendencies the Bombay leaders, like Pherozshah Mehta, Dinshaw Wacha or Gokhale, could not appreciate at all. On the other hand, among the non-Bengali extremists, Lala Lajpat Rai was clearly in favour of restraint and wanted reconciliation between the moderates and the extremists. Even Tilak was not all for a showdown; it was only Ajit Singh in Punjab who was staunchly against any compromise. However, the real issue in all-India politics in 1906–7 was how far the radicalism generated by the swadeshi movement in Bengal was to be incorporated into the future politics of the Congress on an all-India theatre. Already by the end of 1905 political unrest had been reported from 23 districts of the United Provinces, 20 in Punjab, 13 in Madras Presidency, 24 towns in Bombay Presidency and 15 in the Central Provinces; widespread agrarian riots were reported from Rawalpindi and Lahore.[78] In Poona, plague and the interventionist prophylactic official measures had aroused political emotions that tended to radicalise public life—although still at an elite level—and sharpened the discord between Gokhale and Tilak.[79] The Bengal extremists got in touch with the Tilak group in Maharashtra and sought to give the Congress programme a new orientation at the Calcutta Congress of 1906. And here in spite of the opposition of Gokhale and the machinations of Mehta, they scored a resounding victory with the help of the Bengal moderates. Four resolutions were passed in favour of boycott, swadeshi, national education and swaraj, and partition was condemned. It was here that the Extremist Party was born with Tilak as the leader and their main goal was to keep intact the four Calcutta resolutions, which the Bombay moderates were determined to revise at the next session of the Congress.[80]

The 1907 session of the Congress was scheduled to take place at Poona, which was an extremists' stronghold. The moderates, therefore, shifted the venue to Surat. Lala Lajpat Rai, who had been deported, had by then returned from Mandalay and the extremists proposed his name as the next Congress president, while the moderate candidate was Rash Behari Ghosh. But Rai, who did not want a split, refused to accept the nomination and so the ultimate fight between the two contending groups boiled down to the question of either retention or rejection of the four

Calcutta resolutions. Pherozshah Mehta conspired to keep the resolutions out of the Congress agenda, while the extremists decided to oppose the nomination of Rash Behari Ghosh if the resolutions were not retained. The Bengal Congress was already divided, as on the occasion of the Midnapur District Conference, Surendranath Banerjea and Aurobindo Ghosh had parallel sessions. Yet, Banerjea took the initiative to preserve Congress unity and tried to have a reconciliation, without any success, between Gokhale and Tilak. The open session of the Congress at Surat ended in a pandemonium over the election of Rash Behari Ghosh, with shoes flying, chairs toppled and men running for cover. But even after this incident Tilak was willing to reunite the Congress; but Mehta seemed intransigent, as he sought to reconstitute the party by purging the extremist elements, a task which he accomplished at the following Allahabad Convention. The Congress of 1908, known as the Mehta Congress, was attended only by the moderates, who reiterated their loyalty to the Raj. The Bengal model of politics was finally rejected.[81] Congress was certainly weakened at this stage and became an ineffective body. The extremist politics, on the other hand, could not crystallise either into a new political organisation, as Tilak died soon after and Aurobindo Ghosh became more spiritually oriented. The two factions could again come together and the Congress revitalised when Gandhi took the leadership in 1920.

So far as Bengal was concerned, by 1908 political swadeshi was certainly on the decline and was taken over by another trend, i.e., individual attacks against British officials and Indian collaborators. This signified, as Sarkar (1973) points out, a shift from non-violence to violence and also from mass action to elite action, necessitated primarily by the failure of the mass mobilisation efforts. The culture of violence as a mode of political protest was always alive in India even after the suppression of the revolt of 1857. In Maharashtra in 1876–77, Wasudeo Balwant Phadke had gathered around him a band of Ramoshis and other backward classes and engaged them in dacoities to collect money for his more grandiose scheme of an armed revolt against the English. He was caught in 1879 and was deported to Aden where he later died a lonely death.[82] But the revolutionary trend was kept alive in Maharashtra through the physical culture movement and formation of youth clubs, the most well known of which was founded in Poona by the Chapekar brothers, Damodar and Balkrishna. But from here they moved further and in 1897 killed W.C. Rand, the notorious chairman of the Poona Plague Commission, which was allegedly responsible for the atrocities perpetrated by the soldiers during their house searches to identify plague victims. Both of them were later caught and hanged, but the tradition lingered on.[83] In Bengal, militant nationalism developed in the same way since the 1860s and 70s, when the physical culture movement became a craze and *akhras* or gymnasiums were set up everywhere to develop what Swami Vivekananda had described as strong muscles and nerves of steel. As mentioned earlier, this was a psychological attempt to break away from the colonial stereotype of effeminacy imposed on the Bengalees. Their symbolic recovery of masculinity and search for virile heroes remained parts of a larger moral and spiritual training to achieve mastery over body, develop a national pride and a sense of social service, on the basis of ideals preached by Bankim and Vivekananda.[84]

The real story of militant nationalism in Bengal begins from 1902 with the formation of four groups, three in Calcutta and one in Midnapur. The first was the Midnapur Society founded in 1902 and this was followed by the founding of a gymnasium by Sarala Ghosal in Ballygunge Circular Road in Calcutta, the Atmonnoti Samiti by some central Calcutta youths and the Anushilan Samiti by Satischandra Basu in March 1902. The progress of this movement till 1905 was modest; but the beginning of the swadeshi movement in that year brought an upsurge in secret society activities. The Dacca Anushilan Samiti was born in October 1906 through the initiative of Pulin Behari Das. This was followed by an all-Bengal conference of the revolutionaries in December and a revolutionary weekly called *Yugantar* started in the same year. A distinct group within the Calcutta Anushilan Samiti headed by Barindra Kumar Ghosh (Aurobindo's brother), Hemchandra Qanungo and Prafullo Chaki soon started action. The first swadeshi dacoity or robbery to raise funds was organised in Rangpur in August 1906 and a bomb manufacturing unit was set up at Maniktala in Calcutta. Attempts to assassinate oppressive officials and spies, robbery in the houses of wealthy Saha merchants who had earlier refused to stop dealing in foreign goods became the main features of the revolutionary activities since 1907–8. But the abortive attempt at Muzaffarpur on the life of the Presidency Magistrate Kingsford on 30 April 1908 by Khudiram Bose and Prafullo Chaki and the following arrest of the entire Maniktala group, including Aurobindo and Barindra Kumar Ghosh, dealt a great blow to such militant activities.[85]

In terms of direct gains, the revolutionaries achieved precious little; most of their attempts were either aborted or failed. Nor did they believe that assassinations or dacoities would alone bring in India's liberation, as Aurobindo's original idea was to prepare for an open armed revolution. But they also achieved a lot. The hanging of Khudiram and the Maniktala Bomb Conspiracy trial, publicised by the press and immortalised in folk songs, fired the imagination of the entire Bengalee population. C.R. Das, still a briefless barrister, appeared as the defence counsel for Aurobindo and argued that if preaching the principle of freedom was any crime, then the accused was surely guilty. To everybody's surprise, Aurobindo was acquitted; but Barindra and Ullaskar Dutta were sentenced to death and ten others were to be deported for life. On appeal, the death sentences were reduced to life imprisonment; and some other sentences were reduced as well. The movement hereafter went underground and became decentralised, but did not die down. Revolutionary activities by now had acquired legitimacy in popular mind, as many people believed that it was an effective alternative to the earlier mendicant policies of the moderates. When the Morley–Minto Reforms were announced in 1909, many of these people believed it was because of fear generated by revolutionary activities.[86] As one historian argues, the appointment of Lord S.P. Sinha as the law member in the viceroy's executive council was surely the result of pressures generated by violent activities. The partition of Bengal itself was annulled in 1911 and although the measure was presented as a "coronation boon" from George V, it might not have been totally unrelated to such pressures.[87] But there were other administrative calculations too, the most important of which was the transfer of capital from Calcutta to Delhi—a measure that certainly needed to be sugarcoated.[88] This marked the end of Bengali dominance in national politics of India. The Curzonian aim of weakening the Bengali politicians was achieved in a different way and now with less resistance.

But the annulment of partition did not bring an end to militant nationalism, as violence was not generated by partition alone. The centre of activities now moved to Punjab and Uttar Pradesh, where the Bengali revolutionaries were joined by the Punjabis returning from North America, where they had formed the revolutionary Ghadr Party. They organised dacoities throughout north India to raise funds and in 1912 plotted an unsuccessful attempt to assassinate the Viceroy Lord Hardinge. In September 1914 the stranded Punjabi Ghadrites on board the *Kamagata Maru*, clashed with the army at Budge Budge near Calcutta. With the outbreak of World War One even more grandiose schemes of organising armed revolts in the

Indian army with help from Germany or Japan began to appear. Rash Behari Bose operating from Lahore tried to organise an army revolt throughout north India, but failed to evoke any response from the sepoys and ultimately fled to Japan. In Bengal, the revolutionaries united under the leadership of Jatin Mukherjee tried to smuggle in arms from Germany, but the amateurish attempt ultimately ended in an uneven battle with the British police at Balasore in Orissa. The unbound repression of the government at this period, freely using the new wartime Defence of India Act (1915), made violent attacks more and more infrequent.[89] But the spectre of revolutionary violence did not disappear at all and it made the Sedition Committee to draft in 1918 the draconian Rowlatt bills, which inflamed Mahatma Gandhi into action and to initiate a new phase in Indian politics, where the central focus would shift from violence to non-violence, from elite action to mass agitation.

5.4. MUSLIM POLITICS AND THE FOUNDATION OF THE MUSLIM LEAGUE

The mainstream Indian nationalism, which was growing under the aegis of the Indian National Congress—and which, as we have seen previously, failed to maintain its separation from the blooming Hindu nationalism—was first contested by the Muslims. However, in the late nineteenth century, the Muslims were by no means a homogeneous community with a discernible political opinion. In the whole of India, including the princely states, they constituted 19.7 per cent of the population in 1881; but there were significant regional variations in their distribution. In the United Provinces the Muslims constituted a minority, being slightly more than 13 per cent of the population; but in Punjab, on the other hand, they were a majority, accounting for slightly more than 51 per cent of the population; [90] in Bengal, the census of 1872 revealed to everybody's surprise that the Muslims represented nearly half of the population (49.2 per cent).[91] Apart from such dissimilarities in demographic characteristics, there were also other important differences in the position and composition of the Muslim community spread over the subcontinent, such as, most significantly, sectarian differences (Shia-Sunni), linguistic barriers and economic disparities. The colonial authorities while defining the indigenous society for administrative management ignored such demographic incongruities and diversity of status. So also the finer distinctions in regional philosophical orientations of south Asian Islam were ignored and an image of a homogeneous "religiopolitical community" was conjured up. A section of the Muslim population, writes Mushirul Hasan, also "began to see themselves in the colonial image of being unified, cohesive, and segregated from the Hindus". They started homogenising such myths to construct a Muslim community identity that was later enlarged into Muslim nationhood.[92]

The evolution of a politicised Muslim communitarian identity in the late nineteenth century, it is true, was not entirely in response to initiatives from above. But we should nevertheless keep in mind the new institutionalised knowledge of social taxonomy that colonial rule offered and the new public space it created in setting a context for such cultural constructions, which could later be so easily connected to wider political projects. The major premise of colonial cognition of Indian society was the theme of "differentiation",[93] which was traced, mapped and enumerated through various official ethnographic studies and finally, since 1872, through decennial census reports. The Indian colonial census, unlike its British predecessor, made religion its fundamental ethnographic category for ordering and classifying demographic and developmental data. Each census report sought to give concrete and recognisable shape to the religious communities, by discussing the numerical size of such groups, their percentage to the whole population, relative or absolute decline and geographic distribution, indicating their majority or minority status in each region and in the country as a whole. The break-up of literacy and occupational statistics according to religion provided an apparently objective picture of the relative or comparative material and social conditions of each religious community. The result of this census taxonomy was the new concept of "religion as a community". Religion did no longer mean just a set of ideas, but came to be identified with "an aggregate of individuals united by formal official definition", sharing supposedly the same characteristics, and conscious of their comparative demographic as well as socio-economic position vis-à-vis other communities.[94] It was this universalised knowledge which made a difference between pre-colonial localised relations between religious groups and colonial competition and conflict among subcontinental religious communities. For, this colonial knowledge of a redefined religion was incorporated into every structure that the state created, every opportunity that it offered to the colonial subjects—from educational facilities, public employment, representation in local self-governing bodies to entry into the expanded legislative councils. However much the government trumpeted the secular character of this public space, and confine religion to the private, the boundaries remained highly permeable and it was within this context that the relationship between religious groups were reconstituted in the late nineteenth century. As Hindu mobilisation made progress, it also simultaneously sculpted and vilified its 'Other', the Muslims. The latter too began to discover their community identity, informed by their common religion and an invented shared past. How an aggressive Arya Samaj movement contributed to the counter-mobilisation of the Muslims in urban Punjab, we have already seen earlier. In the countryside too Islam penetrated rural politics in the nineteenth century through such intermediaries as the *sajjad nishins*, *pirs* and the *ulama*.[95] However, so far as the all-India Muslim politics was concerned, its leadership and main impetus in the late nineteenth century came primarily from the United Provinces (previously North-Western Provinces and Awadh), and to a lesser extent from Bengal; so it is on these two areas that we will focus more intensively in this section.

So far as the Bengal Muslims were concerned, as it has been shown in some recent studies,[96] they were a highly fragmented group, vaguely united by a common allegiance to the essentials of the Islamic faith. There were considerable economic differences within the community, with a minority of large landed magnates at the top and a majority of poor peasants at the bottom. This also coincided with the significant cultural differentiation between the *ashraf* and the *ajlaf* (or *atrap*) sections within the community. The former were divided into two segments: the urban Urdu-speaking elites and the rural Urdu-Bengali speaking mofussil landlords. At the other end was the Bengali speaking peasantry known as the ajlaf. The two segments represented two distinct cultures. The elites represented a foreign culture: they spoke in Urdu and Hindustani, boasted of foreign racial origin and tried to preserve Delhi or Lucknow court culture. They were averse to manual labour in the same way as the Hindu bhadralok were, and looked at the indigenous Muslims with unabashed contempt. The lesser ashraf or the rural Muslim gentry were, however, closer to the Bengali-speaking peasantry in their language, manners and customs; yet there was very little social interaction between the two groups. The atrap or the ajlaf, on the other hand, were the common mass of peasantry, mainly residing in the swampy low-lying areas of east Bengal. How Islam could spread among the masses of Bengal is a question that has now two plausible historical answers, as opposed to the previous, now rejected, social emancipation theory of conversion of the low caste Hindus. Richard Eaton argues that as the frontiers of cultivation expanded between the sixteenth and the eighteenth centuries in eastern Bengal—away from the core of Brahmanic civilisation—Islam also spread as the "religion of the plough", bringing local people gradually into its fold. This Islamisation did not take place at one stroke, but as a gradual process slowly absorbing the colonisers of the land, who were not yet touched or only just slightly touched by Hinduism. The creation of a Muslim peasantry in Bengal was therefore not the result of any large-scale "conversion", but of gradual incorporation of people residing at the periphery of Brahmanical civilisation.[97] Asim Roy (1983), on the other hand, has argued that under the leadership of a group of "cultural mediators", consisting of a section of Bengali-speaking Muslim literati and religious preachers (pirs), Islam in Bengal in the sixteenth-seventeenth centuries acquired a syncretistic face by borrowing generously from local religious and cultural traditions. This reconstructed Islamic great tradition was more acceptable to the masses, as it resolved the problem of dualism between the Persianised and Arabic Islamic high culture of the ashraf and the Bengali culture of the ajlaf peasants.

Coming to the more modern period, the Muslim community in Bengal, unlike the Hindus, clearly lacked a sizeable educated professional intermediary group, which could close the hiatus between the two sections of their population in the newly instituted colonial public space. This was because of their backward position in educational status both in absolute numbers as well as in relative terms vis-à-vis the Hindus. In 1874–75, the Muslims constituted only 29 per cent of the school-going population in Bengal as against 70.1 per cent Hindus. They had even lesser share at the higher levels of education: in 1875 the Muslims represented 5.4 per cent of the college students, as against 93.9 per cent Hindus; and only 1.50 per cent of the Muslim literates were English-knowing, compared with 4.40 per cent among the Hindus. And this poor representation in education was reflected also in the employment situation: in 1871 the Muslims constituted only 5.9 per cent of the government officials in Bengal proper, while the Hindus accounted for 41 per cent.[98] Many reasons have been offered to explain this Muslim backwardness, such as the vanity of the ashraf as a humiliated ruling class, their economic decline following the Permanent Settlement, supersession of Persian by English as the official language in 1837, their religious aversion to an un-Islamic education etc. But we cannot explain this phenomenon by only looking at the ashraf segment that constituted only a tiny minority within the community. The majority were the poor cultivators who shared the general apathy towards education and whenever they sent their children to school, they preferred the indigenous, less expensive traditional institutions, like the *maktabs* and *madrassahs*. This explains to a large extent the under-representation of the Muslims in Western education. This also indicates that the problems of the Muslim peasantry were different: they constituted a disadvantaged majority in the eastern parts of Bengal where land holding was largely monopolised by the Hindus. The "backwardness" of the two segments of Muslim population had thus been of two different nature; it was only the colonial stereotyping, propounded through books like W.W. Hunter's *The Indian Mussalmans* (1871), which mistakenly presented the image of a homogeneous community, suffering from "backwardness" in education and employment. The interests of the ashraf section were thus presented as the interests of the entire community and it was on this stereotype that Muslim politics was eventually to construct itself.

The situation in north India was slightly different. As it was the centre of Mughal rule, the Muslim elites here constituted a privileged minority, which was gradually losing ground to the Hindus during the British period. There were some large landed magnates, like the Awadh taluqdars, who controlled one-fifth of the land in the United Provinces. Not many of them were however in business, which was largely dominated by the Hindus. But the Muslims were well represented in high administrative jobs since the Mughal days and this predominance continued into the early British period. As late as 1882, the Muslims held as many as 35 per cent of government jobs in UP, with a fair share of high and influential positions as well. But as under British rule English came to replace Persian as the official language, the Muslims began to lose their position of power and influence to the Hindus, who could adapt to the new official environment more quickly. Their position in the subordinate executive and judicial services declined from 63.9 per cent in 1857 to 45.1 per cent in 1886–87 and to 34.7 per cent in 1913, whereas the Hindus improved their representation in these services from 24.1 per cent to 50.3 per cent to 60 per cent during the same time span.[99] In other words, in course of a little more than half a century, the relative position of the two communities in the public services had just been reversed. These north Indian Muslim elites, representing the heritage of Mughal aristocratic culture, were also separated from the Muslim masses, and unlike their Bengali counterparts, they were at odds with the ulama, who exercised considerable influence over the peasantry. The traditional theocratic order was in conflict with the British rule, which had threatened the traditional system and their own predominance. The elites on the other hand had accepted subordination and were trying to adjust to the new social realities of British rule. The Muslims of north India were thus divided along many lines. Francis Robinson has depicted the UP Muslims as "more a multiplicity of interests than a community".[100] David Lelyveld has argued that this was a legacy of the Mughal social structure of asymmetrical hierarchical kinshiplike alliances, linked separately to the imperial dynasty, but rarely experiencing any horizontal solidarity across ethnic, racial or family identities.[101] It was this segmented society which in the late nineteenth century gradually evolved a common identity or a sense of belonging to a *qaum*, with a manifest destiny. In all the regions the Muslims suffered from a sense of relative deprivation in comparison with the Hindus, although this feeling was shared differently by the richer and poorer sections of the community. Gradually, however, when the political mobilisation of the Muslims began, the interests of the peasants came to be subordinated to the interests of the elites, which were projected as the interests of the entire community.

Among the Bengal Muslims a distinct Muslim identity had been developing at a mass level from the early nineteenth century through various Islamic reform movements. These movements rejected the earlier syncretism and sought to Islamise and Arabicise the culture, language and daily habits of the Muslim peasants by purging whatever they thought to be of un-Islamic origin. This gave the lower orders or ajlaf a sense of social mobility. They could think of their mythical foreign or Arabic origin and could feel a sense of identity with the upper-class sharif Muslims. This was developed through various agencies, such as the itinerant *mullahs*, the *bahas* (or religious) meetings and the *anjumans* or local associations. No initiative of the elites was directly involved in the growth of this Muslim consciousness among the masses, but this certainly helped them in political mobilisation and in strengthening their argument about separate Muslim interests.[102] The elite leaders soon linked this new sentiment to their relative backward condition and the need to organise themselves as a political pressure group to demand their just share of the institutional opportunities created by colonial rule. The first Muslim organisation in Bengal was the Mohammedan Association or the Anjuman-i-Islami, established in 1855 with two-fold objective of promoting the interests of the community and preaching loyalty to the British. In a petition to the Lieutenant Governor it demanded "no exclusive privilege, but a fair field" to compete on equal terms with the Hindus. To ensure this it advocated special measure to spread education, expressed loyalty to the Raj and condemned the revolt of 1857.[103]

The essentials of Muslim politics had thus taken shape in Bengal even before the more well known Sayyid Ahmed Khan's movement was started in UP. It soon took the form of a modernisation campaign started around the middle of the nineteenth century. It gathered more momentum in the 1860s and developed two distinct strands. Abdul Latif Khan and his Mohammedan Literary Society (1863) stood for Western education within the traditional Islamic education system, retaining full emphasis on Arabic and Persian learning. Sayyid Amir Ali and his Central National Mohammedan Association (1877–78), on the other hand, advocated a total reorganisation of Muslim education on Western and secular model or total Anglicisation of Muslim education. And although initially the Bengali Muslim elites had demanded a "fair field" and not exclusive privileges, they gradually changed their position and in this they were encouraged by the colonial bureaucracy. Hunter's book in 1871 had put forth the thesis that it was the exclusion of the Muslims from the government-sponsored education system and civil employment that was mainly responsible for greater popular appeal of the anti-British Wahabi and Faraizi movements. A faulty thesis though it was, he advocated on its basis a policy of special government favour for the Muslims in matters of education and employment. The Government of India Resolution of 7 August set the trend by providing increased state assistance for Muslim educational institutions. The policy was further reaffirmed in Lord Northbrook's Resolution of 13 June 1875 and finally endorsed by the Education Commission, which provided for special provision for Muslim education as a matter of justice. The Central National Mohammedan Association (CNMA) in a number of memoranda in 1882 and 1888 also demanded special favour and not just fair justice in matters of employment in government services. The government also endorsed this policy for the political exigency of rallying the Muslims as a counterpoise against the rising tide of Indian nationalism, which was predominantly Hindu in participation. This policy of providing protection to the Muslims to ensure their proper representation in government services was first initiated in a Resolution of July 1885. It received a concrete shape in the circular of 1897, which provided that two-thirds of vacancies in Subordinate Executive Services were to be filled up by nomination to secure a balance between the communities. The policy was finally institutionalised in the partition of Bengal, which created a new province in the Muslim dominated eastern Bengal to ensure for them a greater share of power.[104]

However, all these special concessions were being demanded by the Muslim elites on the basis of numerical superiority of the Muslim community in the population of Bengal as a whole. They became conscious of the political implications of numbers; but this also necessitated social mobilisation across cultural barriers. The easiest way to forge this horizontal solidarity was to harp on the common faith and the mullahs through the local anjumans now carried the urban message to the countryside. Around 1905 almost all major towns in Bengal had local anjumans and by 1909 the CNMA had sixteen branches in the districts. A close collaboration between the educated Muslims and the mullahs was a distinctive feature of these mofussil anjumans. This was more pronounced in the rural anjumans, which were started during the time of the Islamic reformist movements in the early nineteenth century for recruiting volunteers and collecting subscriptions. They retained their religious character, but increasingly came under the influence of the richer gentry leadership, like Nawab Salimullah of Dacca, who had taken a pro-partition stand. These anjumans thus forged a link between the urban elites and the rural masses and thus brought the latter into the larger political conflict.[105]

Extremist politics and Hindu revivalism—the impact of cow killing riots in north India, for example—by reinforcing the social fault-lines further facilitated Muslim mobilisation. The Hindu bhadralok in Bengal often looked down upon the Muslims with contempt. The Hindu *jatras* or rural theatrical performances often indulged in vilification of Muslim historical persona, which was not very lightly taken by the anjumans or the mullahs. The cumulative effect of all these factors was the accumulation of social tension, which ultimately culminated in communal violence. The urban riots, like the Titagarh riot of 1896 and the Talla riot of 1897, were followed by rural riots during the Swadeshi period, like the Ishwarganj riot of May 1906, Comilla riot of March 1907 and the riots of April-May 1907 in Jamalpur and the Dewanganj-Bakshiganj region of Mymensingh. This social separation of the two communities was further politicised by the Swadeshi leaders freely using Hindu religious symbols and coercing Muslim peasants to observe boycott. They unwittingly allowed the movement to grow into a Hindu-Muslim question; instead of having a secular approach to the political issue, they constantly harped that the Muslims were being given extra privileges at the expense of the Hindus. Not all the Muslims were separatist or loyalist at the beginning; but the Swadeshi movement soon put on them the unmistakable stamp of otherness. It was not surprising that in no time the anti-partition agitation appeared in Muslim consciousness as an anti-Muslim campaign. Only the professional and commercial people among them who were centred at Calcutta and whose interests were directly affected by the partition remained the supporters of the movement. The rest of the Bengali Muslim society, both the elites and their peasant followers, had begun to pull in a different direction.

If the anjumans prepared the Bengali Muslims for activities in the colonial public space, in north India in the late nineteenth century a variety of locally instituted bodies, such as anjumans, neighbourhood akhras, festival committees and so on got involved in popular cultural activities that gradually constructed the cultural identities based on a symbolic religious vocabulary that demarcated the boundaries between communities. Contestation over sacred public space or ceremonies led to communal riots between Hindus and Muslims, and there was no dearth of them—in Bareilly in the 1870s, in Agra in the 1880s and finally the cow-protection riots in the 1890s. Such expressions of "relational community"—bound by shared values and symbolic idioms—in a localised public arena, argues Sandria Freitag, could later be enlarged into broader and more abstract "ideological community" that became operational in institutional politics at a subcontinental level.[106] And if such popular cultural activities provided for a behavioral text of identity formation, there were also some other implements of colonial modernity, which provided for the construction of a literary discursive field for the formation of a communitarian ideology or "identity as culture". In north India in the late nineteenth century, as Ayesha Jalal points out, a vibrant regional press and a flourishing Urdu popular poetry were contributing towards the crafting of what she calls a "religiously informed cultural identity" for the Muslims of United Provinces and Punjab. And since poetry was also read in public recitals or *mushairas*, it had the potential to bridge the hiatus between elites and the masses.[107] Such a reconstituted cultural identity—or an "ideological community"—based on imaginatively shared values and interests, could later be deployed in the institutional politics of identity. But so far as the north Indian Muslims were concerned, central to this transformatory process were Sir Sayyid Ahmed Khan and his Aligarh movement.

Sir Sayyid started a modernisation movement among the Muslims and founded for this purpose the Mohammedan Anglo-Oriental College in Aligarh in 1875. As David Lelyveld has shown, his political philosophy revolved round the idea that Indian society was an aggregate of contending groups brought together by a superior power, previously the Mughal emperor, who had now been replaced by Queen Victoria, presiding over a hierarchy of distinct social units. The Muslims as an ex-ruling class were entitled to a special position of authority and power in this new cosmopolitan British empire. But for this they must educate themselves and acquire the new skills which would empower them to assert themselves within the new institutional set up of colonial India. His idea of being a Muslim was not opposed to being an Indian, but he did not visualise India as a nation state based on individual citizenship; for him it was a federation of *qaums* or ethnic communities based on common descent. These groups would enjoy cultural autonomy and share power according to their ancestry and inherited subculture, but not achievement. The Muslims as an ex-ruling class, though a minority, would therefore have a greater representation in the sharing of power and a special relationship with the political order.[108] It was here that his philosophy differed from that of the Indian National Congress, which imagined India as a nation state, based on individual citizen's rights. It was because of this divergence of perceptions that Muslim politics began to drift away from Congress and mainstream nationalism.

Sir Sayyid's Aligarh College, as David Lelyveld further argues, was a "profoundly political enterprise"[109] to construct and consolidate among its Muslim students the mentality of belonging to a qaum and to reach through them the greater social catchment area of north Indian Muslim population. Its curriculum blended Muslim theology with nineteenth century European empiricism that would prepare the new generation of Muslims for the advantages and opportunities of British rule. So far as knowledge was concerned, the Aligarh students did not have much of an edge over others; but what they picked up here was an ethos of solidarity. The other vehicle to spread Sir Sayyid's message was the Mohammedan Educational Conference ('Congress' till 1890) which met every year since 1886, i.e., the year after the Congress was born, at different cities all over India. This was in direct opposition to the Congress which Sir Sayyid thought was an attempt to organise and consolidate the Hindu majority electorate to dominate over the Muslim minority in the new representative bodies and the civil services. This majority-phobia increased further because of the cow-killing riots of 1893, the Hindu demand for legal ban on cow-slaughter and Congress silence about it. The internal problems of the Aligarh College might have also forced Sir Sayyid to take a more radical anti-Congress stand. This particular trend in Muslim politics was patronised by the British bureaucracy. Particularly significant was the role of Theodore Beck, the European principal of the Aligarh College, who formed in 1888 the Indian Patriotic Association to oppose Congress and to plead for government patronage for the Muslims. In 1893 the Mohammedan Anglo-Oriental Defence Association was formed, once again with Beck's encouragement, to check the growing popularity of the Congress and to organise Muslim public opinion against it. So Aligarh movement under Sir Sayyid Ahmed Khan and his Aligarh College developed in opposition to Congress-led nationalism and in loyalty to the British Raj, which was conceived as a legitimate successor to the Mughal empire.

However, Sir Sayyid's leadership was never universally accepted in the north Indian Muslim community. The ulama certainly did not like his thrust towards westernisation, which seemed to threaten their pre-eminence in Muslim society. As opposed to his modernism and rationality, they invoked Islamic universalism and exclusivism. There were men like Jamaluddin al-Afghani who were rabid anti-colonialist and did not like Sir Sayyid's loyalism. He was ridiculed for his imitative Western ways and unabashed championing of specific class interests. By the late 1880s many Muslims in north India were tilting towards the Congress, while in 1887 Badruddin Tyabji of Bombay had become its first Muslim president. By the late 1890s, many of the Urdu newspapers in Punjab were asserting that the Aligarh School "did not represent the Indian Muhammadans".[110] After Sir Sayyid's death in 1898, even the younger generation at Aligarh became restless, as they began to feel that they were losing out because they were not properly organised and hence could not voice their demands effectively. As a result, they gradually began to deviate from the existing tradition of Aligarh politics. For example, the earlier politicians of Sir Sayyid's generation had kept the ulama at arm's length in favour of the Western-educated intelligentsia. The politics of this period was confined to what Lelyveld has called "kachari-linked family groups" who deployed their Muslim identity only in self-defence.[111] But by contrast, the younger leaders like Muhammad Ali and Shaukat Ali, were profoundly influenced by the ulama, like Maulana Abdul Bari, and through their influence they rediscovered the inspiration of Islam as a mobilising force. This resulted in what may be called a gradual Islamisation of Muslim politics. The younger leaders also started deviating from the loyalist stand of Sayyid Ahmed and partly responsible for this was Lieutenant Governor Macdonnell's unsympathetic policies towards the

United Provinces Muslims. He preferred the Hindus to the Muslims, it was alleged, and this preference was reflected in the Nagri Resolution of 18 April 1900, which recognised the Nagri script, along with Persian, for official use in the courts. This sparked off, as mentioned earlier, what is often referred to as the Hindi-Urdu controversy, as language now became a trope for community honour and a focus for mobilisation. And soon to this campaign was added a demand for an all-India Muslim University as a cultural centre of pan-Indian Islam. But the leaders of the older generation, like Mohsin-ul-Mulk, soon backed out of this agitation, as Macdonnell threatened to cut off grants for the Aligarh College. So the younger generation was left alone to protest against discriminatory government policies and in no time they realised the inadequacies of Sayyid Ahmed's loyalist politics; some of them even threatened to join the Congress. So the older leaders and the colonial bureaucracy now felt the urgent need for a political organisation for the Muslims in order to mobilise the community against the Congress and also to offer an independent political platform, as many of the Bengal, Punjab and Bombay Muslim leaders were not prepared to accept Aligarh's leadership.

The Bengali Muslims had been coming closer to their north Indian co-religionists since 1899, when the annual Mohammedan Educational Conference was held at Calcutta. But the events of 1906 brought them even closer, though not entirely on cordial terms. In eastern Bengal the resignation of Lt. Governor Bampfylde Fuller, known for his pro-partition and pro-Muslim sympathies, and the possibility of partition itself being rescinded, made the Bengal Muslim leadership panicky. And then the Secretary of State Morley's budget speech of 1906 indicated that representative government was going to be introduced in India. This alarmed Muslim leaders across the board, as they thought that in the new self-governing bodies they would be swayed by the Hindu majority who were now well organised under the Congress. This provided the context for the Simla deputation of 1 October 1906 to the Governor General Lord Minto. For a long time the prevalent theory was that it was a "command performance", entirely stage-managed by the British, through the European principal of the Aligarh College, W.A.J. Archbald. But recent analyses show that the initiative had come from the Aligarh veterans, like Mohsin-ul-Mulk, the secretary of the Aligarh College, who wanted to assuage the feelings of younger Muslims; and it was hoped that the Bengal Muslims would also join any such deputation. But in the end the grievances of the Bengal Muslims were bypassed for being too sensitive or divisive and no Bengali joined the deputation to Simla. The petition, which the Aligarh leaders drafted, represented only their interests. It depicted the Muslims as a separate community with political interests different from those of the Hindus and therefore having legitimate claim to minority rights to proportional representation in the representative bodies and public employment. The deputation was given a patient hearing by the viceroy, and he also assured the east Bengalees that their rights would not be jeopardised.[112]

The success of the deputation was a tremendous morale booster to Muslim politics; yet mere verbal assurances were hardly expected to satisfy the younger Muslims. They had long been feeling the need for a separate political organisation for themselves; a religious orientation of the movement was also on their agenda, as there has now been, as Lelyveld (1978) describes it, a clear shift of emphasis from qaum (community based on common descent) to *ummah* (community based on allegiance to a common faith). The thirty-five delegates at Simla therefore decided to organise the community for independent political action to secure for themselves a recognition from the government as "a nation within a nation", to use the words of Aga Khan, the leader of the delegation.[113] The next annual Mohammedan Educational Conference was scheduled to be held in December 1906 in Dacca, the capital of the new province of Eastern Bengal and Assam. So it was decided that this opportunity would be taken to launch a new Muslim party. The situation in Dacca was already volatile. The nationalist agitation against the partition of Bengal had gained an unexpected momentum and there was widespread fear among the Bengali Muslims that the government might succumb to the nationalist pressure and annul the partition to the disadvantage of the Muslims. There was already a proposal from Nawab Salimullah of Dacca, the leader of the east Bengali Muslims, about the formation of a political party for the Muslims and this could be an excellent starting point for further discussion. So it was in this Dacca Educational Conference on 30 December 1906 that a new party was launched and it was called the All India Muslim League. Its professed goals were to safeguard the political rights and interests of the Muslims, to preach loyalty to the British and to further the cause of inter-communal amity. The Muslim supporters of the Congress immediately tried to counteract this move, but in vain; the majority of the educated Muslims had already decided to tread along a different path.

Until about 1910 for all practical purposes the All India Muslim League maintained its existence only as an adjunct of the

Mohammedan Educational Conference and then the two bodies were separated. Some scholars like M.S. Jain (1965) think that the League was a logical culmination of the Aligarh movement. Jayanti Maitra, however, believes that the Muslim League was not an outgrowth of the Aligarh movement, but rather the outcome of the political developments among the Bengali Muslims, who were always more politicised than their north Indian counterparts. And after all, it was the Bengal situation of 1906 that had acted as a catalyst in bringing into existence the new Muslim party.[114] But, as Lelyveld mentions, even the Nawab of Dacca believed that the new party represented "the next stage of political life" that first blossomed at Aligarh and it was expected to provide greater opportunity in public institutions for the young educated Muslims.[115] During at least the first decade of its existence, the League remained dominated by the UP Muslims and it established Aligarh's position at the centrestage of all-India Muslim politics. Viqar-ul-Mulk and Mohsin-ul-Mulk became the joint secretaries of a provisional committee that drafted its constitution, which was approved at it next session at Karachi in December 1907. In this way the Aligarh veterans, with the help of some Punjabi leaders, made the League their own organisation and moulded it according to their own ideological preferences. The constitution, for example, ensured that the new organisation would remain under the control of "men of property and influence". This excluded from the League's power structure many of those angry young men under whose pressure the party had been created at Dacca.

Between 1907 and 1909, provincial Muslim Leagues were formed in all the major provinces and they enjoyed liberty to frame their own constitutions. They were not formally controlled by the all-India body, nor could they interfere with the affairs of the central organisation. Hence the provincial Leagues were of varied political complexion and often their policies were at variance with those of the central body. Its London branch was inaugurated in May 1908 and under the leadership of Syed Amir Ali, it played a significant role in shaping the constitutional reform of 1909, the Morley-Minto Reforms.[116] This new act provided for reserved seats for the Muslims in imperial as well as provincial legislatures, in numbers much in excess of their numerical proportions and in keeping with their political importance. This granting of separate electorate for the Muslims thus provided an official legitimacy to their minority status and the separate political identity of the Indian Muslims, the League representing its public face. The subsequent evolution of this

Muslim identity from minority status to nationhood took a long and tortuous trajectory and in the meanwhile the relationship between the League and the Indian National Congress remained on shaky grounds. Between 1920 and 1924 they launched a joint agitation over the issue of Khilafat, but since then their ways progressively drifted apart. We will trace that story further in the subsequent chapters.

NOTES

1. de Barry 1958.II: 115.
2. For more details see Chandra et al. 1989: 115–16.
3. For details see Chandra 1966; and Chandra et al. 1989: 91–101.
4. de Barry 1958.II: 116.
5. Mehrotra 1971: 412.
6. Ghosh 1960: 11.
7. McLane 1977.
8. Ghosh 1960: 11.
9. Lelyveld 1978: 305–8.
10. Chandra et al. 1989: 75.
11. McLane 1977: 325.
12. Sarkar 1992.
13. Partha Chatterjee 1992.
14. Sarkar 1992.
15. Raychaudhuri 1999: 121.
16. A.P. Sen 1993.
17. Raychaudhuri 1989.
18. Kaviraj 1995.
19. For details on this case, see Chandra 1998.
20. Sarkar 2001: 197, 222.
21. Heimsath 1964.
22. A.P. Sen 1993; Sarkar 2001.
23. Wolpert 1962.
24. Sarkar: 2001: 225.
25. Sinha 1995.
26. Heimsath 1964: 173.
27. Van der Veer 1994: 66.
28. McLane 1977: 276–79.
29. Van der Veer 1994: 86–94.
30. McLane 1977: 280–81; for more on Kuka Sikhs, see Oberoi 1994: 194–201.
31. Robb 1992.
32. Yang 1980.
33. Robb 1992.
34. McLane 1977: 322.
35. Robb 1992: 134.

36. Wolpert 1962: 43.
37. McLane 1977: 325.
38. Brass 1974.
39. See Dalmia 1997 for more details.
40. King 1999: 156 and passim.
41. Cashman 1970.
42. Quoted in Wolpert 1962: 80.
43. Ibid.
44. Cashman 1970.
45. Frykenberg 1997.
46. Thapar 1997.
47. Frykenberg 1997.
48. Zavos 2000: 74–75.
49. Nandy 1998: 74.
50. Ibid: 24–25, 28, 103.
51. Raychaudhuri 1989.
52. A.P. Sen 1993: 8–12.
53. Kaviraj 1995.
54. Chatterjee 1986: 75 and passim.
55. Nandy 1998: 24–25.
56. Jaffrelot 1996: 13.
57. Sarkar 1997: 20.
58. Fox 1985: 168–71.
59. See Oberoi 1994 for more details.
60. Ray 1984: 165–70.
61. Goradia 1993: 167–70.
62. Nandy 1998: 24–25.
63. See Chowdhury 1998 for more details.
64. Tripathi 1967: 75 and passim.
65. Partha Chatterjee 1986.
66. Chatterjee 1995.
67. Kaviraj 1995.
68. Neogy 1987.
69. Sarkar 1973: 12–14.
70. Curzon quotations from Sarkar 1973: 15–20; Tripathi 1967: 95–98.
71. Cronin 1977.
72. For details, see Sarkar 1973: 9–20.
73. Ray 1984: 142, 150.
74. Guha 1992: 76–103.
75. Bandyopadhyay 1987: 88.
76. Sumit Sarkar 1984.
77. Tripathi 1967: 139–40.
78. Goradia 1993: 249.
79. Catanach 1984.
80. Ray 1984: 170.

81. Ibid: 173.
82. Hardiman 1993: 52– 53.
83. Wolpert 1962.
84. See Chowdhury 1998.
85. Details in Sarkar 1973.
86. Heehs 1993.
87. For this argument, see Chakrabarti 1992.
88. Neogy 1987.
89. Chakrabarti 1992.
90. Seal 1968: 26.
91. Ahmed 1996: 1–2.
92. Hasan 1996: 193 and passim.
93. Cohn 1986: 284 and passim.
94. Jones 1981: 84 and passim.
05. Gilmartin 1988: 39–72.
96. Ahmed 1996; Roy 1983.
97. Eaton 1993: 306–11.
98. Ahmed 1996: 134–35,153.
99. Robinson 1974: 23, 46 and passim.
100. Ibid: 28.
101. Lelyveld 1978: 20–26, 344.
102. For details, see Ahmed 1996.
103. Maitra 1984: 78–82.
104. For details, see Maitra 1984.
105. For more see Ahmed 1996.
106. Freitag 1989.
107. Jalal 2000: 44–48 and passim.
108. Lelyveld 1978: 311–12, 343–45.
109. Ibid: 317.
110. Jalal 2000: 68, 73, 77, 93–94.
111. Lelyveld 1978: 342.
112. Robinson 1974: 143–47.
113. Quoted in Maitra 1984: 272.
114. Maitra 1984: 279–81.
115. Lelyveld 1978: 338.
116. Robinson 1974: 149–52.

chapter six

The Age of Gandhian Politics

6.1 The Carrots of Limited Self-government, 1909–19

The second half of the nineteenth century, particularly the period after the suppression of the revolt of 1857, is considered to be the high noon of British imperialism in India. A self-confident paternalism tended to turn into a despotism, which was not prepared to accept any self-governing right for the Indians. This imperial idea had a philosophical as well as functional basis. Philosophically, there was what Eric Stokes has called a "Liberal division on India".[1] The division arose on the question of democracy and self-government to the dependent empire. While on the Irish Home Rule question the educated mind in England had gone against the earlier Gladstonian liberalism, utilitarianism in the late nineteenth century developed certain divergent strands. There was on the one hand, an extreme liberal position taken by John Bright and the Manchester School, which became outrightly critical of British rule in India. Taking the middle course were the other liberal utilitarians like John Stuart Mill, who believed that democracy and self-government were essential checks on despotic power, but the doctrine was only suitable for civilised people. India, therefore, had to be governed despotically. But they also inherited the optimism of the eighteenth century Enlightenment that human nature could be changed through proper education. So they conceived the imperial goal as an educative mission: Indians could be entrusted with self-government when they were properly educated for the purpose of self-rule in accordance with the principles of rationalism and natural justice. J. S. Mill had his disciples in India like Macaulay and Lord Ripon, who still believed that the Indians could be given self-governing rights at an appropriate date, when they would be properly educated for this.

There was, however, a third and more authoritarian strand. Both Bentham and James Mill thought that democracy was a checking device against the abuse of power and ultimately a means of registering the will of the majority. But neither had any belief in individual liberty for its own sake; happiness and not liberty was the end of good government. From this, an extreme authoritarian position was derived by Fitzjames Stephen, who succeeded the liberal Macaulay as the law member in the viceroy's council in India. He combined Benthamism with Hobbesian despotism: law and good government, he thought, were the instruments of improvement, and both were meaningless unless backed by power. From this philosophy followed his position on Britain's role in India being the great mission of establishing peace and order conducive to the progress of civilisation, pax Britannica. The task of the British was to introduce essential principles of European civilisation. He rejected the notion that the British had a moral duty to introduce representative institutions in India. It could be conceded if only there was a strong demand from among a sizeable section of the Indians. Stephen, with his immense influence on the Indian civil servants, became the philosopher of authoritarian British imperialism in India in the late nineteenth century. It became the tradition of direct rule, of imperial law, of empire resting on power and an Evangelical sense of duty to initiate improvement and rejecting the notion of buying support with favour to any particular class.[2]

Yet the Government of India had to introduce, though gradually, the principle of representative self-government in the late nineteenth and the early twentieth centuries. The Indian Councils Act of 1861 established limited self-government in Bengal, Madras and Bombay and it was extended to the North-Western Provinces in 1886 and Punjab in 1897. The Act of 1892 increased the number of nominated members in provincial legislative councils. Then there were the Local Self-Government Act of 1882, the Ilbert Bill of 1883, the Morley–Minto Reforms of 1909 and the Montagu–Chelmsford Reforms of 1919. How do we then explain these reforms? The old 'Cambridge School' would refer to its theory of "weak imperialism" and argue that the reforms were because of the functional needs of imperialism. The empire being essentially "weak", politically there was a need for Indian collaborators. Therefore, there was a gradual Indianisation of the civil service and entry of Indians at lower levels of local self-governing institutions. In the British empire, there was strong centralised control, but slackness at the bottom; the devolution of power was essentially to rope in more collaborators.[3] B.R. Tomlinson (1975), on the other hand, has argued about a fiscal crisis of the British Indian empire which left its imperial obligations unfulfilled. So devolution of power was to buy Indian support, as the elected Indian representatives would be better able to raise more revenue and would be more judicious in spending it. This was not a very new idea in itself, as discussion about devolution on financial reasons had started as early as the late nineteenth century. Indeed, opposition to the idea of Indian self-government melted down because of war pressures and financial weaknesses; but it is difficult to explain the reforms solely in terms of fiscal exigencies. A more important reason behind this gradual devolution was the growing strength of Indian nationalism which the Cambridge cluster of historians chose to underestimate.

Intensity of the Swadeshi movement and the spread of extremism had forced upon the administration some new thoughts on constitutional reforms, while militant nationalism reinforced this process. Fresh thinking had started since 1906, as Secretary of State Lord Morley, a liberal scholar, urged Viceroy Lord Minto to balance the unpopular Bengal partition with reforms. Although partition was declared to be a settled fact, there was also a realisation that India could no longer be ruled with a "cast iron bureaucracy". Indians should be given some share of power; they had to be admitted into the legislature, and if necessary, even into the executive council. In the legislatures, more time for budget discussion was to be allowed and amendments to government sponsored resolutions were to be admitted; but at the same time, official majority was to be retained. There were three aspects of this new policy: outright repression on the one hand, concessions to rally the moderates on the other, matched by divide and rule through separate electorates for the Muslims. The discussions on the constitutional reforms were initiated in Morley's budget speech in September 1906. There were some controversies between London and Calcutta, particularly centring round the definition of moderates. By this term, Morley thought of the Congress moderates, while Minto meant the loyal elements outside the Congress, like the rulers of the princely states or the Muslim aristocracy. The post-mutiny policy of alliance with the conservative elements in Indian society was now to be further institutionalised in the face of mounting nationalist pressure.

The Indian Councils Act of 1909 (Morley–Minto Reforms) provided for limited self-government and therefore satisfied none of the Indian political groups. It was the most short-lived of all constitutional reforms in British India and had to be revised within ten years. It did allow somewhat greater power for budget discussion, raising questions and sponsoring resolutions to members of legislative councils, who were to be elected for the first time. The act introduced the principle of election, but under various constraints.

Details of seat allocation and electoral qualifications were left to be decided by the local governments, and this left enough space for bureaucratic manipulation. Special provision was made for additional representation of professional classes, the landholders, the Muslims, as well as European and Indian commerce. Official majority was retained in the Imperial Legislative Council, which would have only 27 elected members out of 60; and out of those 27 seats, 8 were reserved for the Muslim separate electorate. Non-official majorities were provided for in the Provincial Councils, but importance of this non-official majority was reduced by the fact that many of these non-officials were to be nominated by the government. The Bengal provincial legislature was given an elected majority, but four of the elected members were to represent European commercial interests, who were always expected to vote with the government. Finally, the electorate was based on high property qualifications and therefore was heavily restricted. There were disparities too, as income qualifications for the Muslims were lower than those for the Hindus. And above everything, the Government of India was given the general power to disallow any candidate from contesting the election on suspicion of being politically dangerous.

Dissatisfaction with the existing constitution and clamour for more self-governing rights increased during World War One. There was also now greater acceptance of the idea of Indian self-rule in British political circles, and this brought in important changes in British policies too. But the idea of reform perhaps originated in India, where the government had been facing the radical transformation of Indian politics on a day-to-day basis. This experience strengthened the new Viceroy Lord Chelmsford's liberal vision of enunciating the goal of "Indian self-government within the Empire".[4] But as the Government of India's dispatch to the secretary of state in November 1916 argued, this should be offered gradually, in keeping with the rate of diffusion of education, resolution of religious differences and acquisition of political experience. In other words, there was no definite timetable for devolution, but enough safeguards to protect Indians against the tyranny of their own rule.

However, the ultimate goal of transplanting British parliamentary institutions in India had to be declared as the moderates in Indian politics were gradually being sidelined by the radicals. In December 1916 the Congress and the Muslim League for the first time drew up a common constitutional programme at Lucknow. The beginning of the Home Rule agitation and the internment of its leader Annie Besant in April 1917 further radicalised Indian politics, as we shall see. Lord Chelmsford's administration had already allowed a number of concessions to nationalist demands, such as customs duty on cotton imports without a countervailing excise duty, ban on labour emigration etc. Now it was desperate for a declaration of goals for British rule in India, but nothing happened until Edwin Montagu took over as the Secretary of State for India in July 1917. He has been described by a sympathetic historian as "the most liberal Secretary of State since Ripon".[5] Montagu on 20 August 1917 made a historic declaration at the House of Commons that henceforth British policy in India would have an overall objective of "gradual development of self-governing institutions, with a view to the progressive realization of responsible government in India as an integral part of British empire".[6] The declaration, in other words, did not propose the end of empire or independence for India. But the reform proposals were definitely an improvement over the 1909 act, as its main theme was elected majority in the provinces with executive responsibility. But the responsible government was to be realised progressively, thus suggesting an indefinite timetable that could be easily manipulated to frustrate liberal expectations.

Before we jump to any conclusion on whether or not the Montagu–Chelmsford reforms really sought to introduce representative and responsible government in India, we should first examine its provisions. The Government of India Act of 1919 provided for a bicameral legislature at the centre, the council of state and the legislative assembly. The latter would have an elected majority, but no control over the ministers. The viceroy would have a veto in the form of the 'certificate' procedure for pushing the rejected bills. The electorates were considerably enlarged to 5.5 million for the provinces and 1.5 million for the imperial legislature. But on the other hand, despite some theoretical criticism of the principle of separate electorate in the Montagu–Chelmsford Report, communal representation and reservations were not only retained, but also considerably extended. In addition to the Muslims, Sikhs were granted separate electorate too, while seats were reserved for the non-Brahmans in Madras and the 'depressed classes' were offered nominated seats in the legislatures at all levels. However, the most innovative feature of the new act was 'dyarchy', which meant that certain functions of the provincial governments were to be transferred to the ministers responsible to the legislative assemblies, while other subjects were to be kept as 'reserved' for firm bureaucratic control. The departments that were actually transferred were, however, of less political weight, such as education, health, agriculture, local bodies etc. These had limited funds, which would invariably discredit the Indian ministers, while more vital departments, such as law and order, finance etc. were kept under official control. This was to some extent balanced off by the provision of parity of representation between the Europeans and Indians in the provincial executive councils. But the provincial governors too had veto and certificate powers. The revenue resources were divided between the centre and the provinces, with land revenue going to the provinces, and income tax remaining with the centre.

The significance of the reform of 1919 has been assessed variously by different historians. Philip Woods, on the one hand, has argued that the ideas behind the reforms "were crucial in establishing parliamentary democracy in India and, thereby, in beginning the process of decolonisation".[7] For Carl Bridge, on the other hand, these were measures to "safeguard the essentials of the British position" in India.[8] For Tomlinson, it was an attempt to mobilise "an influential section of Indian opinion . . . to support the Raj".[9] The major problem of the reform, as Peter Robb has identified, was its being "limited by ideas of continuing British presence".[10] Many Indians by this time had moved beyond the idea of self-government within the empire. Their new goal was swaraj, which was soon going to be defined as complete independence. The reform therefore failed to satisfy Indian political opinions, and prevent the eventual mass movement. The Cambridge School has in a different way sought to establish a connection between the constitutional reforms of 1909 and 1919 and the emergence of mass politics after World War One. As the electorate was widened, the Indian leaders were forced to operate in a democratic way and seek the support of the masses.[11] This interpretation does not necessarily explain the mass upsurge under Mahatma Gandhi. A major theme of Gandhi's non-cooperation programme launched in December 1920 was the boycott of the new councils. Gandhian philosophy, as we will see, was based on a critique of Western civil society; the mass movement he engineered had an altogether different logic, as his mission was to liberate Indian politics from this constricted arena of constitutionalism.

6.2. THE ARRIVAL OF MAHATMA GANDHI

Nationalist movement in India before the arrival of Mohandas Karamchand Gandhi (soon to be known as Mahatma [great soul] Gandhi) from South Africa in 1915 has been described by Judith Brown as "politics of studied limitations"[12] and by Ravinder Kumar as "a movement representing the classes" as opposed to the masses.[13]

What these descriptions essentially imply is that nationalist politics until this time was participated only by a limited group of Western-educated professionals, whose new skills had enabled them to take advantage of the opportunities offered by the Raj in the form of administrative positions, seats in the district boards or legislative councils. They belonged mainly to certain specific castes and communities, certain linguistic and economic groups, living primarily in the three presidency towns of Calcutta, Bombay and Madras. D.A. Low has described these classes as "the underlings of the British rulers", who were marginally, if at all, interested in any far reaching economic or social change in India. They were more concerned about creating a new elite society and culture for themselves and were influenced by the ideas and ideals of the British aristocracy or the middle classes.[14] Apart from these groups, like the bhadralok of Bengal, the Chitpavan Brahmans of Bombay or the Tamil Brahmans of Madras, the other sections of the society, like the lower-caste Hindus or the Muslims, the landlords and the peasants, both rich and landless, and commercial men of all kinds, showed reluctance to join Congress politics. They lived in Bihar, Orissa, the Central Provinces and Berar as well as in the United Provinces and Gujarat, which could be described as the "backward provinces" so far as Congress politics were concerned. The colonial government, therefore, could take comfort in the fact that Congress was being run as a closed shop by "a microscopic minority".

This early Congress politics was also limited in goals and rather unspectacular in achievements. The moderates after the Surat Split in 1907 demanded colonial self-government, as against the extremist demand of complete independence. Their organisations were seemingly based on personality networks woven around such prominent leaders as S.N. Banerjea, P.M. Mehta or G.K. Gokhale on one side, and Bepin Pal, B.G. Tilak or Lajpat Rai on the other. In popular perception, there appeared to be no difference in principle or conviction between the two groups of leaders, apparently engaged in nothing but fruitless polemics. Both the groups had lost credibility as they had failed to achieve their stated goals. The constitutional politics of the moderates had failed to impress the British government and that was amply reflected in the Morley–Minto Reforms of 1909. Extremism was confined mainly to Bengal, Maharashtra and Punjab, where outbreak of violent activities allowed the government to unleash repression. Deportation and long sentences broke the rank of their leadership and forced the movement to move underground and into further isolation from the people. With extremist leaders like Tilak in prison, the moderate-dominated Congress was immersed in total inactivity. In other words, by 1915–17 both these two varieties of politics had reached an impasse, and when Gandhi came to encounter these politicians, they had very little room to manoeuvre. By contrast, Gandhi as a newcomer to Indian politics was not tainted by the failures of any of these groups. He did not have a vested interest in the political status quo and therefore more prepared to welcome a shift of power from the Western-educated elites to the hands of the masses. He had a clear vision of the pluralist nature of Indian society, but was dedicated to the ideal of a united India. For the younger generation of Indians, frustrated by the eternal squabbles between the moderates and extremists, he offered something refreshingly new. In an age of moral vacuum and physical despondency, he promised a political programme that was also spiritually noble.

In order to understand why Gandhi's philosophy and political programme had a wide popular appeal, it is necessary to have a look at the social and economic environment of India during World War One, as it undoubtedly created a congenial context for his emergence as an undisputed leader of Indian nationalism. The most immediate outcome of war was a phenomenal increase in defence expenditure, which instead of being cut back, kept on rising even after 1919. The result was a huge national debt, which rose by more than Rs. 3 million between 1914 and 1923. This meant heavy war loans and rising taxes and since land revenue had been settled and could not be immediately enhanced, there was more indirect taxation on trade and industry. There were higher customs duties, an income tax, super tax on companies and undivided Hindu business families, excess profit tax and so on. Ultimately the burden of this new taxation fell on the common people, as it resulted in a phenomenal price rise. According to official calculations, price index on an all-India level rose from 147 in 1914 to 281 in 1920 (1873 as the base year).[15] This unprecedented price rise was partly due to indirect taxes, partly due to transport and other economic dislocations. There was underproduction of food crops during the war period, caused by two extraordinary crop failures in 1918–19 and 1920–21, affecting large areas of United Provinces, Punjab, Bombay, Central Provinces, Bihar and Orissa. And when there was already serious shortage of food for home consumption, export of food to feed the army fighting abroad continued. This resulted in near famine conditions in many areas, where the miseries of the people were further compounded by the outbreak of an influenza epidemic. According to the census of 1921, about 12 to 13 million people had lost their lives due to the famine and epidemic of 1918–19, causing a stultification of natural population growth in the country.[16]

Between the years of 1914 and 1923 forced recruitment for the army was going on without interruptions, leading to a steady accumulation of popular resentment in the countryside. More so, because all the sections of rural society had already been affected by the economic impact of war. While prices of industrial and imported goods and food crops were rising, affecting poor peasantry, that of exported Indian agricultural raw materials did not increase at the same pace. The outcome was a decline in export, rising stockpiles and falling acreage for commercial crops, causing a crisis in the market in 1917–19. This adversely affected the richer peasantry. During this period, there was a marked increase in the number of peasant-proprietors being dispossessed and turned into tenants-at-will, and land passing into the hands of the non-cultivating classes. This process was intensive and more clearly visible between 1914 and 1922 in Madras and United Provinces. In some areas the mounting economic distress of the peasantry found expression in organised peasant protests, such as the Kisan Sabha movement in UP which started in 1918.

The other major economic development during World War One was the growth of industries. Due to fiscal requirements, economic necessities and nationalist pressure, there was a change in official policy towards industrialisation, leading to noticeable developments in the jute and textile industries. While the jute industry developed mainly with British capital, it was Indian capital that was involved in the textile industry in Bombay and Ahmedabad. Here the big industrial magnates remained loyal to the British, as they were dependent on exports and on government assistance for keeping the prices of raw cotton low and in dealing with labour unrest. By contrast, the small and middle traders had a series of grievances against the wartime taxes and the fluctuating rupee-sterling exchange rates. The other important result of industrialisation was an expansion of the working class. According to census figures, the number of workers in the organised industries increased by 575 thousand between 1911 and 1921 and this expanding working class was really hard hit by the extraordinary price hike of this period. The wartime and the post-war periods witnessed super profits for businessmen, but declining real wages for the workers. In cities like Lahore or Bombay the average cost of living for workers had increased by 60 to 70 per cent, while wages rose by only 15 to 25 per cent;[17] the situation was the same in the Calcutta jute mills, Jamshedpur steel plants or the Assam tea gardens. The obvious result was what Chelmsford described as a "sort of epidemic strike fever" that affected all the industrial centres in India,[18] a topic which we will discuss in the next chapter.

World War One thus brought in social and economic dislocations for nearly all the classes of Indian population, accomplishing the necessary social mobilisation for an impending mass upsurge. The war also brought disillusionment for the educated youth, long mesmerised by the glitter of the West; suddenly they discovered the ugly face of Western civilisation. It was, therefore, a climate of moral and physical despondency that greeted Gandhi, arriving in India with his background of a successful encounter with the British in South Africa. Gandhi's novel political ideology, as Judith Brown has argued, "appealed to few wholly, but to many partially", as everyone could find in it something to identify with.[19] Unlike the older politicians, he was fully aware of Indian pluralism and took care not to alienate any of the communities or classes. The earlier politicians wanted a hegemony of a nationalist ideology built on ideas borrowed from the West, while Gandhi argued that the ideology must be rooted in India and its ancient civilisation. Popular loyalties in India, in his opinion, were not determined by the institution of class; religion had a stronger influence on popular mind. He therefore successfully used religious idioms to mobilise the masses. But this was not revivalism of the earlier politicians, as he was not referring to history, but to religious morality. His goal was a moral goal, and therefore, a utopian goal—unattainable and ever-elusive. He talked about swaraj as his political goal, but never defined it and therefore could unite different communities under his umbrella type leadership. "Inclusivism" became identified as "Gandhi's unique style of politics",[20] which was based on a recognition of the diversities of India.

Gandhi derived his political ideas from various sources. He drew inspiration from his reading of Western thinkers like Henry David Thoreau, John Ruskin, Ralph Waldo Emerson or Leo Tolstoy. He was equally, if not more, influenced by Vaishnavism and Jainism, as he was exposed to these ideas during his early life in Gujarat.[21] Where Gandhian philosophy differed significantly from those of the earlier nationalist leaders was that he began with a trenchant critique of the "modern" civilisation—a critique which has evoked mixed responses from his later commentators. For Ashis Nandy, he was—like Rabindranath Tagore before him—"a counter modernist critic of the West",[22] which he thought had become diseased because of its disproportionate power and spread; and by arguing this, Gandhi "threatened the internal legitimacy of the ruling culture".[23] For Partha Chatterjee, his philosophy represented a "critique of civil society" or to put it more directly, "a fundamental critique of the entire edifice of bourgeois society".[24] Manfred Steger (2000) has called it a "critique of liberalism", while for Bhikhu Parekh, it is a "Critique of Modern Civilisation", which by way of providing an ideology to confront imperialism also "overlooked some of its great achievements and strengths".[25] Gandhi's *Collected Works* have now run into more than one hundred volumes, and his ideas on various issues had been continually evolving. It is therefore difficult to make an authoritative statement on his philosophy. Within the short space that we have here an attempt will be made only to highlight some important aspects of his political thinking.

In *Hind Swaraj* (1909), a text which is often privileged as an authentic statement of his ideology, Gandhi offered a civilisational concept of Indian nation. The Indians constituted a nation or *praja*, he asserts, since the pre-Islamic days.[26] The ancient Indian civilisation—"unquestionably the best"—was the fountainhead of Indian nationality, as it had an immense assimilative power of absorbing foreigners of different creed who made this country their own. This civilisation, which was "sound at the foundation" and which always tended "to elevate the moral being", had "nothing to learn" from the "godless" modern civilisation that only "propagate[d] immorality". Industrial capitalism, which was the essence of this modern civilisation, was held responsible for all conflicts of interests, for it divorced economic activities from moral concerns and thus provided imperatives for imperial aggression. Indians themselves were responsible for their enslavement, as they embraced capitalism and its associated legal and political structures. "The English have not taken India; we have given it to them." And now the railways, lawyers and doctors, Gandhi believed, were impoverishing the country. His remedy for this national infliction was moral and utopian. Indians must eschew greed and lust for consumption and revert to village based self-sufficient economy of the ancient times. On the other hand, parliamentary democracy—the foundational principle of Western liberal political system and therefore another essential aspect of modern civilisation—did not reflect in Gandhi's view the general will of the people, but of the political parties, which represented specific interests and constricted the moral autonomy of parliamentarians in the name of party discipline. So for him it was not enough to achieve independence and then perpetuate "English rule without the Englishmen"; it was also essential to evolve an Indian alternative to Western liberal political structures. His alternative was a concept of popular sovereignty where each individual controls or restrains her/his own self and this was Gandhi's subtle distinction between self-rule and mere home rule. "[S]uch swaraj", Gandhi asserted, "has to be experienced by each one for himself." If this was difficult to attain, Gandhi refused to consider it as just a "dream". "To believe that what has not occurred in history will not occur at all", Gandhi replied to his critic, "is to argue disbelief in the dignity of man." His technique to achieve it was *satyagraha,* which he defined as truth force or soul force. In more practical terms, it meant civil disobedience—but something more than that. It was based on the premise of superior moral power of the protesters capable of changing the heart of the oppressor through a display of moral strength. Non-violence or ahimsa was the cardinal principle of his message which was non-negotiable under all circumstances.[27]

It is not perhaps strictly correct to say that Gandhi was rejecting modernity as a package. Anthony Parel notes in his introduction to *Hind Swaraj* that this text is presented in the genre of a dialogue between a reader and an editor, "a very *modern* figure", with Gandhi taking on this role.[28] Throughout his career he made utmost use of the print media, editing *Indian Opinion* during his South African days, and then *Young India* and *Harijan* became the major communicators of his ideas. And he travelled extensively by railways while organising his campaigns. Yet, by offering an ideological critique of the Western civilisation in its modern phase, Gandhi was effectively contesting the moral legitimacy of the Raj that rested on a stated assumption of the superiority of the West. So far as his methods were concerned, Partha Chatterjee has argued that they gave Gandhi immense manoeuvrability in terms of real politics. There was an implicit recognition of an existing disjuncture between morality and politics—the concept of ahimsa could bridge this gap. Failures could be explained either in terms of the loftiness of the ideal or in terms of imperfections of human agency.[29] But this ontological space for manoeuvring notwithstanding, this problem of reconciling the principles of non-violence with the realities of nationalist movement proved to be a perpetual "dilemma" that Gandhi had to negotiate with throughout his career as a leader of Indian nationalism, and this dilemma grew stronger over time as the movement intensified.[30]

It will be, however, misleading to suggest that Gandhi was introducing Indians to an entirely new kind of politics. The mass movement organised by Tilak in Maharashtra in the 1890s, the activities of the Punjab extremists and above all the Swadeshi movement in Bengal in 1905–8 had already foreshadowed the coming of agitational politics in India. And so far as mass mobilisation was concerned, the Home Rule Leagues of Tilak and Annie Besant prepared the ground for the success of Gandhi's initial satyagraha movements. Indeed, when in 1914, Tilak was released from prison and Annie Besant, the World President of the Theosophical Society, then stationed in Madras, joined the Congress, they wanted to steer Indian politics to an almost similar direction. But although Tilak was readmitted to Congress in 1915 due to Besant's intervention, they failed to reactivate the party out of its almost decade-long inertia. In frustration, Tilak started his Indian Home Rule League in April 1916 and Besant her own All India Home Rule League in September—both acting at tandem and in cooperation. The Home Rule movement had a simple goal of promoting Home Rule for India and an educative programme to arouse in the Indian masses a sense of pride in the Motherland.[31]

By 1917–18, when the government came down heavily upon the Home Rule Leagues, they had a membership of about sixty thousand all over India, most importantly, in areas like Gujarat, Sind, United Provinces, Bihar and parts of south India, which did not in the past participate in nationalist movement. Yet, although their impact fell on a much wider community outside its direct membership, the Leagues ultimately could not bring in mass agitational politics in India. In Madras, Maharashtra and Karnataka, despite some untouchable support, the Leagues being under Brahman domination, invited the opposition of the non-Brahmans. But more significantly, Annie Besant, who was made the Congress President in 1917, began to take a conciliatory attitude towards the moderates, particularly after the announcement of the Montagu–Chelmsford reform proposals, and put the passive resistance programme on hold. This frustrated the young extremist leaders who provided her main support base and the Home Rule Leagues soon became defunct. Nevertheless, many of the local leaders of Gandhi's early satyagrahas came from Home Rule League background and they used organisational networks created by the Leagues.

While Annie Besant failed, Gandhi succeeded in uniting both the moderates and extremists on a common political platform. In the divided and contestable space of Indian politics, he could effectively claim for himself a centrist position, because he alienated neither and tactically combined the goal of the moderates with the means of the extremists. He adopted the moderates' goal of swaraj, but was "delightfully vague" (to borrow Nehru's expression) about its definition, as any specific definition, he knew, would alienate one or the other group. So each group could interpret it in their own ways. His method of satyagraha looked very much like the passive resistance of the extremists; but his insistence on non-violence alleviated the fears of the moderates and other propertied classes, apprehensive of agitational politics. There was also a rift in the Muslim community around this time, between the Aligarh old guards and the younger generation of Muslim leaders. Gandhi aligned himself with the younger leaders by supporting the khilafat issue. He highlighted its anti-British aspects and underplayed its pan-Islamic tendencies, and thus for the first time united the Hindus and the Muslims in a combined battle against the British.

What was more important, beyond the ranks of these elite leaders, Gandhi could also appeal directly to the Indian peasantry and tap the vast reservoir of popular support among the masses, already afflicted by the dislocations of war. And here he was not constrained by the limitations of the Home Rule leaguers. Judith Brown has argued that Gandhi's rise did not symbolise "a radical restructuring of political life" or opening of modern politics to the "masses"; rather it signified the rise of Western-educated and regional language literate elites of backward areas, in place of the Western-educated leaders of the presidency towns. It was the loyalty networks of these local elite leaders, or the so-called "sub-contractors", which mobilised popular support for Gandhi in the Indian countryside and small towns.[32] Such an interpretation grossly underestimates Gandhi's popular appeal. His simple attire, use of colloquial Hindi, reference to the popular allegory of *Ramrajya* had made him comprehensible to the common people. His charismatic appeal rested on a skilful use of religious symbols and idioms. In popular myths, he was invested with supernatural power, which could heal pain and deliver the common people from their day-to-day miseries. The masses interpreted Gandhi in their own ways, drawing meanings from their own lived experiences, and made him a symbol of power for the powerless.[33] It is difficult to ignore this millenarian aspect of Gandhi's popular appeal; Brown's "sub-contractors" had very little control over this groundswell. And here also lay the main paradox of Gandhian politics, for he wanted not just any mass upsurge, but a "controlled mass movement",[34] which would strictly adhere to his prescribed path. Time and again the masses crossed the boundaries of Gandhian politics and deviated from his ideals, while believing at the same time that they were following their messiah into a new utopian world of *Gandhi Raj*. Gandhi himself, let alone his "sub-contractors", had little control over this mythical messiah imagined by his own followers. Their behaviour he tried to control and when he failed, condemned it as "mobocracy".[35] In this sense, it did signify a radical restructuring of political life in India.

This became quite evident in his three early localised satyagraha movements in Champaran, Kheda and Ahmedabad. At Champaran in Bihar, peasant discontent against the European planters forcing them to produce indigo under the *tinkathia* system (which bound peasants to produce indigo in three twentieth part of their land) had been mounting since the 1860s under the local middle and rich peasant leaders. One of them, Raj Kumar Shukla, travelled to the Lucknow Congress in 1916 and persuaded Gandhi to come to Bihar and lead their movement. Here, the local young educated Congress leaders like Rajendra Prasad or J.B. Kripalani, played little role in mobilising the peasants. These peasant masses spontaneously rallied to the call of the Mahatma, who they believed to be their divinely ordained deliverer. In his name, but without his knowledge, the rich peasant leaders organised the lesser peasantry into violent actions, which Gandhi would not approve of. His intervention, accompanied by telling rumours, broke the barrier of fear in the minds of poor peasants, who now dared to defy the authority of the British Raj and the European planters. But Gandhi would not take this movement beyond its limited goal, which was fulfilled when the Champaran Agricultural Act was passed in November 1918. Yet this legislation neither fully stopped planter oppression, nor quelled peasant protest. The local peasant leaders continued to mobilise support by invoking the name of Gandhi, making this area a strong base for future Gandhian movements.[36] Champaran thus became a nationalist legend, although the local Congress leaders had little sympathy for the protesting peasants, particularly when they stood against the indigenous zamindars. In 1919 when Swami Viswananda organised local peasants against the heavy demands of the Darbhanga Raj and the oppressive behaviour of its amlas, he received no support from the Bihar Congress.[37]

Similarly in 1917 in the Kheda district of Gujarat a variety of factors, such as destruction of crops by late rains, sudden rise in agricultural wages, high rate of inflation and the outbreak of bubonic plague contributed to unusual hardship particularly for the rich Patidar peasants. In a small town of Kathlal in the northern part of the district, a no-revenue campaign was actually started by two local leaders, Mohanlal Pandya and Shankarlal Parikh, with a demand for revenue remission. Through the Gujarat Sabha they got in touch with Gandhi in January 1918, but it was not until 22 March that Gandhi decided to launch a satyagraha in their support. Even then, it was a "patchy campaign", as it affected only a few villages; often the peasants capitulated to government pressure and often they crossed the boundaries of Gandhian politics of non-violence. By April the Bombay government partially fulfilled the peasants' demands by not confiscating the properties of defaulting peasants who could not pay, and in June Gandhi withdrew the campaign. Here too the intervention of the Gujarat Sabha or its educated leaders like Vallabhbhai and Vithalbhai Patel was of little direct consequence, as a movement had already been started and subsequently sustained by the local leaders. Gandhi made a solid political base in the villages of Kheda district; but the support of the villagers was on their own terms. When Gandhi returned with an appeal for recruitment for the army to fight in World War One, peasants rejected it with contempt.[38]

In the middle of the Kheda satyagraha, Gandhi also got involved in the Ahmedabad textile mill strike of February–March 1918. Here his adversaries were the Gujarati millowners, who were otherwise very close to him. The immediate reason for industrial conflict was the withdrawal of plague-bonus, which was being given to dissuade workers from leaving the city in the face of mounting plague-related deaths. This withdrawal came at a time when the workers were already facing hard times from unusual high prices caused by World War One, and there were wildcat strikes and the formation of a weavers' association. Thus when labour got restive in Ahmedabad, Gandhi was invited by Anusuya Sarabhai, a social worker, and his brother Ambalal Sarabhai, the president of the Ahmedabad Millowners' Association, to intervene as an arbitrator and defuse the crisis. But Gandhi's intervention and the formation of an arbitration board proved futile, as millowners demanded a complete strike moratorium as a precondition for any negotiated settlement. On 22 February when the stubborn millowners locked out the weavers, Gandhi decided to champion the workers' cause, but persuaded them to tone down their demand to a wage hike of 35 per cent, instead of their original demand of 50 per cent. He and his Sabarmati ashram volunteers mobilised the workers and held regular meetings where initially thousands attended. But as the impasse continued, the millowners stood their ground and the workers began to lose their morale. Gandhi now used his last weapon of a hunger strike; the intransigent millowners gave in and agreed to send the matter to the arbitration board. Although the workers ultimately got only 27.5 per cent wage rise, this movement went a long way in mobilising and organising the working classes in Ahmedabad, paving the way for the foundation of the Textile Labour Association in February 1920. But neither labour nor capital in Ahmedabad showed any evidence of an ideological commitment to the idea of "arbitration" as a novel Gandhian technique of resolving industrial disputes.[39]

Gandhi gained nationwide popularity by championing these localised causes. Yet, if we look closely at these movements, we will find that on every occasion Gandhi was invited to provide leadership where considerable mass mobilisation had already taken place under local initiative. The masses interpreted Gandhi's message in their own terms and rumours surrounding the powers of this messianic leader served to break the barriers of fear involved in confronting formidable enemies. And everywhere the masses pushed their own agendas, much to the dislike of the elite nationalist leaders in the regions. But in the process all these regions became strongholds of political support for Gandhi, as people here responded eloquently to his later calls for political action. But once again this activism followed trajectories that were vastly divergent from the one desired by the leader.

In the Rowlatt satyagraha of 1919 Gandhi sought to move to a campaign that proposed to involve the entire nation; but here too we witness the same phenomenon, i.e., overwhelming mass support for Gandhi but for reasons and considerations that were different from those of the leader. The movement was aimed against the two bills prepared by a committee under Justice S.A.T. Rowlatt, to provide the government with additional coercive power to deal with political violence. One of the bills was passed in the Imperial Legislative Assembly on 18 March 1919 over the unanimous protests of the Indian members. Ever since the content of the bill was published, Gandhi proposed to resist it with satyagraha. He was opposed to the spirit of the bill, which he described as the distrust for common men. It signified the reluctance of the government to part with arbitrary powers and thus made a mockery of the democratic constitutional reforms. Gandhi's initial programme was, however, modest: along with a few close associates he signed a satyagraha pledge on 24 February to disobey this and similar other unjust laws. On 26 February he issued an 'open letter' to all the Indians urging them to join the satyagraha. He decided to launch a nationwide movement, starting with a general strike or *hartal* on 6 April. But the movement soon lapsed into violence, particularly after Gandhi's arrest on 9 April.

The government had no prior experience of handling such widespread mass agitation. To avoid trouble they arrested Gandhi, but that precipitated a crisis, provoking unprecedented mob fury in areas like Delhi, Bombay, Ahmedabad or Amritsar. Gandhi's trusted volunteers could not control this mass violence and were themselves swayed by it. The government response was varied, as in the event of a complete breakdown of communication, provincial governments reacted according to their own preconceived notions. In Bombay the response was restrained, while in Punjab, Sir Michael O'Dyer unleashed a reign of terror. The worst violent incident was the massacre of Jallianwallabagh in the city of Amritsar on 13 April, where General Dyer opened fire on a peaceful gathering of satyagrahis, killing 379 people, in a bid to break their morale.

By mid-April the satyagraha had started losing momentum, forcing Gandhi to withdraw it. As a political campaign, therefore, it was a manifest failure, since it failed to secure its only aim, i.e., the repeal of the Rowlatt Act. It also lapsed into violence, although it was meant to be non-violent. Gandhi admitted to have committed a Himalayan blunder by offering the weapon of satyagraha to a people insufficiently trained in the discipline of non-violence. But the movement was significant nevertheless, as it was the first nationwide popular agitation, marking the beginning of a transformation of Indian nationalist politics from being the politics of some restricted classes to becoming the politics of the masses. However, having said this, we should also recognise the limits of this Gandhian mass movement. The whole of India literally was not affected and the movement was more effective in the cities than in the rural areas. And here again the strength of the movement was due more to local grievances, like price rise or scarcity of basic commodities, than to protest against the Rowlatt bills, about which there was very little popular awareness. Finally, the effectiveness of the movement depended on the capability of the local leaders to relate local grievances to the national issue of the Rowlatt Act.

In other words, in the absence of any central organisation and an overarching popular consciousness, the importance of regional specificities and salience of local issues and leadership remained too obvious in a movement that is often claimed in the nationalist historiography as the first mass agitation at a national level. Gandhi as yet had no control over the Congress; hence, for organising the movement he set up a Satyagraha Sabha in Bombay and was helped by the Home Rule Leagues. Apart from this, in course of his extensive tours in many parts of India in February-March, he had made personal contacts with local leaders, through whom he now sought to disseminate his message. But the capability and popularity of these leaders, as well as their control over local society varied, as also varied their commitment to Gandhian ideology. While mediation was an important factor at the initial stage of mass mobilisation, the leaders often failed to control mass emotions once these were aroused. As it became apparent soon, such face-to-face leadership was inadequate for organising a nationwide agitation in a vast country like India.[40] The failure of the anti-Rowlatt Act agitation made Gandhi realise the need for an impersonal political organisation such as the Congress. His next step was to take over the Congress leadership.

6.3. KHILAFAT AND NON-COOPERATION MOVEMENTS

After the withdrawal of the Rowlatt satyagraha, Gandhi got involved in the Khilafat movement, in which he saw a splendid opportunity to unite the Hindus and the Muslims in a common struggle against the British. In the early twentieth century, there emerged a new Muslim leadership, which moved away from the loyalist politics of Sir Sayyid Ahmed Khan and the elitism of the older Aligarh generation and looked for the support of the entire community behind them. For these younger leaders there was no basic contradiction between Muslim self-affirmation and Indian nationalism. Certain new issues also emerged around this time, which shook their faith in British patronage. The Muslim university campaign, renewed again after 1910, suffered a setback when the government took a hard line about insisting on strict government control and vetoed the idea of making it an affiliating body. The partition of Bengal was annulled in 1911 and the Muslim League in its Calcutta session in 1912 regretted it. In 1911–12 the Tripolitan and the Balkan Wars appeared as a European conspiracy to weaken the Ottoman empire, which was the last of the Muslim powers in the world. A Turkish Relief Fund was raised and a Red Crescent Medical Mission was sent to Turkey in March 1912. A number of Muslim newspapers and periodicals, such as *Comrade, Hamdard, Zamindar* and *Al Hilal* appeared both in English and in Urdu, reflecting these concerns of the educated Indian Muslims.

Along with a new educated middle-class leadership, the ulama or the Muslim clergy were also emerging as a new political force, or more significantly, as "an important link" between the different Muslim groups in India.[41] Two institutions, i.e., the Dar-al-Ulam at Deoband and the Firangi Mahal at Lucknow, were instrumental in their rise. The Deobandis formed in 1910 the Jamiat-al-Ansar or an old students' association, and in 1913 a Quranic school in Delhi, to reach the wider Muslim community at a time when they were deeply affected, both emotionally and politically, by the Balkan Wars. In Lucknow, the ulama at the Firangi Mahal, who in the eighteenth century represented a rationalist school of Islamic learning, had been taking increasing interest in world Islam since the 1870s.[42] One of them, Abdul Bari, along with the Ali brothers—Muhammad and Shaukat—now opened an All India Anjuman-e-Khuddam-e-Kaaba, to unite all Indians to protect Muslim holy places. The younger Muslim leaders thus closed the distance, which Sayyid Ahmed would prefer to maintain with the ulama, as they were more eager to forge a community of believers or *umma*, as opposed to Sir Sayyid's qaum or a community of common descent.[43]

In the meanwhile, the anti-Congress and pro-government attitude of the Muslim League was also changing with the induction of younger men, like Muhammad Ali, Wazir Hasan or Abul Kalam Azad, into its leadership. Muhammad Ali Jinnah was brought in and he became a bridge between the League and the Congress. These tendencies became more prominent when Britain declared war against Turkey in November 1914. The Muslims refused to believe that it was a non-religious war, as leaders like Ali brothers with pro-Turkish sympathies were soon put behind bars. The Lucknow Pact in 1916 offered a joint League-Congress scheme for constitutional reforms, demanding representative government and dominion status for India. The principle of separate electorate was accepted, and proportional representation in both imperial and provincial legislature was agreed upon. In 1917 the Muslim League supported the Home Rule agitation started by Annie Besant. But the outbreak of communal riots in Bihar, United Provinces and Bengal soon after this rapprochement revealed the continuing disjunction between the masses and their leaders. The latter's lingering faith in constitutional politics suffered a further jolt when the Montagu–Chelmsford Reforms in 1919 totally disregarded the Lucknow Pact and the Muslim University Bill passed in September 1920 provided for a non-affiliating university under strict government control. The defeat of Turkey created the spectre of Islam in danger, an issue that could be used to mobilise mass support. The result of these developments was a shift in Muslim League leadership from the moderate constitutionalists to those who believed in Islamic religious self-assertion and broad-based mass movement. The Delhi session of the Muslim League in December 1918 invited the ulama and gave them public prominence,[44] thus for the first time bringing them directly into the political centrestage.

The context was thus prepared for the beginning of Khilafat movement, the first mass agitation to forge political unity among a divided Indian Muslim community.

Behind the Khilafat movement were the rumours about a harsh peace treaty being imposed on the Ottoman Emperor who was still regarded as the Khalifa or the spiritual head of the Islamic world. The movement, launched by a Khilafat Committee formed in Bombay in March 1919, had three main demands: the Khalifa must retain control over the Muslim holy places; he must be left with his pre-war territories so that he could maintain his position as the head of the Islamic world; and the Jazirat-ul-Arab (Arabia, Syria, Iraq and Palestine) must not be under non-Muslim sovereignty. It was thus a pan-Islamic movement in all its appearance, as the cause had nothing to do with India. But as Gail Minault has shown, the Khilafat was being used more as a symbol, while the leaders actually had little concern about altering the political realities in the Middle East. It was found to be a symbol that could unite the Indian Muslim community divided along many fault-lines, such as regional, linguistic, class and sectarian. To use Minault's words: "A pan-Islamic symbol opened the way to pan-Indian Islamic political mobilization."[45] It was anti-British, which inspired Gandhi to support this cause in a bid to bring the Muslims into the mainstream of Indian nationalism.

Initially the Khilafat movement had two broad trends: a moderate trend headed by the Bombay merchants and a radical trend led by the younger Muslim leaders, like Muhammad Ali, Shaukat Ali, Maulana Azad and the ulama. The former group preferred to proceed through the familiar constitutional path of sending a delegation to the viceroy or ensuring Muslim representation in the Paris Peace Conference. The latter group on the other hand, wanted a mass agitation against the British on the basis of unity with the Hindus. Gandhi took up the Khilafat cause and initially played a mediating role between the moderates and the radicals. The moderates began to lose ground when the delegation headed by Dr Ansari and participated by Muhammad Ali himself, met the viceroy, then Prime Minister Lloyd George and then visited Paris, but returned empty-handed. The radicals then took charge of the movement, as emotions ran high after the publication of the terms of the Treaty of Sevres with Turkey in May 1920. In the same month, the Hunter Commission Majority Report was published, and it did not seem strong enough in condemning General Dyer's role in the Jallianwallabagh massacre. This infuriated Indian public opinion. The Allahabad conference of the Central Khilafat Committee, held on 1–2 June 1920, decided to launch a four stage non-cooperation movement: boycott of titles, civil services, police and army and finally non-payment of taxes. The whole movement was to begin with a hartal on 1 August. Muslim opinion on non-cooperation was still divided and throughout the summer of 1920 Gandhi and Shaukat Ali toured extensively mobilising popular support for the programme. The hartal was a grand success, as it coincided with the death of Tilak, and from then on support for non-cooperation began to rise. Gandhi now pressed the Congress to adopt a similar plan of campaign on three issues: Punjab wrong, Khilafat wrong and swaraj. In an article in *Young India* he announced that through this movement he would bring swaraj in one year. He did not, however, define what this swaraj would actually mean.

The established politicians of the Congress still had their doubts about a non-cooperation programme. As they had no experience in mass agitation, it appeared to be a leap in the dark. There was an apprehension that it might lead to violence which would delay the implementation of the new constitutional reform, since the elections to the reformed councils were scheduled for November 1920. On the other hand, support for Gandhi's proposal for a non-cooperation movement came from the politically backward provinces and groups, which were not hitherto involved in Congress politics. Between September and December 1920 the Congress witnessed a tussle between these two groups, as neither side wanted a split and searched for a consensus. A special session of the Congress was convened at Calcutta on 4–9 September 1920, where Gandhi's resolution on non-cooperation programme was approved over a qualifying amendment from Bepin Chandra Pal of Bengal, and despite stiff opposition from the old guards, like C.R. Das, Jinnah or Pal. The programme provided for surrender of government titles, boycott of schools, courts and councils, boycott of foreign goods, encouragement of national schools, arbitration courts and *khadi* (homespun cloth). The programme was then endorsed at the regular session of the Congress at Nagpur in December 1920. Here too opposition came from Das, who sought to turn the table against Gandhi by proposing a more radical programme. But ultimately a compromise was reached, as Das turned over to Gandhi's side. The resolution accepted all parts of the non-cooperation programme, but it was to be implemented in stages, as directed by the All India Congress Committee. The movement, Gandhi assured, would bring swaraj within one year. If that did not happen or if government resorted to repression, then a civil disobedience campaign was to be launched, involving non-payment of taxes. The resolution also provided for a radical restructuring of the Congress through the constitution of district and village level units to transform the party into a true mass organisation.

Why the veteran Congress leaders accepted Gandhi and his proposal of a mass movement is a matter of conjecture and controversy. Judith Brown thinks that the Nagpur resolution was a victory for Gandhi as he made "no concessions of principle",[46] while Richard Gordon[47] and Rajat Ray[48] think that it was Gandhi who capitulated to Das and accepted many of his proposals. Putting aside these extreme views, we may perhaps argue that in a context of changing balance of power within the Congress, both needed each other. Gandhi's potential as a political organiser had been established and he had access to new areas of political support, which were beyond the reach of the older Congress leaders. Gandhi's support was coming from the Muslim Khilafatists, from the backward regions and backward classes. A populist groundswell, sometimes fuelled by millenarian hopes, and often outside the ambit of the Congress, had been visible in different parts of India. Independent peasant movements had appeared in the Midnapur district of Bengal, in parts of north Bihar, in the Awadh district of Uttar Pradesh and in the Kheda district of Gujarat. This was also the period of labour unrest and trade unionism, marked by a major strike in the Bombay textile industry in January 1919,[49] appearance of the Madras Labour Union in April 1918, some 125 new trade unions and finally the formation of the All India Trade Union Congress in Bombay in November 1920.[50] Within this context, there was an unusually large attendance (14,582) at the Nagpur session of the Congress and most of these new delegates were the supporters of Gandhi. The established leaders were swayed by this huge mass support and accepted the Gandhian creed, although with much hesitation, and not without resistance. On the other hand, Gandhi too needed the Congress leaders, without whom he could not hope to organise a nationwide movement, as his recent experience of Rowlatt satyagraha had clearly demonstrated. His goal was to forge a grand coalition of various classes and communities and in this sense the Nagpur Congress symbolised the emergence of a centrist leadership within the pluralist structure of political India.

The Non-cooperation movement began in January 1921, the initial emphasis being on middle class participation, such as students leaving schools and colleges and lawyers giving up their legal practice. Simultaneously, there were efforts at developing national schools and arbitration courts, raising a Tilak Swaraj Fund of Rs. 10 million and recruiting an equal number of volunteers. Gradually, the movement became more militant, with the beginning of boycott and organisation of public bonfires of foreign cloth. A nationwide strike was observed on 17 November, the day the Prince of Wales arrived in India on an official visit. On that day Bombay witnessed the outbreak of the first violent riot of the movement, targeting the Europeans, Anglo-Indians and the Parsis in the city. Gandhi was incensed; full-scale civil disobedience or a no tax campaign was postponed; it was decided that an experimental no revenue campaign would be launched at Bardoli in Gujarat in February 1922. The venue was carefully chosen, as it was a ryotwari area, with no zamindars and therefore no danger of a no-revenue campaign snowballing into a no-rent campaign tearing apart the fragile coalition of classes. But this never happened, as before that the Non-cooperation movement was withdrawn.

The extent of success of the non-cooperation movement would not definitely give Gandhi total satisfaction. Middle-class participation was not spectacular, as revealed in the figures for school, colleges and court boycotts, while peasant and working class participation was more impressive. Except in Madras, council election boycott was more or less successful, with the polling average being 5–8 per cent. Economic boycott was more intense and successful, as the value of imports of foreign cloth dropped from Rs. 1,020 million in 1920–21 to Rs. 570 million in 1921–22. The import of British cotton piece goods also declined from 1,292 million to 955 million yards during the same period.[51] Partly responsible for this success was trader participation, as the businessmen pledged not to indent foreign cloth for specific periods. During the period 1918–22, while the large industrialists remained anti-non-cooperation and pro-government, the Marwari and Gujarati merchants, aggrieved by the falling exchange rates and the taxation policy of the government, remained "fairly consistently pro-nationalist".[52] However, their refusal to import foreign cloth might have also been due to a sudden fall in rupee-sterling exchange rates that made import extremely unprofitable.[53] Production of handloom, on the other hand, also increased, but no definite statistics are available for that. Together with non-cooperation, there were other associated Gandhian social movements, which also achieved some success. Temperance or anti-liquor campaign resulted in significant drop in liquor excise revenue in Punjab, Madras, Bihar and Orissa. Hindu–Muslim alliance remained unshaken throughout the period, except in the Malabar region. The anti-untouchability campaign, however, remained a secondary concern

majority party in the legislature.[57] In Madras, the movement witnessed from the very beginning a Brahman-non-Brahman conflict, as the Justice Party launched an active campaign against the 'Brahman' Congress and its non-cooperation programme and rallied in support of the Montagu–Chelmsford Reforms. Because of this resistance, the boycott of foreign cloth was also much weaker in the Tamil regions than in other provinces of India.[58] The development of national schools and arbitration courts and khadi did not succeed everywhere either. In Nagpur division, for example, the inadequacy of national schools forced students to get back to government educational institutions. As arbitration courts became defunct, lawyers got back to their usual legal practice.[59] In most areas, khadi was 30 to 40 per cent more expensive than mill cloth, resulting in its unpopularity among the poor people.[60] In many cases, such as in the small towns of Gujarat, mobilisation depended on local issues, like temple politics, control over municipalities or control over educational institutions[61] or in the south Indian towns grievances against rising municipal taxes or the income tax. In Tamilnad, the success of the temperance movement depended on various social motives, such as the Sanskritising tendencies of the upwardly mobile castes and local factionalism.[62] In some other areas, mobilisation to an extent depended on personal influence of local leaders, such as C.R. Das in Bengal, whose personal sacrifices—giving up a lucrative legal practice, for example—inspired the younger generation.[63]

In Punjab, on the other hand, the Akali movement has been described by Richard Fox as representing "the largest and longest application of the Gandhian programme of satyagraha, or non-violent resistance."[64] However, if we look closely at this movement, we will find that it had very little direct relevance to his non-cooperation programme. Tracing its origins from the wider reformist Singh Sabha movement of the late nineteenth century (see chapter 5.2), this particular campaign started in October 1920 when a Siromoni Gurdwara Prabandhak Committee (SGPC) was formed. Its aims were to reform the Sikh gurdwaras and to reclaim control of the Sikh shrines from the hands of the government manipulated loyalist committees that included non-Sikhs. In December, as an auxiliary of the SGPC the Akali Dal was formed to coordinate *jathas* to wrest control of the shrines, the name Akali ("servants of the Eternal God") being derived from the small band of martyr-warriors formed to defend the faith during the time of Ranjit Singh.[65] Already irritated by the administration of martial law and the Jallianwallabagh massacre, the Akalis came to a head-on collision with the government when in early 1921 it took the keys of the Golden Temple at Amritsar and appointed a new manager. When the Akalis protested, the government once more unleashed a repressive regime, and the latter responded with satyagraha. Gandhi and the Congress supported the campaign, which ultimately forced the government to surrender the keys and administration of the temple to the Akalis. But the middle-class Sikh leadership had only selectively adopted the non-cooperation programme and once their limited goal was achieved, did not allow their distinctive religious struggle to be completely appropriated by the Congress agitation.[66]

As urban middle-class enthusiasm soon petered out all over India, business interest was also vacillating. While the larger Indian capitalists opposed the non-cooperation programme from the very beginning, smaller traders and merchants continued to use their networks to promote hartal and generously donated money to the Tilak Swaraj Fund. But they too opposed a total boycott of foreign goods.[67] Attempts to involve the working classes also ran into problems. For instance, an experiment to involve the tea garden labourers in Assam ended up in a disaster at Chandpur which was condemned severely by Gandhi. Dependence on the capitalists prevented the leaders from mobilising the working class, as Gandhi continually insisted that the movement should maintain harmonious capital-labour relationship.[68] In Nagpur and Berar, the Gandhians achieved some influence over the working classes, but this hardly had any significant impact on the overall momentum of the Non-cooperation movement in the region.[69] And where labour unrest turned violent, as in Madras, the local leaders quickly washed their hands off, forcing the striking workers to submit to the authorities. This disheartened the workers so much that when in 1922 the Congress workers wanted again to mobilise them, there was hardly any response.[70] The flagging interest in the urban areas soon shifted the focus of the movement to the countryside. It was here that the movement took widely variable shapes depending on the structures of peasant societies.

The non-cooperation movement was most effective where the peasants had already organised themselves. In Awadh district of UP a radical peasant movement was being organised since 1918–19 against the oppressive taluqdars. This peasant militancy, organised at the grassroots level by local leader Baba Ramchandra, was later harnessed by the UP Kisan Sabha which was launched in February 1918 in Allahabad. By June 1919 the Kisan Sabha had 450 branches and the UP Congress tried to tap into this reservoir of peasant militancy by tagging the movement to the Non-cooperation campaign in the province.[71] In north Bihar too, the Congress movement became most powerful in those areas which witnessed the previous anti-planter agitation, Swami Viswananda's campaign and Kisan Sabha activities.[72] In the Midnapur district of Bengal the Mahishya peasants had been organised in 1919 against the Union Board taxes by a local leader B.N. Sasmal; later on this movement too merged into the non-cooperation campaign.[73] In certain regions of Orissa, like Kanika for example, the existing tradition of peasant *melis* or anti-feudal demonstrations continuing since the nineteenth century, was later on incorporated into the non-cooperation movement.[74] In the Kheda district of Gujarat, the Patidar peasants had already launched a successful no-revenue campaign in 1918 and they were again preparing for another round of stir; this district for obvious reasons, therefore, became the strongest bastion of non-cooperation movement.[75] In south India, between December 1921 and February 1922 there was a "brief and sporadic" no-revenue campaign in the Godavari, Krishna and Guntur districts in the Andhra delta. Here the village officials, through whom the revenue was collected, resigned and the peasants hoping for a collapse of the government, stopped paying the revenue. But when the government instituted an inquiry into their grievances and threatened to arrest the leaders who would not give up, the agitation subsided within weeks. In both these cases, the momentum of the agitations was slowly mounting for quite some time, at least since 1918–19, and these were then integrated into the non-cooperation movement.[76] In other areas, where there was no pre-history of peasant mobilisation, the response of the countryside was rather muted. This shows that it was the internal dynamics of the regions that accounted for the success of the non-cooperation movement, rather than the Congress mobilising an as yet inert peasantry into an organised nationalist campaign.

The Non-cooperation movement remained more under the control of the Congress leaders where there were homogeneous and dominant peasant communities holding sway over lower caste agricultural labourers, such as the Mahishya peasant caste in Bengal or the Patidar peasant caste in Gujarat. Here local leaders had greater control through caste organisations and other community and kinship networks. Even here, the peasants showed considerable self-initiative: the Patidar peasants had started a no-revenue campaign even without the formal approval of the Congress. Then the withdrawal of the movement so disheartened them that when their leaders wanted to mobilise them again in 1922, they simply refused to respond.[77] Such self-initiative was more clearly discernible where no such homogenous peasant groups could be found. In some parts of Orissa, for example, peasants stopped paying rents and forest taxes against the wishes of their local Congress leaders and continued their stir even after its formal withdrawal by the Congress.[78] Elsewhere, in Awadh for example, where there was more cross-caste mobilisation, the peasants were more uncontrolled. They interpreted Gandhi in their own varied ways and tried to combine the nationalist movement with their own struggle against taluqdari oppression. Attacks on taluqdari property increased in the winter of 1921–22 and the Congress found it too difficult to control. Gandhi visited UP and criticised the peasants for turning violent, but with no appreciable results. So the Congress decided to abandon it; Baba Ramchandra was arrested and the movement was severely repressed, but the local Congress did not raise a finger.[79] For the peasants in Gorakhpur, for instance, Gandhi represented a symbol of deliverance from day-to-day oppression. There were rumours all around which showed that to the peasants swaraj meant a millenium, a utopian state where there would be no rent, no revenue, no repayment of loans, no zamindar or taluqdar. It was a situation which the peasants in their imagination had always desired. Gandhi had thus appealed to their imagination and fired them into action.[80] On the other hand, in Punjab after the Amritsar victory the Akali campaign moved to the countryside, wresting control of the Guru-ka-bagh shrine in Novemeber 1922, i.e., long after the non-cooperation movement had been formally withdrawn. By January 1923 they had taken control of about one hundred shrines, and then in September, when the government deposed the ruler of the princely state of Nabha for his alleged support to the Akalis, the latter launched a militant anti-colonial campaign in Jaito for his restoration. During its rural phase the Akali movement at various places crossed the boundary of non-violent movement, and the peasants openly defied the authority of the Raj. Gandhi withdrew his support at this point as he disapproved of the campaign for the deposed Nabha ruler. The government now came down heavily on the Akalis, but ultimately patched up a compromise for fear of affecting the loyalty of the Sikh soldiers. The Gurdwara Reform Act of 1925 restored the control of the shrines to Sikh management. But as the movement was withdrawn, the rural protesters felt betrayed.[81]

Gandhi also appealed to the millennial dreams of the Indian tribal population who got involved increasingly in the wider politics of the nation, although on their own terms. In tribal areas, building on the existing traditions of dissent, local leaders organised movements against various localised grievances. In this sense of course, these movements, apart from a faith in Gandhi, had very little in common with the aims and forms of the Gandhian movements. For example, in the hills of Kumaun and Garhwal in UP, continuing the existing tradition of dhandak or customary protest against the sovereign (see chapter 4.2), Badridutt Pande of Almora organised a militant movement against *utar* or forced labour and forest laws. To contain the *bania raj* of the English, Pande argued, God had sent a saviour in the form of another *bania,* i.e., Gandhi. Although Richard Tucker (1983) has argued that this was modern political conflict reaching the hills for the first time, the specific forms that the movement took, i.e., firing the woods or other acts of incendiarism, showed that it had little connection with the formal structures of the Congress movement.[82] Similarly in the Midnapur district of Bengal, where the Santhal grievances had flared up in 1918 against the forest laws and the Midnapur Zamindari Company, owned by the Europeans, local leaders like Sailajananda Sen could mobilise them again with relative ease in 1921, against their European landlords and the colonial state. However, once the movement turned militant, the Congress became lukewarm in its support; but by that time tribal agitation had acquired its own momentum.[83] In the Gudem Hills of Andhra, another local leader, Alluri Sita Rama Raju, impressed by Gandhi, preached among the hillmen his message of temperance and khadi, but believed that India could be liberated only by force. Building on the existing tradition of fituri (chapter 4.2), he started guerilla warfare in January 1922; but unlike the earlier tradition, he wanted to take his battle beyond the tribal territory of the Gudem region. His attempt failed, as in May 1924 he was captured and executed.[84] But this failed attempt showed, despite Congress antipathy towards such violent upsurges, that tribal populations in India while maintaining their territorial anchorage were also developing a consciousness that connected them to a wider anti-colonial struggle. When the hillmen of Kumaun raised slogans in praise of Gandhi and *Swatantra Bharat* (independent India),[85] they exhibited a consciousness that was evidently broader than what we witnessed in the late nineteenth century (chapter 4.2). However, Congress itself had little to do with this consciousness or its political articulation.

"The Mahatma of his rustic protagonists", writes Shahid Amin, "was not as he really was, but as they had thought him up".[86] In their imagination the real Gandhi and his programme of non-violent non-cooperation were often lost. The imagined Gandhi was endowed with extraordinary occult power: peasants believed him to be a saint who could heal diseases, reward those who would follow him and punish non-believers who would dare to defy his authority.[87] The rumours prevalent among the tribals of Bengal revealed their supreme faith in Gandhi's protective power: if they wore a Gandhi cap or chanted Gandhi's name, they believed, police bullets would not harm them. This broke the barrier of fear and unleashed their energy into unprecedented mass activism. While chanting Gandhi's name, peasants participated in activities, which easily crossed the threshold of Gandhian ideals. The tribal peasants of Bengal looted markets and fisheries and violated forest laws; prisoners broke the prison gates.[88] In north Bihar, where the lower caste poor peasants were the most militant elements, messianic expectations led to a series of market looting incidents, a display of unheard of defiance of authority and bold interference with police action.[89] So when the peasants of Gorakhpur attacked the local police station in Chauri Chaura and burnt alive twenty-two policemen, Gandhi had little option but to withdraw the movement, as it had definitely by then got out of his control.

The local Congress leaders never did approve of these deviations from their authentic version of Gandhian movement, which was meant to dislodge the British without disturbing social harmony. But they had little control over the events. Gandhi was sympathetic to the masses and conceded that "[t]hey often perceive[d] things with their intuition, which we ourselves fail[ed] to see with our intellect." But he did not like their indiscipline and wanted to "evolve discipline out of this habitual indiscipline". And when he failed, he condemned this mass exuberance as "Mobocracy".[90] Therefore, even after the official withdrawal of the movement, it continued in pockets of Bengal, Bihar and Orissa. In several villages in Kheda the no-revenue campaign continued, while in UP another militant peasant movement developed in the form of Eka movement led by the tribal peasants (Pasi). Gandhi had used the Congress organisation for launching what was no doubt the first nationwide mass agitation against colonial rule. It involved the peasants, some workers, tribals and even in some areas the untouchables; but it is doubtful as to what extent they had accepted the Congress creed or internalised Gandhian ideology. Gandhi depended on a provincial leadership that consisted of such prominent personalities, as young Jawaharlal Nehru in UP, C.R. Das in Bengal, Vallabhbhai Patel in Gujarat, Rajendra Prasad in Bihar or C. Rajagopalachari in Madras. These provincial leaders again relied on the local leadership of men like

Baba Ramchandra in Awadh, B.N. Sasmal in Midnapur or Kunwarji Mehta in Bardoli. Through this structure of leadership Gandhi's message reached the masses, but then it was transformed and transfigured in their imagination, as they imputed different meanings into the nationalist movement. The construction of these meanings, which depended on the specific structures of community, the local situations and the nature of existing organisation, determined the extent of mass militancy, which the leadership tried to control, but without success. In other words, the point that needs to be emphasised here is that what passed as a Gandhian mass movement actually contained within it various levels of consciousness informed by different visions of freedom. If the Congress tried to project through this movement a particular programmatic version of nationalism, it is also true that this version was continually contested from within the movement. And this was a feature that marked the subsequent Congress mass movements as well.

6.4. Civil Disobedience Movement

For some time after the withdrawal of the Non-cooperation movement, the Congress was not in a position to launch another round of mass movement. Gandhi since his release from prison in 1924 remained aloof from direct politics and concentrated his energies on constructive programmes, such as the untouchability removal campaign, promotion of the use of *charkha* (spinning wheel) as a mark of self-help, and building up an *ashram* at Sabarmati where he would train a group of ideal satyagrahis. The colonial government considered him to be a spent force, politically. This complacency was also due to the fact that the national consensus, which he had constructed a few years ago, broke down quickly and India witnessed a "crisis of unity". The Congress itself became divided among the "no-changers" and "pro-changers", the former wanting to stick to Gandhian ways, while the latter preferring to revert to constitutional politics. Gradually the constitutionalists became more powerful and under the leadership of C.R. Das and Motilal Nehru launched the Swaraj Party within the Congress. Their ambition was to participate in council politics and wreck the constitution from within. But the swarajists were by no means a stable group or united by all-India loyalty and disciplined to achieve that mission. On the other hand, the growing influence of the Congress Socialists under the young leaders Jawaharlal Nehru and Subhas Chandra Bose eventually led to a Right-Left confrontation within the party.

The short-lived Muslim League-Congress alliance was also jeopardised by the decline of the Khilafat movement. The Muslim League itself became divided among the supporters of joint electorate and separate electorate. Communal riots broke out in Kohat in the North-Western Frontier. In Bengal the Hindu–Muslim pact forged by C.R. Das in 1923 broke down, culminating in a fierce riot in Calcutta in April 1926. It was followed by a series of other riots in eastern Bengal between 1926 and 1931, as "music before mosques" became an emotional issue for rival communal mobilisation in the countryside.[91] In UP between 1923 and 1927 there were eighty-eight riots, leading almost to a complete breakdown of Hindu–Muslim relations.[92] In the election of 1925–26 religious issues were freely exploited by Hindu orthodox groups led by Madan Mohan Malaviya, resulting in the defeat of the secularist Motilal Nehru. As a corollary, Hindu nationalist organisations, like the All India Hindu Mahasabha gained in strength in north and central India; its close and problematic relationship with the Congress tarnished the latter's secular image and led to further alienation of the Muslims from mainstream nationalism.[93] The untouchables too, whom Gandhi called Harijan (God's people), were frustrated as the campaign to ameliorate their conditions received lukewarm response throughout India. They were first organised in 1926 under the banner of an exclusive organisation by Rao Bahadur M.C. Rajah; but in 1930 Dr B.R. Ambedkar organised them into an All India Depressed Classes Congress with a clear anti-Congress agenda (more in chapter 7.2).

However, despite such fissures in organised political life, there were, on the other hand, some significant changes that prepared the ground for another round of mass agitation against the British Raj. First of all, a major crisis for the export-oriented colonial economy culminated in the great depression in the late 1920s. The prices of exportable agricultural cash crops went down steeply—by about 50 per cent in general—affecting the rich peasantry. The prices of some cash crops fell more drastically than others. The price of cotton, for example, grown in Punjab, Gujarat and Maharashtra, fell from Rs. 0.70 per pound in the mid-1920s to Rs. 0.22 in 1930. The price of wheat within a year fell from Rs. 5 to Rs. 3 per maund between 1929 and 1930. The price of rice began to fall a little later, from the beginning of 1931, when the jute market also crashed in Bengal. While the income of the peasantry was going down, the amount of revenue, settled previously in a condition of high prices, remained static, as government was not prepared to allow any remission to accommodate the price fall, still widely believed to be a temporary phenomenon. As landlords remained under pressure to pay revenue, there was no relenting in the pressure of rent on the tenants. And in such a situation debt servicing became a problem, as moneylenders were now more keen in recovering their capital. In many areas the flow of rural credit dried up and the peasants were forced to sell parts of their land to raise the capital to keep cultivation going.[94] However, the situation varied from region to region, and even within the same region such as Bengal, as Sugata Bose has shown, the effect varied widely depending on the structure of peasant society and organisation of production.[95]

This situation helped Congress to mobilise the rich peasants and small holders in various parts of the country, such as Bengal, coastal Andhra or UP. In the latter area, repeated crop failures and shortfall in the production of food crops also added to the miseries of the poor peasants. This led to the organisation of peasant movements outside the Congress, as it was clearly not interested in mobilising such potentially radical lower peasant groups. In Bengal too, poor Muslim, untouchable Namasudra and tribal Santhal peasants mobilised around radical agrarian demands in 1928–29, representing what Tanika Sarkar has described as "a parallel stream of protest".[96] The environment was certainly conducive for a mass agitation if the local Congress leaders could relate the specific grievances of these peasants to the broader national agenda of swaraj. But their major challenge was to reconcile the interests of the richer landowning peasants with the concerns of the labouring agricultural workers and tenants.

The other important development was the emergence of a capitalist class during and in the years immediately following World War One. Fiscal needs forced the Government of India to impose protective tariffs, pushing the prices of imported articles up, and thus helping unintentionally Indian industrialisation. As a result, in the 1920s there was a powerful and conscious Indian capitalist class which organised itself in 1927 under the banner of the Federation of Indian Chambers of Commerce and Industries (FICCI). This was also the time when the Indian bourgeoisie was coming into conflict with the imperial government on many issues. Their usual way of handling the situation was to operate as a pressure group; but increasingly their leaders like G.D. Birla or Purushottamdas Thakurdas and even the moderate Lalji Naranji were coming to the conclusion that they would do better if they sided with the Congress to fight their battle. Many of the captains of Indian industries were the cotton mill owners of western India, who had reached the threshold of endurance as a result of depression and competition from cheap Japanese textiles. By the summer of 1930 the Bombay mill owners were left with record unsold stocks—120,000 bales of cloth and 19,000 bales of yarn.[97] Throwing their lot with the Congress now seemed to be an option worth trying. Congress too began to support many of their demands and made them into national issues, and thus began to attract the capitalist class to its side. But the problem was, there had also been a parallel expansion of the industrial working class and a rise in its political consciousness. The year 1928–29 was the peak period of labour unrest in India, witnessing about 203 strikes spread over all parts of the country. Although the workers often exhibited considerable autonomy of action, one of the major reasons behind this enhanced labour activism was the penetration of communist influence—in eastern India through the Workers' Peasants' Party and in Bombay through the Girni Kamgar Union. By 1930, however, this communist influence declined as the government came down heavily on them with repressive measures, and the Comintern instructed them to keep distance from the Congress-led nationalist movement. This gave the Congress an opportunity to resurrect a broad united front, although working-class support for it was in general weak, except in Bengal, where their fight was against the British capitalists. But still the Congress tried to project itself as a "supra-class entity" and "above interests"[98] and thus sought, although very clumsily, to bring in both the capitalists and the workers under the same banner (more in chapter 7).

Within such a cluttered context of discord and disorder, Indian politics was galvanised again from late 1927 when a Tory government in London appointed an all-white Statutory Commission under Sir John Simon to review the operation of the constitutional system in India. Non-inclusion of Indians in the commission provoked protests from all the political groups in India and resulted in a successful nationwide boycott—participated by both Congress and the Muslim League. When the Simon Commission arrived in the country in early 1928, it was greeted with slogans like "Go Back Simon". Motilal Nehru in this context started negotiating for a joint Hindu-Muslim constitutional scheme as a fitting reply, and at an all parties conference in Lucknow in August 1928 the Nehru Report was finalised. It was a bunch of uneasy compromises and therefore stood on shaky grounds. Its final fate was to be decided at the forthcoming Calcutta Congress in December 1928, and Motilal wanted Gandhi to throw his weight behind the scheme, so that it was accepted smoothly by the Congress. But for Gandhi swaraj was not a constitutional matter that the British could give; for the attainment of proper swaraj, he had been mobilising the masses outside the Congress. If the Nehru Report had been one entry point for Gandhi once again into the Congress-led nationalist politics, the other entry point was the Bardoli satyagraha of 1928.

Bardoli taluka of Surat district in Gujarat was meant to be the site of a no-tax campaign during the Non-cooperation movement. It could not take place as the movement was withdrawn and the peasants complied with the instructions of the Congress leaders to pay up their taxes without resistance. But the local leaders Kunvarji and his brother Kalyanji Mehta carried on their constructive programmes in an area, which was ideally suited to become an important stronghold of Gandhian politics. Its Patidar peasants had been recent immigrants to the area. With less social stratification they were a homogeneous community organised by the Mehtas since 1908 under the banner of the Patidar Yuvak Mandal. The local Kaliparaj tribals were completely under their control, being bound to them through debt-servitude. Here a taluka unit of the Congress was opened, along with a Bardoli Swaraj Sangh, through which the Mehta brothers organised not only the Patidar peasants, but also the Kaliparaj tribals who responded to their constructive work and skilful use of tribal religious symbols. So when the Bombay government in 1927 raised the land revenue by 22 per cent, affecting "a small but dominant landed class", consisting mainly of Patidar, Anavil Brahmans and Baniyas, a good deal of social mobilisation had aleady taken place for the starting of a no-revenue campaign. The Bardoli satyagraha was launched on 4 February 1928 by Vallabhbhai Patel, the president of the Gujarat Congress Committee, with the blessings of Gandhi. Though Patel organised the movement on the spot with the help of local mediators, it was actually Gandhi's movement, as his image was constantly used for political mobilisation, both among the Patidar peasants and Kaliparaj tribals.[99] The movement was widely reported in the national press, as it was a spectacular success. A judicial inquiry was initiated, on the basis of which enhanced revenue rates were cut down, confiscated lands were returned and finally revenue revisions were abandoned, at least for the time being. The success of the Bardoli satyagraha brought Gandhi once again into the limelight. It proved his point that satyagraha was more effective than the constitutional methods.

As Judith Brown has remarked, "Bardoli lifted Gandhi out of the depression";[100] and the Calcutta Congress of December 1928 witnessed his re-emergence as a national leader. By that time the opposition to the Nehru Report had become stronger. It contained a constitutional scheme that proposed dominion status for India, which was opposed by a radical younger group led by Jawaharlal Nehru and Subhas Chandra Bose. Both Nehru and Bose were in favour of complete independence. Even Muslim opposition to the report was increasing, as groups headed by Jinnah and Aga Khan repudiated it. So Gandhi proposed a compromise resolution, which adopted the Nehru Report, but said that if the government did not accept it by 31 December 1930, the Congress would go in for a non-cooperation movement to achieve full independence. Jawaharlal Nehru and Subhas Bosc were still unhappy; but when Gandhi as a further concession cut down the time limit to 1929, the resolution was passed. In the open session also Gandhi's compromise resolution was carried, while Bose's amendment demanding complete independence was lost. Thus Gandhi once again came to dominate the Congress, but as Brown (1977) says, he wanted to assume leadership only on his own terms. So he had a second resolution passed which contained a detailed programme of constructive work. It involved revival of organisational work, removal of untouchability, boycott of foreign cloth, spread of khadi, temperance, village reconstruction and removal of disabilities of women. It was through this constructive programme that Gandhi hoped to achieve true swaraj. But one important issue that this constructive programme did not touch was Hindu–Muslim unity.

Even after the Calcutta Congress, some Congress leaders outside the Nehru-Bose group, like the Liberals, preferred cooperation with the British. The then viceroy, Lord Irwin, also wanted a reconciliation to introduce a constitutional scheme with a dominion status as the ultimate goal. He received the support of the Labour government in power and hence came the "Irwin Offer" of 31 October 1929, proposing a Round Table Conference to settle the issue. Gandhi was reluctant to reject it outright, but negotiations broke down, as the Congress leaders wanted the details of the dominion status to be discussed, and not just the principle. In December public attention shifted to Lahore where the next session of the Congress was going to be held with Jawaharlal Nehru as the president. Many leaders had reservations about starting a movement for full independence, particularly in view of the rising wave of violence spearheaded by revolutionary leaders like Bhagat Singh and others. So when Gandhi arrived in Lahore he had an uphill task and a lot of opposition to encounter; but in spite of everything his preferred resolution was passed. It defined the Congress goal as full independence or "*purna swaraj*" and proposed that as a preliminary to start a civil disobedience movement to achieve it, a boycott of legislature would begin immediately. The All India Congress Committee (AICC) was authorised to start a civil disobedience movement at an appropriate time. But Gandhi, as it seems, had not as yet been able to convince all his critics.

The call for the boycott of legislatures evoked only limited response. Muslim members of the Congress, like Dr Ansari, were unhappy, as communal unity they thought was an essential precondition for the success of a civil disobedience movement. Outside the Congress, the Muslim Conference and the Muslim League condemned the movement as a devise to establish Hindu Raj. Similarly, Sikh support also seemed to have shifted away from Congress. Non-Congress Hindus, like the Hindu Mahasabha and the Justice Party in Madras declared their opposition to civil disobedience. Business groups were apprehensive about the uncertain possibilities of the Lahore resolution, while young Congressmen were pressing for more militant action. Under the circumstances, the celebration of the "Independence Day" on 26 January 1930 evoked little enthusiasm, except in Punjab, UP, Delhi and Bombay. In Bihar, the celebrations resulted in violent clashes between the police and the Congress volunteers. Gandhi had to devise a strategy to break out of this impasse and impute a broader meaning into the word 'independence', as opposed to its narrower political connotation that had such a divisive impact.

On 31 January 1930 Gandhi therefore announced an eleven point ultimatum for Lord Irwin; if these demands were met by 11 March, he declared, there would be no civil disobedience and the Congress would participate in any conference. It was a compromise formula, which included, according to Sumit Sarkar's classification, six "issues of general interest", like reduction of military expenditure and civil service salaries, total prohibition, discharge of political prisoners not convicted of murder, reform of the CID and its popular control and changes in the arms act; three "specific bourgeois demands", like lowering of the rupee-sterling exchange rate to 1s 4d, protective tariff on foreign cloth and reservation of coastal traffic for Indian shipping companies; and two "basically peasant themes", i.e., 50 per cent reduction of land revenue and its subjection to legislative control and abolition of salt tax and government salt monopoly.[101] It was a mixed package to appeal to a wide cross-section of political opinions and unite the Indians once again under one overarching political leadership. Gandhi thus related the abstract concept of independence to certain specific grievances; but of all grievances, salt tax seemed to be the most crucial one for many reasons. It affected all sections of the population and had no divisive implication. It did not threaten government finances or any vested interests and therefore would not alienate any of the non-Congress political elements, nor would provoke government repression. And finally, it could be made into a highly emotive issue with great publicity value.

Irwin was in no mood to compromise, and hence on 12 March began Gandhi's historic Dandi March to the Gujarat seashore where on 6 April he publicly violated the salt law. The march attracted enormous publicity both in India and overseas, and was followed by wholesale illegal manufacture and sale of salt, accompanied by boycott of foreign cloth and liquor. In the next stage would come non-payment of revenue in the ryotwari areas, non-payment of chaukidari taxes in the zamindari areas and violation of forest laws in the Central Provinces. The Congress Working Committee had thus chalked out a programme, which would have less divisive impact on Indian society. But things began to take an abrupt turn towards the end of April, as violent activities and less disciplined mass upsurge began to take place in different parts of India. The most important of these was the armoury raid in Chittagong in Bengal, followed by a spate of violent activities throughout the province. In Peshawar the masses became unruly after the arrest of the local charismatic leader Badsha Khan. Then in mid-May Gandhi himself was arrested. This was followed by a spontaneous textile strike in Sholapur, where the workers went around rampaging government buildings and other official targets in the city. All these encouraged in nearly all parts of India a mass movement that did not merely involve non-cooperation with a foreign government, but actual violation of its laws to achieve complete independence. Even the outbreak of violence in three areas did not immediately lead to withdrawal of the movement. In this sense, the Civil Disobedience movement, as Sumit Sarkar (1983) has argued, witnessed a definite advance of radicalism over the 1920 movement. But at the same time, it was not an unqualified success. There was a discernible absence of Hindu–Muslim unity, no major labour participation and the intelligentsia was not as involved as in the past.

On the other hand, a new feature of the Civil Disobedience movement was a massive business support. They participated, at least during the initial period, in two very fruitful ways: they provided the finance and supported the boycott movement, particularly that of foreign cloth. The value of imported cloth declined from £26 million in 1929 to £13.7 million in 1930.[102] Depression partly contributed to this fall, but it cannot be explained without referring to the merchants' refusal to indent foreign cloth for a specific period. The other most important feature of the Civil Disobedience movement was large-scale women's participation. At almost every stop during the Dandi march, women flocked in thousands to hear Gandhi, and once the movement was launched, they were fully incorporated into it. They participated in the picketing of shops dealing in foreign cloth and liquor, and at places processions participated by one to two thousand women astonished the whole country and bewildered the authorities.[103] These women belonged mostly to the respectable families of the upper castes, such as the Brahman and Marwari families in Berar or the bhadralok and orthodox Marwari and Gujarati trading families in Bengal. Their appearance in the open street and participation in agitational politics did not jeopardise their respectability, as Gandhi's name legitimised such actions as sacred duties to the nation (more in chapter 7).

As in urban areas, in the villages too, in Bengal for example, the peasant women considered it to be a "religious mission" to participate in the Gandhian movement and they belonged mostly to the upwardly mobile peasant castes.[104] For, in the countryside in general, there was more participation from the richer peasantry, whose grievances against high revenue demands were successfully related to the demand for swaraj. Non payment of chaukidari taxes and no-revenue campaign became major features of the movement in parts of Gujarat, UP, Bihar, Orissa and Coastal Andhra; this was accompanied by the boycott movement, widespread illegal manufacture of salt and picketing of liquor shops. And if the general people did not participate in these activities of their own accord, in some places, as in north Bihar, the village-level Congress enthusiasts used "limited violence" and other subtle forms of social coercion to force adherence to their boycott programme.[105]

The government also retaliated with repressive measures; all front ranking leaders and thousands of volunteers were arrested. From September 1930 onwards the movement began to decline. In the urban areas the enthusiasm of the mercantile classes were dampened by the financial losses because of the disruption of day-to-day business. The government also offered them a concession in February 1931 in the shape of a 5 per cent surcharge on imported cotton piece goods. The middle class had been unenthusiastic from the beginning, and now the educated youth felt more attracted to militant nationalism. Bhagat Singh in Punjab, who had assassinated a British officer and thrown bombs at the legislative assembly, and Benoy, Badal and Dinesh in Bengal, who had attacked the Writers' Building in Calcutta, became their heroes. On the other hand, working-class support was non-existent and given their recent radical propensities, Gandhi had reservations about involving them in the movement. One exception was Nagpur, where working-class participation was massive and much more than in the 1921 movement.[106] In the countryside, the enthusiasm of the richer peasantry, such as the Patidars of Gujarat or the Jats of UP, dissipated due to confiscation and sale of properties. On the other hand, drastic fall in agricultural prices resulted in the movement of the lesser peasantry acquiring radical tendencies, such as no-rent campaigns in UP, violation of forest laws and tribal rebellions in parts of Andhra, CP, Maharashtra, Orissa, Bihar, Assam and Punjab. These developments might have serious divisive impact on society which Gandhi certainly wanted to avoid. So the movement was withdrawn through the Gandhi-Irwin Pact of 5 March 1931 and Congress agreed to participate in the Second Round Table Conference to discuss the future constitution of India. Interestingly, peasants in Orissa celebrated the truce as a "victory for Gandhi" and were further encouraged to stop paying taxes and manufacture salt![107]

The compromise of 1931 is, however, the subject of a major controversy in Indian history. It was R.J. Moore (1974) who first pointed out that bourgeois pressure was a significant factor behind the compromise, a point which Sumit Sarkar (1976) developed later to argue that the Indian bourgeoisie played a "crucial" role both in the initial success of the movement as well as in its subsequent withdrawal. This position has been accepted by other historians too across the ideological spectrum, like Judith Brown (1977), Claude Markovits (1985) and Basudev Chatterji (1992). The alliance between Congress and the capitalists, it is argued, was uneasy and vulnerable from the very beginning and now uncontrolled mass movement unnerved the business classes who wanted to give peace a chance. Hence the pressure on Gandhi to return to constitutional politics and the result was the Gandhi–Irwin Pact. But the problem with this thesis is that the business groups hardly represented a homogeneous class in 1931 and did not speak with one voice. As A.D.D. Gordon puts it, the enthusiasm of the industrialists was dampened by the depression, boycott, hartals and the social disruptions, and they wanted either to destroy civil disobedience or broker a peace between Congress and the government. But on the other hand, the marketers and the traders still remained staunch supporters of Gandhi, and their radicalism even increased as civil disobedience made progress.[108] More significantly, as other critics of this theory point out,[109] although business communities supported the movement and could partly claim credit for its early success, they were never in a position to pressurise Gandhi to withdraw the movement. Gandhian Congress was projecting itself as an umbrella organisation, which would incorporate all the different classes and communities. So it was highly unlikely that Gandhi would take such a vital decision only to satisfy the interests of one particular class. We shall return to this topic in the next chapter; for the present, it is important to remember that the most weighty reason for withdrawal of the movement was appearance of radicalism and violence among certain lower classes who refused to remain under the control of local Congress leaders. The movement was moving in wayward directions—or going against the Gandhian creed of non-violence and was tearing apart the fragile unity of the political nation; hence, the compromise and withdrawal.

But the negotiations with the government failed and Gandhi returned empty-handed from the second Round Table Conference in London held in September–December 1931. Congress had boycotted the first session of the conference; the second session deadlocked on the minority issue, as not just the Muslims, but all other minorities, such as the depressed classes (untouchables), Anglo-Indians, Indian Christians and Europeans demanded separate electorates, which Gandhi was adamant not to concede. He came back to India and his only option was a renewal of the battle. There were other compulsions too, as government had already unleashed repression and in a preemptive strike banned the Congress on 4 January 1932. The movement was renewed with greater vigour, but evidently evoked less enthusiasm. The rich peasant groups, who had showed greater militancy during the first phase of the movement, felt betrayed by its withdrawal and remained unstirred in many places, such as coastal Andhra, Gujarat or UP, when the Congress leaders wanted to mobilise them the second time. Some aspects of the Gandhian social programme, such as his crusade against untouchability, simply did not appeal to them, belonging mostly to the higher castes, and even evoked hostile responses.[110] On the other hand, Gandhi's Harijan campaign failed to impress the Harijans themselves. In Marathi-speaking Nagpur and Berar, which had been the strongholds of Ambedkar's *dalit* (untouchable) politics, the untouchables refused to switch their allegiance to the Congress.[111] However, side by side with this apathy and antipathy, there were also signs of more radicalism among certain other sections of the lower peasantry, expressed through salt satyagrahas, forest satyagrahas, non-payment of chaukidari taxes, no-rent and no-revenue campaigns. But these were movements largely outside the ambit of Congress organisation, and so at places Congress leaders tried to exert a moderating influence on them, or where this was not possible, sought to distance themselves from such peasant militancy.[112]

In the urban areas, the business groups were certainly ambivalent. There was an open estrangement between the Congress and the Bombay mill-owners, who under the leadership of Homi Mody warned Gandhi against a renewal of the movement. The other sections of the Indian big business were in a dilemma. Their hope for concessions from the government had been belied; but a renewal of civil disobedience might this time seriously threaten the social status quo, as government was more prepared for a counter offensive. Under the strain of this dilemma, argues Claude Markovits (1985), the unity of the Indian capitalist class broke down. By 1933, the weakening economy and growing violence even crushed the enthusiasm of the staunchest of Gandhian supporters—the Gujarati and Marwari merchants.[113] The urban intelligentsia also felt less inclined to follow the Gandhian path. Picketing of shops was frequently punctuated by the use of bombs, which Gandhi condemned, but failed to stop. The labour remained apathetic and the Muslims often antagonistic. Government repression saw thousands of Congress volunteers behind bars. The movement gradually declined by 1934.

For Congress, however, the Civil Disobedience movement was by no means a failure. It had by now mobilised great political support and gained a moral authority, which were converted into a massive electoral victory in 1937. In this first election under the Government of India Act of 1935, which offered franchise to a larger electorate, Congress achieved absolute majority in five out of eleven provinces, i.e., Madras, Bihar, Orissa, C.P. and U.P., near majority in Bombay and became the single largest party in Bengal, which was a Muslim majority province. For most of the Indians, especially Hindus, it was a "vote for Gandhiji and the yellow box", and it registered their expectation for some real socio-economic changes, promised recently by the Socialists and other left-wing Congress leaders.[114] The subsequent ministry formation in eight provinces (U.P., Bihar, Orissa, C.P., Bombay, Madras, North-West Frontier Province and Assam) was Congress's first association with the apparatus of power. But this office acceptance also symbolised the victory within Congress command structures of the right-wingers who preferred constitutional politics to agitational methods of Gandhi. As D.A. Low has argued,[115] while fighting the British Raj, the Congress itself was becoming the Raj and was gradually drifting away from the Gandhian ideal of swaraj (details in chapter 8.1).

6.5. THE ACT OF 1935, "PAPER FEDERATION" AND THE PRINCES

The Act of 1919 had impressed neither any section of Indian opinion, nor the Conservatives in London. The political agitations made it clear that Congress had to be allowed some share of power, without endangering British control over the central government. So fresh discussions for reform started in the late 1920s, with a parliamentary commission appointed in 1927 under Lord Simon. But when the Simon Commission visited India, it was boycotted by all the political parties as it was wholly European and did not include any Indian member. In October 1929, Lord Irwin made a further concession by making an announcement that full dominion status would be the natural goal of India's constitutional progress; but in view of Conservative opposition at home, it meant really nothing. The report of the Simon Commission was released in June 1930 and it suggested the replacement of dyarchy with full responsible government in the provinces, with the provision of some emergency powers in the hands of the governors; but no change was suggested in the constitution of the central government. Meant to protect imperial control over the centre, the proposal satisfied none of the political groups in India and could not be implemented because of the beginning of Civil Disobedience movement. Irwin again offered as a concession the proposal of a Round Table Conference to discuss the future system of government. But its first session, held in London between November 1930 and January 1931, was boycotted by the Congress. Here the nominated representatives of British India and princely states discussed the need for a federal government of India free of British control. But the conference achieved very little, as the Conservative-dominated National government in power in London was not in a mood to take the federal idea seriously. Gandhi was then persuaded to participate in the Second Round Table Conference in September–December 1931 on the basis of three vague principles of federation, responsible government and reservation and safeguards. But Gandhi's participation proved futile, as negotiations at the Minorities Committee broke down on the issue of separate electorate, now demanded not only by the Muslims, but by the depressed classes (untouchables), Anglo-Indians, Indian Christians and the Europeans too. With the coming of a Tory ministry in Britain in September 1931, British official attitudes hardened even further.[116]

The constitutional history of India again took a dramatic turn when Prime Minister Ramsay Macdonald announced his Communal Award in August 1932. It apportioned representation among communities and extended the provision of separate electorate to the untouchables as well. Gandhi, then in Yeravda jail, saw in it a sinister motive to divide the Hindu society, as the untouchables, he believed, were an integral part of it. The provision of separate electorate, he argued, would politically separate them and would permanently block the path of their integration into Hindu society. He therefore decided to fast unto death to reverse the arrangement. The nation panicked, although some of the depressed classes leaders like M.C. Rajah favoured joint electorate, the most influential of them, Dr B.R. Ambedkar saw in the provision of separate electorate the only hope of securing political representation for the untouchables (for more details see chapter 7.2). But Gandhi, though opposed to separate electorate, was not averse to the idea of reserved seats, and Ambedkar too ultimately agreed to it, as the proposed number of such reserved seats for the depressed classes was increased and a two-tier election system was recommended to ensure proper representation of such classes.[117] This became the basis of the Poona Pact of September 1932, which the government subsequently accepted. The third Round Table Conference in November–December 1932 was largely formal and unimportant, as only 46 out of 112 delegates attended the session. A White Paper in March 1933 set up a Parliamentary Joint Select Committee with a provision merely to consult Indian opinion. The Government of India Act, which ultimately did eventuate in 1935 could therefore hardly satisfy anybody and was criticised equally by Congress as well as the Muslim League.

In the provinces, in place of dyarchy the Act of 1935 provided for responsible government in all the departments. But this was balanced off by wide discretionary powers given to the governors about summoning legislatures, giving assent to bills and administering tribal regions. The governors were also given special power to safeguard minority rights, privileges of civil servants and British business interests. And finally, they could take over and run the administration of a province indefinitely under a special provision. At the centre, the act provided for a federal structure, but it would come into effect only if more than 50 per cent of the princely states formally acceded to it by signing the Instruments of Accession, which would override their previous treaties with the British crown. The act introduced dyarchy at the centre, but subject to various safeguards, and departments like foreign affairs, defence and internal security remained completely under the control of the viceroy. Another feature of this act was the transfer of financial control from London to New Delhi, in response to a long-standing demand of the Government of India for fiscal autonomy. The electorate was enlarged to 30 million; but the high property qualifications only enfranchised 10 per cent of the Indian population. In rural India, it gave voting right to the rich and middle peasants, as they were presumably the main constituency for Congress politics. So the act, suspects D.A. Low, was a ploy to corrode the support base of the Congress and tie these important classes to the Raj. A "competition for the allegiance of the dominant peasant communities", he writes, lay at the heart of the conflict between the Congress and the Raj at this stage.[118] Apart from that, in the bicameral central legislature, members nominated by the princes would constitute 30 to 40 per cent of the seats, thus permanently eliminating the possibility of a Congress majority. Separate electorate was provided for the Muslims and reserved seats for the Scheduled Castes (a new term for the 'depressed classes' or untouchables) in the provincial and central legislatures. Not unjustifiably the Labour opposition argued in London that the act only proposed to protect British interests in India by sharing power with the loyalist elements.

The Act of 1935 did not mention the granting of dominion status promised during the Civil Disobedience movement. However much diehard Conservatives like Winston Churchill might think that the act amounted to Britain's abdication of empire, his colleagues had consciously chosen the federal structure because, as Carl Bridge has argued, it "would act primarily to protect Britain's interests rather than hand over control in vital areas".[119] Its net effect was to divert Congress attention to the provinces, while maintaining strong imperial control at the centre. If any change happened at all, as B.R. Tomlinson has pointed out: "The apex of the system of imperial control moved from London to Delhi."[120] The viceroy was now to enjoy many of the powers previously exercised by the secretary of state and thus Indo-British relationship was provided with a new orientation that would best protect essential imperial interests. The significance of the Government of India Act of 1935 can be best summed up in the words of the then Viceroy Lord Linlithgow himself: "After all we framed the constitution ... of 1935 because we thought it the best way ... to hold India to the Empire."[121]

The provincial part of the 1935 act took effect with the elections of 1937; but a stalemate prevailed at the centre, perhaps as expected by the Tories, because the federal part of the act remained a non-starter, as no one seemed to be really interested in it. The Muslim leaders, first of all, were afraid of Hindu domination and felt that the proposed federal structure was still very unitary. All the representatives of British India to the central legislature were to be elected by the provincial assemblies and this would go against the Muslims who were minorities in all but four provinces. So although they did not oppose federation in public, they certainly preferred decentralisation, with a weak central government, allowing more autonomy for the provincial governments in the Muslim majority provinces.[122] The Congress too did not like the proposed structure of the federation, where one-third of the seats in the federal assembly were to be filled in by the princes, thus tying up the fate of democratic India to the whims of the autocratic dynastic rulers.[123] But the federation scheme ultimately failed because the princes were reluctant to join it. Their main objection was that the act did not resolve the issue of paramountcy. The Government of India as a paramount power still enjoyed the right to intervene in the affairs of their states or even overthrow them if necessary. Their other fear was about joining a democratised federal central government, where the elected political leaders of British India would have little sympathy for their autocratic rules and would provide encouragement to the democratic movements in their territories. Furthermore, the larger states did not want to surrender their fiscal autonomy, while the smaller states complained of their inadequate representation in the legislature.[124] However, these concerns of the princes would become more meaningful if placed in their proper historical context. It will, therefore, be pertinent here to digress a little to tell the story of princely India since the outbreak of World War One.

If the Curzonian policy of interventionist paternalism had strained the relationship between the princes and the Raj at the beginning of the twentieth century, Minto's policy of *laissez faire* again revived the bonhomie. The latter policy was intended to insulate the states from the sweeping political changes of British India and keep their people away from the rising emotions of nationalism.[125] It was this isolation and political quarantine that gradually began to dissolve since the outbreak of World War One. The war once more showed the usefulness of the princes to the empire, as they donated generously to war funds, rendered valuable military services and encouraged army recruitment in their states. At the end of the war, therefore, they wanted a recognition of their services in the shape of greater constitutional restrictions on the domineering tendencies of the Political Department, more guarantee of insularity against the rising political tides in British India, and greater participation in the consultative process of the empire.[126] So when Montagu and Chelmsford initiated their inquiry about postwar constitutional reforms, the princes raised among other issues the demand for a Chamber of Princes, an advisory committee and the right of direct access to the Government of India. The Act of 1919 provided for a 120-member Chamber of Princes, to advise the Raj on all matters relating to the states and their relationship with the paramount power. The composition of its membership remained however a major contentious issue, as ultimately it was decided that all princes with 11 gun-salutes and above will be directly represented, while the smaller princes would elect twelve representatives from among themselves. Inaugurated at the Red Fort in Februrary 1921, and divided from the very beginning by mutual jealousies and squabbles, the Chamber nevertheless formally broke the physical as well as political isolation of the princes.[127]

But contrary to the popular stereotype, the princely states had never been completely insulated from British India, nor were their borders ever nonporous, as both nationalist politics and communal tension continually spilled over from the neighbouring provinces. When, for example, peasant and tribal movements erupted in princely India, such as the Bijonia movement in Mewar or the Bhil movment in Sirohi under the leadership of Motilal, protesting against the jagirdari oppression and the land taxes of the government in 1921–22, they drew inspiration from Gandhi and established connections with the nationalist movement. Indeed Motilal came to be known as a local Gandhi, although Gandhi himself dissociated his name from this movement.[128] Sometimes, the princes also exhibited active interests in the politics of British India. The rulers of Alwar and Bharatpur, for example, became ardent supporters of Hindu nationalism in the early twentieth century and consciously Hinduised their states. They patronised Arya Samaj activities, promoted Hindi in place of Urdu, supported cow protection and suddhi movements and in the process alienated the urban Muslims. The Alwar ruler Jai Singh, celebrated by his subjects as a great patriot, figured prominently in colonial demonology for his conscious nationalist posturing—such as, not shaking hands with Europeans without his gloves on. In Bharatpur, where the local ruler was deposed due to alleged charges of financial irregularities, the combination of Congress, Arya Samaj and the Jat Mahasabha made this region a major centre of nationalism in the entire Rajasthan.[129] But, on the other hand, there were many other princes who remained loyal to the Raj and proved to be its most credible allies when nationalist challenge began to mount. When extremism and violence became powerful in the first decade of the twentieth century and later when the Non-cooperation movement rocked the subcontinent, the princes rendered valuable service in containing the tide in their territories. The visit of the Prince of Wales, boycotted by the Congress, was made somewhat worthwhile because of the warmth and grandeur of princely welcome. In the 1920s, however, popular movements began to appear in all these states in the form of *praja mandals*. These mandals were eventually affiliated to a national body called the All India States' People's Conference, founded in 1927 with its headquarters at Bombay. It raised moderate demands for democratic rights and constitutional changes, to which many of the princes responded with sharp vengeance and massive repression. However, if most of them were sensitive about guarding their autonomy and sovereignty, there were some exceptions too—like Baroda, Mysore, Travancore and Cochin—who had initiated, albeit in limited spheres, some constitutional changes.[130]

There were states—like Mysore or Travancore—where Congress politics had made considerable inroads.[131] But Congress during this whole period scrupulously maintained an official policy of non-interference in the affairs of the states—ostensibly, out of respect for the princes' traditional rights of sovereignty. The only exception was made in 1928 when a Congress resolution urged the princes to "introduce responsible government based on representative institutions" and expressed its "sympathy" and "support" for the "legitimate and peaceful struggle" of the people of the Indian states striving to attain "full responsible government".[132] Such verbal sympathy, however, counted for little for the states' peoples' movements and for the clandestine Congress branches, which were dealt with stiff resistance from most of the princes. Therefore, when the Civil Disobedience movement started, the Raj's princely clients—barring a few exceptions like Bhavnagar, Junagadh or Kathiawar—proved to be as dependable as before in suppressing Congress activities in their respective territories.[133]

So during all these years, the Raj had been using its subordinate allies—representing old and in British perspective, authentic India—

as effective tools against the new forces of nationalism in the provinces. Little was done to induce democratic constitutional changes in the states to bring them at par with the political developments in British India. This made the princes, unprepared to face the future, increasingly more alarmist about the nationalist leaders challenging their internal autonomy of rule.[134] This did not mean that the Raj refrained from intervening in the affairs of the states. Indeed, there were many officers in the Political Department who continually pushed the boundary of the powers of paramountcy, compelling the princes to clamour for an impartial inquiry into their constitutional status. But the Indian States Committee, which was formed in 1928 under Sir Harcourt Butler, scarcely provided in its Report (1929) any solace for the beleaguered princes. It gave them a concession in the form of a promise that paramountcy would not be transferred without their consent to any democratically elected government in British India; but at the same time, it reaffirmed the supremacy of paramountcy with unlimited power—even to suggest constitutional changes in a particular state if there was widespread demand for such reforms. It did push the doctrine of paramountcy, a Political Department officer confessed, "beyond any hitherto accepted limit".[135]

Thus pushed to a tight corner and pressured from both ends, the princes now started taking interest in politics and began to fraternise with some of the moderate politicians. They found in the idea of federation, first proposed in the Motilal Nehru Report of 1928, an ideal way out of their present predicament. By joining an autonomous all-India federation they could escape the "shackles of paramountcy" and at the same time could safeguard their internal autonomy of action. But not all princes were too sure about it, the Maharaja of Patiala being the leader of this faction. Ultimately a mutual agreement—known as the "Delhi Pact"—was brokered on 11 March and was endorsed by the Chamber of Princes on 1 April 1932, projecting federation as a constitutional demand of the princes of India. But the demand was cushioned, as Ian Copland has pointed out, with significant safeguards, which were sure to be rejected by both the British and the nationalists. They wanted, for example, individual seats for all the members of the Chamber of Princes in the upper house of the federal legislature, protection of their existing treaty rights, subjects to be placed under the jurisdiction of the federal government were to be mutually agreed upon by the member states, and above all, a right to secede.[136] The British loved the idea of federation, as in that case the princes could act as counterweight against the nationalist politicians from the provinces; but their idea of federation differed from that of the princes. If in the first Round Table Conference the representatives of princely India deliberated enthusiastically on a federation, by the time of its second session many of them had developed cold feet about the idea. At its Bombay session in late January 1935, the Chamber adopted a resolution, which was highly critical of the federation proposal as it had evolved by that time. When finally the Government of India Act got the royal assent on 2 August 1935, the federation scheme contained in it could hardly satisfy the majority of the princes.[137]

However, Ian Copland (1999) argues that the princes even at this stage were not completely rejecting federation, but were bargaining for a better deal. They wanted the Instrument of Accession to be defined appropriately to address their two major concerns, i.e., recognition of their existing treaty rights and protection of their internal autonomy. Although the new viceroy, Linlithgow, recommended some such changes, intense bureaucratic haggling delayed the process by several years. In the meanwhile, the spectacular political rise of the Congress after the provincial elections of 1937 made the princes panicky. In 1938 the traditional Congress policy of noninterference in the affairs of the states was jettisoned at the Haripura Congress, and in the following months the most vehement peoples' movement under the leadership of the All India States' People's Conference, with the active patronage of the Congress, rocked princely India (for more details of this movement see chapter 8.1). The smaller and middle-sized states were hardly prepared for this kind of popular upsurge and they buckled in, taking a more conciliatory attitude towards the Congress. But the larger states fought back with resolute stubbornness, and they were helped by British troops. To the majority of the princes in 1939, the Congress had thus shown its true colours and could therefore never be trusted again. When in January 1939 Linlithgow finally gave them a revised offer, with some minor concessions, federation to most of them had become an unmitigated evil to be rejected outright. That is what they did at the Bombay session of the Chamber of Princes in June; and then, when the war broke out in Europe in August, the secretary of state, Zetland, promptly put the federal offer in "cold storage".[138]

NOTES

1. For more details, see Stokes 1959: 288.
2. For more details, see Stokes 1959: 288–310; also see chapter 2.1 for more discussion on imperial ideology.

3. Seal 1973.
4. Robb 1976: 3.
5. Woods 1994: 31.
6. Quoted in Desika Char 1983: 457.
7. Woods 1994: 42.
8. Bridge 1986: 5.
9. Tomlinson 1976a: 10.
10. Robb 1976: 268.
11. Seal 1973.
12. Brown 1972: 28.
13. Kumar 1971: 4.
14. Low 1968: 1.
15. Brown 1972: 125.
16. For more details, see Balabushevich and Dyakov 1964.
17. Kumar 1983.
18. Quoted in Sarkar 1983: 174.
19. Brown 1972: 46.
20. Dalton 1993: 21.
21. Basham 1971: 17–42.
22. Nandy 1994a: 2–4.
23. Nandy 1998: 100–2.
24. Chatterjee 1984b: 162 and passim.
25. Parekh 1989b: 34.
26. Parel 1997: 53.
27. Quotations from Gandhi 1997: 39, 52, 66–67, 71–74, 116.
28. Parel 1997: 50; emphasis in original.
29. Chatterjee 1986.
30. Steger 2000.
31. Owen 1968: 174.
32. Brown 1972: 356.
33. See Amin 1989.
34. Sarkar 1983: 225.
35. See Guha 1993: 107; Amin 1996: 13.
36. Details in Pouchepadass 1999.
37. Henningham 1982.
38. Details in Hardiman 1981: 85–113.
39. Details in Patel 1987: 37–51.
40. Owen 1971.
41. Hasan 1985: 24.
42. For more on Firangi Mahal, see Robinson 2001.
43. Lelyveld 1978.
44. Robinson 1974: 262.
45. Minault 1982: 11.
46. Brown 1972: 296–97, 302.
47. Gordon 1973: 150.
48. Ray 1984: 262.

49. Kumar 1983: 213–39.
50. Sarkar 1983: 174–75.
51. Ibid: 206–7.
52. Gordon 1978: 159.
53. Bhattacharya 1976.
54. Quoted in Zelliot 1988: 185.
55. Details in Amin 1996:14–17.
56. See Wood 1987; Panikkar 1989; Dhanagare 1991.
57. Arnold 1977.
58. Irschick 1969: 183, 197–98.
59. Baker 1979: 78.
60. Bhattacharya 1976: 1832.
61. Hardiman 1981.
62. Baker and Washbrook 1975; Arnold 1977.
63. Broomfield 1968: 204–5.
64. Fox 1985: 78.
65. Ibid: 80.
66. Tuteja 1999: 180–81.
67. Bhattacharya 1976.
68. Ray 1984: 284.
69. Baker 1979: 75.
71. Arnold 1977.
71. For details, see Siddiqi 1978; Kumar 1984; Pandey 1982.
72. Henningham 1983.
73. Ray 1984; Sanyal 1988a.
74. Pati 1993: 62–66.
75. Hardiman 1981.
76. Baker and Washbrook 1975.
77. Hardiman 1981: 157.
78. Pati 1993: 65 and passim.
79. Pandey 1982.
80. Amin 1989.
81. Fox 1985: 90–93.
82. Guha 1991.
83. Dasgupta 1994.
84. Arnold 1986b.
85. Guha 1994: 86.
86. Amin 1996: 196–97.
87. Amin 1989.
88. Sarkar 1984.
89. Henningham 1983.
90. Quotations in Ranajit Guha 1992: 107–8, 111.
91. Das 1991b.
92. Brown 1977: 10.
93. Hasan 1985.
94. Rothermund 1992: 79–96.

95. Bose 1986: 144.
96. Sarkar 1987a: 37.
97. Rothermund 1992: 140, 160.
98. Bhattacharya 1986.
99. Shah 1974.
100. Brown 1977: 32.
101. Sarkar 1983: 284–85.
102. Ibid: 293.
103. Forbes 1988.
104. Tanika Sarkar 1984: 98.
105. Henningham 1982: 112–15.
106. Baker 1979: 86.
107. Pati 1993: 75.
108. Gordon 1978.
109. Bhattacharya 1986; Mukherjee 1986 and Tripathi 1991.
110. Stoddard 1977.
111. Baker 1979: 88.
112. Pandey 1978.
113. Gordon 1978: 235.
114. Sarkar 1983: 349.
115. Low 1977: 14.
116. For details, see Bridge 1986: 43–91.
117. Kumar 1987a.
118. Low 1977: 24.
119. Bridge 1986: ix.
120. Tomlinson 1976a: 30.
121. Quoted in Bridge 1986, title page.
122. Tomlinson 1976a: 25.
123. Moore 1970: 77–78.
124. Tomlinson 1976a: 24–25.
125. Copland 1982: 241.
126. Copland 1999: 32–35.
127. Ramusack 1978: 77–93.
128. Vidal 1997: 113–56.
129. Mayaram 1997: 53–97.
130. Ramusack 1978.
131. For Mysore, see Manor 1977 and for Travancore, Jeffrey 1978b.
132. Quoted in Ramusack 1978: 181.
133. Ibid.
134. Manor 1978: 310– 16.
135. Quoted in Copland 1999: 70.
136. For details, ibid: 108–10.
137. See ibid for details.
138. Ibid: 181 and passim.

chapter seven

Many Voices of a Nation

7.1. Muslim Alienation

The mainstream Indian nationalism—as it was developing gradually since the late nineteenth century under the aegis of the Indian National Congress—was contested incessantly from within the Indian society. What we find as a result is a series of alternative visions of nation, represented by a variety of minority or marginal groups, who constantly challenged and negotiated with the Congress. The Muslims of India, as already noted (chapter 5.4), were the first to contest this version of nationalism and almost from the beginning many of them did not consider the Indian National Congress to be their representative. Between 1892 and 1909 only 6.59 per cent of the Congress delegates were Muslims. Muslim leaders like Sayyid Ahmed Khan clearly considered it to be the representative of the majority Hindus. He was not anti-nationalist, but favoured a different conception of nation. For him the nation was a federation of communities having entitlement to different kinds of political rights depending on their ancestry and political importance and the Muslims, being an ex-ruling class had a special place within the framework of the new cosmopolitan British empire. This was in sharp contrast to the Congress vision of nation consisting of individual citizens. The prospect of the introduction of representative government created the political threat of a majority domination, which led to the formation of the All India Muslim League in 1906. This was the beginning of a search for distinctive political identity—not a quest for separate homeland—with a demand for the protection of their political rights as a minority community through the creation of separate electorate. The granting of this privilege of separate electorate by the colonial state in the Morley–Minto reform of 1909 elevated them to the status of an "all-India political category", but positioned them as a "perpetual minority" in the Indian body politic.[1] These structural imperatives of representative government henceforth began to influence the relationship between the Congress and the Muslim League.

A brief period of compromise with the Congress followed the signing of the Lucknow Pact in 1916, which recognized the Muslim demand for separate electorate. But soon all such arrangements became irrelevant, as the whole structure of Indian politics was changed by the coming of Gandhi and the advent of the masses into the previously enclosed arena of nationalist politics. Gandhi by supporting the Khilafat movement, which used a pan-Islamic symbol to forge a pan-Indian Muslim unity, went a long way in producing unprecedented Hindu–Muslim rapport (chapter 6.3). But the movement died down by 1924 due to internal divisions and finally, because of the abolition of the Caliphate through a republican revolution in Turkey under Kemal Pasha. But what is important, the Khilafat movement itself contributed further to the strengthening of Muslim identity in Punjab and Bengal. Frequent use of religious symbols by the overzealous ulama, who were pressed into service, highlighted the Islamic self of the Indian Muslims. It was indeed from the Khilafat movement that a serious communal riot erupted in Malabar in 1921. So this Muslim mobilisation under the banner of Khilafat, as Christophe Jaffrelot (1996) has argued, generated a sense of inferiority and insecurity among the Hindus, who in emulation of their aggressive Other now started counter-mobilisation. The Arya Samaj started a militant suddhi campaign in Punjab and UP and the Hindu Mahasabha launched its drive towards Hindu *sangathan* (organisation) in 1924; the Rastriya Swayam Sevak Sangh, an overtly aggressive Hindu organisation, was also born in the same year. The inevitable result of such mobilisation along community lines was the outbreak of a series of riots between the Hindus and the Muslims in the 1920s, affecting practically all parts of India.[2] An exasperated Gandhi lamented in 1927 that the resolution of the problem of Hindu–Muslim relations was now beyond human control, and had passed on to the hands of God.[3]

How do we explain this rapid deterioration of Hindu–Muslim relations in the wake of the decline of Khilafat movement? Gyanendra Pandey (1985) has argued that in the 1920s there had been a remarkable shift in the Congress conceptualisation of nationalism. There was now a distinct tendency to delegitimise religious nationalism by relegating religion to the private sphere. Congress leaders like Jawaharlal Nehru in their public pronouncements emphasised a secularist view of Indian nation, which was conceived to be above community interests. A binary opposition was visualised between nationalism and communalism and therefore, whoever talked about community were dubbed as anti-nationalists or communalists. This eliminated the likelihood of accommodating the community identities within a composite nationhood and destroyed all possibilities of a rapprochement between the Congress and the Muslim League. The Muslims at this juncture, as Ayesha Jalal argues, "required a political arrangement capable of accommodating cultural differences." They looked for "shared sovereignty"; they were not against a united India, but contested Congress's claim to indivisible sovereignty.[4]

The public pronouncements of Congress secularism came at a time when religious identity was being articulated practically at every sphere of public life by both the Muslims as well as Hindus. So far as the latter were concerned, unlike the earlier nationalist leaders who used Hindu revivalist symbols but remained within the Congress framework, the present leaders of the Hindu Mahasabha decided to operate as a separate pressure group within the Congress, trying constantly to marginalise the secularists and destroy any possibility of an understanding with the Muslims. There went on within the Congress, as Jaffrelot (1996) shows, a constant contest between two rival concepts of nationalism, one based on the idea of composite culture, i.e., nation above community, and the other founded on the idea of racial domination of the Hindus, more particularly, of the subordination of the Muslims. What was significant, the protagonists of the former often gave way to or made compromises with those of the latter, giving ample reasons to the Muslims to be suspicious about the real intent of Congress politics.

This contestation was visible very clearly in the arena of institutional politics, which the Swarajist group within the Congress, under the leadership of Motilal Nehru and C.R. Das, had decided to re-enter, with Gandhi's endorsement, following the withdrawal of the Non-cooperation movement. At the municipal level, in UP, the alliance between the swarajists and the khilafatists won most of the seats in 1923 on a note of communal harmony. But their support base was systematically undercut by the Hindu Mahasabha under Madan Mohan Malaviya, whose actions contributed to further Hindu-Muslim tension that resulted in riots in Allahabad and Lucknow in 1924. In the next municipal election of 1925, the swarajists lost all seats to the Hindu Mahasabhites. In the Muslim majority province of Punjab, communal tension escalated in the wake of the Municipal Amendment Act of 1923, which by providing additional seats for Muslims reduced the Hindus to a minority in the municipal boards. With the blessings of Malaviya and the Hindu Mahasabha, the local Hindus took up cudgels against Muslims and so intense was the communal hatred that when Gandhi came to Lahore in December

1924 to restore harmony, the local Hindus gave him a cold shoulder. On the Muslim side, leaders like Muhammad Ali, who favoured communal harmony and once visualised India as a federation of faiths, were now marginalised; and leaders like Dr Kitchlew who were once staunchly in favour of Hindu-Muslim unity, now turned uncompromisingly against any communal reconciliation.[5]

At the Central Legislative Assembly, Mohammad Ali Jinnah, elected by the Bombay Muslims, appeared as the most prominent spokesman of the Muslims. Jinnah's preference for constitutional methods and abhorrence for agitational politics had driven him away from Gandhian Congress. But now after the withdrawal of Non-cooperation, when Congress once again reverted to constitutionalism under the swarajists, he was willing to cooperate with them. His 'Independent Party' formed an alliance with the swarajists and together they came to be known as the Nationalist Party in the Assembly. But at the same time, he focused on reviving the Muslim League at its Lahore session in 1923; decided to work on a new constitutional arrangement for India, and for that purpose, wanted to renegotiate the Lucknow Pact with the Congress. Although swarajists were willing, the Mahasabhites like Malaviya, B.S. Moonje and Lajpat Rai were not, and they successfully torpedoed all efforts at reconciliation. Even the Bengal Pact, which C.R. Das had negotiated with the local Muslims, was rejected at the Coconada session of the Congress in December 1923 on the ground that a national issue could not be resolved on a provincial basis.[6]

In the meanwhile, outside the arena of institutional politics, mobilisation of Hindus around the claim of a right to play music before mosques was gathering momentum in various parts of the country. From the late nineteenth century, indeed, as mentioned earlier (chapter 5.4), ever since the colonial state started defining a new public sphere, contest over sacred space, such as a dispute over the route of a religious procession, was fast becoming the bone of communal contention and a mode of defining communal identities in India.[7] And now, as the public contest for contending community rights became sharper, as over the cow slaughter/protection issue in the 1890s, "ritual space" came to be "defined by acoustic range"[8] and became a major symbol of communal mobilisation throughout India. Gandhi described this tradition of playing music in public as a non-essential aspect of Hinduism. But in a war of symbols, such non-essentials became non-negotiable demands for those wanting to mobilise communities along religious lines. This issue was used in UP, Punjab and Bengal to consolidate Hindu solidarity, and in CP and Bombay to divert attention from the rising tide of anti-Brahmanism. This "music before mosque" not only sparked off a series of violent riots between 1923 and 1927, but also in the election of 1926 it became an emotive issue dividing the electorate along communal lines.

Within the Congress, swarajists like Motilal Nehru were now being increasingly sidelined and they succumbed to pressure to nominate pro-Mahasabha candidates. There was not a single Muslim among the Congress candidates in Bengal or Punjab in 1926; elsewhere all the Congress Muslim candidates lost. The majority of the elected Congress members were those with known pro-Hindu sympathies. A resolution condemning separate electorate for Muslims was just prevented from being passed at the Guwahati Congress by timely intervention of Gandhi and Nehru. But the process of renegotiating the Lucknow Pact was finally derailed by the Mahasabhites at the All Parties Conference at Delhi in January 1928. It is not difficult to understand why Muslim support for Congress further diminished around this time. Aligarh Muslims now became afraid of being swamped by Hindus. Shaukat Ali ruefully observed in 1929 that "Congress ha[d] become an adjunct of Hindu Mahasabha".[9] Muslim alienation from Congress politics was then boldly inscribed in their large-scale abstention from the Civil Disobedience and the Quit India Movements.

This Muslim alienation —often stigmatised in Indian historiography as "communalism"—is a contentious issue among historians. One way to explain it is to dismiss it as "false consciousness" of a self-seeking petty bourgeoisie and misguided workers and peasants, who mistakenly saw their interests through the communal mirror and sought to safeguard them with constitutional privileges. Their frustration increased in the years after 1929, as depression constricted opportunities, leading to more tension, conflicts and violence.[10] On the other hand, it is also to a large extent true that the imperatives of representative government—the granting of separate electorate and conferment of minority status by the colonial state—contributed to the forging of an all-India Muslim political identity. It is, therefore, explained in terms of Islamic ideas of representation founded on ascriptive criteria, i.e., Muslims liked to be represented by Muslims alone, and not by those who were not members of their community.[11] While dismissal of communalism as a false consciousness does not take us anywhere so far as understanding of this political vision is concerned, the latter argument about a hegemonic Islamic ideology is also problematic. This explanation is essentially based on the assumption of a substantive ideological consensus within the Muslim community, which has been questioned by a number of historians.[12]

The Muslims were not a political community yet, not even in the late 1930s. There had been positional differences and ideological contestation within Muslim politics from its very beginning. Even in the 1930s, Muslim politics remained caught in provincial dynamics, as their interests in Bengal and Punjab, where they were a majority, were different from those of others in the minority provinces. In Bengal, the Krishak Praja Party under A.K. Fazlul Huq mobilised both the Muslim and lower caste Hindu peasants on class based demands, and competed with the Muslim League, after its revival in 1936, for Muslim votes.[13] In Punjab, the Unionist Party led by Fazl-i-Husain, Sikandar Hayat Khan, as well as the Jat peasant leader Chhotu Ram, appealed to a composite constituency of Muslim, Hindu and Sikh rich landlords and peasant producers—who had benefited from the Punjab Land Alienation Act of 1900—and had a complete control over rural politics.[14] The All India Muslim League, on the other hand, was until 1937, as Ayesha Jalal puts it, "little more than a debating forum for a few articulate Muslims in the minority provinces and had made no impact on the majority provinces".[15] In the election of 1937, both the regional parties did well, while Muslim League had a dismal performance throughout India. The resounding victory of the Congress in this election and the arrogance that it bred, however, gradually brought all these divergent groups together under the banner of a revived and revitalised Muslim League under the leadership of Jinnah.

As partners of the Raj, as R.J. Moore (1988) has shown, the Muslims had politically gained a lot in the 1920s and 1930s. The doctrine of separate electorate was now firmly enshrined in the Indian constitution. They had wrested power from the Congress in the majority provinces of Bengal and Punjab. And two other Muslim majority areas, Sind and the North-West Frontier Province, had been elevated to full provincial status. All these came to be threatened by the Congress victory in the 1937 elections. Not only did Congress refuse to enter into any coalition government in the minority provinces like UP to share power with the Muslim League, but Jawaharlal Nehru declared with supreme arrogance that there were now only two parties in the Indian political scene, the Raj and the Congress. From now on, there was a steady Congress propaganda against separate electorate and a constant vilification of the Muslim League as unpatriotic and reactionary. In view of the electoral debacle of the

Muslim League, Nehru launched his Muslim Mass Contact campaign to bring in the Muslim masses into Congress fold. But the endeavour failed as the Hindu Mahasabhites sabotaged it from within.[16] The Muslims, particularly in the minority provinces, had now ample reasons to be afraid of Hindu domination. There were numerous complaints of discrimination against Muslims by the Congress ministries. Whether true or imagined, these reflected the Muslim sense of missing out from the patronage distribution system created by the new constitutional arrangement of 1935.[17] The class approach in Congress policies, and its emphasis on individual citizenship, in other words, failed to satisfy the community-centric concerns of the Muslims

It was this collective sense of fear and dissatisfaction, which was politically articulated by Jinnah, who came back to India in 1934, after a short period of self-imposed exile in London, to take up the leadership of the Muslim League. But between 1934 and 1937 Jinnah was still willing to cooperate with the Congress at the centre with a view to revising the federal constitutional structure provided by the Act of 1935.[18] The election results, however, put him in a disadvantageous position, as Congress could now comfortably choose to ignore him. What Jinnah wanted at this stage was to make the Muslim League an equal partner—a third party—in any negotiation for the future constitution of India. The passage of the Shariat Application Act in 1937, with spirited advocacy by Jinnah in the Central Legislative Assembly, provided a symbolic ideological basis for Muslim solidarity on a national scale, transcending all divisive internal political debates.[19] He launched a mass contact campaign and pressed the ulama into service, while the emotionally charged Aligarh students further galvanised the campaign. In November 1939 when the Congress ministries resigned in protest against India being drawn into World War Two without consultation, Jinnah decided to celebrate it as a "Deliverance day". By December 1939 the Muslim League membership had risen to more than 3 million[20] and Jinnah had projected himself as their "sole spokesman".

Within this political context of estrangement and distrust, another idea gradually germinated and that was the notion of Muslim nationhood. In 1930 Sir Muhammad Iqbal, as president of the Muslim League, had proposed the constitution of a centralised territory for Islam within India, by uniting the four provinces of Punjab, North-West Frontier Province, Sind and Baluchistan. The idea was further elaborated by the Cambridge student Rahmat Ali, who in 1933 vaguely talked about 'Pakistan' to be constituted of the four Muslim provinces and Kashmir. It was, however, at the Karachi meeting of the Sind branch of the Muslim League, presided over by Jinnah himself, that a resolution was passed which mentioned the need for "political self-determination of the two nations, known as Hindus and Muslims"[21] and asked the Muslim League to think of appropriate measures to realise it. It was the first declaration of the "two nation" theory, but it was not separatism yet; the two federations of Hindus and Muslims were meant to be united through a common centre. Since then, public discussions went on about the practicality of a constitutional arrangement that could give shape to this abstract notion, with intellectual inputs coming from a variety of Muslim leaders, from the Sindhi leader Abdoola Harun, Dr Syed Abdul Latif, Abdul Bashir of the Pakistan Majlis in Lahore, to the prominent Aligarh scholars, Professor Syed Zafarul Hasan and Dr M.A.H. Qadri. Finally, the Lahore resolution of the Muslim League in March 1940 formally proclaimed the Muslims as a nation. It did not mention partition or Pakistan, but only talked about "Independent states" to be constituted of the Muslim majority provinces in an unspecified "future".[22] The resolution, in other words, only signalled the transformation of Indian Muslims from a 'minority' to a 'nation', so that no future constitutional arrangement for India could any more be negotiated without their participation and consent. The central plank in Jinnah's politics henceforth was to be a demand for 'parity' between the Hindus and the Muslims in any such arrangement.

The road from this declaration of nationhood to the actual realisation of a separate sovereign state in 1947 was long and tortuous. It may suffice here to mention that this conceptualisation of a Muslim nation was not the imagining of Jinnah alone or of a select group of articulate intellectuals. It was legitimated by thousands of ordinary Muslims who joined the processions at Karachi, Patna or Lahore, participated in the hartals, organised demonstrations or even took part in riots between 1938 and 1940.[23] And their alienation was born of provocations from the militant Hindu nationalists, as well as constant sneering by an intransigent secularist leadership of the Congress. For Muslim leaders, who in 1921 saw no conflict between their Indianness and Muslim identity, recognition of their separate Muslim nationhood became a non-negotiable minimum demand in the 1940s. And gradually these sentiments were shared by a wider Muslim population. Indeed, as Achin Vanaik has argued, "the Congress-led National Movement cannot escape most of the responsibility" for this emergence of a separate Muslim identity, at a period when an anti-colonial pan-Indian national identity was in the making.[24]

7.2. NON-BRAHMAN AND DALIT PROTEST

The other important social groups in India who also expressed their dissent from this Congress version of nationalism, were the non-Brahman castes and the untouchable groups. The latter, from around the 1930s, began to call themselves dalit or oppressed. The term more appropriately signified their socio-economic position in Hindu India, than the colonial terms "depressed classes", replaced after 1936 by "Scheduled Castes", or the Gandhian term "Harijan" (meaning God's people). As the term dalit indicates, any understanding of their protest needs to begin from a discussion of the evolution of caste system as a mode of social stratification and oppression in India. Anthropologists and social historians have considered it to be the most unique feature of Indian social organisation expressed in two parallel concepts of varna and jati. The fourfold division of varna was the ancient most social formation dating back to about 1000 BC, when the "Aryan" society was divided into Brahmans or priests, Kshatriyas or warriors, Vaishyas or farmers, traders and producers of wealth, and the Sudras who served these three higher groups. Untouchability as a fully developed institution appeared sometime between the third and sixth centuries AD, when the untouchables came to constitute a fifth category, known variously by terms like Panchamas, Ati-sudras or Chandalas.[25]

However, this varna division had little relevance to subsequent social realities, providing nothing more than "a fundamental template"[26] within which social ranks were conceptualised across regions. For actual social organisation, more important were the numerous jatis that were vaguely referred to as castes, a term derived from the Portuguese word *castas*. Jatis as occupational groups, which number more than three thousand in modern India[27] were emerging side by side with the varnas, and often they were again further subdivided on the basis of professional specialisation. Some anthropologists would call those smaller groups subcastes, while Iravati Karve (1977) would consider them as castes and the larger groups as "caste-clusters". Without going further into this debate over nomenclature, we may identify jatis or castes as occupational groups, whose membership was determined by birth, and whose exclusiveness was maintained by stringent rules of endogamy and commensality restrictions. Each and every caste was ascribed a ritual rank, which located its members in an elaborate hierarchy that encompassed the entire society.

What determined this rank is again a subject of intense controversy. Structural anthropologists like Louis Dumont (1970) believed, that this ranking system was essentially religious, as in Indian society the sacred encompassed the secular, making the Brahman priest more powerful than the Kshatriya king. In this cultural environment, social rank was determined by a purity-pollution scale: the Brahman, being the embodiment of purity, was located at the top of the scale and the untouchables being impure were at the bottom, while in the middle there were various groups with varying grades of purity/impurity. However, later social historians have argued that ritual rank was never unconnected with the power structure; the crown was never that hollow as it was made out to be by some colonial ethnographers.[28] In this situation, factors like nature of occupation and distance from the centre of power etc determined the ritual rank—in other words, there was close positive correlation between power, wealth and rank. This was a social organisation, which Gail Omvedt has described as the "caste-feudal society", marked by "caste/class confusion".[29] However, it was not exactly a class system in disguise. It was not a dichotomous system, but a system of gradation, with "a great deal of ambiguity in the middle region",[30] where various peasant castes competed with each other for superiority of status.

Within this scheme of things, members of each caste were assigned a moral code of conduct—their dharma—the performance or non-performance of which—or their karma—determined their location in caste hierarchy in next life. Although this implies a rigid social order enjoined by scriptures, the reality of caste society differed significantly from this ideal. For dharma was not always universally accepted and its hegemony was from time to time contested from within, most significantly in the medieval bhakti movement, which questioned the ritualistic foundation of religious and social life and emphasised simple devotion (bhakti) in its place.[31] Apart from that, opportunities for limited social mobility often led to positional changes and readjustments. Colonisation of wasteland, rise of warrior groups, emergence of new technology or new opportunities of trade at various stages of history helped groups of people to improve their economic and political status, and to translate that into higher ritual ranks in the caste hierarchy.[32] Indeed, the system could survive for so many centuries because it could maintain such a "dynamic equilibrium"[33] and absorb shocks from below.

Colonial rule disengaged caste system from its pre-colonial political contexts, but gave it a new lease of life by redefining and revitalising it within its new structures of knowledge, institutions and policies.[34] First of all, during its non-interventionist phase, it created opportunities, which were "*in theory* caste-free".[35] Land became a marketable commodity; equality before law became an established principle of judicial administration; educational institutions and public employment were thrown open to talent, irrespective of caste and creed. Yet the very principle of non-intervention helped maintain the pre-existing social order and reinforced the position of the privileged groups. Only the higher castes with previous literate traditions and surplus resources, could go for English education and new professions, and could take advantage of the new judicial system.[36] Moreover, in matters of personal law, the Hindus were governed by the *dharmashastra*, which upheld the privileges of caste order.[37] As the Orientalist scholars, immersed in classical textual studies, discovered in the caste system the most essential form of Hindu social organisation, more and more information was collected through official ethnographic surveys, which gave further currency to the notions of caste hierarchy. Furthermore, the foremost of such colonial ethnographers, Herbert Risley, following Alfred Lyall and the French racial theorist Paul Topinard, now provided a racial dimension to the concept of caste, arguing that the fair-skinned higher castes represented the invading Aryans, while the darker lower castes were the non-Aryan autochthons of the land.[38]

This racial stereotype and the scriptural view of caste were gradually given enumerated shape, and above all an official legitimacy, through the decennial census classification of castes, which Susan Bayly has described as the "single master exercise of tabulation" of the entire colonial subject society.[39] When Risley became the Census Commissioner in 1901, he proposed not only to enumerate all castes, but also to determine and record their location in the hierarchy of castes. To the Indian public this appeared to be an official attempt to freeze the hierarchy, which had been constantly, though imperceptibly, changing over time. This redefined caste now became what Nicholas Dirks has called the "Indian colonial form of civil society".[40] Voluntary caste associations emerged as a new phenomenon in Indian public life, engaging in census based caste movements, making petitions to census commissioners in support of their claims for higher ritual ranks in the official classification scheme.[41] Ironically, caste thus became a legitimate site for defining social identities within a more institutionalised and apparently secularised public space.

These caste associations, where membership was not just ascriptive but voluntary, gradually evolved into tools of modernisation in colonial India. Their goals shifted from sacred to secular ones and, as Lloyd and Susanne Rudolf have put it, they tried "to educate ... [their] members in the methods and values of political democracy".[42] What contributed to this development was another set of colonial policies that imposed a particular pattern on political modernisation in India. Initially, it was some princely states like Mysore or Kolhapur which in the late nineteenth and early twentieth centuries introduced the system of caste based reservation of certain proportions of public employment for people of non-Brahman birth, in order to compensate them for their past losses. Gradually, the colonial administration too discovered the gap between the high caste Hindus and others, particularly the untouchables, now described as the "depressed classes". It took on the latter as its special ward and initiated a policy of "protective discrimination" in their favour. It meant provision of special schools for their education and reservation of a share of public employment for such candidates and finally, provision for special representation of these classes in the legislative councils. This provision was initially through nomination in the Act of 1919, and then through the announcement of separate electorate in the Communal Award of 1932. What all these measures resulted in was a relatively greater dispersal of wealth and power across caste lines. There were now larger discrepancies between caste prescribed status and caste irrelevant roles, and this limited social mobility led to several contradictory responses

First of all, there were signs of "Westernisation". Because of improved communications, there was greater horizontal solidarity among the caste members, who formed regional caste associations. There was also a growing realisation of the significance of the new sources of status, i.e., education, jobs and political representation and awareness that those new sinews of power were monopolised by the Brahmans and the upper castes. This led to organised demands for more special privileges and reservation from the colonial state. This involved conflict and contestation, particularly when the education of the dalit groups was concerned, as the colonial bureaucracy, despite the much-publicised policy of supporting dalit education, often showed ambivalence in the face of caste Hindu opposition. It required the dalit groups to protest—like the Mahar students in Dapoli in Maharashtra sitting on the verandah of the local municipal school—to actually induce the colonial civil servants to take measures to ensure their educational rights. In this particular case, however, they were ultimately allowed to sit in a classroom, but at a distance from the caste Hindu students.[43] These efforts at "Westernisation" were not therefore just attempts at imaging themselves in the light of their colonial masters, but to claim their legitimate rights to education and other opportunities from a reluctant state bureaucracy. On the other hand, these upwardly mobile groups also engaged in a cultural movement, which noted sociologist M.N. Srinivas (1966) has called the process of "Sanskritization". As status was still being defined and expressed in the language of caste—which enjoyed both official legitimacy and social currency—the upwardly mobile groups sought to legitimise their new status by emulating the cultural and ritual practices of the upper castes. This was one of the reasons why customs like sati, prohibition of widow remarriage, child marriage—the performance of which was regarded as hallmarks of high caste status—were in the nineteenth century being more widely practised by the upwardly mobile lower peasant groups. Ironically, what this behaviour signified was an endorsement of the caste system, and seeking a positional readjustment within the existing ritual hierarchy. However, not all castes at all times followed this same behavioural trajectory.

There were movements which instead of seeking positional changes within the caste system, questioned the fundamentals of this social organisation, the most notable of them being the non-Brahman movements in western and southern India and some of the more radical movements among the dalit groups. The non-Brahman movement started in Maharashtra under the leadership of an outstanding leader of the Mali (gardener) caste, Jotirao Phule, who started his Satyasodhak Samaj (Truthseekers' Society) in 1873. Phule argued that it was Brahman domination, and their monopoly over power and opportunities that lay at the root of the predicament of the Sudra and Ati-sudra castes. So he turned the Orientalist theory of Aryanisation of India (see chapter 2.1) upside down.[44] The Brahmans, he argued, were the progeny of the alien Aryans, who had subjugated the autochthons of the land and therefore the balance now needed to be redressed and for achieving that social revolution, he sought to unite both the non-Brahman peasant castes as well as dalit groups in a common movement. But in the 1880s and 1890s, there were certain subtle shifts in the non-Brahman ideology, as Phule focused more on mobilising the Kunbi peasantry. There was now more emphasis on the unity of those who laboured on the land and a contestation of the claim by the Brahman-dominated Poona Sarvajanik Sabha that they represented the peasantry. This shift of focus on the Kunbi peasants also led to the privileging of the Maratha identity which was dear to them, and an assertion of their Kshatriyahood, which, as Rosalind O'Hanlon has argued, "seemed at times perilously close to a simple Sanskritising claim".[45] Phule tried to overcome this problem by claiming that these Kshatriyas, who were the ancestors of the Marathas, lived harmoniously with the Sudras and assisted them in resisting Aryan assaults. But this emphasis on Kshatriyahood also led to a diminution of interest in the mobilisation of dalits. In other words, while this Kshatriya identity was constructed to contest the Brahmanical discourse that ascribed to them an inferior caste status, it also inculcated an exclusivist ethos that separated them from the dalit groups who were once treated as brothers-in-arms in a previous tradition inspired by Phule's own inclusive message. Ironically, such indigenous constructions of identity also impacted on colonial stereotyping, as the dalit Mahars and Mangs were no longer treated as "martial races", i.e., of Kshatriya lineage (for more on this theory see chapter 2.4), and therefore were excluded from military service from 1892.[46]

The non-Brahman movement in Maharashtra, as Gail Omvedt (1976) has shown, developed at the turn of the century two parallel tendencies. One was conservative, led by richer non-Brahmans, who reposed their faith in the British government for their salvation, and after the Montagu–Chelmsford reforms of 1919, organised a separate and loyalist political party, the Non-Brahman Association, which hoped to prosper under the benevolent paternal rule of the British. But the movement also had a radical trend, represented by the Satyasodhak Samaj, which developed a "class content" by articulating the social dichotomy between the "*bahujan samaj*" or the majority community or the masses, and the "*shetji-bhatji*"—the merchants and Brahmans. Although opposed initially to the Brahman-dominated Congress nationalism, by the 1930s the non-Brahman movement in Maharashtra was gradually drawn into the Gandhian Congress. The power of nationalism, the growing willingness of the Congress to accommodate non-Brahman aspirations, the leadership of the young Poona-based non-Brahman leader Kesavrao Jedhe and his alliance with N.V. Gadgil, representing a new brand of younger Brahman Congress leadership in Maharashtra, brought about this significant shift. In 1938 at Vidarbha, the non-Brahman movement of the Bombay Presidency formally decided to merge into Congress, providing it with a broad mass base.[47]

If in western India the non-Brahman movement was associated with the Kunbis and the Maratha identity, in Madras Presidency it was associated with the Vellalas and a Dravidian identity. It arose in a late nineteenth century context where the Brahmans constituting less than three per cent of the population monopolised 42 per cent of government jobs. Advanced in their English education, they valorised Sanskrit as the language of a classical past, and showed a public disdain for Tamil, the language of the ordinary people.[48] This motivated the Vellala elite to uphold their Dravidian identity. For some time the Christian missionaries like Rev Robert Caldwell and G.E. Pope were talking about the antiquity of Dravidian culture. Tamil language, they argued, did not owe its origin to Sanskrit, which had been brought to the south by the colonising Aryan Brahmans, while the Vellalas and other non-Brahmans could not be described as Sudras, as this was a status imposed on them by the Brahman colonists trying to thrust on them their idolatrous religion.[49] The non-Brahman elite appropriated some of these ideas and began to talk about their Tamil language, literature and culture as an "empowering discourse" and to assert that caste system was not indigenous to Tamil culture.[50] This cultural movement to construct a non-Brahman identity—which began like its western Indian counterpart with an inversion of the Aryan theory of Indian civilisation—always had as its central theme an emotional devotion to Tamil language, which could bring disparate groups of people into a "devotional community".[51] On the political front the movement followed a familiar trajectory that began with the publication of a 'Non-Brahman Manifesto' and the formation of the Justice Party in 1916, as a formal political party of the non-Brahmans. It opposed the Congress as a Brahman dominated organisation, and claimed separate communal representation for the non-Brahmans as had been granted to the Muslims in the Morley–Minto reform. This demand, supported by the colonial bureaucracy, was granted in the Montagu-Chelmsford reform of 1919, as it allocated twenty-eight reserved seats to the non-Brahmans in the Madras Legislative Council. Opposed to the Congress and to its programme of non-cooperation, the Justice Party had no qualm in contesting the election in 1920, which the Congress had given a call for boycott. As a result, the council boycott movement (see chapter 6.3) had no chance of success in Madras, where the Justice Party won 63 of the 98 elected seats, and eventually came to form a government under the new reforms.

The formation of a ministry in 1920 was the high point in the career of the Justice Party, and also the beginning of its decline. It was a movement patronised mainly by richer landowning and urban middle class non-Brahmans, like the Vellalas in the Tamil districts, the Reddis or Kapus and Kammas in the Telugu districts, the Nairs in Malabar and the trading Beri Chettis and Balija Naidus scattered all over south India.[52] Soon after assumption of office, these elite members of the Justice Party became engrossed in using and abusing their newly gained power, gave up their reformist agenda and became less interested in the plight of the untouchables. The latter as a result, under the leadership of M.C. Rajah, left the party in disgust. The decline in popular base which thus began, ultimately culminated in their electoral defeat in 1926 at the hands of the swarajists. Many non-Brahmans thereafter left the party and joined the Congress, which regained its power. This was reflected adequately in the success of the Civil Disobedience campaign in 1929–30. The Quit India movement of 1942 (see chapter 8.1) finally took the wind out of its sails; in the election of 1946, the Justice Party did not even field a candidate.

But if the Justice Party gradually paled into political insignificance, another more radical and populist trend within the non-Brahman movement emerged in south India around this time in the "Self-Respect" movement, under the leadership of E.V. Ramaswamy Naicker, "Periyar". Once an enthusiastic campaigner for the non-cooperation programme, he left the Congress in 1925, believing that it was neither able nor willing to offer "substantive" citizenship to the non-Brahmans.[53] He was incensed by Gandhi's pro-Brahman and pro-varnashram dharma utterances during his tour of Madras in 1927 and constructed a trenchant critique of Aryanism, Brahmanism and Hinduism, which he thought created multiple structures of subjection for Sudras, Adi-Dravidas (untouchables) and women. So before self-rule what was needed was self-respect, and its ideology was predicated upon a sense of pride in—though not an uncritical valorisation of—the Dravidian antiquity and Tamil culture and language. Indeed, Ramaswamy had reservations about privileging Tamil, as this could alienate the other non-Tamil speaking Dravidians of south India. Yet, Tamil language remained at the centre of the movement, sometimes creating tension between 'Tamil' and 'Dravidian' identities.[54] The movement, however, was more clear in identifying its oppositional Other, as it mounted scathing attacks on the Sanskrit language and literature, being the cultural symbols of Aryan colonisation of the south. The story of the *Ramayana* was inverted to make Ravana an ideal Dravidian and Rama an evil Aryan. Unlike Justice Party, this ideology was more inclusive in its appeal. What is significant, the Self-Respect movement also drew its inspiration from and gave more currency to the earlier writings of the Adi Dravida intellectuals like Iyothee Thass and M. Masilamani. Both were publishing since the first decade of the twentieth century numerous articles against the caste system, Brahman domination and Indian nationalism.[55] During the 1930s, as the Congress gradually became more powerful, the non-Brahman movement became more radical and populist in its appeal, with more emphasis on the boycott of

Brahman priests, more and more incidents of public burning of *Manusmriti* and attempts to forcibly enter temples which denied access to low caste people.

Eugene Irschick (1969) has shown how the non-Brahman movement in Madras gradually took the shape of an articulate Tamil regional separatism, particularly when in 1937 the Congress government under C. Rajagopalachari proposed to introduce Hindi as a compulsory school subject in the province. There were huge demonstrations in the city of Madras, identifying Hindi as an evil force trying to destroy Tamil language and its speakers, and with this the Tamil language movement spread from elite circles into the masses.[56] This political campaign slowly propelled into a demand for a separate land or "Dravida Nad". In August 1944, the Justice Party, of which Ramaswamy was now the president, changed its name into Dravida Kazhagam (DK), with its primary objective supposedly being the realisation of a separate non-Brahman or Dravidian land. But in its essence, E. V. Ramaswamy's concept of nation, as M.S.S. Pandian has recently claimed, was "not constrained by the rigid territoriality of the nation-space". He visualised "equal and free citizenship for the oppressed in the anticipatory mode", i.e., in a relentless struggle, and for him "Dravidian" was "an inclusive trope" for all the oppressed people living across the territorial and linguistic boundaries.[57] In other words, the social equality movement nurtured a millennial hope of a society that would be free of caste domination, untouchability or gender discrimination.[58]

Dalit protests in India in the late nineteenth and early twentieth centuries followed somewhat different—but not entirely dissimilar—trajectories. As the Christian missionaries started working among the dalits and the colonial government sponsored special institutions for the spread of education among them, not only was a small educated elite group created among these classes, but in general a new consciousness was visible among the masses as well. However, it should be emphasised here that the colonial bureaucracy, as we have noted earlier, often vacillated in implementing the professed public policies on dalit education and it required the dalit groups to protest and assert themselves to get their rights to education protected. Similarly, the Christian missionaries were not always the aggressive agents of improvement among the dalits, as they too often succumbed to the pressures of an intolerant traditional society and an ambivalent bureaucracy. It is often believed that one way of protesting against the caste system was conversion to Christianity, as dalits took recourse to this method in large numbers in some parts of south India.[59] But conversion itself was not a signifier of liberation, as often the converted dalits were appropriated back into the existing structures of local society. What was really significant was the message of self-respect that the missionaries and the new education inculcated in these groups. Some of the articulate sections among them successfully integrated that message into their own local tradition of bhakti and constructed an ideology of protest against the degradations of caste.[60] This led to the emergence of organised caste movements among various dalit groups all over India, such as the Ezhavas or Iravas[61] and Pulayas of Kerala,[62] Nadars of Tamilnad,[63] Mahars of Maharashtra,[64] Chamars of Punjab,[65] UP[66] and Chattisgarh in central India,[67] Balmikis of Delhi,[68] and the Namasudras of Bengal,[69] to name only a few.

Without denying the distinctiveness of each movement, we may discuss here some of the shared features of these dalit protests. What some of these organised groups (not all) tried first of all, was to appropriate collectively some visible symbols of high ritual status, such as wearing of sacred thread, participation in ritual ceremonies such as community pujas, and entering temples from where they were historically barred by the Hindu priests. A number of organised temple entry movements took place in the early twentieth century, the most important of them being the Vaikkam satyagraha in 1924–25 and the Guruvayur satyagraha in 1931–33 in Malabar,[70] the Munshiganj Kali temple satyagraha in Bengal in 1929[71] and the Kalaram temple satyagraha in Nasik in western India in 1930–35. Apart from such religious rights, the organised dalit groups also demanded social rights from high caste Hindus, and when denied, they took recourse to various forms of direct action. For example, when the higher castes resisted the Nadar women's attempt to cover their breasts like high caste women, this resulted in rioting in Travancore in 1859. The issue remained an irritant in the relationship between the Ezhavas and Nairs and again led to disturbances in 1905 in Quilon. In Bengal, when the high caste Kayasthas refused to attend the funeral ceremony of a Namasudra in 1872, the latter for six months refused to work in their land in a vast tract covering four eastern districts. In Maharashtra, the celebrated Mahar leader, Dr B.R. Ambedkar organised in 1927 a massive satyagraha with ten to fifteen thousand dalits to claim the right to use water from a public tank in Mahad under the control of the local municipality.

This social solidarity and the spirit of protest were to a large extent the result of a resurgence of bhakti among the untouchables during this period. A number of protestant religious sects, like the

Sri Narayana Dharma Paripalana Yogam among the Ezhavas or the Matua sect among the Namasudras, inculcated the message of simple devotion and social equality, and thus interrogated the fundamentals of Hindu social hierarchy. A few religious sects emphasised the fact that the dalits were indeed the original inhabitants of the land subjugated by the intruding Aryans. So now they had to be accepted as they were, without requiring any changes in their culture or way of life, be compensated for their past losses and be given back all their social rights. This self-assertion or endeavour to reclaim lost social grounds was quite evident in the Ad Dharam movement among the Chamars of Punjab or the Adi Hindu movement among the Chamars and other urbanised dalits of UP. On the other hand, some religious movements went even further. The Satnampanth among the Chamars of Chattisgarh manipulated ritual symbols to construct their superiority over the Brahmans,[72] while the Balahari sect among the untouchable Hadis of Bengal went on to imagine an inverted ritual hierarchy where the Brahmans were located at the bottom and the Hadis at the top.[73]

Although many of these movements did not last long, their implications were quite subversive for Hindu society, as not only did they unite dalits around the message of a commonly shared brotherhood, they also indicated their defiance of the Hindu notions of hierarchy and untouchability. This tendency to repudiate Hindu theology as a disempowering and subordinating ideology for the dalits came to an explosive high point when in December 1927 Dr Ambedkar in a public ceremony burnt a copy of *Manusmriti*, the most authentic discursive text authorising untouchability. In 1934 he wrote to temple satyagrahis at Nasik about the futility of temple entry or seeking redress for their grievances within a Hindu religious solution. What he suggested instead, was a "complete overhauling of Hindu society and Hindu theology", and advised the dalits to "concentrate their energy and resources on politics and education."[74]

This tendency to seek a secular or political solution to the problems of their social and religious disability was indeed a prominent feature of the movement of the backward castes during the early decades of the twentieth century. For many of these dalit associations, not just integration of public institutions, but caste based reservation in education, employment and legislatures as a compensation for historical injustices became a non-negotiable minimum demand. And in this, they found patronage from the colonial state, since "protective discrimination" became a regular feature of colonial public policy since the 1920s. From the official standpoint, this was partly to redress social imbalances, but partly also to divide and rule. At the actual field level, it is true, the colonial bureaucracy often did not implement this policy, and in the name of maintaining social equilibrium supported the local conservative elites' opposition to the entry of dalit students into public schools.[75] Yet, for the first time, there was in place such a public policy to promote their education, and there were always some bureaucrats who would be prepared to lend them a sympathetic ear. This brought the dalits closer to the government and estranged them from the Congress. The final solution of their problem, many of the dalits now believed, lay in the provision for separate electorate for them, which the Congress opposed tooth and nail.

This dalit alienation from Congress politics was also to a large extent the result of Congress approach to the question of caste and untouchability. In its eagerness to avoid socially sensitive issues, it ignored the question till 1917 and then took it up only when dalit leaders had organised themselves and were about to steal the initiative from the Congress.[76] Brahman domination and social conservatism of the early Congress, which we have discussed earlier (chapters 4.4 and 5.2), were much to blame for this inaction. But other than this, the mental gap with the untouchables also widened as many of the Hindu nationalist groups, unlike the earlier reformists, now openly tried to glorify and rationalise caste system as a unique social institution of ancient India that united disparate groups of Indians in harmonious solidarity.[77] For the dalits, however, this solidarity meant a subterfuge for ensuring subordination. These attempts to define Indian national identity in terms of Hindu tradition isolated them as they had developed a different perspective about Indian history. If the Hindu nationalists imagined a golden past, for the dalits it was the dark age marked by untouchability and caste discrimination, in contrast to the golden present, when the British made no distinction of caste and had thrown away the rules of Manu that sanctioned caste disabilities.[78]

Gandhi for the first time had made untouchability an issue of public concern and the 1920 Non-cooperation resolution mentioned the removal of untouchability as a necessary pre-condition for attaining swaraj. But his subsequent campaign for the welfare of the Harijans after the withdrawal of the Non-cooperation movement, could neither arouse much caste Hindu interest in the reformist agenda nor could satisfy the dalits. He condemned untouchability as a distortion, but until the1940s upheld *varnashram* dharma or caste system as an ideal non-competitive economic system of social division of labour as opposed to the class system of the West.[79] This theory could not satisfy the socially ambitious groups among the untouchables as it denied them the chances of achieving social mobility. For the eradication of untouchability too, Gandhi took essentially a religious approach: temple entry movement, initiated by caste Hindus as an act of penance, and the idealisation of "Bhangi", the self-sacrificing domestic sweeper, were his answers to the problem. This campaign significantly undermined the moral and religious basis of untouchability, but, as Bhikhu Parekh has argued, failed to deal with its "*economic* and *political* roots". It dignified the untouchables, but failed to empower them.[80] The dalit leaders argued that if they were given proper share of economic and political power, the gates of temples would automatically open for them. The Gandhian approach, in other words, failed to satisfy dalit leaders like Ambedkar who preferred a political solution through guaranteed access to education, employment and political representation. Ambedkar (1945) later charged Gandhi and Congress for obfuscating the real issue and the demand for a separate political identity for the dalits became a sticky point in the relationship between the dalit political groups and the Congress.

Although the first meeting of the Akhil Bharatiya Bahishkrut Parishad (or All India Depressed Classes Conference) held at Nagpur in May 1920 under the presidency of the Maharaja of Kolhapur, was the modest beginning,[81] the actual pan-Indian dalit movement at an organised level started at the All India Depressed Classes Leaders' Conference held at the same city in 1926. Here the All India Depressed Classes Association was formed, with M.C. Rajah of Madras as its first elected president. Dr Ambedkar, who did not attend the conference, was elected one of its vice-presidents. Ambedkar later resigned from this association and in 1930 at a conference in Nagpur, founded his own All India Depressed Classes Congress. As for its political philosophy, in his inaugural address Ambedkar took a very clear anti-Congress and a mildly anti-British position, thus setting the tone for the future course of history.[82]

It was in his evidence before the Simon Commission in 1928 that Ambedkar had first demanded separate electorate—in the absence of universal adult franchise—as the only means to secure adequate representation for the dalits. During the first session of the Round Table Conference, he moved further towards this position, as many of his comrades were in its favour.[83] Following this, on 19 May 1931, an All India Depressed Classes Leaders' Conference in Bombay formally resolved that the depressed classes must be guaranteed "their right as a minority to separate electorate".[84] It was on this point that Ambedkar had a major showdown with Gandhi at the second session of the Round Table Conference in 1931, as the latter opposed it for fear of permanently splitting the Hindu society. Nor was there a consensus among the dalits over this issue. The M.C. Rajah group was staunchly in favour of joint electorate and the Working Committee of their All India Depressed Classes Association in February 1932 deplored Ambedkar's demand for separate electorate and unanimously supported joint electorate with the Hindus, with provision of reservation of seats on the basis of population. An agreement, known as the 'Rajah-Munje Pact', was also reached to this effect between Rajah and Dr B.S. Munje, the president of the All India Hindu Mahasabha. The dalit leadership, in other words, was divided "down the middle" over the electorate issue.[85]

The differences persisted when the Communal Award in September 1932 recognised the right to separate electorate for the untouchables—now called the Scheduled Castes—and Gandhi embarked on his epic fast unto death to get it revoked. Ambedkar now had little choice but to succumb to the moral pressure to save Mahatma's life and accepted a compromise, known as the Poona Pact, which provided for 151 reserved seats for the Scheduled Castes in joint electorate. For the time being, it seemed as if all conflicts had been resolved. There was a nationwide interest in temple entry movement and Gandhi's Harijan campaign. Even, there was cooperation between Gandhi and Ambedkar in relation to the activities of the newly founded Harijan Sevak Sangh. The provisions of the pact were later incorporated into the Government of India Act of 1935. Although there were many critics of the pact at that time, Ravinder Kumar has argued that it represented a triumph for Gandhi who prevented a rift in India's body politic and offered a nationalist solution to the untouchability problem.[86]

But disunity reappeared very soon, as Congress and Ambedkar again began to drift apart. While Gandhi's Harijan Sevak Sangh was involved in social issues, the other Congress leaders had little interest in his mission. They needed a political front to mobilise dalit voters to win the reserved seats in the coming election. For this purpose, they founded in March 1935 the All India Depressed Classes League, with Jagjivan Ram, a nationalist dalit leader from Bihar, as the president. But still in the election of 1937 the Congress won only 73 out of 151 reserved seats all over India. Subsequently, situations changed in different areas in different ways, depending on the nature of commitment the local Congress leaders had towards the Gandhian creed of eliminating untouchability. In the non-Congress provinces like Bengal, the leaders were more sensitive to electoral arithmetic and assiduously cultivated the friendship of the dalit leaders.[87] But in the eight provinces where the Congress formed ministries and remained in power for nearly two years, they performed in such a way that not just critics like Ambedkar were unimpressed, but even those dalit leaders like M.C. Rajah of Madras who once sympathised with the Congress, were gradually alienated.[88]

Ambedkar in 1936 founded his Independent Labour Party, in a bid to mobilise the poor and the untouchables on a broader basis than caste alone—on a programme that proposed "to advance the welfare of the labouring classes".[89] In the election of 1937, his party won spectacular victory in Bombay, winning eleven of the fifteen reserved seats. The Ambedkarites also did well in the Central Provinces and Berar. But from this broad-based politics of caste-class cluster, Ambedkar gradually moved towards the more exclusive constituency of the dalits. He also became a bitter critic of the Congress, as in the 1930s the "secularist" approach of leaders like Nehru and their persistent refusal to recognise "caste as a political problem" most surely alienated the dalit leadership.[90] The difference between the two groups now rested on a contradiction between two approaches to nationalism, the Congress being preoccupied with transfer of power and independence, and the dalits being more concerned with the conditions of citizenship in a future nation-state. Ambedkar was prepared to join the struggle for swaraj, he told the Congress. But he made one condition: "Tell me what share I am to have in the Swaraj".[91] Since he could not get any guarantee, he preferred to steer clear of the Congress movement. In July 1942 he was appointed the Labour Member in the viceroy's council. At a conference from 18 to 20 July 1942 in Nagpur, he started his All India Scheduled Caste Federation, with its constitution claiming the dalits to be "distinct and separate from the Hindus". Leaders like Rajah were now only too happy to join this new exclusive dalit organisation.

This statement of dalit dissent and their claim of a separate identity came just a few days before the beginning of the Quit India movement (8–9 August), which the Muslims had also decided to stay away from. But unlike Muslim breakaway politics, dalit self-assertion did not go very far, and their politics was soon appropriated by the Congress in the late 1940s. This happened due to various reasons. First of all, not all dalits believed in this politics, particularly at a period when Gandhian mass nationalism had acquired an unprecedented public legitimacy. The Scheduled Caste Federation neither had the opportunity nor time or resources to build up a mass organisation that could match that of the Congress at a time when the Gandhian reformist agenda, and later the revolutionary programme of the communists, were constantly corroding its support base. Finally, the imperatives of the transfer of power process left very little elbow room for the dalit leadership to manoeuvre, compelling them to join hands with the Congress. In the election of 1946, like all other minor political parties—including the Hindu Mahasabha and the Communist Party—the Scheduled Caste Federation was practically wiped off, wining only 2 of the 151 reserved seats for the dalits. The overwhelming majority of these seats went to the Congress, which was at that time riding on the crest of a popularity wave generated by the Quit India movement and later the anti-INA trial agitation (see chapter 8). On the basis of the election results, the Cabinet Mission that visited India in 1946 to negotiate the modalities of transfer of power came to a conclusion that it was Congress, which truly represented the dalits and would continue to do so in all official fora. Ambedkar responded furiously to this "crisis of representation" and staged a mass satyagraha to prove his popular support. But the agitation did not last long due to lack of organisation. So, with official patronage withdrawn, and the direct action failing, he was left with no political space where he could project the separate identity of the dalits or fight for their citizenship.[92]

At this historic juncture—just on the eve of independence—the Congress endeavoured to absorb dalit protest, by offering nomination to Ambedkar for a seat in the Constituent Assembly and then by choosing him for the chairmanship of the constitution drafting committee. Under his stewardship, the new Indian constitution declared untouchability illegal, and he became after independence the new law minister in the Nehru cabinet. Thus, as Eleanor Zelliot describes the scenario, "[a]ll the varying strains of Gandhi-Congress-Untouchable situation seemed to come together".[93] But this moment of integration was also fraught with possibilities of rupture. Soon Ambedkar realised the futility of his association with the Congress, as its stalwarts refused to support him on the Hindu Code Bill. He resigned from the cabinet in 1951 and then on 15 October 1956, barely a month and a half before his death, he converted to Buddhism, along with three hundred and eighty thousand of his followers. This event is often celebrated as an ultimate public act of dissent against a Hinduism that was beyond reform. But what needs to be remembered here is that Ambedkar actually redefined Buddhism, criticised its canonical dogmas and foregrounded its radical social message, so that it could fit into the moral role which he envisaged for religion in Indian society.[94] It is for this reason that his particular reading of Buddhism could be seen by the dalits as the basis of a new world view and a socio-political ideology, which contested the dominant religious idioms of the society and the power structure that continually reinforced and reproduced them.

7.3. BUSINESS AND POLITICS

From politics of the communities we may now turn to politics of the classes. Since the late nineteenth century, the Indian capitalist class, more specifically an industrial bourgeoisie, was gradually becoming more matured and influential in politics. Till the end of World War One for various reasons the number of registered industrial enterprises had been steadily rising,[95] while developments in the interwar period further strengthened their position. The factors which facilitated a modest Indian industrial development, despite an obstructing colonial presence, were many, such as a growing tendency towards import substitution in consumer goods, shifting of attention towards the domestic markets, growth in internal trade, shifting of traditionally accumulated capital through trade, moneylending and landowning to industrial investments and the outflow of foreign capital creating a space for indigenous entrepreneurs. By 1944, nearly 62 per cent of the larger industrial units employing more than one thousand workers, and 58 per cent of their labour force were controlled by the Indian capital. And in the smaller factories, which constituted 95.3 per cent of the industrial sector, the control of the Indian capital, as Aditya Mukherjee has emphasised, was "absolute".[96] This development happened as Indian capital moved into areas hitherto not developed by foreign capital, such as sugar, paper, cement, iron and steel etc. Indian capital also intruded into areas so long dominated by expatriate capital, such as finance, insurance, jute, mining and plantation. But it also consolidated its position in its traditional areas of strength, such as cotton. Indeed, most spectacular was the rise of the cotton industry, which was now catering for the domestic consumers, reducing Manchester's market share to less than 40 per cent by 1919.[97]

As mentioned already, this modest growth in Indian industrialisation took place not because of colonial rule, but in spite of it (chapter 2.5). The earlier generation of Indian businessmen, too dependent on foreign capital, were prepared to accept its domination, and with it the realities of a discriminatory colonial state. But the newer generation of industrialists, coming from an expanded social base, were more matured and less prepared to surrender their rights. To consolidate their position, they began to organise themselves, and so the Bengal National Chamber of Commerce in 1887 and the Indian Merchants' Chamber in Bombay in 1907 came into existence. But the question is, what really at this stage was the political attitude of the Indian business community towards nationalism vis-à-vis imperialism. Historians seem to be divided on this issue. Bipan Chandra, on the one hand, thinks that the "Indian capitalist class had developed a long-term contradiction with imperialism while retaining a relationship of short-term dependence on and accommodation with it".[98] In the long run the capitalists desired the end of imperial exploitation and the coming of a nation-state; but their structural weaknesses and dependence on the colonial government dictated a prudent strategy of combining pressure with compromise. They preferred a nationalist movement within safe and acceptable limits, not guided by left-wing radicals, but in the reliable hands of right-wing moderates. This position is further developed by Aditya Mukherjee, who has talked about a "multi-pronged" capitalist strategy to overthrow imperialism and maintain capitalism.[99] They were afraid of organised labour, left-wing radicalism and mass movement; but as safeguards against these, they did not surrender to imperialism. They evolved a class strategy to guide the nationalist movement into the path of constitutionalism, patronise the right-wingers and thus follow a Congress, which would remain under a "bourgeois ideological hegemony".[100]

As opposed to this Marxist view, which looks at the capitalists as a matured class with a well-defined anti-imperialist ideology, other historians are less sure about it. Basudev Chatterji, for example, is more direct: "Politically", he thinks, "Indian business groups were overwhelmingly loyalist".[101] A.D.D. Gordon, looking at the Bombay business groups, makes a distinction between the merchants and the industrialists; while the former, he thinks, were more nationalist, the latter were the "traditional allies of government".[102] Claude Markovits (1985) too has observed similar rifts, but over a longer period also rapprochement and shifts in the political attitudes of the different groups of Indian businessmen towards nationalism and Congress. So far as the colonial authorities were concerned, as Rajat Ray has observed, the Indian businessmen were both "co-operating and opposing at the same time", and thus their attitudes preclude any "clear-cut generalisation".[103] On the whole, argues Dwijendra Tripathi, business politics was guided by a "pragmatic approach" to issues as they arose, maintaining the policy of "equidistance" or avoiding a tilt either in favour of Congress or government for fear of antagonising or alienating either of them. Talking of a capitalist "grand strategy", he thinks, is to make an "overstatement".[104] In other words, what appears from these writings is that the Indian businessmen hardly constituted a "class for itself" in the first half of the twentieth century. They did not pull together, had divided interests, clash of ideas and contradictions in strategies; during this period it is difficult to talk about their politics in generalised terms. We will, therefore, try to understand these complexities, instead of attempting to identify a unified capitalist ideology or political strategy towards nationalism or imperialism.

World War One and the period immediately after it brought mixed fortunes for the Indian business communities. While the industrialists prospered due to wartime developments, the merchants suffered due to currency fluctuations and high taxes. The rupee collapsed in December 1920, threatening the Indian importers with a possible loss of nearly 30 per cent on their previous contracts; but this helped the Indian exporters and mill owners. The high wartime taxation affected everybody, but the particular changes in the income tax law hurt the indigenous joint family businesses, as their accounting system did not fit in well with the requirements of filling tax returns under the new law.[105] Although the Marwari and Gujarati traders were aggrieved with the government's taxation and currency policies, the industrialists and big businessmen were less concerned, as the government was also trying hard to buy their support. The Montagu–Chelmsford Reforms in 1919 introduced the system of "interest representation", thus giving Indian business—along with labour—representation in the central and provincial legislatures.[106] Other than that, the Fiscal Autonomy Convention in 1919 and the promise of a policy of "discriminatory protection" after 1922 brought the hope of protective tariffs.[107] Therefore, when mass nationalism started with the advent of Gandhi, it evoked mixed responses from India's business communities.

Some of the Marwari and Gujarati merchants and new entrepreneurs, who were deeply religious, were drawn irresistibly towards Gandhi as they could find common ground in his Jain and Vaishnava philosophy. His emphasis on non-violence was reassuring against any kind of political radicalism; and his "trusteeship" theory legitimised wealth. Thus although Gandhian ideology was not based on capitalist interests, some of its concepts were attractive to them. Hence, they happily contributed for Gandhi's constructive programmes and some big businessmen like G.D. Birla or Jamnalal Bajaj became his close associates.[108] But there were some irritants as well; particularly Ahmedabad mill owners like Ambalal Sarabhai was not entirely happy with his leadership style in the labour strike of 1918 (see chapter 6.2). But Gandhi somehow overcame this barrier, as the Indian businessmen realised very well that it was only he who could prevent the Congress from becoming anti-capitalist.[109] Yet, when the Rowlatt satyagraha started in 1919, the industrialists remained skeptical, although the merchants of Bombay supported overwhelmingly. When Gandhi was arrested in April there was a complete business strike in the Bombay city. When the Non-cooperation movement started, the cotton merchants again supported the boycott movement and donated generously to the Tilak Swaraj Fund.[110] But many industrialists on the other hand remained silent, or opposed mass agitation outright. An Anti-Non-cooperation Society was started in Bombay with the blessings of Purushottamdas Thakurdas and funds from R.D. Tata. The split in the business community was visible nowhere more clearly than in Bombay, where the dominance of the industrialists in the Indian Merchants' Chamber came under threat twice in 1920 and 1921—first time on the issue of council boycott and then on the question of presenting an address to the visiting Prince of Wales whom Congress wanted to be boycotted.[111] Clearly the merchants were on the side of the Congress and the Congress too needed their support, as without them the boycott movement had little chance of success.

After 1922, however, due to the deteriorating economic conditions all sections of the Indian business community were drawn more closely to the side of nationalism, the industrialists included. The wartime boom collapsed in 1921–22 and was followed by a slump in the industry throughout the 1920s. The non-saleability of goods and large unsold stocks were accompanied by rising labour costs. The situation for the Bombay cotton mill owners was further worsened by their dependence on imported yarn and the growing competition from cheap Japanese goods that started inundating Indian markets from around this time, pushing prices further down. The prices of cotton mill shares plunged sharply between 1920 and 1923,[112] sending shivers down the spines of many industrialists. Their major grievance at this stage was against the 3.5 per cent excise duty on cotton, for the abolition of which they now joined hands with the swarajists in the legislative assembly. The duty was abolished in December 1925, but that did not solve the problems of the cotton mill owners. In 1926 eleven mills were closed and 13 per cent of the workforce became unemployed. In January 1927, a majority report of the Indian Tariff Board recommended an increase in import duties from 11 to 15 per cent on all cotton manufactures other than yarn. But the decision was put on hold by the Government of India because of vehement opposition of the Lancashire lobby.[113]

In the 1920s, the Indian industrialists were not only being rebuffed by the Government of India that remained insensitive to their economic problems under pressure from London; but their relationship with expatriate capital in India too was gradually deteriorating both in Calcutta and Bombay. As Maria Misra (1999) has shown, ever since the reforms of 1919, the attitudes of the British capitalists in India, insistent on their racial exclusivism and autonomy, hardened towards their Indian counterparts, as they were averse to granting any concessions either to Indian politicians or businessmen. In 1921 the European trading organisations formed an apex body called the Associated Chambers of Commerce (ASSOCHAM). In response, in 1927 the Indian capitalists, despite their differences and clash of interests, formed their own organisation, the FICCI, with Purushottamdas Thakurdas at its helm. The battle lines were further drawn as the depression touched India with all its fury in 1929. This time it was interpreted in terms of the failures of government policies; the agricultural prices plummeted and the situation was worsened by conservative fiscal and monetary policies. The government, now in a desperate financial situation, needed additional sources of revenue and looked once again to cotton duties. In the Cotton Protection Act of March 1930, the cotton duties were raised from 11 per cent to 15 per cent, but were limited only to non-British goods, thus giving preference to Lancashire. This introduction of the system of imperial preference irked the Indian industrialists and drew widespread protest from the nationalists, with a number of them resigning from the legislative assembly, including Birla and Thakurdas.

The other irritant was the currency policy of the government and the artificially fixed high rupee-sterling exchange rate of 1s 6d prescribed by the Hilton–Young Commission in 1926. The government tried to maintain this high exchange value of rupee in order to ensure the flow of remittances from India and to maintain India's creditworthiness. The high rate favoured the English exporters to India to the disadvantage of the Indian importers; it also affected adversely, it was argued, the agricultural producers and the industrial workers. In September 1931, Britain went off gold standard with rupee linked to the sterling at the rate of 1s 6d. The resultant release and outflow of domestic gold from India helped Britain, but did not benefit Indian interests. Business groups demanded a lower rate of 1s 4d as best suited to Indian economic recovery and a Currency League was formed in 1926 in Bombay, with the blessings of Gandhi and Patel. This currency debate, in other words, was drawing the businessmen and the Congress closer together on a common platform against the government. Traditionally, the business groups favoured constitutionalism and "pressure group politics" and this explains why they maintained their distance from the Non-cooperation movement in 1920–21.[114] But as Congress reverted to constitutionalism, the representatives of the Indian business also came closer to the swarajists and started cooperating with them in the legislative assembly on various national economic issues. For instance, issues such as revision of government purchase policy, the repeal of the cotton excise duty, raising of duties on cotton piece-goods against Japanese competition, opposition to the system of imperial preference and the currency policy. Businessmen also donated generously to Gandhi's constructive programmes and to the swarajists' campaign funds.[115] Yet, many of them still had their lingering doubts about throwing their lot in favour of agitational politics under a Gandhian Congress.

Although depression had made their condition desperate and created, according to Sumit Sarkar,[116] some kind of a "groundswell of opinion" in favour of participating in the Civil Disobedience movement, this drift, as Markovits (1985) points out, was by no means simple or without complexities. To many of them, agitational politics was still too risky a proposition—a possible fertile ground for civil unrest and Bolshevism; yet others believed that it was their only chance to wrest some concessions from an insensitive government. They were heartened when Lord Irwin announced his proposal in November 1929 for a Round Table Conference which promised a constitutional resolution of India's problems. But their hopes were dashed by Congress intransigence, as its Lahore resolution, passed in December, demanded *purna swaraj* or complete independence, which sounded too radical to the business groups. The other provision of the resolution repudiating debt had serious repercussions in the share market in Bombay and the Indian securities market in London, and therefore, was not quite palatable to the business groups either. Yet, they remained with the Congress, according to many historians, for fear of communism and the threat of continued labour unrest. This period witnessed a series of strikes in 1928 and 1929, under the leadership of trade unions like Girni Kamgar Union, which increasingly came under communist leadership. The red scare prompted Dorabji Tata to offer a desperate proposal to form an Indo-European political organisation of the capitalists to contain communism. It was stopped through the intervention of Birla and Thakurdas and thus an open rift with the nationalists was averted. Although in 1929, the government came down heavily against the communists in the Meerut Conspiracy Case, still the only hope of the Indian capitalists to win their battle against communism was an All India Trade Union Congress (which had been formed in 1920) under the sober influence of Gandhi.

Thus for various reasons, by the beginning of 1930 all sections of the Indian business community had been drawn towards the Congress. And the Congress too was sensitive to their conditions and interests. So when Gandhi announced his 11 point ultimatum to Irwin, it contained three specific capitalist demands—a rupee-sterling exchange rate of 1s 4d, protection for cotton industry and reservation of coastal shipping for the Indian companies (see chapter 6.4). But as the Civil Disobedience movement started, the business response once again was mixed. The traders and marketeers were more enthusiastic: they contributed funds and participated in the boycott movement. It was, indeed, the cloth merchants, particularly the importers, who contributed most to the success of the boycott movement by refusing to indent foreign goods for specific periods. The mill owners, on the other hand, were nervous and offered little concrete support, while some Bombay industrialists like the Tatas, who depended on government orders, remained skeptical. But complete neutrality would have been suicidal; so the FICCI supported the principles of the movement and condemned police brutalities.

The practicalities of the boycott movement also resulted in clashes of interests between the Congress and the mill owners. Gandhi's idea of boycott was to replace foreign cloth with khadi; although he was willing to accept some amount of profiteering by the Indian mill owners, but this had to be contained within limits. So the Congress in 1928 devised certain rules, and the mills that agreed to abide by them were classified as swadeshi mills, not to be boycotted. But the rules were too stringent for the mill owners and therefore they had to be relaxed in 1930 and lengthy negotiations followed between the Congress and the Ahmedabad and Bombay mill owners. In the end, by March 1931, only eight mills still refused to accept the pledge of swadeshi; others signed the pledge, but rarely cared to go by the rules.[117] And whatever enthusiasm the mill owners had for

Civil Disobedience, it clearly evaporated by September 1930, when they found themselves saddled with huge unsold stocks. The growing civil unrest not only hampered day-to-day business; it struck terror in the minds of the big business about the loss of respect for authority and the spectre of a social revolution. They clearly now wanted to get back to constitutionalism, and leaders like Birla and Thakurdas preferred to play the role of honest brokers between the Congress and the government. If Gandhi signed the truce with Irwin because of a "host of other factors", as Aditya Mukherjee has claimed,[118] business pressure was certainly one of them—and an important one.

In February 1931, just before the Gandhi–Irwin Pact was signed in March, the Government of India had offered an important concession to cotton mill owners by raising duties by a further 5 per cent on cotton piecegoods, and this time without giving preference to Lancashire.[119] But this did not mean that the business leaders were bought off. At the second Round Table Conference, where Gandhi represented the Congress, and the FICCI delegation was led by Birla and Thakurdas, the latter strictly adhered to the Gandhian line in all negotiations on economic matters.[120] Yet, they did not certainly like to revert to agitation when the constitutional negotiations failed in London. When the Congress launched the second Civil Disobedience movement in January 1932, business support was clearly not forthcoming, although there was no consensus on this matter either. The political pressure around this time split the business community into several warring factions. The Bombay business was split into four groups, with some like Tata and Sir Homi Mody openly condemning Civil Disobedience. At the all-India level, big business was split into three factions: the Ahmedabad mill owners supporting the movement, the Bombay mill owners along with some lobbies in Calcutta and in the south opposing it, and some prominent FICCI leaders like Birla and Thakurdas constantly vacillating.[121]

The fractious nature of business politics became more evident when the government announced the proposal for an Imperial Economic Conference at Ottawa in 1932. Its purpose was to foster imperial economic cooperation, by establishing "a *new* specialization of production between and within different industries in the empire".[122] The FICCI leaders were initially enthusiastic about cooperating with the government on this issue, but a distrustful Viceroy Willingdon turned down the hands of friendship and instead sent an Indian business delegation comprising confirmed loyalists and second rate business leaders. As a result, the Ottawa

Agreement of August 1932, although it promised some real benefits to Indian business, was greeted with a hostile reaction from the FICCI and the nationalists. But the condemnation was not unanimous, as Bombay big business began to take a more conciliatory attitude to British capital and preferred to ally with British companies against competition from non-British goods. On labour policy, leaders like Tata and Mody even preferred to collaborate with expatriate capital, and formed in 1933 the Employers' Federation of India. But this experiment did not go much further, as British businessmen in India were less enthusiastic about collaborating with their Indian counterparts.[123]

The political opinion of the Indian big business was clearly divided at this juncture on the issues of imperial preference and nationalism and this became manifest once again around the Lees–Mody Pact of October 1933. Under the leadership of Mody the Bombay cotton mill owners, who produced coarse cotton, were prepared to accept preference for Lancashire, but the Ahmedabad mill owners were not, as they more directly faced competition from Lancashire in the market for finer cotton goods. Yet, despite their protest, the pact was signed inviting condemnation from the nationalists as well as all the business organisations, except the Bombay big business. But as the split in the business community widened, it also became clear that business lobbies on their own had little power to change any government policy. This was evident when the Reserve Bank bill was passed and sugar excise duties were imposed in 1934 despite business protests. This created a compulsion to retain links with the Congress, despite reservations about its confrontational stance and agitational politics.

So when the Civil Disobedience movement was formally suspended by Gandhi in April 1934, the decision was welcomed by the Indian business community, who were relieved by the return of constitutionalism to Indian politics. Loyalty was duly rewarded by the government, as the TISCO got the Steel Protection bill passed in the assembly, and the Bombay textile industry benefited from the Indo-Japanese treaty providing for a quota system for the sale of Japanese goods in India. The major dilemma, however, was for those who had sided with the Congress, as they were alarmed by the rise of socialism under Jawaharlal Nehru, Subhas Bose and Jayaprakash Narayan, who formed in October 1934 their Congress Socialist Party. However, as Aditya Mukherjee (1986) has emphatically argued, this red scare did not throw them into the arms of imperial authorities. Their strategy to contain socialism was to patronise the right-wingers within the Congress, i.e., people like "Vallabhbhai, Rajaji and Rajendrababu" who were, in the words of Birla, "all fighting communism and socialism"[124]—and finally, to throw in their lot behind Gandhi. The Gandhians too were eager to get capitalist support and their financial backing in their bid to regain control of the Congress. In the election of 1934, business finance was a crucial factor behind Congress victory.

The major interests of the capitalists at this juncture were to keep the Congress within the bounds of constitutional politics and to clip its socialist wings. For this, they were even prepared to meddle in the internal politics of the Congress. The 'Bombay Manifesto', signed in 1936 by twenty-one Bombay businessmen, contained an open indictment of Nehru's preaching of socialist ideals, which were deemed prejudicial to private property, and to the peace and prosperity of the country. Although it did not evoke support from any other section of the business community, it strengthened the hands of the moderates within the Congress, like Bhulabhai Desai and G.B. Pant, who put pressure on Nehru to tone down his socialist utterances. The Congress decision to participate in the election of 1937 and accept office thereafter brought the capitalists closer to it. Even skeptics like Mody, in the context of continually deteriorating economic conditions, now drifted closer to the nationalists. But although business finance once again became a crucial factor behind the spectacular victory of the Congress in the election of 1937, the party was far from under capitalist domination.

Indeed, when the Congress formed ministries in eight provinces, it evoked jubilation and expectations from both labour and capital, and the party had to continually balance between the two contradictory interests. During the first two years in office, trade union activities and labour unrest increased phenomenally in the Congress-ruled provinces, particularly in Madras and the United Provinces and the Congress ministries had to adopt a number of resolutions implementing the labour welfare programmes, which it had promised during the election. This irritated the capitalists no doubt, but what further added to it were the conservative economic and fiscal policies of the provincial governments. Faced with financial stringency, these governments had very little choice but to increase taxes, like the property tax or sales tax, which the business did not quite like. They now closed ranks and this alarmed the Congress high command. Therefore, by the spring of 1938, there was a remarkable change in Congress policies, as it tried to placate capitalist interests. The most authentic manifestation of this shift was in its labour policy, which resulted in the passage of the notorious Bombay Trades Disputes Act, passed in November 1938. It aimed at preventing both strikes and lockouts, but was tilted heavily in favour of the capitalists. This new anti-labour mood was visible in other provinces too, where industrial disputes gradually began to decline from 1939. This marked shift in Congress ideology and policy towards industrial relations dispelled capitalist fear and brought about a rapprochement between the two. But once again, it is difficult to generalise about business attitudes, as some businessmen in the United Provinces and Madras still had their reservations about Congress, while the Muslim businessmen on the whole remained alienated.[125]

Throughout this period and after, the Indian businessmen on the whole maintained a strategic relationship with the Congress. Most of them were not averse to nationalism; but they preferred constitutionalism and feared insurrectionary revolutions. Just four days before the launching of the Quit India movement some leading industrialists of the country, like Thakurdas, J.R.D. Tata and Birla wrote to the viceroy that the immediate solution to the Indian crisis lay in the "granting of political freedom to the country . . . even during the midst of war".[126] But when the Quit India movement actually started with this same demand, they were extremely reluctant to support and assured the viceroy of their opposition to it. However, once the storm was over, they returned once again to the side of the Congress and when the negotiations for the transfer of power began there was even more eagerness to cooperate. The Congress too after the defeat of the Quit India movement came under the control of a conservative leadership, which preferred collaborating with the capitalists and remain strictly within the path of constitutionalism.

Equally significant is the fact that some of the business leaders actively participated in the economic planning process initiated by the socialist thinking of Jawaharlal Nehru. When the Congress under the presidency of Subhas Bose constituted its first National Planning Committee in 1938, it included prominent business leaders like Purushottamdas Thakurdas, A.D. Shroff, Ambalal Sarabhai and Walchand Hirachand. Interestingly, two of them—Thakurdas and Hirachand—were the signatories to the 'Bombay Manifesto' of 1936 that had expressed serious disapprobation of Nehru's socialist ideals. In the changed circumstances, however, the commitment of the Indian business to the idea of planning was further evinced when in 1944 they independently produced what is known as the 'Bombay Plan'. Its eight signatories represented "a wide cross-section of India's business world"[127] and it anticipated in a real sense the Five Year plans and the industrial policies of the future Congress governments.

Thus, throughout the period under review the relationship between the Indian capitalists and the Congress remained strategic, issue based, and even pragmatic. The former's commitment to nationalism was not certainly above business interests, and support for Congress was strictly conditional. But they were neither loyalists nor unpatriotic; and they agreed, despite reservations, with many aspects of the Congress programme. In this complex, continually evolving, multi-faceted relationship, it is difficult to identify any consistent ideology.

7.4 WORKING CLASS MOVEMENTS

The gradual industrialisation of India did not only bring the Indian capitalists into the foreground of public life, it also created an industrial working class. The growth of tea plantations in northeastern and southern India and the beginning of an infant iron and steel industry since the early nineteenth century, the commencement of railway construction from the middle of the nineteenth century, mining in eastern India from the same period, and the spectacular growth of two industries, the jute industry in and around Calcutta and the cotton industry in Bombay and Ahmedabad since the time of World War One (see chapter 2) saw the formation of an industrial working class in the organised sector in India. There was a vast increase in the size of the working class in the late nineteenth and the early twentieth centuries. According to census figures, in a population of 303 million, the number of workers in the organised industry was about 2.1 million in 1911; to this another five hundred and seventy five thousand were added between 1911 and 1921. In addition to these, there were workers in the so-called 'informal sectors', such as those who worked as casual labourers in docks and markets or as domestic servants, about whom we have very little information.

This growth in the size of the urban industrial working class was sustained by a continual rural-urban migration, caused, according to some historians, by the 'push' factors. The rural poor were pushed out of their villages because an overstretched agrarian economy could no longer support a surplus labour force. The growing numbers of "landless laborers and submarginal peasants constituted a large part of the potential labour force for the Bombay cotton mills", argued Morris D. Morris.[128] And in eastern India, in the words of Ranajit Das Gupta, the "ruined artisans, labourers failing to get adequate employment ... in the rural economy, agriculturists unsettled by the changes taking place in the agricultural economy and unskilled people" constituted "the majority of the working mass employed in the jute mills". However, he also concedes that "a sizeable proportion" of them belonged to "land-holding peasant groups".[129] The stereotype has been further questioned in recent times, for example, by Arjan de Haan (1995), who finds in eastern India a multiplicity of factors, including attractions for industrial employment and the lure of urban living—and not just "'push' of shortage of land"—as motivations behind labour migration. The motivations varied from person to person; people both with and without land migrated. And in most cases, it was cyclical migration, as most of these migrants retained their regular connections with the villages, went back to their ancestral homes either at harvesting times or during the marriage or festival seasons, and regularly sent money to their families. Rajnarayan Chandavarkar has argued that migration to cities and retaining connections with their villages were for them a matter of "conscious choice", as it was seen as a means to repay their debts, hold on to their lands and improve their position and status in village society.[130] Moreover, the uncertainties of urban living were offset by the psychological reassurance provided by their continuing connections with an ancestral village "home".[131]

In the urban industrial neighbourhoods, therefore, these migrant labourers instead of developing a working-class consciousness maintained a cultural dual self of a peasant and an industrial worker and remained divided among religious groups and castes. The demographic composition of the working-class neighbourhoods looked exactly like that of the villages where they came from; their village ties, in other words, operated in the urban-industrial settings as well. Apart from the spatial segregation of religious groups in the working-class *mohallas*, their community identity manifested itself in their observance of caste oriented commensality restrictions, in their dress codes and in their slogans which frequently used overt religious idioms.[132] Even at work, various departments in an industry were manned exclusively by members of particular religious communities or social groups.[133] Often, the higher castes got the better jobs, while lower castes and the untouchables got the low paid and risky jobs.[134] Thus this working class from the very beginning remained differentiated and hierarchised and this happened, according to some historians, because of a structured recruitment system.

Unlike the European situation, in India there was no random or open recruitment from among a proletarianised peasantry; recruitment was usually made through jobbers. Known as *sardars* in eastern and western India or *mistri* in the north, they were appointed from among the labourers themselves. From the employers' point of view, given the fluctuating demand for labour, the jobbers ensured a steady supply of labour. For the workers, in view of the extremely temporary nature of employment, the jobbers were a source of patronage, as they provided jobs, helped them in finding shelter and guaranteed them access to credit at times of unemployment. The sardars had their own preferences in terms of village, community and caste ties and thus wove around them social networks of mutual dependence. These were articulated in various forms in the working class neighbourhoods in the cities and the workers being in a most vulnerable position had to depend on these ties as sources of patronage and security. And therefore, as Morris has argued, the jobbers not only hired workers, they also had "uncontrolled power in the administration of labor discipline".[135]

Some modern researchers, however, have questioned this overemphasis on the role of sardars. The clustering of communities in certain departments happened also because of particular recruitment policies of the employers, who were often guided by colonial stereotypes.[136] And if religious and ethnic categorisation mattered so much, gender inequities were far more deeply entrenched in Indian industrial policies. As Samita Sen has shown, in the Bengal jute mills certain jobs were identified as particularly "suitable" for women, because of their family engagements and reproductive role. And these were usually the unskilled and therefore low-paid jobs.[137] So, in other words, for getting employment the workers had to depend on a whole set of ideological preferences and personal connections, and the sardars were only a part of that network.[138] While the workers depended on the sardars, they also defied the latter's authority and turned against them when the patrons failed to deliver or did something against their interests. There were several strikes and agitations against sardars in the Calcutta jute mills in 1919–20, which explodes the "myth of sardari power".[139] On the other hand, far from always serving the interests of the employers and ensuring shopfloor discipline, sometimes sardars themselves became organisers of working-class agitations, as it happened in the Calcutta jute mills in 1929 and 1937.[140] In western India too, the sardar's agency was constrained by various other focuses of power within the neighbourhood and in the workplace and the growth of working class politics in the 1920s and 1930s definitely resulted in a diminution of their social influence. As Chandavarkar argues, the sardars were a part of an informal network of social interdependence; the sardari system was in fact the result of "actions and autonomous organisations of rural migrants", not just a creation of the employers to control the workforce.[141]

However, what can hardly be denied is the fact that these migrant workers remained embedded in their community relationships and organisations, and this, it has been pointed out, hindered the growth of a class consciousness. That does not, of course, mean that they were not conscious of their social situation. As Dipesh Chakrabarty has shown,[142] they were perfectly aware of their poverty, conscious of the power relations in the factory and dissatisfied about their subordination in jobs. There were instances of incendiarism and attempts to turn the power structure in the factory upside down. Yet, their anti-employer mentality, their sense of identity as workers or poor people were often enmeshed with other narrower and conflicting identities. Hence the religious and caste divisions kept the working class divided horizontally, and often the employers took advantage of this to weaken industrial action. In the Madras textile strike in 1921, for example, the Adi-Dravidas or the untouchables were used as strike breakers against the caste Hindu and Muslim unionists.[143] Communal riots between the Hindu and Muslim workers occurred regularly in the industrial neighbourhoods, the Talla riot in Calcutta, which took place on 29 June 1897 over the demolition of a mosque, is just a glaring example of that. The workers' actions, it is argued, were thus motivated more by "community" consciousness than class consciousness, which can be explained, according to Chakrabarty, in terms of their "precapitalist culture".[144] This was most evident in the limited growth of trade unionism, although there was no dearth of industrial actions: "so much militancy, yet so little organization", Chakrabarty argues, constituted a "paradox" of working class history.[145] This happened because the concept of trade union as a "bourgeois-democratic organisation" was alien to the cultural space of the Indian workers.[146] Even their relationship with the middle-class trade union leaders was locked in a hierarchical structure—the "*babu*-coolie relationship".[147] No wonder that a more sophisticated class consciousness did not emerge under such circumstances.

However, if we give up our expectations that the Indian industrial workers ought to have evolved a working-class consciousness like that of their European counterparts, we may perhaps look at their history in a different way and discover the more interesting nuances of their politics. In Madras, for example, the Adi-Dravidas became strike breakers more because compared with caste Hindus and Muslims they were economically much too vulnerable due to their total dependence on wages for survival.[148] In many cases what appeared as "communal riots" were not entirely communal in character. In many of the riots, including the Talla riot, the principal targets of attack were the police, and there were instances of cooperation across religious lines.[149] And like Calcutta, in Kanpur too, in riots like the Plague disturbances of 1900 or the Machli Bazar riot of 1913, the main grievance was against an intruding state.[150] The former was caused, as in the similar Bombay or Calcutta disturbances of 1898, by the enforcement of Plague regulations that compromised the religious codes of privacy and the latter by the demolition of a mosque by road construction projects. On the other hand, it should also be noted that the workers often used their informal community ties and religious institutions like mosques or gurdwaras to forge inter-communal class solidarities to further their class interests and demands and at times of confrontation used religious idioms and slogans to boost flagging morale.[151] However, at the other end of the spectrum, there is no reason to assume uncritically that the working-class mentality was always governed by their religion. The levelling effects of the urban workplace also led to the undermining of older loyalties and to the bonding of new connections. Even, as Janaki Nair finds among the workers at the Kolar Gold Fields in Mysore, "the growing tide of rationalism and atheism won many converts".[152]

In the face of low wages, improper working conditions and often subhuman living environment, the usual mode of workers' response was what one scholar has described as "disaggregated resistance", meaning withdrawal and absenteeism[153] of which there had been plenty of instances throughout the industrial scene. But other than that, there had also been a series of successful strikes in Indian industries despite very limited growth of trade unionism. And this happened because of the informal community ties mentioned earlier. The Bombay textile workers struck eight times between 1919 and 1940, each time their industrial action lasted for more than one month and in 1928–29 lasted for more than one year.[154] And not just in Bombay, such strikes took place in Ahmedabad (1918, 1923, 1935, 1937), in Sholapur (1920, 1928, 1934, 1937), in Calcutta (1920–21, 1929, 1937), in Jamshedpur (1920, 1922, 1928, 1942), in Nagpur (1934), in Madras (1918, 1921), in Coimbatore (1938) and in the railways (1928, 1930). It was actually through these moments of confrontation, as we shall see later, that trade unions were actually born. It is, therefore, in this complex matrix of community, class and workers' collective action, that we will have to locate their relationship with the colonial state and nationalism.

The workers' attitudes to colonial state were shaped by their earlier experience with the authorities in the villages. There they encountered the landlord-state combination, while in the industrial centres they witnessed another version of that same alliance dominating their daily lives.[155] The employers' organisations like the Indian Jute Mills Association in Calcutta were dominated by the Europeans; the Bombay Mill Owners' Association, though controlled by the Indian capitalists, was still viewed as an extension of that same alien imperialist culture. This was largely because of the latter's European lifestyle, their free social mixing with the European mill owners, and the pro-employer policies of the state which further contributed to such images.[156] There were, of course, legislations, like the Bengal Factory Acts of 1881 or 1911, regulating the age of employment and working hours. But the employers flouted them with impunity with the active connivance of the state and the workers continued to work for long hours, were paid low wages and lived in squalid conditions.[157] In the coalfields of eastern India, the collieries actually acted as the "industrial variant of the zamindary estate", with the zamindary managers being invariably Europeans. The usual practice was to bind the miners in service tenancy arrangements, under which a small plot of land was given to them in exchange for their labour in the mines. In 1908 the Chota Nagpur Tenancy Act prohibited such service arrangements. But it continued unabated until the depression made it obsolete in the 1930s, and the local colonial officials saw nothing wrong with that deliberate infringement of law.[158] Similarly, in the Assam tea gardens where the hated indentured system was abolished in 1926, the "extra-legal" practice of "reindenturing" the labourers continued without any intervention from the state.[159]

In the 1920s, although only for a while, the colonial state and also some employers realised the usefulness of trade unions as legitimate channels of negotiations. This was in response to the granting of representation to the labour in the legislative councils in the Act of 1919, later this principle being extended to municipalities as well. So this change of attitude was much less a change of heart, and more the pursuance of a "notion of containment".[160] In Bombay, after the general textile strike of 1928, and throughout the 1930s, the state showed only unmitigated hostility towards the trade unions and working class activism.[161] Not only were a number of anti-labour legislations passed in 1934, 1938 and 1946 to contain working class militancy and trade union activities, but also frequent use of police became a handy tool to break strikes and ensure labour discipline. This happened at every industrial centre throughout India, where the police, being the only visible representative of the state, appeared in the eyes of the workers as the long hand of tyranny.

That Indian workers remained divided among them, competed with each other and did not join the trade union movements, was largely because of this employer-state collusion. Both at industry and factory levels, workers were victimised, intimidated, coerced, often physically attacked for attempting to combine and at the event of a strike, due to an oversupply of labour, the employers could easily dismiss the striking workers. And in all these, the state was always on their side. These factors, as Chandavarkar has argued, constrained the growth of trade unionism. Even larger unions like the Bombay Textile Labour Union or the Ahmedabad Textile Labour Association (ATLA) were vulnerable to pressures from the employers and the state.[162] The Madras Labour Union was temporarily crushed in 1921 by the British textile magnates, the Binnys, with rather overt assistance from the provincial bureaucracy.[163] The TISCO management, whenever it found an opportunity, tried to crush the Jamshedpur Labour Association (JLA), even though it was actively patronised by the Congress leaders, and was known for its loyalty to the employers; and in this, the local colonial administration was always with the management.[164] Even the goondas or hooligan elements, who were as a matter of routine patronised by the employers and hired as strike breakers, were protected by the local police officials as institutionalised tools of violence.[165] There were, in other words, serious obstacles that prevented and even discouraged workers from combining.

But despite such impedance and limited trade unionism, labour unrest, as mentioned earlier, began to grow from the late nineteenth century. In the 1890s, a series of strikes took place in the jute mills in Calcutta because of the new workplace discipline, denial of holidays on the occasion of religious festivals like Bakr Id and the active intervention of the state to enforce such restrictions.[166] There was greater unrest towards the closing years of World War One due to wartime decline in real wages (see chapter 6.2), leading to a series of strikes, the most important of them being the Ahmedabad textile strike in March 1918 led by Gandhi himself and the Bombay textile strike in January 1919. These industrial actions are often described as 'spontaneous' movements with no centralised leadership, no coordination among the strikers, no programme and no organisation—something like "a working class *jacquerie*".[167] Like the western Indian cotton mills, the Calcutta jute mills also witnessed unprecedented labour unrest around this time: there were 119 strikes in 1920, followed by 152 in 1921.[168] If things began to improve a little from 1922, the onset of depression worsened the situation once again. To overcome the crisis, the Bombay mill owners had resorted to rationalisation policies, causing retrenchment, wage losses and higher workloads. This magnified the problems of the mill-hands to such an extent that they could no longer be dealt with at individual mill level and resulted in an industry-wide general textile strike in 1928–29.[169] Rationalisation policies also resulted in a serious industrial action by twenty-six thousand TISCO workers in Jamshedpur in 1928.[170] In the Calcutta jute mills, prescription of long working hours by the IJMA resulted in a general strike in 1929 involving 272 thousand workers.[171] The working class militancy had by now reached a proportion when it could no longer be ignored by the established political groups.

The Indian National Congress from the very beginning took an ambivalent position vis-à-vis the working class. During the Swadeshi period there were isolated attempts to organise labour strikes in European owned industries and railways. But the nationalist leaders hardly took any initiative to mobilise the workers. Where a congenial situation was created by the "spontaneous" action of the working class, they only intervened to harness it to their own movement.[172] By 1918, as strikes began and the working class asserted itself, it became increasingly difficult for Congress to ignore them. So in 1919 at its Amritsar session it adopted a resolution urging the provincial committees to "promote labour unions throughout India".[173] But by this time it had also developed a close relationship with the big business. So in the labour front, Congress could afford to be more articulate only where European capitalists were involved, such as the railways, jute mills or the tea gardens; and they exerted a moderating influence where the Indian capitalists were affected, like the Jamshedpur steel plants or the textile industry in Bombay and Ahmedabad. The workers were often asked to sacrifice their present day needs for the future of the nation, as a strike affecting Indian business was portrayed as likely to perpetuate foreign economic domination. The workers' unresolved grievances were to be met once the swaraj was attained. From the 1920s these dilemmas of the Congress were very clearly visible, often inviting articulate, even violent, disapproval of the workers themselves.

Some of the Congress leaders did from time to time participate in strikes, such as Gandhi in the Ahmedabad textile strike in 1918 or Subhas Bose in the Jamshedpur steel strike in 1928–29; others got involved in trade union movement, such as V. V. Giri in Madras or Guljarilal Nanda in Ahmedabad. But they did so as individuals, often to increase their own popularity as nationalist leaders. Some of them were involved in the formation of the All India Trade Union

Congress (AITUC), which was constituted in 1920 to elect an Indian delegation to the International Labour Organisation. Although number of trade unions affiliated to it began to increase in the 1920s, its national existence remained "largely fictional", except in 1929 when there was a communist threat of take over.[174] Gandhi's aversion to AITUC was well known, as he asked the ATLA, ever loyal to him, not to join it. Making "use of labour strikes for political purposes", he argued, would be a "serious mistake".[175] Since 1918, he was developing the philosophy of harmonious capital-labour relationship expressed in the rhetoric of family bonds. The Non-cooperation resolution adopted by the Congress in 1920, therefore, talked about oppression of workers by foreign agents, but failed to mention that the Indian employers also perpetrated similar atrocities.[176] As a result, the management in Indian owned industries regarded trade unions dominated by Congress leaders, like the ATLA or the JLA, as the more desirable legitimate channels of negotiations. Seth Mangaldas of the Ahmedabad Millowners' Association thought that the "primary duty" of such labour organisations was to inculcate "a sense of discipline among its members", thus increasing productivity. The workers, on the other hand, often had little faith in such organisations. In Ahmedabad, there were series of strikes in 1921–22 which the union failed to control, while after the failure of the 1923 strike, in which the union had taken the initiative, the membership of the ATLA rapidly declined.[177] In Jamshedpur, after the strike of 1928, the JLA leader Subhas Bose had to be escorted by Gurkha police, as his own supporters turned against him because of the compromise settlement he had arrived at with the TISCO management.[178]

Yet, despite organisational apathy from the Congress, the working class in various parts of the country participated overwhelmingly in the nationalist movement. Their direct participation in the Gandhian agenda was selective, but what was important, they often integrated the nationalist agitation into their own struggles and industrial actions. The strike waves in the Bengal industrial centres in 1920–21 were directly motivated by the new spirit and enthusiasm generated by the Khilafat-Non-cooperation movement.[179] The strikes in the Assam tea gardens, the Assam-Bengal Railways and the steamship employees at Chandpur in May 1921 were also directly related to this movement.[180] In Ahmedabad, during the latter part of Non-cooperation movement there was at least one strike per month in the textile industry, and some of them were organised around quite radical demands.[181] The striking workers in the Madras cotton mills run by the Binnys invited the Congress Non-cooperators to give them leadership.[182] The strikes of the North-Western Railways in 1919 and 1920 were also inspired by the Congress movement. The Civil Disobedience movement too generated similar responses. The industrial workers participated in the boycott movement; there were strikes in the Great Indian Peninsular (GIP) Railway in 1930, and the Dockworkers struck in 1932.[183] In Chota Nagpur in 1930, the workers began to wear Gandhi caps and attended nationalist meetings in thousands, despite the fact that the Congress leaders had scandalously mishandled the Golmuri Tinplate strike in 1929.[184] By linking up the strikes with the nationalist movement the workers sought greater legitimacy for their own struggles, in which Congress as a party took little interest. And rarely the Congress leaders themselves were directly responsible for organising these strikes. In Bengal, for example, in only 19.6 per cent of all strikes between 1918 and 1921 any "outsiders" were actually involved; others took place through workers' own initiative.[185] Sometimes, workers' own nationalism surpassed that of the Congress leaders in its radicalism and militancy. In 1928 the Calcutta session of the Congress was taken over for two hours by thirty thousand workers who passed resolutions for the complete independence of India and for a labour welfare scheme.[186]

Gandhi disapproved of this autonomous labour militancy and after the Chandpur tragedy in May 1921 (see chapter 6.3) seriously reprimanded the Bengal Congress leadership for their misadventure in trying to harness this militancy in the cause of nationalism. "We seek not to destroy capital or capitalists", he reasoned, "but to regulate the relations between capital and labour".[187] The same argument resonated in Jawaharlal Nehru's statement in 1929. As the President of the AITUC, he reminded everybody that Congress was "not a labour organisation", but "a large body comprising all manner of people".[188] Although the Congress Socialists showed greater sympathy for labour, the compulsion to remain an umbrella organisation representing the interests of all the classes prevented Congress from integrating the working classes more closely into its movement. Compulsions to seek labour votes in the provincial elections of 1937 forced the Congress to include in its election manifesto some promises for labour welfare programmes. Its subsequent victory, therefore, aroused great enthusiasm and expectations among the working classes, as a number of trade union leaders became labour ministers in Congress cabinets. Trade union membership increased by 50 per cent during this time, leading to a spectacular rise in industrial unrest in 1937–38, causing panic among the Indian industrialists. This only resulted in a decisive anti-labour shift in Congress policies, which we have discussed in the earlier section.

It may be noted here that in a non-Congress province like Bengal, the Congress leaders were only too happy to support the general jute mill strike in 1937, as it was an ideal opportunity to discredit the Fazlul Huq ministry and to hit at the "white bosses" of the IJMA. Nehru even went so far as to claim it to be "a part of our freedom movement".[189] Yet at the same time, in the Congress provinces like Bombay, Madras and UP, their governments were using similar strong-arm tactics to control industrial unrest. The same Nehru, known for his socialist leanings, during the Kanpur textile strikes of 1937, while condemning the victimisation of workers also defended the mill manager's "right to dismiss a worker who does not do his work well."[190] By this point, the Congress appeared to be too closely allied with the Indian capitalists, the passage of the Bombay Trades Disputes Act in 1938 being an unmistakable marker of that growing friendship. All parties except Congress condemned it and the passage of the bill was immediately greeted with a general strike in Bombay.

One of the obvious results of this Congress dilemma was the increasing influence of the communists in the labour front. The Workers and Peasants Party in Bengal, organised by middle-class communist leaders, began to mobilise mill workers from around 1928 in the Calcutta industrial belt.[191] The jute mill strike in 1929 gave rise to the Bengal Jute Workers' Union, and the strike of 1937 to the Bengal Chatkal Mazdoor Union, both organised by educated bhadralok communist leaders, some of them trained in Moscow.[192] In Bombay, the Girni Kamgar Mahamandal was developed among the Bombay cotton mill workers through the bonus disputes in the textile mills in 1924; the Bombay Textile Labour Union was born through the strikes in the following year. And finally, the militancy generated by the general textile strike in 1928 resulted in the ascendancy of the Girni Kamgar Union, now overtly dominated by the communists. However, as Chandavarkar has argued, this "[w]orking class support for the communists did not . . . arise simply from a fusion of shared antagonisms towards the capitalist class and the state".[193] Their consistent opposition to the state was of course one reason behind the popularity of the communists. But being outsiders and excluded from the workplace, they also had to take account of the existing social relations among the workers in their neighbourhoods, and present themselves as alternative sources of patronage and power, which the workers could rely upon. The development of the new institutional structures and legal frameworks made the services of such outsiders more vitally important to the workers than those of the traditional jobbers or neighbourhood organisations. The communist trade unions also utilised community ties and informal social networks. In Kanpur, for example, in the 1930s, the emerging communist leadership of the Kanpur Mazdoor Sabha specifically targeted the Muslim workers alienated by the Congress and the Arya Samaj.[194] In Ahmedabad too, the communist dominated Mill Mazdoor Sangh drew its support from the Muslim workers dissatisfied with the Gandhiite ATLA. Religious ties were frequently used to organise strikes by these communist trade unions, which thus appeared as class orientated organisations operating essentially within the hierarchical cultural milieu of the Indian workers.

This communist penetration into the labour front and the series of strikes that followed in the wake of the trade depression in the middle of the 1920s precipitated a crisis for them in 1928–29. The government offensive against the communists came in the form of two legislations in Bombay. The Public Safety Bill and the Trades Disputes Act of April 1929—which virtually banned strikes—were passed without any Congress opposition. A major crack down on the communists came in March 1929 when 31 top labour leaders were arrested and tried for conspiring against King-Emperor in the notorious Meerat Conspiracy Case. The case continued for four years and ended in long jail sentences for all the leaders, who were thus sent behind bars till the late 1930s. But the labour upsurge under communist leadership did not die down, as a second wave of general strikes in cotton mills, jute mills and the GIP Railways were organised in 1929–30. Yet, the communists were weakened no doubt, as the workers' allegiance to them was neither permanent nor unconditional. Their decision to dissociate themselves from the Congress under a fiat from Comintern in 1928 cost the Indian communists dearly, as the Civil Disobedience movement soon diverted mass attention to Gandhi and the Congress.

There was a communist revival around 1933–34, after the Civil Disobedience movement was withdrawn and the Comintern in the summer of 1935 mandated in favour of a united front strategy. The Congress socialists also began to collaborate with the communists and the results were increasing working class enthusiasm and militancy around 1937–38, manifested in another strike wave across the country. This consolidation of communist position among the working classes was perhaps one reason why the provincial Congress governments became so sternly anti-labour at this stage. The ban on the Communist Party was lifted in 1942, as it supported British war efforts, since Soviet Union was now involved in it. But communist endeavours to consolidate popular support for the "Peoples' War" did not succeed. The workers' allegiance to them in the past was largely because of their continued resistance to the state. Since their role now reversed, "their fortunes [also] began to wane",[195] as the Quit India movement drew huge mass support. Although the communists in the 1940s took control of a few trade unions and came to dominate the AITUC, in real terms this did not indicate their rising popularity, as very few workers were actually unionised. In 1942, the AITUC had a membership of only 337,695.[196] In 1952 at a convention of the AITUC, the communist leader Indrajit Gupta acknowledged that about 95 per cent of the jute mill workers were not unionised yet.[197] But that did not mean that these workers were unable to perceive of their relationship with the colonial state, the capitalist class and nationalism. They were neither unresponsive to, nor dissociated from the nationalist or leftist politics organised by educated middle-class politicians; but their support was conditional, not absolute. There were, to reiterate our point once again, various meanings of freedom for different groups of people and these variegated forms of consciousness continually contested and interacted with each other within the dynamics of the national movement.

7.5. WOMEN'S PARTICIPATION

The colonial discourses on India from very early on were gendered, as the colonised society was feminised and its "effeminate" character, as opposed to "colonial masculinity", was held to be a justification for its loss of independence.[198] The "women's question" figured prominently in these discourses as Western observers, like James Mill, used it to construct a "civilizational critique of India". The degraded condition of Indian women was taken as an indicator of India's inferior status in the hierarchy of civilisations.[199] It is no wonder therefore that the status of women became the main focus of the reforming agenda of the modernising Indian intellectuals of the nineteenth century. In their response to the damning critique of the West, they imagined a golden past where women were treated with dignity and honour; they urged reforms of those customs, which they considered to be distortions or aberrations. Thus female infanticide was banned, sati was abolished and widow remarriage was legalised. In all cases reforms were legitimated by referring to the shastras and no women were ever involved in the reform movements. It will be misleading to suggest that these male reformers lacked sympathy or compassion for their womenfolk. But they treated them as subjects of their modernising project and could not imagine them to be their conscious equals claiming agency for their own emancipation (for details, see chapter 3.1). And then, this reformism brought forth a virulent Hindu backlash when the Age of Consent Bill in 1891 sought to push the age for consummation of marriage for women from 10 to 12. The proposed reform, by trying to restrain the conjugal rights of a husband over his wife, invaded what was hitherto recognised as the only remaining site of autonomy for "native masculinity". The child bride therefore became a symbol of Hindu glory; the control over her was the indigenous male privilege that could not be allowed to be tampered with by an alien state (for more details see chapter 5.2). Thus the nineteenth century ended in a shift from a modernising project to a Hindu conservative assertion of patriarchal control over the women's domain, which now constituted an essential part of the nationalist agenda.

It is difficult to defend an indigenist argument that the condition of women was better in pre-colonial India. Indeed, women's status in ancient India was never static or uniform: in the words of Romila Thapar, it varied widely from "a position of considerable authority and freedom to one of equally considerable subservience".[200] Their plight began to deteriorate decisively with the development of peasant societies and the evolution of states. In Hindu society the central organising principle of caste hierarchy came to be integrally connected to the ideology of patriarchy; both Sudras and women were debarred from access to Vedic ritual rites. While the public space became the sphere of activities for men, women were confined to the household. The ancient Hindu lawgiver Manu prescribed a permanent dependent status for women, to be protected by their fathers, husbands and sons at different stages of their lives. Coming down to more immediate pre-colonial period, an eighteenth century text indicates that women were groomed to become good wives, serve their husbands as their supreme gods, and expected to give birth to sons. If they became widows, they were meant to spend their lives in strictest discipline of celibacy, cherishing memories of their dead husbands.[201] However, if this was a fact of life, it was also true on the other hand, that seclusion of women was not a universal practice, as there is evidence of high public visibility of women, both rich and poor, in certain regions in the eighteenth century. The royal courts of the Mughal successor states were no strange places for ambitious and powerful women, some of whom exerted considerable political influence. The ideal of secluded womanhood came to be universalised only in the nineteenth century.[202]

The Muslim society too put similar restrictions on women. In the nineteenth century, there were two reform movements among the Indian Muslims: one was Islamic revivalism spearheaded by the ulama, and the other a modernisation campaign led by the educated middle classes. Both these movements, as Azra Asghar Ali has argued, "constructed *sharif* culture almost as a private polity", with the status of women being central to it, as an indicator of the "progress" of the Muslim community as a whole.[203] It is no wonder, therefore, that the sharif Muslims in Bengal shuddered at the thought of their women transgressing the norms of purdah (a Persian word, literally meaning curtain).[204] For both Hindu and Muslim women, this metaphor of purdah did not merely mean their physical seclusion behind the veil or the walls of the zenana (the women's quarter in the inner part of the house). It meant, according to one scholar, "multitudes of complex social arrangements which maintain[ed] *social* and not just physical distance between the sexes".[205] It "entailed an all-encompassing ideology and code of conduct based on female modesty which determined women's lives wherever they went."[206] In other words, even when they stepped out of their houses, which they increasingly did from the mid-nineteenth century, their movements and conduct were to be contained within these ethical parameters. By the nineteenth century, the ideal of purdah had become universalised for both Muslim and Hindu women and for both elites and commoners, although in its practical implications it acted differently for different groups.

In the nineteenth century as the women's question became a part of the discourses of progress and modernity, a movement for female education started as a part of the colonised males' search for the "new woman". The agency for the spread of education lay with three groups of people, as Geraldine Forbes has classified them: "the British rulers, Indian male reformers and educated Indian women".[207] The initiative was taken in Calcutta by men like Radhakanta Deb and the School Book Society and later by Keshub Chandra Sen and the Brahmo Samaj, in western India by Mahadev Govind Ranade and Prarthana Samaj, in north India by Swami Dayanand and his Arya Samaj and in Madras by Annie Besant and the Theosophical Society. So far as Indian educated women were concerned, we may mention the endeavours of Pandita Ramabai in western India, Sister Subbalaksmi in Madras and Begum Rokeya Sakhawat Hossain among the Muslim women in Bengal. As for the education of Muslim women in other parts of the country, certain families like the Bilgramis in Hyderabad, the Tyabjis in Bombay and the Mians in Lahore, or a few organisations like Anjuman-i-Himayat-i-Islam, the Anjuman-i-Islam or the Nizam's government in Hyderabad took significant initiatives. The colonial government from the administration of Lord Dalhousie (1848–56) also took particular interest in female education. J.E. Drinkwater Bethune, the law member in the governor general's council opened in 1849 what eventually became the most well known girls' school in Calcutta. Between then and 1882 when the Hunter Commission was appointed, female education in India had progressed very little, as 98 per cent of women in the school-going age remained uneducated. Hence the commission recommended liberal grants-in-aid and special scholarships for women's education. During the next two decades significant improvements were seen in women's enrolment in both universities and secondary schools, although compared to the total female population of the country the figures still remained insignificant.[208]

However little might have been the rate of progress, the fact remains that at the turn of the century a number of women in middle class Indian households were educated, either formally or informally. But this did not improve the conditions of their social existence very remarkably. The answer to this puzzle may be found if we look at the motivations behind the education movement, which was never the emancipation of women. The colonial government wanted female education as it wanted the Indian civil servants to be married to educated wives, so that they did not have to face the psychological trauma of a split household. Also English educated mothers were expected to breed loyal subjects.[209] The educated Indian middle-class males, on the other hand, dreamt of the Victorian ideal of companionate marriage. In Bengal, the educated *bhadramahila* (gentlewoman) appeared as the ideal companion to the enlightened Hindu bhadralok. This new concept of womanhood was a fine blending of the self-sacrificing Hindu wife and the Victorian helpmate. Education thus far from being emancipatory, further confined women to idealised domestic roles as good wives and better mothers.[210] If ignorant and uneducated women were perceived as impediments to progress or modernisation or bad for the welfare of the family, children, community and nation, "wrongly educated or over-educated" women, negligent of household chores—or more precisely, westernised women—were considered to be threats to the cherished moral order.[211] And although there were some differences, the Muslim bhadramahila also shared significant common grounds with their

Hindu counterparts.[212] The goal of the Muslim educators of women, as Gail Minault argues, was "to create women who would be better wives, better mothers and better Muslims".[213]

Voices of protest from within the Indian womanhood against such public stereotyping were rare, but not altogether absent. In 1882, Tarabai Shinde, a Marathi woman from Berar, published a book entitled, *A Comparison Between Women and Men*. In this she protested against the fact that in a new colonial society men enjoyed all the rights, opportunities and benefits of change, while women were blamed for all the evils and were still bound by the old strictures of *pativrata* (duty to husband). Yet, ultimately, Tarabai was no rebel; what she claimed for Indian women was more respect and dignity in a happy home and the enlightenment that the colonial state had supposedly promised.[214] But there were other rebels—like Pandita Ramabai—who challenged more directly the new role model of educated but compliant wives. She was a Brahman woman who remained unmarried for a long time; she was well versed in the ancient shastras, married a man from a Sudra caste defying the restrictions on hypergamy, then became a widow with an infant daughter, refused to withdraw herself from public life, went to England to study medicine, and there converted to Christianity, went to America and raised money for a widows' home in Bombay which was later shifted to Poona. As she asserted her independent choice and crossed the boundaries that Indian patriarchy had set on the freedom of women, she was equally criticised by the reformers and damned by the conservatives, as both considered her to be a social threat.[215] But then, Shinde or Ramabai were exceptions; most educated women knew and minded their boundaries very well. For, if the indigenous elite, attached to the middle-class gender ideology of Victorian England, tended to privatise the women's spheres, the colonial state too wanted to confine women to domesticity. For it was there that they would be safe both for themselves and for the state. Both the customary Hindu and Islamic personal laws which the courts upheld and the new statutory laws which the state promulgated, sanctified the rights of the patriarchal family and constricted the freedom of choice for women. It was in this area, as Rosalind O'Hanlon argues, that there was a "broad degree of consensus" between the colonial state and the nationalist male elites.[216]

This valorisation of 'domesticity' for Indian womanhood impacted also on the conditions of women in peasant families as well as lower class women in urban industrial environments. It is often supposed that among the lower caste labouring women the restrictions on their freedom were less rigorous. But from the early nineteenth century, this began to erode under the influence of "Sanskritization", as the lower castes began to appropriate the 'respectable' norms of gender relations. Purity of women became an index of the status of a caste; seclusion of women therefore became a cherished ideal, if not always a practical goal. For example, more and more lower and middle order castes began to enforce celibate ascetic widowhood on their women, as it became a symbol of high status—indeed, a means to social mobility—both in Bengal[217] and in Maharashtra.[218] In the numerous peasant movements of the nineteenth and early twentieth centuries, women only "remained conspicuous by their absence".[219] In the cultural space, the ideal of chaste and reformed womanhood gradually marginalised and nudged out the indigenous forms of women's popular culture,—their songs, farces and theatrical performances—which used to offer them a space for autonomy. Although belatedly, the women from the lower strata also "had to grasp the logic of an altered social world" and conform to the ideal that was imposed from above.[220]

So far as women's work was concerned, although they did participate in agricultural activities, from the late nineteenth century more and more socially mobile peasant families began to confine their women to household work. As they were idealised as wives and mothers, their household responsibilities came to be regarded as sacred duties and were thus emptied of any economic value. Many of those who participated in various crafts began to lose their vocation with the advancement of mechanisation in the early twentieth century. In Bengal, for example, women employed in rice husking began to lose out with the coming of rice-mills, which became predominantly male domains.[221] When men migrated to cities in search of industrial employment, they left their families back home. When women migrated, it was usually under extreme poverty, when rural resources failed to support them any longer. In the early twentieth century considerable number of women were working in the cotton and jute mills, in tea plantations and in the coalmines. But here too the dominant ideology of domesticity affected their conditions. Their reproductive role was considered to be more important than wage labour. Their income was regarded as "supplementary" to family income and therefore of less importance. This argument of domesticity was sponsored by the state and reformers, and used by the capitalists in the cotton mills of Bombay[222] and the jute mills of Calcutta[223] to stereotype women workers as devoid of skills and commitment. These constructs could then be deployed to justify lower wages for women or to retrench them first at the time of rationalisation. In the mines and plantations of eastern India too, women were given less wages than their male counterparts and were always considered as parts of family units.[224] The female workers protested vehemently against this deprivation of rights and inequality. But nothing changed, as even the trade unions valued more their motherhood, than their economic rights and freedom.

When modern nationalism developed in the second half of the nineteenth century, it addressed the women's question within these restrictive parameters of domesticity. As reformism gave way to valorisation of tradition through various iconic representations of nation, the Hindu woman became an ideal emblem of the moral order that symbolised the spirit of India, supposedly uncontaminated by the polluting influence of the West. Partha Chatterjee has argued that the nationalist construction of the public and private spaces equated them with the material/spiritual dichotomy. The "world" or the public space, a typically male domain, was the site of the contest and negotiation with the modernising colonial state, while the "home" was the inner domain of sovereignty—which was beyond colonisation—where women were perceived as the protector and nurturer of the spiritual essence of Indian national identity.[225] This nationalist construction of difference in the gender specific models of modernisation removed the earlier dilemmas of reformism, but did not "resolve" the women's question, as expected by Chatterjee. It indeed opened up new areas of contestation and negotiation for women, as many of them did not accept the attribution of passivity and in the first half of the twentieth century began to claim agency for creating their own autonomous space of action, without however being overtly defiant of the boundaries set by nationalism's historical project.

If women's issues did not figure in the nationalist discourse of the early twentieth century, it was because all other forms of emancipation were being perceived as conditional on national liberation. The Congress until 1917 did not directly address the women's question—just as it did not deal with the untouchability issue—because it was unsure of itself and was oversensitive about the fragility of an incipient nation. However, as extremism gained in strength in Bengal, the nationalists there appropriated the already privileged cultural concept of "motherhood" as an empowering and authentic symbol of indigenous cultural distinctiveness. The nationalist imagining of their country as "motherland"—as opposed to the concept of fatherland in Europe—was initiated when in 1875 the famous

Bengali intellectual Bankim Chandra Chatterjee wrote the song *Bande Mataram* (Hail Mother), which was later incorporated and contextualised in his novel *Anandamath* (1882). In this novel, he portrays three images of mother-goddess: 'mother as she was', 'mother as she is' and 'mother as she will be'. The three representations were enough to fire the imagination and dedication of her nationalist devotees and permanently inscribed the metaphor of mother-goddess in Indian nationalist discourse. The song was first sung by Rabindranath Tagore at the Calcutta session of the Congress in 1896. A few years later during the Swadeshi movement, the Bengali extremist leader Aurobindo Ghosh discovered the potential of the imagery that could excite patriotism and a national awakening. And from now on almost every nationalist leader, from Bepin Chandra Pal[226] to Jawaharlal Nehru[227] used this metaphor of motherhood to signify the country and the nation.

In the early nationalist reconstruction of mother-goddess, the familiar image of a nurturing and affectionate Bengali mother was mixed with the concept of *shakti* or primal power that was variously represented in Hindu cosmology as Goddesses Durga or Kali who destroyed the demons and protected the innocent. Gradually, however, this aggressive aspect was toned down, as the mother was imagined to be the epitome of the cultural essence of Indian spiritualism. In nationalist iconography, Abanindranath Tagore's painting of *Bharat Mata* or "Mother India" (c.1904–5) came to symbolise this new image. Here the mother-goddess is more serene and genteel, offering protection and prosperity; it was "an image that was both human and divine", both familiar and transcendental.[228] Whether this imagery of motherhood was just a "cultural artifact" of militant nationalism[229] or emanated from genuine conviction in mother-nature equation[230] is a matter of debate. What is important however is the discursive implication of this metaphor for the status of women in Indian society. Jasodhara Bagchi has argued that this ideology of motherhood by "creating a myth about her strength and power", took away from women their "real power", confined them exclusively to their reproductive role and thus deprived them of access to education and occupation, or in other words, to all possible avenues to their real empowerment.[231]

Indeed, in the Swadeshi movement, whatever participation women had, it was within this accepted gender ideology that prescribed home as the rightful arena of activities for women. They boycotted British goods and used swadeshi, crushed their glass bangles and observed non-cooking days as a ritual of protest. Interestingly, the most powerful imagery that was used to mobilise women's support in Bengal around this time was Lakshmi, the goddess of prosperity, who had allegedly left her abode because of partition, and who had to be brought back, protected and looked after.[232] There were of course some remarkable exceptions, like Sarala Debi Chaudhurani, who got involved in a physical culture movement for the Bengali youth or a few women who participated in the revolutionary movement. But in the latter case, their involvement was mostly of a supportive or "indirect" nature, that of giving shelter to fugitive revolutionaries or acting as couriers of messages and weapons.[233] This nature of participation thus did not abruptly breach the accepted norms of feminine behaviour or signify their empowerment.

The period after World War One witnessed the rise of two eminent women in Indian politics. Annie Besant, the president of the Theosophical Society and a founder of the Home Rule League, was elected president of the Congress in 1917. The same year, Sarojini Naidu, the England-educated poet who had been delivering patriotic speeches at Congress sessions since 1906, led a delegation to London to meet Secretary of State Montagu to demand female franchise. The following year she moved a resolution at the Congress session demanding equal eligibility for voting rights for both men and women. In 1925, she too was elected president of the Congress. But despite being "inspirational figures", these two leaders could neither evolve an ideology for women's emancipation, nor could carve out for them a niche in nationalist politics.[234]

So it was only with the advent of Gandhi that we see a major rupture in this story of women's involvement in the nationalist movement. Gandhi, in conceptualising the ideal Indian womanhood, shifted the focus from motherhood to sisterhood, by negating women's sexuality. It was in South Africa that he had realised the power of self-less sacrifice that women could offer and decided to harness it in the service of the nation. But his clarion call to women was couched in a language full of religious metaphors that did not appear to be subversive of the traditional values about femininity. Sita-Damayanti-Draupadi were his role models for Indian women. Although taken from Indian mythology, these symbols were reconstituted and loaded with new meanings. These women were represented as no slaves of their husbands, but extremely virtuous, and capable of making supreme sacrifice for the welfare of their family, society and the state. Particularly important was the example of Sita, as the British could conveniently be equated with the demon king Ravana. However, while addressing Muslim women, Gandhi would scrupulously avoid such allegorical references to *Ramayana* and would simply ask them to make sacrifice for their country and for Islam. He accepted what he called the "natural division of labour" between the sexes and believed that women had a duty to look after the hearth and home. But from within their ordained spheres, they could serve the nation by spinning, by picketing at foreign cloth and liquor shops and by shaming men into action.[235] For him, men and women were equal, but had different roles to play and in this, as Sujata Patel has forcefully argued, Gandhi remained within the Indian middle-class tradition of conceptualising womanhood. He accepted women's biological weakness, but turned that weakness into power by glorifying their strength of soul. He did not seek to invert the doctrine of two "separate spheres" of private and public space, but redefined political participation by creating space for politics in home. In other words, what Gandhi did was "an extraction and reformulation of received social ideas in moral terms".[236]

It was first in South Africa in 1913 that Gandhi had for the first time involved women in public demonstrations and realised the huge political potential of the Indian womanhood.[237] Back in India, during the Rowlatt satyagraha of 1919 he again invited women to participate in the nationalist campaign; but it was withdrawn before any significant advancement in this direction could take place. When the Non-cooperation movement started in 1921, Gandhi initially prescribed a limited role for women, i.e., that of boycott and swadeshi. But women claimed for themselves a greater active role. In November 1921 a demonstration of a thousand women greeted the Prince of Wales in Bombay. And then in December, Basanti Devi, the wife of the Bengal Congress leader C.R. Das, his sister Urmila Devi and niece Suniti Devi, stunned the nation by participating in open demonstration on the streets of Calcutta and by courting arrest. Gandhi was concerned about their physical safety and chastity, but endorsed their move, as it had a tremendous demonstration effect. Similar movements took place in other parts of the country, and this involved not just women from respectable middle-class families. Gandhian appeal was now seemingly reaching down also to the marginalised women—the prostitutes and *devdasis* (temple women), for example—although Gandhi himself was not too keen to involve them.[238] It was during the Civil Disobedience movement that the floodgates were really opened. Gandhi once again did not want to include women in his original core group of volunteers on the Dandi march. But on his way he addressed meetings attended by thousands of women and when the movement actually took off, thousands of others participated in the illegal manufacture of salt, picketing foreign cloth and liquor shops and took part in processions. The movement, so far as women's participation was concerned, was most organised in Bombay, most militant in Bengal and limited in Madras. In north India, in cities like Allahabad, Lucknow, Delhi and Lahore, hundreds of women from respectable families shocked their conservative menfolk by openly participating in nationalist demonstrations. Some women in Bengal got involved in violent revolutionary movement, and this time, unlike the Swadeshi period, they were not in supportive roles; they were now actually shooting pistols at magistrates and governors.[239]

The trend that was set in the 1930s continued into the 1940s, as women's active role in the public space became accepted in society. It is not difficult to see why women responded to Gandhi's appeal, which made women's service to nation a part of their religious duty. His insistence on non-violence and emphasis on the maintenance of a respectable image of women satyagrahis did not breach the accepted norms of feminine behaviour and as a result, men felt confident that their women would be safe in Gandhi's hands. There was less resistance because, in the ultimate analysis, women participated because their male guardians wanted them to. In most cases, women who joined the nationalist struggle came from families where men were already involved in Gandhian movements. So in their case, their public role was an extension of their domestic roles as wives, mothers, sisters or daughters. Their politicisation therefore did not lead to any significant change in their domestic or family relations. Most of these women came from Hindu middle class respectable families. Although in some areas rural women did take part in the agitations, women's participation remained predominantly an urban phenomenon, and here too emphasis on respectable image kept the lower class and marginal women like prostitutes out. So far as Muslim women were concerned, many of them participated in the Khilafat-Non-cooperation movement in 1921. But if this helped towards weakening of the rigours of purdah, its total abolition was out of question; because for Muslims, it was a symbol of their cultural distinctiveness.[240] On the other hand, if a handful of women actually crossed the socially constituted boundary of feminine modesty by involving in violent revolutionary action, they were heavily censored by a disapproving society. Such "strong traditionalist moorings", argues Tanika Sarkar, explains why this politicisation was possible and why it failed to promote to any significant extent social emancipation of women in India.[241] The Congress and its leaders were simply not interested in women's issues and except for allowing some symbolic presence, never included women in any decision making process. A frustrated Sarala Debi Chaudhurani therefore had to lament that Congress wanted them to be "law-breakers only and not law-makers".[242]

However, having said all this, we have to acknowledge as well that hundreds of women from respectable families marching in files on the streets of India, going to jails, suffering indignity there, and coming back to their families with no stigma attached, signified a remarkable change in Indian social attitudes. And as for agency, as Sujata Patel has succinctly put it, "it is difficult to separate analytically which proceeded first: women's participation or Gandhi's advocacy of this."[243] It may also be pointed out that without being openly deviant, some of these women were slowly pushing the boundaries of their autonomy by manipulating available cultural metaphors, like for example, the "extended family". Bi Amman, the elderly mother of Shaukat and Muhammad Ali, participated in the Khilafat-Non-cooperation movement after a whole life behind purdah. At a mass meeting in Punjab, she lifted her veil and addressed the crowd as her children. A mother did not require a veil in front of her children; the whole nation by implication was thus incorporated into her "extended fictive family".[244] Her rhetoric did not subvert the ideology of purdah; her practice effectively extended its boundary. On the other hand, it is highly unlikely that all those thousands of women who actually participated in the Civil Disobedience movement had actually secured their guardians' prior permission. And even if they did, there are numerous historical examples to show that "once mobilised, women moved on their own".[245] Time and again they disobeyed Gandhian injunctions that set limits to their activism.

But did this activism and politicisation of women promote a feminist consciousness in colonial India? So far as the wider society was concerned, the answer should be clearly no. But for those women who actually participated in the nationalist struggle, and for their more enlightened middle-class women leaders, life could perhaps never be the same again. A burgeoning women's literature of this period indicates that the private/public dichotomy was increasingly being blurred in their consciousness, and that they were resentful of the existing gender asymmetry in their society.[246] But despite such contestation and "transgressions of 'desirable' codes", as Janaki Nair puts it, these middle class/high caste women also broadly "consented to . . . [the] hegemonic aspirations" of the nationalist patriarchy.[247]

Among the Muslim women too, there was the rise of a new "feminist" Urdu literature in the early twentieth century that contested the traditional boundaries and ideologies of gender relations. But it also refrained from advocating any "dramatic change" and privileged "the image of the Muslim community" over everything else.[248] Such contradictions were more clearly visible in the space created by the growing number of women's organisations of the time. From the beginning, women's participation in politics took place from a variety of women-only organisations, which constituted in Gail Pearson's terminology an "extended female space", that lay somewhere in between the segregated family household and the wider public arena.[249] These organisations ranged from various local social organisations, girls' educational institutions to a number of political bodies, such as the Rashtriya Stree Sangha or the Des Sevika Sangha, which acted as auxiliary bodies of the Congress. Then in the early twentieth century, there came into existence a number of women's organisations, which operated more actively in the public arena and focused more directly on women's political and legal rights.

At the all-India level, the first to appear in Madras in 1917 was the Women's Indian Association, started by enlightened European and Indian ladies, the most important of them being Margaret Cousins, an Irish feminist, and Annie Besant. In 1925 the National Council of Women in India was formed as a branch of the International Council of Women, and Lady Mehribai Tata remained its main spirit during the early years. Then in 1927 the most important of these organisations, the All India Women's Conference came into existence, initially as a non-political body to promote women's education, with Margaret Cousins as the main inspirational figure. Eventually however, it got involved in nationalist politics and lobbied for all sorts of women's rights, from franchise to marriage reform and the rights of women labourers.[250] At the provincial level too, various organisations started functioning around this time for a multitude of women's issues. Sarala Devi Chaudhurani's Bharat Stree Mahamandal, which had its first meeting in Allahabad in 1910, opened branches all over India to promote women's education. In Bengal in the 1920s, as Barbara Southard (1995) has shown, the Bangiya Nari Samaj started campaigning for women's voting rights, the Bengal Women's Education League demanded compulsory elementary and secondary education for women and the All-Bengal Women's Union campaigned for a legislation against illicit trafficking of women.

However, instead of mobilising mass agitations in support of these issues, these women's organisations petitioned the government and appealed to the nationalists for support. The government intervened reluctantly, if at all, and often preferred compromise formulae, as it believed that the majority of Indian women were not yet ready to use their rights properly. For example, the Montagu–Chelmsford Reform in 1919 left undecided the question of women's franchise, which was to be determined later by the provincial legislatures. The nationalists, on the other hand, seemed more sympathetic to the women's question since the 1920s, as they needed their participation in the nation-building project. Women too privileged this "process of universalization"[251] by placing nationalism before women's issues. As a reward, all the provincial legislatures between 1921 and 1930 granted voting right to women, subject of course to usual property and educational qualifications. The Government of India Act of 1935 increased the ratio of female voters to 1:5 and gave women reserved seats in legislatures. The Congress and the women's organisations did not like the idea of reservation and had preferred instead universal adult franchise. However, once provided they accepted it and this helped a number of women to launch their legislative careers after the election of 1937.[252] On the other hand, unlike the Age of Consent bill of 1891, the Child Marriage Restraint Act or the Sarda Act of 1929, which proposed to fix the minimum age of marriage for females at fourteen and males at eighteen, was passed with overwhelming nationalist support. Apart from that, in the central and provincial legislatures a whole range of bills were passed in the 1930s to define women's right to property, inheritance and divorce, to restrain dowry and control prostitution. But did all these legislations improve gender relations and the quality of life for women in India? If we take the Sarda Act as a test case, we find that soon both the government and the nationalists found it impossible to implement; before long the Sarda Act was dead for all practical purposes.[253]

To get back to our earlier point, the developments of the early twentieth century—the birth of a new consciousness, new organisations and the politicisation of women—did bring in some remarkable changes for some women—the more enlightened, middle class and urban variety, who had effectively claimed for themselves a niche in the public space. Towards the end of the colonial period many of them were in higher professions like medicine and law, earning lucrative salaries and enjoying social respect. But they too constantly juggled between their new public roles and the onerous demands of housewifery and childcare, without much audible protest. And for the rest of the Indian womanhood, the changes were even less spectacular. This happened because the efforts of the women's organisations and activists remained constrained by what Geraldine Forbes in her most perceptive account of *Women in Modern India* (1998) has described as the "framework of a social feminist ideology" (p.189). It recognised certain public role for women, but accepted at the same time the social, biological and psychological difference between sexes. The nationalist teleological construction of essential Indian womanhood remained privileged in their agenda, which itself was subsumed by that of nationalism.

However, as Forbes further argues,[254] this limiting social ideology and the dominance of the women's organisations which upheld it, came to be seriously challenged in the 1940s, when women across class and religious lines began to claim a more active role for themselves in the public space and fought as comrade-in-arms with their male counterparts in the last phase of the struggle for freedom. This female activism was visible most significantly in the Quit India movement of 1942, in which almost at the very beginning nearly all the front-ranking male Congress leaders were put in prison (details in chapter 8.1). In a contingency like this some prominent women leaders took upon themselves the responsibility of coordinating the movement in the face of unprecedented police repression. Sucheta Kripalani co-ordinated the non-violent resistance, while Aruna Asaf Ali gave leadership to the underground revolutionary activities—and this she did by politely turning down Gandhi's advice to surrender.[255] However, the most important aspect of this movement was the participation of a large number of rural women taking their own initiative to liberate their country. This engagement of rural women was further enlarged with the lifting of the ban on the Communist Party in 1942. Back in the 1920s and 1930s many middle-class educated women had joined the communist movement, and had participated in mobilising the working classes, in organising industrial actions and in campaigning for the release of political prisoners. By 1941 the girls' wing of the All-India Students Federation had about 50,000 members. In 1942 some of the leftist women leaders in Bengal organised a Mahila Atmaraksha Samiti or Women's Self-Defence League, mobilised rural women through it, and organised relief work during the Bengal famine of 1943.[256]

This involvement of women in the communist movement was expanded to a new level when the Tebhaga movement began in Bengal in 1946 under communist-led kisan sabhas with the sharecroppers' demand for two-thirds share of the produce (details in chapter 8.2). It saw widespread autonomous action of the "proletariat and semi proletariat women", belonging to dalit and tribal communities. Through their own initiative they formed *Nari Bahinis* or women's brigades and resisted the colonial police with whatever weapon they could lay their hands on. In the uneven contest that followed a number of them became martyrs.[257] Similarly in Andhra, where the Telangana movement continued from 1946 to 1951 against the Nizam of Hyderabad and feudal oppression (details in chapter 8.2), women fought side by side with men for better wages, fair rent and greater dignity. By highlighting certain gender specific issues, the Communist Party made special efforts to mobilise women, as without their support the movement could not sustain itself for such a long period. However, in most cases they joined on their own, acted as couriers of secret messages, arranged shelter and few of them took up guns and became participating members of the *dalams* (revolutionary units). But although this movement created for peasant women a new space for militant action, they were not treated as equals even by the communist leaders. The party leadership—just like their counterparts in Bengal—preferred only supportive and secondary roles for women, could not think of women outside the conventional structures of gender relations, i.e., family and marriage, and therefore, could not trust them with guns in the actual battlefield. More significantly, it was women who were considered to be the sources of problems when it came to the issue of maintaining sexual morality and discipline within the ranks of the rebels.[258]

Outside the country, around the same, time, an experiment to involve Indian women in actual military action had been initiated by Subhas Chandra Bose. Back in 1928, he had been instrumental in raising under the leadership of "Colonel" Latika Ghosh a Congress women's volunteer corps that had marched on the streets of Calcutta in full uniform. When in 1943 he raised an expatriate army in Southeast Asia, known as the Indian National Army (INA) (details in chapter 8.1), he decided to add a women's regiment, which he called the Rani of Jhansi Regiment, named after Rani Lakshmi Bai, the legendary heroine of the revolt of 1857. In October 1943, the training camp was opened for the new regiment, which was joined by about fifteen hundred women from elite as well as working class Indian families of all religions and castes living in Southeast Asia. They were given full military training and were prepared for combat duties. When at the initial stages they were assigned non-combat roles, the ranis protested to their leader, and were later engaged in the actual war operations in the Imphal campaign of 1945. This campaign, however, went seriously wrong and put an end to the whole experiment, as the INA had to retreat in the face of the advancing British army. Ideologically, this experiment of having women in arms was not perhaps a radical departure, as Bose too believed in and sought to invoke the "spiritual power" of the "mothers and sisters" of India. But it certainly amounted to a significant enlargement of women's role in nationalist politics from the passive role model of mythic Sita to that of the heroic activism of historic Rani of Jhansi fighting as comrade-in-arms with male soldiers.[259]

At another plane, the emergence of the 'Pakistan' movement in the 1940s opened up for the Muslim women of the subcontinent a new space for political action. In the 1930s they had been participating in a united front with their Hindu sisters to claim women's rights, such as female suffrage. But the division appeared in 1935 on the issue of reservation of women's seats on a communal basis. Some of the Muslim leaders of the All India Women's Conference, as Begam Shah Nawaz recollects in her autobiography, refused to "accept joint electorates when their men were not prepared to do so".[260] Thus broader political alignments—or men's politics—influenced women's movements as well. The Muslim League also sought to universalise its politics and in 1938 started a women's sub-committee to involve Muslim women. As the Pakistan movement grew in momentum, more and more of them were sucked into it as election candidates, as voters and as active demonstrators in street politics, particularly in Punjab and the North-West Frontier Province. Many of them were ordinary women for whom this political participation was itself a "liberating experience". True, this moment of emancipation was so short-lived that it could hardly bring in any actual change in their daily existence. But it signified nevertheless, an acceptance of a public role for women in Muslim society.[261]

Thus, increasingly in the 1940s Indian women across class, caste and religious barriers claimed agency in their participation in the anti-imperialist and democratic movements. But, as Kumari Jayawardena points out, they "did not use the occasion[s] to raise issues that affected them as women."[262] Their own goals were subordinated to those of national liberation, community honour or class struggle. The concept of feminism itself created a lot of confusion; it was either considered as a Western import subversive of the cultural essence of Indian nationhood or as an undesirable digression from the more important cause of the freedom struggle.[263] Some leading nationalists like Jawaharlal Nehru believed that once political freedom was achieved, the women's question would resolve itself automatically.[264] Patriarchal concerns continued to be a major dilemma for the communist leadership as well. In Tebhaga movement, a women's leadership could emerge only when the leadership of the Communist Party "abstained".[265] The trade unions in general, although they mobilised working class women, ignored women's issues, which were "subsumed within male or general working-class interests".[266] If the boundaries were blurred in course of militant action, they were re-established quickly afterwards without failure. Can we imagine what a woman like Swarajyam, described as "the legendary heroine of Telangana", was doing a few years after the withdrawal of the movement? In the words of her husband: "she is cooking and she is eating. What else?" If the women of Telangana came out of their homes because the movement promised them equality, they soon found out that the metaphor of family was being continually emphasised by the communist leadership whose preference always was to place women within that traditional boundary.[267]

On the other hand, the Pakistan movement did involve some Muslim women in public action, but the partition experience once again reinforced the traditional ashraf ideal of Muslim womanhood, to be protected within the domestic sphere. Any transgression of this boundary would lead to immorality, irreliogiosity and dishonour for the community.[268] Indeed, partition violence brought the worst moment for subcontinental womanhood, both Hindu and Muslim, as they became the objects of male construction of community honour. Women's sexuality became the territory that could either be conquered or be destroyed to deny the enemy the glory of conquering it. As Ritu Menon and Kamla Bhasin put it, they were caught in a "*continuum of violence*", where they had the choice either to be raped, mutilated and humiliated by men of the 'Other' community or to commit suicide, instigated by their own family members and kinsmen, to prevent the honour of their community from being violated by the enemy. Instances of such collective suicide were disturbingly many,[269] while on the other hand, in course of a few months of partition madness seventy-five to one hundred thousand women were abducted or raped.[270] Those who survived, lived with an indelible memory of shame, which they have endured in silence in deference to the honour of their community and family.

Thus, as it seems, the women's question in colonial India hardly received the priority it deserved. Although some women became conscious and actively participated in the political struggles, and also identified themselves in many ways with the emerging nation (s), feminism had not yet been incorporated into the prevailing ideologies of liberation. The honour and interests of the community and nation still prevailed over the rights of women. But that does not mean that no woman ever dreamed of 'freedom' in a way contrary to the dominant patriarchal convention upheld by their nationalist leaders, community elders or party bosses.

NOTES

1. Jalal 1987: 86.
2. Pandey 1992:234.
3. Hasan 1985: 213.
4. See Jalal 2000: 422 and passim.
5. Details in Page 1982.
6. Hasan 1985: 207.
7. Freitag 1989.
8. Datta 1999: 246.
9. Quoted in Hasan 1985: 210.
10. Chandra 1993.
11. Shaikh 1989.
12. Hasan 1996; Jalal 1997.
13. Chatterjee 1984a; Murshid 1995.
14. Talbot 1988.
15. Jalal 1994: 19–20.
16. Hasan 1988.
17. Hasan 1993.
18. See Jalal 1994.
19. Gilmartin 1988: 172–73.
20. Moore 1988: 122.
21. Quoted in Moore 1988: 113.
22. Jalal 1994: 58.
23. Talbot 1996b.
24. Vanaik 1997: 31.
25. Jha 1986.
26. Raheja 1994: 95.
27. Sanyal 1981: 17.
28. Dirks 1987.
29. See Omvedt 1994: 42–44 and passim.
30. Beteille 1991: 43.
31. Chatterjee 1989.
32. See Silverberg 1968; Srinivas 1968; Sanyal 1981.
33. Lynch 1969: 12.
34. Dirks 1992.
35. Srinivas 1966: 90; italics in original.
36. Galanter 1984.
37. Cohn 1987.
38. Bandyopadhyay 1990; Trautmann 1997; Susan Bayly 1999.
39. Susan Bayly 1999: 124.

40. Dirks 1989: 51.
41. Carroll 1978.
42. Rudolf and Rudolf 1967: 33.
43. Constable 2000.
44. Omvedt 1971.
45. O'Hanlon, 1985: 265.
46. Constable 2001.
47. Omvedt 1976: 245–47.
48. Pandian 1994.
49. Irschick 1969: 277–81.
50. Pandian 1994.
51. For more on this, see Ramaswamy 1997: 62–66.
52. Irschick 1969: 176.
53. Pandian 1993.
54. Ramaswamy 1997: 64.
55. For more details, see Geetha and Rajadurai 1998: 43–108.
56. Ramaswamy 1997: 62, 65.
57. Pandian 1999: 286–307.
58. Geetha and Rajadurai 1998: 514, 523 and passim.
59. Mendelsohn and Vicziany 1998: 78–79.
60. Constable 1997: 337–38; 2000: 416–22.
61. Jeffrey 1974.
62. Saradamoni 1980.
63. Hardgrave 1969.
64. Zelliot 1992.
65. Juergensmeyer 1982.
66. Gooptu 1993.
67. Dube 1998.
68. Prashad 2000.
69. Bandyopadhyay 1997a.
70. Details in Menon 1994.
71. Bandyopadhyay 1997a: 145–52.
72. For details, see Dube 1998.
73. Chatterjee 1989.
74. Quoted in Zelliot, 1992: 95.
75. See Constable 2000.
76. Zelliot 1988.
77. Susan Bayly 1999: 163–79.
78. Bandyopadhyay 1990: 155–56.
79. Susan Bayly 1999: 251.
80. Parekh 1989a: 209, 249. Italics in original.
81. Omvedt 1994: 147.
82. Bandyopadhyay 2000.
83. Gore 1993: 111.
84. Quoted in Galanter 1984: 31.
85. Mendelsohn and Vicziany 1998: 105.

86. Kumar 1987a: 98–99.
87. Bandyopadhyay 1997a: 179–209.
88. Bandyopadhyay 2000: 899–900.
89. Quoted in Omvedt 1994: 193.
90. Susan Bayly 1999: 260.
91. Quoted in Omvedt 1994: 216.
92. For details, see Bandyopadhyay 2000.
93. Zelliot 1992: 172–73.
94. Rodrigues 1993.
95. Tripathi 1991: 87.
96. Mukherjee 1986: 245–46.
97. Bagchi 1972; Ray 1979.
98. Chandra 1979: 145.
99. Mukherjee 1986: 265.
100. Ibid: 275.
101. Chatterji 1992: 319.
102. Gordon 1978: 156.
103. Ray 1979: 292.
104. Tripathi 1991: 118.
105. Gordon 1978: 161–66.
106. Bhattacharya 1986.
107. Chatterji 1992.
108. Ray 1979: 295–97.
109. Tripathi 1991: 94.
110. Bhattacharya 1976.
111. Gordon 1978: 170–71.
112. Ibid: 176.
113. Chatterji 1992: 274, 281–87.
114. Bhattacharya 1986.
115. Tripathi 1991: 98–102.
116. Sarkar 1985: 95.
117. Markovits 1985:72–73.
118. Mukherjee 1986: 281.
119. Markovits 1985: 78.
120. Tripathi 1991: 109.
121. Markovits 1985: 834.
122. Chatterji 1992: 369.
123. Misra 1999: 172.
124. Quoted in Tripathi 1991: 112.
125. For details, see Markovits 1985: 180–81.
126. Quoted in Mukherjee 1986: 271–72.
127. For details, see Ray 1979: 332–37.
128. Morris 1965: 41.
129. Das Gupta 1994: 35, 45.
130. Chandavarkar 1998: 66.
131. Joshi 1985: 252.

132. Ibid: 252–59.
133. For examples, see Joshi 1981: 1827; Simmons 1976: 459; Nair 1998: 102.
134. Patankar and Omvedt 1979: 411–12.
135. Morris 1965: 142.
136. Joshi 1981: 1827; Nair 1998: 102.
137. Sen 1999: 89–93 and passim.
138. de Haan 1995.
139. Datta 1993: 70–71.
140. Goswami 1987: 572–73.
141. Chandavarkar 1998: 67.
142. Chakrabarty 1989: 186–89.
143. Murphy 1977.
144. Chakrabarty 1989: 218.
145. Ibid: 123.
146. Ibid: 132.
147. Ibid: 145.
148. Murphy 1977: 319.
149. Basu 1998.
150. Joshi 1985: 265.
151. Simeon 1995: 332.
152. Nair 1998: 118.
153. Simeon 1995: 326–27.
154. Chandavarkar 1998: 68, 75.
155. Ghosh 2000: 85–86.
156. Rajat Ray 1979: 310.
157. See Ghosh 2000: 89–94.
158. Simmons 1976: 463–70.
159. Das Gupta 1994: 149.
160. Ghosh 1994: 2025.
161. Chandavarkar 1994: 406.
162. Chandavarkar, 1998.
163. Murphy 1977: 291.
164. Bahl 1995: 373.
165. Simeon 1995: 330.
166. Basu 1998.
167. Kumar 1983: 219.
168. Datta 1993: 58.
169. Chandavarkar 1994: 407.
170. Bahl 1995: 319.
171. Goswami 1987: 560.
172. Sumit Sarkar 1984: 279.
173. Quoted in Bahl 1988: 3.
174. Chandavarkar 1998: 95.
175. Quoted in Bahl 1988: 6.
176. Sen 1977: 222.
177. Patel 1987: 58–62.

178. Bahl 1995: 315–16.
179. Datta 1993.
180. Ray 1984: 277–84.
181. Patel 1987: 52, 56.
182. Murphy 1977: 307–11.
183. Chandavarkar 1994: 417.
184. Simeon 1995: 134.
185. Gourlay 1988: 35–36.
186. Bahl 1988: 22.
187. Quoted in Ray 1984: 284.
188. Quoted in Chandavarkar 1994: 414.
189. Quoted in Basu 1994: 86.
190. Quoted in Bahl 1995: 381.
191. Sarkar 1987a: 69–72.
192. Chakrabarty 1989: 126–27.
193. Chandavarkar 1994: 411 and passim.
194. Joshi 1985: 272, 277.
195. For details, see Chandavarkar 1998: 320.
196. Desai 1959: 195.
197. Chakrabarty 1989: 116.
198. Sinha 1995: 18.
199. Chakrabarty 1994: 54.
200. Thapar 1975: 7.
201. Leslie 1989: 273–304.
202. O'Hanlon 1994: 21–22, 48–49.
203. Azra Asghar Ali 2000: xiii.
204. Amin 1995: 112.
205. Jeffrey 1979: 4.
206. Engels 1996: 2.
207. Forbes 1998: 60.
208. For details see ibid: 44–45.
209. See ibid: 60–61.
210. For details, see Borthwick 1984; Murshid 1983.
211. Samita Sen 1993: 234.
212. Amin 1995: 109.
213. Minault 1998: 215.
214. O'Hanlon 1994: 7.
215. Chakravarti 1998: 303–42.
216. O'Hanlon 1994: 51.
217. Bandyopadhyay 1995: 11–12.
218. Chakravarti 1998: 52.
219. Sarkar 1984: 94.
220. Banerjee 1990: 130.
221. Mukherjee 1983, 1995.
222. Kumar 1983.
223. Sen 1999.
224. Engels 1996: 207–11.

225. Chatterjee 1993: 116–34.
226. Bose 1997: 52–55 and passim.
227. Prakash 1999: 206.
228. Guha-Thakurta 1992: 255.
229. Sarkar 1987b: 2011.
230. Bose 1997: 54.
231. Bagchi 1990: WS65–66.
232. Engels 1996: 28–29.
233. Ray 1995: 184–89.
234. Forbes 1988: 63.
235. Kishwar 1985.
236. Patel 2000: 305 and passim.
237. Brown 1989: 56–57.
238. Patel 2000: 312.
239. Details in Forbes 1998: 124–56.
240. Minault 1981: 8.
241. Tanika Sarkar 1984: 101.
242. Quoted in Forbes 1998: 143.
243. Patel 2000: 297.
244. Minault 1981: 12–13.
245. Kasturi and Mazumdar 1994: 51.
246. Ray 1995: 212.
247. Nair 1994: 89.
248. Azra Asghar Ali 2000: 247.
249. Pearson 1981: 177.
250. Details in Basu and Ray 1990.
251. Pearson 1981: 177.
252. Pearson 1983.
253. Forbes 1998: 89.
254. Ibid: 222.
255. Aruna Asaf Ali 1991: 142.
256. Jayawardena 1986: 105–6.
257. Custers 1986: WS-101.
258. Lalita, et al. 1989: 16–17, 262–68 and passim; Kannabiran and Lalitha 1990.
259. For details, see Lebra 1971, 1986; Hills and Silverman 1993.
260. Quoted in Aruna Asaf Ali 1991: 131.
261. Aruna Asaf Ali 2000: 197–205.
262. Jayawardena 1986: 108.
263. Ibid: 2.
264. Forbes 1998: 193.
265. Custers 1986: WS-97.
266. Sen 1999: 19.
267. Lalita, et al. 1989: 263, 272 and passim.
268. Jalal 2000: 564–66.
269. Menon and Bhasin 1998: 57 and passim; italics in original.
270. Butalia 2001: 208.

chapter eight

Freedom with Partition

8.1. Quit India Movement

The demise of the Civil Disobedience movement around 1934 resulted in serious dissension within the Congress, in the same way as it had happened after the withdrawal of the earlier Non-cooperation campaign. While Gandhi temporarily withdrew from active politics, the socialists and other leftist elements—the most important of them being Jayaprakash Narayan, Achhut Patwardhan, Asoke Mehta, Yusuf Mehrali, Narendra Dev and Minoo Masani—formed in May 1934 the Congress Socialist Party (CSP). His sympathies for socialism notwithstanding, Nehru never formally joined this group, whose "ideology", in the words of Sumit Sarkar, "ranged from vague and mixed-up radical nationalism to fairly firm advocacy of Marxian 'scientific socialism'."[1] The CSP, which rapidly gained in strength in provinces like UP, was meant to operate from within the Congress and try to change its orientation towards a socialist programme as well as contain the dominance of the conservative 'right' wingers. However, soon the divide within the Congress centred on two issues, i.e., council entry and office acceptance. The rift came to a head, but was somehow avoided at the Lucknow Congress in 1936. Here the majority of the delegates, led by Rajendra Prasad and Vallabhbhai Patel, with the blessings of Gandhi, came round to the view that participation in the elections and subsequent acceptance of office in the provinces under the Act of 1935 would help boost the flagging morale of the Congress, at a time when direct action was not an option. The AICC meeting (August 1936) in Bombay decided in favour of contesting the election, but postponed the decision on office acceptance until the election was over. The results of the election in 1937, for which both the right and left-wingers campaigned jointly, were outstanding for the Congress (see chapter 6.4) and this was followed by the AICC sanctioning office acceptance in March by overriding the objections of Nehru and other CSP leaders. Gandhi by taking one of his remarkable compromise positions endorsed the decision, while reposing his faith in non-violence and constructive programme from outside the legislatures. Nehru's opposition hinged on the argument that by running the provincial governments, the Congress would be responsible for "keeping the imperialist structure functioning" and thereby would be letting down the masses whose "high spirits" the Congress itself had once helped in boosting up.[2] Within a few years he was to be proved prophetic!

The Congress won the election in 1937 by targeting the newly enfranchised voters who included sections of the industrial working class and sections of the peasantry, including some of the dalits. But the achievements of the Congress ministries during the next two years frustrated all these groups. We have noted earlier (chapter 7.2) how dalits and their leaders were not impressed by the few caste disabilities removal and temple-entry bills that constituted the token legislative programmes of the Congress ministries, offering nothing more than mere window dressing. We have also noticed (chapter 7.4) how Congress victory had aroused the hopes and aspirations of the industrial working class, leading to increased labour militancy and industrial unrest in Bombay, Gujarat, UP and Bengal, at a time when the Congress was being decisively drawn into a closer friendship with the Indian capitalists. This resulted in a perceptible anti-labour shift in Congress attitudes, epitomised in the passage of the Bombay Trades Disputes Act in 1938. Equally significant were the developments on the peasant front, where the rising militancy before the elections were harnessed by the Congress to win the race; but later it found it difficult to rise up to the expectations of its *kisan* (peasant) voters who were hoping for some radical changes in the existing agrarian relations.

The Kisan Sabha movement started in Bihar under the leadership of Swami Sahajanand Saraswati who had formed in 1929 the Bihar Provincial Kisan Sabha (BPKS) in order to mobilise peasant grievances against the zamindari attacks on their occupancy rights. Initially, the BPKS, by Sahajanand's own admission, was meant to promote class harmony, so that the escalating landlord-tenant friction did not jeopardise the nationalist broad front. But when it was revived again in 1933, it increasingly came under the influence of the socialists, so that by 1935 it adopted abolition of zamindari as one of its programmes. By this time the BPKS membership had risen to thirty-three thousand.[3] It is also important to remember that this kisan movement sought to construct a broad front of the peasantry. Although the rich occupancy tenants provided it with the leadership and its main support base, it attracted a fair amount of participation from the middle and poorer peasants as well.[4] Around the same time the Kisan Sabha movement also gained in momentum in central Andhra districts under the leadership of the CSP activist N.G. Ranga. He organised a number of peasant marches in 1933–34, and under his stewardship at the Ellore Zamindari Ryots Conference in 1933 the demand was raised for the abolition of zamindari. In 1935 Ranga and E.M.S. Namboodripad tried to spread the peasant movement to other linguistic regions of Madras Presidency, organised a South Indian Federation of Peasants and Agricultural Labour and initiated the discussion for an all-India peasant body.[5] Also in the neighbouring province of Orissa, which was created in 1936 under the new constitutional arrangements, the Utkal Kisan Sangha had been formally established in 1935 under the leadership of the Congress socialists, who were organising, in the coastal districts of Cuttack, Puri and Balasore, militant peasant movements around some radical demands. In its very first conference, abolition of zamindari was given a programmatic expression in one of its resolutions.[6]

All these radical developments on the peasant front culminated in the formation of the All India Kisan Sabha (AIKS) at the Lucknow session of the Congress in April 1936, with Sahajanand Saraswati elected as its first president. The Kisan Manifesto, which was adopted in August, contained radical demands, such as the abolition of zamindari, graduated income tax on agricultural income, granting of occupancy rights to all tenants and scaling down of interest rates and debts. A number of CSP leaders and communists—following the 1935 Comintern decision to follow a 'united front' strategy—joined the AIKS and helped in consolidating the movement where it already existed, such as UP, Bihar and Orissa, and also in extending the movement to other provinces, such as Bengal, where a provincial Kisan Sabha was started in March 1937. It was also because of its CSP members that the AIKS remained a part of the Congress and maintained close relationship with the provincial Congress committees. The Congress too was given a more radical orientation by its socialist members; in the Faizpur session in December 1936 the Congress finally adopted an Agrarian Programme. There was also a marked shift towards the democratic and anti-feudal movements in the princely states. The All India States Peoples' Conference, which had been formed in 1927 to coordinate nationalist movement in the native states, so far received apathetic treatment from the Congress. Indeed, the 1934 Bombay Congress had specifically resolved to follow a non-interventionist policy in the states. But this began to change from 1936 when Nehru attended the fifth session of the States Peoples' Conference and stressed the need for mass movement. In October 1937 the AICC resolved to provide moral and material support to the peoples' movements in the states. But Gandhi still remained cautious; he did not like this shift and wanted the whole policy to be reviewed at the next Congress session at Haripura.

Obviously, this ascendancy of the 'left' within the Congress was not liked by the 'right' wingers like Vallabhbhai Patel, Bhulabhai Desai, C. Rajagopalachari or Rajendra Prasad, who still preferred constitutional politics to radical agitation, and also by the committed Gandhians who believed in constructive programme. However, with the election approaching, they could hardly ignore the organisational bases created by the provincial kisan sabhas, and under leftist pressure in some provinces they agreed to include abolition of zamindari in their election manifesto. In the election of 1937 the socialists and the right-wing leaders acted in unison, and reaped its benefits in the spectacular Congress victories, which were quite unexpected in some provinces. So when after July 1937 the Congress ministries began to take over office in the eight provinces, it was hailed by the rural masses as an emancipatory experience marked by the institution of an alternative authority.

But while the ministry formation raised great expectations and brought in greater militancy among the peasantry, it also brought the right-wingers back to power and they now tried to retrieve the Congress from the clutches of the socialists. In the province of Bihar, where the Kisan Sabha began to organise a powerful peasant movement around the issue of *bakasht* land where permanent tenancies had been converted into short-term tenancies in recent years, the conservative Congress leadership renegotiated their alignment with the landlords and entered into formal "agreements" with them. When the proposed tenancy legislations of the Congress were significantly watered down because of landlord pressure, the peasants were not impressed and they staged in 1938–39 a militant movement under the leadership of the Kisan Sabha for the restoration of the bakasht lands. The movement that spread over large parts of Bihar, was strongest in the Reora and Manjihiawan regions of the Gaya district, in Chapra in Sahabad, in Barahiya Tal in Monghyr and among the Santal bataidars in the Kosi Diara region. Participation cut across caste and class barriers, bringing in both dalit and poorer landless agricultural workers, along with the richer Bhumihar and Rajput peasantry. In its basic ideological thrust, the movement was "reformist", as claimed by Stephen Henningham,[7] as it did not threaten the zamindari system, but only sought to restore some pre-existing rights, and did not take recourse to any radical action, such as a no-rent campaign or withholding of debt repayment. But at the popular level there was enough evidence that the peasants in rural Bihar were successfully challenging the authority of the landlords. The panicky zamindars therefore activated the Congress government to use its coercive power; the repression by the landlords' musclemen and the police force went on in tandem, gradually bringing in the demise of the movement. The Bihar Congress now tried to distance itself from the Kisan Sabha, preventing its members from associating with it.[8]

In UP too the Kisan Sabha activists were disillusioned with the Congress ministry that significantly blunted the teeth of a 1938 tenancy legislation, which was originally expected to reduce rents by half. The UP Kisan Sabha leaders like Narendra Dev and Mohanlal Gautam mobilised peasant demonstrations against the ministry; but such protestations remained contained and isolated because of the influence exerted by Nehru.[9] In Orissa also the kisan leaders were frustrated when the Congress ministry allowed pro-landlord amendments to the proposed tenancy legislation; and even this diluted legislation was blocked by the governor until there was a mammoth Kisan Day rally on 1 September 1938. In the neighbouring princely states of Nilgiri, Dhenkanal and Talcher, where peasant movements had been organised by the local praja mandals, unrestrained repression was unleashed by the *durbars*, with the active patronage of the British Resident. The Orissa Congress silently watched it, following its old non-interventionist policy.[10] By this time the Congress had been completely taken over by the right-wing leaders and their ire against the kisan sabhas was rising. In October 1937 the AIKS had adopted the red flag as its official banner. In its 1938 annual conference it denounced the Gandhian principle of class collaboration and proclaimed that an agrarian revolution would be its ultimate goal. A resolution at the Haripura session in February 1938 prohibited Congressmen from becoming members of the kisan sabhas, but its implementation was left to the provincial bodies.[11]

Another significant territory where the dilemmas of the Congress leadership were becoming highly visible was princely India. Throughout the 1920s and 1930s, the Congress chose not to intervene in the affairs of the princely states, respecting the rights of the traditional rulers over their subjects. Left to themselves, the local people of the states organised themselves into praja mandals, raised moderate demands for constitutional changes and democratisation and later affiliated to an all-India body called the All India States Peoples'

Conference (AISPC), founded in 1927. Although the states could never remain totally insulated from the political waves of British India, the princes remained steadfast loyalists to their imperial protectors, trying to keep the nationalist agitation at bay. In the late 1930s, therefore, the Congress left-wingers, like Bose and Nehru, became more insistent on the desirability of greater intervention in the princely states, in order to bring them at par with the political developments in British India.[12] The right-wingers too now possibly, as surmised by Ian Copland (1999), began to dream of power at the proposed federal centre, and for that they required the princes to nominate their representatives from among people close to the praja mandals. Such a confluence of ideas and ambitions resulted in a significant policy shift at the Haripura Congress in 1938, where a resolution was adopted to support the peoples' movements in the states; although no organisational assistance was to be provided, individual leaders could participate, under the overall leadership of a special subcommittee of the Congress Working Committee. In February 1939, Nehru accepted the presidency of the AISPC and the Tripuri Congress endorsed the scheme of joint action. As a result of this evolving situation, in late 1938 and early 1939 many of the princely states witnessed an unprecedented escalation of popular agitation, spearheaded by the local praja mandals, clandestine Congress branches and outside political leaders from British India. Significant agitation took place in Mysore, Jaipur, Rajkot, Travancore, Kashmir and Hyderabad—Gandhi himself taking a leading role in Rajkot.[13] While some states like Mysore and Rajkot became more conciliatory and made token concessions, the larger states resisted the pressure resolutely, with help coming, although belatedly, from the British authorities. As a result of such confrontational line up, peaceful demonstrations soon deteriorated into numerous acts of violence, and later into communal conflicts in southern Deccan, forcing Gandhi to withdraw the movement in April 1939. The situation was again back to normal by autumn.[14] As mentioned earlier (chapter 6.5), the major political fall out of this sudden flare up was the stiffening of princely opposition to the proposed federation idea of the Act of 1935.

On the other end too, the issue of federation became the cause of a major rift between the Congress old guards and their left-wing critics and it came to a head in the period between the Haripura Congress in March 1938 and the Tripuri Congress in March the following year. It centred on the re-election of the Congress president Subhas Chandra Bose, whose militant anti-federation stand had irked the conservatives. Bose contested the election defying Gandhi's wishes, and emerged victorious defeating Gandhi's own candidate, Pattabhi Sitaramayya. As B.R. Tomlinson describes it, the election "was fought out in ideological terms—'right' versus 'left', 'pro-Federation' versus 'anti-Federation', 'pro-Ministry' versus 'anti-Ministry'".[15] Gandhi took it as his personal defeat and twelve of the fifteen members of the Working Committee resigned immediately. The showdown came at the Tripuri Congress where a resolution was passed censoring Bose for raising allegations against the Gandhians that they would sell out on the federation issue. Gandhi asked him to constitute his own Working Committee and refused all cooperation. Bose tried to patch up a compromise but failed, and ultimately at the AICC meeting in Calcutta in April 1939 he resigned and was quickly replaced by Rajendra Prasad. Bose then formed his own Forward Block, as a left party within the Congress; but it did not gain much strength outside his own province of Bengal. When he staged a protest against the AICC decision to ban Congressmen from participating in civil disobedience without the prior permission of provincial Congress committees, the Working Committee at Gandhi's insistence punished him for indiscipline; in August 1939 he was removed from all Congress positions—notably the presidency of the Bengal PCC—and was banned from holding any executive office for three years. Later in January 1940, Gandhi wrote to C.F. Andrews describing Subhas as "my son"—but a "spoilt child of the family" who needed to be taught a lesson for his own good.[16] Bose's virtual expulsion, however, did not mean that Congress was about to fall apart, although it definitely signified a reassertion of authority by the right-wingers. The socialists were weakened within the Congress, but could not be completely weeded out. Although some members at this stage clearly preferred autonomy, the AIKS still remained a part of the Congress. But the expectations and militancy that its members had once generated among the masses, had been clearly dampened by the conservative policies of the Congress ministries. The Congress itself began to lose its popularity as indicated in the drastic fall in its membership, from 4.5 million in 1938–39 to 1.4 million in 1940–41.[17] It was this sense of popular frustration combined with a growing militant mood that prepared the ground for the next round of mass movement in India in 1942.

The outbreak of World War Two in September 1939 brought in new variables in Indian politics. The war brought changes in British policies and changes in Congress strategies too. Viceroy Lord Linlithgow associated India with England's declaration of war against Germany without consulting any Indian opinion. The Congress Working Committee made it clear that it was going to support war efforts only if the British gave some concessions on two key issues: a post-war independence pledge and an immediate national government at the centre. But what Linlithgow offered on 14 October fell far short of that. In protest Congress ministries resigned between 29 and 30 October 1939. Jinnah and the Muslim League celebrated the occasion as a "day of deliverance"; dalit leader Ambedkar supported them and the Home government thought of capitalising on this rift. The war at this stage was still distant from the shores of India, yet many Congress leaders were alive to the issue of resisting fascism and therefore were keen to support British war efforts, provided some constitutional concessions were promised. But the London government was not prepared to offer anything that might bind its hands in any post-war negotiations on constitutional issues. So Linlithgow's August (1940) offer of dominion status in an unspecified future, a post-war constitutional consultative body, expansion of the viceroy's executive council to include some Indians and the provision of a War Advisory Council fell far short of Congress expectations. In the meanwhile, the Japanese intervention and rapid Japanese victories since December 1941 brought war closer to India: between December 1941 and March 1942 Hong Kong, Borneo, Manila, Singapore, Java, Rangoon, Sumatra and Andaman and Nicobar Islands fell into Japanese hands in quick succession. Colombo was bombed on 5 April, followed by the bombing of two Indian coastal towns of Vizagapatnam and Coconada. Indian support for war efforts was now clearly necessary, and so was urgently needed some discussion on the constitutional future of India. At least that was what the American President Franklin Roosevelt and the Chinese leader Chiang Kai Shek had been telling Winston Churchill, who had taken over as the premier of a coalition War Cabinet in London in May 1940. So the Cripps Mission came to India in March-April 1942; but before it could disentangle the constitutional knot, Churchill called it back. What led to the failure of the Mission we will discuss in detail later in the chapter; but the failure prepared the ground for Congress action against what many Indians now believed to be an imperial war, which they had been unnecessarily dragged into against their wishes.

Initially the war had evoked mixed reactions from Congress politicians. While some leaders like Nehru were alive to the need of supporting the war against fascism, other leftist leaders were itching for action against British war efforts; but they were no longer in a position to force the issue on the Congress. On the other hand, some leaders like Rajagopalachari still firmly believed in the effectiveness of parliamentary politics and wanted to make the best of the existing constitutional arrangement. Gandhi was ambivalent: at one stage he believed that war was against his principle of non-violence; then, he promised the viceroy all support in his war efforts, and for that became a target of criticism from his own followers in the Congress. Ultimately, at the Ramgarh Congress in May 1940, he agreed to launch civil disobedience; but this would be "individual satyagraha" by volunteers personally selected by Gandhi for this purpose, and they would only offer anti-war speeches. The movement was by no means a success and in the meanwhile the Japanese came closer to the borders of India, while the British remained intransigent about promising any constitutional changes. In 1942 there was a remarkable change in Gandhi's attitude and he seemed to be in an unusually militant mood. As the possibility of a Japanese invasion became real, Gandhi refused to accept that the Japanese could be the liberators and believed that India in the hands of the Indians was the best guarantee against fascist aggression. Meanwhile, the war had its obvious impact on the economic and social life of the Indians, many of whom had reached the threshold of their tolerance and were ready for a final showdown with British imperialism.

The economic impact of war was initially beneficial to various groups of Indians. As commodity prices rose, it benefited industrialists, merchants and rich peasants producing for the market; it took away the bad effects of the depression and for the peasants, it reduced the pressure of rent. But in 1942 the main problem caused by the war was what Max Harcourt has described as "a scarcity crisis", resulting from mainly a shortfall in the supply of rice. Between April and August the price index for food grains rose by sixty points in north India. This was partly because of bad seasonal conditions and partly due to the stoppage in the supply of Burmese rice and the stringent procurement policy of the British.[18] While the higher food prices hit the poor, the rich were hurt by excess profit tax, forcible collection of war funds and coercive sale of war bonds. This situation created a popular mentality of panic, as British power clearly seemed to be desperate and on the verge of imminent collapse. This was confirmed by the streams of refugees who came back from Malay and Burma, bringing with them horror stories of not only Japanese atrocities, but also of how British power collapsed in Southeast Asia and British authorities abandoned the Indian refugees to their fate, forcing them to traverse hostile terrains on foot, enduring hunger, disease and pain. There was a widespread fear that if Japan invaded, the British would do the same in India. And that seemed no longer a distant possibility, as the British initiated a harsh 'denial policy' in coastal Bengal by destroying all means of communications, including boats and cycles, paying very little compensation. From May 1942 American and Australian soldiers began to arrive in India and soon became the central figures in stories of rape and racial harassment of civilian population. Rumours were rife, both fed by the Axis propaganda machine, and by Subhas Bose's *Azad Hind* Radio, broadcast from Berlin from March 1942 (more in chapter 8.2). By the middle of the year there was a widespread popular belief in India that British power was going to collapse soon and therefore it was the opportune moment for a fight to the finish and to liberate India from nearly two hundred years of colonial rule.

Gandhi was not slow to feel this popular mood of militancy and realised that the moment of his final engagement with the Raj had arrived. "Leave India to God", Gandhi wrote in May 1942. "If that is too much, then leave her to anarchy. This ordered disciplined anarchy should go, and if there is complete lawlessness, I would risk it".[19] He briskly set aside all opposition from within the Congress against direct action, coming mainly from Nehru and Rajagopalachari, and prepared the party for the final struggle, "the biggest fight in my life".[20] In July, the Congress Working Committee approved of a draft resolution on mass—as opposed to individual—civil disobedience. The "Quit India" resolution, adopted by the AICC in Bombay on 8 August 1942, proposed to begin this mass civil disobedience under Gandhi's direction, if power was not immediately handed over to the Indians. On this occasion, Gandhi delivered his famous "Do or Die" speech, arguing that this was the final battle—a "fight to the finish"—and so the Indians must win independence or give up their lives for it. This fired the imagination of an already rankled Indian population, expecting a breakdown of the established authority. As Gyanendra Pandey puts it, Gandhi provided them with a "psychological break", by asserting that everyone should henceforth consider themselves as "free man or woman", and should choose their own course of action if the leaders were arrested.[21] His fear proved to be true, as all front-ranking leaders of the Congress, including Gandhi, were arrested in the early morning of 9 August and this was followed by unprecedented mass fury that goes by the name of "August Revolution" in nationalist legends. The unusual intensity of the movement surprised everyone. Viceroy Linlithgow described it as "by far the most serious rebellion since 1857".[22] It was violent and totally uncontrolled from the very beginning, as the entire upper echelon of the Congress leadership was behind bars even before it began. And therefore, it is also characterised as a "spontaneous revolution", as "no preconceived plan could have produced such instantaneous and uniform results".[23]

The history of the Quit India movement as revealed in recent studies shows that it was not just an impulsive response of an unprepared populace, although the unprecedented scale of violence was by no means premeditated by the Congress leadership, as was claimed by the government. First of all, the last two decades of mass movement—which in the recent past had been conducted on a much more radical tone under the leadership of the various associated and affiliated bodies of the Congress, like the AITUC, CSP, AIKS and the Forward Block—had already prepared the ground for such a conflagration. The Congress leaders before 9 August had drafted a twelve-point programme which not only included the usual Gandhian methods of satyagraha, but a plan to promote industrial strikes, holding up of railways and telegraphs, non-payment of taxes and setting up of parallel government. Several versions of this programme were in circulation among Congress volunteers, including the one prepared by the Andhra Provincial Congress Committee, which contained clear instructions for such subversive action. However, compared to what actually happened, even this was a cautious programme! But then, as the movement progressed, the AICC continued to issue "Instructions to peasants" which outlined the course of action anticipating what was to eventuate in the later months of the movement.[24] On the question of non-violence, Gandhi this time was remarkably ambivalent. "I do not ask from you my own non-violence. You can decide what you can do in this struggle", said Gandhi on 5 August. Three days later on the 8th, speaking on the AICC resolution, he urged: "I trust the whole of India to-day to launch upon a non-violent struggle." But even if people deviated from this path of non-violence, he assured: "I shall not swerve. I shall not flinch".[25] In other words, the issue of non-violence seemed to have been of lesser importance in 1942 than the call for "Do or Die" or the invitation to make a final sacrifice for the liberation of the nation.[26] The people accepted the challenge and interpreted it in their own ways and these interpretations were to some extent influenced by the lower level, often unknown, Congress leaders and students, who took over the leadership after the national and provincial leaders were all arrested between 9 and 11 August. There is no denying that the Congress and Gandhi at this important historical juncture enjoyed unquestionable symbolic legitimacy in popular mind—whatever happened, happened in their name. But Congress as an organisation and Gandhi as a person had little control over these happenings. In the words of Gyanendra Pandey, Gandhi was "the undisputed leader of a movement over which he had little command."[27]

Sumit Sarkar has identified three phases of the Quit India movement.[28] It initially started as an urban revolt, marked by strikes, boycott and picketing, which were quickly suppressed. In the middle of August, the focus shifted to the countryside, which witnessed a major peasant rebellion, marked by destruction of communication systems, such as railway tracks and stations, telegraph wires and poles, attacks on government buildings or any other visible symbol of colonial authority and finally, the formation of "national governments" in isolated pockets. This brought in severe government repression forcing the agitation to move underground. The third phase was characterised by violent activities, which primarily involved sabotaging of war efforts by dislocating communication systems and propaganda activities by using various means, including a clandestine radio station run by hitherto unknown Usha Mehta from "somewhere in India". Not only the educated youth participated in such activities, but also bands of ordinary peasants organised such subversive actions by night, which came to be known as the "Karnataka method". What is important, these groups enjoyed enormous popular support and patronage, so that the definition of "underground" in British official parlance virtually got expanded to cover the entire nation, as no Indian could anymore be trusted by the authorities. As time passed, underground activities came to be channeled into three streams, with a radical group under the leadership of Jayaprakash Narayan organising guerrilla warfare at India-Nepal border, a centrist group led by Congress Socialists like Aruna Asaf Ali mobilising volunteers throughout India for sabotage activities, and a Gandhian group led by Sucheta Kripalani and others emphasising non-violent action and constructive programme.[29] In the Quit India movement there was use of violence at an unprecedented scale and the government used it as a justification for repression. The wartime emergency powers were taken advantage of to use the army for the first time—as many as fifty-seven battalions of British troops were deployed to crush what was essentially a civilian agitation. Churchill could defend this swift and ruthless repression and silence a critical world opinion by citing the needs of war. By the end of 1942, the "August Revolution" had been thoroughly crushed, with nearly ninety-two thousand people arrested by the end of 1943.

However, the whole of India did not convulse in the same way, as the intensity of the movement varied from region to region. If we compare the regional details revealed in recent studies, the movement would evidently appear to have been most powerful in Bihar where the Kisan Sabha had done major preparatory organisational groundwork. Here the conflagration started at Patna city, where students took the initiative to mobilise a mammoth rally at the Secretariat on 11 August and tried to hoist a Congress flag atop the Assembly building. The student initiative was soon appropriated by the masses, who burnt railway stations, municipal buildings and post offices and the local police seemed powerless, until the army was called out on the 12th. In Jamshedpur, the movement started with a strike of the local constabulary on the 9th, a strike in TISCO on the 10th and again on the 20th, when about thirty-thousand workers took part. In Dalmianagar too there was a labour strike on the 12th, and on both these occasions complicity of the management was suspected by the administration. However, more important was the peasant revolt that took place in the following week in practically every district of Bihar. Under the initiative of students, thousands of ordinary peasants attacked and looted local treasury buildings and railway stations, killed unarmed European officers in public, thus ceremonially destroying the physical presence of colonial authority. Isolated police thanas were taken over and destroyed when the lower level village police and local civilian administrators vacated their posts without resistance. The movement was covertly supported by the zamindars and merchants who supplied funding and participation came from across caste barriers. The most significant example of lower caste participation here was the formation of a parallel government in Barh by the Gops and Dusadhs, who formed their own "Raj" and started levying taxes. The peasant movement in Bihar was ruthlessly suppressed by the British army, which was given a free hand to torture and burn down entire villages. The movement hereafter went underground and was coordinated from around 1943 by a new organisational structure called the *Azad Dastas* or guerrilla bands, which operated mainly in south Bihar, conducting raids on ammunition depots, treasuries and other government offices. Some of the CSP leaders like Jayaprakash Narayan tried to maintain control over the Dastas, but the latter soon developed links with the professional dacoit gangs of low caste landless peasants and indulged in what has been described as "social crime". The CSP at this stage began to distance itself from the Dastas and the movement was finally suppressed in 1944.[30]

In eastern UP, in districts of Ghazipur and Azamgarh the arrival of student volunteers from the Banaras Hindu University (BHU)—even rumour of their arrival—galvanised the local peasantry into action, destroying railway tracks and stations and burning papers in the Court of Ward office. However, in many places in these districts, like the Sherpur-Mohammadabad region—as Gyanendra Pandey puts it—the "message of destruction" and the Gandhian principle of non-violence "co-existed uneasily", as some committed Gandhian leaders sought to maintain its non-violent purity.[31] The mass insurrection was much more intense in the district of Ballia, where British rule ceased to exist for a few days; but here too contradictions weakened the movement. The story was not much dissimilar, as student leaders arriving from BHU and Allahabad University—the latter in a hijacked *Azad* (liberty) train—inspired the peasantry into action. Several thousands of them attacked and looted the railway station and a military supply train at Bilthara Road on 14 August, took over the thana and tahsil buildings at Bansdih town four days later, with the local station officer and tahsildar offering no resistance, and the local Congress leader trying to establish a parallel administration. And then on 19 August, a huge crowd besieged the Ballia town, forcing its Indian District Magistrate to burn all currency notes in the treasury and free all political prisoners. The released Gandhian leader Chittu Pande hereafter took control of the movement and was proclaimed the *Swaraj Ziladhish* or Independent District Magistrate, who did not however know what to do next. So when on the following day the army arrived, the leaders all fled and the whole town of Ballia lay deserted. The Quit India movement here thus came to a rather "anti-climactic end" due to a lack of leadership.[32]

In contrast to Bihar and eastern UP, the Quit India movement was less instantaneous and intense, but more prolonged in other regions of India. In Bengal, the movement took place in Calcutta and in the districts of Hugli, Bankura, Purulia, Birbhum and Dinajpur—in the latter district marked by the participation of Santals and dalit groups like Rajbansis and Paliyas. But it was undoubtedly strongest in Tamluk and Contai (Kanthi) subdivisions of Midnapur where, as Hitesranjan Sanyal has commented, "national movement had by 1930 become a part of the popular culture among peasants.";[33] and they had been further organised in recent past by the Krishak Sabhas and Forward Block. Since April 1942, in the coastal areas of Midnapur the government destroyed nearly eighteen thousand boats in pursuance of its 'denial policy', and this not only deprived the peasants of their vital means of communication, but also impacted very badly on the local economy. And the problem was further complicated by general price rise and stringent procurement policy. So when in August local Congress volunteers and students started mobilising peasants for an open rebellion, they found a fertile ground. Quit India in Midnapur started from around 8 September, with orchestrated attacks on several police thanas by crowds ranging from ten to twenty thousands. By the 30th, British administration almost collapsed in these two subdivisions, bringing in the army with a mandate to torture, rape and ruthlessly suppress the movement. The situation was further complicated by a devastating cyclone and tidal wave on 16 October killing nearly fifteen thousand people. The local district officer refused relief as a retaliatory measure; so the Congress organised alternative relief camps and thus became more popular. What is more important, the Congress now moved on to establish parallel national governments: in Contai the *Swaraj Panchayat* was started in November, while in Tamluk the *Tamralipta Jatiya Sarkar* was inaugurated on 17 December. The latter had a trained volunteer corps or *Bidyut Bahini*, a women's volunteer corps or *Bhagini Sena*, and a mouthpiece, *Biplabi.* It organised relief work, settled 1,681 cases in arbitration courts, ran the civil administration, clashed with powerful loyalist zamindars, merchants and local officials and despite ruthless repression, continued to function until August 1944 when Gandhi gave a call to end the rebellion. The *Kanthi Swaraj Panchayat* was also disbanded around this time.[34]

In neighbouring Orissa too the movement was strongest where the Kisan Sangha and the praja mandals had already mobilised the peasantry in previous agrarian movements. It started as usual in cities like Cuttack, with hartals and strikes in educational institutions and then spread to the countryside, mainly in the coastal districts of Cuttack, Balasore and Puri. Here the peasants were inspired by rumours of an "impending doom" and attacked all visible symbols of colonial authority, in open defiance of which they rescued prisoners from police stations, stripped local policemen of their uniforms, stopped paying chowkidari taxes and in some areas attacked zamindari cutcheries and extorted paddy from moneylenders. This rural revolt in the districts, marked by participation from across caste barriers, was however virtually over by October-November under pressure of police repression and collective taxes. In the princely states of Nilgiri and Dhankanal, where tribal and dalit peasants violated forest laws and were mobilised by praja mandal leaders in mammoth demonstrations, collective taxes were imposed and repression was supervised by the British Political Agent. However, in the state of Talcher, the Quit India took a novel form. Here the local praja mandal leaders, in a bid to end the rule of the local raja and his patron the British Raj, decided to establish a "*chasi-mulia raj*" on a programme of "popular peasant utopia", with promises of food, shelter and clothes for everyone. By 6 September the new raj had established its authority over most of the state and men from various directions now closed in towards the town of Talcher in order to destroy the centre of power. Here on the 7th, the demonstrators were machine-gunned from air using RAF planes and this was followed by ruthless repression; but in spite of that guerrilla warfare in this region continued until about May 1943. The dreams of an alternative raj were also present in Malkangiri and Nawrangpur, where the charismatic leader Laxman Naiko assembled tribal and non-tribal peasants in his attacks on liquor and opium shops, and declared proudly in crowded meetings that British Raj had ended and had been replaced by Gandhi Raj which no longer required payment of "shandy" and forest dues. This movement too was crushed by the end of September by troops called in from the neighbouring state of Bastar.[35]

The experiment to establish alternative national governments was indeed most successful in Maharashtra, where the Satara *Prati Sarkar* (parallel government) emerged out of the organisational bases created by the non-Brahman movement. In the early twentieth century it was this movement which had mobilised the bahujan samaj in anti-caste and anti-feudal agitation and in the 1930s it had forged links with nationalism and Congress (see chapter 7.2). In late 1942 when the initial outburst of violent sabotage activities subsided under pressure of army repression, the young and educated members of the bahujan samaj in the district of Satara decided to form a prati sarkar which was formally established between February and June 1943, significantly, when the Quit India movement had almost died down in other provinces. It had elaborate organisational structures, with a volunteer corps or *Seba Dal* and village units or *Tufan Dals*, with Nana Patil as the central inspirational figure. It was involved in various activities and these included running the peoples' courts or *nyayadan mandals*, implementing constructive programmes and conducting armed sabotage activities. And in contrast to the Azad Dastas of Bihar, it fought hard battles to destroy local dacoit gangs in the rugged ravines of Satara in order to establish its own authority and legitimacy. Although dominated by middle ranking Kunbi peasants, it equally attracted— because of its anti-feudal and anti-caste orientation—significant participation and support from poorer dalit peasants. It gained support from Congress socialists, but the prati-sarkar could never be hegemonised by the Congress. So when in August 1944 Gandhi gave a call for surrender, unlike their Midnapur counterparts, most of the members of the Satara Prati Sarkar decided to defy Mahatma's instruction and stuck to his earlier call for "do or die". This parallel government continued to function until the election of 1946, despite various British attempts to repress it.[36]

Among other parts of western India, the Quit India movement was most powerful in the districts of Kheda, Surat and Broach in Gujarat and in the princely state of Baroda. It was here that Congress had a stronghold from the days of Non-cooperation movement and the leader of the Gujarat PCC, Vallabhbhai Patel himself was believed to have prepared a blueprint for sabotage activities before being arrested in Bombay. The movement started in the cities of Ahmedabad and Baroda, with labour strikes, hartals and rioting, using various community structures, such as the exclusive caste enclaves of *pols* and mahajans or unions of traders. In Ahmedabad a parallel "Azad Government" was established and here the industrialists—expecting the Congress to become the party in power soon—expressed sympathy with the nationalist cause. They did nothing to end the industrial strike, which went on for nearly three and half months on pure political demands, rather than on any economic claim for higher wages. The revolt in the countryside, which went on from September to December, followed the usual pattern of sabotage activities as elsewhere. But one major dissimilarity with the past movements in this region was the absence of any no-revenue campaign this time, as the rich Patidar peasantry did not want to risk confiscation of their properties at a time when they had prospered due to recent price hikes. Another significant feature was that although tribal peasants in many places participated in the movement, the dalit Baraiya and Pattanvadiya peasants, dissatisfied with the Patidar-dominated Congress ministry, actively opposed Quit India in Kheda and Mehsana districts. In Broach, Surat and Navsari districts, however, there was rural unity across caste and class lines, and British rule as a result disappeared from this region, until it recovered again through ruthless repression that only made Gandhian Congress more popular.[37]

The Quit India movement, as we find from the detailed regional studies, was intense and robust in some regions, less forceful but more prolonged in others. In some regions like Madras Presidency, it was fairly moderate, not only because leading figures of Madras politics like Rajagopalachari opposed the movement, but because of various other factors, such as the strength of constitutionalism, absence of the socialists, opposition of the Kerala communists, indifference of the non-Brahmans and a strong southern challenge to a political campaign dominated by the north.[38] But what was more significant, there were important social groups who consciously stayed away from the movement. The most important of them were the Muslims who stood aloof from the campaign almost in all regions and therefore, the Muslim League, which did not approve of the movement, could claim that it represented the majority of the Indian Muslims. But although their abstention was nearly universal, the Muslims did not oppose Quit India actively, except perhaps in some parts of Gujarat, and there was no major incident of communal conflict throughout the whole period. On the other hand, Dr B.R. Ambedkar, the leader of the dalits, who had joined the viceroy's executive council as a labour member just before the onset of the campaign, also did not support it. But once again, although many of his supporters did not join, we have evidence of dalit participation in the Quit India movement in various regions and cross-caste unity was never a rare occurrence in this campaign (as shown earlier). It is also important to remember that the Hindu Mahasabha too condemned the Quit India movement as "sterile, unmanly and injurious to the Hindu cause" and stalwart Hindu leaders like V.D. Savarkar. B.S. Munje and Shyama Prasad Mukherjee wholeheartedly supported British war efforts that were allegedly being wrecked by the Congress campaign. But despite this official line, a strong group of Mahasabha members led by N.C. Chatterjee seemed eager to participate in it and under their pressure the Mahasabha Working Committee had to adopt a face saving but vague resolution stating that defence of India could not be supported unless freedom of India was recognised with immediate effect.[39] The other Hindu organisation, RSS, which until now had its main base in Maharashtra, remained aloof as well. As the Bombay government noted in a memo: "the Sangh has scrupulously kept itself within the law, and in particular, has refrained from taking part in the disturbances that broke out in August 1942."[40]

The Communist Party of India, following the involvement of Soviet Russia in the war in December 1941, became another important political group which did not support Quit India movement because of their "Peoples' War" strategy. The British government, then anxious to find any group that could embarrass the Congress and support war efforts, promptly withdrew the ban on the CPI that had been in place since 1934 and the latter now started preaching in favour of war efforts to contain fascism. However, despite this official line, there is ample evidence to show that many individual communists were swayed by the patriotic emotions of the day and actively participated in the Quit India movement.[41] And on the other hand, the trade unions and kisan sabhas, which the communists controlled, began to lose their popularity and support, as the leaders found it difficult to convince their followers the logic of supporting a distant war by subverting a campaign for their own freedom. It is possible to argue that when the dalit peasants or other poorer classes participated in the Quit India movement, their motivation was different from those of the educated youth and the middle peasant castes. But it is too simplistic to describe the movement as a "dual revolt",[42] because despite variance in vision, the different classes and communities were also united in common action against the British. Watching Patna city on 11 August, a confounded communist leader Rahul Sankrityayana observed in utter astonishment that the "leadership had passed on to the *ricksha*-pullers, *ekka*-drivers and other such people whose political knowledge extended only this far—that the British were their enemies".[43] It was this commonly shared dominant tone of anti-imperialism that united everyone in 1942 and in the villages it even overshadowed the anti-feudal tendencies that appeared from time to time in different parts of the country. The Quit India movement by promising immediate freedom from an oppressive imperial order had thus captured the imagination of a significant section of the Indian population, notwithstanding their differing perceptions of freedom.

The Quit India movement also provided important lessons for the Congress. First of all, the defeat discredited the left-wingers who had been demanding action. Gandhi, on the other hand, was in a dilemma. Congress volunteers were justifying violence by referring to his own dictum that it was justifiable in self-defence. He did not condone violence, but did not formally condemn it either; instead, he held the government responsible for the outbreak of violence. Indeed, neither he nor any other Congress leaders had any control over the people and the volunteers, nor any of them had anticipated the kind of response the Quit India movement had generated. To the Indian masses in 1942, Gandhi and Congress were symbols of liberation, not sources of ideological constraint. Gandhi's twenty-one day fast commencing on 10 February 1943 restored symbolically his centrality in the movement once again, but not as a controlling figure; nor did he insist on the surrender of the underground leaders.

Even after his release in 1944, when he gave a call to surrender, not everyone listened. He too was full of praise for those who had evidently deviated from his path of non-violence. "I am one of those"—he told Nana Patil of Satara Prati Sarkar fame—"who feel that the violence of the brave is better than the non-violence of the cowardly!"[44] But the Congress high command, now dominated by the right-wingers, strongly disapproved of this popular militancy and wanted to return to a regime of discipline and order and therefore, urged for a negotiated settlement rather than confrontation. The Congress after the movement steadily drifted away from the path of agitation and leaned towards constitutionalism. Thus by way of fighting the Raj, as D.A. Low had once argued, the Congress itself was in the process of becoming the Raj.[45] The British Raj too learned important lessons. They realised first of all, that it was difficult to tackle such militant mass movements without the wartime emergency powers. When war would be over, keeping India by force against such opposition would be an expensive proposition in every sense and hence there was greater readiness to accept a negotiated settlement for a respectable and ordered withdrawal. In these negotiations Congress was to figure prominently, as it was the only political structure that had the potential to mobilise such a mass movement and it was supposed to be the only organisation that could provide India with a stable government.

8.2 THE TURBULENT FORTIES

Notwithstanding the fact that there was a grand convergence of multiple streams of protest at the historical conjuncture of 1942 and that gave Congress immense political legitimacy, it is still difficult to deny that contesting visions and agendas of emancipation existed within India's national struggle against imperialism. We may now turn to some such alternative visions before going into the story of the final withdrawal of colonial rule. When the war broke out in Europe and the Congress was still vacillating in its response, its renegade leader Subhas Chandra Bose was arguing that the Indians were losing a rare opportunity, for they must take advantage of the empire's weakest moment. He was convinced in 1939, when disciplinary action was taken against him, that it was the result of "Right-consolidation"; and now this hesitation to initiate a mass movement against the Raj was because of the same right-wing leaders who were "out of touch with the new forces and the new elements that ... [had] come into existence in the last few years".[46] He, therefore, travelled alone across India to stir a movement, but did not get much enthusiastic response. Back in Bengal, he forged a link with the Muslim League, and decided to launch a civil disobedience movement to destroy the Holwell monument that stood in Calcutta as a reminder of a Black hole tragedy which most people believed did never happen and was invented only to tar the memory of Siraj-ud-daula, the last independent ruler of Bengal. It was a campaign that had an obvious appeal to the Muslims and thus could further strengthen the Hindu-Muslim pact in Bengal. But before it could start, he was arrested by the British on 3 July 1940 under the Defence of India Act. The Holwell monument was later removed, but Bose remained incarcerated until he threatened to start a hunger strike in December.[47] He was then released unconditionally, but kept under constant surveillance. In the meanwhile, war progressed in Europe, and Bose believed that Germany was going to win. Although he did not like their totalitarianism or racism, he began to nurture the idea that the cause of Indian independence could be furthered with the help of the Axis powers and started exploring various possibilities. Finally, in the midnight of 16–17 January 1941 he fled from his Elgin Road residence in Calcutta incognito as an upcountry Muslim. He travelled to Kabul and then through Russia on an Italian passport; by the end of March he reached Berlin.[48]

Subhas Bose met Goebbels and Hitler in Berlin, but did not receive much help from them. He was allowed to start his *Azad Hind* Radio and was handed over the Indian POWs captured in North Africa to start an Indian Legion, but nothing beyond that. Particularly, he could not get an Axis declaration in favour of Indian independence, and after German reverses at Stalingrad, that became even more difficult.[49] But in the meanwhile, a new stage of action was being prepared for him in Southeast Asia, where the Japanese were taking real interest in the cause of Indian independence. India originally did not figure in the Japanese policy of Greater East Asia Co-prosperity Sphere, under which the Japanese proposed to help Asians gain independence from Western imperialism. But by 1940 Japan had developed an India policy and the following year sent Major Fuziwara to Southeast Asia to contact expatriate Indians who were organising themselves into the Indian Independence Leagues under the leadership of men like Pritam Singh. Then in December 1941, Captain Mohan Singh, a young officer of the Punjab Regiment of the British Indian Army who had surrendered to the Japanese in the jungles of Malaya, agreed to cooperate with Fuziwara to raise an Indian army with POWs to march alongside the Japanese to liberate India. In June 1942, a united Indian Independence League, representing all Indians in Southeast Asia, was born as a civilian political body having controlling authority over the army. To chair this body, Rash Behari Bose, a veteran Bengali revolutionary then living in Japan, was flown in. By September, the INA was formally in existence. But its relationship with the Japanese was still far from satisfactory, as "Japanese duplicity" now became more than apparent.[50] General Tojo, the Japanese prime minister, made a declaration in the Diet supporting Indian independence. But beyond that, the Japanese were only prepared to treat INA as a subsidiary force, rather than an allied army. As Mohan Singh insisted on autonomy and allied status, he was removed from command and put under arrest. Rash Behari Bose tried to hold the banner for some time, but he was then too aged for the task. By the beginning of 1943 the first INA experiment virtually collapsed.

As Mohan Singh had often mentioned to the Japanese, the INA movement needed a new leader and outside India only one person could provide that leadership, and that was Subhas Chandra Bose. The Japanese now seriously considered the proposition and negotiated with the Germans to bring him to Asia. At last, after a long and arduous submarine voyage, in May 1943 Bose arrived in Southeast Asia and immediately took control of the situation, with Japanese assurance of help and equal treatment. In October, he established a Provisional Government of Free India, which was immediately recognised by Japan and later by eight other governments, including Germany and Fascist Italy. And he became the supreme commander of its army, the *Azad Hind Fauj* (Free India Army) or the Indian National Army, which recruited around forty thousand men by 1945[51] and had a women's regiment named after the legendary Rani of Jhansi of 1857 fame (see chapter 7.5). The Provisional Government declared war on Great Britain and its chief ambition was to march—as an allied army with the Japanese—through Burma to Imphal (in Manipur) and then to Assam, where the Indian people were expected to join them in an open rebellion to liberate their mother-country. But the ill-fated Imphal campaign, which was finally launched on 8 March 1944 by Japan's Southern Army accompanied by two INA regiments, ended in a disaster. The reasons were many, as Joyce Lebra enumerates them: the lack of air power, breakdown in the chain of command, disruption of the supply line, the strength of Allied offensive, and finally for the INA, lack of cooperation from the Japanese. The retreat was even more devastating, finally ending the dream of liberating India through military campaign. But Bose still remained optimistic, thought of regrouping, and after Japanese surrender, contemplated seeking help from Soviet Russia. The Japanese agreed to provide him transport up to Manchuria from where he could travel to Russia. But on his way, on 18 August 1945 at Taihoku airport in Taiwan, he died in an air crash, which many Indians still believe never happened.[52]

But if INA's military campaign was over after a last valiant engagement at Mount Popa in Burma, its political impact on India was yet to unfold itself. After their surrender, the twenty thousand INA soldiers were interrogated and transported back to India. Those who appeared to have been persuaded or misled by Japanese or INA propaganda—classified as "Whites" and "Greys"—were either released or rehabilitated in the army. But a few of them at least—the most committed and categorised as "Blacks"—were to be court martialled. Not to try them would be to give indication of weakness; and to tolerate 'treason' would be to put the loyalty of the Indian army at risk. So altogether ten trials took place, and in the first and most celebrated one at Red Fort in Delhi, three officers—P.K. Sahgal, G.S. Dhillon and Shah Nawaz Khan—were charged of treason, murder and abetment of murder. The trial would take place in public, as this was expected to reveal the horrors that these INA men had perpetrated and that, the government hoped, would swerve public opinion against them. But as the events subsequently unfolded, the government, it seemed, had completely miscalculated the political fallout of the INA trials. As the press censorship was lifted after the war, the details of the INA campaign were revealed every day before the Indian public and these officers appeared as patriots of the highest order—not by any means traitors—and the demand for discontinuing the trials grew stronger by the day. The Congress leaders, many of them just released after long incarceration since the Quit India days, could hardly ignore this issue that so profoundly touched popular emotions. The election was round the corner and the INA trials could be an excellent issue. Subhas Bose might have been a renegade leader who had challenged the authority of the Congress leadership and their principles. But in death he was a martyred patriot whose memory could be an ideal tool for political mobilisation. So the AICC meeting in September 1945 decided to defend the accused in the INA trial—the "misguided patriots"—and announced the formation of a Defence Committee, consisting of some legal luminaries of the day, like Tej Bahadur Sapru, Bhulabhai Desai, Asaf Ali, and also Jawaharlal Nehru, donning the barrister's gown after about a quarter of a century. In the subsequent days, as the election campaign set in, Nehru and other Congress leaders addressed numerous public meetings with large gatherings. And there two issues figured prominently: one was the government excesses and the martyrs of 1942 and the other was INA trial.[53]

The government, however, remained firm. The first trial opened on 5 November and continued for two months, and in course of that time India erupted into "a mass upheaval", as Nehru later described it. "Never before in Indian history", he admitted, "had such unified sentiments been manifested by various divergent sections of the population."[54] There were many factors that led to this mass upsurge. The trial took place at Red Fort which appeared to be the most authentic symbol of British imperial domination, as here took place in 1858 the trial of Bahadur Shah II, the last Mughal emperor and the acclaimed leader of the 1857 revolt. Furthermore, as trial progressed, its reports appeared in the press, leading to more awareness and to some extent more emotionalisation of the sacrifices made by the INA soldiers. All political parties, like the Congress Socialists, Akali Dal, Unionist Party, Justice Party, Rashtriya Swayam Sevak Sangh, Hindu Mahasabha and even the Muslim League wanted the trials to be discontinued. Individual communists enthusiastically participated in the demonstrations, although their party vacillated in its response. And by a strange coincidence, the three accused belonged to three different religions: one Hindu, one Sikh and one Muslim! The demonstrations, therefore, showed signs of remarkable communal harmony. An INA week was celebrated between 5 and 11 November, while the INA Day was observed on 12 November in cities across the country. People from all walks of life participated in the campaign, attended protest meetings, donated money to the INA relief fund, closed shops and other commercial institutions and in some places refrained from celebrating diwali. And the movement touched even the remotest places like Coorg, Baluchistan and Assam.[55] Violence erupted first on 7 November when the police opened fire on the crowd at a protest demonstration in Madura. Then between 21 and 24 November, rioting broke out in various parts of the country, starting from Bose's own Calcutta. Here, first of all, American and British military establishments were attacked; but then the rioting took a general anti-British tone, with students clashing with the police and being joined later by the striking taxi drivers and tramway labourers. They exhibited unprecedented communal harmony, with the demonstrators flying simultaneously the Congress, League and Communist flags. Order could be restored after three days, with 33 people dead and 200 injured. The Calcutta riot was soon followed by similar demonstrations in Bombay,

Karachi, Patna, Allahabad, Banaras, Rawalpindi and other places, or in other words, all over the country.[56]

The government's determination now wavered. In the trial, the defence tried to argue that people fighting for freedom of their country could not be tried for treason. But despite that, they were found guilty as charged; but the commander-in-chief remitted their sentence and set them free on 3 January 1946. The three officers came out of the Red Fort to a hero's welcome at public meetings in Delhi and Lahore, that celebrated a moral victory against the British. But it was not all over yet. On 4 February, in another trial, Captain Abdur Rashid—who preferred to be defended by a Muslim League Defence Committee, rather than by the Congress[57]—was sentenced to seven years rigorous imprisonment. It sparked off another explosion in Calcutta between 11 and 13 February, this time called initially by the student wing of the Muslim League, but later joined by the members of the communist-led Student Federation and industrial workers. Once again demonstrations followed, with Congress, League and red flags flying simultaneously, and large meetings were organised, where League, Communist and Congress leaders addressed the crowd. A general anti-British sentiment pervaded the city, which was paralysed by transport strikes, industrial action and pitched street battles with British troops. Order was again restored after three days of brutal repression that had eighty-four people killed and three hundred injured. To a historian who participated in the demonstrations as a student leader, the situation looked like an "Almost Revolution". The fire soon spread to east Bengal and the spirit of revolt affected other parts of the country as well, as sympathetic protest demonstrations and strikes took place in practically all major cities of India.[58]

Since the middle of 1945 the British were expecting a mass upheaval in India any way. But what really perturbed them was the impact of the INA trials on the loyalty of the army, which in post-Quit India days was their only reliable apparatus of rule. General Auchinleck, the commander-in-chief, remitted the sentence of the three INA officers because, as he later explained to senior British officers, "any attempt to force the sentence would have led to chaos in the country at large and probably to mutiny and dissention in the army culminating in its dissolution."[59] The growing political consciousness among the army personnel during and after the war had already been a cause of concern for the authorities. What further contributed to it was the INA trial and the growing sympathy for the INA soldiers who were almost universally regarded as patriots, rather than "traitors". The members of the RIAF, as well as some other army personnel in various centres openly donated money to the INA relief fund and on some occasions attended protest rallies in full uniform. In January 1946, the RIAF men went on strike in support of their various grievances. But what really posed a real grave challenge to the Raj was the open mutiny in the Royal Indian Navy (RIN) in February 1946.

It all started in Bombay on 18 February when the naval ratings in HMIS Talwar went on hunger strike against bad food and racial discrimination. Soon the rebellion spread to other naval bases all over India and to some ships on the sea where sympathetic strikes took place. At its peak, seventy-eight ships, twenty shore establishments and twenty thousand ratings were involved. What was really remarkable was the extent of fraternisation between the naval ratings and common people that was visible during these few days in various cities of India—a phenomenon that had immense revolutionary potential. Bombay went on strike on 22 February in sympathy, and here public transport system was paralysed, roadblocks were raised, trains were burnt, shops and banks were closed and industrial workers went on strike. Here too the navy rebels used three flags simultaneously as they went round rampaging the city. A Maratha battalion was called in to bring peace to Bombay. By 25 February the city was quiet again, but by then 228 civilians were dead and 1,046 were injured. Similar hartals took place in Karachi on 23 February and in Madras on the 25th; in both cities several ratings and civilians died in police firing. Sympathetic, but less violent, one day strikes were also reported from Trichinopoly and Madurai; workers' strikes took place in Ahmedabad and Kanpur. The RIAF men and some army personnel also went on strike at different centres.[60] There was, in other words, enough reason for the government to be perturbed.

The RIN mutiny was, however, short lived, but it had dramatic psychological repercussions. Although it did not immediately lead to an open revolt in the Indian army, such a possibility could never be ruled out. An official inquiry commission later revealed that "majority of ratings [were] politically conscious" and were profoundly influenced by the INA propaganda and ideals.[61] The sympathetic strikes in the air force and army indicated very clearly that the Indian Army was no longer the same "sharp sword of repression" which the British could use as before, if a popular outburst of the 1942 proportions took place again. To what extent this revelation forced upon the British a change of policy in favour of transfer of power is debatable. For, the Congress, which could alone give leadership to such an upsurge, was not interested in the radical and violent potential of the happenings of 1945–46. To its leadership, the INA officers were patriots, but "misguided"; they could be taken back into the Congress, as Sardar Patel announced at a meeting in Calcutta, only if they "put their swords back into the scabbard".[62] When the RIN mutiny took place, socialists like Aruna Asaf Ali sympathised with the rebels; but Gandhi condemned the violence and Patel persuaded the ratings to surrender. To Patel the preferences were clear: "discipline in the Army cannot be tampered with.... We will want Army even in free India".[63] In other words, for Congress the days of struggle were over; it was now looking forward to its new career as the ruling party. For, after the war it was clear to everyone that the British would like to hand over power to Indians sooner rather than later. Leaders like Nehru were anticipating in late 1945 that "Britain would leave India within two to five years".[64] So it was time to negotiate for a peaceful transfer of power.

But if Congress was not prepared to risk another battle in 1945–46, the communists were. Not only did they participate actively in the urban riots in Calcutta and Bombay, where they had by now prepared a solid base among the industrial workers, they now organised some militant peasant movements in various parts of India, involving the poor peasants and sharecroppers. Ever since the Seventh World Congress of the Communist International in Moscow gave its verdict in 1935 in favour of a united front strategy in India, the Indian communists started functioning through the Congress. In Bengal, the "ex-detenus", once incarcerated for violent activities, started communist propaganda and sought to capture the Bengal Provincial Kisan Sabha (BPKS). Through this organisation they started mobilising the peasantry in northern, eastern and central Bengal around radical agrarian issues such as payment of tolls at village marts collected by the Union Boards, illegal abwabs (taxes) imposed by the zamindars, abolition of the zamindari system, and finally the sharecroppers' demand for a two-thirds share of the produce.[65] By 1940 the BPKS was almost totally under the control of the communists, and its membership had shot to thirty-four thousand from mere eleven thousand three years ago. Communist activities and kisan mobilisation picked up further momentum once the ban on the CPI was lifted in 1942. Although the Quit India movement temporarily stole the wind off its sails, the popularity of the BPKS does not seem to have been affected at all; by May 1943 it had 124,872 members.[66]

One reason for the popularity of the communists by mid-1943 and subsequently, was perhaps the aftermath of the devastating Bengal famine of that year. Amartya Sen is "inclined to pick a figure around 3 million as the death toll of the Bengal famine".[67] Paul Greenough would put it somewhere "between 3.5 and 3.8 million",[68] while the more recent estimate of Tim Dyson and Arup Maharatna puts it at 2.1 million as the figure for excess deaths caused by the Bengal famine.[69] Even if we go by the most conservative estimate, the famine was a catastrophe of such magnitude that history of the subcontinent had never known before. Bengali public opinion was unanimous that it was a "man-made" famine. There were a few natural factors of course, like a devastating cyclone in Midnapur; but that alone did not cause the famine. As Greenough points out, the per capita entitlement of rice was gradually going down in Bengal over a long period. In 1943 it reached a crisis point due to multiple factors, such as the breakdown of an already vulnerable rice marketing system, which had for long remained completely unsupervised and uncontrolled, leading to hoarding and speculation. What added to this were a government procurement policy that prioritised official and military requirements over local needs of subsistence and the wartime stresses, like the 'denial policy', the refugee influx from Burma into Chittagong and the disappearance of imported rice from Burma. The relief operations failed miserably; while the government tried to save Calcutta at the expense of the countryside, the Marwari Relief Committee and the Hindu Mahasabha relief committees targeted only the middle classes. The peasantry, the worst sufferers of the famine, had nowhere to go. It is true that this unusual scarcity of food caused by the exorbitant price of rice—that shot beyond the reach of the ordinary people—did not cause any food riot in Bengal; instead, the violence, as Greenough argues, turned "inward" and "downward" destroying all conventional relationships of patronage and dependency.[70]

The communists responded adequately to the food situation. They held meetings at various parts of Bengal criticising the government's food policy and undertook—through BPKS and Mahila Samitis—extensive relief work in the villages of the presidency and Rajshahi divisions, i.e., in north and central Bengal, where they became instantly popular among the poor peasants and sharecroppers. In 1943 the BPKS membership reached 83,160—the highest among all the provincial Kisan Sabhas in the country.[71] Although they preferred a conciliatory policy at this stage—under the People's War strategy—the involvement of poor peasants often got BPKS engaged in clashes with zamindars, grain dealers and other vested interests. This gradually prepared the ground for the Tebhaga movement in support of a longstanding demand of the sharecroppers for two-thirds share of the produce, instead of the customary half. At the end of the war, in view of the rising popular unrest, the Communist Party too started shifting grounds and moved towards a more belligerent line. In a resolution adopted on 5 August 1946 it declared that the "Indian freedom movement has entered its final phase". So what was needed was a "joint front of all patriotic parties" to stage a "national democratic revolution" that would ensure "all power to the people".[72] Against this backdrop, in September 1946 the BPKS decided to launch the Tebhaga movement and soon it spread to a wide region where peasants harvested the paddy and took it to their own *khamar* (storehouse) and then invited the landlords to come and take their one-third share. Although north Bengal districts were the worst affected by this sharecroppers' agitation, contrary to popular notion, as Adrienne Cooper has shown, Tebhaga movement touched a wider region, covering almost every district in eastern, central and western Bengal. Here the peasants carved out their tebhaga *elaka* or liberated zones, where they instituted alternative administrations and arbitration courts. The Muslim League ministry, then in power in Bengal, responded by proposing a Bargadar Bill in January 1947, apparently conceding the sharecroppers' demand; but it was soon dropped because of opposition from within the Muslim League and from the Congress. From February the movement began to spread rapidly, provoking an angry response from the government. The peasants bravely fought police repression and resisted landlords' lathiyals, but soon it became such an uneven battle that the BPKS decided to retreat, although in some pockets peasants resolved to continue without their leaders.[73]

One may observe in this peasant movement some of the earlier features like the strength of community ties that predominated previous peasant struggles (noted in chapters 3.2 and 4.2). The sharecroppers belonged mainly to tribal and dalit groups, such as the Rajbansis and Namasudras, and the BPKS had built its organisation on the foundation of such community structures.[74] Sugata Bose has, however, noticed in this movement of the late colonial period greater class consciousness, concerns about individual rights and preponderance of economic issues that often tended to fracture older community loyalties, as Rajbansi and Muslim sharecroppers often did not feel inhibited in attacking Rajbansi and Muslim jotedars.[75] But it was not a revolutionary movement either, claiming land for the tillers, which remained only a distant goal to cement a delicate alliance between various classes of peasantry. It was a partial movement that gave precedence to the sharecropper's demand. It was therefore participated by the sharecroppers and poor peasants in large numbers, supported and sometimes led by the middle peasants. Its impact on Bengal agrarian relations was far reaching. But above all, it showed that in a political environment already vitiated by communal riots, the peasants were still capable of aligning across the religious divide.[76] However, it was also true that the same peasants on other occasions participated in communal riots. Class and community were thus so intimately intertwined in peasant consciousness and identity that it is analytically difficult to separate one from the other. Such elements of continuity suggest that these peasant responses were more conjunctural—instigated by their immediate grievances, ideological mediation and historical environment—rather than indicative of any sharp turn in colonial peasant history. And this is a pattern that we will observe in other communist-led mass movements as well.

In western India, the Maharashtra Kisan Sabha took up the cause of the Varli tribal agricultural labourers in Umbargaon and Dahanu talukas in Thana district. Their main grievance was against forced labour (*veth*) performed for the landowners and moneylenders at a time when prices of daily necessities had been pushed up by war. In 1944 the Varlis of Umbargaon on their own staged an unsuccessful strike to demand a minimum daily wage of twelve annas (1 rupee = 16 annas) for agricultural work such as grass cutting and tree felling. The strike failed, but hereafter the Kisan Sabha started organising the Varlis and at a conference in May 1945 decided to launch a more prolonged movement for the abolition of forced labour and claiming a minimum wage of twelve annas. The movement spread quickly in the Umbargaon taluka where forced labour was stopped and debt-serfs were released, and then it spread to the nearby Dahanu taluka with similar results. In October, as the grass-cutting season approached, the movement entered its second phase when the Kisan Sabha called for a strike to claim a minimum wage of Rs 2–8 for cutting five hundred lbs of grass. The landlords responded with intimidation, court cases and appeals to district administration for help. In one incident on October 11, when the police opened fire on a peaceful gathering, five Varlis died defending the red flag, which had by now become the symbol of their unity and an icon of their liberation. The strike was nearly complete and forced many landlords—though not all—to yield to their demands. But that did not end the Varli's struggle. In October 1946 the movement was again renewed, this time with an additional demand for a minimum daily rate of Rs 1–4 for forest work, which the timber companies were not prepared to offer. The near total peaceful strike continued for over a month and finally on 10 November in an agreement with the Kisan Sabha, the Timber Merchants Association agreed to pay the minimum wage.[77] The movement thus ended in a great victory for the tribal Varlis who were mobilised by the Kisan Sabha around specific economic grievances. This did not mean however that their community identity played a less important role, as the red flag had now acquired a magical significance to become a new iconic representation of their tribal solidarity.

In the south, the communists entrenched themselves and established their undisputed sway over peasant unions in the villages of north Malabar during the early forties, when the region suffered from acute food shortages and near famine conditions. During the People's War phase they preferred a conciliatory policy, sought to renegotiate the agrarian relations and tried to construct what Dilip Menon has called a "conjunctural community of landowners and cultivators".[78] But this fragile truce broke down in 1946 in a context of postwar stress and scarcity, as the landlords became more aggressive in collecting rent in kind, evicting defaulting peasants and asserting their rights over wastelands and forests. The Kerala Communist Party also allowed a more belligerent line for the peasants at this stage. It was never that violent as in Bengal, but throughout the 1946–47 period peasant volunteers here fought with the landlords and the Malabar Special Police to prevent collection of rents at times of scarcity, to stop the sale of rice in open markets for excess profits and to bring wastelands under cultivation.[79]

However, it was further south in the princely state of Travancore that the most violent popular upsurge led by the communists took place in October1946 at Punnapra-Vayalar near the industrial city of Alleppye. Here the growth of coir industry after World War One saw the emergence of a large working class and their unionisation under communist leadership by mid-1940s. In 1946, the government of the princely state, in view of the impending withdrawal of the British, started working towards asserting the independence of Travancore by imposing an undemocratic constitution, allegedly based on "American model". While the local Congress seemed to be conciliatory to the Diwan, the Communist Party decided to make it an issue. As this situation coincided with food scarcity and a lockout in the coir industry, the workers were exasperated, and were joined by agricultural workers, boatmen, fishermen and various other lower occupational groups. On 24 October they attacked a police outpost at Punnapra, killing three policemen and thereafter violence spread rapidly to other areas. The government retaliated the next day, when the military attacked and killed 150 communist volunteers at a camp in Vayalar and another 120 at Menessary. The movement then died down quickly, as the communist leaders went underground and repression was unleashed. Robin Jeffrey has argued that the "revolt had nothing at all to do with communal or caste issues" and was a "product of an organised, disciplined working class". But the fact remains that about 80 per cent of the participants belonged to the low ranking—but socially organised—Ezhava caste, and this certainly provided an element of solidarity among the ranks of the rebels.[80]

It was in Hyderabad—another southern princely state—that the most prolonged and radical peasant movement under communist leadership took place from mid-1946. Here, agrarian relations under the autocratic rule of the Nizam resembled, in the words of D.N. Dhanagare, "a page from medieval, feudal history", where the jagirdars, *pattadars* (landowners), deshmukhs and deshpandes (revenue collectors) held complete sway over the rural society.[81] Further to that, commercialisation of agriculture and introduction of cash crops brought in the *sahukars* (moneylenders), growing land alienation and increasing number of agricultural labourers. Particularly in the 1940s, the falling prices continuing from the depression years affected the small landowning pattadars and rich peasants, while poorer peasants resented the oppressive practice of forced labour or *vetti* and food scarcity of the postwar period. This created the groundwork for an armed peasant insurrection, which took place in Telangana, i.e., the eight Telugu speaking districts of Hyderabad, with the nearby Andhra delta of the British ruled Madras Presidency providing a secure base. Here the communists had started mobilising the peasantry since mid-1930s through certain front organisations, such as the Andhra Conference in Telengana and the Andhra Mahasabha in the delta region. The movement started in Nalgonda district in July 1946 with an attack on a notorious landlord and within a month it spread to a wide region in Nalgonda, Warangal and Khammam districts. The demands of the movement were many, as they were meant to forge a class alliance between the Kamma and Reddy small pattadar and rich peasant leadership of the communist movement, and the poorer untouchable Mala, Madiga and tribal peasants and landless labourers who were gradually being drawn into the movement. These included demands for wage increases and abolition of vetti, illegal exactions, eviction and the recently imposed grain levy. The movement at this initial stage was, however, less organised and more "spasmodic" in nature.[82]

In June 1947 the Nizam announced that after the withdrawal of the British, Hyderabad would maintain its independence and would not join the Indian union. As this meant the continuation of the anti-quated medieval rule, the local Congress decided to launch a satyagraha, and the communists, despite their reservations, joined in and hoisted national flags in various parts of the state. But the alliance soon broke down, as the movement was not going anywhere, while the Majlis Ittehad-ul-Musalmin, an outfit of the minority Muslim aristocracy, now recruited its own armed bands, called the *Razakars*, and with the endorsement of the Nizam unleashed a reign of terror in the Telangana countryside. To resist repression, the peasants under communist leadership now began to form volunteer guerrilla squads called *dalams*, began to seize wastelands and surplus land from big landlords and redistribute them, and formed village republics or 'soviets' in areas considered to be liberated zones. When on 13 September 1948 the Indian army entered Hyderabad, it meant the end of the Nizam's dream of independence and his army, police and the Razakar bands surrendered immediately. But this did not mark the end of the Telangana insurrection, which now entered its second phase, as the Communist Party, despite some opposition from within, decided to continue the struggle, which was claimed to be heralding a People's Democratic Revolution in India. The Indian army also launched its "Police Action" against the communist guerrillas and the uneven battle continued until October 1951, when the movement was formally withdrawn.[83]

The Telangana movement was perhaps the most widespread, most intense and most organised peasant movement in the history of colonial India. According to one estimate, the movement involved peasants in "about 3,000 villages, covering roughly a population of 3 million in an area of about 16,000 square miles." It mobilised ten thousand village squad members and about two thousand guerrilla squads, and managed to redistribute about 1 million acres of land. About four thousand communist cadres or peasant volunteers were killed, while about ten thousand were jailed and many more thousands harassed and tortured.[84] This sheer scale also makes it clear that there were more complexities in the movement than these statistics apparently suggest. Dhanagare has shown that it was based on very broad class and communal alliances, which often proved vulnerable. The class alliance began to flounder after the seizure of land began and the land-ceiling question was settled in favour of rich peasants.[85] Also in occupying land, there was more enthusiasm about commons land, wasteland and forests, than about the surplus land of the landlords. Although dalit groups formed a sizeable section of the participants, their role, as Gail Omvedt asserts, was mainly "a subordinate one", as the communist leadership almost routinely ignored the issues of caste oppression and untouchability.[86]

In all these peasant movements organised by the communists and Kisan Sabhas, there is evidence of autonomous peasant initiative, either in taking action before the middle-class leaders actually arrived or in defying the latter's cautionary directives.[87] What these conflagrations, therefore, indicate is the existence of widespread popular discontent among all classes of peasantry in postwar India, which the Communist Party decided to channelise, albeit in certain specific regions. And if the peasantry was restive, the industrial working classes had become restless too, because of the inflation and post-war retrenchment. The wave of strikes in Indian industries reached its peak in 1946 when more than 12 million man-days were lost and this figure was more than three times higher than in the previous year. And apart from industries, workers struck at the Post and Telegraph Department and in the South Indian Railways and North-Western Railways.[88] This general environment of disquiet did not, however, lead to any nationwide mass movement. But that does not mean that all those moments of rebellion were meaningless or those hundreds of lives were sacrificed in vain. After the war it was clear that the British were going to leave India. But that decision, one may argue, was to a large extent prompted by this environment of inquietude. There was a growing realisation that now it would be more difficult to deal with a mass upsurge or to hang on to the empire by force, as disaffection had also trickled into the army ranks. Hence there was a greater urge to negotiate for an ordered transfer of power, so that India might at least remain within the Commonwealth and the British economic and strategic interests were protected. We may now turn to that story.

8.3 TOWARDS FREEDOM WITH PARTITION

The historiography of decolonisation in India, as Howard Brasted and Carl Bridge point out, is polarised on the question whether freedom was seized by the Indians or power was transferred voluntarily by the British "as an act of positive statesmanship".[89] That British decision to quit was partly based on the ungovernability of India in the 1940s is beyond doubt. It is difficult to argue that there was a consistent policy of devolution of power, which came to its logical culmination in August 1947 through the granting of self-government in India. We have already seen (chapter 6) that the constitutional arrangements of 1919 and 1935 were meant to secure British hegemony over the Indian empire through consolidation of control over the central government, rather than to make Indians masters of their own affairs. Even in the 1950s the British foreign office and colonial office were contemplating ways and means of protecting economic and strategic interests in Asia and Africa against the recent upsurge of nationalism. There was, however, also a sad acknowledgement that in view of the rising tide of political resistance it would be impossible to reverse the constitutional process that inevitably gravitated towards the demission of empire.[90] So it is unlikely that the British left India voluntarily in 1947 in pursuance of a well-designed policy of decolonisation or that freedom was a "gift" to the Indians.

When World War Two broke out, India was considered to be the most important strategic point for the defence of the British empire in the Middle East and Southeast Asia. So London's major concern at that time was to mobilise Indian agricultural, industrial and manpower resources to war efforts and for that reason to maintain a strong grip over Indian affairs and not to concede anything that might signal British weakness. The rapid advance of the Germans in the European front made Indian cooperation in war efforts even more crucial; but on the other hand, in May 1940 Winston Churchill became the prime minister in a coalition War Cabinet and he was a patriotic champion of the empire. During this period, as R.J. Moore has argued, British policy towards India was caught between two polarities: "Churchillian negativism and Crippsian constructiveness".[91] Churchill represented the perspective of the Conservative reformer who acknowledged the need for granting self-government to India at some stage in future, but preferred to postpone it as long as possible.[92] Sir Stafford Cripps, on the other hand, represented on the War Cabinet Britain's Labour Party, which was committed to Indian independence for a long time. In a meeting with Nehru in 1938 in London, he and Clement Attlee had agreed on the idea of an Indian Constituent Assembly, elected on the basis of universal adult franchise, drafting its own constitution.[93] But when the question came to offering some tangible constitutional concessions to Indian political opinion in 1940, Churchill dominated the show and edited the final version of the announcement in such a way that all major concessions were dropped.[94] It was no wonder that the 'August offer' (1940) by Viceroy Linlithgow could not satisfy the Congress.

But apart from Labour colleagues, Churchill had other problems too, as some of his allies did not like the idea of empire. Particularly hostile was the American public opinion, and it could not be easily cast aside, as since the Lend Lease Act Britain had become too dependent on the United States for conducting the war. So Franklin Roosevelt finally had him to sign the Atlantic Charter in August 1941, which acknowledged the right to self-determination for all people of the world. But it was open to interpretation and in Churchill's conservative interpretation, it was meant only to be applicable to the European people subjugated by Nazi Germany, and not to their colonial subjects. A few months later, he announced arrogantly that he had "not become His Majesty's Chief Minister in order to preside over the liquidation of the British Empire".[95]

The rapid progress of the Japanese army in Southeast Asia, however, shattered British prestige and dented its self-confidence. Indian collaboration was now more urgently needed, and the allies like Roosevelt and Chiang Kai Shek wanted the Indian problem to be sorted out on a priority basis. The Labour members in the cabinet therefore insisted that something had to be done about India in the line of their 1938 agreement. It was decided that Cripps would go to India to negotiate with the Indian political parties on a declaration that very much resembled the previous August offer. Cripps Mission which came to India in March–April 1942 promised Indian self-determination after the war; India then might opt out of the Commonwealth, but had to enter into a treaty to safeguard British economic and strategic interests; there would be an elected Constituent Assembly to which the princes could also nominate their representatives; the provinces could secede from the union if they so wished and this gave tacit recognition to Muslim League's Pakistan demand; and more immediately, Indians would become members of the viceroy's executive council in order to prop up war efforts. Congress rejected the proposal, as it did not want to shoulder responsibilities without real power and also wanted some control over defence. Cripps could not persuade them, as he did not get either the cooperation of the viceroy or the support of his prime minister.[96] It is also argued that Churchill did not sincerely wish the Mission to succeed; he merely wanted to show the world—and more particularly, his allies—that something was being done to resolve the Indian political imbroglio.[97] The failure of the Mission, as we have noted earlier, prepared the ground for a total confrontation between the Raj and the Congress. But although a failure, the Mission signified an important shift in British policy. It announced Indian independence after the war, within or outside the empire, to be the ultimate goal of British policy; and that unity would no longer be a precondition for independence.[98] It was on these two essential conceptual pillars that post-war British policy of decolonisation was to evolve, although in 1942 there was not yet any political consensus on them.

During the last years of World War Two and immediately after it the global political situation as well as the objective conditions in India changed so drastically that they gravitated almost inevitably towards India's independence. "Whatever pre-war tendencies may have existed", argues John Darwin, "the pattern of post-war decolonization was profoundly influenced by the course and impact of the war."[99] In India, the Quit India movement and its brutal repression ruptured the relationship between the Raj and the Congress and destroyed whatever goodwill the former might have had among the majority of Indian population. The Bengal famine and the wartime food scarcity in other regions further damaged the moral foundations of the Raj. The subsequent agitation surrounding the INA trials showed that no resolution of the Indian question was possible without the participation of the Congress, which could neither be sidelined nor coerced into silence. Meanwhile, in global politics too the balance of power had tilted decisively in favour of the United States. Britain emerged victorious from the war with its empire in tact. But although there was no dearth of desire to maintain the old imperial system of power, it simply did not have—being dependent on a United States loan—the financial capacity to shoulder the responsibilities of a world power. The interest of Franklin Roosevelt in India's national movement, on the other hand, remained as a constant pressure on an otherwise intransigent Churchill. And after the war, worldwide anti-imperialist sentiments, generated by the very struggle against Nazi Germany and enshrined in the United Nations Charter and its strict trusteeship rules, made empire morally indefensible.

Britain's imperial relations with India had also undergone profound changes in the meanwhile. India performed three imperial functions: it provided a market for British exports, was a remitter of sterling and a source of military strength to protect the British empire. But since the 1930s London had little control over Indian monetary and fiscal policies: protective tariffs had already been imposed and wartime procurement policies led to an evaporation of India's sterling debt, replaced by Britain's rupee debt to India. India's relevance to imperial defence was also coming under close scrutiny. India was traditionally considered to be a strategic asset for maintaining control over Britain's world empire, particularly in the Middle East and Southeast Asia. But it was now doubtful as to how long that would be viable, as already there was stiff opposition against the use of British Indian Army for post-war restoration of the Dutch and French empires in Indonesia and Indochina. Military expenditure had been another key issue. In 1938 it was found that the Indian army needed modernisation, and the government of India was unable to bear the expenditure. So under an agreement in November 1939 it was decided that the bulk of this expenditure would be borne by the British government, which would also bear the cost of the Indian army fighting on foreign soil outside India. As the war broke out, Indian army had to be deployed in the Southeast Asian front and it became increasingly difficult to transfer cash during wartime; as a result, Britain's debt to India started piling up, so that by 1946 Britain owed India more than £1,300 million, almost one-fifth of Britain's GNP.[100] But this did not mean that Britain decided to leave because, as Tomlinson has surmised, India was no longer considered to be one of her "imperial assets" and was regarded as "a potential or actual source of weakness".[101] Even during the war there was optimism at the Whitehall that the sterling balances would be an advantage, rather than problem, for it would serve as pent up demand for British export industries and could be used to supply capital goods to India, which would boost employment during the crucial post-war reconstruction period in Britain.[102] One may further point out, that this financial situation arose because of the increasing nationalist pressure for more resources and budgetary allocation for the development of their own country, rather than for servicing the empire. If the current situation could reveal anything at all to the imperial managers, it was that India had now certainly become less manageable as a colony—that henceforth it could only be kept under control at a heavy cost, both financial and military. Britain's interest in India could now best be safeguarded by treating it as an independent nation, through informal rather than formal control. The massive Labour victory in July 1945 created a congenial atmosphere for such a political change.

Much indeed has been said about the significance of Labour victory in the history of Indian independence. B.N. Pandey, for example, has argued that the Labour Party, particularly the new Prime Minister Clement Attlee, the new Secretary of State Lord Pethick-Lawrence and Stafford Cripps, now the President of the Board of Trade, were long committed to the cause of Indian independence. Now with decisive majority in the House of Commons the time arrived for them to redeem their pledge.[103] Contemporary observers like V. P. Menon went further to suggest that a Labour victory was indeed the "main factor responsible for the early transfer of power."[104] More recently, Howard Brasted and Carl Bridge have described "15 August 1947" as "Labour's Parting Gift to India".[105] Other historians, however, are more skeptical about post-war Labour attitude to empire in general and to India in particular. R.J. Moore, for example, has talked about Labour's "imperialist inheritance" which proved to be an "impediment" in fulfilling its promise of Indian self-government.[106] John Darwin has shown that although Labour had been committed to Indian independence since its 1935 election manifesto, the attitudes of Attlee and Cripps had undergone an "ideological sea change" during the war. And after the war the new Labour government "turned out to be remarkably unradical in its approach to foreign, defence and imperial policy.", as no one was averse to having an empire or would dislike the glory of being a great power.[107] India in this context seemed much too significant for defence and economic interests to warrant an early withdrawal, and powerful interest groups pulled the government in that direction. So what Labour government proposed, as we shall soon find out, was nothing radical that went beyond what was offered by the Cripps Mission in 1942. What was dominant now in British imperial thinking vis-à-vis India was the need for a reorientation of the relationship in an orderly way within the structures of dominion status and the Commonwealth of Nations—which in a way had become a new expression for empire—so that it could serve as a model for other colonies in Asia and Africa and could safeguard long-term British interests and influence, if not power.[108] Subsequent developments towards a rapid withdrawal were only in response to the political situation in India, which considerably narrowed down the available options.

The major obstacle to an unruffled transfer of power in India was the Hindu–Muslim divide, which by now had become quite apparent at the negotiating fora, despite some signs of harmony at the barricade lines. The 1940 Lahore resolution had elevated the Indian Muslims from the status of a 'minority' to that of a 'nation' and subsequent developments projected M.A. Jinnah as their "Sole Spokesman" (see chapter 7.1). Recognition of this national identity of the Muslims and their right to self-determination, as well as 'parity' of representation with the Hindus at the centre now became the non-negotiable minimum demands for Jinnah and the Muslim League. Jinnah rejected the Cripps proposal precisely because it did not recognise the Muslims' right to self-determination and equality as a nation; just the right for the provinces to secede from the Indian union was not enough.[109] As the Congress chose the collision course and launched the Quit India movement, the British found useful allies in Jinnah and the Muslim League, as Churchill openly described "Hindu-Muslim feud as the bulwark of British rule in India".[110] Between 1942 and 1943 League ministries were installed in Assam, Sind, Bengal and the North-West Frontier Province through active maneuvring by the British bureaucracy. The demand for Pakistan was, however, still not well defined at this stage. At the constitutional front, what Jinnah wanted was autonomy for the Muslim majority provinces in a loose federal structure, with Hindu-Muslim parity at the central government, the minority Hindus in the Muslim majority provinces serving as security for the Muslim minorities elsewhere.

The Congress tried to meet Muslim demands through top level political negotiations. In April 1944 C. Rajagopalachari proposed a solution: a post-war commission would be formed to demarcate the contiguous districts where the Muslims were in absolute majority, and there a plebiscite of the adult population would decide whether they would prefer Pakistan; in case of a partition there would be a mutual agreement to run certain essential services, like defence or communication; the border districts could choose to join either of the two sovereign states; the implementation of the scheme would wait till after full transfer of power. In July 1944 Gandhi proposed talks with Jinnah on the basis of the 'Rajaji formula', which indeed amounted to an acceptance of Pakistan demand. But Jinnah did not agree to this proposal and Gandhi–Jinnah talks in September 1944 broke down. In Gandhi's view, the talks failed because of fundamental differences in perspectives: while he looked at separation as within the family and therefore preferred to retain some elements of partnership, Jinnah wanted complete dissolution with sovereignty.[111] It is difficult to tell, however, whether Gandhi's perception was true or Jinnah at this stage was not contemplating partition, but was fighting for his principal demand for the recognition of parity between Hindus and Muslims as two equal nations, whatever their numbers might have been.

This issue surfaced again in June 1945 when Churchill permitted Wavell—the previous commander-in-chief who had in 1943 replaced Linlithgow as the new viceroy—to start negotiations with the Indian leaders. Wavell had a clear understanding that "India after the war will become a running sore which will sap the strength of the British empire". India would be ungovernable by force, because a policy of ruthless repression would not be acceptable to the British public. So "some imaginative and constructive move" needed to be taken immediately, in order "to retain India as a willing member of the British Commonwealth".[112] During his visit to London in March 1945 he finally convinced Churchill of the desirability of a Congress-League coalition government in India as a preemptive measure to forestall the political crisis he predicted after the war. He, therefore, convened a conference at Simla to talk about the formation of an entirely Indian executive council, with the viceroy and commander-in-chief as the only British members. Caste Hindus and Muslims would have equal representation, while the Scheduled Castes would also be separately represented; and doors would be open for discussion of a new constitution. But the Simla conference of 25 June–14 July 1945 crashed on the rock of Jinnah's demand for parity. He claimed for Muslim League an exclusive right to nominate all the Muslim members of the cabinet. Congress refused to accept it, for that would amount to an admission that Congress was a party only of the caste Hindus. Ironically, at that time, Maulana Abul Kalam Azad was the Congress president! Wavell called off the meeting, as a coalition government without the League would not work.

Ayesha Jalal has argued that at no point between 1940 and the arrival of the Cabinet Mission in 1946 did either Jinnah or Muslim League ever coherently define the Pakistan demand.[113] But it was this very vagueness of the demand that made it an excellent instrument for a Muslim mass mobilisation campaign in the 1940s, the primary objective of which was to construct a Muslim national identity transcending class and regional barriers. In addition to its traditional constituency, i.e., the landed aristocracy, Muslim politics during this period began to attract support from a cross-section of Muslim population, particularly from professionals and business groups for whom a separate state of Pakistan would mean elimination of Hindu competition. And to this was added the political support of the leading ulama, pirs and maulavis who lent this campaign a religious legitimacy.[114] Muslim politics at a national level was now being institutionalised and Jinnah gradually emerged as its authoritative leader, establishing his control over the provincial branches of the League. Those provincial groups or leaders, who did not toe his line, like A.K. Fazlul Huq and his Krishak Praja Party (KPP) in Bengal or Sir Sikander Hyat Khan and his Unionist Party in Punjab, were systematically pulled down and politically marginalised. Both Huq and Khan were censored in July 1941 when they agreed to join—without Jinnah's approval—the Viceroy's National Defence Council, which in terms of its membership structure did not recognise the Muslim claim of parity.[115] During the closing years of the war, both the KPP and the Unionist Party were gradually shoved out of the political centrestage in the Muslim majority provinces of Bengal and Punjab where Pakistan demand became an ideological rallying symbol that helped overcome the various fissures within a heterogeneous Muslim community.

To get to the details of the Bengal story first, Fazlul Huq and his KPP had thrown here a major challenge to the Muslim League in the 1937 election; but soon after the election, they came to terms with the League by forming a coalition government with them. Huq soon began to lose popularity, as he gravitated more towards zamindar and rich peasant interests and reneged on a number of election promises given to the tenant and poor peasant constituencies of the KPP. He joined the League in 1937 and was given the honour of introducing the Lahore Resolution in 1940. But he never fully endorsed Jinnah's politics and in 1941, when reprimanded by him, Huq resigned both from the National Defence Council and from the Muslim League, with a stinging letter of complaint against the authoritarian leadership style of Jinnah. Although he later retracted his steps, his relationship with the Bengal League members remained strained, particularly when later that year he formed a coalition government with the Hindu Mahasabha, with Shyama Prasad Mukherjee as the co-leader. This Progressive Coalition ministry was ultimately toppled in March 1943 with the active connivance of the Bengal Governor and a Muslim League ministry was then installed under the leadership of Khwaza Nazimuddin. This boosted League's image, local branches of the Muslim League were opened throughout Bengal and a mass mobilisation campaign was launched.[116] This campaign was however more symbolic and emotional than programmatic. 'Pakistan' was presented as "a peasant utopia" which would bring in liberation for the Muslim peasantry from the hands of the Hindu zamindars and moneylenders. As a result, by the mid-1940s, Pakistan as an ideological symbol of Muslim solidarity gained almost universal acceptance among the Muslim peasants.[117] Abul Hashim, the Bengal League leader travelled extensively throughout east Bengal countryside campaigning for Pakistan and his draft manifesto, that outlined the moral, economic and political objectives of the movement, also appealed to the Muslim middle classes, particularly the students. The Nazimuddin ministry had to resign in March 1945; but by then the Muslim League in Bengal had emerged as the only mass based political party of the Muslims.[118] This meant a virtual political death of the KPP, many of its younger progressive members having already joined the League, which by now had become, to quote Taj Hashmi, "everything to everybody".[119] This popularity was translated into a massive election victory in 1946, with the League winning 93 per cent of Muslim votes in the province and 119 of the 250 seats in the assembly. This was the inevitable result of an election campaign that had been turned into "a religious crusade", as the Congress President Maulana Azad later complained.[120]

In Punjab the structure of politics was sharply divided along rural-urban lines; while the Unionist Party held sway over rural politics, the Muslim League acquired a base among the urban Muslims. But the Unionist Party was in control, as Punjab landowners accounted for 60 per cent of its much restricted electorate, organised along agricultural 'tribal' constituencies.[121] The Unionists after the 1937 election formed a coalition ministry in Punjab with Sir Sikander Hyat Khan as the premier. But Sikander soon came to terms with Jinnah through what is called the Jinnah–Sikander Pact of 1937. Although the alliance was full of tensions, this gave the Unionists some sort of legitimacy among the Punjabi Muslim population, while Jinnah found a springboard to further his mission to project Muslim League as the centre of South Asian Muslim politics. Sikander also contributed to the organisation of the 1940 Lahore conference and to the drafting of the resolution. But he never fully accepted 'Pakistan' as a separatist demand. "If Pakistan means unalloyed Muslim raj in the Punjab", he announced in the Punjab Assembly in March 1941, "then I will have nothing to do with it".[122] But Sikander died suddenly in December 1942 and his mantle fell on relatively inexperienced Malik Khizr Hyat Khan Tiwana. Jinnah continuously pressurised him for more and more political leverage, first to form a Muslim League Assembly Party and then to rename the coalition government as "Muslim League Coalition Ministry". When Khizr refused to oblige and stood his ground, he was expelled from the Muslim League in April 1944.[123] Hereafter, Jinnah launched a well orchestrated mass campaign to popularise the idea of Pakistan in rural Punjab, with the help of some of the disgruntled elements in the Unionist Party, the young enthusiasts of the Punjab Muslim Students Federation and the *sajjad nishin*s (custodians of *sufi* shrines) who were now pressed into the political service of Islam. He even befriended the Communist Party, which supported the Pakistan demand. When the *pir*s with their huge rural influence, issued *fatwa*s, support for Pakistan became an individual religious responsibility of every Muslim. As the election of 1946 approached, the entire power structure of the Punjabi Muslim community—from the rural magnates and the landowning *jaildar-lambardar* class which previously supported the Unionist Party to the ordinary Muslim peasants in western Punjab—all drifted towards the Muslim League. The wartime scarcity and food procurement policy also contributed to this groundswell.[124]

If the League undercut the Unionist support base in the west, the Congress did the same in east Punjab; the Akalis mobilised too. So in the election of 1946, the Unionist Party got just 18 of the 175 seats in the Punjab Assembly; Congress got 51, the Akalis 22 and the Muslim League 75, almost sweeping the rural Muslim constituencies. But this did not immediately mean the demise of the Unionist Party, as Khizr now cobbled together another coalition ministry with the Congress and the Akalis—much to the chagrin of the Muslim League.[125] However, although still kept away from power, the election results for Muslim League certainly signalled a popular acceptance of Pakistan as a religious definition of state and community by the Punjabi Muslims. The Muslim League also did reasonably well in the election in the other Muslim majority province of Sind and in the whole of India it got 74.7 per cent of votes in the Muslim constituencies.[126] Although the electorate was heavily restricted (about 10 per cent of the population), this was interpreted as a popular mandate for Pakistan. An unfettered Hindu raj or Pakistan, Jinnah had announced in an election meeting: "That is the only choice and only issue before us".[127] The League, claims Anita Inder Singh, had thus "presented the elections as a plebiscite for Pakistan"[128] and the victory certainly made it the only constitutionally legitimated representative of the Indian Muslims—the centre of the South Asian Muslim political universe, as Jinnah had dreamed of it. The election of 1946 also brought a popular mandate for Congress, which won majorities in every province except Bengal, Sind and Punjab, winning 80.9 per cent of votes in the general constituencies. For Congress too the issue was singular: "only one thing counts", announced its election manifesto, "the freedom and independence of our motherland, from which all other freedoms will flow to our people".[129]

These election results also marginalised all other non-Muslim political parties, like the Communist Party winning only eight seats, the Hindu Mahasabha with only three seats and Dr Ambedkar's All India Scheduled Castes Federation bagging just two of the 151 seats reserved for such castes. This was undoubtedly the outcome of the wave of patriotism generated by the Quit India movement, from which Congress had emerged with unprecedented legitimacy as the representative of the Indian political nation. And then it successfully tied up its election campaign with the INA agitation, a strategy in which S. Gopal has smelled "a touch of escapism".[130] But it was a movement that attracted almost universal approbation of all sections of the Indian population and by supporting it Congress remained at the forefront of a situation that created immense possibilities for the future of India. Although it is difficult to establish any direct link between the INA agitation, the subsequent naval mutiny and the political turmoil they generated with any immediate and perceptible change in imperial policy,[131] it is quite probable, as P.S. Gupta has surmised, that the situation, particularly the more mass based INA agitation, "led to the sending of a Cabinet Mission".[132]

However, on 19 February 1946—the day after the RIN mutiny broke out in Bombay—when Clement Attlee announced the proposed visit of a Cabinet Mission, as R.J. Moore has shown, the uppermost concern in official mind was that of imperial defence, and for that purpose a united India was considered to be in Britain's best interests.[133] The three-member mission that visited India between March and June 1946, was headed by Lord Pethick-Lawrence, the Secretary of State for India, and included Sir Stafford Cripps, now the President of the Board of Trade, and First Lord Admiralty Mr A.V. Alexander. Its brief was to discuss two issues—the principles and procedures for the framing of a new constitution for granting independence, and the formation of an interim government based on widest possible agreement among Indian political parties. But agreement proved to be elusive, as the two major political parties in India had now become more intolerant about their contradictory political agendas. Between 7 and 9 April 1946, the Muslim League Legislators' Convention in Delhi defined Pakistan as "a sovereign independent state" consisting of the Muslim majority provinces of Bengal and Assam in the northeast and the Punjab, North-West Frontier Province, Sind and Baluchistan in the northwest.[134] On the other hand, on 15 April Maulana Azad, the Congress president, declared that complete independence for a united India was the demand of the Congress.[135] The Cabinet Mission rejected the proposal of a sovereign Pakistan with six provinces as a non-viable concept and offered instead, on 16 May—after wide consultation across the political spectrum—a three tier structure of a loose federal government for the Union of India, including both the provinces and the princely states. There would be a Union government at the top, in charge only of defence, foreign affairs and communications and with right to raise revenue to render those functions; all residual powers would be vested in the provincial governments, which would be free to form groups; each group could also have their own executives and legislatures and could decide what provincial subjects to take on. A Constituent Assembly was to be elected by the recently constituted provincial assemblies to draft a constitution for the whole of India; it would first meet at the Union level and then split into three sections: Section A would consist of the Hindu majority provinces, Section B of the Muslim majority provinces in the north-west and Section C would include Bengal and Assam. The princely states would be given, through negotiations, adequate representation at the Central Constituent Assembly. After a constitution was finally settled for all the three levels (Province, Group and Union), the provinces would have the right to opt out of any particular group, but not from the Union; they could also reconsider the constitution after an interval of ten years. In the meanwhile, an Interim Government would look after the day-to-day administrative matters. The final goal, as Pethick-Lawrence announced, would be to "accord . . . independence whether within or without the British Commonwealth" as Indians would choose of their free will.[136]

Agreement on the Cabinet Mission proposal looked likely when on 6 June Muslim League accepted it on the assumption that "the basis and the foundation of Pakistan" had been "inherent" in the plan and this would ultimately lead to "the establishment of complete sovereign Pakistan".[137] Why Muslim League accepted the Cabinet Mission plan, which in its preamble categorically rejected the Pakistan demand, is a subject of contradictory interpretations. For Ayesha Jalal, the Mission plan was a perfect "way forward for . . . Pakistan Jinnah was after", for he never really wanted partition; and the Muslim League reiterated Pakistan demand as its ultimate goal only as a face saver.[138] For Asim Roy too, the resolution suggested that Jinnah was still willing to "accept something less than what almost everyone else knew as Pakistan".[139] For R.J. Moore, however, the very rhetoric of acceptance signalled that it was "an attempt to turn the scheme to advantage, without compromising in principle".[140] Congress, however, had other reservations. Its first priority had been independence of India, which the Mission argued would follow only after the drafting of a constitution. It also did not like Assam and North-West Frontier Province, where Congress had won majorities in recent elections, to be grouped with the other Muslim majority provinces. The Sikh majority areas in Punjab were another cause of anxiety. Also it wanted additional power for the central government to intervene in crisis situations or extreme breakdown of law and order. Therefore, although the Congress Working Committee on 25 June and the AICC on 6 July announced conditional approval of the long term plan offered by the Cabinet Mission, within a few days Nehru, the newly elected president, declared in a press conference on 10 July that Congress had "agreed to nothing else" other than participation in the Constituent Assembly and most probably the group system would collapse as the NWFP and Assam would not agree to it.[141] The short-term plan to constitute an interim government also fell through on the sticky issue of parity, as Congress wanted to include a Muslim candidate among its nominees. For Jinnah it was the ultimate betrayal by the Congress. On 29 July the League Working Committee withdrew its earlier approval of the Mission's long term plan and gave a call for "direct action". For Qa'id-i-Azam, who believed throughout his life in constitutional politics, the day finally arrived to "bid goodbye to constitutional methods"[142] and prepare his Muslim nation for agitational politics.

This popular agitation for Pakistan was to commence from 16 August 1946, which was chosen as the "Direct Action Day", and it was on this very day that all hell was let loose on Calcutta. The Muslims were meant to observe the day through nationwide hartal, protest meetings and demonstrations to explain the meaning of Pakistan and the reasons for rejecting the Cabinet Mission plan. With a League ministry in power, the day was expected to be observed with much fanfare in Bengal. It was declared a public holiday and a large public rally was arranged at the Ochterlony Monument in Calcutta, where the premier, H.S. Suhrawardy gave a hint that the army and police had been "restrained". What followed next has gone down in history as the "Great Calcutta Killing". The Muslim crowd on their way back began to attack Hindus and their properties; the Hindus fought back; and this craziness went on unfettered for four days, killing four thousand people and injuring ten thousand more. As Suranjan Das (1993) has argued, this was not unexpected, given the political polarisation of provincial politics since the notorious Dacca riots of 1941. If the Muslim League mobilised the masses around the ideological symbol of Pakistan, the Hindu Mahasabha had also raised the slogan of Hindu *rashtra* (state) and launched a mass mobilisation campaign.[143] In a detailed study Joya Chatterji has shown that since the late 1930s the Hindu organisations in Bengal, like the Hindu Sabha, Bharat Sebashram Sangha and the Hindu Mahasabha were trying to convert the "the putative 'Hindu family' into a single harmonious whole" and by the mid-1940s they were preparing for an ultimate showdown by giving their volunteer groups "pseudo-military training".[144] This was the period, which witnessed, to quote Das, the "convergence of elite and popular communalism", creating a general environment of distrust and tension between the Hindus and the Muslims, that finally exploded in August 1946. As a "chain reaction" to the Calcutta carnage, riots broke out in the districts of Chittagong, Dacca, Mymensingh, Barisal and Pabna. But the worst came in October in the two southeastern districts of Noakhali and Tippera. If in Calcutta the two communities shared the casualties almost equally, here the Hindus were mostly on the receiving end, as Muslim peasants, in very systematically orchestrated attacks, destroyed Hindu property, raped their women and killed several thousands of them.[145]

It was not just Bengal that witnessed such communal polarisation at a mass level. Christophe Jaffrelot (1996) has shown that almost the entire north Indian Hindi belt was experiencing the same communal build up in the 1940s. If the Muslim minorities organised themselves around the rallying symbol of Pakistan and were raising disciplined paramilitary volunteer organisations as the Muslim National Guard,[146] the Hindus did not fall behind in organising and simultaneously stigmatising their "threatening Others". This can be gauged from the growing popularity of the overtly Hindu nationalist organisation, the Rashtriya Swayamsevak Sangh (RSS), which focussed primarily on the social and psychological construction of the Hindu nation. The number of its volunteers (*swayamsevaks*) rose from forty thousand in 1938 to seventy-six thousand in 1943 to six hundred thousand by the beginning of 1948. More interesting is the regional distribution of this disciplined and well-drilled volunteer corp. The RSS was most strong in Bihar, the Bombay region, the Central Provinces, Greater Punjab (including Delhi and Himachal Pradesh) and UP. Here the RSS appealed to the students and youth, who were attracted to paramilitary training, were distrustful of Gandhian methods, and nurtured deep anti-Muslim feelings. And the organisation was generously patronised by the Hindu Mahasabha leaders, the Arya Samajis and the maharajas of certain princely states where Muslim minorities had of late become articulate and militant.[147] It was no wonder, therefore, that the communal fire that was kindled in Calcutta soon engulfed the whole of the subcontinent. Riots began in Bombay from 1 September, in Bihar from 25 October and in Garhmukteswar in UP from November—and in all these places Hindus were primarily in the offensive.[148] The news of the killing of Muslims travelled with survivors to such far off lands as the North-West Frontier Province where a Congress government was in power, facing a civil disobedience campaign by local Muslims. The Pathan code of honour made them identify with their victimised community and the cycle of vengeance continued. Pathan tribesmen, instigated by local pirs, began to attack local Hindus and Sikhs from December 1946 in Dera Ismail Khan and Tonk. Their primary target was property rather than life; yet, by April 1947 over a hundred Hindus and Sikhs were killed. The worst communal inferno ravaged Punjab since March 1947. Trouble started brewing when the Unionist ministry, on the advice of Governor Jenkins, banned the Muslim National Guard—and also the RSS—in January. This led to the launching of a civil disobedience movement by the League, which organised protest demonstrations and processions, participated by hundreds of thousands of ordinary Muslim men and also women. The ministry ultimately resigned on 2 March in the face of mounting discontent, plunging the region into chaos and disorder. The chief target of Muslim attack was Hindu property; the latter retaliated as well and Muslims lost about four thousand shops and houses in just one week in March 1947. And then in the following three months, according to official accounts, about thirty-five hundred people died in Punjab and properties worth Rs. 150 million were damaged.[149] But this was nothing in view of what was yet to come to Punjab in the wake of partition, and in that mindless mayhem "all communities", to quote Ian Talbot, "had blood on their hands".[150]

Viceroy Wavell had in the meanwhile managed to constitute an Indian interim government without the Muslim League. A Congress dominated government was sworn in on 2 September 1946 with Jawaharlal Nehru as the prime minister. But it came to a complete impasse when in late October the League was also persuaded to join. Nehru sat helplessly while his country was torn asunder by civil war. On 9 December the Constituent Assembly started meeting, but the League decided to boycott it, as Congress refused to accommodate its demand for sectional meetings drafting group constitutions. Only one man still tried to change the course of history! Gandhi almost single-handedly tried to bring back public conscience. He moved alone fearlessly into the riot-torn places—from Noakhali to Calcutta to Bihar to Delhi. His presence had a miraculous effect, but this personal effort failed to provide a permanent solution. At the age of seventy-seven, Gandhi was now a lonely figure in Indian politics; as S. Gopal succinctly describes it, "His role in the Congress was similar to that of a head of an Oxbridge college who is greatly revered but has little influence on the governing body".[151] By March/April 1947, against his explicit wishes, many of the Congress leaders had more or less reconciled themselves to the idea of conceding Pakistan and accepting freedom with partition as a preferable option to the continuing communal violence. However, this was tinged with optimism that this partition would be temporary and, as Nehru wrote on 29 April, "ultimately there will be a united and strong India".[152] In a resolution on 8 March the Congress Working Committee decided in favour of "division of the Punjab into two Provinces" in order to separate the Muslim from non-Muslim areas. The resolution proposed that the provinces could join the Union and accept the constitution on an entirely voluntary basis; appealed to the Muslim League to participate in the Constituent Assembly proceedings; and demanded immediate recognition of the Interim Government as a Dominion Government.[153]

For the British, now with significantly scarce resources, the available political options shrank even further when communal violence erupted in India. Back in 1946 when the Cabinet Mission was deliberating, Viceroy Wavell had proposed a "Breakdown Plan", i.e., in case of disagreement, the British should withdraw to the six Pakistan provinces leaving the Congress to deal with the rest of India. But the plan was then rejected, as it was found to be dishounourable for Britain to leave without a universally agreed arrangement for the transfer of power. But again in September Wavell predicted that British rule would not last beyond the spring of 1948 and again proposed a "Breakdown Plan" of phased withdrawal by that date. Attlee and Earnest Bevin did not like his "defeatist" attitudes and decided to replace him with Lord Mountbatten in December. But they could hardly postpone the withdrawal any longer, for as Attlee confessed in January 1947: "It would be quite impossible ... for a few hundred British to administer against the active opposition of the whole of the politically minded of the population."[154] So on 20 February he declared that power would be transferred by June 1948 to such authority or in such a way as would seem most reasonable and be in the best interests of the Indian people. Mountbatten arrived in New Delhi on 22 March with plenipotentiary powers and a clear mandate to expedite the process of withdrawal. He realised on his very arrival that it was virtually impossible to hand over power to a united India. On the contrary, there is also a view that it was his "forced march" to the demission of power that further heightened communal tension and made partition inevitable.[155] In the middle of

April he produced what is known as 'Plan Balkan'. It proposed the partition of Punjab and Bengal and handing over power to the provinces and sub-provinces, which would be free to join one or more of group Constituent Assemblies on the basis of self-determination, while the Interim Government would remain until June 1948. Demission of power to the provinces and the absence of a strong centre would certainly lead to Balkanisation of India.[156] It is therefore not surprising that Nehru rejected these proposals on the ground that "[i]nstead of producing any sense of certainty, security and stability, they would encourage disruptive tendencies everywhere and chaos and weakness".[157] Jinnah cast them aside too, as he was not yet prepared to accept the partition of Punjab and Bengal which would give him only a "truncated or mutilated, moth-eaten Pakistan".[158]

The alternative plan that Mountbatten proposed was to transfer power to two successor Dominion governments of India and Pakistan. Nehru, who was opposed to the idea of dominion status was won over, although according to his biographer, he accepted it only as an "interim arrangement".[159] And as for partition, he is reported to have confessed later about the "truth", that "we were tired men and we were getting on in year too. . . . We saw the fires burning in the Punjab and heard everyday of the killings. The plan for partition offered a way out and we took it."[160] On 3 June Mountbatten announced his new plan and proposed to advance the date of transfer of power from June 1948 to 15 August 1947. The plan provided for the partition of Bengal and Punjab; the Hindu majority provinces which had already accepted the existing Constituent Assembly would be given no choice; while the Muslim majority provinces, i.e., Bengal, Punjab, Sind, North-West Frontier Province and Baluchistan would decide whether to join the existing or a new and separate Constituent Assembly for Pakistan; this was to be decided by the provincial assemblies; there would be a referendum in the North-West Frontier Provinces, and in case of Baluchistan, the Quetta municipality and the tribal representatives would be consulted. Nehru, Jinnah and Sardar Baldev Singh on behalf of the Sikhs endorsed the plan the following day[161] and thus began the fast march to transfer of power.

But partition still remained a contentious issue. Neither Jinnah nor Muslim League ever defined the rights of non-Muslims in future Pakistan, and this omission, as Jalal points out, proved to be a "fatal defect" of their scheme,[162] causing anxieties in religious minorities in Punjab and Bengal. In Punjab, since the 1930s the Akali Dal had been speaking of a separate land for the Sikhs. Such demands were reiterated after the Lahore resolution of the Muslim League in 1940. For the first time the proposal of a "Khalistan", consisting of territories from Jammu to Jamrud, as a buffer state between Pakistan and India was floated. The Shiromoni Akali Dal opposed such separatist claims, but its anxiety to preserve the territorial integrity of the Sikh community increased once the Pakistan proposal was given serious consideration by the Cripps Mission and in the Rajagopalachari formula of the Congress. As a pre-emptive strike to prevent the possiblility of their perpetual subjugation to Muslim majority rule, they now began to talk of a distinct Sikh land in eastern and central parts of Punjab, taking Chenab River as the dividing line. This territorial vision of Sikh identity took various expressions, such as "Azad Punjab" in 1942 or a "Sikh state" in 1944; but none of these claims were separatist per se. For example, the Memorandum of the Sikh All Parties Committee to the Cripps Mission asserted their determination to resist "the separation of the Punjab from the All India Union". After the abortive Gandhi-Jinnah talks, and in response to the Rajaji formula which they all detested, the Akali leader Master Tara Singh announced in no uncertain words that "the Sikhs could not be forced to go out of India—into Pakistan". Once the talk of Pakistan became more serious, particularly in the election of 1946, the Akalis decided to move into strategic alliance with the Unionists and later formed a coalition government with them. Before the Cabinet Mission in 1946, Tara Singh on their behalf once again asserted that they were opposed to Pakistan, but if that eventuality occurred, Punjab would like to remain a separate state, with options to federate with either India or Pakistan.[163] The relationship between the Muslims and the Sikhs deteriorated further following the resignation of the Khizr ministry and outbreak of violence since March 1947. The Akali Dal, patronised by the Maharaja of Patiala, now started mobilising jathas for the defence of Sikh life, property and the holy shrines, and more significantly, called for partition of Punjab—a demand, which was ultimately accepted by the Congress in its 8 March resolution. But when partition was agreed upon in the 3 June proposal on the basis of population, the Sikhs found that they were about to lose significant properties and important shrines in the Muslim majority divisions of west Punjab. So a group, prompted by a few British advisers, now began to advocate a third line, that of opting for Pakistan and having an autonomous Sikh region there, and thus retaining the unity of the Sikh community, at least as a powerful minority. But given the hostile attitude of Jinnah and the existing communal relationship, such an alternative to partition seemed impossible to most of the Sikhs.[164]

In Bengal, on the other hand, a group within the Bengal Muslim League, led by H.S. Suhrawardi and Abul Hashim, began to advocate since May 1947 a proposal for a 'United Sovereign Bengal', and received the support of the local Congress stalwart Sarat Bose. But in a communally charged environment, most of the Bengali Hindus believed that the move was nothing but a ploy to have a greater Pakistan that would incorporate the economically rich western Bengal, particularly the city of Calcutta.[165] The proposal was virtually dead when the "well-orchestrated campaign" that the Hindu Mahasabha and the local Congress had launched since April 1947 picked up momentum, advocating the partition of Bengal and constructing a Hindu homeland by retaining the Hindu majority areas in a separate province of West Bengal within the Indian Union. The movement was spearheaded by the Hindu bhadralok, who had constructed by now, in the words of Joya Chatterji, a "notional 'Hindu identity'" and were trying to seize political initiative once again to determine their own destiny.[166] But it was also supported and participated by significant non-elite elements as well, particularly some of the dalit groups in north and east Bengal, who also visualised, like their bhadralok leaders, a real threat of perpetual domination by a Muslim majority in a future Pakistan.[167]

By late June partition of India was a fait accompli. The Bengal Assembly on 20 June and the Punjab Assembly on 23 June decided in favour of partition: west Punjab and east Bengal would go to Pakistan and the rest would remain in India. Shortly following this, Sind, Baluchistan and then the North-West Frontier Province—against the wishes of the popular Gandhian leader Abdul Gaffar Khan—opted to join Pakistan. Mountbatten's next task was to appoint two Boundary Commissions—one for Bengal and one for Punjab—both under Sir Cyril Radcliffe, to delineate the international frontiers within a strict time frame of not more than six weeks. And the boundaries that the Radcliffe Award prescribed, even the viceroy admitted, were sure to "cause anguish to many millions of people" on both sides.[168] The India Independence Act was ratified by the Crown on 18 July and was implemented on 14/15 August 1947. Power was handed over through meticulously planned rituals and ceremonies, some of which, as Jim Masselos comments, reflected the British attitude of giving up the empire, and some the Indian assumption of sovereignty.[169] Pakistan became independent on 14

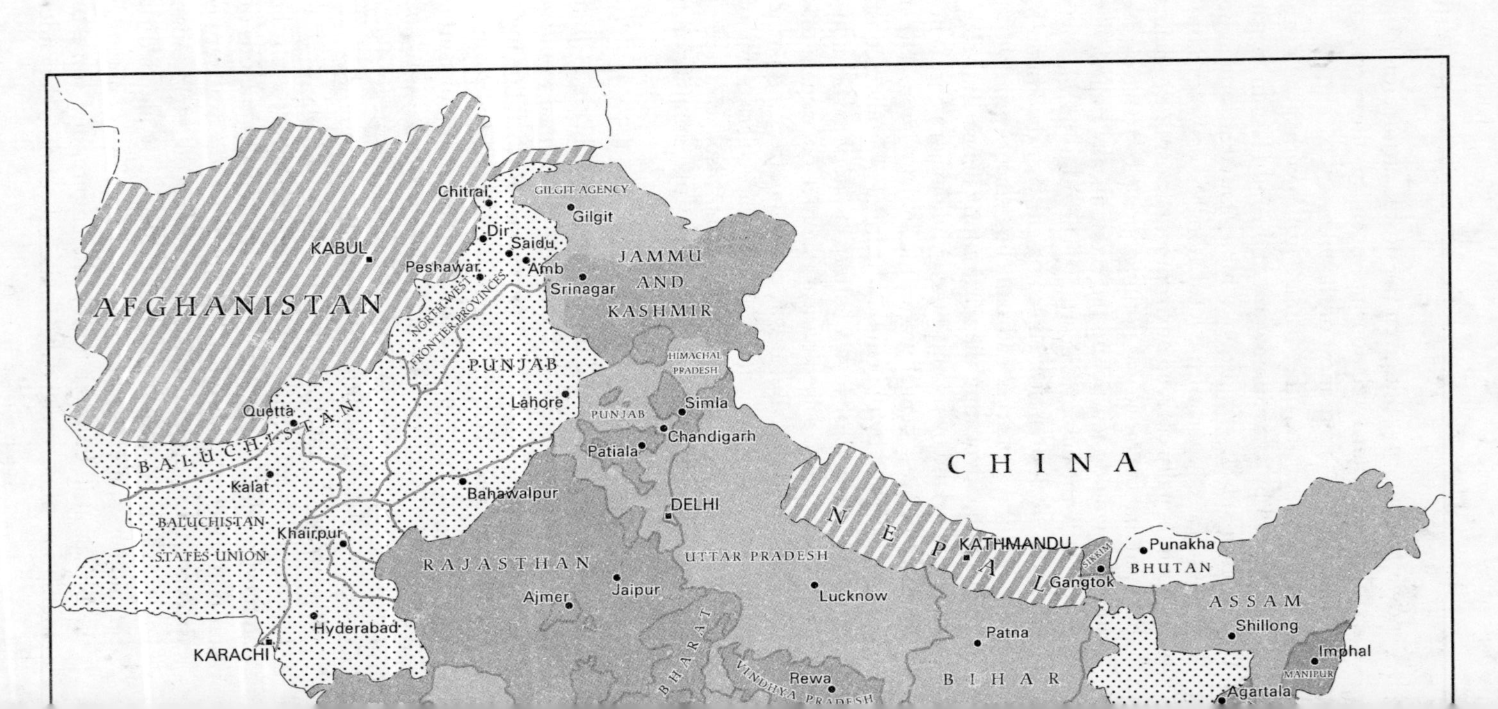

AFGHANISTAN
KABUL
Chitral
Dir
Saidu
Amb
Peshawar
NORTH-WEST FRONTIER PROVINCES
GILGIT AGENCY
Gilgit
JAMMU AND KASHMIR
Srinagar
PUNJAB
Lahore
HIMACHAL PRADESH
Simla
PUNJAB
Chandigarh
Patiala
DELHI
Quetta
BALUCHISTAN
Kalat
BALUCHISTAN STATES UNION
Khairpur
Bahawalpur
Hyderabad
KARACHI
RAJASTHAN
Ajmer
Jaipur
UTTAR PRADESH
Lucknow
BHARAT
VINDHYA PRADESH
Rewa
CHINA
NEPAL
KATHMANDU
SIKKIM
Gangtok
Punakha
BHUTAN
ASSAM
Shillong
Patna
BIHAR
Imphal
MANIPUR
Agartala

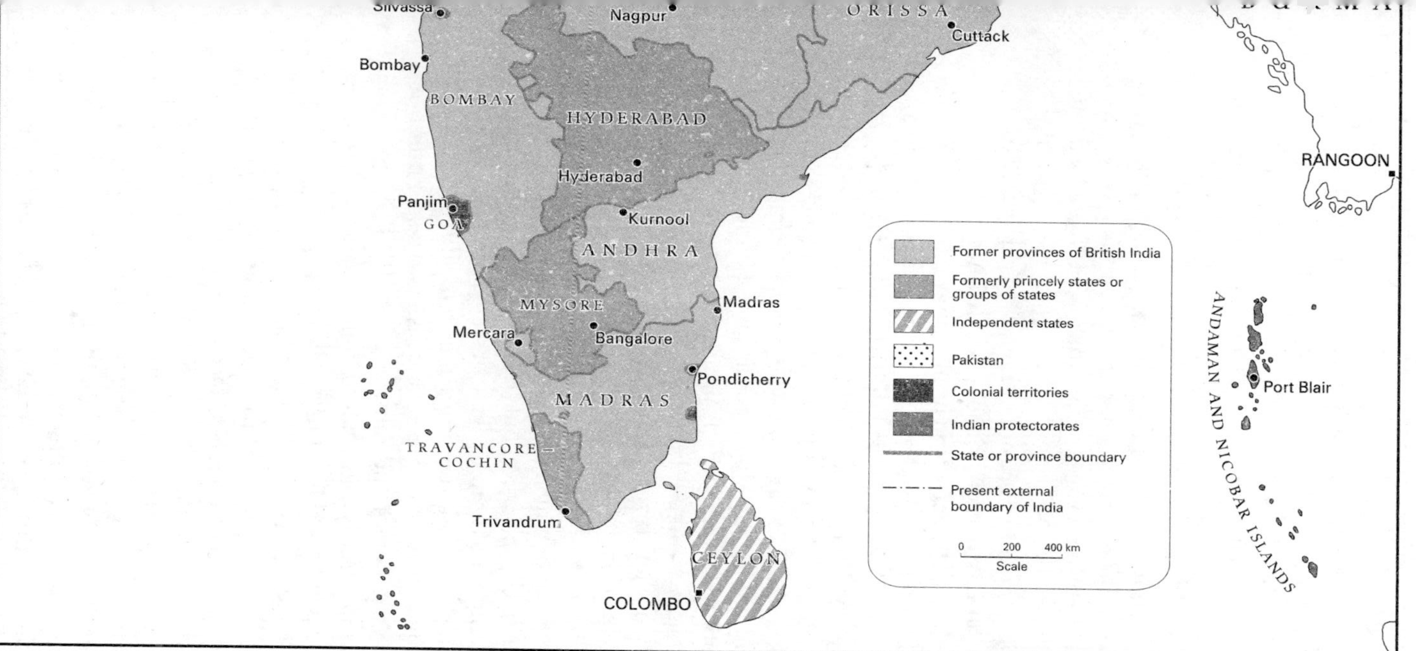

MAP 5: India in 1947

August, when in a brief ceremony at Karachi, the newly designated capital, Mountbatten handed over power by reading a King's message, and Jinnah took over as the first governor general of the Dominion of Pakistan. That night the Indian Constituent Assembly met in a special session, where at the stroke of midnight Nehru delivered his now famous "Tryst with Destiny" speech. When the rest of the world was fast asleep, as he put it in his exemplary flamboyant style, India awoke to life and freedom. The next day he was sworn in as free India's first prime minister and the country plunged into celebrations.

But there were many who were not in a mood to celebrate. To register his opposition to partition, Gandhi decided not to participate in any celebration and spent the day in fasting and prayer. The nationalist Muslims felt betrayed too, as the publication in 1988 of the thirty pages of Maulana Azad's book *India Wins Freedom* (1957)—the pages which remained sealed for thirty years—revealed that he was not in a celebratory mood either. Also unhappy were the Hindu nationalists like Veer Savarkar, who had once campaigned for *Akhand Hindustan* (undivided India), and so the Hindu Mahasabha and the RSS launched a campaign against the celebrations. But the feeling of uncertainty was most dominant in the minds of the minorities, particularly in Punjab and Bengal, where they suddenly found themselves entrapped in an alien land or indeed in an enemy territory.[170] What followed in a little while was the worst-case scenario of communal violence and human displacement that the history of the subcontinent has ever known: about 1 million people were killed and seventy-five thousand or more women were raped. Trains full of dead bodies travelled across the border in both directions; more than 10 million people were displaced and began to taste bitter freedom amidst the squalor of the refugee camps.[171] The most well known victim of this frenzy was Gandhi himself, assassinated on 30 January 1948 by a militant Hindu nationalist.

For many Indians freedom thus came with a sense of loss caused by the partition, while to many Muslims in Pakistan, particularly to their state ideologues, partition itself meant freedom. It is no wonder, therefore, that 'Partition' happens to be the most contested discursive territory of South Asian historiography; just the sheer volume of the literature that has been produced in this field is staggering.[172] We do not have space here to delve into the details of this historiography, other than highlighting a few major trends. This historiography begins its career with a focus on the elite, the leaders of the two principal parties, the Congress and the Muslim League being the chief actors in this drama of truly epic proportions. For some Pakistani historians, first of all, the partition was a liberatory experience, a logical culmination of a long historical process that had started in the nineteenth century by Sayyid Ahmed Khan and others, when the South Asian Muslims began to discover their national identity that was articulated later in the complex subcontinental politics of the 1940s.[173] For Aitzaz Ahsan, partition was "A Primordial Divide"—"a Divide that is 50 years young and 5,000 years old".[174] As Akbar Ahmed argues, the concept of Pakistan was "irresistible and widespread among the Muslims". In 1947 they "forced a separation" and thus claimed for themselves "a separate history of their own".[175] And the chief architects of this history were Jinnah and the leaders of the Muslim League. As opposed to this position, there are other important works, which have questioned the inevitability and legitimacy of partition. The works of Uma Kaura (1977), Stanley Wolpert (1984), Anita Inder Singh (1987), R.J. Moore (1988), Ian Talbot (1988), Mushirul Hasan (1993, 1997) and more recently Sucheta Mahajan (2000), have argued consistently over the period—despite some differences in emphases, nuances and semantics—that Congress, i.e., its leaders, had stood all along until the very end for a secular united India. But it was Jinnah and his Muslim League—which from 1940 began to advocate the 'two nation theory'—who were ultimately responsible for the sad but avoidable vivisection of the subcontinent. Jinnah's alienation from the Congress began after 1937, and if he was a little flexible as regards the definition and specifics of the Pakistan demand until Britain announced its decision to quit, "it was always on the cards".[176] This interpretation, in other words, rests on two fundamental assumptions—which Asim Roy has described as the "two partition myths"—i.e., "'The League for Partition' and 'the Congress for unity'"[177] A recent 'revisionist' history has forcefully challenged these two shibboleths of the familiar partition narratives.

When Pakistan was ultimately created, it contained 60 million Muslims, leaving behind another 35 million in non-Muslim India. So Ayesha Jalal (1985) launched her 'revisionist' critique by raising an all-important question: "how did a Pakistan come about which fitted the interests of most Muslims so poorly?" (p. 4) In her view, the Lahore Resolution, which neither mentioned 'Partition' nor 'Pakistan', was Jinnah's "tactical move"—his "bargaining counter" to have the claim of separate Muslim nationhood accepted by the Congress and the British (pp. 57–58). The ideal constitutional arrangement he preferred for India at this stage was a weak federal structure, with strong autonomy for the provinces, with Hindu–Muslim parity at the centre. His optimism was that Congress, keen on a strong unitary centre, would ultimately concede his demand to avoid his more aggressive scheme of separation, which "in fact [he] did not really want" (p. 57). But that Congress or the British would never accept partition under any circumstances was a mistaken assumption. Congress in the end did accept partition and thus Jinnah was beaten in his own game of wits. Asim Roy, in a supportive article for Jalal, therefore, came up with a rather strong emotive statement that "it was not the League but the Congress who chose, at the end of the day, to run a knife across Mother India's body".[178] However, this interpretative model, as pointed out by many, attaches even more importance to "High Politics" than the one it seeks to displace; it relies too much on Jinnah's agency and allows too much space to the inner depths of his speculative mind. Even though we agree that Jinnah might have first floated the idea of Pakistan as a "bargaining counter"—and even Sumit Sarkar admits that[179]—it is doubtful if he had the same bargaining autonomy once the mass mobilisation campaign began in 1944 around this emotive symbol of Muslim nationhood. Jalal has rectified this imbalance in her analysis in her second book, which focuses on a wider Muslim quest for *Self and Sovereignty* (2000). Here she traces the evolution of a "religiously informed cultural identity" of the north Indian Muslims from the late nineteenth century and its enlargement into a claim of nationhood. But this assertion of nationhood, she affirms, did not become a demand for exclusive statehood until the late summer of 1946. Her discussion of popular mentality, it seems, still does not go beyond the newspaper reading and poetry appreciating public; the non-literate Muslims on the streets of Lahore or the peasants in the Bengal countryside remain largely excluded from this narrative until the riots break out in 1946. But the Pakistan movement, as we have already noted, had started embracing a wider public from a much earlier period, as it "meant all things to all people";[180] once the riots started the campaign only reached the point of no return.

However, it will be equally fallacious to argue that Jinnah did not lead, but was led by Muslim consensus, for, as Mushirul Hasan has demonstrated, consensus there was none. In Hasan's view "the two-nation idea" was itself "grounded . . . in the mistaken belief" about such Muslim unanimity.[181] At the political level, the League was equally "faction-ridden and ideologically fragmented" as the Congress was, and at the popular level, even at the height of communal distrust and conflict, there were sizeable sections of Muslim population who were not mentally reconciled to the idea of partition and even did not consider the religious divide as an insurmountable problem. And many of those who joined the partition campaign were actually manipulated by a highly orchestrated campaign imposed from above.[182] In his ultimate analysis, it was the "colonial government [which] *created* a [Muslim] community in its own image and allowed its war-time ally, the League, to transform a segmented population into a 'nation' or a 'juridical entity'".[183] However, this does not mean that Pakistan movement lacked popular support at least during the penultimate years of the Raj.

Some of the recent works have focused on these popular aspects of the partition history. In a significant later study, Ian Talbot has shown how in Punjab the League took the Pakistan campaign "from the drawing room on to the streets", how "[h]undreds of thousands of Muslims" celebrated various special 'Days', participated in demonstrations, processions and strikes, and finally battled in the communal riots in the name of Pakistan, and thus "legitimized the Muslim League's claims."[184] In Bengal too, the earlier work of Shila Sen and the more recent works of Taj Hashmi have argued that the "Pakistan movement was mass based and democratic", as it could successfully involve the east Bengali Muslim peasantry by offering them a utopian vision of a promised land.[185] In the 1940s the Muslim rioters in Bengal attacked their Hindu adversaries with such overtly political slogans as "*Pakistan ki jai*" (victory to Pakistan), and this indicated a considerable politicisation of the crowd along communal lines.[186] Similarly, the Hindus mobilised too, as the growing popularity of the RSS in the Hindi belt, as Jaffrelot argues, was "undoubtedly linked to the circumstances of Partition".[187] It has already been mentioned that Joya Chatterji (1995) has demonstrated how the Bengali bhadralok launched a campaign for partition and sought to involve the non-bhadralok classes as well. And many of the latter, particularly some dalit groups in the north and eastern districts actively responded to that call, as they were eager to carve out a niche for themselves in the emerging power structure of post-colonial India.[188] The Pakistan movement, as it appears from these works, was hardly an elite affair anymore.

In leftist historiography this question of communalism and partition have come up in different ways. For Bipan Chandra and his colleagues, partititon took place because of the "surging waves of Muslim communalism" since 1937 and mainly "because of the long-term failure of the Congress to draw the Muslim masses into the national movement". The Congress leaders owned up their "failure" and accepted partition "as an unavoidable necessity in the given circumstances".[189] For Sumit Sarkar, however, this "communalism" had not yet been normalised in Indian public life. Indeed, there was more communal harmony at the barricade lines—as evidenced in the popular agitations, peasant struggles and industrial actions of the 1940s—than at the negotiating table.[190] The Congress leadership, instead of harnessing these popular emotions and risking another round of mass movement, accepted the tempting alternative of an early transfer of power, with partition as a necessary price for it. For Sarkar the communal riots that broke out from August 1946 do not form a part of this popular politics. The subaltern historians, on the other hand, Gyanendra Pandey for example, have argued that the conventional elitist partition historiography has been seriously constrained by its self-imposed aim of "establishing the 'causes' of Partition".[191] It is for Partha Chatterjee a non-question, as it was all decided by the "all-India players" and it is "historically inaccurate" to suggest, at least for Bengal, that the partition campaign involved any significant mass participation.[192] Pandey, therefore, redirects his historical gaze away from the 'causes', to "the meaning of Partition for those who lived through it, the trauma it produced and the transformation that it wrought".[193] In his view, the "'truth' of the partition" lay in the violence it produced, and he, therefore, endeavours to unravel how this violence is "conceptualised and remembered by those who lived through partition—as victims, aggressors or onlookers".[194]

But Pandey is certainly not alone in this new discursive terrain. It needs to be mentioned here that the agenda of partition historiography has significantly shifted grounds in recent years from its previous preoccupation with causes to a greater interest in the experiences. This is proved by the recent spate of publications focusing on the memories of partition, on the creative literature that recaptures this traumatic experience and on the visual representations of that "epic tragedy".[195] Historians are now evidently less concerned about causes, and more introspective about the "afterlife" or "aftermath" of partition in South Asia.[196] In other words, they look at how partition impacted on post-colonial history and politics, how partition memory defines community identities and affect inter-community relations, thus emphasising a historical continuity. They self-consciously deny the year 1947 and the foundation of the two nation-states the privilege of being treated as "the end of all history".[197]

Apart from partition, another thorny issue that figured prominently in this episode of transfer of power in India was the fate of

565 princely states after the lapse of British Paramountcy. The British Crown, through informal pledges and formal treaties, had committed itself to defending the states in lieu of their surrendering some political rights. But the Labour government decided to wriggle out of that obligation in view of the altered political realities and the practical difficulties of defending the states after the transfer of power to British India. So the Cabinet Mission announced on 12 May 1946 that Paramountcy would end with the demission of power and the rights surrendered would return to the states. These would be free to enter into either a federal relationship with the successor state(s) in British India or such other political arrangement with them as they would think best suited to their interests. The declaration, therefore, by default, gave an understanding to the princes that they would have the option to remain independent. Nothing was done to rectify this in Mountbatten's 'Plan Balkan', which simply stated that the states would have the liberty to join one or the other confederation of provinces or could stand out independently. In the 3 June declaration, the policy towards the states remained unchanged.[198] But then Mountbatten realised that Congress leadership, particularly Nehru and Patel, did not like the idea of independence for the princely states, as this would not only disrupt law and order, but would seriously jeopardise India's future economic development. So he now decided to persuade the princes to accede to India by surrendering rights only in three areas, i.e., communication, diplomacy and defence, where they did not previously enjoy any right. Patel, who was now heading the new State Department, agreed to accept the scheme, provided the viceroy could offer him "a full basket of apples".[199]

But that was a tough task, as already by early June the rulers of a few larger states, like Bhopal, Travancore, Kashmir and Hyderabad had expressed their desire to choose independence. A beleaguered viceroy was left with little choice other than resorting to arm twisting, if he had to persuade Congress to accept dominion status and partition. In the end, as Ian Copland has suggested, "accession was facilitated by pressure—subtle, gentlemanly but relentless pressure from the viceroy and his ministers".[200] Yet he failed to deliver the full basket. Although by 15 August 1947, the majority of the princes had signed—with a profound sense of betrayal—the Instrument of Accession (IoA) to India, there were some adamant rebels as well. Kashmir and Hyderabad chose to remain independent, Junagadh signed an IoA to join Pakistan, while few other smaller states failed to return the signed documents by the due date. So it was ultimately the strong-arm tactics of Sardar Patel and his deputy V.P. Menon that secured the integration of India. They emphasised the anomalies of the IoA that such anachronistic monarchical enclaves could not survive in the newly independent democratic India. In course of next two years all the princes were pressured to renegotiate their IoA, surrender their rights, open up to constitutional changes and democratisation—in lieu of fat Privy Purses and sometimes prestigious sinecures in foreign diplomatic missions—and the states were eventually merged into the contiguous provinces. As for the rebels, Junagadh's ruler was forced to escape to Pakistan. Maharaja Hari Singh of Kashmir had to accede to India and sign an IoA in October 1947 in the face of a Pathan invasion, thus preparing the context for the first Indo-Pak war of 1948. And finally, the Indian tanks rolled into Hyderabad in September 1948 to smash the Nizam's ambitious dream of independence.[201]

The integration of princely India has been a subject of intense controversy. Ian Copland (1993, 1999), for example, has raised serious and justified questions about the ethics, morality and legality of the unilateral repudiation of the Crown's treaty obligations; he has also chastised Mountbatten for his early indifference to and later overbearing treatment of the princes. The methods used by Patel to bring in the flippant rebels into his basket have appeared to be of "dubious legality" to Judith Brown.[202] But for some other historians, James Manor, for example, the demise of the princely states was historically inevitable, for those archaic autocratic regimes were already relics of the past and did not deserve another lease of life. "The paradox of two different Indias", writes Manor, "was clearly destined to pass away".[203] In new independent India, few shed tears for the hapless princes, whose luck had now clearly run out.

Demission of power in India did not, however, immediately mean the end of Britain's imperial ambitions, as the old notion of empire now evolved into the more dynamic concept of the Commonwealth of Nations, where old colonies would be "in no way subordinate in any aspect of domestic or external affairs", but would be "freely associated and united by common allegiance to the Crown".[204] Mountbatten took it as a personal mission to persuade India to accept dominion status and remain within the Commonwealth. India in 1947 found its hands forced to some extent when Pakistan accepted the Commonwealth membership; but the new constitution, promulgated on 26 January 1950, proclaimed India a Republic. However, British "pragmatism", as D. George Boyce has argued, managed to overcome this challenge to the "Crown, so central to the whole

Empire and Commonwealth identity".[205] India agreed and was allowed to remain in the Commonwealth, despite its republican status—the whole idea of Commonwealth thus being reconstituted. The new Dominions of India and Pakistan were integrated into the Sterling Area and Dollar Pool, and Britain's control over their sterling balances gave her immense bargaining power.[206] At the time of independence British investment accounted for 80 per cent of total foreign investment in India, and in 1948–49 more than 25 per cent of India's foreign trade was with Britain.[207] In other words, even after independence Britain retained a significant stake in and a good deal of control over the economies and development plans of her ex-colonies. It is no wonder, therefore, that the thorniest issue in Indo-British relationship, i.e., that of sterling balances arising from Britain's creditor status to India, was continually "fudged" in post-colonial negotiations, and finally "became resolved by default".[208] However, this dependence and control gradually waned, due to deliberate government policies in India and the changing directions of its trade, as well as Britain's declining role as an international financial power. But there were other areas—particularly when we come to the actual nitty-gritty of managing and administering the new nation-state—where we certainly find elements of "continuity rather than striking change", as Judith Brown has claimed.[209] This is evident in India's adopting the Westminster system of parliamentary democracy and inheriting the existing structures of bureaucracy, police, army and the judiciary, with all their associated ideals, regalia and rituals. However, the most fundamental shift that occurred in 1947 was in the location of power, i.e., in the "emergence of India as a sovereign state", which historian Ravinder Kumar has claimed in his celebratory mood to be "one of the crucial events of the 20th century".[210]

NOTES

1. Sarkar 1983: 332.
2. Damodaran 1992: 36 and passim.
3. Ibid: 98–102.
4. Henningham 1982: 144.
5. Sarkar 1983: 333, 340.
6. Pati 1993: 86–88.
7. Henningham 1982: 166–67.
8. Damodaran 1992: 124, 138 and passim.
9. Tomlinson 1976a: 96–97.
10. Pati 1993: 98–108.

11. Sarkar 1983: 364.
12. Ramusack 1978: 181–82.
13. For the Rajkot movement, see Wood 1978: 240–74.
14. For details, see Copland 1999: 163–70.
15. Tomlinson 1976a: 127.
16. Quoted in Gordon 1990: 403.
17. Chakrabarty 1997: 12.
18. Harcourt 1977: 338.
19. Quoted in Pati 1993: 160.
20. Pandey 1988b: 129.
21. Ibid: 131.
22. Quoted in Sarkar 1983: 391.
23. Hutchins 1973: 217, 240.
24. Gupta 1997, 2: 2068–77.
25. Quoted in Sanyal 1988b: 30.
26. Greenough 1983.
27. Pandey 1988a: 5.
28. Sarkar 1983: 394.
29. Hutchins 1973: 245, 250–51.
30. Damodaran 1992, 1998.
31. Pandey 1988b: 134.
32. Mitra 1988: 180 and passim.
33. Sanyal 1988b: 31.
34. Sanyal 1988b; Chakrabarty 1997.
35. Details in Pati 1993.
36. Details in Omvedt 1988.
37. See Hardiman 1988.
38. Arnold 1988.
39. Chakrabarty 1997: 24–26.
40. Quoted in Anderson and Damle 1987: 44.
41. Pandey 1988a: 9; Chakrabarty 1997: 28.
42. Henningham 1983.
43. Quoted in Pandey 1988b: 139.
44. Quoted in Omvedt 1988: 223.
45. Low 1977: 14.
46. Quoted in Gordon 1990: 400, 406.
47. Chakrabarty 1990: 63–65.
48. Details of the journey in Gordon 1990: 415–28.
49. Lebra 1971: 108–10.
50. Fay 1993: 145.
51. Ibid: 526.
52. Lebra 1971: 174–99.
53. Mahajan 1987: 68–71.
54. Quoted in Gordon 1990: 552.
55. Mahajan 1987: 72–73; 2000: 80–86.
56. Ghosh 1969: 215–16; Sarkar 1983: 421.

57. Fay 1993: 497–98.
58. Chattopadhyay 1976; 1987.
59. Quoted in Ghosh 1969: 232.
60. Mahajan 1987: 76–80; 2000: 92–98.
61. Ghosh 1969: 235.
62. Quoted in Fay 1993: 503.
63. Quoted in Sarkar 1983: 425.
64. Quoted in Mahajan 2000: 73.
65. Cooper 1988: 133–40.
66. Majumdar 1993: 60.
67. Sen 1980: 202.
68. Greenough 1982: 309.
69. Dyson and Maharatna 1991: 296.
70. Greenough 1982: 85–138, 264–71.
71. Gupta 1997, 2: 2086.
72. Quoted in Sen 1972: 35.
73. Cooper 1988: 166–96.
74. Ibid: 255–60.
75. Bose 1986: 263–73; 1993: 151, 164, 172–74.
76. Sen 1972: 78–85.
77. Details in Parulekar 1979: 569–92.
78. Menon 1994: 177.
79. Ibid: 157–89.
80. Jeffrey 1981: 102, 121 and passim.
81. Dhanagare 1991: 183.
82. Ibid: 183–95.
83. Ibid: 196–207.
84. Sundarayya 1979: 532–34.
85. Dhanagare 1991: 202.
86. Omvedt 1994: 310–12.
87. For such evidence see Cooper 1988: 144, 191–96; Jeffrey 1981: 102–3; Parulekar 1979: 569–71; Dhanagare 1991: 194; Rao 1979: 518.
88. Mahajan 2000: 108–95.
89. Brasted and Bridge 1994: 94–5.
90. Boyce 1999: 118–19.
91. Moore 1979: 44.
92. Low 1997: 307.
93. Moore 1983: 6.
94. Ibid: 9.
95. Quoted in Holland 1985: 53.
96. Moore 1983: 11–12.
97. Sarkar 1983: 386–88.
98. Moore 1988: 10.
99. Darwin 1988: 33.
100. Tomlinson 1976b: 344.

101. Tomlinson 1985: 158.
102. Zachariah 1998: 190, 195.
103. Pandey 1969: 172.
104. Menon 1957: 436.
105. Brasted and Bridge 1990.
106. Moore 1983: 18–31.
107. Darwin 1988: 71–72 and passim.
108. Boyce 1999: 141.
109. Shaikh 1993: 95.
110. Quoted in Moore 1979: 28.
111. Singh 1987: 109–11.
112. Moon 1973: 97–98.
113. Jalal 1985: 59.
114. Hasan 1997: 70–77, 91–99.
115. Moore 1988: 123.
116. Details in Sen 1976.
117. Hashmi 1992: 248–56; 1999.
118. Das 1991b: 164–65.
119. Hashmi 1992: 249.
120. Kuwajima 1998: 144.
121. Talbot 1996a: 61.
122. Quoted in Gilmartin 1988: 184.
123. Talbot 1996a: 111.
124. Gilmartin 1988: 186–221.
125. Talbot 1996a: 148–49.
126. Kuwajima 1998: 167–68.
127. Quoted in ibid: 134.
128. Singh 1987: 136.
129. Kuwajima 1998: 131, 167.
130. Gopal 1975: 307.
131. Mahajan 2000: 97–104.
132. Gupta 1987: 9.
133. Moore 1983: 63–64.
134. Pirzada 1970, 2 513.
135. Mansergh 1977, 7: 285.
136. Ibid: 582–92.
137. Ibid: 837–38.
138. Jalal 1985: 201–2.
139. Asim Roy 1993: 120.
140. Moore 1983: 122.
141. Ibid: 158.
142. Quoted in Wolpert 2000: 344.
143. Das 1991b: 161–88.
144. Joya Chatterji 1995: 191–240.
145. Das 1991b: 189–203.
146. Talbot 1996b: 57–76; Hasan 1997: 87–91.

147. Jaffrelot 1996: 66–79.
148. Sarkar 1983: 433–34.
149. Menon and Bhasin 1998: 37.
150. Talbot 1996b: 45–50.
151. Gopal 1975: 343.
152. Quoted in ibid: 343–44.
153. Mansergh 1980, 9: 899–901.
154. Quoted in P. S. Gupta 1987: 13.
155. Krishan 1983: 22–26; Holland 1985: 83.
156. Moore 1983: 246–47.
157. Quoted in Philips 1970: 20.
158. Quoted in Moore 1983: 260.
159. Gopal 1975: 356.
160. Mosley 1961: 248.
161. Tan and Kudaisya 2000: 80.
162. Jalal 2000: 403.
163. For details, see Banga 1999: 192–95 and passim; Grewal and Banga 2000.
164. Tan and Kudaisya 2000: 115–19.
165. Gordon 1989: 580–85; Chakrabarty 1993.
166. Joya Chatterji 1995: 220–59.
167. Bandyopadhyay 2001.
168. Tan and Kudaisya 2000: 96–100.
169. Masselos 1990: 38.
170. For details of the celebrations and counter-celebrations, see Tan and Kudaisya 2000: 29–77.
171. Figures from Hasan 2000a: 343.
172. For a list, see Neogy 1998.
173. Kumar 1987b: xiv–xvi.
174. Ahsan 2000: 287–88.
175. Ahmed 1997:113.
176. Moore 2000: 393.
177. Asim Roy 1993: 102.
178. Ibid: 104.
179. Sarkar 1983: 380.
180. Ahmed 1997: 109.
181. Hasan 1993: 33 and passim.
182. Hasan 1997: 53–99; 2000a: 350 and passim.
183. Hasan 1997: 98; italics in original.
184. Talbot 1996b: 23–53.
185. Sen 1976:196–97; Hashmi 1999: 27; also 1992.
186. Das 1991a: 45.
187. Jaffrelot 1996: 75.
188. Bandyopadhyay 2001.
189. Chandra et al. 1989: 500–4.
190. See Sarkar 1985.

191. Pandey 1994: 207.
192. Chatterjee 1997: 37–38.
193. Pandey 1994: 205.
194. Pandey 1997: 2037.
195. See, for example, Hasan 1995, 1997, 2000b; Samaddar 1997; Menon and Bhasin 1998; Butalia 1998; Kaul 2001.
196. See Tan and Kudaisya 2000.
197. Pandey 1991: 559.
198. Copland 1993: 387–92.
199. Hodson 1969: 368.
200. Copland 1999: 257.
201. Details in ibid: 257–68.
202. Brown 1994: 346.
203. Manor 1978: 323.
204. Mansergh 1948: 22.
205. Boyce 1999: 142.
206. Zachariah 1998: 200–2.
207. Banerji 1978: 200.
208. Tomlinson 1985: 157.
209. Brown 1994: 349.
210. Kumar 1987b: xiii.

chapter nine

After Independence and Partition

9.1. The Transition

The end of colonial rule in 1947 was undoubtedly a defining moment of modern South Asian history. India achieved Independence at midnight of 14–15 August 1947; her astrologers had previously identified this moment to be the most auspicious for her future historical trajectory. Jawaharlal Nehru, the prime minister in the interim government, proudly announced in his "Tryst with Destiny" speech: "At the stroke of the midnight hour, when the world sleeps, India will awake to life and freedom. A moment comes, which comes but rarely in history, when we step out from the old to the new, when an age ends, and when the soul of a nation, long suppressed, finds utterance."[1] Pakistan was born on the previous day, and thus the territory that was once the British Indian empire was now partitioned and made initially into two dominions—both straddling towards their historic destinies as sovereign nation-states. What happened in August 1947 in the subcontinent needs therefore to be treated as a twin process—Independence and Partition—both affecting the future trajectories of the two nations.

In India, this meant of course the end of nearly two hundred years of British rule, for which the Indian National Congress and various other political groups had been fighting for about half a century. So naturally there was euphoria on the streets of the capital New Delhi, as well as in the provinces. The celebrations started from 11 p.m. on 14 August when the Constituent Assembly met under the chairmanship of Rajendra Prasad, followed by the presentation of the emblems of the new nation—the flag and the anthem. The Constituent Assembly had previously accepted the new flag, which had been the Congress flag since 1930, with a minor change—the *charkha* (spinning wheel) was replaced by the *chakra* (wheel of life). The nation, as Nehru argued, could now stand under the same flag with which they had fought against foreign rule. As for the anthem, the Constituent Assembly preferred Rabindranath Tagore's "Jana Gana Mana" over the familiar "Bande Mataram", which, it was apprehended, might offend the Muslims. Thus, at the moment of arrival the founding fathers carefully chose the emblems of the new nation, which they expected to be secular, inclusive and democratic, as well as closely associated with the legacy of the Congress.

On the streets people were ecstatic that night and the following day. In New Delhi, in the morning of 15 August, Jawaharlal Nehru was sworn in as the first prime minister of free India. In the evening more than a million people came to watch the parade at Kings Way, where the national flag was hoisted and the government buildings were illuminated. A million people marched on the streets of Bombay that morning, and some of them even took possession of the Secretariat Building. In Calcutta about 200,000 people broke the police cordon and rushed into the Governor House and later the Assembly House, in a bid to reclaim what was once the most sacred and secluded spaces of the Raj. Numerous functions were held all over the country, where national flags were unfurled, the national anthem was sung and patriotic speeches were delivered.[2] It was a special day—out of the ordinary—for most of the Indians.

But on that day not everyone was in a mood to rejoice, as freedom also arrived with the pain of Partition. Mahatma Gandhi, then in Calcutta trying to stop communal riots, spent the day in prayer and fasting as an act of penance. The Hindu Mahasabha, which wanted *Akhand Hindustan* (united India) but later supported bifurcation of Bengal to keep its Hindu-majority western districts in India, boycotted the celebrations as a protest against Partition. The Muslim League decided to join, but Muslims being a minority—like their Hindu counterparts in Pakistan—lived in a state of anxiety about an uncertain future. The communists too decided to keep away from the celebrations as a protest against Partition and the communal riots.

Freedom at the moment of arrival thus evoked mixed emotions. As we have seen earlier, the idea of freedom in India had grown exponentially through the encounter with colonial rule. As the freedom struggle progressed, the issue of individual freedom came to be subordinated to the concept of collective freedom, the nation taking precedence over all other identities, like class, caste or gender.[3] Until recently, the historiography of Indian nationalism located the final moment of its fulfilment in the formation of the nation-state. But the history of nationalism during the British period was not just the prehistory of the nation-state, but a phase in a continuing process of nation-building. If we identify the nation as a space for contestation (see chapter 4.1), that contest continued into the postcolonial period. There was tension in the ways national freedom was being conceptualised by myriad groups of people who constituted the grand nationalist coalition. While some saw in the attainment of political sovereignty the immediate fulfilment of the goals of the freedom struggle, others preferred to expand the meaning of freedom to incorporate also the notions of economic and social freedom for the people. In 1947, as Nehru reminded his countrymen, the immediate goal of political freedom had been achieved, but the greater challenge was to ensure for every citizen the freedom from poverty, ignorance, disease and inequality. And it was this challenge which caused anxiety, as there was no agreement yet on how to grapple with it.

Bipan Chandra and his colleagues in their *India After Independence* argued that independent India started her journey with a foundational political consensus: "Starting off with a broad social consensus on the basic contours of the India that was to be built—on the values of nationalism, secularism and democracy and the goals of rapid economic development and radical social change—was a great advantage. These values and goals, and the road to their achievement had been mapped over more than seventy years by the national movement."[4] We have however argued previously that what had appeared in the pluralist society of India during the colonial period was a polyphonic nationalism, within which different melodies were played, but all of them harmonised—sometimes uneasily, and never losing their distinctiveness—at various historical conjunctures, in common opposition to colonial rule or in disapprobation of various aspects of its unwholesome impact. But beyond that anti-colonial consensus there was hardly any agreement on what the future trajectory of the nation would be. The process of nation-building was thus far from over in 1947, as the relationship between those divergent voices and visions with the structures of the nation-state continued to be the central problematic of postcolonial history. Nehru tried to initiate a policy of reconciliation by making his cabinet fairly broad-based through the incorporation of the Dalit leader Dr B.R. Ambedkar as the law minister and Dr S.P. Mukherjee of the Hindu Mahasabha as the minister of industry and supply. But the differences were far from resolved, and therefore freedom in 1947 did not mean a clinical break with the colonial past.

But there are divergent historical views on the nature of such continuity. D.A. Low, for example, has seen such continuity in "innumerable British-type institutions" that were left behind.[5]

In India one could easily point out the continuation of the old structures of civil service, police, army and the judiciary as evidence of that temporal bridge with the colonial past. Holden Furber has therefore argued that compared to Pakistan, India was particularly fortunate to have "inherited much of the machinery of the former central government and did not have to establish *de novo* either a national capital or a national government".[6] This Commonwealth view of decolonisation—which is also a very statist vision—sees in the history of postcolonial India more evidence of continuity than any fundamental epistemological rupture. As Judith Brown has argued, such continuity was manifest in the pageantry, rituals, regalia and the institutions of governance, and above all, in India's supposedly uninterrupted linear movement towards political modernity.[7] This was not evidently the kind of freedom that Mahatma Gandhi would have preferred. In his *Hind Swaraj* (1909) he had warned that India might end up with English rule without the Englishmen. His and many other nationalists' expectation was that the process of decolonisation would involve a complete reversal of the colonial past. But possibly such a total reversal has never happened anywhere in the world in the history of decolonisation. However, it was not entirely a story of continuity either.

As Dipesh Chakrabarty has argued, the process of decolonisation as "a historical process" was "necessarily clumsy, complicated, and inherently incomplete (that is, fragmentary)".[8] In this sense freedom was not a moment of complete rupture, but symbolised a process of transference and adaptation—a process of hybridisation through which the meanings of freedom would be expanded exponentially. Srirupa Roy has therefore described this process as "continuity yet change".[9] It was a dialogic process between the colonial past and the postcolonial present, a dialogue that has not ended yet. And this dialogue took place at many levels, as the nation was hardly a homogenous entity, and lived in what Partha Chatterjee has called the "heterogeneous time of modernity".[10] Ted Svensson has however recently argued that it was more a "rupture" than "continuity", because the "new political orders were to a large extent newer than what most scholars would like to admit". It was only the experience of decolonisation and Partition which gave the new the appearance of old.[11] To understand the nature of this complicated and ambiguous process of decolonisation we summarise below some of these early trends in uncertainties and anxieties as well as achievements of postcolonial India.

9.2. PARTITION AND REFUGEES

As freedom came with Partition, the immediate anxiety of everyone was about the award of the Boundary Commissions formed under Sir Cyril Radcliffe. The commissions in Punjab and Bengal consisted of two Muslim and two non-Muslim judges in each case, both overseen by Sir Cyril, who had no experience of India and was entrusted with the responsibility of drawing the international boundary within a very short span of time. The deciding factor would of course be religious demography of each district ("contiguous majority areas"), but other factors, such as rivers as natural boundaries, administrative units, economic viability, railway and road connections and infrastructural facilities such as the canal system in the Punjab were also to be taken into consideration. Both parties—Hindus and Muslims—presented their cases in legalistic terms through their counsels. The Sikhs, as a third party in Punjab, further complicated the situation, as demographically they were scattered throughout the region, and they demanded that all their holy shrines should be in East Punjab in India. In this legal wrangling often rational decisions were sacrificed for political considerations, while everyone knew that the census figures of 1941, on which decisions were to be based, were hopelessly faulty. So the boundary lines drawn hastily were bound to be problematic, and leave many people unhappy. The viceroy knew that, and so postponed the announcement of the award until after the formal transfer of power and celebrations were over.

In the award, West Punjab, which went to Pakistan, received 62,000 square miles of territory and 15,800,000 people (according to the 1941 census figures), of whom 11,850,000 were Muslims. East Punjab that remained in India received 37,000 square miles of territory, with a population of 12,600,000, of whom 4,375,000 were Muslims. In the east, West Bengal that remained in India received a territory of 28,000 square miles and a population of 21,200,000, of whom 5,300,000 were Muslims, while East Bengal, which was to constitute East Pakistan, received 49,400 square miles of territory and 39,100,000 people, of whom 27,700,000 were Muslims. Following a referendum in July 1947, the district of Sylhet was transferred to East Bengal from Assam, which was left with no direct rail link with the rest of India. The district of Khulna with a Muslim population of 49.3 per cent was given over to Pakistan for no apparent reason, as was the primarily tribal region of Chittagong Hill Tracts. On the other hand, largely Muslim majority areas in Malda, Nadia and Murshidabad districts were added to West Bengal. Economically,

Pakistan became more agriculture-based, while mineral resources and industries remained in India.[12] But more seriously, on both sides of the border there were sizeable sections of populations who could be described as "minorities"—about 42 million (later reduced to 35 million) Muslims in India and 20 million non-Muslims in Pakistan. Their future hung in the balance and they suffered from mounting anxiety as the new boundary was announced and many of them felt like aliens in enemy territory while being in their own homes.

Freedom it is said had different meanings for different people in the subcontinent. To the political elite in Pakistan, Partition itself was freedom—freedom from the political domination of the Hindu majority. In India, while a few rejoiced the arrival of freedom, others—the refugees and the minorities—paid the heaviest price of Partition. The subcontinent was soon plunged into large-scale violence, which in modern terms could only be described as a serious case of ethnic cleansing in recent history. The worst cases of violence took place in Punjab, where about four-and-half a million Hindus and Sikhs arrived in East Punjab, while five-and-half a million Muslims departed for West Pakistan between August and November 1947.[13] The refugees arrived at various places: in Delhi alone, as Gyanendra Pandey enumerates, about 500,000 non-Muslim refugees—primarily Hindu and Sikh—arrived in 1947–48. And some became refugees in their own land, as thousands of Muslims in Delhi sought shelter in the refugee camps at Old Fort and Humayun's Tomb to escape from the violence that had been unleashed; eventually 330,000 Muslims left the city for Pakistan.[14] On the other side, when Bengal was partitioned, 42 per cent of its non-Muslim population were left in East Pakistan; by June 1948, according to Prafulla Chakrabarty's calculation, about 1.1 million of them had migrated to West Bengal.[15] This was despite the fact that the level of violence was relatively low in Bengal than in Punjab.

These displaced people were "refugees" in the sense that they were not leaving their homes voluntarily, and the two governments did not organise any orderly exchange of population. In fact the governments actively tried to stop this movement of people from regions other than Punjab.[16] And even in Punjab, as Neeti Nair has recently shown, many Hindus never expected that they would have to leave their homes. But "August 15 heralded a new kind of freedom in the Punjab. In Lahore, a gurdwara was burnt with at least 13 Sikhs inside while Muslim police and troops did nothing. In Amritsar city, a Sikh crowd paraded naked Muslim women, some of whom were raped and then burnt."[17] So the people of Punjab ultimately had to leave their homes, as the level of violence and insecurity was unprecedented. And this was obviously a two-way traffic: when Hindu and Sikh refugees arrived from West Punjab, it required a Muslim exodus from India to accommodate them in the latter's empty houses.[18]

On the other hand, as long caravans of thousands of refugees began their uncertain journeys across the border, rival groups took revenge on one another. A joint Military Evacuation Organisation was quickly formed with the arrangement that the Pakistani army would protect the Muslim refugees and the Indian army would do the same for the Hindu and Sikh refugees, and together they would oversee a virtual exchange of population in Punjab. But despite that violence continued, as trains were stopped and passengers were butchered indiscriminately and mercilessly. Often trains would "arrive at their destinations carrying only corpses".[19] Women became particular targets of this violence, as their body became the symbol of their community's honour. They were abducted, raped and murdered by the males of the opposing community trying to trample on the collective honour of their "Other". In a situation like this men sometimes preferred to kill their own female family members to protect them from violation by their rival community.[20] While memories of this violence and the experiences of displacement continued to rancour in the minds of the refugees for a long time and shaped their worldviews and sense of belonging to their new nation state, the Indian government struggled to get these refugees resettled and define the terms of their citizenship.[21]

Refugee resettlement proved to be a major problem for the government as the pattern of influx varied across the regions. The Government of India immediately established an Emergency Committee of the Cabinet to deal with the situation in Delhi and a Ministry of Relief and Rehabilitation was set up to look after the refugees.[22] In Punjab where the outbreak of violence was one-time and catastrophic, there was an immediate large-scale influx of displaced people; according to the report of the Ministry of Rehabilitation, about five million of them had arrived in India from West Pakistan by October 1948.[23] In this situation the notion of "evacuee property" to be protected by the state for any future return of the refugees became an empty rhetoric, as there was no political will to force the refugees to vacate the occupied Muslim houses. This, as Zamindar has argued, made the return of the refugees impossible.[24] Some of these refugees were accommodated in refugee camps, which were run until 1949. Later the rural refugees were resettled with land, agricultural loans and housing subsidies. For urban refugees industrial and vocational training schemes were provided, and grants were offered to start small businesses or industries. Industrial homes were set up for widows in cities like Amritsar. And housing colonies were constructed for urban refugees; many of them were also compensated for the properties they left behind in Pakistan. In all, both the East Punjab and the national government mobilised massive resources for refugee rehabilitation, although it was still not adequate in many cases. And there were also differential entitlements to such benefits, as refugees with social and cultural capital, e.g., class and caste status and political connections, often got the better deal, while the Dalit refugees were given short shift.[25]

In Bengal the process was much more prolonged and complicated, as initially in 1947–48 only a relatively small group of high-caste, landed or middle-class Hindus, who could arrange exchange of property or jobs, migrated to West Bengal. According to the rehabilitation ministry until July 1949 only 1.3 million people had migrated from East Pakistan.[26] Some of them resettled themselves; others set up "squatter colonies" by forcibly taking over unoccupied land.[27] But the problem arose when a larger peasant migration from East Pakistan took place after fresh outbreak of violence in Khulna in December–January 1949–50. In retaliation, there were anti-Muslim riots in West Bengal in February that resulted in about one million Muslims leaving for East Pakistan. This led to further spread of anti-Hindu violence throughout East Bengal. By 1951, following the disturbances in Khulna, about 1.5 million Hindu refugees had arrived in West Bengal.[28] But the Indian government never believed that the violence they were allegedly fleeing from was serious enough to warrant such large-scale migration and hence these migrants did not deserve the status of refugees. They were temporarily sheltered in refugee camps, but Prime Minister Nehru seriously thought of sending them back.[29]

With that view, on 8 April 1950 Nehru signed with his Pakistani counterpart Liaquat Ali Khan what is known as the Delhi Pact on minorities. It was meant to restore communal peace in both countries through appointment of ministers from minority communities in both Pakistan and India and at both central and provincial levels. Minority Commissions were to be formed in West Bengal, Assam and East Bengal. Commissions of Inquiry were to be instituted in both the Bengals to find out the causes behind the recent riots and to recommend measures to prevent recurrence of such incidents in the future. An agency was to be created to recover and rehabilitate "abducted" women. Refugees were to be encouraged to return to their original homes, and measures were to be taken to restore their properties on return.[30] The main purpose of the pact was "to speed up the restoration of confidence among minorities in the two Bengals and Assam".[31] For the Government of India this was necessary not just to reassure the minorities in India, but primarily to prevent fresh migration from East Bengal, and more importantly, to encourage a reverse migration. Some aspects of the Delhi Pact, like the absurd idea of recovering abducted women, have been criticised by historians.[32] But its main failure was in its inability to restore confidence among the refugees to go back. Very few actually went back, and those who did, found their properties already taken over as enemy property. The pact was severely attacked by Hindu nationalists like S.P. Mukherjee, who resigned along with his Hindu Mahasabha colleague K.C. Neogy, from the Nehru cabinet in protest. For them the ongoing refugee problem could only be solved through a transfer of population, seizure of certain territories from Pakistan to rehabilitate the displaced people, or in outright reversal of Partition.[33]

The debates and political controversies that arose around the riots and the pact revealed that the Indian nation was still deeply divided on the minority question, particularly on the issue of citizenship of the Muslims who chose to remain in India. Although India had chosen to be secular, there was serious ambivalence about the place of religious minorities within the new nation-state. Many people believed that Partition had permanently demarcated the communal political space of the subcontinent, where the Muslims belonged to Pakistan, and India belonged to the Hindus. Suspicion about Muslim loyalty and questions about their full citizenship were raised not just by the Hindu nationalist groups, but also by influential leaders of the Congress and powerful members of the bureaucracy.[34] Mushirul Hasan has given evidence to show that they were the powerful men who actually ran the state and this was despite the Congress having passed a resolution at Jaipur in 1948 professing the aim of building "this great country as a democratic secular state".[35] At an ontological level, the Muslims continued to be socially alienated and physically ghettoised in cities like Delhi or Calcutta, where Hindu Partition refugees arrived in large numbers and Muslims became refugees in their own land. They often came to be described as "fifth columnists" and their neighbourhoods came to be known as "miniature Pakistans".[36]

However, against such tendencies Nehru relentlessly pursued the secularist agenda of the Congress. The traditionalist elements within the Congress were also weakened with Sardar Patel's death in December 1950 and Nehru taking over as Congress president by defeating the traditionalist Purushottamdas Tandon in 1951. This established Nehru's undisputed sway over the Congress party and the government, as he combined in himself the two positions of party president and prime minister.[37] In his Congress presidential address in October 1951 and later in the election campaign Nehru identified communalism and poverty as the nation's two principal enemies.[38] The Congress victory in the first national election of 1951–52 set the country on what came to be known as the Nehruvian path of secularism and socialism (more on this in section 9.4). But the processes of Partition and decolonisation had also left other residual problems for the new nation-state to handle in its initial years.

9.3. KASHMIR, HYDERABAD AND THE COMMUNISTS

The other major problem facing India immediately in the wake of Independence and Partition concerned the fate of the princely states, which under existing monarchical systems, remained the backwaters of politics in a new India. By signing instruments of accession (IoAs) to join the Indian Union, the princes had only surrendered their power on three subjects, i.e., defence, foreign affairs and communications, and had thereby retained some residual powers of governance. Shortly after 1947, Vallabhbhai Patel and V.P. Menon therefore wanted to have a "final solution" to the problem of the princely states. In the words of Ian Copland, "[t]his project, which took about two years, involved, in more or less chronological order (although the processes overlapped), the amalgamation of the states into larger administrative units and/or merger with the erstwhile provinces, their rapid democratisation, and their total subordination to the federal centre."[39] This meant cajoling them to surrender their residual powers, accept democratic change, and finally embrace the new Constitution of India as their own. Many of the princes were pensioned off with tax-free "privy purses" and other benefits; some were given largely ceremonial positions in foreign missions. But that did not mean that all of them had happily joined what Menon described as a peaceful revolution.[40] Some of them resisted, and in their cases the state power was unhesitatingly unleashed. Of those who resisted, we may mention here three cases, i.e., Junagadh, Kashmir and Hyderabad.

Of these, the Muslim ruler of Junagadh—one of the Kathiawar states completely surrounded by Indian territory—had opted to sign an IoA with Pakistan, disregarding Mountbatten's rule of territorial contiguity. His subjects rose in revolt against him, and the Indian government resorted to a blockade of his territory, forcing the ruler to flee to Pakistan. Hereafter, the Indian armed forces took control of the state, and held a referendum in February 1948, in which the people of Junagadh almost unanimously opted for union with India. A year later, Junagadh was merged with the province of Saurashtra and allotted seven members in the Saurashtra legislative assembly. This rounded off the process of its integration into the India Union, which Pakistan continued to contest.[41]

The Kashmir situation on the other hand was more complex and directly related to the history of Partition. As Sumit Ganguly has argued, the crux of the problem lay in the "competing visions of state construction in South Asia".[42] In 1947, the Muslim-majority princely state of Kashmir remained geographically contiguous with Pakistan with strong trade links with her. So Pakistan legitimately believed that it had a natural claim on the state. For Jinnah and the Muslim League, Pakistan without Kashmir would be "incomplete", while for Nehru and the Congress, integration of Kashmir would buttress India's secular credentials.[43] Since 1846, Kashmir had been ruled by a Hindu Dogra chief, Maharaja Gulab Singh, as a "Hindu state", to the total exclusion of the Muslim majority from any share of political power. His descendent Maharaja Hari Singh also ruled Kashmir with the help of a small Brahman–Dogra elite, who controlled political power as well as most of the fertile agricultural land. But he faced a democratic political agitation launched by the All Jammu and Kashmir National Conference under the leadership of Sheikh Muhammad Abdullah, demanding rights for the Muslims and asserting a Kashmiri regional nationalism or *Kashmiriyat*.[44]

At the time of transfer of power, while Pakistan's claim to Kashmir was supported by the Muslim Conference—a breakaway group of the National Conference—the National Conference itself, enjoying the support of 75 per cent of the local Muslims, took a different course of action. In May 1946, fearing the prospect of an independent Dogra autocratic rule, it launched a "Quit Kashmir" movement based on a broad communal coalition with the local Hindu Pandits, and got closer to the Indian National Congress. Abdullah, who had developed a personal friendship with Nehru since 1938,[45] was put in jail for his opposition to Dogra rule, while the maharaja, faced with such challenges, refused to sign any IoA. Meanwhile, communal trouble from Punjab spread to Kashmir and the existing feeble administration failed to control it. So allegedly to avenge the atrocities on their co-religionists, the Pathan tribesmen from the North-West Frontier Province, with covert assistance from the Pakistani administration, entered western Kashmir in October 1947. The maharaja's tiny army and civil administration collapsed after a brief resistance, and he appealed to the Indian government for help. The latter agreed to help only if the maharaja signed an IoA to join India, which he did. And immediately after this the Indian army landed at Srinagar airport and brought the situation under control. But this also ushered in a protracted conflict with Pakistan, which saw Kashmir as its legitimate part and intervened militarily. Full-scale war between the Indian and Pakistani armies started from November 1947. While the Indian army established control over much of the Kashmir Valley, Ladakh and Jammu, the Pakistani army occupied about one-third of the territory of the state, which it called "Azad Kashmir". Thus by December 1947 Kashmir was virtually bifurcated, and India decided, on the advice of Lord Mountbatten, to take the case to the United Nations (UN) for a multilateral solution.[46]

When Prime Minister Nehru decided to take the Kashmir issue to the UN, he believed that India had a strong legal case based on Kashmir's accession to India being signed by the maharaja, and supported by the National Conference, representing the majority of the Muslim population in the valley. He complained of an illegal Pakistani aggression, first indirect and then direct. Pakistan on the other hand contested the legality of the accession, which it believed was extracted through pressure.[47] But more importantly, at this global forum the issue was caught in Cold War politics and became subservient to Britain's strategic interests in the region.[48] As a result, the UN failed to take a firm decision or deliver any tangible solution that would be acceptable to both the parties. In April 1948, it set up a five-nation commission to find a solution to the Kashmir issue. By 1949, it came to a patchy agreement by which both India and Pakistan agreed to a ceasefire. The resolution asked Pakistan to "vacate its aggression" and India to reduce its troops to a level sufficient only for maintaining law and order; and after that a plebiscite was to take place to decide the fate of Kashmir. But that plebiscite never took place as India demanded that all the tribesmen and Pakistani troops withdraw first before such a plebiscite could take place, while Pakistan agreed to withdraw its troops only after the plebiscite had taken place and conditional on its outcome. By the 1960s, as Ganguly argues, the UN and the world lost interest in the Kashmir issue,[49] which remained as a festering wound in the India-Pakistan relations causing two subsequent wars—the Indo-Pak War of 1965 and the Kargil War of 1999.

The situation in Hyderabad was just the reverse, as it was a Hindu-majority state under a Muslim ruler—the nizam—supported by an oppressive Muslim oligarchy. It was geographically landlocked, economically dependent on India, and surrounded by Indian territory. Yet, the nizam in 1947 preferred independence and refused to sign any IoA. Considering Hyderabad's geographical position—being the main corridor of communication between south and north India—and its demographic composition, many in India considered the nizam's claim of independence to be absurd and prejudicial to India's security. So the Government of India rejected the nizam's *firman* resuming independence after the departure of the Britisn. The internal politics in Hyderabad also became complicated at this stage (as already mentioned in chapter 8), as the Telangana movement took a bizarre turn. The alliance between the Congress and the communists broke down, the peasant insurgency escalated, and Razakar oppression increased. Within this context of a continually deteriorating political situation, the Government of India, through Vallabhbhai Patel, negotiated with the nizam and his representatives, continually raising their demands to that of complete accession and the establishment of a representative government in Hyderabad, which the Muslim elite stubbornly resisted. Finally, on 13 September 1948, on the pretext of maintaining the law and order situation in south India, the Indian army intervened and took control of Hyderabad without much resistance.

But the communist-led peasant insurgency in Telangana continued to create the most complex problem for the infant Indian state. In December 1947, the CPI declared that the Indian independence was fake, their new slogan proclaiming "*ye azadi jhooti hai*". The Congress and its leader Jawaharlal Nehru were considered to be the stooges of Anglo-American imperialism and the feudal elements within the country, and a movement to replace them was considered to be the only way to achieve real independence.[50] The CPI held its Second Congress in Calcutta between 28 February and 6 March 1948, where it adopted its "Political Thesis", which formally declared that the national government established on 15 August 1947 was indeed the major enemy of the Indian people and therefore needed to be replaced. To accomplish this, the party decided to follow what popularly came to be known as the "B.T. Randive line" (after the name of its general secretary), or the path of promoting in India a "People's Democratic Revolution". Its aim would be "to bring about those fundamental changes in our political and social structure without which there can be no freedom and no prosperity for our people. The present state will be replaced by a people's democratic republic—a republic of workers, peasants and oppressed middle classes."[51] After this, not only the Telangana insurgency continued (details in chapter 8), it was extended to other parts of India, notably to West Bengal, which witnessed a renewal of the Tebhaga movement in the countryside and an urban insurgency in Calcutta and the surrounding industrial areas.[52]

Why the communists decided to carry on with the insurgency at this stage is a question that historians have tried to answer in various ways. Bipan Chandra and his colleagues think that the communists decided to go this way because of intense factionalism within the party and their inability to properly assess the nature of the political situation in India at that time.[53] Ramachandra Guha also thinks that the CPI leadership, encouraged by the initial successes of the Telangana movement, mistook the "scattered disillusionment with the Congress" as revolutionary potential, and thought that this "would be the beginning of Red India".[54] To put it in a wider political perspective, one may point out that ever since communal riots and partition politics started in 1946, the CPI leaders struggled to evolve a strategy to address the situation. Their political aim to unite the Congress and the League in a united struggle against the British Empire ultimately ended in what Shashi Joshi and Bhagwan Josh have called "an exercise in absurdity". By deploying their secularist theories they could not grapple with the communal situation of the period, and consequently failed to evolve an appropriate policy.[55] And then, as T.J. Nossiter has argued, the political scenario in post-Partition India was changing at such a fast pace that it put further pressure on the CPI leadership, while no directive was immediately forthcoming from Moscow. At the same time, some leaders sincerely believed that there was a real revolutionary possibility in the unfolding political situation, and they did not want to let that opportunity slip off their grip.[56] As Javeed Alam has argued, the Indian communists looked at the bourgeois state as the real enemy, and believed that a "class-based mobilisation directed against the state...[was] enough to transform the outlook of toiling people into revolutionary consciousness." In short, the "Hyderabad way" was thought to be better than the "Kashmir way".[57] The policy of class struggle and armed insurgency against the state run by a collaborationist bourgeoisie was considered to be the best way to shift the attention of the masses away from the politics of communal conflict that had engulfed the country after Partition.

It is also necessary to remember that the late 1940s and the early 1950s constituted the period that witnessed remarkable communist successes in Asia—in China, Malaya, Indonesia, Philippines and

Burma. This encouraged the Indian communists too, as they received endorsement of Moscow, which announced in September 1947 in a conference in Poland its "A. Zhdanov thesis" of encouraging more activism on the part of the international communist parties. This was Moscow's answer to the Marshall Plan.[58] Emboldened by this situation, the CPI purged leaders like P.C. Joshi, who was general secretary of the party until January 1948 and advocated cooperation with the Nehru government, and geared up for armed insurgency, which posed perhaps the most serious domestic problem for the Indian state in the initial years after Independence.

But the movement did not go very far, as it mostly remained localised in Hyderabad and West Bengal, and even here mass support was sporadic and conditional, as people were not prepared to abandon the Congress so soon after Independence. And the government also decided to deal with it sternly, using the usual repressive tools inherited from the earlier regime. While in Telangana the Indian army continued its "police action" against the communist insurgents, in West Bengal a new Security Act was passed in January 1948 to imprison without trial the leaders of the CPI, which was banned in March. Under such pressure, the party remained divided between a politburo that preferred a "Russian line" and the Andhra leaders who wanted a "Chinese line", and the debate became particularly bitter after the failure of a proposed railway strike on 9 May1949. By the end of September 1950 a stringent internal critique of both the strategies came from three front ranking leaders, Ajoy Ghosh, S.A. Dange and S.V. Ghate, who argued that neither strategy took notice of the objective conditions in India. The result was a significant shift in the CPI policy endorsed at the Third Party Congress in Calcutta in October 1951. It announced a new "tactical line", withdrawing the Telangana movement, agreeing to forge a broad front between the peasants, workers and the middle classes, and deciding to participate in the forthcoming general election of 1951–52.[59] The Indian communists thus moved from an insurrectionist strategy to constitutional democracy.

9.4. CONSTITUTION AND DEMOCRACY

The Constituent Assembly of India, presided over by the Congress stalwart Dr Rajendra Prasad, had started deliberating since 9 December 1946, and in little over three years it delivered a new constitution for India, which was passed on 24 January 1950.[60] It has been claimed, and rightly so, that the constitution was "a working out of the principle of popular sovereignty that was conceived and validated during the prolonged mass mobilizations that characterized the anti-colonial revolution."[61] But this anti-colonial movement in its late colonial institutionalised phase was dominated by the Congress, and hence the majority of the members of the Constituent Assembly were representatives of the Congress party, coming from the usual social classes that the party leadership was constituted of, i.e., primarily upper-caste Hindus, who were either zamindars or professionals. An attempt to make it more broad-based was made through the appointment of Dr B.R. Ambedkar, a Dalit leader and an accomplished lawyer, as the chairman of the Drafting Committee of the Constituent Assembly. But on the whole, the Constituent Assembly, which decided through consensus, remained almost completely monopolised by the Congress, and therefore reflected the ideological principles that it stood for, such as nationalism, democracy and secularism. There were three overriding concerns of the Constituent Assembly: unity of the nation, need for social engineering, and ensuring India's place in the world.[62] In other words, the future path that the new constitution was to chart for India was derived mainly from the ideological legacies of the nationalist movement that had remained under the hegemony of the Congress over the last thirty years. On 26 January 1950, the new constitution came into effect and India was declared a "Sovereign Democratic Republic". But as an element of continuity, she remained a member of the Commonwealth, as London agreed to bend the rules to retain a republican India within this imperial family of nations.

There were other elements of continuity as well, as the Indian Constitution was largely derived from an Anglo-American model. The most important aspect of this continuity was its dependence on previous colonial legislation, particularly the Government of India Act of 1935. The colonial government had been gradually introducing limited self-government through successive reform acts—the Indian Councils Act of 1909 (popularly known as Morley–Minto reforms) and the Government of India Act of 1919 (popularly known as Montague–Chelmsford reforms)—to associate a section of the Indians with its rule. The most liberal of these reforms was the Act of 1935, which expanded the electorate (although still based on high property and educational qualifications) and provided for provincial autonomy and a federal structure, while retaining crucial emergency powers in the hands of the executive to keep the reins of control in British hands. The Constitution of independent India lifted some 250 clauses straight out of this Act,[63] but it also incorporated changes that suited the preferences of the Congress and the realities of Indian politics as perceived by its leaders. For example, the principle of federalism which the 1935 Act had provided for, but which remained a non-starter because of resistance of the princes (see chapter 8), was retained, but was significantly watered down by the founding fathers who preferred to have emergency powers at the disposal of a strong central government, because they feared that otherwise ethnic and regional dissensions might jeopardise the fragile unity of the nascent state.[64] The constitution allows the central government to take over power in a state if national interests are threatened by war, external aggression or armed rebellion (Article 352), or if the constitutional machinery allegedly fails (Article 356). In other words, being conscious of the pluralist nature of Indian society they were out to build a strong nation through the power of a centralised state that somehow weakened all other corporate social institutions. The idea of a territorial state as the natural habitat of the nation was thus firmly established through the Constitution, which was expected to accomplish the unfinished task of national integration.[65]

In a society that lacked homogeneity, the framers of the Constitution did not want to leave popular sovereignty directly in the hands of the people; it was to be exercised through a "proceduralized" state.[66] The Preamble to the Constitution laid the foundation of a strong state that privileged the idea of "justice"—also derived from the legacy of the anti-colonial struggle. It was to be implemented through the "Directive Principles of State Policy" that promised equity and justice for all disparate social groups that constituted the nation. As Mithi Mukherjee has argued, unlike Western constitutions that enshrined the idea of individual freedom, the Indian constitution made the philosophy of "justice as equity" the "sovereign legislative principle", which was given precedence over the notions of freedom and individual rights enumerated in the "Fundamental Rights" for citizens. In future if there was a conflict between the two principles of "justice" and "freedom", the framers of the Constitution expected the former to prevail. Rights and freedom of citizens were not considered to be absolute, and could be curbed in exceptional situations for greater good as determined by the Parliament.[67] While this arrangement was deemed necessary for the uplift of different groups of people—many of them disadvantaged—it also implied the vision of "an activist and capacious state" entrusted with the duty of active social engineering.[68] Thus, as Mukherjee has summed up, "it was the institution of the Parliament—like the British colonial state before it—that would be the primary agent of a new society, where the people themselves were merely passive recipients of the beneficence of the state rather than agents of their future."[69]

Such continuities of principle from an earlier tradition also resulted in contradictions in rules of governance. By the time India achieved independence, the Congress had developed an internal structure of governance, which was democratic in nature. And therefore, when the Constituent Assembly debated the future governing structure of the state, there was an immediate consensus in favour of parliamentary democracy based on universal adult franchise.[70] For Sunil Khilnani, it was this common democratic experience shared by all sections of the Indian population that ultimately sustained India's unity.[71] Yet, despite this support for popular democracy, the Constitution also retained discretionary emergency powers for the executive to control unrest and steamroll dissensions. And the Nehruvian state used them in various forms (such as the Preventive Detention Act or Security Act providing for detention without trial) on a variety of occasions, particularly when the communist insurgency rattled it in the initial years. In Paul Brass's view, these measures betrayed a distrust of the masses.[72] Other historians have argued that in postcolonial India while electoral democracy was upheld and celebrated, there was a marked reluctance on the part of the state to tolerate the right to direct democratic protest or civil disobedience.[73] In other words, as Granville Austin has argued, for years to come, the goals of the Constitution and the realities of Indian politics created sets of contradictions for both the government and the citizenry that belonged to a variety of classes and communities.[74]

There were other areas of contradiction too. Within the Constituent Assembly there was a consensus that the new state of India would be secular—but secularism had many meanings. Ultimately the Constitution showed deference to the Gandhian ideal of equal respect for all religions, but this was also tempered by a fear of communalism. The Constitution therefore provided freedom of religious practices for all citizens, but incorporated no safeguards to protect the political rights of the minorities through proportional representation. The Minorities Sub-Committee decided to do away with the principle of separate electorates in the name of democracy, secularism and nationhood. The proposal of reservation of seats in the legislatures and government services for the religious minorities was dropped on the ground that in post-Partition India such a provision would encourage communalism and impede national integration. Nehru argued that "this doing away with this reservation business...shows that we are really sincere about this business of having a secular democracy".[75] But this did not satisfy leaders like Ambedkar who thought that Indian nationalism had developed an odd doctrine where "[a]ny claim for the sharing of power by the minority...[was] called communalism while the monopolising of the whole power by the majority...[was] called Nationalism."[76] Although the Constituent Assembly could more easily brush aside the concerns of the Muslims, those of the untouchables demanded greater attention for obvious political reasons. The minority question was therefore resolved by providing safeguards for groups that suffered from economic and social backwardness, but withdrawing it for those who wanted protection of their religious and cultural identities. Untouchability was declared illegal; and the provision of reservation was retained, though only temporarily for ten years, for the Scheduled Castes and Scheduled Tribes, in view of their historic backwardness.[77]

But Ambedkar's frustration with the Hindu orthodoxy was not over yet, as it came to the surface a few days later through the debate over the Hindu Code Bill. The proposed legislation was to streamline personal laws for the Hindus governing such matters as marriage, divorce, adoption, succession, property rights for women, etc. It was being discussed by Indian lawmakers since 1941 as it was widely felt that some sort of uniformity was required in this area as personal laws were being interpreted and enforced in widely divergent ways in different parts of India. In 1944–45, a committee under Sir Benegal Narsing Rau, a judge of the Calcutta High Court, was given the charge of formulating a comprehensive Hindu code. Independence and Partition delayed the process; but immediately after Independence, the Constituent Assembly appointed a Select Committee under the chairmanship of Ambedkar—who was also the law minister—to draft a Hindu code bill, which was finally submitted to the government in August 1948. The effort has been criticised by Madhu Kishwar as reflective of a colonial modernist mindset desiring to bring in social reform from above through the power of the state, as the bill would have the effect of freezing and universalising the legal system without any proper justification.[78] It was nonetheless a comprehensive bill touching all aspects of personal law, and particularly giving larger rights to Hindu women in matters of adoption and succession to property. And it was here that it struck a hornet's nest.

It was particularly the third draft of the bill prepared by Ambedkar, which proposed to give equal right to Hindu women to share their parents' property, which attracted the ire of the conservative Hindus within and outside Parliament and threatened to divide the Congress party. When it came up for debate in Parliament in the summer of 1951, eighty-five official amendments and over 300 private amendments were submitted for discussion.[79] It was a bitter debate with modernists like Nehru and Ambedkar on one side and those who valued the Hindu extended family above everything on the other.[80] Soon it became clear that the bill was not going to be passed, and Prime Minister Nehru decided to shelve it, although he declared it to be a temporary measure. In disgust, Ambedkar resigned from the cabinet and decided to go on his own in the next election as the leader of his All India Scheduled Caste Federation. After the election of 1951–52, the bill was divided into four components and passed separately: the Hindu Marriage Act was passed in 1955; the Hindu Succession Act, the Hindu Minority and Guardianship Act and the Hindu Adoption and Maintenance Act were all passed in 1956. In these new Acts the rights of women were so watered down that Kishwar labels them as "something of a fraud on women".[81]

However, with the new Constitution in force, the more urgent concern for the political elite was the first ever general election based on universal adult franchise. The Representation of People Act was passed in April 1950 and an autonomous Election Commission was constituted with Sukumar Sen, a Bengali ICS officer, as the chief election commissioner. Half of the population or nearly 176 million people over the age of twenty-one years were registered as voters—a marked improvement over the 1935 Act which had enfranchised only about 11 per cent of the population.[82] These new voters, legally conceptualised as free, unattached and uncoerced individual citizens, exercising their freedom of choice, were to constitute the "people" or the backbone of Indian democracy.[83] They were to elect about 500 members of the popular house of Parliament (called Lok Sabha or House of the People) and about 4,000 members to the state (or provincial) legislatures—in all, voting was to take place for about 4,500 seats. The elections were therefore not only a novel political experience for the majority of the Indian people; it also presented an enormous administrative challenge for the state, which had never conducted an election at such a massive scale. As Ramachandra Guha enumerates,

> 224,000 polling booths were constructed, and equipped with 2 million steel ballot boxes to make which 8,200 tonnes of steel were consumed; 16,500 clerks were appointed...to type and collate the electoral rolls by constituency; about 380,000 reams of paper were used for printing the rolls; 56,000 presiding officers were chosen to supervise the voting, these aided by another 280,000 helpers;

224,000 policemen were put on duty to guard against violence and intimidation.[84]

The voting procedure was also extremely complicated. Some of the seats were two-seat constituencies, where one seat was reserved for either Scheduled Castes or Scheduled Tribes. With 85 per cent of the electorate being illiterate, the procedure had to be made visual by allocating each party a distinctive symbol and placing a separate ballot box for each party in the polling booths. This meant a voter had to cast her/his vote three times—each time stamping on a separate ballot paper against the right symbol of the preferred candidate and putting the paper in the right ballot box with the symbol of their chosen candidate. This could be a daunting task for voters who were voting for the first time in their lives.

In a broadcast to the nation on 22 November 1951, Prime Minister Nehru rightly described the first general election as a "great adventure".[85] Ambedkar was also unsure about it: "An ancient people like the Indians who have no roots in democracy are made the judges and asked to choose the party and put it in charge of the Government."[86] Many in the West also thought that democracy would not suit the Indians who were more used to despotic rule. Nehru on one occasion expressed his doubt as to whether or not it had been a prudent decision to offer franchise to an illiterate electorate. But he nevertheless reiterated that this was the best alternative and launched a vigorous election campaign.[87] His Congress party, the inheritor of the legacy of the freedom struggle, had the best chance of winning the election, not just because it could muster a massive amount of resources and use a large party network, but also because its political opposition was hopelessly fragmented and disorganised.

Rajni Kothari has described the party system in post-Independence India as "a system of *one party dominance*", where the Congress was the "*party of consensus*" and the opposition consisted of "*parties of pressure*", because none of the latter was capable of offering a viable alternative government.[88] On the right of this political spectrum was the Hindu Mahasabha which had suffered a severe political setback in the wake of the assassination of Mahatma Gandhi on 30 January 1948 by Nathuram Godse, alleged to have had previous connections with the Hindu Mahasabha and the RSS. The public outrage that followed led to a severe clampdown on both these groups by the Government of India. Apart from state control, there was also a huge popular backlash against the Hindu political organisations and their leaders.[89] They could not recover from this crisis when the election approached. Its leadership remained hopelessly divided, and its election manifesto with the promise of "establishing Hindu Raj in Bharat"[90] could hardly attract the citizens of a new India. Its most prominent leader Dr S.P. Mukherjee had resigned, and at a conference in Delhi on 21 October 1951 formed a new political party called the Bharatiya Jana Sangh. He claimed it to be a non-communal party aiming to build a broad-based democratic opposition to the Congress, which was increasingly becoming authoritarian and corrupt. But in the end it could not offer any effective alternative ideology or programme, and without a mass support base became dependent on the RSS.[91] The Jana Sangh therefore could not distinguish itself from the Mahasabha, and as a result, in this election the Hindu Mahasabha, the Jana Sangh and the Ram Rajya Parishad (another small Hindu nationalist party) competed with each other and the Congress for votes.

The Congress's main opposition, however, came from within its own organisational structure. First, the socialists, who were operating within the Congress since 1934 as the Congress Socialist Party, decided to secede under the leadership of Jayaprakash Narayan and Ashok Mehta. Their separation as a protest against the Congress's move towards the right and its growing authoritarian tendencies was announced at a meeting in Nashik on 28 March 1948. Then Gandhian leaders like Acharya J.B. Kripalani and others wanted to reform the Congress from within; but after Kripalani's defeat at the hands of Purushottamdas Tandon for the post of party president in 1950, their frustration became public as repeated attempts to reform and unite the party failed. Kripalani resigned from the Congress on 16 May 1951, and at a convention in Patna on 14 June announced the formation of a new party called the Kissan Mazdoor Praja Party—or Praja Party for short.

Kripalani's critique, despite his recent defeat in the party election, was probably not driven by mere personal agenda as speculated by some historians.[92] It was a voice of dissent that was joined by many other Gandhian leaders from across the country, such as Triloki Singh and the People's Congress in Uttar Pradesh, Professor N.G. Ranga and his Andhra Praja Party, and Dr P.C. Ghosh and his Krishak Mazdoor Praja Party in West Bengal. Theirs was a critique that was ethical and moral, though not ideological. They were vocal against what they considered to be the disturbing tendency of the post-Independence Congress drifting away from the cherished Gandhian goal of "*Krishak-praja-mazdoor raj*". They were also worried about the growing authoritarian attitude of many of its leaders and their rampant corruption in public life. But ideologically they remained committed to the Congress philosophy and Gandhian ideals, which they proposed to implement through their policies. As a result of this ideological conflation, when the election approached, they could hardly distinguish themselves from the Congress. Its professed objective to establish "a free, democratic, casteless and classless society by peaceful means" sounded very much like the Jaipur resolution of the Congress (1948). And they disastrously failed to provide a concrete programme for translating that vague ideal into positive reality.[93]

If the Socialist Party and the Praja Party were roughly at the centre of the political spectrum, on the left the only major opposition to the Congress came from the CPI which had lately decided to give up the path of armed insurgency and fight the election to take over control of the state. However, their organisation was mostly limited to parts of southern and eastern India where the recent insurgency had been most powerful, and here they could use their well-disciplined party apparatus for electioneering purposes. But they also suffered from a major handicap, as many of their leaders were still in jail and the Congress government was in no mood to release these political prisoners before the election, although some of them were incarcerated without trial.[94] There were several minor leftist parties like the Forward Bloc, Revolutionary Socialist Party, All India Kisan Sabha, Peasants' and Workers' Party, Bolshevik Party of India among others. But they remained hopelessly divided. Sarat Bose, who had resigned from the Congress and formed his own Socialist Republican Party in August 1947, tried to bring all these non-communist leftist parties into an all-India coalition called the United Socialist Organisation of India, which he hoped would be a leftist alternative to the Congress. But he could hardly reconcile the differences—both ideological and personal—between these disparate groups, and hence the dream of a united leftist opposition to the Congress died with his death on 20 February 1950.[95]

So the Congress had very little opposition to fear. To buttress that nearly invincible position, Nehru conducted a vigorous election campaign through a whirlwind tour of the country commencing from 1 October 1951. In all, he travelled 25,000 miles in course of nine weeks, addressing election meetings in remote corners of the country.[96] He identified two enemies of the nation—"communalism" and "poverty"—and had two themes of his election campaign—"history" and "stability". As the Congress was the inheritor of the legacy of the freedom struggle, it was the only party that could legitimately claim the right to govern the new nation-state. And it was the only party that could deliver a stable administration.[97] The national media was an open partisan of the Congress, as wherever Nehru spoke, the speeches made front-page headlines in newspapers all over the country, thus taking his messages to the drawing rooms of the literate provincial voters everyday.[98] Obviously, the opposition had to contest this particular construction of history and argue that it was not the Congress which had won India her freedom. But such contestation also made the opposition election campaign look very negative—it seemed as if its only agenda was to dislodge the Congress from power.

This first election in independent India went on for about five months between October 1951 and February 1952. It was only in Nagaland that the Naga National Council had organised a complete boycott of the election, with not a single candidate filing nomination and not a single vote being cast.[99] But elsewhere, it was received with much enthusiasm, with about 60 per cent of the eligible voters casting their votes. This made Nehru ecstatic: "My respect for the illiterate voter has gone up and whatever doubts I might have had about adult suffrage are gone and the faith I put in our people has increased."[100] This tribute was also because they had delivered his expected results. In India as a whole, the Congress won absolute majority in seventeen out of the twenty-two states; it remained the single largest party, but failed to win majorities in Orissa, Patiala and East Punjab States Union (PEPSU), Madras and Travancore-Cochin.[101] At the centre, in the Lok Sabha, the Congress got absolute majority, but it was not an unambiguous victory. As Ramachandra Guha calculates, in Parliament, the Congress won 364 of the 489 seats, or 74.4 per cent of the seats, but got only 45 per cent of the votes polled; in the states, it won 68.6 per cent of the seats with 42.4 per cent of votes polled. In other words, more than 50 per cent of the electorate had voted against the Congress, and several of its prominent leaders were defeated.[102] But an even more significant outcome of this election was the emergence of the CPI as the largest opposition party in Parliament where along with its allies it won twenty-seven seats. Among the states, in Madras the CPI got fifty-nine seats, in Hyderabad forty-two seats, and in Travancore-Cochin thirty-two seats; in all these states, the Congress failed to get absolute majorities. In West Bengal, the CPI got twenty-eight seats in the state legislature, and five out of the nine seats it contested for the Lok Sabha. In a way, the results of the first election indicated the way the structure of Indian politics was to evolve over the next two decades.

9.5. The Nehruvian State and its Policies

Although the results of the first election were not unambiguous, in a first-past-the-post system it was a commendable victory for Nehru and the Congress. And this victorious journey continued for the next three elections in which the Congress won about 45 per cent of the votes, but 75 per cent of the seats in Parliament. And until 1967, the Congress ruled in almost every state, with the only exceptions being Jammu and Kashmir, Kerala and Nagaland.[103] Nehru and the Congress interpreted this electoral verdict as an unquestionable mandate to proceed with their preferred vision of the future trajectory of the nation. And this future trajectory for Nehru, as many historians and political commentators have argued, was towards modernity. The goal of the nation, as Nehru defined it in a 1963 article in *Foreign Affairs*, was to achieve "political democracy and economic justice". The massive exercise of the first election, he proudly announced, had already made India "the largest functioning democracy in the world". In terms of economy, Nehru argued, she strived to achieve socialism "without adhering to any doctrinaire definition of the word". This meant effective planning through the democratic process for extensive land reforms, industrialisation, and development of various infrastructural facilities like power plants, transport projects, irrigation dams, etc.[104] The result of this policy of modernisation, as Partha Chatterjee has argued, was the evolution of a "developmental state intervening in the economy, planning and guiding its growth and trying directly to promote the welfare of the population."[105]

The idea of planning, however, was not new, as in 1938 the Congress had established its own National Planning Committee with Nehru as the chairman. It functioned up to 1940, and then briefly in 1945, and recommended that India's prime economic need was rapid industrialisation. It had also suggested that India should strive for economic development in a planned way to achieve socialistic goals, and thus prepared the grounds for the setting up of a Planning Commission after Independence in 1950, with the prime minster as its chairman. It formulated India's First Five Year Plan for the period 1951–52 to 1955–56. According to P.C. Mahalanobis, the statistical advisor to the Planning Commission, and actually the chief architect of planning in India, the main aim of planning was to be the eradication of poverty through continuous economic development by using scientific and technical knowledge. Towards the end of the First Five Year Plan period, on 21 December 1954 the Lok Sabha passed a resolution stating that "the objective of our economic policy should be a socialistic pattern of society and towards this end the tempo of economic activity in general and industrial development in particular should be stepped up to the maximum possible extent."[106] The Congress party at its annual session in January 1955 again reiterated its faith in socialism;[107] but what actual form this socialism would take and how it would be achieved were still matters of debate and experimentation. While the Gandhian ideal of village economy was not completely or openly jettisoned, the main focus of planning gradually moved towards development of large capital goods industries with the mantra of import-substitution.

In India, agriculture still accounted for nearly half of the net national product, and its backward state was the major reason behind her mass poverty. At the time of Independence, out of a total geographical area of 800 million acres, only about 300 million acres were annually cultivated; and only 17 per cent of this cultivated land was irrigated, while the rest was entirely dependent on rainfall. While the quantum of yield per acre varied significantly between irrigated and un-irrigated lands, the slightest failure of the monsoon resulted in acute food shortages and near-famine conditions in many areas, requiring import of food.[108] As the largest segment of the population depended on agriculture, the root cause of rural poverty was uneven ownership of land. In an article in 1950, the economist Daniel Thorner observed: "The typical Indian peasant now is not an independent proprietor but a landless labourer or a debt ridden tenant."[109] About 40 per cent of them were wage labourers, and another 30 per cent rented or owned tiny patches of land, while the agricultural surplus was appropriated by a small group of absentee landlords and other intermediaries.[110] So the first crying need of the day was effective land reform, and for this purpose in December 1947, the Congress appointed an Agrarian Reforms Committee, which for a year investigated the post-World War II agrarian situation in the country, and came up with a policy recommendation to eliminate intermediary interests between the state and the tillers of land. This would increase the income of the tenant, and would therefore work as an incentive to invest to increase agricultural productivity. An advisory board of the Planning Commission formed in August 1950 was to review this agrarian policy with a view to create economic land holdings, examine the role of village panchayats (councils), and ensure the relationship between land reforms and agricultural productivity.[111]

Nehru thought that the best way to move forward to enhance agricultural productivity was through cooperative farming by peasants holding 1–2 acres of land; he did not like large-scale capital intensive farming or the collective farming model.[112] Such efforts were to be coordinated through the "community development" schemes or the *Panchayati Raj* on Gandhian model. As Nehru defined it, this meant "decentralization in favour of village-elected councils which... [were to be] given authority and resources to carry out schemes of development."[113] It was in 1959 that Andhra Pradesh and Rajasthan first introduced this decentralised system of local self-government with a three-tier institutional set-up. At the bottom was the village panchayat; above it was the *samiti* consisting of the heads of village panchayats covering an area inhabited by about 60,000 people; and at the top was the *zilla parishad*, or district council, consisting of samiti presidents. The area of the zilla parishad coincided with the area of the community development blocks created under the First Five Year Plan. Each block was assigned agricultural, educational and social welfare officers who were supposed to collectively promote development in villages within the blocks. By the early 1960s, the scheme was rapidly expanded to about half a million villages. Although in most parts of the country the panchayats continued to be dominated by rich high-caste landlords, in some areas such local self-governing institutions also provided for empowerment of the lower-caste peasants who in some cases even came to control a few samitis.[114]

But what rural development really needed was land reform, particularly ceiling on agricultural property holding, and the obstacles in the path of such agrarian reform were many. First, the Indian Constitution had made the subject of agriculture and land reforms the responsibility of the state legislatures. By early 1951, most of the states except West Bengal had either introduced or passed laws to reform the tenurial structures. In Bombay and Madras, where the ryotwari system prevailed, the laws were to protect the interests of the tenants. Elsewhere, bills were introduced to abolish zamindari, but it required close to four billion rupees to pay compensation to the dispossessed landlords. The central government made it clear to the states that it could not provide any financial assistance, and this delayed the implementation of the reforms. In the meanwhile, the bills were challenged in courts, as they allegedly violated the fundamental right to own private property guaranteed by the Constitution.

This led to a long battle between the judiciary and the legislatures; while the judiciary used Part III of the Constitution relating to Fundamental Rights, the government evoked Part IV on Directive Principles of State Policy to bring in the desired nationalisation programme. To resolve the standoff the Nehru government passed the Constitution (First Amendment) Act in 1951 to amend Article 31 and introduce the Ninth Schedule to make all land reform legislation immune from judicial review.[115] As Nehru boldly put it, the Act, which received presidential assent on 18 June, was simply "to take away, and I say so deliberately, to take away the question of zamindari and land reform from the purview of the courts."[116] But even that did not solve the problem, as implementation was delayed and impeded by continued obstruction by the landowning classes who had their influence over the administration as well as on the political establishment. Many of them avoided the land ceiling simply by transferring their excess lands to other family members. Some surplus land was recovered through the *bhoodan* or voluntary land donation campaign initiated by the veteran Gandhian leader Vinoba Bhave in 1951. In 1954, he started a *gramdaan* campaign encouraging people to donate entire villages. But in most cases the poor peasants received the surplus barren and unproductive lands through such land redistribution campaigns, which they had to cultivate without any infrastructural support or resources.[117] This lack of land reforms was accompanied by under-investment in agriculture. The proportion of planned investment in agriculture declined from 27 per cent in the First Plan to 18 per cent in the Third Plan.[118] The decline continued until the mid-1960s when the economy reached its crisis point—"the worst ever during the post-Independence period"[119] —with serious food shortages resulting in total dependence on food imports from the USA.

The government sought to handle the situation through the introduction of high yield variety (HYV) seeds—known as "miracle seeds"—developed in Mexico and the Philippines, and through the adoption of the New Agricultural Strategy as a part of the Fourth Five Year Plan. The experiment, known as the "Green Revolution", was expected to solve India's problem of food scarcity and produce a surplus. During the first phase of its implementation between 1966 and 1971, it was a great success as food production increased phenomenally and imports declined. But in the second phase, between 1972 and 1975, food production began to decline due to bad weather, and picked up again in 1975–76. On the whole, however, the growth rate in food production over the entire Green Revolution period remained lower than the pre-HYV years. Additional public investment in agricultural infrastructure remained marginal. The new technology involved greater use of pesticides and weedicides with their adverse environmental effects. Socially, it increased inequality in the countryside, as only the rich farmers could take advantage of the new technologies. Moreover, the new seeds were more effective for the production of wheat, and not for other food crops like rice, which was the staple diet in most other parts of India. And so the wheat growing areas like Punjab, Haryana and western UP, which were also better irrigated, prospered more than the other areas. The Green Revolution thus further exacerbated the regional disparities in living standards and created a new powerful interest group of rich farmers.[120]

The Planning Commission's attention during all these years remained primarily focused on industrialisation. When India achieved Independence, she had very few industries, the only exception being the cotton textile industry which alone competed at the global level. Less than 1 per cent of the total population were employed in modern factories.[121] But being rich in mineral resources, she had tremendous potential: she had the world's largest deposits of iron ore, virtual monopoly of mica mining, and ranked seventh among the world's coal-producing countries. But the First Five Year Plan (1951–56) had modest goals. With an outlay of only 20 billion rupees in planned expenditure to generate economic growth, it recognised the complementarity of the private and the public sectors.[122] While its focus was more on manufacturing consumer goods rather than capital goods, some modern factories in the public sector, some large river projects for irrigation and power generation, and a few institutes for technological and scientific research were established. In comparison, the Second Five Year Plan (1956–61) was really ambitious, as its aim was to achieve full employment within ten years; and this could be achieved by investing in heavy industries producing capital goods. As production of steel was considered to be the index of development, three steel plants, each producing more than a million tonne of steel per year, and a heavy machine-building industry were to be set up within the plan period. It was decided that on an average 30–35 per cent of investment should go to capital goods industries, providing import substitution, while the present rate was only 10 per cent.[123] Thus the basic focus of India's economic development now shifted decisively from the Gandhian model of village economy based on agriculture and small-scale handicraft industries to large-scale industrialisation to be achieved with public investment through deficit financing, indirect taxation and foreign aid. Socialism, however, continued to be the main rhetoric of the discourse of economic planning.

There were many apparent contradictions in this discourse. The Second Plan, for example, reiterated that it would go by the

Industrial Policy Declaration of 1948 which had stipulated that the task of industrialisation would be undertaken within the public sector and recommended a strict licensing and regulatory regime.[124] However, the 1948 policy also left a wide space for the private sector by announcing that India would have a mixed economy, and state ownership would be limited to certain specific sectors only, like railways, ordnance, atomic energy, coal, iron and steel, aircraft manufacturing, shipbuilding, telephone and telegraph materials, and minerals.[125] In 1951, the Industries (Development and Control) Act was passed, establishing a regulatory regime for private industries owned by both indigenous and foreign capital.[126] But despite such restrictions, the private sector in India, dominated by small groups of financiers and businessmen, often controlled by family groups, was never squeezed out of existence; on the contrary, it actually flourished. The government's position on the private sector was further defined in the Second Plan, as the Industrial Policy Resolution which accompanied the plan reiterated that only the "basic and strategic" industries would be reserved for the public sector, while in other areas the private sector would have a free hand.[127] Private enterprise further benefited from the protectionist policies of the government, characterised by import restrictions, foreign exchange regulations, and a licensing regime that prevented foreign competition in the name of economic nationalism.

Some historians have therefore argued that the connection between socialism and Nehruvian economic planning was more tenuous and rhetorical than substantive.[128] And this did not bring in prosperity for the Indian people. By the time of the Fourth Five Year Plan the weaknesses of this planning process became apparent. While the private sector could not be properly regulated, the restrictive behaviour of the licensing bureaucracy discouraged new enterprise. The public sector suffered from inefficiency; there was decline in public investment and too much dependence on foreign aid. The overall growth rate of the Indian economy was only 3.5 per cent between 1951 and 1980—often disparagingly called the "Hindu rate of growth". And adjusted against population growth, it was only a modest 1.3 per cent per year, with significant regional and sectoral imbalances.[129]

If pulling India out of poverty and underdevelopment was a major challenge for the Nehru government, keeping India united was certainly another. After the Kashmir and Hyderabad issues were settled, it had to deal with the remaining European colonial enclaves in India. The French handed over its possessions through persuasion, but the Portuguese proved to be more intransigent. When passive resistance was started in Goa in 1955 by Indian and Goan volunteers, the Portuguese unleashed repression resulting in the killing of a number of satyagrahis. Ultimately, the Indian army intervened in 1961, and thus ended this last vestige of European colonial rule in India, and as Nehru noted: "After that the independence of India was complete."[130] But while territorial integration was achieved, maintaining the unity of India and reorganising a pluralist society into an integrated administrative unit now proved to be a challenge, as controversies over the issue of a national language and linguistic regionalism had begun to raise their heads side by side.

While the British had used English as the official language throughout the empire, at the time of Independence in 1947, there were eleven major languages in India, each spoken by more than a million people. In this pluralistic situation, the question now arose about having a "national" or "official" language, replacing English, and thus asserting India's cultural identity and independence. For the sake of national integration, Gandhi had recommended the use of Hindustani as the national language of the country. Nehru too had recognised the potential of Hindustani—"not... too Sanskritised, not too Persianised" — to become the national language.[131] After Independence, however, the demand was to make the more Sanskritised Hindi, spoken extensively in north India, the "national" language of the country. But the proposal invited serious resentment and resistance from the non-Hindi speaking southern and eastern regions. Ultimately, the Constituent Assembly came up with a compromise solution: Hindi was to be the "official" language, but only after fifteen years; until then English was to continue as the language of the Union, while the provinces were free to use their regional languages, which were to be listed in the Eighth Schedule of the Constitution. This situation was further clarified by Parliament in 1963 through the Official Languages Act which stated that Hindi was to become the official language in India from 1965 as stipulated in the Constitution, but as a concession to the non-Hindi speakers also accorded the status of "associate additional official language" to English. But even this did not quell the suspicion and resistance of the non-Hindi speakers, especially in south India, where riots broke out in late 1964 and early 1965. Ultimately, the issue was resolved through the Official Languages (Amendment) Act of 1967, which basically provided a bilingual (English–Hindi) solution for any official communication between the centre and the states, and also a multilingual concession by recognising regional languages in provincial administration and in public service examinations.[132]

But there were also other complexities arising from this linguistic pluralism. The Congress in its 1920 session in Nagpur had decided to recognise regional linguistic identities and divided India into twenty-one linguistic units for its organisational purposes.[133] But the British had constituted administrative units without any consideration for linguistic homogeneity; and as a result, administrative units like the Madras Presidency contained four linguistic groups—Tamil, Telugu, Kannada and Malayalam—leading to varying senses of domination and relative deprivation. Hence, when the Constituent Assembly met in 1946, there were demands for linguistic reorganisation of the provinces. But now the Congress, which in 1920 had recognised the regional languages, opposed the demand for linguistic states in the interest of national unity. In June 1948, a Linguistic Provinces Commission was set up under the chairmanship of S.K. Dar, and it delivered its report in December. What is significant, despite huge public support in favour of creating the four southern linguistic provinces of Andhra, Kerala, Karnataka and Maharashtra, the Dar Commission opposed such a move in the interest of national integration. In December 1948, the Congress established its own high-powered Linguistic Provinces Committee, with Jawaharlal Nehru, Vallabhbhai Patel and Pattabhi Sitaramayya as its members. Its report—which is known as the JVP Report—also opposed the creation of linguistic provinces for the sake of national unity. Their preference was for composite states with no particular parochial identities, but constituted on the basis of administrative convenience and economic viability.[134] But they also recognised the popular pressures for linguistic provinces, to which the central government had to ultimately give in.

The first demand for a linguistic province was raised by the Telugu-speaking people of Andhra. On 16 August 1951, Swami Sitaram, a Gandhian leader, started a fast unto death in support of the demand for a separate Andhra state. While he broke his fast after thirty-five days, the movement was renewed on 15 December 1952. And this time another Gandhian leader, Pottti Sriramulu, ultimately lost his life after fasting for fifty-six days. This caused a political furore and violent clashes broke out in several places. On 19 December, the Government of India finally gave in and announced its decision to create the new state of Andhra, which was inaugurated on 1 October 1953. But despite linguistic unity, Andhra was hardly a homogenous region, as there were significant economic, geographic and cultural differences between the coastal districts known as the Circars and the southern districts known as Rayalaseema. And when Hyderabad came in, the Telugu-speaking people of Telangana could hardly identify with the other regional groups, and opposed the idea of "Vishalandhra". In other words, while a new state was inaugurated, the tensions within remained unresolved. While the situation in Kerala and Karnataka were relatively straightforward, in the case of Maharashtra, the Marathi-speaking people of Vidarbha were not comfortable about the idea of "Samyukta Maharashtra".[135]

Under popular pressure a States' Reorganisation Commission was constituted in 1953. While recommending the formation of "sizeable composite" states with self-sustaining economies, it ultimately gave in to the demand for linguistic states. But it did so rather "half-heartedly", as many linguistic demands were not considered. The States' Reorganisation Act of 1956 constituted fourteen states, but many of these states still contained sizeable linguistic minorities and regional economic imbalances. The continued preference of the Nehruvian government for a centralised administration provoked dissident voices of ethnic, regional and linguistic sub-nationalisms in Punjab, Assam and Kashmir, tribal insurgencies in the north-east, and cultural self-assertion of the Tamils in the south. There were fresh demands for the formation of new states. While until the 1970s linguistic demand continued to be the guiding principle for the creation of new states, later, ethnic identity and administrative and financial viability came to be considered as the new criteria for state formation.[136] In 1960, Bombay was split into Gujarat and Maharashtra; and in 1966, Punjab was reconstituted into Punjab, Haryana and Himachal Pradesh. The issue of ethnic identity became particularly significant in north-east India, where the Nagas led the charge first by not voting in the first general election, then by showing their back to the prime minister during his visit in 1953, and finally by starting an insurgency, forcing the Government of India to concede to the demand for a separate state of Nagaland in 1960, inaugurated in 1963.[137] Other states in the north-east followed gradually, with more claims still remaining unresolved. In 1972, Meghalaya, Manipur and Tripura were accorded statehood, Mizoram and Arunachal Pradesh being made union territories (to be made full-fledged states later).[138] In 2014, Telangana became the twenty-ninth state of the Indian Union, apart from the seven union territories (directly governed by the Union government), with a relatively greater acceptance of a federal spirit (more about that later).

In the 1963 article in *Foreign Affairs*, which we have already referred to, Nehru had argued that two policies had guided India since Independence. They were "democratic planning for development

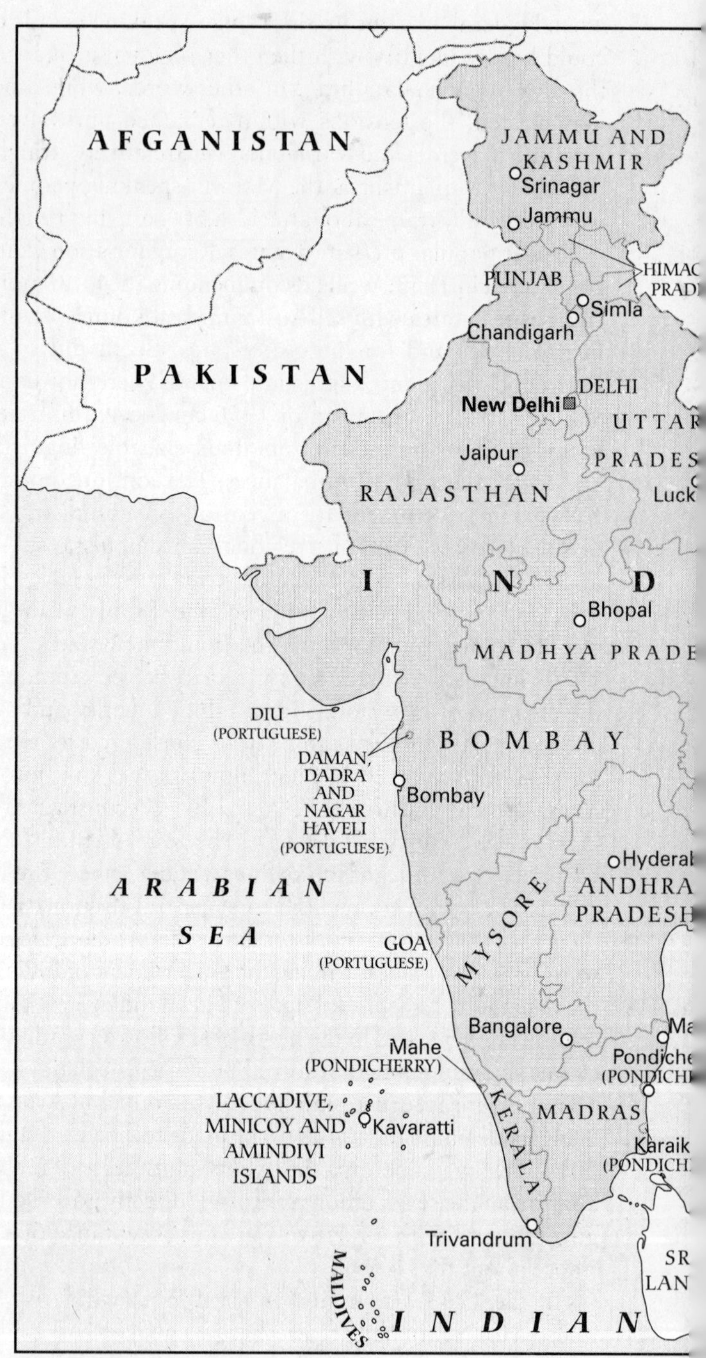

Map 6: India in 1956

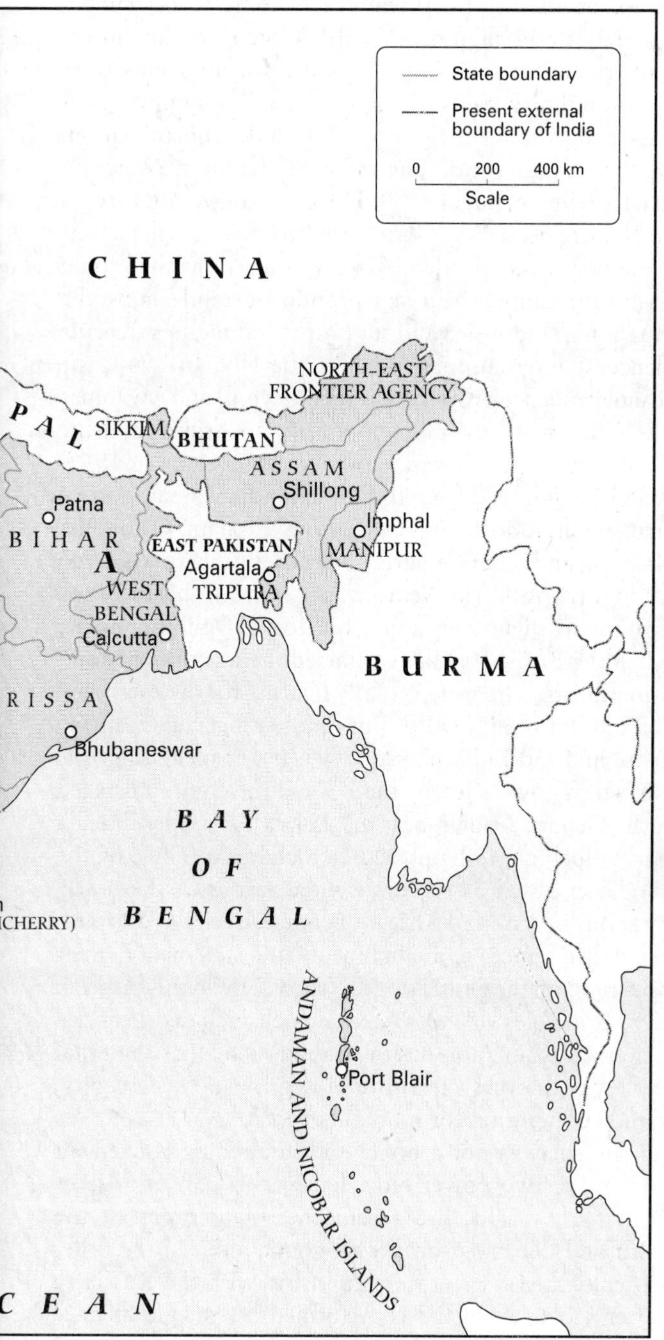
State boundary
Present external boundary of India
0
200
400 km
Scale
CHINA
NORTH-EAST FRONTIER AGENCY
PAL
SIKKIM
BHUTAN
ASSAM
Shillong
Patna
Imphal
BIHAR
EAST PAKISTAN
MANIPUR
A
Agartala
WEST BENGAL
TRIPURA
Calcutta
BURMA
RISSA
Bhubaneswar
BAY OF BENGAL
ICHERRY)
ANDAMAN AND NICOBAR ISLANDS
Port Blair
CEAN

at home and, externally, a policy which has come to be named, rather inadequately, 'non-alignment'." He defined non-alignment as a "policy of friendship toward all nations, uncompromised by adherence to any military pacts."[139] For him, non-alignment was rhetoric for asserting the identity of a newly independent nation; in his words: "Essentially, 'non-alignment' is freedom of action which is a part of independence."[140] Hence in terms of foreign policy, under Nehru's leadership India tried to position herself as the leader of the newly independent Afro-Asian nations that could potentially form a third bloc. She took a prominent stand against the Dutch reoccupation of Indonesia and supported Indonesia's struggle for independence at international fora like the UN. In 1948, she welcomed the independence of Sri Lanka (then Ceylon) and Myanmar (then Burma). Nehru was also a champion of Pan-Asianism, as he convened a conference of the Asian nations in New Delhi in 1949, demanding Dutch withdrawal from Indonesia. India was supportive of freedom struggles in Indochina (constituting Vietnam, Cambodia and Laos), Malaysia and different parts of Africa. But there were also contradictions in this position as Nehru was not favourably disposed towards the communists who were giving him lots of trouble at home. So in 1950 when the British in Malaya started their "police action" against the communists, who were actually fighting for their national freedom, India did not utter a word. But on the other hand, during the Korean War in 1950 India played a significant mediating role between the Western powers led by the US and the communists led by China. In the Geneva Conference of 1954, which ended French colonial rule in Indochina, India played a crucial role. Thus, by the early 1960s India emerged as the undisputed leader of the newly independent nations of Asia and Africa (of course, barring Pakistan), many of whom had accepted "non-alignment" as a statement of their independent position on the global stage. Nehru defined this position in terms of five principles or *Panchsheel*, which included peaceful co-existence, non-agression, non-interference in each other's internal affairs, respect for each other's territorial integrity and sovereignty, and equality and cooperation for mutual benefit.[141]

But non-alignment was not a policy of maintaining convenient equidistance from the two power blocs led by the USA and USSR in a Cold War-torn world. India remained a member of the Commonwealth and depended on US economic aid. On the other hand, she also cultivated a friendly relationship with the Russians, particularly after 1954, when the USA formed a strategic alliance with Pakistan. In 1956, while India expressed strong opposition to

Anglo-French intervention in Egypt after the nationalisation of the Suez Canal, she remained rather ambivalent on Russian intervention in Hungary.[142] From the very beginning, India tried to maintain cordial relation with communist China, being one of the earliest nations to recognise the People's Republic of China in December 1949. She did not protest—almost approved—when the Chinese army entered Tibet in 1950, and in 1954 signed with China an "Agreement on Trade and Intercourse in the Tibet Region of China". In June 1954, the Chinese premier Zhou Enlai visited New Delhi; in October Nehru went to Beijing. Indo-Chinese friendship was celebrated through the slogan of "*Hindi-Chini bhai bhai*".[143]

But the euphoria did not last very long, and the relationship began to sour once India offered asylum to the fugitive Tibetan religious leader Dalai Lama and the Tibetan refugees fleeing from Chinese crackdown. The Chinese saw it as a conscious effort to undermine their hold over Tibet, and against this backdrop, from 1959 the 2,500 miles of disputed boundary line between the two countries began to surface in diplomatic discussions. While India wanted to stick to the MacMahon Line drawn by the British in 1914 as the boundary between the two countries, China objected to it. Nehru misunderstood the new "militant, leftward course" of the Chinese foreign policy during this period,[144] and possibly overestimated the strength of the Indian army. Pressured by the opposition and a patriotic press at home, he took an aggressive stance, resulting in a disastrous military engagement with China in October–November 1962 that ended in a complete humiliation for India. China easily overwhelmed an ill-equipped Indian army, and ended the conflict through a unilateral declaration of ceasefire. India's territorial losses were minimal, but the loss of credibility on the world stage was huge.[145]

Since the debacle of 1962, criticism of Nehru's leadership began to mount both within and outside the Congress; and with failing health, he could never recover from this setback. After Nehru's death on 27 May 1964, India's search for security and her endeavour to equip her defence forces continued, and in this respect her policy of non-alignment was of little help. She sought military assistance from the Western world, particularly from the US, but did not get much response, as the US now was already aligned with Pakistan. On top of that, in 1964 China became a nuclear power. In this context, India's search for security precipitated a drift towards the USSR, which provided her MiG-21 fighter planes and other weapons, and diplomatic support at the UN Security Council. After the second

India-Pakistan war over Kashmir in 1965, which ended in a stalemate, the USSR offered to mediate, and the Tashkent Agreement of 1966 brought back peace to the subcontinent as the two parties agreed to restore status quo ante. The third war with Pakistan in 1971, under the leadership of Nehru's daughter, Prime Minister Indira Gandhi, was in response to the Pakistani regime's genocide in East Pakistan, resulting in about ten million refugees moving into India. The subsequent intervention of the Indian army led to the breaking away of East Pakistan, which emerged as the new nation-state of Bangladesh. But at this critical juncture India found herself pitted against a powerful alliance of Pakistan, USA and China, and this prompted Indira Gandhi to sign a semi-military friendship treaty with the USSR in 1971. Non-alignment as a preferred principle of Indian foreign policy was now finally abandoned.

9.6. DECLINE OF THE "CONGRESS SYSTEM"

Despite Jawaharlal Nehru's emphasis on the traditional principles of ethical good government to be intertwined with the Western concept of centralised bureaucratic administration, corruption in the polity could not be curbed, and this gradually led to the decline of Congress as the only political alternative at the centre. This dominance of one party and its preferred models of development and governance—or the "Congress system" as the renowned political scientist Rajni Kothari has called it—began to crumble even before the death of Nehru. And its consequences can be best summarised in Kothari's words:

> Corruption, centralization and arrogance of central authority, erosion of the party and the rise of a ruling class consisting of rich peasants, feudal lords, an all-pervasive civil service, a sprawling public sector, and a business class presiding over an urban-industrial-mafia power nexus, a lot of these a result of state policies and Nehru's own imported vision about the "temples of new India", all began before his reign came to an end.[146]

Although one could argue that history has often been unduly harsh on Nehru,[147] it can hardly be denied that the Congress had already become unpopular during his lifetime. Unkind words of criticism began to be aired when the first no-confidence motion against his government was introduced in the Lok Sabha in 1963.[148] And once his charismatic leadership was over, the Congress began its fast downhill slide. After his death, the Congress high command had Lal Bahadur Shastri elected as the new prime minister. But he died soon in January 1966, immediately after signing the Tashkent Pact that brought the second India-Pakistan war to a close. After that, Nehru's daughter Indira Gandhi was brought to the helm; an election was due in the following year.

The election of 1967 was preceded by two years of drought, serious food shortages, industrial recession, devaluation of the rupee, and growing dissatisfaction with the performance of the Congress governments in different states. The support of traditional vote banks like the Muslims, who had supported Congress in the past few elections, began to shift to non-Congress opposition parties due to the frustrations of the last two decades, the outbreak of communal riots in the mid-1960s, and the persuasion of special interest groups.[149] As a result, the Congress suffered severe reverses in this election. Although it retained a slim majority in the Lok Sabha by winning 283 seats, it still lost nearly 60 seats and lost power in half of the states. Non-Congress governments were formed in Tamil Nadu, Kerala, Punjab, Haryana, Uttar Pradesh, Madhya Pradesh, Bihar, Orissa and West Bengal. However, none of these state governments were single-party governments, but coalitions of several parties. In other words, this did not as yet signal the rise of any single alternative party to the Congress. As Rajni Kothari has argued, although the "dominant party model" had started to disintegrate, at this stage it only gave way to "a more differentiated structure of party competition".[150] The Congress could hardly be written off yet, as Indira Gandhi won from the Rae Bareli constituency and formed a new government at the centre. But it was her ascendancy, which precipitated the real internal crisis for the Congress.

At this juncture, the old guard of the Congress—known as the Syndicate—led by veteran leaders like Morarji Desai, S. Nijalingappa and K. Kamaraj, tried to wrest control of the party and the government, setting them off on a collision course with Prime Minister Gandhi. This open conflict between the party bosses and the government took place around the presidential election in 1969, when Indira Gandhi and most of her parliamentary party colleagues supported the independent candidate V.V. Giri, a veteran labour leader who was then functioning as the acting president, against the official Congress candidate Neelam Sanjiva Reddy, the speaker of the Lok Sabha. Following Giri's victory—despite a Congress whip in favour of Reddy—Indira Gandhi was expelled from Congress. The Congress parliamentary party was asked to elect a new leader, but the majority of its members chose Mrs Gandhi as their leader, thus finalising the split in the party.[151]

The new breakaway group known as the Congress (Requisition)—as opposed to the old party that came to be known as the Congress (Organisation)—now claimed to be the real inheritor of the Congress heritage, and gave an ideological colour to the intra-party strife by identifying the Syndicate leaders as conservatives who worked for the rich and powerful and against the Congress goal of socialism. Mrs Gandhi further reinforced her populist image through a reform programme initiated in 1969 that included nationalisation of fourteen banks, discontinuance of privy purses for the princes, and introduction of land ceiling. The political instability that prevailed in many non-Congress states, the conservatism of the old Congress leaders and Mrs Gandhi's decisive action in relation to some of her bold policies at home made her appear as a strong leader. And this resulted in an impressive victory for Congress (R) in the Lok Sabha election in 1971, winning 350 seats and virtually restoring that same dominance which the undivided Congress enjoyed between 1952 and 1967. And the spectacular victory in the Bangladesh war (1971) further consolidated that hold on power.[152]

But this victory failed to contain growing opposition to the Congress, now further fuelled by the arrogance of Mrs Gandhi, who centralised all powers in her hands. Nehru's developmental ideology gave way to a new "rhetoric of state socialism", while the Congress (R) became "far more centralized, statist and focused on a single leader".[153] On the other hand, increasing prices and growing unemployment, coupled with corruption and abuse of power by politicians and bureaucrats alike, led to mass discontent towards the middle of the 1970s. This growing unpopularity of the Congress was confirmed in an electoral debacle in the Gujarat assembly election in June 1975. The Janata Morcha, a loose coalition of a few disgruntled groups under the leadership of Morarji Desai and Jayaprakash Narayan, defeated the ruling Congress party by twelve seats.[154] But before this coalition could form a government, some momentous changes were to take place in Indian politics.

On 12 June 1975, in a landmark judgement the Allahabad High Court declared Mrs Gandhi's election from the Rae Bareli parliamentary constituency invalid due to corrupt electoral practices, and debarred her from holding any public office for six years. Justice Jagmohal Lal Sinha dismissed many other charges but found her guilty on two counts: using a government servant (the prime minister's private secretary) and the state government officials in organising her election campaign. But instead of resigning immediately, Mrs Gandhi decided to appeal to the Supreme Court. On 24 June, the Supreme

Court granted her a "conditional stay" of the Allahabad High Court decision: she could continue as prime minister, speak in Parliament, but could not vote. While this was an embarrassing situation for Mrs Gandhi, on 25 June, Jayaprakash Narayan gave a call for a civil disobedience movement to force her to resign. Without taking any further chances she decided to resort to authoritarian rule: in the early hours of 26 June, most of the important opposition leaders including Jayaprakash Narayan and Morarji Desai were arrested under the Maintenance of Internal Security Act that had been enacted during the Bangladesh War. On the same day, invoking Article 352 of the Indian Constitution, President Fakhruddin Ali Ahmed, on the prime minister's advice, declared a state of emergency.[155]

Under the Emergency, while all fundamental rights and legal remedies for citizens were suspended, a "Twenty Point Programme" was announced for the eradication of mass poverty. It included such populist measures as abolition of bonded labour, liquidation of rural indebtedness, land ceiling, and higher wages for landless labourers. On the other hand, some draconian social measures like forced mass sterilisation, spearheaded by her son Sanjay Gandhi, was carried through with the use of excessive force. The twenty-one-month long Emergency is thus remembered as the darkest period for Indian democracy. By 4 August 1975, more than 50,000 political leaders were arrested and held without trial;[156] media freedom was seriously curbed, and the Constitution was amended to give Mrs Gandhi retrospective reprieve from electoral corruption charges. But no hegemony is ever so complete that it leaves no space for resistance. As Mrs Gandhi needed political legitimacy for her rule, she called an election in 1977, presumably completely misjudging the public mood. The opposition parties like Congress (O), Jana Sangh, Bharatiya Lok Dal and the Socialist Party immediately merged to form the new Janata Party, which went into seat adjustments with other opposition parties like the CPI (Marxist) and Akali Dal, while there were also defections from the ruling Congress party. A slow groundswell of silent opposition had in the meanwhile swept the country, and it finally managed to overthrow Mrs Gandhi from power in this election. It was a massive victory for the opposition: the Janata Party and its allies won 328 seats and came to form the first non-Congress government at the centre under Morarji Desai. Indian democracy proved to have become mature and resilient.

But the change was not a lasting one, as the new loose coalition could not offer a stable alternative government. In January 1978, Mrs Gandhi brought about another split in the Congress, now forming

Congress (Indira), which subsequently won state elections in Andhra Pradesh and Karnataka in February. In November, she got back to Parliament through a bye-election from Karnataka. While Mrs Gandhi was thus staging a slow comeback, the dissensions within the Janata coalition also began to surface, causing defections, and forcing Morarji Desai to resign, and Charan Singh taking over with the support of Congress (I). This support, however, was soon withdrawn, forcing a fresh election in January 1980, in which Congress (I) came back to power with a thumping victory. Mrs Gandhi henceforth tried to consolidate all power in her own hands. This centralisation meant curbing of internal democracy within the party, as all decisions regarding policy and appointments flowed from her or from people close to her. There were attempts to weaken the opposition parties through creating dissensions and encouraging defections, as well as imposing stricter control over the state governments. In terms of policies, there was now a conservative shift to woo Hindu votes and offer more freedom to the private sector in the economy. These political tendencies continued till her death in October 1984, and also under her son Rajiv Gandhi who took over her mantle.[157]

An "unintended result of the excessive centralization of power by Mrs Gandhi", argues James Manor, was the rise of the regional political parties between 1977 and 1984. The period witnessed "freer competition between political parties but also greater instability in the party system and within many parties."[158] The trend certainly had started some time ago, from around 1967 when the Dravida Munnetra Kazhagham (DMK) had replaced the Congress in Tamil Nadu. Since then the most important of these regional parties that emerged were the Akali Dal in Punjab, the Telugu Desam Party in Andhra Pradesh, the Asom Gana Parishad in Assam, and later the splinter group of DMK, the All India Anna Dravida Munnetra Kazhagam (AIADMK) in Tamil Nadu. In a sense the Communist Party of India (Marxist) also emerged as a regionally powerful party in West Bengal, Tripura and Kerala. However, all these parties faced internal dissensions, and struggled to protect their state governments against relentless pressures from the centre.

Another result of these centralising tendencies was the rise of militant sub-nationalism and insurgency in Punjab and Assam. A radical group within the Akali Dal, initially patronised by the Congress, demanded sovereignty for a separate Khalistan. Indira Gandhi's strong-arm tactics to deal with them, epitomised by the attack on the Sikh holy shrine Golden Temple in Amritsar in June 1984, was followed by her own assassination by her Sikh bodyguards in October and an anti-Sikh retaliatory riot in Delhi, in which allegedly a number of Congress leaders were complicit. Rajiv Gandhi tried to control the situation by signing an "accord" with the moderate Akali leader H.S. Longowal. Although Longowal himself was assassinated soon after, the Akali Dal won the assembly election in 1985, and emerged as a strong regional party.[159] On the other hand, insurgency in Assam initially started in 1979 as a protest against illegal migration from Bangladesh, but eventually picked up issues of ethnic sub-nationalism, such as protection of Assamese language and culture and grievances against years of regional underdevelopment. Once again, Rajiv Gandhi signed an "accord" in 1985 to bring the Assam conflict to an end. The leaders of the All Assam Students Union, who once spearheaded the movement against immigration, soon formed a political party, the Asom Gana Parishad, and won the assembly election in December 1985. But the "accord" did not end the Assam problem, as the continued neglect of the centre now led to a more militant movement by the United Liberation Front of Assam, which wanted to liberate Assam from Delhi's rule with the force of arms. Ultimately, the Indian state suppressed the insurgency, "by using [both] persuasive and coercive means at its disposal".[160]

This did not mean an end to all ethnic sub-nationalist movements in India; but such movements ultimately have not been able to subvert either the unity of the Indian Union or its democratic political structure. As Atul Kohli has argued, "in an established multicultural democracy of the developing world [such] ethnic conflicts...come and go". Indian democracy has shown its resilience and the Indian state its capacity to absorb, accommodate—and if necessary, repress—such movements, as their trajectories usually resemble an "inverted 'U' curve".[161] At the same time, such movements have also contained the aggressive homogenising tendencies of the state, impelled it to respect cultural pluralism, and thus ensured greater harmony between the state and civil society.

As for national politics, in the parliamentary election of 1984, Rajiv Gandhi, who had been hastily brought to power by an embattled Congress after Mrs Gandhi's assassination, won a landslide victory; but that victory was to a large extent due to a sympathy wave generated by the brutal killing of his mother. Subsequently, Rajiv steered the party to a more conservative position. On the one hand, he began to woo Hindu voters and allowed the *Ram janmabhoomi* controversy to fester. The Babri Masjid in Ayodhya, a small town in Uttar Pradesh, was believed to have been built in the sixteenth century by the first Mughal emperor Babur by demolishing a temple commemorating the birthplace of the Hindu god and mythical king, Rama. In 1986, a district judge allowed the padlock to the site to be removed to allow Hindu worshippers to start their pujas.[162] In November 1989, the Congress government allowed the laying of the foundation stone of the *Ram Mandir* at the disputed site, and thus initiated what later became a major political controversy of contemporary India.[163] On the other hand, Rajiv also planned to win over the Muslim conservatives. When in the Shah Bano case the Supreme Court granted alimony to a divorced Muslim woman, the Rajiv government sought to overturn it by passing a law that gave precedence to Islamic laws in personal matters for Muslims over the civil laws of the land. In the economic field too he started moving towards the private sector and liberalisation of the restrictive licensing regime. In foreign policy, he sent an Indian peacekeeping force to Sri Lanka to intervene in their civil war between the Sinhala majority and the Tamil nationalists led by the Liberation Tigers of the Tamil Eelam (LTTE). As Rajiv centralised all power in his hands and ruled with the aid of close confidantes, the government became embroiled in corruption scandals, the most notable of them being the allegation of multi-million rupees bribery in the Bofors gun deal. Electoral reverses for the Congress began soon after.[164]

The regional parties and the leftists had already begun to take over power in the states, and they now altered the balance of power at the centre in the parliamentary election of 1989. This election truly ended the Congress system and ushered in a new era of coalition politics which was to continue in India for the next twenty-five years. It brought in a minority government led by the Janata Dal, a new party formed by Vishwanath Pratap Singh after his resignation from the Congress. This National Front government was supported by the leftists on the one hand and the Bharatiya Janata Party (BJP) on the other, and therefore remained highly vulnerable. While the period of one-party domination by the Congress was now truly and permanently over, the alternative government was hardly stable, as another election was held within two years. Midway through this election campaign, Rajiv Gandhi was assassinated on 21 May 1991 by Tamil terrorists, apparently exacting a price for sending peacekeeping forces to Sri Lanka. In the election, Congress did not win an absolute majority, but formed a minority government with the help of the leftists, with P. V. Narasimha Rao as the prime minister.[165]

Apart from the steady decline of the Congress, the other important development in the political history of this period was the gradual rise of the BJP in the 1990s as a champion of a reinvented Hindu nationalism and also as an alternative national party. The movement to assert *Hindutva* (Hindu identity) focused on the Babri Masjid issue mentioned above. The demand to demolish the mosque and construct a temple at the site was raised before the election of 1989, and supported by other Hindu organisations like the Rashtriya Swayamsevak Sangh and the Vishwa Hindu Parishad—together known as the "Sangh Parivar". It gathered further momentum during the time of the National Front government. V.P. Singh tried to divide the Hindu constituency by proposing to implement the Mandal Commission report that not only promised to continue the reservation policy for the Scheduled Castes and Scheduled Tribes, but proposed to extend it to the Other Backward Classes (OBCs) or the Shudra castes of the fourfold Hindu *varnashrama* system. It was supposed to break what Gail Omvedt has called the "twice-born monopoly of jobs", particularly in the public sector, where the Dalit and Shudra castes were historically under-represented.[166] It provoked a severe caste-Hindu backlash, and riots broke out on the streets of many big cities, seriously challenging the BJP's rhetoric of Hindu unity. But it failed to stem the tide of Hindutva. The mosque was ultimately razed to the ground on 6 December 1992 by hundreds of volunteers, known as *kar sevaks*.[167] On the one hand, while the demolition was followed by widespread communal riots in various parts of the country, it also contributed to the growing popularity of the BJP, which improved its position in the subsequent Lok Sabha elections. It the 1996 election, it emerged as the single largest party and under the leadership of Atal Behari Vajpayee formed a government at the centre that only lasted for thirteen days. Then, after a period of instability, the Lok Sabha was dissolved and fresh elections held in 1998, in which the BJP again came out as the single largest party, and formed a government with the support of some regional parties. This National Democratic Alliance (NDA) government lasted for thirteen months until the AIADMK withdrew its support. In the election that followed in October 1999, the BJP at the head of a much more stable NDA won 303 seats and formed a government that lasted the full term until 2004.

It has been argued that the BJP rose to prominence because it successfully gave voice to the deeply held sense of frustration and grievances of the people against the state and the Congress party. In other words, people supported the BJP for diverse reasons, which were often unrelated to faith or communal hostility. Rama in this context was a unifying symbol for those who felt strongly against the divisiveness of the Mandal Commission and the minority policies of the successive Congress governments that only paid lip service to secularism. And paradoxically, this unificatory symbol itself was in a way a gift of the Congress governments. The serialisation of the Indian epics, *Ramayana* and the *Mahabharata* in the state-controlled electronic media, prompted by the political decisions of an insecure Congress party, provided cultural imageries which the Sangh Parivar could easily appropriate for mass mobilisation. In short, the failures of the successive post-colonial Congress governments are often held responsible for the rise of Hindu nationalism since the 1980s.[168] However, emotions of Hindutva alone, it seemed, were not sufficient to satisfy millions of poor Indians; the NDA was voted out of power in the 2004 election as the poor rural voters sent out a powerful message about the more pressing economic problems facing the nation. Indian democracy, as in 1977, once again delivered a significant political change. The Congress came back to power again, but only as a part of a larger coalition called the United Progressive Alliance (UPA). In the states, various regional parties continued to rule.

The other major political development of the 1990s was what Yogendra Yadav has called the "second democratic upsurge", meaning a significantly higher rate of participation by "the socially underprivileged" groups in electoral politics. In other words, this marked the political rise of the *bahujan samaj*, which included the Dalits, Adivasis, OBCs, Muslims, other religious minorities and women.[169] This did not only mean a higher voters' turnout from among these groups at the time of elections. As single party domination waned and political competition increased, it also meant a tendency among these groups to politically organise as a possible means of empowerment. The OBCs rallied under the Janata Dal, and later its successor Samajwadi Party (SP), while the Dalits mobilised under the banner of the Bahujan Samaj Party (BSP), established by Kanshi Ram in 1984. Inspired by Ambedkarite ideology, the BSP had one blunt message: "We have a one point programme—take power."[170] Power they did indeed take in Uttar Pradesh in 1993, first as a junior member in a coalition with the SP; but when this alliance fell in 1995, the BSP formed its own government in alliance with the BJP under the chief ministership of Mayawati, a Dalit Jatav woman, who became the first Dalit woman to reach such a high echelon of power in India. Mayawati's clever strategies of political mobilisation through the use of Dalit cultural icons and oral traditions led to an unprecedented consolidation of Dalit power in Uttar Pradesh. In the 1996 elections, the BSP got 20 per cent of votes in Uttar Pradesh, with fifty-nine seats in the state legislative assembly and five seats in the Lok Sabha.[171] It was now a party of national importance.

Within the competitive political context of the 1990s, the assertion of caste identities by the Dalit and the OBCs was seen in opposition to a homogenised Hindu identity.[172] The lower caste self-assertion was widely expected to provide a basis for modernisation and struggle against communalism and the hierarchical order in contemporary Indian society.[173] But the formation of the BSP government in 1995 with the support of the BJP and the renewal of that political alliance in 2002 belied that expectation. Such a political alignment was either denigrated as opportunism or explained as "a compulsion of electoral politics".[174] Gail Omvedt described the BSP's politics as "genuine assertion and...a step forward", but it stopped short of being transformatory, thus allowing the Hindutva wave to take over.[175] It was also explained as Dalit refusal to be bound by the secular-communal binary, which was created, as Kancha Ilaiah has argued, to obfuscate the process of "Mandalisation" that promised empowerment of the Dalits.[176] No matter how we try to explain it, it is nonetheless remarkable that in an age of political competitiveness, the BSP quickly acquired the art of coalition politics and learnt to negotiate with rival social groups, including the Brahmans, in order to get into and retain political power that remained until recently a "twice-born monopoly", to use Omvedt's expression. In the wake of the decline of the Congress, it is undoubtedly a significant development in north Indian politics, following the pattern in south India where, as M.S.S. Pandian has shown for the Tamil region, the non-Brahmans had already arrived in politics even earlier.[177]

But this era of coalition politics as well as the dominance of the Congress system both seemingly came to a final end with the sixteenth Lok Sabha election of 2014, which resulted in a spectacular comeback for the BJP-led NDA and an equally catastrophic defeat for the Congress. To many commentators this looked like a paradigm shift in Indian politics, as for the first time after the 1984 election a single political party—the BJP under its leader Narendra Modi—won an absolute majority in the Lok Sabha, getting 281 of the 543 seats, thus being able to govern alone. This election thus effectively ended the need for coalition politics, though in effect the coalition arrangement of the NDA was maintained through token inclusion of ministers from its constituent partners, the Shiv Sena, Telugu Desam Party, Akali Dal and Lok Janshakti Party. On the other hand, the Congress was reduced to an all-time low—winning just 44 seats, and thus being denied even the position of the leader of the opposition. However, one needs to remember also that this election result did not necessarily signify the re-establishment of one-party dominance, as the rise of the BJP has been largely a northern and western Indian phenomenon, while a significant number of states in the south, east and the north-east either remained less influenced by the BJP or voted for regional parties.

While the wider implications of this most recent political change remain outside the purview of this book, we may discuss briefly how various aspects of Nehruvian policies were coming under increasing attack from various quarters over the last few decades. We may start with the Nehruvian policy of high industrialism of building large dams and heavy industries which came under serious scrutiny and criticism from the 1970s from the environmentalists and other social activists. This led to a number of important social movements, such as the Chipko ("Hug the tree") movement in the Himalayas to protect trees against industrial exploitation and uncontrolled commercial logging. It was started in April 1973 by a social worker, Chandi Prasad Bhatt through his Dashauli Gram Swarajya Mandal, and was taken forward by a Gandhian activist Sunderlal Bahuguna who organised a series of protests between 1977 and 1980 to bring the adverse effects of deforestation caused by industrialism to the attention of the world. Another important example of a movement led by the environmentalists was the Narmada Bachao Andolan ("Save Narmada Movement") against a proposed large dam (Sardar Sarovar Dam) on the Narmada River to generate hydroelectricity, supply drinking water, and provide irrigation facilities. As this project was about to displace thousands of villagers—mainly Adivasis and Dalits—without proper rehabilitation programmes, a movement was started in 1985 in a Gandhian non-violent way by social activists Baba Amte and Medha Patkar.[178] While the environmentalist protesters were subjected to state repression and harassment and the Supreme Court allowed the construction of the dam only on condition of proper rehabilitation of the displaced people, their struggle for justice for the villagers in Maharashtra, Madhya Pradesh and Gujarat still continues. However, despite this limited success in the face of powerful state opposition, what remains important about this movement is the philosophy that it stands for: as the official website of the Andolan claims, it seeks to "challenge the dominant model of development (of which Sardar Sarovar dam is a prime example) that holds out the chimerical promise of material wealth through modernisation but perpetuates an inequitous distribution of resources and wreaks social and environmental havoc."[179]

But if socialism was at least a shibboleth of Nehruvian development policy in the early years of the republic, in the 1990s that idea came to be further undermined, discredited and finally abandoned under multiple pressures. India was until now, in the opinion of the International Monetary Fund (IMF), "one of the most heavily regulated economies in the world".[180] It is true that this policy of planned development, overseen by a corrupt bureaucracy, had failed to alleviate the miseries of India's growing population that was soon to cross the one billion mark. Faced with a serious balance of payments crisis in 1991, Prime Minister Narasimha Rao and his academically inclined finance minister, Dr Manmohan Singh initiated a policy of economic liberalisation in order to fulfil the conditions required by the IMF for getting a loan. This policy, which was later continued enthusiastically by the NDA and the UPA governments as well, has been described as "a watershed in India's economic history".[181] It meant the easing of the licensing regime, lowering of import tariffs, actively soliciting foreign direct investments, reducing the number of industries reserved for the public sector, rationalising the taxation system, reducing subsidies, and attempts to reform labour legislations. India thus made a significant paradigm shift from economic nationalism to globalisation, an impressed World Bank calling it a "quiet economic revolution".[182]

This new policy, which has been followed by Congress, NDA and two successive UPA governments, has brought mixed results for India. First of all, the economy experienced a high annual rate of growth: on the whole it remained in the range of 6–6.5 per cent during the period between 1991 and 2009; it was more than 9 per cent between 2005 and 2008, but dropped to about 5 per cent in 2012–13. This rate has been significantly higher than the previous rates that we have mentioned earlier. Within the economy, the service sector enjoyed a higher rate of growth than manufacturing and agriculture.[183] In short, this high growth was fuelled by the development of the service sector industries like the IT, with a growing share of the world's outsourcing business and the financial institutions. It benefited a burgeoning middle class, which developed a seemingly unlimited appetite for global consumer goods. And therefore, unlike many other countries, it was this domestic consumption—not exports—which powered India's economic growth. India offered a large market, and therefore attracted the attention of many multinational corporations, all wanting to have a share of the pie. But on the other hand, as the manufacturing sector did not expand as it should have, it was growth without jobs for the masses. Those new signs of "India shining" have not been shared by the poor peasants, many of whom have committed suicide. Despite such employment-generating schemes as National Rural Employment Guarantee Scheme, initiated in 2005 to provide guaranteed employment for 100 days at a minimum wage, poverty alleviation has not progressed at a desired rate. According to government statistics, only 27 per cent of the population lived in poverty in 2004–05 as compared with 50 per cent in 1977–78. But this rate of poverty reduction is a good deal less than expected given the high rate of economic growth. In 2009, India was the tenth largest economy in the world in terms of GDP, and fourth largest in terms of purchasing power parity; but in 2010 she ranked 132nd in the world in per capita income and 122nd in Human Development Index. And as all economists agree, income inequality has steadily increased over the last few decades. As economist R. Nagaraj concludes: "India's development story, therefore, is one of *growth acceleration with polarization: modest poverty reduction with marginal gains in tangible human welfare.*"[184]

The level of poverty has remained alarmingly high particularly in areas populated by the Adivasi groups. Concerns for environment and battle for access to vital mineral resources have further complicated the story of India's economic growth. The issue of food security, once thought to have been resolved, has resurfaced, and steps are being taken to address it through legislation promising "right to food". This uneven development has created serious social imbalances and political tensions in the country, such as a militant Maoist movement in large parts of India, as not all the regions and social groups have equally shared the benefits of the recent economic bonanza.

On the other hand, a sizeable part of India's budget is still spent on defence; in 2013–14 India allocated Rs 2.24 trillion—a 10 per cent increase over the previous year—to maintain her 1.4 million strong armed forces.[185] Regionally, the real challenge of her foreign policy in the twenty-first century, and the most potent threat to her security, continues to be her relationship with Pakistan over the issue of Kashmir. With the beginning of militant insurgency in the late 1980s, encouraged and aided by the Pakistani army, India got embroiled in a protracted proxy war in Kashmir, while an actual but short war was fought over Kargil in 1999. A major consequence of this prolonged conflict has been the nuclearisation of the region. It was Indira Gandhi's Congress government, which had taken the first step by undertaking an underground nuclear explosion in May 1974. It was the BJP-led NDA government, which decided to weaponise that nuclear capability by detonating three devices in May 1998; Pakistan responded with its own devices within three weeks.[186] However, condemned by the world and pushed by the USA, the two neighbours got back to the negotiating table; but the peace process has progressed haltingly. The emotive power of religious nationalisms in both countries has made the peace process all the more difficult. On top of that, daring terrorist attacks in India—such as the assault on the Indian Parliament on 13 December 2001 or the mayhem in Mumbai in November 2008, allegedly masterminded from Pakistan—have not helped to ease the tension in bilateral relationship, despite periodic initiatives from both sides.

But globally India has adjusted well to a post-Cold War unipolar world. It is true that following the nuclear tests in 1998, her relationship with the West had gone through a tough phase. Her persistent refusal on ideological grounds to sign the restrictive Nuclear Non-proliferation Treaty and the Comprehensive Test Ban Treaty brought in economic and technological sanctions. But in the context of India's recent economic growth and the opening up of her vast market to foreign direct investment, the West gradually began to take her *de facto* nuclear weapon state status and her aspirations to become a world power seriously. Following US involvement in Afghanistan and the war on terrorism, India became important to its strategic interests. In August 2008, India therefore succeeded in negotiating a nuclear deal with the USA, known as the US-India Civil Nuclear Agreement.[187] This ended India's nuclear isolation for three decades and allowed her to purchase nuclear fuel and technology from the US for her civil nuclear installations.

At the same time India has also begun to look more closely towards Asia through the "Look East" policy, initiated in 1992 by the Narasimha Rao government. Thus one may say that while Nehru's idea of non-alignment was completely jettisoned in a new world order, his dream of Pan-Asianism has been reinvented. In the past, India's participation in regional networks of collaboration—such as the South Asian Association for Regional Cooperation (SAARC), formed in 1986 by seven South Asian nations—has been rather reluctant, as she did not exert much influence in that organisation. But with China's growing influence in the Asia-Pacific region, India's strategic interests in this area have led her to engage more closely with the Association of South East Asian Nations (ASEAN). India became its sectoral partner in 1992, a dialogue partner in 1995, and a summit partner in 2002. She also became a dialogue partner of the Pacific Islands Forum in 2002, and a member of the East Asia Summit from 2005.[188] This growing involvement in the Asia-Pacific region, particularly in its various multilateral organisations, was no doubt prompted by India's strategic interests in the South China Sea region and her apprehension about the growing power of China. But it is also in consonance with her ambition to position herself not only as a regional big power, but as a significant world power too, with an aspiration to secure a permanent seat on the UN Security Council. More importantly, with economic liberalisation India needed to integrate more closely into the world marketplace, and ASEAN seemed to be a convenient gateway for that. Therefore, in August 2009 India signed a trade agreement with the ASEAN.[189] Economic interests have also brought her into greater collaboration with the other important network of developing nations called the BRICS, an acronym that stands for Brazil, Russia, India, China and South Africa, some of the fastest growing economies of the world.

Thus, India's search for greatness, which started in 1947, still continues, albeit haltingly, in the twenty-first century. It has been an intrepid journey through many obstacles inherited from a colonial past, but undertaken—with some success and some failures—with unbounded optimism and undaunted aspiration. Despite going through many vicissitudes of history, India still remains a vibrant pluralist democratic nation with its many pulsating voices.

NOTES

1. "Great speeches of the twentieth century", Jawaharlal Nehru, theguardian.com, Tuesday 1 May 2007 00.06 BS, http://www.theguardian.com/theguardian/2007/may/01/greatspeeches, accessed on 14 May 2014.
2. Tan and Kudaisya 2000.
3. Kaviraj 2011: 75–81.
4. Chandra etal 1999: 1.
5. Low 1991: 14ff.
6. Furber 1949: 86.
7. See for example, Brown 1994: 349.
8. Chakrabarty 2007a: 3.
9. Roy 2007: 27.
10. Chatterjee 2004: 7, 12, 29, 34, 36.
11. Svensson 2013: 24, 34.
12. Spate 1947.
13. Oberoi 2006: 51.
14. Pandey 1997.
15. Chakrabarti 1999: 1.
16. Oberoi 2006: 47ff.
17. Nair 2011: 208.
18. Zamindar 2007: 19–20ff.
19. Oberoi 2006: 51.
20. For memories of violence, see Butalia 2000, Pandey 2001, and others.
21. For the experience of refugees, see Chatterji 2007, Zamindar 2007, Kaur 2007, Nair 2011, Roy 2012.

22. Zamindar 2007: 21.
23. Report on the Working of Ministry of Rehabilitation 1949–50: 5.
24. Zamindar 2007: 120–21.
25. Talbot 2011: 118–19; Kaur 2007: 131-33.
26. Report on the Working of Ministry of Rehabilitation 1949–50: 5.
27. See for details see Chakrabarti 1999, Chatterji 2007, Roy 2012.
28. Chatterji 2007: 112, Table 3.1; see also Chatterji 2005: 228–29.
29. See for details, Roy 2012.
30. See Bandyopadhyay 2012 for details.
31. *The Statesman*, 17 August 1950.
32. Menon and Bhasin 1993.
33. Bandyopadhyay 2012.
34. Pandey 1999.
35. Hasan 1999: 136–52.
36. For moving details, see Pandey 1997, Chatterji 2005, Zamindar 2007: 79–94.
37. See Guha 2007: 132–33.
38. *The Statesman*, 19 October 1951.
39. Copland 1999: 262.
40. For details, see Copland 1999:261–68;
41. See for details, Furber 1951: 359, Copland 1999: 260–62.
42. Ganguly 2013: 331.
43. Ganguly 1997: 8.
44. See for details Rai 2004.
45. Rai 2004: 280–81.
46. See for details, Ganguly 1997: 8–13.
47. Talbot 1949.
48. See for details, Dasgupta 2002.
49. Ganguly 2013: 333.
50. Chandra et al. 1999: 203–04.
51. Basu 1997, V: 643.
52. See for details, Bandyopadhyay 2012: 105–20.
53. Chandra et al. 1999: 203 and passim.
54. Guha 2007: 96–97.
55. Joshi and Josh 1994: 335 and passim.
56. Nossiter 1988: 16-17, 128–29.
57. Alam 1991: 25–73.
58. Masani 1954: 89.
59. See for details, Alam 1991 and Bandyopadhyay 2012.
60. For a comprehensive history on the making of the constitution, see Austin 1966.
61. Sen 2007: 36.
62. See Mehta 2007: 15ff.
63. Chakrabarty 2008: 3.
64. Brass 2000: 62–70.
65. Chakrabarty 2008: 8.
66. For a discussion on this, see Sen 2007: 39, 111–12ff.

67. Mukherjee 2010: 185–99.
68. Mehta 2007: 21ff.
69. Mukherjee 2010: 199.
70. Tudor 2013: 30-31.
71. Khilnani 1997: 6ff.
72. Cited in Chakrabarty 2008: 6.
73. See Chakrabarty 2007b.
74. Austin 1999: 14.
75. Quoted in Jha 2002: 3179.
76. For the quote and Ambedkar's view on minorities, see Tejani 2013.
77. For more discussion on the Constituent Assembly debates on the minority issue, see Bajpai 2000.
78. Kishwar 1994: 2147.
79. B.E.H.F. 1952.
80. Majumdar 2007: 231.
81. Kishwar 1994: 2146. Also see Majumdar 2007.
82. For more on the enormity of this exercise, see Guha 2007: 134.
83. For more discussion on this, see Gilmartin 2007.
84. Guha 2007: 134.
85. Quoted in Bandyopadhyay 2012: 154.
86. B. R. Ambedkar, "The Scheduled Castes: Claim to Clear-cut Policy and Programme", *The Statesman,* 23 December 1951.
87. Bandyopadhyay 2012: 156.
88. Kothari 2002: 40. Italics original.
89. Jaffrelot 1993: 87.
90. *Election Manifesto 1951*, Akhil Bharat Hindu Maha Sabha: 8.
91. Graham 1990: 54 and passim.
92. See Chandra, et al. 1999: 201.
93. For details see Bandyopadhyay 2012: 130–36.
94. See Bandyopadhyay 2009.
95. For details see Bandyopadhyay 2012: 137–43.
96. Guha 2007: 139.
97. *The Statesman*, 19 October 1951.
98. See, Karkhanis 1981: 89.
99. Chatterjee 1997: 23.
100. *The Statesman*, 18 February 1952.
101. *The Statesman*, 12 February 1952.
102. Guha 2007: 146.
103. Chatterjee 1997: 10–11.
104. Nehru 1963: 455–56.
105. Chatterjee 1997: 12.
106. Mahalanobis 1955: 7.
107. Frankel 1978: 117.
108. Mahalanobis 1955: 10.
109. Thorner 1950: 97
110. Thorner 1950: 98
111. Bekker 1951.

112. Frankel 1978: 118–19.
113. Nehru 1963: 456.
114. See for details Weiner 1962.
115. For a history of the protracted constitutional battle, see Austin 1999: 67–92.
116. Quoted in Austin 1999: 88.
117. Zachariah 2004: 195–96.
118. Tomlinson 1993: 179.
119. Dasgupta 1977: 241.
120. For details see Dasgupta 1977, Brass, 1990: 280, Chatterjee 1997: 22.
121. Thorner 1950: 98.
122. Tomlinson 1993: 171.
123. Mahalanobis, 1955: 16–20
124. Ibid: 125.
125. Tomlinson 1993: 169.
126. Ibid: 171.
127. Ibid: 177.
128. Zachariah 2004: 151ff.
129. Brass 1990: 276, 281, Nagaraj 2013: 192.
130. Nehru 1963: 454.
131. Quoted in Zachariah 2004: 208.
132. For details see Brass 1990: 157–68
133. Windmiller 1954: 297.
134. Majeed 2003: 83.
135. For details see Windmiller 1954.
136. Majeed 2003: 87–88.
137. Zachariah 2004: 210.
138. Chatterjee 1997: 23–24.
139. Nehru 1963: 455–56.
140. Nehru 1963: 457.
141. See for details, Zachariah 2004: 198–204.
142. Nayar 2013: 314.
143. See for details, Zachariah 2004: 204–05.
144. See for details, Dutt 1984: 15–16.
145. Sáez 2013: 322–23.
146. Kothari 1998: 28–29.
147. See Guha 2005.
148. Guha 2007: 343–45.
149. Quraishi 1968.
150. Quoted in Manor 1997: 98.
151. See for details Hardgrave 1970.
152. Weiner 1971.
153. Chatterjee 1997: 22–23.
154. Park 1975: 1003.
155. For details, see Park 1975.
156. Park 1975: 1008

157. For a masterly summary of the political history of this period, see Chatterjee 1997: 27–31.
158. Manor 1997: 106.
159. Chatterjee 1997: 32–33.
160. Baruah 1997: 496ff.
161. Kohli 1997: 342–43.
162. For the story of the Babri Mosque–Ramjanmabhumi issue, see Srivastava 1991.
163. Hasan 2000: 150.
164. For a detailed account of the Rajiv Gandhi period, see Nalapat 2000.
165. See details in Chatterjee 1997: 34–36.
166. Omvedt 1990: 2196
167. For more details see Gopal 1991.
168. See the essays in Ludden 1996.
169. Yadav 2000: 120–21 and passim.
170. Quoted in Hasan 2000: 155.
171. Hasan 2000: 148, 158–59.
172. Sarkar 1996.
173. Upadhyay 1992, Kothari 1994.
174. Shah 2001: 35.
175. Omvedt 2011: 156–57.
176. Ilaiah 1998: 283, 285.
177. Pandian 2007: 6ff.
178. Guha 1991, 1998.
179. http://www.narmada.org/introduction.html, accessed on 15 July 2014.
180. Quoted in Nayar 1998: 335.
181. Nayar 1998: 335.
182. Quoted in Nayar 1998: 335.
183. Nagaraj 2013: 192, 194.
184. Nagaraj 2013:189, 196–97. Italics original.
185. Laxman K. Behera, "IDSA Comment: India's Interim Defence Budget 2014-15: An Appraisal", http://www.idsa.in/idsacomments/IndiasInterimDefenceBudget2014-15_lkbehera_230214, accessed on 4 May 2014.
186. For India's nuclear policy, see Bajpai 2013.
187. For details, see "The U.S.-India Nuclear Deal", Council on Foreign Relations, http://www.cfr.org/india/us-india-nuclear-deal/p9663, accessed on 4 May 2014.
188. For a discussion on "Look East" policy, see Grare and Mattoo 2003.
189. For details on the FTA, see Pal and Dasgupta 2009.

Appendix
Chronology of Modern Indian History

1600	Royal Charter for English East India Company
1612	First English factory at Surat in western India
1613	Mughal emperor Jahangir grants trading rights to the English company
1616	Sir Thomas Roe visits the Mughal imperial court.
1618	Roe secures more farmans (imperial orders) granting liberal trading rights to the English company.
1639	Foundation of Fort St. George at Madras
1651	English factory at Hughli in eastern India.
1698	The English obtain zamindari (landowning) rights in Kolikata, Sutanuti and Gobindapur in eastern India.
1717	Mughal emperor Farruksiyar grants duty free trading rights to the English company.
1744–48	First Anglo-French War
1750–54	Second Anglo-French War
1756–63	Seven Years' War in Europe Third Anglo-French War in India—elimination of French competition.
1756	Nawab of Bengal captures Calcutta from the English
1757	Battle of Plassey—a new Nawab of Bengal under the protection of the English Beginning of the political influence of the English East India Company
1765	Grant of diwani (revenue collecting rights) for Bengal, Bihar and Orissa (eastern India) to the English company.
1767–69	First Anglo-Mysore War
1772	Warren Hastings appointed as the governor
1773	The Regulating Act
1774	Warren Hastings becomes Governor General of India Supreme Court established in Calcutta
1775–82	First Anglo-Maratha War

1780–84	Second Anglo-Mysore War
1783	Fox's India bills
1784	Pitt's India Act
1785	Resignation of Warren Hastings
1786	Lord Cornwallis becomes the new governor general
1790–92	Third Anglo-Mysore War
1793	The Permanent Settlement of land revenue in Bengal
1798	Lord Wellesley becomes governor general
1799	Fourth Anglo-Mysore War
1803–5	Second Anglo-Maratha War
1814–16	Anglo-Gurkha War
1817–19	Third Anglo-Maratha War
1828	Lord William Bentinck appointed governor general
1829	Prohibition of sati (self-immolation by widows)
1833	Renewal of the Company's Charter
	Abolition of the Company's monopoly trading rights
1835	Lord Macaulay's Minute on Indian Education
1839–42	First Anglo-Afghan War
1845–46	First Anglo-Sikh War
1848	Lord Dalhousie appointed governor general
1848–49	Second Anglo-Sikh War
1853	Railways opened from Bombay to Thana
1856	Annexation of Awadh
1857–58	Mutiny and the Revolt
1858	Establishment of Crown rule in British India
1859	Indigo rebellion
1861	Indian Councils Act
1876–77	Delhi Durbar—Queen Victoria proclaimed the Empress of India
1878	Second Anglo-Afghan War
	Vernacular Press Act to control 'seditious' vernacular press
1883	The Ilbert bill controversy
1885	Foundation of the Indian National Congress
1891	Age of Consent Act
1892	Indian Council's Act
1893	Hindu–Muslim riots over cow-killing
1899	Lord Curzon becomes viceroy
1905	Partition of Bengal
	Swadeshi movement
1906	Foundation of the All India Muslim League
1909	Morley–Minto Reforms

1911	Partition of Bengal annulled
1912	Imperial capital moves from Calcutta to Delhi
1914	World War One begins
1915	Gandhi returns to India
1916	Lucknow Pact between Indian National Congress and the Muslim League
	The Home Rule Leagues formed
1919	Montagu–Chelmsford Reforms
	Anti-Rowlatt Act movement under Gandhi's leadership
	Punjab (Jallianwallabagh) massacre
1920	Gandhi takes over leadership of the Indian National Congress
1921	Khilafat and Non-cooperation movements under Gandhian leadership
1922	Non-cooperation movement withdrawn after Chaurichaura violence
1923	Swaraj Party candidates enter the legislative councils
1928	Visit of the Simon (Indian Statutory) Commission
	All Parties conference
	Motilal Nehru report on the future constitution of India
1929	Lahore Congress and the resolution to fight for *purna swaraj* (full independence)
1930	Civil Disobedience movement under Gandhi's leadership
	First Round Table Conference at London to discuss a future constitution for India
1931	Gandhi–Irwin Pact
	Withdrwal of Civil Disobedience Movement
	Second Round Table Conference participated by Gandhi ends in a failure
1932	Banning of the Congress
	Second phase of the Civil Disobedience Movement
	The Communal Award and the Poona Pact
	Third Round Table Conference ends in a failure
1934	Civil Disobedience Movement called off.
1935	Government of India Act
1937	Inauguration of provincial autonomy
	Elections under the new act
	Congress ministries in eight provinces
1939	World War Two begins
1940	Lord Linlithgow's August offer of dominion status
	Muslim League adopts Lahore resolution

1942	Cripps Mission ends in a failure
	Quit India Movement
1944	Gandhi–Jinnah talks
1945	Victory of Labour Party in England
	Trial of the Indian National Army prisoners; widespread protests
1946	Mutiny in Royal Indian Navy
	Cabinet Mission to India
	Interim government under Jawaharlal Nehru
	Hindu–Muslim riots
1947	Clement Atlee's declaration to hand over power by June 1948
	Mountbatten Plan to hand over power to two national governments of India and Pakistan
	India Independence Act
	Transfer of power to Pakistan and India
	Communal violence and mass migration in the Punjab
	First Indo–Pak war over Kashmir
1948	Assassination of Mahatma Gandhi (30 January)
	Indian army takes control of Hyderabad
1949	A new constitution of India adopted and signed
1950	New constitution comes into force
	India becomes a republic
	Communal violence and mass migration in Bengal
	Delhi Pact on minorities
1951–56	First Five Year Plan
1951	Constitution (First Amendment) Act
	Gandhian leader Vinoba Bhave initiates *bhoodan* (voluntary land donation) campaign
1952	Congress victory in first national election
1953	New state of Andhra inaugurated
1955–56	Watered-down components of Hindu Code Bill passed
1956	Fourteen states constituted under States Reorganisation Act
1956–61	Second Five Year Plan
1959	*Panchyati Raj* (local self-government) first introduced in Andhra and Rajasthan
1961	Indian army expels Portuguese from Goa
1962	Sino–Indian War
1963	Official Languages Act
1964	Death of Jawaharlal Nehru (27 May)
1965	Second Indo–Pak war over Kashmir

1966–71	Fourth Five Year Plan; first phase of the 'Green Revolution'
1967	Congress suffers severe reverses in national election
1969	Indira Gandhi initiates populist reform programme
1971	Congress (R) wins Lok Sabha election
	Third Indo–Pak war over Bangladesh
1974	First nuclear test carried out
1975	Allahabad High Court declares Indira Gandhi's election invalid (12 June)
	Jayaprakash Narayan calls for civil disobedience movement to force her resignation (25 June)
	Opposition leaders arrested and state of Emergency declared (26 June)
1977	Congress suffers electoral defeat by Janata Party and allies
1980	Congress (I) returns to power
1984	Assassination of Indira Gandhi (31 October)
	Anti-Sikh riots in Delhi
	Congress under Rajiv Gandhi wins landslide election victory
1989	Election results in minority government led by the Janata Dal
1991	Assassination of Rajiv Gandhi (21 May)
	Congress forms minority government after election
	Policy of economic liberalisation initiated
1992	Babri Masjid in Ayodhya destroyed (6 December)
1996	BJP emerges from election as single-largest party and forms short-lived government
1998	Nuclear tests carried out
1999	BJP forms stable National Democratic Alliance (NDA) government
	Third (fourth overall) Indo–Pak war over Kashmir (Kargil War)
2004	Congress returns to power at head of United Progressive Alliance (UPA) government
2005	National Rural Employment Guarantee Act
2014	Telengana becomes twenty-ninth state of the Indian Union
	BJP-led NDA wins decisive victory in sixteenth Lok Sabha election

Bibliography

Ahmed, A. 1997. *Jinnah, Pakistan and Islamic Identity: The Search for Saladin*. London, New York: Routledge.

Ahmed, R. 1996. *The Bengal Muslims, 1871–1906: A Quest for Identity.* Paperback edition. Delhi: Oxford University Press.

Ahsan, A. 2000. The Partition in retrospect: A primordial divide. In *The Partition in Retrospect*, ed. A. Singh, 287–310. New Delhi: Anamika.

Alam, J. 1991. State and the making of communist politics in India, 1947–57. *Economic and Political Weekly* 26 (45): 2573–77, 2579–83.

Alam, M. 1974. The zamindars and the Mughal power in Deccan, 1685–1712. *The Indian Economic and Social History Review* 11 (1): 74–91.

———. 1986. *The Crisis of Empire in Mughal North India: Awadh and Punjab, 1707–48*. Delhi: Oxford University Press.

———. 1991. Eastern India in the early eighteenth century "crisis": Some evidence from Bihar. *The Indian Economic and Social History Review* 28 (1): 43–71.

Alam, M., and S. Subrahmanyam. 1998. Introduction to *The Mughal State, 1526–1750*. Delhi: Oxford University Press.

Alavi, Seema. 1995. *The Sepoys and the Company: Tradition and Transition in Northern India, 1770–1830*. Delhi: Oxford University Press.

Ali, Aruna Asaf. 1991. *The Resurgence of Indian Women*. London: Sangam Books.

Ali, Azra Asghar. 2000. *The Emergence of Feminism among Indian Muslim Women, 1920–1947*. Karachi: Oxford University Press.

Ali, B. Sheik. 2000. Developing agriculture: Land tenure under Tipu Sultan. In *Confronting Colonialism: Resistance and Modernization under Haidar Ali and Tipu Sultan*, ed. Irfan Habib, 161–64. New Delhi: Tulika.

Ali, Imran. 1988. *The Punjab under Imperialism, 1885–1947*. Princeton, NJ: Princeton University Press.

Aloysius, G. 1997. *Nationalism without a Nation in India*. Delhi: Oxford University Press.

Ambedkar, B.R. 1945. *What Congress and Gandhi Have Done to the Untouchables*. Bombay: Thacker & Co. Ltd.

Amin, S. 1989. Gandhi as Mahatma: Gorakhpur district, eastern UP, 1921–22. In *Subaltern Studies: Writings on South Asian History and Society*, vol. 3, ed. R. Guha, 1–61. Paperback edition. Delhi: Oxford University Press.

———. 1996. *Event, Metaphor, Memory: Chauri Chaura, 1922–1992*. Paperback edition. Delhi: Oxford University Press.

Amin, Sonia Nishat. 1995. The early Muslim bhadramahila: The growth of learning and creativity, 1876 to 1939. In *From the Seams of History: Essays on Indian Women*, ed. Bharati Ray, 107–48. Delhi: Oxford University Press.

Anderson, B. 1983. *Imagined Communities: Reflections on the Origin and Spread of Nationalism*. London: Verso.

Anderson, W. K., and S. D. Damle. 1987. *The Brotherhood in Saffron: The Rashtriya Swayamsevak Sangh and Hindu Revivalism*. New Delhi: Vistaar Publications.

Arnold, David. 1977. *The Congress in Tamilnad: Nationalist Politics in South India, 1919–1937*. New Delhi: Manohar.

———. 1986a. *Police Power and Colonial Rule: Madras, 1859–1947*. Delhi: Oxford University Press.

———. 1986b. Rebellious hillmen: The Gudem-Rampa risings, 1839–1924. In *Subaltern Studies: Writings on South Asian History and Society*, vol. 1, ed. Ranajit Guha, 88–142. Paperback edition. Delhi: Oxford University Press.

———. 1988. Quit India in Madras: Hiatus or climacteric. In *The Indian Nation in 1942*, ed. G. Pandey, 207–22. Calcutta: K.P. Bagchi & Co.

Athar Ali, M. 1966. *Mughal Nobility under Aurangzeb*. Bombay: Asia Publishing House.

———. 1975. The passing of empire: The Mughal case. *Modern Asian Studies* 9 (3): 385–96.

———. 1993. The Mughal polity—A critique of revisionist approaches. *Modern Asian Studies* 27 (4): 699–710.

Austin, Granville. 1966. *The Indian Constitution: Cornerstone of a Nation*. New Delhi: Oxford University Press.

———. 1999. *Working a Democratic Constitution: The Indian Experience*. New Delhi: Oxford University Press.

Bagchi, A. K. 1972. *Private Investment in India, 1900–1939*. Cambridge: Cambridge University Press.

———. 1976a. De-industrialization in India in the nineteenth century: Some theoretical implications. *Journal of Development Studies* 12 (2): 135–64.

———. 1976b. Deindustrialization in Gangetic Bihar, 1809–1901. In *Essays in Honour of S.C. Sarkar*, ed. B. De. New Delhi: People's Publishing House.

———. 1987. *Evolution of the State Bank of India*. Vol. 1, pt 1. Bombay: Oxford University Press.

Bagchi, J. 1990. Representing nationalism: Ideology of motherhood in colonial Bengal. *Economic and Political Weekly*, October 20–27: WS-65–71.

Bahl, Vinay. 1988. Attitudes of the Indian National Congress towards the working class struggle in India, 1918–1947. In *Congress and Classes: Nationalism, Workers and Peasants*, ed. K. Kumar, 1–33. New Delhi, Manohar.

———. 1995. *The Making of the Indian Working Class: The Case of the Tata Iron and Steel Co., 1880–1946*. New Delhi, Thousand Oaks, London: Sage Publications.

Bajpai, R. 2000. Constituent assembly debates and minority rights. *Economic and Political Weekly* 35 (21/22): 1837–45.

Baker, C. J., and D. A. Washbrook. 1975. *South India: Political Institutions and Political Change, 1880–1940.* Delhi: Macmillan.

Baker, D.E.U. 1979. *Changing Political Leadership in an Indian Province: The Central Provinces and Berar, 1919–1939.* Delhi: Oxford University Press.

Balabushevich, V. V., and A. M. Dyakov, eds. 1964. *A Contemporary History of India.* New Delhi: People's Publishing House.

Ballhatchet, K. 1980. *Race, Sex and Class under the Raj.* London: Weidenfeld and Nicholson.

Bandopadhyay, A. 1992. *The Agrarian Economy of Tamilnadu, 1820–1855.* Calcutta: K.P. Bagchi & Co.

Bandyopadhyay, S. 1987–88. Protest and accommodation: Two caste movements in eastern and northern Bengal, c. 1872–1937. *The Indian Historical Review* 14 (1–2): 219–33.

———. 1990. *Caste, Politics and the Raj: Bengal, 1872–1937.* Calcutta: K.P. Bagchi & Co.

———. 1995. Caste, widow-remarriage and the reform of popular culture in colonial Bengal. In *From the Seams of History: Essays on Indian Women,* ed. Bharati Ray, 8–36. Delhi: Oxford University Press.

———. 1997a. *Caste, Protest and Identity in Colonial India: The Namasudras of Bengal*, 1872–1947. Richmond, Surrey: Curzon Press.

———. 1997b. From subjects to citizens: Reactions to colonial rule and the changing political culture of Calcutta in mid-nineteenth century. In *History, Literature and Society: Essays in Honour of S.N. Mukherjee,* ed. Mabel Lee and Michael Wilding, 9–32. New Delhi: Manohar.

———. 2000. Transfer of power and the crisis of dalit politics in India, 1945–47. *Modern Asian Studies* 34 (4): 893–942.

———. 2001. Mobilizing for a Hindu homeland: Dalits, Hindu nationalism and partition in Bengal (1947). In *The Unfinished Agenda: Nation-Building in South Asia*, ed. M. Hasan and N. Nakazato, 151–95. New Delhi: Manohar.

———. 2012. *Decolonization in South Asia: Meanings of Freedom in Post-independence West Bengal, 1947–52*, New Delhi: Orient BlackSwan.

Banerji, A. K. 1978. *India and Britain, 1947–68: The Evolution of Post-Colonial Relations.* Columbia: South Asia Books.

Banerjee, S. 1990. Marginalization of women's popular culture in nineteenth-century Bengal. In *Recasting Women: Essays in Indian Colonial History,* ed. Kumkum Sangari and Sudesh Vaid, 127–79. New Brunswick, NJ: Rutgers University Press.

Banga, I. 1978. *Agrarian System of the Sikhs: Late Eighteenth and Early Nineteenth Centuries.* New Delhi: Manohar.

———. 1999. The Sikhs and the prospect of 'Pakistan'. In *The Khalsa over 300 Years,* ed. J.S. Grewal and I. Banga, 190–99. New Delhi: Tulika.

Barnett, Richard. 1980. *North India between Empires: Awadh, the Mughals, and the British, 1720–1801.* Berkeley, Los Angeles, London: University of California Press.

Barrier, N.G. 1993. The Punjab disturbances of 1907: The response of the British government in India to agrarian unrest. In *Peasant Resistance in India, 1858–1914,* ed. David Hardiman, 227–58. Paperback edition. Delhi: Oxford University Press.

Baruah, S. 1997. Politics of subnationalism: Society versus state in Assam. In *State and Politics in India*, ed. P. Chatterjee, 496–520. New Delhi: Oxford University Press.

Basham, A. L. 1971. Traditional influences on the thoughts of Mahatma Gandhi. In *Essays in Gandhian Politics: The Rowlatt Satyagraha of 1919,* ed. R. Kumar, 17–42. Oxford: Clarendon Press.

Basu, Aparna. 1974. *The Growth of Education and Political Development in India, 1898–1920.* Delhi: Oxford University Press.

Basu, Aparna, and Bharati Ray. 1990. *Women's Struggle: A History of the All-India Women's Conference, 1927–1990.* New Delhi: Manohar.

Basu, J. (ed.). 1997. *Documents of the Communist Movement in India*, vols V–VI. Calcutta: National Book Agency Ltd.

Basu, Nirban. 1994. *The Working Class Movement: A Study of Jute Mills of Bengal, 1937–47.* Calcutta: K.P. Bagchi & Co.

Basu, Subho. 1998. Strikes and 'communal' riots in Calcutta in the 1890s: Industrial workers, bhadralok nationalist leadership and the colonial state. *Modern Asian Studies* 32 (4): 949–83.

Bayley, D. H. 1969. *The Police and Political Development in India.* Princeton, NJ: Princeton University Press.

Bayly, C. A. 1975. *The Local Roots of Indian Politics: Allahabad, 1880–1920.* Oxford: Clarendon Press.

———. 1983. *Rulers, Townsmen and Bazars: North Indian Society in the Age of British Expansion, 1770–1870.* Cambridge: Cambridge University Press.

———. 1986. Editor's concluding note: Eric Stokes and the uprising of 1857. In *The Peasant Armed: The Indian Rebellion of 1857*, by Eric Stokes, 226–43. Oxford: Clarendon Press.

———. 1987. *Indian Society and the Making of the English Empire.* The New Cambridge History of India, vol. 2.1. Cambridge: Cambridge University Press.

———. 1989. *Imperial Meridian: The British Empire and the World, 1780-1830.* London: Longman

———. 1998. *Origins of Nationality in South Asia: Patriotism and Ethical Government in the Making of Modern India.* Delhi: Oxford University Press.

———. 1999. The second British empire. In *The Oxford History of British Empire*. Vol. 5, *Historiography*, ed. R.W. Winks, 54–72. Oxford, New York: Oxford University Press.

Bayly, Susarn 1999. *Caste, Society and Politics in India from the Eighteenth Century to the Modern Age.* The New Cambridge History of India, 4.3. Cambridge: Cambridge University Press.

Beaglehole, T. H. 1966. *Thomas Munro and the Development of the Administrative Policy in Madras, 1792–1818.* Cambridge: Cambridge University Press.

B.E.H.F. 1952. Social reform in India: The Hindu Code Bill. *The World Today* 8 (3): 123–32.

Bekker, K. 1951. Land reform legislation in India. *The Middle East Journal* 5 (3): 319–36.

Beteille, Andre. 1991. *Society and Politics in India: Essays in Comparative Perspective*. London and Atlantic Highlands, NJ: Athlone Press.

Bhabha, Homi. 1990. Introduction: Narrating the nation. In *Nation and Narration*, ed. Homi Bhabha, 1–7. London and New York: Routledge.

Bhadra, Gautam. 1985. Four rebels of Eighteen-Fifty-Seven. In *Subaltern Studies: Writings on South Asian History and Society*, vol. 4, ed. R. Guha, 229–75. Delhi: Oxford University Press.

———. 1994. *Iman O Nishan* [Honour and the Flag], Calcutta: Subarnarekha.

Bhattacharya, Neeladri. 1992. Colonial state and agrarian society. In *The Making of Agrarian Policy in British India, 1770–1900*, ed. B. Stein, 113–49. Delhi: Oxford University Press.

Bhattacharya, P. 1975. Rammohun Roy and Bengali prose. In *Rammohun Roy and the Process of Modernization in India,* ed. V.C. Joshi, 195–223. New Delhi: Vikas.

Bhattacharya, S. 1971. *Financial Foundations of the British Raj.* Simla: Indian Institute of Advanced Study.

———. 1976. Cotton mills and spinning wheels: Swadeshi and the Indian capitalist class, 1920–22. *Economic and Political Weekly*, 20 November, 11 (47): 1828–32.

———. 1982. Regional economy (1757–1857): Eastern India. In *The Cambridge Economic History of India,* vol. 2, ed. Dharma Kumar, 270–332. Cambridge: Cambridge University Press.

———. 1986. The colonial state, capital and labour: Bombay, 1919–1931. In *Situating Indian History for Sarvepalli Gopal,* ed. S. Bhattacharya and R. Thapar, 171–93. Delhi: Oxford University Press.

———. 1989. *Ouponibeshik Bharater Arthaniti 1850–1947* [Economy of Colonial India, 1850–1947]. Calcutta: Ananda Publishers, 1396 BS.

———. 1998. Introduction to *The Contested Terrain: Perspectives on Education in India*. Hyderabad: Orient Longman.

Borthwick, M. 1978. *Keshub Chunder Sen: A Search for Cultural Synthesis.* Columbia: South Asia Books.

———. 1984. *The Changing Role of Women in Bengal, 1849–1905.* Princeton: Princeton University Press.

Bose, Sugata. 1986. *Agrarian Bengal: Economy, Social Structure and Politics, 1919–1947.* Cambridge: Cambridge University Press.

———. 1993. *Peasant Labour and Colonial Capital: Rural Bengal since 1770.* The New Cambridge History of India, vol. 3.2. Cambridge: Cambridge University Press.

———. 1997. Nation as mother: Representations and contestations of 'India' in Bengali literature and culture. In *Nationalism, Democracy and Development: State and Politics in India*, eds. S. Bose and A. Jalal, 50–75. Delhi: Oxford University Press.

Bose, Sugata, and Ayesha Jalal. 1998. *Modern South Asia: History, Culture, Political Economy.* London and New York: Routledge.

Boyce, D.G. 1999. *Decolonisation and the British Empire, 1775–1997.* Basingstoke: Macmillan.

Brass, Paul. 1974. *Language, Religion and Politics in North India.* London: Cambridge University Press.

———. 1990. *The Politics of India since Independence.* Cambridge: Cambridge University Press.

———. 2000. The strong state and the fear of disorder. In *Transforming India: Social and Political Dynamics of Democracy*, eds. F.R. Frankel, Z. Hasan, R. Bhargava and B. Arora, 60–88. New Delhi: Oxford University Press.

Brasted, H.V., and C. Bridge. 1990. '15 August 1947': Labour's parting gift to India. In *India: Creating a Modern Nation*, ed. J. Masselos, 1–35. New Delhi: Sterling Publishers.

———. 1994. The transfer of power in South Asia: An historiographical review. *South Asia,* New Series, 17 (1): 93–114.

Bridge, Carl. 1986. *Holding India to the Empire: The British Conservative Party and the 1935 Constitution.* New Delhi: Sterling.

Brittlebank, K. 1997. *Tipu Sultan's Search for Legitimacy: Islam and Kingship in a Hindu Domain.* Delhi: Oxford University Press.

Broomfield, J. H. 1968. *Elite Conflict in a Plural Society: Twentieth-Century Bengal.* Berkeley and Los Angeles: University of California Press.

Brown, Judith M. 1972. *Gandhi's Rise to Power: Indian Politics, 1915–1922.* Cambridge: Cambridge University Press.

———. 1977. *Gandhi and Civil Disobedience: The Mahatma in Indian Politics, 1928–1934.* Cambridge: Cambridge University Press.

———. 1989. *Gandhi: Prisoner of Hope.* New Haven and London: Yale University Press.

———. 1994. *Modern India. The Origins of an Asian Democracy.* 2nd ed. New York: Oxford University Press.

Butalia, Urvashi. 1998. *The Other Side of Silence: Voices from the Partition of India.* Delhi: Penguin Books India.

———. 2001. An archive with a difference: Partition letters. In *The Partitions of Memory: The Afterlife of the Division of India,* ed. Suvir Kaul, 208–41. New Delhi: Permanent Black.

Cain, P. J., and A. G. Hopkins. 1993. *British Imperialism: Innovation and Expansion, 1688–1914.* London and New York: Longman.

Calkins, P. B. 1970. The formation of a regionally oriented ruling group in Bengal, 1700–1740. *Journal of Asian Studies* 29 (4): 799–806.

Carroll, Lucy. 1978. Colonial perceptions of Indian society and the emergence of caste(s) associations. *Journal of Asian Studies* 37 (2): 233–50.

———. 1983. Law, custom, and statutory social reform: The Hindu Widows' Remarriage Act of 1856. *The Indian Economic and Social History Review* 20 (4): 363–88.

Cashman, R. 1970. The political recruitment of God Ganapati. *The Indian Economic and Social History Review* 7 (3): 347–73.

Catanach, I. J. 1970. *Rural Credit in Western India, 1875–1930*. Berkeley, Los Angeles and London: University of California Press.

———. 1984. Poona politics and the plague. *South Asia* 7 (2): 1–18.

———. 1993. Agrarian disturbances in nineteenth-century India. In *Peasant Resistance in India, 1858–1914*, ed. David Hardiman, 184–203. Paperback edition. Delhi: Oxford University Press.

Chakrabarti, P. K. 1999. *The Marginal Men: The Refugees and the Left Political Syndrome in West Bengal*. Calcutta: Naya Udyog.

Chakrabarty, B. 1990. *Subhas Chandra Bose and Middle Class Radicalism: A Study in Indian Nationalism, 1928–1940*. Delhi: Oxford University Press.

———. 1993. The 1947 united Bengal movement: A thesis without synthesis. *The Indian Economic and Social History Review* 30 (4): 467–88.

———. 1997. *Local Politics and Indian Nationalism: Midnapur, 1919–1944*. New Delhi: Manohar Publishers and Distributors.

———. 2008. *Indian Politics and Society since Independence: Events, Processes and Ideology*. London and New York: Routledge.

Chakrabarty, D. 1989. *Rethinking Working Class History: Bengal, 1890–1940*. Princeton: Princeton University Press.

———. 1994. The difference-defferal of a colonial modernity: Public debates on domesticity in British India. In *Subaltern Studies: Essays in Honour of Ranajit Guha*, vol. 8, ed. David Arnold and David Hardiman, 50–88. Delhi: Oxford University Press.

———. 1998. Minority histories, subaltern pasts. *Economic and Political Weekly*, 28 February, 473–79.

———. 2000. *Provincializing Europe: Postcolonial Thought and Historical Difference*. Princeton and Oxford: Princeton University Press.

———. 2007a. Introduction. In *From the Colonial to the Postcolonial: India and Pakistan in Transition*, eds. D. Chakrabarty, R. Majumdar and A. Sartori. New Delhi: Oxford University Press.

———. 2007b. "In the Name of Politics": Sovereignty, Democracy, and the Multitude in India. In *From the Colonial to the Postcolonial*, eds. D. Chakrabarty, R. Majumdar and A. Sartori, 31–54. New Delhi: Oxford University Press.

Chakrabarty, R. 1985. *Vaishnavism in Bengal, 1486–1900*. Calcutta: Sanskrit Pustak Bhandar.

Chakrabarti, H. 1992. *Political Protest in Bengal: Boycott and Terrorism, 1905–1918*. Calcutta: Papyrus.

Chakravarti, U. 1998. *Rewriting History: The Life and Times of Pandita Ramabai*. New Delhi: Kali for Women.

Chandavarkar, Rajnarayan. 1994. *The Origins of Industrial Capitalism in India: Business Strategies and the Working Classes in Bombay, 1900–1940*. Cambridge: Cambridge University Press.

———. 1998. *Imperial Power and Popular Politics: Class, Resistance and the State in India, c. 1850–1950*. Cambridge: Cambridge University Press.

Chandra, Bipan. 1966. *The Rise and Growth of Economic Nationalism in India*. New Delhi: People's Publishing House.

———. 1979. *Nationalism and Colonialism in Modern India.* New Delhi: Orient Longman.

———. 1993. *Communalism in Modern India.* 2nd revised ed. New Delhi: Vikas Publishing House.

Chandra, Bipan, Mridula Mukherjee and Aditya Mukherjee. 1999. *India after Independence: 1947–2000.* New Delhi: Penguin Books.

Chandra, Bipan, Mridula Mukherjee, Aditya Mukherjee, K.N. Panikar and Sucheta Mahajan. 1989. *India's Struggle for Independence.* New Delhi: Penguin Books India.

Chandra, Satish. 1973. *Parties and Politics at the Mughal Court.* Bombay: People's Publishing House.

———. 1991. *The Eighteenth Century in India: Its Economy and the Role of the Marathas, the Jats, the Sikhs and the Afghans.* Revised edition. Calcutta: K.P. Bagchi & Co.

———. 1993. *Mughal Religious Policies: The Rajputs and the Deccan.* New Delhi: Vikas Publishing House.

Chandra, Sudhir. 1998. *Enslaved Daughters: Colonialism, Law and Women's Rights.* Delhi: Oxford University Press.

Charlesworth, Neil. 1972. The myth of the Deccan riots. *Modern Asian Studies* 6 (4): 401–21.

———. 1982. *British Rule and the Indian Economy, 1800–1914.* London and Basingstoke, Macmillan.

———. 1985. *Peasants and Imperial Rule: Agriculture and Agrarian Society in the Bombay Presidency, 1850–1935.* Cambridge: Cambridge University Press.

Chatterjee, Partha. 1984a. *Bengal, 1920–1947: The Land Question.* Calcutta: K.P. Bagchi & Co.

———. 1984b. Gandhi and the critique of civil society. In *Subaltern Studies: Writings on South Asian History and Society*, vol. 3, ed. Ranajit Guha. Delhi: Oxford University Press.

———. 1986. *Nationalist Thought and the Colonial World: A Derivative Discourse?* London: Zed Books.

———. 1989. Caste and subaltern consciousness. *In Subaltern Studies: Writings on South Asian History and Society*, vol. 6, ed. Ranajit Guha, 169–209. Delhi: Oxford University Press.

———. 1992. A religion of urban domesticity: Sri Ramakrishna and the Calcutta middle class. In *Subaltern Studies: Writings on South Asian History and Society,* vol. 7, ed. P. Chatterjee and G. Pandey, 40–68. Delhi: Oxford University Press.

———. 1993. *The Nation and Its Fragments: Colonial and Postcolonial Histories.* Princeton, N.J.: Princeton University Press.

———. 1995. History and nationalization of Hinduism. In *Representing Hinduism: The Construction of Religious Traditions and National Identity,* ed. V. Dalmia and H. von Stietencorn, 103–28. New Delhi, Thousand Oaks, London: Sage Publications.

———. 1997a. *The Present History of West Bengal: Essays in Political Criticism.* Delhi: Oxford University Press.

———. 1997b. Introduction: A political history of independent India. In *State and Politics in India*, ed. Partha Chatterjee, 1–40. New Delhi: Oxford University Press.

———. 2004. *The Politics of the Governed: Reflections on Popular Politics in Most of the World*. New Delhi: Permanent Black.

Chatterji, B. 1992. *Trade, Tariffs and Empire: Lancashire and British Policy in India, 1919–1939*. Delhi: Oxford University Press.

Chatterji, J. 1995. *Bengal Divided: Hindu Communalism and Partition, 1932–1947*. Cambridge: Cambridge University Press.

———. 2005. Of graveyards and ghettos: Muslims in partitioned West Bengal 1947–67. In *Living Together Separately: Cultural India in History and Politics*, eds. Mushirul Hasan and Asim Roy, 222–49. New Delhi: Oxford University Press.

———. 2007. *The Spoils of Partition: Bengal and India, 1947–1967*. Cambridge: Cambridge University Press.

Chattopadhyay, B. 2000. *Crime and Control in Early Colonial Bengal, 1770–1860*. Calcutta: K.P. Bagchi & Co.

Chattopadhyay, G. 1976. The almost revolutions: A case study of India in February 1946. In *Essays in Honour of S.C. Sarkar*, ed. B. De, 427–50. New Delhi: People's Publishing House.

———.1987. Bengal students in revolt against the Raj, 1945–46. In *Myth and Reality: The Struggle for Freedom in India, 1945–47*, ed. A.K. Gupta, 152–71. New Delhi: Manohar.

Chaudhuri, B. B. 1967. Agrarian economy and agrarian relations in Bengal (1859–1885). In *The History of Bengal (1757–1905)*, ed. N.K. Sinha, 237–336. Calcutta: Calcutta University Press.

———. 1975. The land market in eastern India, 1793–1940. Pt 1. *The Indian Economic and Social History Review* 12 (1): 1–42.

———. 1982. Agrarian relations: Eastern India. In *The Cambridge Economic History of India*, vol. 2, ed. Dharma Kumar, 86–177. Cambridge: Cambridge University Press.

———. 1996. The process of agricultural commercialisation in Eastern India during British rule: A reconsideration of the notions of "Forced Commercialisation" and "Dependent Peasantry". In *Meanings of Agriculture: Essays in South Asian History and Economics*, ed. Peter Robb, 71–91 Delhi: Oxford University Press.

Chaudhuri, S. B. 1957. *Civil Rebellion in the Indian Mutinies*. Calcutta: The World Press.

Chaudhuri, K. N. 1978. *The Trading World of Asia and The English East India Company*. Cambridge: Cambridge University Press.

Chaudhury, Sushil. 1995. *From Prosperity to Decline: Eighteenth-Century Bengal*. Delhi: Manohar.

———. 2000. *The Prelude to Empire: Plassey Revolution of 1757*. New Delhi: Manohar.

Chowdhury, Indira. 1998. *The Frail Hero and Virile History: Gender and the Politics of Culture in Colonial Bengal*. Delhi: Oxford University Press.

Chowdhry, P. 1995. Popular perceptions of widow-remarriage in Haryana: Past and present. In *From the Seams of History: Essays on Indian Women*, ed. Bharati Ray, 37–66. Delhi: Oxford University Press.

Cohen, Stephen P. 1971. *The Indian Army: Its Contribution to the Development of a Nation*. Bombay: Oxford University Press.

Cohn, Bernard S. 1986. The command of language and the language of command. In *Subaltern Studies: Writings on South Asian History and Society*, vol. 4, ed. Ranajit Guha, 276–329. Delhi: Oxford University Press.

———. 1987. *An Anthropologist among the Historians and Other Essays*. Delhi: Oxford University Press.

———. 1992. Representing authority in Victorian India. In *The Invention of Tradition*, ed. E. Hobsbawm and T. Ranger, 165–210. Canto edition, Cambridge: Cambridge University Press.

Constable, P. 1997. Early dalit literature and culture in late nineteenth and early twentieth century western India. *Modern Asian Studies* 31(2): 317–38.

———. 2000. Sitting on the school verandah: The ideology and practice of 'untouchable' educational protest in late nineteenth-century western India. *The Indian Economic and Social History Review* 37 (4): 383–422.

———. 2001. The marginalization of a *dalit* martial race in late nineteenth and early twentieth-century western India. *Journal of Asian Studies* 60 (2): 439–78.

Cooper, A. 1988. *Sharecropping and Sharecroppers' Struggle in Bengal, 1930–1950*. Calcutta: K.P. Bagchi & Co.

Copland, I. 1982. *The British Raj and the Indian Princes*. Bombay: Orient Blackswan.

———. 1993. Lord Mountbatten and the integration of the Indian States: A reappraisal. *The Journal of Imperial and Commonwealth History* 21 (2): 385–408.

———. 1999. *The Princes of India in the Endgame of Empire, 1917–1947*. Cambridge: Cambridge University Press.

Cronin, R. P. 1977. *British Policy in Bengal, 1905–1912: Partition and the New Province of Eastern Bengal and Assam*. Calcutta: Firma K. L. Mukhopadhyay.

Custers, P. 1986. Women's role in Tebhaga movement. *Economic and Political Weekly*, Review of Women Studies, 23 October, 31 (43): WS-97–104.

Dale, S. 1975. The Mappila outbreaks: Ideology and conflict in nineteenth-century Kerala. *Journal of Asian Studies* 35 (1): 85–97.

Dalmia, Vasudha. 1997. *The Nationalization of Hindu Traditions: Bharatendu Harschandra and Nineteenth-Century Banaras*. Delhi: Oxford University Press.

Dalton, D. 1993. *Mahatma Gandhi: Nonviolent Power in Action*. New York: Columbia University Press.

Damodaran, Vinita. 1992. *Broken Promises: Popular Protest, Indian*

Nationalism and the Congress Party in Bihar, 1935–1946. Delhi: Oxford University Press.

———. 1998. Azad Dastas and dacoit gangs: The Congress and underground activity in Bihar, 1942–44. In *Turbulent Times: India, 1940–44*, ed. B. Pati, 108–37. Mumbai: Popular Prakashan.

Darwin, J. 1988. *Britain and Decolonisation: The Retreat from Empire in the Post-War World*. Basingstoke: Macmillan.

Das, S. 1991a. Communal violence in twentieth-century colonial Bengal: An analytical framework. In *Communalism in India*, ed. K.N. Panikkar, 36–50. New Delhi: Manohar.

———. 1991b. *Communal Riots in Bengal, 1905–1947*. Delhi: Oxford University Press.

Dasgupta, A. 1967. *Malabar in Asian Trade, 1740–1800*. Cambridge: Cambridge University Press.

———. 1979. *Indian Merchants and the Decline of Surat, c.1700–1750*. Wiesbaden: Steiner.

Das Gupta, A. K. 1992. *The Fakir and Sannyasi Uprising*. Calcutta: K.P. Bagchi & Co.

Dasgupta, B. 1977. India's Green Revolution. *Economic and Political Weekly* 12 (6/8), Annual Number: 241–60.

Dasgupta, C. 2002. *War and Diplomacy in Kashmir*. New Delhi: Sage Publications.

Dasgupta, S. 1994. Adivasi politics in Midnapur, c. 1760–1924. In *Subaltern Studies: Writings on South Asian History and Society*, vol. 4, ed. Ranajit Guha, 101–35. Paperback edition. Delhi: Oxford University Press.

Das Gupta, Ranajit. 1994. *Labour and Working Class in Eastern India. Studies in Colonial History*. Calcutta: K.P. Bagchi & Co.

Datta, Partho. 1993. Strikes in the greater Calcutta region, 1918–1924. *The Indian Economic and Social History Review* 30 (1): 57–84.

Datta, Pradip Kumar. 1999. *Carving Blocs: Communal Ideology in Early Twentieth-Century Bengal*. New Delhi: Oxford University Press.

De Barry, W. T. ed. 1958. *Sources of Indian Tradition*, 2 Vols. New York and London: Columbia University Press.

de Haan, Arjan. 1995. Migration in eastern India: A segmented labour market. *The Indian Economic and Social History Review* 31 (1): 51–93.

Derbyshire, Ian. 2001. The building of India's railways: The application of western technology in the colonial periphery, 1850–1920. In *Railways in Modern India*, ed. I.J. Kerr, 268–303. New Delhi: Oxford University Press.

Derret, J. D. M. 1968. *Religion, Law and the State in India*. London: Faber and Faber.

Desai, A. R. 1959. *Social Background of Indian Nationalism*. 3rd edition. Bombay: Popular Book Depot.

Desika Char, S. V. 1983. *Readings in the Constitutional History of India, 1757–1947*. Delhi: Oxford University Press

Dewey, C. 1993. *Anglo-Indian Attitudes: The Mind of the Indian Civil Service*. London and Rio Grande: The Hambledon Press.

Dhanagare, D. N. 1991. *Peasant Movements in India, 1920–1950*. Delhi: Oxford University Press.

Dirks, Nicholas B. 1987. *The Hollow Crown: Ethnohistory of an Indian Kingdom*. Cambridge: Cambridge University Press.

———. 1989. The invention of caste: Civil society in colonial India. *Social Analysis,* September 25: 42–52.

———. 1992. Castes of mind. *Representations,* Winter: 56–78.

Dobbin, C. 1972. *Urban Leadership in Western India: Politics and Communities in Bombay City, 1840–1885*. London: Oxford University Press.

Duara, P. 1995. *Rescuing History from the Nation: Questioning Narratives of Modern China.* Chicago and London: Chicago University Press.

Dube, Saurabh. 1998. *Untouchable Pasts: Religion, Identity, and Power among a Central Indian Community, 1780–1950.* New York: State University of New York Press.

Dumont, Louis. 1970. *Homo Hierarchicus.* London: Paladin

Dutt, V.P. 1984. *India's Foreign Policy.* New Delhi: Vikas Publishing House.

Dyson, T., and A. Maharatna. 1991. Excess mortality during the Bengal famine: A re-evaluation. *The Indian Economic and Social History Review,* 28 (3): 281–97.

Eaton, R. M. 1978. *Sufis of Bijapur: Social Roles of Sufis in Medieval India.* Princeton: Princeton University Press.

———. 1993. *The Rise of Islam and the Bengal Frontier, 1204–1760.* Berkeley, Los Angeles, London: University of California Press.

Embree, A. T. 1962. *Charles Grant and British Rule in India.* London: George Allen and Unwin Ltd.

———. 1963. *1857 in India: Mutiny or War of Independence?* Boston: D. C. Heath & Company.

Engels, Dagmar. 1996. *Beyond Purdah? Women in Bengal, 1890–1939.* Delhi: Oxford University Press.

Fay, Peter W. 1993. *The Forgotten Army: India's Armed Struggle for Independence, 1942–1945.* Ann Arbor: University of Michigan Press.

Fisher, Michael H. 1991. *Indirect Rule in India: Residents and the Residency System, 1764–1858.* Delhi: Oxford University Press.

———. 1993. Introduction to *The Politics of the British Annexation of India, 1757–1857.* Delhi: Oxford University Press.

Forbes, Geraldine. 1988. The politics of respectability: Indian women and the Indian National Congress. In *The Indian National Congress: The Centenary Hindsights*, ed. D.A. Low, 54–97. Delhi: Oxford University Press.

———. 1998. *Women in Modern India.* The New Cambridge History of India, vol. 4.2. Cambridge: Cambridge University Press.

Frankel, F.R. 1978. *India's Political Economy, 1947–1977.* Princeton, NJ: Princeton University Press.

Fox, Richard G. 1985. *Lions of the Punjab: Culture in the Making.* Berkeley, Los Angeles, London: University of California Press.

Freitag, Sandria B. 1989. *Collective Action and Community: Public Arenas and the Emergence of Communalism in North India.* Berkeley, Los Angeles, Oxford: University of California Press.

Frykenberg, R. E. 1997. The emergence of modern "Hinduism" as a concept and as an institution: A reappraisal with special reference to South India. In *Hinduism Reconsidered*, ed. G.D. Sontheimer and H. Kulke, 82–107. New Delhi: Manohar.

Fuchs, S. 1992. *Godmen on the Warpath: A Study of Messianic Movements in India.* New Delhi: Munshilal Manoharlal Publishers Pvt. Ltd.

Fukazawa, H. 1982. Agrarian relations: Western India. In *The Cambridge Economic History of India,* vol. 2, ed. Dharma Kumar, 177–206. Cambridge: Cambridge University Press.

Furber, H. 1949. Constitution-making in India. *Far Eastern Survey* 18 (8): 86–89.

———. 1951. The Unification of India, 1947–1951. *Pacific Affairs* 24 (4): 352–71.

Gadgil, Madhav, and Ramchandra Guha. 1993. State forestry and social conflict in British India. In *Peasant Resistance in India, 1858–1914*, ed. David Hardiman, 259–95. Paperback edition. Delhi: Oxford University Press.

Gallagher, J., G. Johnson and A. Seal. eds. 1973. *Locality, Province and Nation: Essays on Indian Politics, 1870 to 1940.* Cambridge: Cambridge University Press.

Gallagher, J., and R. Robinson. 1953. The imperialism of free trade. *Economic History Review,* 2nd ser., 6 (1): 1–15.

———. 1961. *Africa and the Victorians: The Official Mind of Imperialism.* London: Macmillan.

Galanter, M. 1984. *Competing Equalities: Law and Backward Classes in India.* Berkeley and Los Angeles: University of California Press.

Gandhi, M. K. 1997. *Hind Swaraj and Other Writings.* Edited by A.J. Parel. Cambridge: Cambridge University Press.

Ganguly, S. 1997. *The Crisis in Kashmir: Portents of War Hopes of Peace.* Cambridge: Cambridge University Press.

———. 2013. The Indo-Pakistani Conflict. In *Routledge Handbook on Indian Politics*, eds. Atul Kohli and Prema Singh, 331–38. London and New York: Routledge.

Gardner, Brian. 1971. *The East India Company; A History.* London: Rupert Hart-Davis.

Geertz, Clifford. 1994. Primordial and civic ties. In *Nationalism,* ed. J. Hutchinson and A.D. Smith, 29–34. New York: Oxford University Press.

Geetha, V., and S.V Rajadurai. 1998. *Towards a Non-Brahmin Millennium: From Iyothee Thass to Periyar.* Calcutta: Samya.

Ghosh, K. K. 1969. *The Indian National Army: Second Front of the Indian Independence Movement.* Meerut: Meenakshi Prakashan.

Ghosh, P. 1994. Colonial state and colonial working conditions; Aspects of the experience of Bengal jute mill hands, 1881–1930. *Economic and Political Weekly,* 30 July, 29 (31): 2019–27.

———. 2000. *Colonialism, Class and a History of the Calcutta Jute Mill hands, 1880–1930*. Chennai: Orient Longman.

Ghosh, P. C. 1960. *The Development of the Indian National Congress, 1892–1909*. Calcutta: Firma K. L. Mukhopadhyay.

Ghosh, S. C. 1995. *The History of Education in Modern India, 1757–1986*. Hyderabad: Orient Longman.

Gilmartin, D. 1988. *Empire and Islam: Punjab and the Making of Pakistan*. Berkeley, Los Angeles, London: University of California Press.

———. 2007. Election Law and the "People" in Colonial and Postcolonial India. In *From the Colonial to the Postcolonial*, eds. D. Chakrabarty, R. Majumdar and A. Sartori, 55–82. New Delhi: Oxford University Press.

Gooptu, Nandini. 1993. Caste and labour: Untouchable social movements in urban Uttar Pradesh in the early twentieth century. In *Dalit Movements and the Meanings of Labour in India,* ed. Peter Robb, 277–98. Delhi: Oxford University Press.

Gopal, S. 1953. *The Viceroyalty of Lord Ripon, 1880–1884*. London: Oxford University Press.

———. 1975. *Jawaharlal Nehru: A Biography, 1889–1947*. Vol. 1. London: Jonathan Cape.

———. (ed.). 1991. *Anatomy of a Confrontation: The Babri Masjid-Ramjanmabhumi Issue*. New Delhi: Penguin.

Goradia, N. 1993. *Lord Curzon: The Last of the British Moghuls*. Delhi: Oxford University Press.

Gordon, A. D. D. 1978. *Businessmen and Politics: Rising Nationalism and a Modernising Economy in Bombay, 1918–1933*. New Delhi: Manohar.

Gordon, L. A. 1974. *Bengal: The Nationalist Movement, 1876–1940*. New York, London: Columbia University Press.

———. 1990. *Brothers against the Raj: A Biography of Sarat and Subhash Chandra Bose*. New Delhi: Viking Penguin.

Gordon, Richard. 1973. Non-cooperation and council entry, 1919 to 1920. In *Locality, Province and Nation: Essays on Indian Politics, 1870 to 1940*, ed. J. Gallagher, G. Johnson, and A. Seal, 123–53. Cambridge: Cambridge University Press.

Gordon, S. 1969. Scarf and sword: Thugs, marauders, and state-formation in eighteenth-century Malwa. *The Indian Economic and Social History Review* 6 (4): 403–29.

———. 1993. *The Marathas, 1600–1818*. The New Cambridge History of India, vol. 2.4. Cambridge: Cambridge University Press.

Gore, M. S. 1993. *The Social Context of an Ideology: Ambedkar's Political and Social Thought*. New Delhi, Thousand Oaks, London: Sage.

Goswami, O. 1985. Then came the Marwaris: Some aspects of the changes in the pattern of industrial control in eastern India. *The Indian Economic and Social History Review* 22 (3): 225–49.

———. 1987. Multiple images: Jute mill strikes of 1929 and 1937 seen through other's eyes. *Modern Asian Studies* 21 (3): 547–83.

Gough, Kathleen. 1979. Indian peasant uprisings. In *Peasant Struggles in India*, ed. A.R. Desai, 85–128. Bombay: Oxford University Press.

Gourlay, S. N. 1988. Nationalists, outsiders and labour movement in Bengal during the non-cooperation movement, 1919–21. In *Congress and Classes: Nationalism, Workers and Peasants*, ed. K. Kumar, 34–57. New Delhi: Manohar.

Graham, B.D. 1990. *Hindu Nationalism and Indian Politics: The Origins and Development of the Bharatiya Jana Sangh*. Cambridge: Cambridge University Press.

Grare, F., and A. Mattoo eds. 2003. *Beyond the Rhetoric: The Economics of India's Look East Policy*. New Delhi: Manohar.

Greenough, Paul R. 1982. *Prosperity and Misery in Modern Bengal: The Famine of 1943–1944. New York: Oxford University Press.*

———. 1983. Political mobilization and the underground literature of the Quit India Movement, 1942–44. *Modern Asian Studies* 17 (3): 353–86.

Grewal, J. S. 1990. *The Sikhs of the Punjab*. The New Cambridge History of India, vol. 2.3. Cambridge: Cambridge University Press.

Grewal, J. S., and I. Banga. 2000. Pakistan, Khalistan and Partition. In *The Partition in Retrospect*, ed. A. Singh, 159–77. New Delhi: Anamika.

Guha, N. 1985. *Pre-British State System in South India, Mysore, 1761–1799*. Calcutta: Minerva.

Guha, Ramchandra. 1991. *The Unquiet Woods: Ecological Change and Peasant Resistance in the Himalaya*. Delhi: Oxford University Press.

———. 1994. Forestry and social protest in British Kumaun, c. 1893–1921. In *Subaltern Studies: Writings on South Asian History and Society*, vol. 4, ed. Ranajit Guha, 54–100. Paperback edition. Delhi: Oxford University Press.

———. 1998. Mahatma Gandhi and the Environmental Movement in India. In *Environmental Movements in Asia*, eds. A. Kalland and G. Pearson, 65–82. Richmond, Surrey: Curzon.

———. 2005. Verdicts on Nehru: Rise and Fall of a Reputation. *Economic and Political Weekly* 40 (19): 1958–62.

———. 2007. *India after Gandhi: The History of the World's Largest Democracy*. London: Macmillan.

Guha, Ranajit. 1963. *A Rule of Property for Bengal: An Essay on the Idea of Permanent Settlement*. Paris: Mouton & Co.

———. ed. 1982. *Subaltern Studies: Writings on South Asian History and Society,* vol. 1. Delhi: Oxford University Press.

———. 1992. Discipline and mobilize. In *Subaltern Studies: Writings on South Asian History and Society,* vol. 7, ed. P. Chatterjee and G. Pandey, 69–120. Delhi: Oxford University Press.

———. 1993. Neel-Darpan: The image of a peasant revolt in a liberal mirror. In *Peasant Resistance in India, 1858–1914,* ed. David Hardiman, 60–110. Paperback edition. Delhi: Oxford University Press.

———. 1994. *Elementary Aspects of Peasant Insurgency in Colonial India*. second impression. Delhi: Oxford University Press.

Guha, Sumit 1992. Society and economy in the Deccan, 1818–1850. In *The Making of Agrarian Policy in British India, 1770–1900*, ed. B. Stein, 187–214. Delhi: Oxford University Press.

———. 1999. *Environment and Ethnicity in India, 1200–1991*. Cambridge: Cambridge University Press.

Guha-Thakurta, Tapati. 1992. *The Making of a New "Indian" art: Artists, Aesthetics and Nationalism in Bengal, c.1850–1920*. Cambridge: Cambridge University Press.

Gupta, A. K. ed. 1987. *Myth and Reality: The Struggle for Freedom in India, 1945–47*. Delhi: Manohar.

Gupta, B. K. 1962. *Siraj-ud-daullah and the East India Company, 1756–1757: Background to the Foundation of British Power in India*. Leiden: E.J. Brill.

Gupta, P. S. 1987. Imperial strategy and the transfer of power, 1939–51. In *Myth and Reality: The Struggle for Freedom in India, 1945–47*, ed. A.K. Gupta, 1–53. Delhi: Manohar.

———. 1997. *Towards Freedom: Documents on the Movement for Independence in India, 1943–1944*. 2 Vols. Delhi: Oxford University Press.

Habib, Irfan. 1963. *The Agrarian System of Mughal India*. London: Asia Publishing House.

———. 2000. Introduction: An essay on Haidar Ali and Tipu Sultan. In *Confronting Colonialism: Resistance and Modernization under Haidar Ali and Tipu Sultan*. New Delhi: Tulika.

———. (ed.) 1999. *Confronting Colonialism: Resistance and Modernization under Haidar Ali and Tipu Sultan*. New Delhi: Tulika.

Harcourt, M. 1977. Kisan populism and revolution in rural India: The 1942 disturbances in Bihar and east United Provinces. In *Congress and Raj: Facets of the Indian Struggle, 1917–47*, ed. David A. Low, 315-48. London: Heinemann.

Hardgrave, R.L. 1970. The Congress in India: Crisis and Split. *Asian Survey* 10 (3): 256–62.

Hardiman, David. 1981. *Peasant Nationalists of Gujarat: Kheda District, 1917–1934*. Delhi: Oxford University Press.

———. 1988. The Quit India movement in Gujarat. In *The Indian Nation in 1942*, ed. G. Pandey, 77–122. Calcutta: K.P. Bagchi & Co.

——— . 1993. Introduction to *Peasant Resistance in India, 1858–1914*. Delhi: Oxford University Press.

———. 1996. *Feeding the Baniya: Peasants and Usurers in Western India*. Delhi: Oxford University Press.

Hardgrave, Robert L. 1969. *The Nadars of Tamilnad*. Berkeley and Los Angeles: University of California Press.

Hasan, Mushirul. 1985. Religion and politics in India: The Ulama and the Khilafat movement: Communal and revivalist trends in Congress. In *Communal and Pan-Islamic Trends in Colonial India*, ed. Mushirul Hasan, 17–42. New Delhi: Manohar.

———. 1988. The Muslim mass contact campaign: Analysis of a strategy of political mobilization. In *Congress and Indian Nationalism: The Pre-Independence Phase*, ed. R. Sisson, and S. Wolpert, 198–222. Berkeley and Los Angeles: California University Press.

———. 1993a. Introduction to *India's Partition: Process, Strategy and Mobilization*. Delhi: Oxford University Press.

———. ed. 1993b. *India's Partition: Process, Strategy and Mobilization*. Delhi: Oxford University Press.

———. ed. 1995. *India Partitioned: The Other Face of Freedom*. 2 Vols. New Delhi: Roli Books.

———. 1996. The myth of unity: Colonial and national narratives. In *Making India Hindu: Religion, Community and the Politics of Democracy in India*, ed. D. Ludden, 185–208. Delhi: Oxford University Press.

———. 1997. *Legacy of a Divided Nation: India's Muslims since Independence*. Boulder, Colorado: Westview Press.

———. 2000a. Memories of a fragmented nation: Rewriting the histories of India's partition. In *The Partition in Retrospect*, ed. A. Singh, 339–60. New Delhi: Anamika.

———. ed. 2000b. *Inventing Boundaries: Gender, Politics and the Partition of India*. Delhi: Oxford University Press.

Hasan, S. N. 1969. Zamindars under the Mughals. In *Land Control and Social Structure in Indian History*, ed. R.E. Frykenberg, 17–31. Madison: University of Wisconsin Press.

Hasan, Z. 2000. Representation and Redistribution: The New Lower Caste Politics of North India. In *Transforming India: Social and Political Dynamics of Democracy*, eds. F.R. Frankel, Z. Hasan, R. Bhargava and B. Arora, 146–75. New Delhi: Oxford University Press.

Hashmi, T. I. 1992. *Pakistan as a Peasant Utopia: The Communalization of Class Politics in East Bengal, 1920–1947*. Boulder, Colorado: Westview Press.

———. 1999. Peasant nationalism and the politics of Partition: The class-communal symbiosis in East Bengal, 1940–47. In *Region and Partition: Bengal, Punjab and the Partition of the Subcontinent*, ed. I. Talbot and G. Singh, 6–41. Karachi: Oxford University Press.

Hawley, J. S. 1994. Introduction to *Sati, the Blessing and the Curse*, ed. J.S. Hawley, 3–26. New York, Oxford: Oxford University Press.

Heehs, P. 1993. *The Bomb in Bengal: The Rise of Revolutionary Terrorism in India, 1900–1910*. Delhi: Oxford University Press.

Heimsath, C. H. 1964. *Indian Nationalism and Hindu Social Reform*. Princeton: Princeton University Press.

Henningham, Stephen. 1982. *Peasant Movements in Colonial India: North Bihar, 1917–1942*. Canberra: Australian National University.

———. 1983. Quit India in Bihar and the Eastern United Provinces: The Dual Revolt. In *Subaltern Studies: Writings on South Asian History and Society*, vol. 2, ed. Ranajit Guha, 130–79. Delhi: Oxford University Press.

Hills, C., and Daniel C. Silverman. 1993. Nationalism and feminism in late colonial India: The Rani of Jhansi regiment, 1943–1945. *Modern Asian Studies* 27 (4): 741–60.

Hodson, H. V. 1969. *The Great Divide: Britain, India, Pakistan*. London: Hutchinson.

Holland, R. F. 1985. *European Decolonization, 1918–1981: An Introductory Survey*. Basingstoke: Macmillan.

Hunter, W. W. 1899–1900. A *History of British India*. 2 Vols. London: Longmans Green.

Hurd, J. 1982. Railways. In *The Cambridge Economic History of India*, vol. 2, ed. Dharma Kumar, 737–61. Cambridge: Cambridge University Press.

Hutchins, F. G. 1967. *The Illusion of Permanence: British Imperialism in India*. Princeton, NJ: Princeton University Press.

———. 1973. *India's Revolution: Gandhi and the Quit India Movement*. Cambridge: Harvard University Press.

Ilaiah, K. 1998. Towards the Dalitisation of the Nation. In *Wages of Freedom: Fifty Years of the Indian Nation State*, ed. P.Chatterjee, 267–91. Delhi: Oxford University Press.

Inden, Ronald. 1990. *Imagining India*. Oxford: Clarendon Press.

Ingram, Edward. 1981. *Commitment to Empire: Prophecies of the Great Game in Asia, 1797–1800*. Oxford: Clarendon Press.

Irschick, Eugene F. 1969. *Politics and Social Conflict in South India: The Non-Brahman Movement and Tamil Separatism, 1916–1929*. Berkeley and Los Angeles: University of California Press.

———. 1994. *Dialogue and History: Constructing South India, 1795–1895*. Berkeley, Los Angeles, London: University of California Press.

Islam, S. 1979. *The Permanent Settlement in Bengal: A Study of Its Operation, 1790–1819*. Dacca: Bangla Academy.

———. 1988. *Bengal Land Tenure: The Origin and Growth of Intermediate Interests in the Nineteenth Century*. Calcutta: K.P. Bagchi & Co.

Jaffrelot, Christophe. 1996. *The Hindu Nationalist Movement and Indian Politics 1925 to the 1990s*. London: Hurst & Company.

Jain, M. S. 1965. *The Aligarh Movement: Its Origin and Development, 1858–1906*. Agra: Sri Ram Mehra.

Jalal, Ayesha. 1985. *The Sole Spokesman: Jinnah, the Muslim League and the Demand for Pakistan*. Paperback edition. Cambridge: Cambridge University Press.

———. 1997. Exploding communalism: The politics of Muslim identity in South Asia. In *Nationalism, Democracy and Development: State and Politics in India*, ed. Sugata Bose and Ayesha Jalal, 76–103. Delhi: Oxford University Press.

———. 2000. *Self and Sovereignty: Individual and Community in South Asian Islam Since 1850*. London and New York: Routledge.

Jayawardena, Kumari. 1986. *Feminism and Nationalism in the Third World*. London and New Jersey: Zed Books Ltd.

Jeffrey, Patricia. 1979. *Frogs in a Well: Indian Women in Purdah*. London: Zed Press.

Jeffrey, R. 1974. The social origins of a caste association, 1875–1905: The founding of the S. N. D. P. Yogam. *South Asia* 4: 39–59.

———, ed. 1978a. *People, Princes and Paramount Power: Society and Politics in the Indian Princely States*. Delhi: Oxford University Press.

———. 1978b. Travancore: Status, class and the growth of radical politics, 1860–1940. In *People, Princes and Paramount Power: Society and Politics in the Indian Princely States*, ed. R. Jeffrey, 136–69. Delhi: Oxford University Press.

———. 1981. India's working class revolt: Punnapra-Vayalar and the communist "Conspiracy" of 1946. *The Indian Economic and Social History Review* 18 (2): 97–122.

———. 1994. *The Decline of Nair Dominance: Society and Politics in Travancore, 1847–1908*. New Delhi: Manohar.

Jha, S. 2002. Secularism in the Constituent Assembly Debates, 1946–1950. *Economic and Political Weekly* 37 (30): 3175–80.

Jha, V. 1986–87. Candala and the origin of untouchability. *The Indian Historical Review* 13 (1–2): 1–36.

Johnson, G. 1973. *Provincial Politics and Indian Nationalism: Bombay and the Indian National Congress, 1880–1915*. Cambridge: Cambridge University Press.

Jones, Kenneth W. 1976. *Arya Dharm: Hindu Consciousness in Nineteenth-Century Punjab*. New Delhi: Manohar.

———. 1981. Religious identity and the Indian census. In *The Census in British India: New Perspectives*, ed. N.G. Barrier, 73–101. New Delhi: Manohar.

———. 1994. *Socio-Religious Reform Movements in British India*. The New Cambridge History of India, vol. 3.1. Cambridge: Cambridge University Press.

Joshi, Chitra. 1981. Kanpur textile labour: Some structural features of formative years. *Economic and Political Weekly*, Special Number, November 16 (44–46): 1823–38.

———. 1985. Bonds of community, ties of religion: Kanpur textile workers in the early twentieth century. *The Indian Economic and Social History Review* 22 (3): 251–80.

Joshi, S., and B. Josh. 1994. *Struggle for Hegemony in India 1920–47: Culture, Community and Power*, vol. III: 1941–47. New Delhi, Thousand Oaks, London: Sage Publications.

Juergensmeyer, Mark. 1982. *Religion as Social Vision: The Movement against Untouchability in Twentieth-Century Punjab*. Berkeley and Los Angeles: University of California Press.

Kannabiran,V., and K. Lalitha, 1990. The magic time: Women in the Telengana People's struggle. In *Recasting Women: Essays in Indian Colonial History*, ed. Kumkum Sangari and Sudesh Vaid, 180–203. New Brunswick, NJ: Rutgers University Press.

Karim, A. 1963. *Murshid Quli Khan and His Times*. Dacca: Asiatic Society of Pakistan.

Karkhanis, S. 1981. *Indian Politics and the Role of the Press*. New Delhi: Vikas Publishing House.

Karve, Irawati. 1977. *Hindu Society—An Interpretation*. 3rd ed. Poona: Deccan College.

Kasturi, L., and V. Mazumdar. 1994. Introduction to *Women and Indian Nationalism*. New Delhi: Vikas.

Kaul, Suvir, ed. 2001. *The Partitions of Memory: The Afterlife of the Division of India*. New Delhi: Permanent Black.

Kaur, R. 2007. *Since 1947: Partition Narratives among Punjabi Migrants of Delhi*. New Delhi: Oxford University Press.

Kaura, U. 1977. *Muslims and Indian Nationalism: The Emergence of Demand for India's Partition, 1928–1940*. New Delhi: South Asia Books.

Kaviraj, N. 1982. *Wahabi and Farazi Rebels of Bengal*. New Delhi: People's Publishing House.

Kaviraj, S. 1995. *The Unhappy Consciousness: Bankimchandra Chattopadhyay and the Formation of Nationalist Discourse in India*. Delhi: Oxford University Press.

———. 2011. *The Enchantment of Democracy and India*. Ranikhet: Permanent Black.

Kawai, Akinobu. 1986–87. *"Landlords" and Imperial Rule: Change in Bengal Agrarian Society, c.1885–1940*. 2 Vols. Tokyo: Institute for the Study of Languages and Cultures of Asia and Africa, Tokyo University of Foreign Studies.

Keay, John. 1991. *The Honourable Company: A History of the English East India Company*. London: HarperCollins.

Kerr, I. J. 2001a. Reworking a popular religious practice: The effects of railways on pilgrimage in nineteenth- and twentieth-century South Asia. In *Railways in Modern India*, ed. I.J. Kerr, 304–27. New Delhi: Oxford University Press.

———, ed. 2001b. *Railways in Modern India*. New Delhi: Oxford University Press.

Khaldun, T. 1986. The great rebellion. In *Rebellion, 1857: A Symposium*, ed. P.C. Joshi, 1–70. Calcutta: K.P. Bagchi & Co.

Khan, A. M. 1969. *The Transition in Bengal, 1756–1775*. Cambridge: Cambridge University Press.

Khilnani, S. 1997. *The Idea of India*. London: Hamish Hamilton.

King, Christopher R. 1999. *One Language Two Scripts: The Hindi Movement in Nineteenth-Century North India*. Paperback edition. Delhi: Oxford University Press.

Kishwar, Madhu. 1985. Gandhi on women. *Economic and Political Weekly*, 5 October, 20 (40): 1691–702.

———. 1994. Codified Hindu law: Myth and reality. *Economic and Political Weekly* 29 (33): 2145–61.

Kling, B.B. 1966. *The Blue Mutiny: The Indigo Disturbances in Bengal, 1859–1862*. Philadelphia: University of Pennsylvania Press.

———. 1976. *Partner in Empire: Dwarkanath Tagore and the Age of Enterprise in Eastern India*. Berkeley, Los Angeles, London: University of California Press.

Kohli, Atul. 1997. Can democracies accommodate ethnic nationalism? Rise and decline of self-determination movements in India. *Journal of Asian Studies* 56 (2): 325–44.

Kolff, D. 1990. *Naukar, Rajput and Sepoy: The Ethnohistory of the Military Labour Market in Hindustan.* Cambridge: Cambridge University Press.

Kopf, D. 1979. *The Brahmo Samaj and the Shaping of the Modem Indian Mind.* Princeton: Princeton University Press.

Kothari, R. 1974. The Congress system revisited: A decennial review. *Asian Survey* 14 (12): 1035–54.

———. 1994. Rise of the Dalits and the renewed debate on caste. *Economic and Political Weekly* 29 (26): 1589–94.

———. 1998. The democratic experiment. In *Wages of Freedom: Fifty Years of Indian Nation-State*, ed. P. Chatterjee, 23–36. Delhi: Oxford University Press.

———. 2002. The Congress "System" in India. In *Parties and Politics in India*, ed., Z. Hasan 39–55. New Delhi: Oxford University Press.

Krishan, Y. 1983. Mountbatten and the Partition of India. *History* 68: 22– 38.

Kumar, Dharma. 1965. *Land and Caste in South India: Agricultural Labour in Madras Presidency in the Nineteenth Century*. Cambridge: Cambridge University Press.

———. 1982. Agrarian relations: South India. In *The Cambridge Economic History of India,* vol. 2, ed. Dharma Kumar, 207–41. Cambridge: Cambridge University Press.

Kumar, K. 1984. *Peasants in Revolt: Tenants, Landlords, Congress and the Raj in Oudh, 1886–1922.* New Delhi: Manohar.

Kumar, Radha. 1983. Family and factory: Women workers in the Bombay cotton textile industry, 1919–1939. *The Indian Economic and Social History Review* 20 (1): 81–110.

Kumar, Ravinder. 1968. *Western India in the Nineteenth Century*. London: Routledge and Kegan Paul.

———. 1971. Introduction to *Essays in Gandhian Politics: The Rowlatt Satyagraha of 1919*. Oxford: Clarendon Press.

———. 1983. *Essays in the Social History of Modern India.* Delhi: Oxford University Press.

———. 1987a. Gandhi, Ambedkar and the Poona Pact, 1932. In *Struggling and Ruling: The Indian National Congress, 1885–1985*, ed. J. Masselos, 87–101. New Delhi: Sterling Publishers.

———. 1987b. Introduction to *Myth and Reality: The Struggle for Freedom in India, 1945–47*, ed. A.K. Gupta. Delhi: Manohar.

Kuwajima, S. 1998. *Muslims, Nationalism and the Partition: 1946 Provincial Elections in India.* New Delhi: Manohar.

Lalita, K., Stree Shakti Sanghatana. 1989. "*We Were Making History...*" *Life Stories of Women in the Telengana People's Struggle*. London: Zed Books.

Lawson, P. 1993. *The East India Company: A History.* London and New York: Longman.

Lebra, Joyce C. 1971. *Jungle Alliance*. Singapore: Donald Moore for Asia Pacific Press.

———. 1986. *The Rani of Jhansi: A Study in Female Heroism in India.* Honolulu: University of Hawaii Press.

Lelyveld, David. 1978. *Aligarh's First Generation: Muslim Solidarity in British India.* Princeton, NJ: Princeton University Press.

Leonard, K. I. 1971. Hyderabad political system and its participants. *Journal of Asian Studies* 30 (3): 569–82.

———. 1979. The "Great Farm" theory of the decline of the Mughal empire. *Comparative Studies in Society and History* 21: 151–67.

Leslie, I. Julia. 1989. *The Perfect Wife: The Orthodox Hindu Woman According to the Stridharmapaddhati of Tryambakayajvan.* Delhi: Oxford University Press.

Loomba, Ania. 1998. *Colonialism/Postcolonialism.* London and New York: Routledge.

Low, David A. 1968. Introduction to *Soundings in Modern South Asian History.* London: Weidenfeld and Nicolson.

———. 1977. Introduction: The climactic years, 1917–47. In *Congress and the Raj,* ed. David A. Low. London: Heinemann.

———. 1991. *Eclipse of Empire*, Cambridge: Cambridge University Press.

———. 1997. *Britain and Indian Nationalism: The Imprint of Ambiguity.* Cambridge: Cambridge University Press.

Ludden, D. 1985. *Peasant History in South India.* Princeton, NJ: Princeton University Press.

———. 1996. *Making India Hindu.* New Delhi: Oxford University Press.

———. 1999. *An Agrarian History of South Asia.* The New Cambridge History of India, vol. 4.4. Cambridge: Cambridge University Press.

Lynch, Owen. 1969. *The Politics of Untouchability: Social Mobility and Social Change in a City of India.* New York: Columbia University Press.

Mahajan, Sucheta. 1987. British policy, nationalist strategy and popular national upsurge, 1945–46. In *Myth and Reality: The Struggle for Freedom in India, 1945–47*, ed. A.K. Gupta, 54–98. New Delhi: Manohar.

———. 2000. *Independence and Partition: The Erosion of Colonial Power in India.* New Delhi: Sage Publications.

Mahalanobis, P.C. 1955. The Approach of Operational Research to Planning in India. *Sankhya: The Indian Journal of Statistics* 16 (1–2): 3–130.

Maitra, J. 1984. *Muslim Politics in Bengal, 1855–1906: Collaboration and Confrontation.* Calcutta: K.P. Bagchi & Co.

Majeed, A. 2003. The Changing Politics of States' Reorganization. *Publius* 33 (4): 83–98.

Majeed, Javed. 1992. *Ungoverned Imaginings: James Mill's The History of British India and Orientalism.* Oxford: Clarendon Press.

Majumdar, A. 1993. *Peasant Protest in Indian Politics: Tebhaga Movement in Bengal.* New Delhi: NIB Publishers.

Major, A. J. 1996. *Return to Empire: Punjab under the Sikhs and British in the Mid-Nineteenth Century.* New Delhi: Sterling Publishers.

Majumdar, N. 1960. *Justice and Police in Bengal, 1765–1793: A Study of the Nizamat in Decline*. Calcutta: Firma K. L. Mukhopadhyay.

Majumdar, R. 2007. Family values in transition: Debates around the Hindu Code Bill. In *From the Colonial to the Postcolonial: India and Pakistan in Transition*, eds. D. Chakrabarty, R. Majumdar and A. Sartori, 223–40. New Delhi: Oxford University Press.

Majumdar, R.C. 1963. *The Sepoy Mutiny and the Revolt of 1857*. 2nd ed. Calcutta: Firma K. L. Mukhopadhyay.

Malik, Z. U. 1977. *The Reign of Muhammad Shah, 1719–1748*. Bombay: Asia Publishing House

Mani, Lata. 1990. Contentious traditions: The debate on sati in colonial India. In *Recasting Women*, ed. Kumkum Sangari and Sudesh Vaid, 88–126. New Brunswick, NJ: Rutgers University Press.

———. 1998. *Contentious Traditions: The Debate on Sati in Colonial India*. Berkeley, Los Angeles and London: University of California Press.

Manor, J. 1977. *Political Change in an Indian State: Mysore, 1917–1955*. New Delhi: Oxford University Press.

———. 1978. The demise of the princely order: A reassessment. In *People, Princes and Paramount Power: Society and Politics in the Indian Princely States*, ed. R. Jeffrey, 306–28. Delhi: Oxford University Press.

———. 1997. Parties and the party system. In *State and Politics in India*, ed. P. Chatterjee, 92–124. New Delhi: Oxford University Press.

Mansergh, N. 1948. *The Commonwealth and the Nation*. London: Royal Institute of International Affairs.

——— (ed.). 1970–83. *The Transfer of Power, 1942–47*. 12 vols. London: Her Majesty's Stationery Service.

Markovits, C. 1985. *Indian Business and National Politics, 1931–1939*. Cambridge: Cambridge University Press.

Marshall, P. J. 1968. *Problems of Empire: Britain and India, 1757–1813*. London: George Allen and Unwin Ltd.

———. 1975a. British expansion in India in the eighteenth century: A historical revision. *History* 60 (198): 28–43.

———. 1975b. Economic and political expansion: The case of Oudh. *Modern Asian Studies* 9 (4): 465–482.

———. 1976. *East Indian Fortunes: The British in Bengal in the Eighteenth Century*. Oxford: Clarendon Press.

———. 1987. *Bengal: The British Bridgehead. Eastern India, 1740–1828*. Cambridge: Cambridge University Press.

———. 1998. The British in Asia: Trade to Dominion, 1700–1765. In *The Oxford History of the English Empire*. Vol. 2, *The Eighteenth Century*, ed. P.J. Marshall, 487–507. London and New York: Oxford University Press.

———. 1999. The first British empire. In *The Oxford History of British Empire*. Vol. 5, *Historiography*, ed. R.W. Winks, 43–53. Oxford, New York: Oxford University Press.

Masani, M.R. 1954. *The Communist Party of India: A Short History*. London: Derek Verschoyle.

Masselos, Jim. 1990. "The magic touch of being free": The rituals of independence on 15 August. In *India: Creating a Modern Nation,* ed. Jim Masselos, 37–53. New Delhi: Sterling Publishers.

Mayaram, Shail. 1997. *Resisting Regimes: Myth, Memory and the Shaping of a Muslim Identity.* Delhi: Oxford University Press.

McCully, B. T. 1966. *English Education and the Origins of Indian Nationalism.* Gloucester, Mass.: Peter Smith.

McGuire, John. 1983. *The Making of a Colonial Mind: A Quantitative Study of the Bhadralok in Calcutta, 1857–1885.* Canberra: Australian National University Press.

McLane, J. R. 1977. *Indian Nationalism and the Early Congress.* Princeton, NJ: Princeton University Press.

McLeod, W. H. 1968. *Guru Nanak and the Sikh Religion.* Oxford: Clarendon Press.

———. 1976. *The Evolution of the Sikh Community.* Oxford: Clarendon Press.

Mehrotra, S. R. 1971. *The Emergence of the Indian National Congress.* Delhi: Vikas.

Mendelsohn, Oliver, and Marika Vicziany. 1998. *The Untouchables: Subordination, Poverty and the State in Modern India.* Cambridge: Cambridge University Press.

Menon, Dilip. 1994. *Caste, Nationalism and Communism in South India, Malabar, 1900–1948.* Cambridge: Cambridge University Press.

Menon, Ritu, and Kamla Bhasin. 1993. Recovery, Rupture, Resistance: Indian State and Abduction of Women during Partition. *Economic and Political Weekly* 28 (17): WS2–WS11.

———. 1998. *Borders and Boundaries: Women in India's Partition.* New Brunswick: Rutgers University Press.

Menon, V.P. 1957. *The Transfer of Power in India.* Calcutta: Orient Longman.

Metcalf, Thomas R. 1965. *The Aftermath of Revolt: India, 1857–1870.* Princeton, NJ: Princeton University Press.

———. 1979. *Land, Landlords and the British Raj: Northern India in the Nineteenth Century.* Berkeley, Los Angeles, London: University of California Press.

———. 1994. *Ideologies of the Raj.* The New Cambridge History of India, vol. 3.4. Cambridge: Cambridge University Press.

Minault, Gail. 1981. Introduction: The extended family as metaphor and the expansion of women's realm. In *The Extended Family: Women and Political Participation in India and Pakistan,* ed. Gail Minault. Delhi: Chanakya Publications.

———. 1982. *The Khilafat Movement: Religious Symbolism and Political Mobilization in India.* Delhi: Oxford University Press.

———. 1998. *Secluded Scholars: Women's Education and Muslim Social Reform in Colonial India.* Delhi: Oxford University Press.

Misra, B. B. 1959. *The Central Administration of the East India Company, 1773–1834.* Manchester: Manchester University Press.

———. 1977. *The Bureaucracy in India: An Historical Analysis of Development up to 1947.* Delhi: Oxford University Press.

———. 1978. *The Indian Middle Classes: Their Growth in Modern Times.* Delhi: Oxford University Press.

Misra, Maria. 1999. *Business, Race and Politics in British India, c.1850–1960.* Oxford: Clarendon Press.

Mitra, C. 1988. Popular uprising in 1942: The case of Ballia. In *The Indian Nation in 1942*, ed. G. Pandey, 165–84. Calcutta: K.P. Bagchi & Co.

Moon, P., ed. 1973. *Wavell: The Viceroy's Journal.* London: Oxford University Press.

Moore, R. J. 1970. The Making of India's Paper Federation, 1927–35. In *The Partition of India: Policies and Perspectives, 1935–1947*, ed. C.H. Philips and M.D. Wainwright, 54–78. London: George Allen and Unwin Ltd.

———. 1974. *The Crisis of Indian Unity, 1917–1940.* Delhi: Oxford University Press.

———. 1979. *Churchill, Cripps and India, 1939–45.* Oxford: Clarendon Press.

———. 1983. *Escape from Empire: The Attlee Government and the Indian Problem.* Oxford: Clarendon Press.

———. 1988. *Endgames of Empire: Studies of Britain's Indian Problem.* Delhi: Oxford University Press.

———. 2000. Historical writing on India in the 1940s. In *The Partition in Retrospect,* ed. A. Singh, 383–96. New Delhi: Anamika.

Moore Jr., Barrington. 1966. *Social Origins of Dictatorship and Democracy.* Boston: Beacon Press.

Morris, M. D. 1965. *The Emergence of an Industrial Labor Force in India: A Study of the Bombay Cotton Mills, 1854–1947.* Berkeley and Los Angeles: University of California Press.

———. 1968. Towards a reinterpretation of nineteenth-century Indian economic history. *The Indian Economic and Social History Review* 5 (1): 1–15.

Mosley, L. 1961. *Last Days of the British Raj.* London: Weidenfeld and Nicholson.

Mukherjee, A. 1986. The Indian capitalist class: Aspects of its economic, political and ideological development in the colonial period, 1927–47. In *Situating Indian History for Sarvepalli Gopal*, ed. S. Bhattacharya and R. Thapar, 239–87. Delhi: Oxford University Press.

Mukherjee, Mithi. 2010. *India in the Shadows of Empire: A Legal and Political History, 1774–1950.* New Delhi: Oxford University Press.

Mukherjee, Mukul. 1983. Impact of Modernisation on Women's Occupations: A Case Study of the Rice-husking Industry of Bengal. *The Indian Economic and Social History Review* 20 (1): 27–46.

———. 1995. Women's Work in Bengal, 1880–1930: A Historical Analysis. In *From the Seams of History: Essays on Indian Women*, ed. Bharati Ray, 219–52. Delhi: Oxford University Press.

Mukherjee, N. 1962. *The Ryotwari System in Madras, 1792–1827.* Calcutta: Firma K. L. Mukhopadhyay.

Mukherjee, N., and R.E. Frykenberg. 1969. The Ryotwari system and social organization in Madras presidency. In *Land Control and Social Structure in Indian History*, ed. R.E. Frykenberg, 217–26. Madison, Milwauki and London: University of Wisconsin Press.

Mukherjee, Rudrangshu. 1982. Trade and empire in Awadh, 1765–1804. *Past and Present* 94: 85–102.

———. 1984. *Awadh in Revolt, 1857–1858: A Study of Popular Resistance*. Delhi: Oxford University Press.

———. 1998. *Spectre of Violence: The 1857 Kanpur Massacres*. New Delhi: Viking.

Mukherjee, S. N. 1968. *Sir William Jones: A Study in Eighteenth-Century British Attitudes to India*. Cambridge: Cambridge University Press.

———. 1993. *Calcutta: Essays in Urban History*. Calcutta: Subarnarekha.

———. 1996. *Citizen Historian: Explorations in Historiography*. New Delhi: Manohar.

Murphy, E. D. 1977. Class and Community in India: The Madras Labour Union 1918–21. *The Indian Economic and Social History Review* 14 (3): 291–321.

Murshid, Ghulam. 1983. *Reluctant Debutante: Response of Bengali Women to Modernisation, 1849–1905*. Rajshahi: Rajshahi University Press.

Murshid, Tazeen M. 1995. *The Sacred and the Secular: Bengal Muslim Discourses, 1871–1977*. Calcutta: Oxford University Press.

Nagaraj, R. 2013. India's economic development. In *Routledge Handbook on Indian Politics*, eds. A. Kohli and P. Singh, 189–203. London and New York: Routledge.

Nair, Janaki. 1994. On the question of agency in Indian feminist historiography. *Gender and History* 6 (1): 82–100.

———. 1998. *Miners and Millhands: Work, Culture and Politics in Princely Mysore*. New Delhi, Thousand Oaks, London: Sage Publications.

Nair, N. 2011. *Changing Homelands: Hindu Politics and the Partition of India*. Ranikhet: Permanent Black.

Nakazato, Nariaki. 1994. *Agrarian System in Eastern Bengal, c.1870–1910*. Calcutta: K.P. Bagchi & Co.

Nalapat, M.D. 2000. The last Nehru: A retrospective: A decade after Rajiv's Fall. *Economic and Political Weekly* 35 (6): 427–31.

Nandy, Ashis. 1994a. *The Illegitimacy of Nationalism: Rabindranath Tagore and the Politics of Self*. Delhi: Oxford University Press.

———. 1994b. Sati as profit versus sati as spectacle: The public debate on Roop Kanwar's death. In *Sati, the blessing and the Curse*, ed. J.S. Hawley, 131–49. New York, Oxford: Oxford University Press.

———. 1998. *The Intimate Enemy*, in *Exiled at Home*, Delhi: Oxford University Press.

Natarajan, L. 1979. The Santhal insurrection, 1855–56. In *Peasant Struggles in India*, ed. A.R. Desai, 136–47. Bombay: Oxford University Press.

Nayar, B.R. 1998. Political structure and India's economic reforms of the 1990s. *Pacific Affairs* 71 (3): 335–58.

———. 2013. India and the World: The Vicissitudes of Mutual Adjustment. In *Routledge Handbook on Indian Politics*, eds. A. Kohli and P. Singh, 311–19. London and New York: Routledge.

Nehru, J. 1963. Changing India. *Foreign Affairs* 41 (3): 453–65.

Neogi, G. 1998. Was Partition the costliest price for Independence? A historiographic critique. In *India's Partition: Preludes and Legacies*, ed. Ramakant and R. Mahan, 54–83. Jaipur and New Delhi: Rawat Publications.

Neogy, A.K. 1987. *Partitions of Bengal.* Calcutta: A. Mukherjee & Co.

Nightingale, P. 1970. *Trade and Empire in Western India, 1784–1806.* Cambridge: Cambridge University Press.

Nossiter, T.J. 1988. *Marxist State Governments in India.* London and New York: Pinter Publishers.

Nurullah, S., and J.P. Naik. 1971. *A Students' History of Education in India (1800–1965).* 5th ed. Calcutta: Macmillan.

Oberoi, H. 1994. *The Construction of Religious Boundaries: Culture, Identity, and Diversity in the Sikh Tradition.* Chicago: The University of Chicago Press.

Oberoi, P. 2006. *Exile and Belonging: Refugees and State Policy in South Asia.* New Delhi: Oxford.

O'Hanlon, Rosalind. 1985. *Caste, Conflict and Ideology: Mahatma Jotirao Phule and Low Caste Protest in Nineteenth-Century Western India.* Cambridge: Cambridge University Press.

———. 1991. Issues of widowhood: Gender and resistance in colonial western India. In *Contesting Power: Resistance and Everyday Social Relations in South Asia,* ed. D. Haynes and G. Prakash, 62–108. Delhi: Oxford University Press.

———. 1994. *A Comparison between Women and Men: Tarabai Shinde and the Critique of Gender Relations in Colonial India.* Madras: Oxford University Press.

Omissi, David. 1994: *The Sepoy and the Raj: The Indian Army, 1860–1940.* London: Macmillan.

Omvedt, Gail. 1971. Jotirao Phule and the ideology of social revolution in India. *Economic and Political Weekly,* 11 September, 6 (37): 1969–19.

———. 1976. *Cultural Revolt in a Colonial Society: The Non Brahman Movement in Western India: 1873 to 1930.* Bombay: Scientific Socialist Education Trust.

———. 1988. The Satara Prati Sarkar. In *The Indian Nation in 1942,* ed. G. Pandey, 223–62. Calcutta: K.P. Bagchi & Co.

———. 1990. "Twice Born" Riot against democracy. *Economic and Political Weekly* 25 (39): 2195–2197, 2199–2201.

———. 1994. *Dalits and the Democratic Revolution: Dr Ambedkar and the Dalit Movement in Colonial India.* New Delhi, Thousand Oaks, London: Sage.

———. 2001. Ambedkar and After: The Dalit Movement in India. In Dalit Identity and Politics, ed. G. Shah. New Delhi, Thousand Oaks, London: Sage Publications.

Oommen, T. K. 2000. Conceptualising nation and nationality in South Asia. In *Nation and National Identity in South Asia,* eds. S.L. Sharma and T.K. Oommen, 1–18. New Delhi: Orient Longman.

Owen, H. F. 1968. Towards nationwide agitation and organisation: The Home Rule Leagues, 1915–18. In *Soundings in Modern South Asian History*, ed. D.A. Low, 159–95. London: Weidenfeld and Nicolson.

———. 1971. Organizing for the Rowlatt Satyagraha of 1919. In *Essays in Gandhian Politics: The Rowlatt Satyagraha of 1919*, ed. R. Kumar, 64–92 Oxford: Clarendon Press.

Page, David. 1982. *Prelude to Partition: The Indian Muslims and the Imperial System of Control, 1920–1932*. Delhi: Oxford University Press.

Pal, P., and M. Dasgupta. 2009. The ASEAN–India Free Trade Agreement: An assessment. *Economic and Political Weekly* 44 (38): 11–15.

Panda, Chitta. 1996. *The Decline of the Bengal Zamindars: Midnapore, 1870–1920*. Delhi: Oxford University Press.

Pandey, B. N. 1969. *The Break-up of British India*. London: Macmillan.

Pandey, Gyanendra. 1978. *The Ascendancy of the Congress in Uttar Pradesh, 1926–34: The Imperfect Mobilization*. Delhi: Oxford University Press.

———. 1982. Peasant revolt and Indian nationalism: The peasant movement in Awadh, 1919–1922. In *Subaltern Studies: Writings on South Asian History and Society*, vol. 1, ed. Ranajit Guha, 143–97. New Delhi: Oxford University Press.

———. 1983. Rallying round the cow: Sectarian strife in the Bhojpuri region, c. 1888–1917. In *Subaltern Studies: Writings on South Asian History and Society*, vol. 2, ed. Ranajit Guha, 60–129. Delhi: Oxford University Press.

———. 1988a. Introduction: The Indian nation in 1942. In *The Indian Nation in 1942*, ed. G. Pandey. Calcutta: K.P. Bagchi & Co.

———. 1988b. The revolt of August 1942 in eastern UP and Bihar. In *The Indian Nation in 1942*, ed. G. Pandey, 123–64. Calcutta: K.P. Bagchi & Co.

———. 1991. In defence of the fragment: Writing about Hindu-Muslim riots in India today. *Economic and Political Weekly*, Annual Number, 26 March (11–12): 559–72.

———. 1992. *The Construction of Communalism in Colonial North India*. Delhi: Oxford University Press.

———. 1994. The prose of otherness. In *Subaltern Studies: Essays in Honour of Ranajit Guha*, vol. 8, ed. David Arnold and David Hardiman, 188–221. Delhi: Oxford University Press.

———. 1997. Community and violence: Recalling Partition. *Economic and Political Weekly*, 9 August, 32 (32): 2037–45.

Pandian, M. S. S. 1993. "Denationalising" the past: "Nation" in E.V. Ramaswamy's political discourse. *Economic and Political Weeekly*, 16 October, 28 (42): 2282–87.

———. 1994. Notes on the transformation of "Dravidian" ideology: Tamilnadu, c. 1900–1940. *Social Scientist* 22 (5–6): 84–104.

———. 1997. Partition and Independence in Delhi, 1946–47. *Economic and Political Weekly* 32 (36): 2261–72.

———. 1999a. Can a Muslim be an Indian? *Comparative Studies in Society and History* 41 (4): 608–29.

———. 1999b. "Nation" from its margins: Notes on E. V. Ramaswamy's 'Impossible' nation. In *Multiculturism, Liberalism and Democracy*, ed. R. Bhargava, A. K. Bagchi and R. Sudarshan, 286–307. New Delhi: Oxford University Press.

———. 2001. *Remembering Partition: Violence, Nationalism and History in India*. Cambridge: Cambridge University Press.

Pandian, M.S.S. 2007. *Brahmin and Non-Brahmin: Genealogies of the Tamil Political Present*. Delhi: Permanent Black.

Panikkar, K. N. 1989. *Against Lord and State: Religion and Peasant Uprisings in Malabar, 1836–1921*. Delhi: Oxford University Press.

———. 1995. *Culture, Ideology, Hegemony: Intellectuals and Social Consciousness in Colonial India*. New Delhi: Tulika.

Parekh, Bhikhu. 1989a. *Colonialism, Tradition and Reform: An Analysis of Gandhi's Political Discourse*. New Delhi, Newbury Park, London: Sage Publications.

———. 1989b. *Gandhi's Political Philosophy: A Critical Examination*. Notre Dame, Indiana: University of Notre Dame Press.

Parel, Anthony J. 1997. Introduction to *Hind Swaraj and Other Writings*, by M.K. Gandhi. Cambridge: Cambridge University Press.

Park, R.L. 1975. Political crisis in India 1975. *Asian Survey* 15 (11): 996–1013.

Parulekar, S. V. 1979. The liberation movement among Varlis: The struggle of 1946. In *Peasant Struggles in India*, ed. A.R. Desai, 569–96. Delhi: Oxford University Press.

Patankar, B., and Gail Omvedt. 1979. The dalit liberation movement in the colonial period. *Economic and Political Weekly*, Annual Number, 14 February (7–8): 409–24.

Patel, S. 1987. *The Making of Industrial Relations: The Ahmedabad Textile Industry, 1918–1939*. Delhi: Oxford University Press.

———. 2000. Construction and reconstruction of woman in Gandhi. In *Ideals, Images and Real Lives: Women in Literature and History*, ed. Alice Thorner and M. Krishnaraj, 288–321. Hyderabad: Orient Longman.

Pati, Biswamoy. 1993. *Resisting Domination: Peasants, Tribals and the National Movement in Orissa, 1920–50*. New Delhi: Manohar.

Peabody, Norbad. 1996. Tod's Rajast'han and the boundaries of imperial rule in nineteenth-century India. *Modern Asian Studies* 30 (1): 185–220.

Pearson, Gail. 1981. Nationalism, universalization, and the extended female space in Bombay city. In *The Extended Family: Women and Political Participation in India and Pakistan*, ed. Gail Minault, 174–91. Delhi: Chanakya Publications.

———. 1983. Reserved seats—women and the vote in Bombay. *The Indian Economic and Social History Review* 20 (1): 47–66.

Pearson, M. N. 1976. Sivaji and the decline of the Mughal empire. *Journal of Asian Studies* 35 (2): 221–35.

Peers, Douglas M. 1995. *Between Mars and Mammon: Colonial Armies and the Garrison State in Early Nineteenth-Century India*. London, New York: I. B. Tauris.

Perlin, F. 1985. State formation reconsidered. *Modern Asian Studies* 19 (3): 415–80.

Philips, C. H. 1970. Introduction to *The Partition of India: Policies and Perspectives, 1935–1947*. London: Allen & Unwin Ltd.

Pinch, William R. 1996. *Peasants and Monks in British India*. Berkeley, Los Angeles, London: University of California Press.

Pirzada, S. S., ed. 1970. *Foundations of Pakistan: All-India Muslim League Documents, 1906–1947*. Vol. 2. Karachi: National Publishing House.

Potter, D. C. 1986. *India's Political Administrators, 1919–1983*. Oxford: Clarendon Press.

Pouchepadass, J. 1974. Local leaders and the intelligentsia in the Champaran satyagraha (1917): A study in peasant mobilization. *Contributions to Indian Sociology,* New Series, 8: 67–87.

———. 1999. *Champaran and Gandhi: Planters, Peasants and Gandhian Politics*. New Delhi: Oxford University Press.

Prakash, Gyan. 1992. Introduction to *The World of the Rural Labourer in Colonial India*. Delhi: Oxford University Press.

———. 1999. *Another Reason: Science and the Imagination of Modern India*. Princeton, N.J.: Princeton University Press.

Prakash, Om. 1976. Bullion for goods: International trade and the economy of early eighteenth-century Bengal. *The Indian Economic and Social History Review* pp.3.

———. 1988. *The Dutch East India Company and the Economy of Bengal, 1630–1720*. Delhi: Oxford University Press.

Prashad, Vijay. 2000. *Untouchable Freedom: A Social History of a Dalit Community.* Delhi: Oxford University Press.

Qaisar, A. J. 1965. Distribution of the revenue resources of the Mughal empire among the nobility. *Proceedings of the Indian History Congress*. Allahabad Session.

Quraishi, Z.M. 1968. Electoral strategy of a minority pressure group: The Muslim Majlis-E-Mushawarat. *Asian Survey* 8 (12): 976--87.

Raheja, G. G. 1994. Caste System. In *Encyclopedia of Social History,* ed. P.N. Stearns, 94–96. New York and London: Garland Publishing, Inc.

Rai, M. 2004. *Hindu Rulers, Muslim Subjects: Islam, Rights, and the History of Kashmir*. London: Hurst & Co.

Ramaswamy, Sumathi. 1997. *Passions of the Tongue: Language Devotion in Tamil India, 1891–1970*. Berkeley, Los Angeles, London: University of California Press.

Ramusack, Barbara N. 1978. *The Princes of India in the Twilight of Empire: Dissolution of a Patron-Client System, 1914–1939*. Columbus: Ohio State University Press.

———. 1990. From symbol to diversity: The historical literature on women in India. *South Asia Research* 10 (2): 139–57.

Rao, C. R. 1979. The postwar situation and beginning of armed struggle. In *Peasant Struggles in India*, ed. A.R. Desai, 517–31. Delhi: Oxford University Press.

Ray, Bharati. 1988. *Hyderabad and British Paramountcy, 1858–1883*. Delhi: Oxford University Press.

———. 1995. The freedom movement and feminist consciousness in Bengal, 1905–1929. In *Front the Seams of History: Essays on Indian Women*, ed. Bharati Ray, 174–218. Delhi: Oxford University Press.

Ray, R. 1979. *Change in Bengal Agrarian Society, 1760–1850*. New Delhi: Manohar.

Ray, Rajat K. 1975. Introduction to *Rammohun Roy and the Process of Modernization in India*, ed. V.C. Joshi, 1–20. New Delhi: Vikas.

———. 1979. *Industrialization in India: Growth and Conflict in the Private Corporate Sector, 1914–47*. Delhi: Oxford University Press.

———. 1980. Three interpretations of Indian nationalism. In *Essays in Modern Indian History*, ed. B.R. Nanda, 1–41. Delhi: Oxford University Press.

———. 1984. *Social Conflict and Political Unrest in Bengal, 1875–1927*. Delhi: Oxford University Press.

———. 1988. The retreat of the Jotedars. *The Indian Economic and Social History Review* 25 (2): 235–47.

———. 1993. Race, religion and realm: The political theory of the "Reigning India Crusade", 1857. In *India's Colonial Encounter: Essays in Memory of Eric Stokes*, ed. N. Gupta and M. Hasan, 133–82. Delhi: Manohar.

———. 1994. Introduction to *Entrepreneurship and Industry in India, 1800–1947*. Delhi: Oxford University Press.

———. 1998. Indian society and the establishment of British supremacy, 1765–1818. In *The Oxford History of the English Empire*. Vol. 2, *The Eighteenth Century*, ed. P.J. Marshall, 508–29. London and New York: Oxford University Press.

———. 2001. *Exploring Emotional History: Gender, Mentality and Literature in the Indian Awakening*. New Delhi: Oxford University Press.

Ray, Rajat K., and Ratnalekha Ray. 1973. The dynamics of continuity in rural Bengal under the British imperium. *The Indian Economic and Social History Review* 10 (2): 103–28.

———. 1975. Zamindars and jotedars: A study of rural politics in Bengal. *Modern Asian Studies* 9 (1): 81–102.

Raychaudhuri, Tapan. 1969. Permanent Settlement in operation: Bakarganj district, East Bengal. In *Land Control and Social Structure in Indian History*, ed. R.E. Frykenberg, 163–74. Madison, Milwauki and London: The University of Wisconsin Press.

———. 1979. Indian nationalism as animal politics. *The Historical Journal* 22 (3): 747–63.

———. 1982. The state and the economy: The Mughal India. In *The Cambridge Economic History of India*, vol. 1, ed. Tapan Raychaudhuri and Irfan Habib, 172–93. Cambridge: Cambridge University Press.

———. 1989. *Europe Reconsidered: Perceptions of the West in Nineteenth-Century Bengal*. Delhi: Oxford University Press.

———. 1995. The pursuit of reason in nineteenth-century Bengal. In *Mind*

Body and Society: Life and Mentality in Colonial Bengal, ed. R.K. Ray, 47–64. Calcutta: Oxford University Press.

———. 1999. *Perceptions, Emotions, Sensibilities: Essays on India's Colonial and Post-Colonial Experiences*. Delhi: Oxford University Press.

Reeves, P. D. 1991. *Landlords and Governments in Uttar Pradesh: A Study of Their Relations until Zamindari Abolition*. Bombay: Oxford University Press.

Richards, J. F. 1975. *Mughal Administration in Golconda, 1687–1727*. Oxford: Oxford University Press.

———. 1976. Imperial crisis in the Deccan. *Journal of Asian Studies* 35 (2): 237–56.

———. 1993. *The Mughal Empire*. The New Cambridge History of India, vol. 1.5. Cambridge: Cambridge University Press.

Robb, P. G. 1976. *The Government of India and Reform: Policies toward Politics and the Constitution, 1916–1921*. Oxford: Oxford University Press.

———. 1992. *The Evolution of British Policy towards Indian Politics, 1880–1920*. New Delhi: Manohar.

———. 1997. *Ancient Rights and Future Comforts: Bihar, the Bengal Tenancy Act of 1885 and British Rule in India*. Richmond, Surrey: Curzon Press.

Robinson, F. 1974. *Separatism among Indian Muslims: The Politics of the United Provinces' Muslims, 1860–1923*. Cambridge: Cambridge University Press.

———. 2001. *The 'Ulama of Farangi Mahall and Islamic Culture in South Asia*. London: C. Hurst.

Rodrigues, V. 1993. Making a tradition critical: Ambedkar's reading of Buddhism. In *Dalit Movements and the Meanings of Labour in India*, ed. Peter Robb, 299–338. Delhi: Oxford University Press.

Rothermund, D. 1970. *The Phases of Indian Nationalism and Other Essays*. Bombay: Nachiketa Publications.

———. 1992. *India in the Great Depression, 1929–1939*. New Delhi: Manohar.

Roy, Asim. 1983. *The Islamic Syncretistic Tradition in Bengal*. Princeton: Princeton University Press.

———. 1993. The high politics of India's partition: The revisionist perspective. In *India's Partition: Process, Strategy and Mobilization*, ed. M. Hasan, 102–32. Delhi: Oxford University Press.

Roy, H. 2012. *Partitioned Lives: Migrants, Refugees, Citizens in India and Pakistan, 1947–1965*, New Delhi: Oxford University Press.

Roy, S. 2007. *Beyond Belief: India and the Politics of Postcolonial Nationalism*. Durham, NC: Duke University Press.

Roy, Tapti. 1993. Visions of the rebels: A study of 1857 in Bundelkhand. *Modern Asian Studies* 27 (1): 205–28.

Roy, Tirthankar. 1993. *Artisans and Industrialization: Indian Weaving in the Twentieth Century*. Delhi: Oxford University Press.

———. 1999. *Traditional Industry in the Economy of Colonial India*. Cambridge: Cambridge University Press.

———. 2000. *The Economic History of India, 1857–1947*. New Delhi: Oxford University Press.

Rudolph, Lloyd I., and Susanne H. Rudolph. 1967. *The Modernity of Tradition—Political Development in India*. Chicago and London: The University of Chicago Press.

Sáez, L. 2013. India in Asia: Geostrategic and economic considerations. In *Routledge Handbook on Indian Politics*, eds. Atul Kohli and Prema Singh, 320–30. London and New York: Routledge.

Said, Edward W. 1978. *Orientalism*. London & Henley: Routledge and Kegan Paul.

Samaddar, R., ed. 1997. *Reflections on Partition in the East*. New Delhi: Vikas Publishing House.

Samanta, A. 2002. *Malarial Fever in Colonial Bengal, 1820–1939*. Kolkata: Firma K. L. M. Pvt. Ltd.

Sanyal, H. 1981. *Social Mobility in Bengal*. Calcutta: Papyrus.

———. 1988a. Congress in southwestern Bengal: The anti-union board movement in eastern Medinipur, 1921. In *Congress and Indian Nationalism: The Pre-Independence Phase*, ed. R. Sisson and S. Wolpert, 352–76. Delhi: Oxford University Press.

———. 1988b. The Quit India movement in Medinipur district. In *The Indian Nation in 1942*, ed. G. Pandey, 19–76. Calcutta: K.P. Bagchi & Co.

Sarkar, J. N. 1932–50. *Fall of the Mughal Empire*. 4 Vols. Calcutta: M.C. Sarkar & Sons.

Sarkar, Jagadish N. 1976. *A Study of Eighteenth-Century India*. Vol. 1. *Political History (1707–1761)*. Calcutta: Saraswat Library.

Sarkar, S. C. 1981. *Bengal Renaissance and Other Essays*. 2nd ed. New Delhi: People's Publishing House.

Sarkar, Sumit. 1973. *Swadeshi Movement in Bengal, 1903–8*. New Delhi: People's Publishing House.

———. 1975. Rammohun Roy and the break with the past. In *Rammohun Roy and the Process of Modernization in India*, ed. V. C. Joshi, 46–68. New Delhi: Vikas.

———. 1976. The Logic of Gandhian nationalism: Civil Disobedience and the Gandhi-Irwin Pact, 1930–31. *Indian Historical Review*. Reprinted in *A Critique of Colonial India*, 86–115. Calcutta: Papyrus, 1985.

———. 1983. *Modern India, 1885–1947*. New Delhi: Macmillan.

———. 1984. Condition and nature of subaltern militancy: Bengal from swadeshi to non-co-operation, 1905–1922. In *Subaltern Studies: Writings on South Asian History and Society*, vol. 3, ed. R. Guha, 271–320. Delhi: Oxford University Press.

———. 1985. *A Critique of Colonial India*. Calcutta: Papyrus.

———. 1992. "Kaliyuga", "Chakri" and "Bhakti": Ramakrishna and his times. *Economic and Political Weekly*, 18 July, 27 (29): 1543–66.

———. 1997. *Writing Social History*. Delhi: Oxford University Press.

———. 2000. Orientalism revisited: Saidian frameworks in the writing of modern Indian history. In *Mapping Subaltern Studies and the Postcolonial*, ed. V. Chaturvedi, 239–55. London, New York: Verso.

Sarkar, Tanika. 1984. Politics and women in Bengal: The conditions and meaning of participation. *The Indian Economic and Social History Review* 21 (1): 91–101.

———. 1987a. *Bengal, 1928–1934: The Politics of Protest*. Delhi: Oxford University Press.

———. 1987b. Nationalist Iconography: Image of women in nineteenth-century Bengali literature. *Economic and Political Weekly*, 21 November, 22 (47): 2011–15.

———. 1996. Indian nationalism and the politics of Hindutva. In *Making India Hindu*, ed. D. Ludden, 270–93. New Delhi: Oxford University Press.

———. 2001. *Hindu Wife, Hindu Nation: Community, Religion and Cultural Nationalism*. London: Hurst & Co.

Saradamoni, K. 1980. *Emergence of a Slave Caste: Pulayas of Kerala*. Delhi: People's Publishing House.

Satyanarayana, A. 1990. *Andhra Peasants under British Rule: Agrarian Relations and the Rural Economy, 1900–1940*. New Delhi: Manohar.

Scott, James C. 1985. *Weapons of the Weak: Everyday Forms of Peasant Resistance*. New Haven: Yale University Press.

Seal, A. 1968. *The Emergence of Indian Nationalism: Competition and Collaboration in the Later Nineteenth Century*. Cambridge: Cambridge University Press.

———. 1973. Imperialism and nationalism in India. In *Locality, Province and Nation: Essays on Indian Politics, 1870 to 1940*, ed. J. Gallagher, G. Johnson and A. Seal, 1–27. Cambridge: Cambridge University Press.

Sen, Asoke. 1977. *Iswar Chandra Vidyasagar and His Elusive Milestones*. Calcutta: Riddhi.

Sen, A. K. 1980. Famine mortality: A study of the Bengal famine of 1943. In *Peasants in History: Essays in Honour of Daniel Thomer*, ed. E.J. Hobsbawm, W. Kula, A. Mitra, K.N. Raj and I. Sachs, 194–220. Calcutta: Oxford University Press.

Sen, A. P. 1993. *Hindu Revivalism in Bengal, 1872–1905*. Delhi: Oxford University Press.

Sen, S. N. 1957. *Eighteen Fifty-Seven*. New Delhi: The Publication Division, Ministry of Information and Broadcasting, Government of India.

Sen, S. P. 1971. *The French in India, 1763–1816*. 2nd ed. New Delhi: Munshiram Manoharlal.

Sen, Samita. 1993. Motherhood and mothercraft: Gender and nationalism in Bengal. *Gender and History* 5 (2): 231–43.

———. 1999. *Women and Labour in Late Colonial India: The Bengal Jute Industry*. Cambridge: Cambridge University Press.

Sen, Sarbani. 2007. *Popular Sovereignty and Democratic Transformations: The Constitution of India*. New Delhi: Oxford University Press.

Sen, Shila. 1976. *Muslim Politics in Bengal, 1937–47*. New Delhi: Impex India.

Sen, Sudipta. 1998. *Empire of Free Trade: The East India Company and the Making of the Colonial Marketplace*. Philadelphia: University of Pennsylvania Press.

Sen, Sukomal. 1977. *Working Class of India: History of Emergence and Movement, 1830–1970*. Calcutta: K.P. Bagchi & Co.

Sen, Sunil. 1972. *Agrarian Struggle in Bengal, 1946–47*. New Delhi: People's Publishing House.

Sengupta, K. K. 1974. *Pabna Disturbances and the Politics of Rent, 1873–1885*. New Delhi: People's Publishing House.

———. 1979. Peasant struggle in Pabna, 1873: Its legalistic character. In *Peasant Struggles in India*, ed. A.R. Desai, 179–88. Bombay: Oxford University Press.

Shah, G. 1974. Traditional society and political mobilization: The experience of Bardoli satyagraha (1920–1928). *Contributions to Indian Sociology*, new ser., 8: 89–107.

———. (ed.). 2001. *Dalit Identity and Politics*. New Delhi, Thousand Oaks, London: Sage Publications.

Shaikh, F. 1989. *Community and Consensus in Islam: Muslim Representation in Colonial India, 1860–1947*. Cambridge: Cambridge University Press.

———. 1993. Muslims and political representation in colonial India: The Making of Pakistan. In *India's Partition: Process, Strategy and Mobilization*, ed. M. Hasan, 81–101. Delhi: Oxford University Press.

Siddiqi, A. 1973. *Agrarian Change in a Northern Indian State: Uttar Pradesh, 1829–1833*. Oxford: Clarendon Press.

———. 1982. The Business World of Jamsetjee Jeejeebhoy. *The Indian Economic and Social History Review* 19 (3–4): 301–24.

Siddiqi, M. H. 1978. *Agrarian Unrest in North India: United Provinces,1918–1922*. New Delhi: Vikas.

Silverberg, J., ed. 1968. *Social Mobility in the Caste System in India*. The Hague: Mouton.

Simeon, D. 1995. *The Politics of Labour Under Late Colonialism: Workers, Unions and the State in Chota Nagpur, 1928–1939*. New Delhi: Manohar.

Simmons, C. P. 1976. Recruiting and organizing an industrial labour force in colonial India: The case of the coal mining industry, c. 1880–1939. *The Indian Economic and Social History Review* 13 (4): 455–82.

Singh, A., ed. 2000. *The Partition in Retrospect*. New Delhi: Anamika.

Singh, A. I. 1987. *The Origins of the Partition of India, 1936–1947*. Delhi: Oxford University Press.

Singh, K. 1963–66. *A History of the Sikhs*. 2 vols. Princeton: Princeton University Press.

Singh, K. S. 1983. *Birsa Munda and His Movement, 1874–1901: A Study of a Millenarian Movement in Chota Nagpur.* Calcutta: Oxford University Press.

Singh, R. P. 1998. British educational policy in nineteenth-century India: A nationalist critique. In *The Contested Terrain: Perspectives on Education in India*, ed. S. Bhattacharya, 99–121. Hyderabad: Orient Longman.

Singha, Radhika.1998. *A Despotism of Law: Crime and Justice in Early Colonial India*. Delhi: Oxford University Press.

Sinha, M. 1995. *Colonial Masculinity: The "Manly Englishman" and the "Effeminate Bengali" in the Late Nineteenth Century.* Manchester & New York: Manchester University Press.

Sinha, N. K. 1962. *Economic History of Bengal.* Vol. 2. Calcutta: Firma K. L. Mukhopadhyay.

Sinha, P. 1978. *Calcutta in Urban History.* Calcutta: Firma K. L. Mukhopadhyay.

Skaria, A. 1999. *Hybrid Histories: Forests, Frontiers and Wildness in Western India.* Delhi: Oxford University Press.

Southerd, B.1980. The political strategy of Aurobondo Ghosh: The utilization of Hindu religious symbolism and the problem of political mobilization in Bengal. *Modern Asian Studies* 14 (3): 353–76.

———. 1995. *The Women's Movement and Colonial Politics in Bengal, 1921–1936.* New Delhi: Manohar.

Spangenberg, B. 1976. *British Bureaucracy in India: Status, Policy and the I.C.S. in the Late Nineteenth Century.* Columbia: South Asia Books.

Spate, O.H.K. 1947. The Partition of the Punjab and of Bengal. *The Geographical Journal* 110 (4/6): 201–18.

Spear, P. 1965. *The Oxford History of Modern India, 1740–1947.* Oxford: Clarendon Press.

Spear, T. G. P. 1973. *Twilight of the Mughals.* Oxford: Clarendon Press.

Srinivas, M. N. 1966. *Social Change in Modern India.* Berkeley and Los Angeles: University of California Press.

———. 1968. Mobility in the Caste System. In *Structure and Change in Indian Society*, ed. M. Singer and B.S. Cohn, 189–200. Chicago: Aldine Publishing Co.

Srivastava, S. 1991. *The Disputed Mosque: A Historical Inquiry.* New Delhi: Vistaar Publications.

Steger, M. 2000. *Gandhi's Dilemma: Non-violent Principles and Nationalist Power.* New York: St. Martin's Press.

Stein, Burton. 1985. State formation and economy reconsidered. *Modern Asian Studies* 19 (3): 387–413.

———. 1989a. *Vijaynagara.* The New Cambridge History of India, vol. 1.2. Cambridge: Cambridge University Press.

———. 1989b. *Thomas Munro: The Origins of the Colonial State and His Vision of Empire.* Delhi: Oxford University Press.

———. 1992. Introduction to *The Making of Agrarian Policy in British India, 1770–1900.* Delhi: Oxford University Press.

Stoddard, B. 1977. The structure of Congress politics in coastal Andhra, 1925–37. In *Congress and the Raj*, ed. D.A. Low, 109–32. London: Heinemann.

Stokes, E. 1959. *The English Utilitarians and India.* Oxford: Clarendon Press.

———. 1978. *The Peasant and the Raj.* Cambridge: Cambridge University Press.

———. 1980. *The Peasants and the Raj: Studies in Agrarian Society and Peasant Rebellion in Colonial India.* Paperback edition. Cambridge: Cambridge University Press.

———. 1982. Agrarian Relations: Northern and Central India. In *The Cambridge Economic History of India,* vol. 2, ed. Dharma Kumar, 36–86. Cambridge: Cambridge University Press.

———. 1986. *The Peasant Armed: The Indian Rebellion of 1857*. Edited by C.A. Bayly. Oxford: Clarendon Press.

Subramanian, Lakshmi. 1995. *Indigenous Capital and Imperial Expansion. Bombay, Surat and the West Coast*. New Delhi: Oxford University Press.

———. 2001. "East Indian Fortunes": Merchants, companies and conquest, 1700–1800: An exercise in historiography. In *Bengal: Rethinking History. Essays in Historiography*, ed. S. Bandyopadhyay, 39–63. Delhi: Manohar.

Sundarayya, P. 1979. Hyderabad State—Its Socio-Political Background: The Communist Movement in Andhra: Terror Regime, 1948–51; Entry of Indian Army and Immediately After. In *Peasant Struggles in India*, ed. A.R. Desai, 537–68. Delhi: Oxford University Press.

Sutherland, L. 1952. *The East India Company in Eighteenth-Century Politics*. Oxford: Clarendon Press.

Svensson, T. 2013. *Production of Postcolonial India and Pakistan: Meanings of Partition*, London and New York: Routledge.

Talbot, Ian. 1988. *Provincial Politics and the Pakistan Movement*. Karachi: Oxford University Press.

———. 1996a. *Khizr Tiwana, the Punjab Unionist Party and the Partition of India*. Richmond, Surrey: Curzon.

———. 1996b. *Freedom's Cry: Popular Dimension in the Pakistan Movement and Partition Experience in North-West India*. Karachi: Oxford University Press.

———. 2011. Punjabi refugees' rehabilitation and the Indian state: Discourses, denials and dissonances. *Modern Asian Studies* 45 (1): 109–30.

Talbot, I., and G. Singh, eds. 1999. *Region and Partition: Bengal, Punjab and the Partition of the Subcontinent*. Karachi: Oxford University Press.

Talbot, P. 1949. Kashmir and Hyderabad, *World Politics* 1 (3): 321–32.

Tan, T. Y., and G. Kudaisya. 2000. *The Aftermath of Partition in South Asia*. London and New York: Routledge.

Taylor, P. J. O. ed. 1996. *A Companion to the "Indian Mutiny" of 1857*. Delhi: Oxford University Press.

———, 1997. *What Really Happened During the Mutiny: A Day-by-Day Account of the Major Events of 1857–1859 in India*. Delhi: Oxford University Press.

Tejani, S. 2013. The Necessary Conditions for Democracy: B.R. Ambedkar on Nationalism, Minorities and Pakistan. *Economic and Political Weekly* 48 (50): 111–19.

Thapar, R. 1975. Looking back in history. In *Indian Women*, ed. D. Jain, New Delhi: Publication Division, Ministry of Information and Broadcasting, Government of India.

———. 1997. Syndicated Hinduism. In *Hinduism Reconsidered*, ed. G. Sontheimer and H. Kulke, 54–81. New Delhi: Manohar.

Thorner, D. 1950. Problems of economic development in India. *Annals of the American Academy of Political and Social Science* 268: 96–103.

Tomlinson, B. R. 1975. India and the British empire, 1880–1935. *The Indian Economic and Social History Review* 12 (4): 337–65.

———. 1976a. *The Indian National Congress and the Raj, 1929–1942: The Penultimate Phase*. London: Macmillan.

———. 1976b. India and the British empire, 1935–47. *The Indian Economic and Social History Review* 13 (3): 331–49.

———. 1979. *The Political Economy of the Raj, 1914–1947: The Economics of Decolonization in India*. London and Basingstoke: Macmillan.

———. 1981. Colonial firms and the decline of colonialism in eastern India. *Modern Asian Studies* 15 (3): 455–86.

———. 1985. Indo-British relations in the post-colonial era: The sterling balances negotiations, 1947–49. *The Journal of Imperial and Commonwealth History* 13 (3): 142–62.

———. 1993. *The Economy of Modern India, 1860–1970*. The New Cambridge History of India, vol. 3.3. Cambridge: Cambridge University Press.

Trautmann, Thomas R. 1997. *Aryans and British India*. Berkeley, Los Angeles, London: University of California Press.

Tripathi, A. 1967. *The Extremist Challenge*. Calcutta: Orient Longman.

Tripathi, D. 1991. Congress and the industrialists (1885–1947). In *Business and Politics in India: A Historical Perspective*, ed. by D. Tripathi, 86–123. Delhi: Manohar.

Tucker, R. 1976. Hindu traditionalism and nationalist ideologies in nineteenth-century Maharashtra. *Modern Asian Studies* 10 (3): 321–48.

———. 1977. *Ranade and the Roots of Indian Nationalism*. Bombay: Popular Prakashan.

Tudor, M. 2013. The historical inheritance of India's democracy. In *Routledge Handbook on Indian Politics*, eds. Atul Kohli and Prema Singh, 23–36. London and New York: Routledge.

Tuteja, K. L. 1999. Akalis and the non-cooperation movement. In *The Khalsa over 300 Years*, ed. J.S. Grewal and I. Banga, 174–82. New Delhi: Tulika.

Upadhyay, P.C. 1992. The Politics of Indian Secularism. *Modern Asian Studies* 26 (4): 815–53.

Van der Veer, Peter. 1994. *Religious Nationalism: Hindus and Muslims in India*. Berkeley, Los Angeles, London: University of California Press.

Van Schendel, Willem. 1985. Madmen of Mymensingh: Peasant resistance and the colonial process in eastern India, 1824 to 1833. *The Indian Economic and Social History Review* 22 (2): 139–73.

———. 1991. *Three Deltas: Accumulation and Poverty in Rural Burma, Bengal and South India*. New Delhi: Sage Publications.

Vanaik, Achin. 1997. *The Furies of Indian Communalism: Religion, Modernity and Secularization*. London, New York: Verso.

Vicziany, M. 1979. The deindustrialization of India in the nineteenth century: A methodological critique of Amiya Kumar Bagchi. *The Indian Economic and Social History Review* 16 (2) 105–46.

Vidal, D. 1997. *Violence and Truth: A Rajasthani Kingdom Confronts Colonial Authority*. Delhi: Oxford University Press.

Vishwanath, L. S. 1998. Efforts of colonial state to suppress female infanticide. *Economic and Political Weekly*, 9 May 33 (19): 1104–12.

Viswanathan, Gauri. 1989. *Masks of Conquest: Literary Study and British Rule in India.* New York: Columbia University Press.

Visweswaran, Kamala. 1997. Small speeches, subaltern gender: Nationalist ideology and its historiography. In *Subaltern Studies: Writings on South Asian History and Society*, vol. 9, ed. S. Amin and D. Chakrabarty, 83–125. Paperback edition. Delhi: Oxford University Press.

Washbrook, D. A. 1976. *The Emergence of Provincial Politics: The Madras Presidency, 1870–1920.* Cambridge: Cambridge University Press.

———. 1981. Law, State and Agrarian Society in Colonial India. *Modern Asian Studies* 15 (3): 649–721.

Watson, I. B. 1980. *Foundation for Empire: English Private Trade in India, 1659–1760.* Delhi: Vikas.

Weiner, M. 1962. The struggle for equality in India. *Foreign Affairs* 40 (4): 644–52.

———. 1971. The 1971 elections and the Indian party system. *Asian Survey* 11 (12): 1153–66.

Whitcombe, E. 1982. Irrigation. In *The Cambridge Economic History of India*, vol. 2, ed. D. Kumar, 677–737. Cambridge: Cambridge University Press.

Windmiller, M. 1954. Linguistic regionalism in India. *Pacific Affairs* 27 (4): 291–318.

Wink, A. 1986. *Land and Sovereignty in India: Agrarian Society and Politics under the Eighteenth-Century Marat ha Svarajya.* Cambridge: Cambridge University Press.

Wolpert, S. 1962. *Tilak and Gokhale: Revolution and Reform in the Making of Modern India.* Berkeley and Los Angeles: University of California Press.

———. 1984.*Jinnah of Pakistan.* New York: Oxford University Press.

———. 2000. *A New History of India.* 6th ed. New York: Oxford University Press.

Wood, C. 1987. *The Moplah Rebellion and Its Genesis.* New Delhi: People's Publishing House.

Wood, J. R. 1978. Rajkot: Indian nationalsm in the princely context: The Rajkot satyagraha of 1938–39. In *People, Princes and Paramount Power: Society and Politics in the Indian Princely States*, ed. R. Jeffrey, 240–74. Delhi: Oxford University Press.

Woods, P. 1994. The Montagu-Chelmsford Reforms (1919): A re-assessment. *South Asia* 17 (1): 25–42.

Yadav, Y. 2000. Understanding the second democratic upsurge: Trends of Bahujan participation in electoral politics in the 1990s. In *Transforming India: Social and Political Dynamics of Democracy*, eds. F.R. Frankel, Z. Hasan, R. Bhargava and B. Arora, 120–45. New Delhi: Oxford University Press.

Yang, Anand A. 1980. Sacred symbol and sacred space in rural India: Community mobilization in the "Anti-Cow Killing" riot of 1893. *Comparative Studies in Society and History* 20: 576–96.

———. 1989. *The Limited Raj: Agrarian Relations in Colonial India, Saran District, 1793–1920*. Berkeley, Los Angeles, London: University of California Press.

———. 1998. *Bazaar India: Markets, Society, and the Colonial State in Bihar*. Berkeley, Los Angeles, London: University of California Press.

Zachariah, B. 1998. Imperial economic policy for India, 1942–44. In *Turbulent Times India, 1940–44*, ed. Biswamoy Pati, 185–213. Mumbai: Popular Prakashan.

———. 2004. *Nehru*. New York, London: Routledge.

Zamindar, V.F-Y. 2007. *The Long Partition and the Making of Modern South Asia: Refugees, Boundaries, Histories*. New York: Columbia University Press.

Zavos, J. 2000. *The Emergence of Hindu Nationalism in India*. New Delhi: Oxford University Press.

Zelliot, E. 1988. Congress and the untouchables, 1917–1950. In *Congress and Indian Nationalism*, ed. R. Sisson and S. Wolpert, 182–97. Delhi: Oxford University Press.

———. 1992. *From Untouchable to Dalit: Essay on Ambedkar Movement*. New Delhi: Manohar Publishers and Distributors.

Ziegler, Norman P. 1998. Rajput loyalties during the Mughal period. In *Kingship and Authority in South Asia*, ed. J.F. Richards, 241–84. Delhi: Oxford University Press.

Index